# POLICE POWER
*and Individual Freedom*

# POLICE POWER
## *and Individual Freedom*

THE QUEST FOR BALANCE

*edited by CLAUDE R. SOWLE*

ALDINE PUBLISHING COMPANY / CHICAGO

First published 1962
ALDINE PUBLISHING COMPANY
64 East Van Buren Street
Chicago 5, Illinois

Library of Congress Catalog Card Number 62-10632

Printed in the United States of America

# Introduction

In a free society, few disagree with the basic principle that police and judicial inter-ference with individual freedom should be permitted only under the most necessitous circumstances. Such a principle, however, is not self-executing. And, not surprisingly, general agreement usually dissolves whenever a serious attempt is made to define those situations in which the individual's right to be let alone should give way to the state's duty to preserve the security of the community.

Four of the areas of criminal law administration in which the debate has become most heated — arrest and detention, search and seizure, police interrogation, and self-incrimination — were chosen by Northwestern University School of Law in 1960 as the principal problems for discussion at its International Conference on Criminal Law Administration. The goal of the Conference, which was a part of the Law School's centennial celebration, was to bring to bear upon these four problem areas the greatest possible breadth of viewpoint and depth of insight. To this end, the Law School, with the aid of a grant from the Ford Foundation, brought to the Conference leading criminal law scholars and practitioners from the United States and from seven foreign countries.

The papers prepared and delivered by the Conference participants were subsequently published in four parts by the *Journal of Criminal Law, Criminology and Police Science*. For purposes of convenience and wider dissemination, they are now collected here under one cover. It is our hope that all who concern themselves in the years ahead with the vexing problems of criminal law enforcement in a free society will find aid and direction in this valuable and unprecedented collection of information and exchange of viewpoint.

In connection with the publication of these papers, I wish to express deep apprecia-tion to my colleague, Professor Fred E. Inbau, for his counsel and guidance. It was Professor Inbau who conceived the idea for the International Conference and directed its planning and execution. I am also indebted to Dean John Ritchie of Northwestern University Law School for his aid and encouragement. Also, a special note of thanks is due to my wife, Kathryn D. Sowle, a Research Associate in the School of Law at Northwestern and Assistant to the Editor of the *Journal of Criminal Law, Criminology and Police Science*. Her help in connection with the preparation of the manuscripts for publication was invaluable.

CLAUDE R. SOWLE

# Contents

# PART ONE

# Police Detention and Arrest Privileges

Four general questions were posed for consideration by the Conference participants in the preparation of their papers dealing with arrest and detention:

(1) In the absence of sufficient grounds for an arrest, should the police have a right to stop and question a person as to his identity and reason for being where he is, if the appearance or conduct of that person has reasonably aroused police suspicion?

(2) Should the police be permitted to search such a person for weapons or for incriminating evidence?

(3) If police practices of this nature are to be legally sanctioned, what limitations should be imposed?

(4) With respect to police arrest statutes generally, should more freedom be granted to the police in recognition of their contentions that existing laws are obsolete and hamper police attempts to meet the public demand for adequate police protection?

The papers dealing with these questions and related problems are reproduced in the following pages. At the outset, Professor Frank J. Remington of the University of Wisconsin presents a summary of the American law of arrest and detention. Next appear two papers dealing with policy questions which were prepared by the American participants in the Conference who discussed arrest and detention, Professor Caleb Foote of the University of Pennsylvania and O. W. Wilson, now Superintendent of Police in Chicago, Illinois, and, at the time of the Conference, Professor of Police Administration and Dean of the School of Criminology of the University of California. The final papers in Part I are reports by the seven foreign authorities concerning the status of police powers of arrest and detention in their countries.

# The Law Relating to "On the Street" Detention, Questioning and Frisking of Suspected Persons and Police Arrest Privileges in General

FRANK J. REMINGTON

Traditionally, all of these issues presented for discussion at this session of the Conference have been dealt with by the law as a single problem of arrest despite the fact that there are obviously important differences between questioning or frisking on the one hand and taking a person into custody for purposes of prosecution on the other hand. This over-simplified "single problem" approach of the law has had unfortunate consequences. The failure of the law to deal adequately with some important law enforcement problems has left enforcement officials without sufficient guidance, thus creating unnecessary risks both for the officer and for the citizen with whom he deals. It is obvious that clear definition of the scope of legitimate power is important for the officer as well as for persons whose interests would be endangered by its abuse. Explanation for inadequacies in current law comes, in part, from the way the law has developed.

Almost without exception, legal rules defining the power of police officers have been developed on a case by case basis. Putting aside the Uniform Arrest Act, which has been adopted by only three states,[1] no legislature has attempted an adequate formulation of police power in relation to issues like the right to stop and question, the right to frisk and the right to take a person into custody.[2]

Such legislation as there is is largely sporadic, usually adopting common law principles and making them applicable to certain designated types of police officers. Case law development is itself not undesirable provided the appellate court gets important issues presented to it in proper perspective. Such presentation has been lacking in this field.[3]

An officer may stop and question a suspect under circumstances in which the officer knows he will be in danger if the suspect is armed. Current police practice under such circumstances is to frisk the suspect.[4] If a gun is found, its admissibility may be in issue in states which exclude evidence which is obtained illegally. The basic issue is whether police have the right to frisk a suspect whom they have no right to arrest. This is not the issue which is presented to the appellate court, however. Typically, the prosecution will argue that an arrest was made and the frisking was incidental to the arrest. The defense will argue that there were no grounds for arrest. However the case is decided, the principal issue, the right to frisk a suspect in the absence of an arrest, is avoided. The law and practice continue, therefore, to fail to reflect each other's influence.

---

[1] DEL. CODE ANN., tit. 11, §1902 (1958); N. H. REV. STAT. ANN. 594.2 (1960); R. I. GEN. LAWS, tit. 12, c. 7. For a discussion of the act, see Warner, *The Uniform Arrest Act*, 28 VA. L. REV. 315 (1942).

[2] The American Law Institute has currently under consideration a project to formulate a Model Law of Arrest, Search and Seizure.

[3] Apparently the case law development may be thought adequate so far as the development of the law of torts is concerned. See HARPER & JAMES, THE LAW OF TORTS §3.18, at 275 (1956): "The law of arrest represents the compromise between two conflicting interests of the highest order—the interest in personal liberty and the interest in apprehension of criminals. It represents one of the most successful efforts of the common law to accommodate itself both to the needs of society and of its individual members."

[4] See for example, 2 LOS ANGELES POLICE DEP'T DAILY TRAINING BULLETIN 126 (1950). The practice in Philadelphia is discussed in Note, *Philadelphia Police Practice and the Law of Arrest*, 100 U. PA. L. REV. 1182, 1203 (1952).

Even the issue of the right to stop and question a suspect is typically avoided with the result that this most common, most important law enforcement practice is neither condemned nor sanctioned in most jurisdictions. For example, in a recent case in the United States Supreme Court the majority of the Court held that the issue of the right to stop and question is identical with the issue of the right to take a person into custody.[5] While the law might properly take the position that there is no right to stop and question a suspect unless adequate grounds for arrest exist, this conclusion ought not be based upon the uncritical assumption that the questions lack important differences.

The individual who desires to challenge the right of a law enforcement officer to stop and question, frisk, or arrest him can do so by bringing a tort action against the officer. Typically, the cause of action will be for the intentional tort of false imprisonment. If the officer is to escape liability he must do so upon one of two grounds: (a) there was no confinement without the consent of the plaintiff and thus no imprisonment at all; or (b) the officer was privileged to confine the plaintiff under the existing circumstances. The only privilege category generally recognized is the privilege which an officer has to make a lawful arrest.[6] In this situation counsel for the police officer is therefore likely

to argue either that there was no confinement without consent or that adequate grounds for an arrest existed and thus the conduct was privileged. Whatever the decision of the court, the central problem is avoided. There still is no basis for knowing whether there are circumstances in which an officer can confine a suspect for a short period of time in order to question him when the person does not consent and there are not adequate grounds to make an immediate arrest. As a consequence current practice continues without effective guidance from the law.

Generalization is thus made difficult by the ambiguity brought about by the failure of current law to deal adequately with important current enforcement problems like the right to stop and question a suspect or to frisk a suspect thought to be armed and dangerous. The English, if one may judge from Lord Justice Devlin's writings,[7] take pride in their ability to have a responsible law enforcement program with a minimum of formal written legal rules. In the United States it is generally assumed that the written rule of law is an essential method of controlling the exercise of governmental power, and that the principle of government by law requires that reliance upon legal rules be the dominant method of control. Although this is so, a careful look at the law of arrest discloses a situation of ambiguity so great that there are wide areas of discretion largely untouched by legal rules. As a consequence, there is in fact a delegation of immense power and responsibility to law enforcement agencies whose actions are left largely uncontrolled by the formal legal system.

One other preliminary matter should be mentioned. In talking about the law of arrest, one cannot help but envy those foreign participants who are here from countries where there is a single uni-

---

[5] Henry v. United States, 361 U.S. 98 (1959). Compare Mr. Justice Burton, concurring in Brinegar v. U.S., 338 U.S. 160, 179 (1949): "Government agents are commissioned to represent the interests of the public in the enforcement of the law and this requires affirmative action not only when there is reasonable ground for an arrest or probable cause for a search, but when there is reasonable ground for an investigation."

[6] The dilemma created by attempting to make the concept of "arrest" fit all situations in which police conduct interferes with individual liberty is apparent in the literature. It is often asserted that the term "arrest" refers to a privilege which may be asserted as a defense in an action for false imprisonment or battery against an officer. In this context arrest is said to require a purpose to take the arrested person before a court. See for example HARPER & JAMES, THE LAW OF TORTS §3.18, at 285 (1956). On the other hand, it is sometimes assumed that calling police behavior an arrest is essential if the officer is to be held liable for his misconduct. See Note, *Philadelphia Police Practice and the Law of Arrest*, 100 U. PA. L. REV. 1182, 1186 (1952): "By a literal application of the narrower definition, a search of the person, detention for questioning and in-

vestigation and wholesale round-ups of suspects would not be arrests. *This means that the police may engage in such activities without being subject to the sanctions for an unlawful arrest.*" (Emphasis added.)

People v. Esposito, 194 N.Y.S. 326, 332 (1922): "Any restraint of liberty is an arrest."

[7] DEVLIN, THE CRIMINAL PROSECUTION IN ENGLAND (New Haven: Yale University Press, 1958).

form law throughout the entire jurisdiction. It is difficult when dealing with 50 separate states and the federal government to avoid generalizations so broad that they overlook significant local variations. On the other hand, concentration upon detailed local variations is not possible here. Therefore it is, I think, helpful to try to generalize, even at the risk of over-generalization, in order to provide a framework for the discussions which will follow.

## THE LAW OF ARREST

### Arrest With a Warrant

In the United States an arrest may be made with or without a warrant. An arrest warrant may be issued by a magistrate on a showing of probable cause to believe that the suspect is guilty of a crime.[8] In most states, the warrant may be issued on the basis of information and belief.[9] In theory the issuance of warrants is a judicial function,[10] although in some states a warrant may be issued by the prosecuting attorney.[11] In practice it is

[8] A.L.I. CODE OF CRIMINAL PROCEDURE §2 (1931).

[9] In some states information and belief is clearly sufficient to support the issuance of a warrant. See for example WIS. STAT. §954.02 (1957). In other states, there seems to be a requirement of direct information similar to that required for a search warrant.

Perhaps the most accurate generalization is that the officer applying for the warrant must either have actual knowledge or must disclose to the magistrate the source of his information so that the magistrate can make an independent assessment of its adequacy. Giordenello v. United States, 357 U.S. 480 (1958).

[10] Giordenello v. United States, 357 U.S. 48 (1958): ". . . inferences from the facts [are to be] drawn by a neutral and detached magistrate instead of being judged by the officer engaged in the often competitive enterprise of ferreting out crime."

[11] See for example WIS. STAT. §954.01 (1957). There is no clear concensus as to what function the warrant should serve. This was pointed out thirty years ago by Alfred Bettman in his REPORT ON PROSECUTION FOR THE NATIONAL COMMISSION ON LAW OBSERVANCE AND ENFORCEMENT at p. 88 where, in commenting upon prior surveys, he says: "None of the surveys, however, searchingly face, either in the gathering of the data or in the discussion, this problem of whose function it should be to determine the institution of prosecution and what should be the working methods and principles which govern its administration. Should the clerk of court be the official in whom this function is placed, using clerical methods, or the prosecuting attorney using methods appropriate to that office, or the magistrate using methods of a judicial nature?"

largely a ministerial function, performed as a matter of routine by a clerk, with nothing which could properly be called judicial review of the decision to arrest.

The warrant is utilized today primarily where it serves some administrative function such as making a record of the decision to arrest where the suspect's whereabouts are unknown, or where he is outside the county or the state and the warrant is a prerequisite to an arrest by officers of the other jurisdiction. The warrant may also be issued prior to arrest when the decision to prosecute actually precedes the decision to arrest. This is true, for example, in non-support and in bad check cases where the prosecutor actually makes the decision as to whether the criminal process ought to be invoked, and this decision, reflected by the issuance of a warrant, precedes the arrest. This occurs also in cases involving difficult legal questions like sale of obscene literature or negligent homicide. In these cases, the police may prefer that, before the offender is taken into custody, a legally trained official make the decision as to whether the crime has been committed. However, the common situation is one where the police act first, by arresting a suspect, and then present the case to the prosecutor for his decision as to whether to proceed further. In this situation, the arrest is typically made without a warrant.

### Arrest Without a Warrant

In dealing with the law relating to arrest without a warrant, a distinction must be drawn between an arrest for a felony and an arrest for a misdemeanor.

The law relating to felonies is more consistent and easier to state. Generally it may be said that an arrest may be made for a felony whenever a police officer has reasonable grounds to believe that a felony has been committed and that the person to be arrested has committed it.[12] There is indication in some legislation that it is proper to arrest a person who has in fact committed a felony, apparently without regard to whether the officer has knowledge which makes it reasonable for him to

[12] A.L.I. CODE OF CRIMINAL PROCEDURE §21 (1931); Perkins, *The Law of Arrest*, 25 IOWA L. REV. 210, 233 (1940). CAL. PENAL CODE §836.

conclude that the individual has committed a felony.[13] It is clear, however, that the fact that the person is actually guilty of the felony will not justify a *search* if there are no reasonable grounds to believe him guilty of the felony at the time the arrest is made.[14] Probably the effect of these statutes is to preclude tort liability on the part of the officer when the arrested person is in fact guilty though the officer has no reasonable basis for concluding this at the time of the arrest.[15] This is another instance of the failure to make important distinctions; here, the statutes neglect the difference between the power of the officer to make an arrest and the right of an individual to a civil recovery against the officer. To assert that a person who is actually guilty of a felony has no right of recovery against an arresting officer does not require the enactment of legislation giving an officer the power to arrest a person, actually guilty, where there are no reasonable grounds to justify the officer's belief.

It is more difficult to generalize about the situation in regard to the law relating to misdemeanor arrests. There are at least three identifiable views:

(1) An arrest for a misdemeanor may be made without a warrant only when a misdemeanor amounting to a breach of the peace is committed in the presence of the officer.[16] It is typically held that an offense is committed "within the presence" when the officer can detect its commission by the use of his senses, including the senses of hearing and smelling as well as seeing the elements of the offense.[17]

(2) The law of some jurisdictions provides a somewhat broader right of arrest, allowing an arrest for *any* misdemeanor, not only a breach of

peace, committed in the presence of the officer.[18]

(3) Finally, some few states allow an officer to arrest for a misdemeanor whenever he has reasonable grounds to believe that a misdemeanor has been committed. Typically these statutes require a further showing that the officer had reasonable grounds to believe that an arrest was necessary in order to prevent additional harm or to prevent the escape of the person reasonably suspected of having committed the misdemeanor.[19]

This general legislation is, in most states, modified by specific legislation either increasing or contracting a power of arrest depending on what kind of officers are involved and in some instances depending upon what kind of offense the arrested person is suspected of having committed.[20]

## The Right of the Police to Stop and Question a Suspect

It is obvious that an officer may ask an individual a question and not subject himself to a risk of liability provided that he does not confine or restrain the individual without his consent.[21] More difficult is the question whether the officer can, under circumstances where grounds for arrest are lacking, by force or display of authority confine or restrain an individual for a brief period of time for the purpose of questioning him.

There is no doubt that it is common police practice to stop and question suspects as to whom there are no sufficient grounds for arrest.[22] In

---

[13] See for example A.L.I. CODE OF CRIMINAL PROCEDURE §21(b) (1931): "When the person to be arrested has committed a felony, although not in the presence of the officer."

[14] People v. Brown, 45 Cal.2d 640, 290 P.2d 528 (1955).

[15] HARPER & JAMES, THE LAW OF TORTS §3.18, at 280 (1956).

[16] RESTATEMENT, TORTS §121 (1934), stating the common law view.

[17] McBride v. U.S., 284 Fed. 416 (5th Cir. 1922); Dilger v. Commonwealth, 88 Ky. 550, 11 S.W. 651 (1889).

[18] A.L.I. CODE OF CRIMINAL PROCEDURE §21(a) (1931); CAL. PENAL CODE §836.

[19] WIS. STAT. §954.03 (1957).

[20] For a careful study of the situation in one state, see Comment, *Arrest Without Warrant in Wisconsin*, 1959 WIS. L. REV. 489.

[21] Note, *Arrest—Stopping and Questioning as an Arrest*, 37 MICH. L. REV. 311 (1938). The police may properly ask a person to accompany them to the station, and if the suspect consents there is no confinement without consent. Gunderson v. Struebing 125 Wis. 173, 104 N.W. 149 (1905).

[22] Note, *Philadelphia Police Practice and the Law of Arrest*, 100 U. PA. L. REV. 1182, 1205 (1952). Although the practice is well known, it is difficult to document. Police manuals often ignore the problem or deal with the matter ambiguously, in this respect probably reflecting the ambiguity of current law. A study of 26 police manuals from cities of varying size shows the following results:

some instances this can be justified on the basis of some statutory privilege, other than arrest, such as the privilege to stop a vehicle for the purpose of examining a driver's license.[23] In many instances, however, there is no specific statutory privilege, and thus the issue remains as to whether the police have the right to stop and question a suspect, without his consent, in the absence of grounds for an arrest. Despite the importance of

the question in day-to-day enforcement, it is difficult to give a clear answer in most jurisdictions.[24] The problem has been largely ignored by commentators[25] and dealt with ambiguously by most courts, in part at least because it is assumed that the issue is whether there were adequate grounds for arrest.[26] In a recent case,[27] the United States Supreme Court was urged to give explicit recognition to the right of police to stop and question persons suspected of crime. The government argued that

"Being stopped by a police officer for purposes of inquiry may at times cause some inconvenience to the person stopped, but that temporary

(1) Thirteen of the manuals make no reference to questioning suspicious persons.

(2) Six of the manuals assume the necessity for questioning but do not attempt to define when questioning is proper.

(3) Seven of the manuals assume the necessity for questioning and make an effort to define the circumstances in which questioning should be conducted. Illustrative of these is the Denver, Colorado, manual: "4. Patrol Procedures.... 17 Suspicious persons and known criminals should be carefully observed and interrogated if circumstances warrant such action.... 18 A suspicious person is one whose actions, appearance, or very presence in certain places at late or unusual hours would normally excite the suspicions of an ordinarily prudent person. An officer armed with knowledge gained by experience and guided by information concerning the amount and type of crime being committed on his beat, or in his precinct, would be justified if he were more suspicious than the ordinary citizen."

See similar provisions in: (a) Honolulu, Hawaii, RULES AND REGULATIONS OF THE POLICE DEPT. under Duties of the Policeman: #17, 19, and 33, p. 57; (b) Topeka, Kansas, POLICE DEPT. MANUAL OF REGULATIONS under "Duties of the Patrolman" §7, p. 52; (c) Detroit, Michigan, REVISED DETROIT POLICE MANUAL, 1958, Ch. 16 (arrest) §25; (d) Harrisburg, Pa., RULES AND REGULATIONS OF BUREAU OF POLICE p. 29 under "Valuable Information for Policemen"; (e) Salt Lake City, POLICE DEPT. MANUAL, Ch. 14 #38; (f) MILWAUKEE POLICE DEPT. RULES AND REGULATIONS, Rule 29, §24, Rule 14, §§17, 18.

Police training material tends to be unduly limited in its objective, instructing the officer how to question but not when it is proper to question. There are, however, exceptions, as in LOS ANGELES POLICE DEPT. DAILY TRAINING BULLETIN 123 (1958): "There is no hard and fast rule which will determine when a field interrogation should be made. The decision to interrogate must be based on the circumstances of each individual case. Generally, the circumstances will involve time, place, appearance, and actions of a person. When one or more of these elements appears to be out of the ordinary, it may indicate that an interrogation should be made."

See also MILWAUKEE POLICE TRAINING SCHOOL BULLETIN, "Field Interrogation" (1954).

[23] Perkins, *The Law of Arrest*, 25 IOWA L. REV. 201, 207 (1940); DONIGAN & FISHER, KNOW THE LAW 228 *et seq.* (1957).

[24] Warner, *The Uniform Arrest Act*, 28 VA. L. REV. 315, 319 (1942). One reason for the failure to deal with the issue is suggested by Kaufman, J. in United States v. Bonanno, 180 F. Supp. 71, 78 (S.D.N.Y. 1960): "I believe the relative dearth of authority in point can be explained by the fact that few litigants have ever seriously contended that it was illegal for an officer to stop and question a person unless he had 'probable cause' for a formal arrest."

The right of an officer to stop and question a suspect is not dealt with in the RESTATEMENT OF TORTS or treatises in that field presumably because the question is seldom dealt with in appellate litigation.

[25] There are apparently only two efforts to deal explicitly with the issue: Note, *Arrest—Stopping and Questioning as an Arrest*, 37 MICH. L. REV. 311 (1938); DONIGAN & FISHER, KNOW THE LAW 228 *et. seq.* (1957). See also Waite, *The Law of Arrest*, 24 TEX. L. REV. 275, 279 (1946), and Warner, *The Uniform Arrest Act*, 28 VA. L. REV. 315, 318 (1942), both of whom assert that a detention for purposes of questioning is probably illegal unless grounds for arrest exist. In Perkins, *The Law of Arrest*, 25 IOWA L. REV. 201, 261 (1940), it is said that an officer ought to have the right to question when sufficient grounds for arrest exist. In BRISTOW, FIELD INTERROGATION 6 (1958), it is said that an officer may question anyone who arouses suspicion.

[26] In Henry v. United States, 361 U.S. 98 (1959), F.B.I. agents stopped a vehicle in which suspects whom the agents had under surveillance were riding. The government and the majority of the Court assumed that the legality of the stopping had to be determined according to whether adequate grounds for arrest existed at the time of the stopping. Justice Clark, joined by Chief Justice Warren, took the position that there were adequate grounds for further investigation which justified stopping the vehicle: "The earlier events certainly disclosed ample grounds to justify the following of the car, the subsequent stopping thereof, and the questioning of petitioner by the agents. This interrogation, together with the sighting of the cartons and the labels gave the agents indisputable probable cause for the search and arrest." *Id.* at 106.

[27] Rios v. United States, 364 U.S. 253 (1960).

inconvenience is normally minor compared to the importance of such reasonable inquiry to effective law enforcement. Without the power, for example, to stop a suspiciously-acting automobile to ask questions, the police might be forced to spend fruitless hours investigating actions which the occupant, had the police been able to ask him questions, could readily have explained as being entirely innocent. In a fair balancing of the interest at stake, we submit that the rights of the person questioned are adequately protected by his privilege not to answer and that the police, having reasonable grounds for inquiry, ought not to be foreclosed from at least the opportunity, by asking questions, to determine whether further investigation is necessary."[28]

The court dealt with the issue with traditional ambiguity, returning the case to the trial court to determine when the arrest was made without giving explicit attention at all to the issue of whether a right to stop and question exists apart from arrest and, if it does, within what kinds of limitations. The prosecution's suggestion that the test should be "reasonable grounds for inquiry" was neither accepted nor rejected.[29]

State courts are in disagreement as to whether there is a right to detain a person for purposes of questioning prior to arrest. The issue has been most often dealt with in California, where the courts have typically recognized the right to question.[30] Some other state courts have had less occasion to consider the question but have given some indication that police may stop and question under circumstances in which an arrest would be improper.[31] Finally, a group of state court decisions reject the right to detain for questioning unless there are grounds for arrest.[32]

Questioning by an officer may produce sufficient additional information to justify an arrest. It is not clear whether a refusal to answer can be given weight in determining whether grounds for arrest exist.[33] The answer would seem to depend upon whether a court considers the privilege against self-incrimination to apply to on-the-street-questioning and, if it does, whether it requires excluding a refusal to answer from the issue of arrest as well as from the issue of guilt or innocence. Here, too, current law is ambiguous.[34] A refusal to answer seems relevant as a matter of substantive law in vagrancy cases where being "unable to account for his presence" is an element of the offense.[35]

---

[28] Brief for United States, p. 11, Rios v. United States, 364 U.S. 253 (1960).

[29] The fact that the case was returned to the trial court to determine when the arrest was made may imply that the prior stopping and questioning were proper, assuming the officer did not intend, at that time, to take the suspect into custody. Yet this is not made explicit, and it is not at all clear what test the trial judge should apply in determining when the arrest took place.
This issue was dealt with more explicitly in United States v. Bonanno, 180 F. Supp. 71 (S.D.N.Y. 1960), where Judge Kaufman stated, "Not every temporary restriction of absolute freedom of movement is an illegal police action demanding suppression of all resultant evidence."

[30] The leading case, upon which later decisions rely, is Gisske v. Sanders, 9 Cal. App. 13, 98 Pac. 43 (1908).

See also People v. Simon, 45 Cal.2d 645, 290 P.2d 531 (1955); People v. Jones, 1 Cal. R. 210, —— Cal. App. 2d —— (1960); People v. Jackson, 164 Cal. App. 2d 759, 331 P.2d 63 (1958); People v. Ambrose, 155 Cal. App. 2d 513, 318 P.2d 181 (1957); People v. Blodgett, 46 Cal.2d 114, 293 P.2d 57 (1956); People v. Martin, 46 Cal.2d 106, 293 P.2d 52 (1956); People v. West, 144 Cal. App. 2d 214, 300 P.2d 729 (1956); People v. Jiminez, 143 Cal. App. 2d 671 (1956).

[31] People v. Henneman 367 Ill. 151, 10 N.E.2d 649 (1937); People v. Mirbelle, 276 Ill. App. 533 (1934); State v. Hatfield, 112 W. Va. 424, 164 S.E. 518 (1932); State v. Zupan, 155 Wash. 80, 283 Pac. 671 (1929); Pena v. State, 11 Tex. Cr. 218 (1929); State v. Gulcznski, 32 Del. 120, 120 Atl. 88 (1922).

[32] People v. Esposito, 118 Misc. 867, 194 N.Y. Supp. 326 (1922); Arnold v. State, 255 App. Div. 422, 8 N.Y.S.2d 28 (1938); People v. Tinston, 6 Misc.2d 485, 163 N.Y.S.2d 544 (1951); Commonwealth v. Balanzo, 261 Pa. 507 (1918); Commonwealth v. Doe, 109 Pa. Sup. 187, 167 A.2d 241 (1953); Travis v. Bacherig, 7 Tenn. App. 638 (1928); Shirey v. State, 321 P.2d 981 (Okla. Cr. 1958), noted in Bandy, *Power of Police Officer to Detain for Investigation*, 11 OKLA. L. REV. 320 (1958).

[33] In People v. Simon, 290 P.2d 531 (Cal. 1955), the court said: "There is, of course, nothing unreasonable in an officer's questioning persons outdoors at night . . . and it is possible that in some circumstances even a refusal to answer would, in the light of other evidence, justify an arrest . . . ."

[34] See MORGAN, MAGUIRE & WEINSTEIN, CASES AND MATERIALS ON EVIDENCE 763 n.3 (1957).

[35] WIS. STAT. §947.02(2) (1957).

## The Right to Frisk a Suspect

If the right to stop and question a suspect is recognized, then it follows that the officer ought to be allowed to frisk, under some circumstances at least, to insure that the suspect is not possessed of a dangerous weapon which would put the safety of the officer in peril.[36]

Certainly it is current practice to frisk some suspects as to whom there are not sufficient grounds for arrest. The Training Bulletin of the Los Angeles Department states:

"Although persons may appear to be logical suspects for interrogation, they often prove to be innocent of any crime. Unless the interrogation is to be more than a casual conversation, an officer should not place his hands on the person questioned. However, if there is any reason to believe that a suspect is armed, he should be searched immediately for offensive weapons. It is seldom advisable to make a 'wall shakedown' immediately upon contacting an individual, unless he is known to be, or suspected of being, an armed or dangerous criminal. After a short explanation, the average innocent citizen will usually be able to comprehend the reason for a field interrogation, but he will seldom be convinced of the necessity for a 'wall shakedown.' "[37]

Usually courts which have recognized a privilege to stop and question a suspect have also recognized the right of the officer to frisk the suspect if the officer has reason to believe him dangerous.[38] This is specifically provided for in the Uniform Arrest Act.[39] On the other hand, it is frequently assumed that frisking is illegal unless, at the time, there were sufficient grounds for arrest.[40]

## Limitations Upon the Right to Stop, Question, and Frisk

There is increasing concern with the question of when it is proper to subject an individual to the inconvenience of a reasonable investigation to determine whether he is guilty of crime. If it is assumed that there is no right to question, for example, unless there are grounds for arrest, then the issue is resolved. But, if it is assumed that there is a right to question in situations where there is no right of arrest, these situations must then be defined. No one, I think, would assert that questioning should be completely indiscriminate.

[36] See Hall, *Police and Law in a Democratic Society*, 28 IND. L. J. 133, 158 (1953); Note, *Philadelphia Police Practice and the Law of Arrest*, 100 U. PA. L. REV. 1182, 1204 (1952).

[37] LOS ANGELES POLICE DEPARTMENT DAILY TRAINING BULLETIN 126 (1958). Typically police manuals are ambiguous as to when a right to frisk exists, often reflecting the ambiguity of the law. Often it is not clear whether the right is said to exist only where an arrest could be made. See ATLANTA, GA., POLICE DEP'T. RULES AND REGULATIONS, Rule 539, p. 65; SAN FRANCISCO RULES AND PROC. POLICE DEP'T. 12–13; MICH. STATE POLICE, RULES AND REGULATIONS, p. 35 sec. 5; DETROIT, MICH., REV. DETROIT POLICE MANUAL (1958) ch. 16, sec. 41; RALEIGH, N.C., MANUAL POLICE DEP'T. ch. 8, §2. Training materials stress methods of frisking, without treating the issue of when it is proper to frisk. See PHILA. POLICE ACADEMY TRAINING PAMPHLETS, vol. 6, pamphlets 2, 11, and 16; CHICAGO POLICE DEP'T. INSTRUCTOR'S MANUAL—POLICE TRAINING DIVISION (1958); PEACE OFFICERS' TRAINING SCHOOL REPORT (Kansas) (1960) at pp. 19–20.

[38] See for example Gisske v. Sanders, 9 Cal. App. 13, 98 Pac. 43 (1908): "The officers did nothing which the plaintiff did not desire, except the examination of his person to see if he carried concealed weapons. This, however, was a precaution which the officer might well take under the circumstances of the meeting and the conduct of the plaintiff whether the plaintiff was under arrest or not."

See also People v. Martin, 46 Cal.2d 106, 293 P.2d 52 (1956); People v. Jones, 1 Cal. R. 210, —— Cal. App. 2d —— (1960); People v. Jackson, 164 Cal. App. 2d 759, 308 P.2d 38 (1958); People v. Brittain, 149 Cal. App. 2d 201 (1957); People v. Jiminez, 143 Cal. App. 2d 671, 300 P.2d 38 (1956).

[39] Warner, *The Uniform Arrest Act*, 28 VA. L. REV. 315, 324–327 (1942): "Section 3. Searching for Weapons. Persons Who Have Not Been Arrested. A peace officer may search for a dangerous weapon any person whom he has stopped or detained to question as provided in section 2, whenever he has reasonable ground to believe that he is in danger if the person possesses a dangerous weapon."

[40] See People v. Esposite, 194 N.Y. Supp. 326 (1922); People v. DiDanna, 210 N.Y. Supp. 135 (1925). See CAL. PENAL CODE §833 (1958). This statute authorizes frisking where grounds for arrest exist even though an arrest has not been made. It casts some doubt upon earlier California cases which held that frisking was proper in some circumstances where grounds for arrest did not exist.

Perhaps the test should depend upon the seriousness of the suspected offense. This has been suggested by Mr. Justice Jackson:

"If we assume, for example, that a child is kidnapped and the officers throw a roadblock about the neighborhood and search every outgoing car, it would be drastic and undiscriminating use of the search. The officers might be unable to show probable cause for searching any particular car. However, I should candidly strive hard to sustain such an action, executed fairly and in good faith, because it might be reasonable to subject travelers to that indignity if it was the only way to save a threatened life and detect a vicious crime. But I should not strain to sustain such a roadblock and universal search to salvage a few bottles of bourbon and catch a bootlegger."[41]

It is not an easy task to develop a verbal formula to describe the probability of guilt requisite for stopping and questioning, assuming the objective is less than the "reasonable grounds to believe" typically required for arrest, but more than the mere good faith suspicion of the officer. Development of an adequate formula is particularly difficult if the sliding scale suggested by Justice Jackson is followed. The Uniform Arrest Act proposes "reasonable ground to suspect."[42] In *Rios v. United States*,[43] the government argued that questioning should be proper where an officer has "reasonable grounds for inquiry."[44] The need is for a test clear enough for day-to-day enforcement and adequate enough to reflect the need to balance the nature of the interference with the individual involved against the risk created by the suspected conduct. The obvious difficulty of the task does not justify the easy alternative of ignoring the issue.

## MAJOR CURRENT ISSUES

There are a number of very important current

[41] Brinegar v. United States, 338 U.S. 160, 183 (1948).
[42] Warner, *The Uniform Arrest Act*, 28 VA. L. REV. 315, 320 (1942).
[43] 364 U.S. 253 (1960).
[44] Brief for United States, p. 11, Rios v. United States, 364 U.S. 253 (1960).

issues relating to the right of police to detain, to frisk and to arrest persons suspected of crime. It may be helpful to try to enumerate these issues, some of which have already been discussed:

(1) Can a suspect be detained for purposes of questioning on the basis of less evidence of guilt than is necessary to justify his arrest? If so, how much evidence of guilt is needed to make it proper for an officer to stop and question a suspect? This important law enforcement issue too often has been ignored entirely or dealt with ambiguously.

(2) How great a probability of guilt should the law require before allowing the police to make an arrest without a warrant? It is safe to assume that the "in presence" requirement involves the highest probability of guilt of the alternatives, since the officer must actually observe something which he reasonably concludes to be a crime being committed in his presence. If he is to arrest for a misdemeanor not committed in his presence, he must get a warrant. This requirement would have meaning if there were in fact a judicial review of his decision to arrest; but where the issuance of the warrant is in ministerial function, it is not apparent what purpose is served by this process except perhaps a delay in the decision to arrest and, as a result, more reflection than would take place if the arrest were made immediately. Statutes allowing police to arrest upon reasonable grounds to believe the suspect guilty of any crime have been in existence sufficiently long to make it possible to assess their effect in current administration and to make meaningful evaluation of the alternatives.

(3) Does the "reasonable ground to believe" requirement for arrest necessitate as much evidence of guilt as is required to charge a person with a crime and hold him for trial? Some courts have at least implied that the requirements are the same. For example, the United States Supreme Court said in the *Mallory* case:

"Presumably, whomever the police arrest they must arrest on "probable cause." It is not the function of the police to arrest, as it were, at large and to use an interrogating process at police headquarters in order to determine whom they should charge before a committing magistrate."[45]

However, subsequent to the *Mallory* case, a majority opinion of the Court of Appeals for the District of Columbia, in applying the *Mallory* Rule, assumed the contrary to be true:

"A vital factor to bear in mind is that as these steps progress the burden of the law enforcement agency increases. What may constitute probable cause for arrest does not necessarily constitute probable cause for a charge on arraignment."[46]

The issue is an obviously important one, in terms of both the standard for arrest and the right of police to interrogate a suspect between the time of his arrest and his initial appearance before a magistrate. As to some offenses, there is no problem. For example, an arrest is not made for non-support unless there is adequate evidence to warrant charging and conviction. As to other offenses, however, a difficult problem does exist. For example, it is not uncommon to arrest a number of suspects in an armed robbery case under circumstances in which it would not be proper or desirable to charge each person arrested.[47] In this kind of situation it has been thought proper by most police agencies to arrest on the basis of less evidence than is needed to warrant charging and holding for trial. On the whole, the situation is characterized by unnecessary ambiguity.

(4) When, assuming a person is to be subjected to criminal prosecution, is it necessary to take him into custody immediately? This question is resolved by those statutes which require, in addition to reasonable ground to believe that a misdemeanor has been committed, a showing that there were reasonable grounds to believe that further damage or escape would result unless an arrest were immediately made.[48] However, the "in presence" statutes, although requiring a high probability of guilt, do not in any way require a

showing that immediate custody is necessary. Thus a person who fails to come to a complete stop at a stop sign may be taken into custody though he is a well-known member of the community, and though it is apparent that neither further harm nor escape would be at all likely. Typically an arrest would be made in such a situation only where the officer desired to make a search and used the arrest to legitimize the search. Whatever the merits of allowing a search in such a situation, the obvious consequence is to distort the law of arrest.

Statutes authorizing the use of a summons in lieu of arrest have apparently not been much utilized in practice, in some states at least. Knowledge of why this is so would be helpful in devising workable substitutes for arrest in situations where immediate custody is unnecessary.

(5) What function should the warrant of arrest serve? There is abundant evidence that in current practice the warrant does not serve as a judicial review of the decision to arrest. It is, therefore, important to known precisely what function it does serve and, on the basis of this knowledge, to re-examine legal requirements relating to the issuance and execution of the warrant.

(6) Do police have a right to release a person, once arrested, without charging him? His release may be made because there is insufficient evidence to convict; because subsequent investigation has disclosed the innocence of the person arrested; because charging will not accomplish anything worthwhile, as, for example, in the case of the drunk who is arrested and released when sober;[49] because the arrested person agrees to serve as an informant; or, because the arrest itself has served a deterrent purpose without the necessity of further official action.

It is often asserted that the police must bring an arrested person before a magistrate and that a failure to do so renders the arrest unlawful.[50]

---

[45] Mallory v. United States, 354 U.S. 449, 456 (1957).
[46] Goldsmith v. United States, 277 F.2d 335 (D.C. Cir. 1960).
[47] *Ibid.*
[48] WIS. STAT. (1957) §954.03.

[49] Hall, *Law of Arrest in Relation to Contemporary Social Problems*, 3 U. CHI. L. REV. 345, 354 (1936).
[50] For an able analysis of how the issue of release by the police should be handled in tort, see Bohlen & Shulman, *Effect of Subsequent Misconduct on Lawful Arrest*, 28 CALIF. L. REV. 841 (1928).

Yet the practice is clearly to the contrary, and recent legislative proposals frequently contain provisions legitimizing this practice.

(7) How much discretion should police have in determining what conduct should be subjected to the criminal process, and how should the exercise of that discretion be controlled?[51] It is obvious that arrests are not made for every offense which comes to the attention of the police. So great has been the proliferation of criminal statutes that arrest of all violators would cause a breakdown of the criminal justice system. There must therefore be a limitation upon the number of persons subjected to the criminal process. As a practical matter, this limitation must take place, in large part, at the arrest stage since this is ordinarily the first official decision relating to the offender's conduct. The power and responsibility which this discretion gives police is immense. Too often the existence of this discretion is denied and its

exercise is, therefore, left without guidance and control from the legal system.

These are obviously difficult problems which cannot easily be solved. Adequate solution requires detailed knowledge of current arrest practices and the consequences of those practices in current administration. This is an objective of the American Bar Foundation's Survey of the Administration of Criminal Justice in the United States.[52] The results of the pilot phase of this survey will be published in a year or two.[53] Other research efforts are now in the planning stage. The American Law Institute has tentative plans to prepare a Model Law of Arrest, Search and Seizure which certainly must face these issues and make an effort to resolve them.

Whatever the difficulties, existing legislation can certainly be made more adequate. Police agencies deserve clearer guidance in the discharge of their law enforcement responsibility than is afforded by the law today.

---

[51] See Williams, *Turning a Blind Eye*, 1954 CRIM. L. REV. (N.Y.) 271, where the following view is expressed: "And so to demand that he [the policeman] should exercise some sort of discretion, and refrain from enforcing certain laws is neither fair nor correct. In the first place, it demands of him a judgment and a sense of responsibility which is scarcely reflected in our treatment of him when we fix his salary in relation to that of other public officers. But, more important, such a process must inevitably subject all police activity to the personal likes and dislikes of individual policemen."

For a contrary view see Dunning, *Discretion in Prosecution*, 1 POLICE J. 39, 47 (1928): "But if they [the police] believe that the prosecution is not necessary as an example and warning to others, they may legitimately consider whether the offender may be saved from a repetition of his offense by treating him otherwise than by prosecution."

See also ARNOLD, THE SYMBOLS OF GOVERNMENT 160 (Yale University Press, 1935), where the view is ex-

pressed that discretion in the police is inherent in current administration: "However, so far as the effect of the number of criminal laws on policemen or the prosecutor is concerned, they are more apt to be a help than a hindrance. Such persons are trying to apprehend individuals who at the time happen to be considered dangerous to society, and the wider the selection of laws which they have, the more chance there is of conviction."

[52] The entire cost of the project has been covered by a grant from the Ford Foundation in the amount of $445,000. For a description of the general aims of the research see Remington, *Criminal Justice Research*, 51 J. CRIM. L., C. & P. S. 7 (1960).

[53] For an analysis of some of the data relating to police discretion see Goldstein, *Police Discretion Not To Invoke the Criminal Process: Low Visibility Decisions in the Administration of Justice*, 69 YALE L. J. 543 (1960).

# Police Arrest Privileges in a Free Society: A Plea for Modernization

O. W. WILSON

My title, "Police Arrest Privileges in a Free Society," is merely one summation of the dilemma presented by the fact that you cannot have complete, absolute freedom in a free society when some people are confined or their freedom of movement and conduct is restricted. Doctor Samuel Johnson, some two hundred years ago, stated the dilemma and emphasized its apparent insolubility when he said: "The danger of unbounded liberty and the danger of bounding it have produced a problem in the science of government which human understanding seems hitherto unable to solve." The subjects under discussion in this International Conference seem to indicate that Johnson was being unduly optimistic when he modified his statement by the insertion of the word, "hitherto."

It is my intention, in discussing police arrest privileges, to consider both the danger of unbounded liberty and the danger of bounding it, in the belief that a fair compromise is possible between the two—a compromise that will be to the advantage of a free society. The discussion will be within the framework of our Constitution; its amendment or violation is not proposed. This exclusion of the constitutional guarantees from the discussion cannot be absolute, however, for the reason that the reasonableness of search and seizure is often dependent upon the validity of the arrest.

Our free society has created a system designed to identify and apprehend the person who commits a crime and to give him a fair trial in which the truth of his guilt or innocence is to be established. This system is based on the principle that guilty persons should be adjudged guilty. The trial court is as ethically bound to ascertain the guilt of the guilty as it is to ascertain the innocence of the innocent. Rules that exclude material and relevant facts bearing on the guilt or innocence of the defendant are inconsistent with this principle and with the oath to tell the truth, the whole truth, and nothing but the truth. Since an invalid arrest may result in the exclusion of material and relevant facts, the liberalization of arrest privileges would lessen the likelihood of the exclusion of truth, and would also facilitate the apprehension of criminals and lessen the physical hazards of the police.

The rules that establish the validity of arrest, as well as the other police arrest privileges under discussion, should be established by legislation, as was proposed in 1942 by the Interstate Crime Commission in its Uniform Arrest Act. The courts may then rule on their constitutionality. The decisions would probably be favorable; the provisions of the Uniform Act have not been declared unconstitutional in any of the states that have adopted them.

## THE PROBLEM

Both unbounded liberty and its restriction place basic human rights in jeopardy. Unbounded liberty jeopardizes the security of life and property and, indeed, the security of our free society. Were this not so, there would be no need to place any restrictions on liberty. Restricting liberty, on the other hand, jeopardizes the basic human right to freedom in movement and conduct.

The problem, then, is to prescribe restrictions which will provide an acceptable degree of security without unduly infringing upon individual freedom. The restrictions on liberty now under discussion are adjusted by increasing or decreasing police arrest privileges. They must be so regulated that the price paid in inconvenience and restraint has an equal compensating value in the advantages of greater security. To keep the scales of justice in balance, the advantages to a free society resulting from a reasonable degree of security in one pan must hold in precise equilibrium the other containing the disadvantages that result from restrictions.

This means compromise; some liberty must be sacrificed for the sake of security. A compromise is a modification of opposing views so that they may blend to the mutual satisfaction of the opponents. The opponents in the issue under discussion are not the assailant and his victim but instead law abiding citizens who differ in their appraisals of the danger of unbounded liberty on the one hand and the danger of bounding it on the other. The issue is not simplified by the fact that both groups would like to have at the same time both complete security and complete liberty. The impossibility of achieving both desires simultaneously is recognized, and each group makes a compromise it believes will provide a suitable balance between maximum security and minimum restriction on liberty. Were the appraisals by the groups identical, the problem would be solved. Since opposing groups make different appraisals, a reconciliation of the opposing views must be sought.

## WHO SHOULD ARBITRATE?

Compromise is a characteristic of a free society, the strength of which is derived from consolidating the most acceptable features of opposing views into a workable system. In compromise, each side appraises what it gains in advantage against what it loses in disadvantage; there is then a measure of give and take. The appraisal in a free society is participated in by the citizens with the legislature serving as the arbitrator to say, "This is the way it will be." This democratic process enables citizens to have their desires implemented by law.

In the absence of legislation bearing on some aspect of police arrest privileges, the appellate courts may make decisions that are as binding in their effect as legislative enactments. The process which results in an appellate decision is markedly different from the legislative process. The issue before the court relates to the rights of the appellant, who has been judged guilty by the most liberal system of criminal justice found anywhere in the world. The court considers whether the rights of the appellant have been violated, not by organized society, but by a policeman whose actions are often viewed with distaste because all of the facts which may have justified the action are not on the record. The court ponders the alleged infringement of the rights of the convicted person as a legal abstraction and feels obliged to consider the question as it would apply were the individual innocent. Finally, the desires of the general public for some reasonable measure of security and for a redress of the wrong done to the innocent victim of the criminal are not made known nor are they readily available to the court.

The issue before us does not jeopardize the integrity of the Constitution. Instead, it involves an appraisal of relative dangers, of advantages arrayed against disadvantages, which result from restrictions on liberty imposed by police arrest privileges. Statesmen representative of the people seem better qualified to make fair appraisals of public needs than appellate judges who, by virtue of their positions, are not so responsive to the desires of the public. The fundamental question is not a legal one after its constitutionality has been established. Instead, it is a philosophical problem in the science of government.

## APPRAISAL OF THREATS TO SECURITY

It is apparent that equilibrium in the scales of justice may necessitate adjustment of the weight in one pan to compensate for a change in weight in the other. Should reasonable security be jeopardized by an increase in criminality, further restrictions on liberty may be justified. On the other hand, a society that has minimum criminality may enjoy maximum liberty.

An accurate and valid comparison of the crime

frequency of this country with that of other countries is not possible today, but analysis and fair interpretation of available statistics lead to the conclusion that our country is among those having the highest crime rates. This fact in itself is apparently not alarming to a people accustomed to excel in industrial production, in standard of living—and in liberty.

Some cause for concern is found, however, in that the extent of criminality in our country is not remaining constant at this excessively high level. Instead, it is increasing at an alarming rate year by year. For example, the frequency of those crimes categorized by the F.B.I. as "Part I crimes" increased four times more rapidly than the population of this country during the first seven years of this decade.

In 1958, the F.B.I. adopted a new crime index which differed from the previously used Part I crimes by the exclusion of negligent manslaughter, statutory rape, and larceny under $50. This new and more accurate index revealed that crime increased five times more rapidly than population from 1957 to 1958.

Reports for the first nine months of 1959 from cities with a total population of 69 million showed an overall decrease of 1% in the number of crimes from the comparable 1958 statistics. It seems unwise to conclude from these incomplete figures, however, that the upward crime trend has been halted.

During the past decade, the police of this country have been strengthened in number, in training, and in equipment. They are better organized and are using more progressive procedures to prevent crime and to apprehend criminals than ever before in their history. Crime increases during the past decade have not resulted from a decrease in police effectiveness; they must be accounted for by other factors.

The effectiveness of a free society in controlling criminals may be measured in part by its success in convicting defendants. Comparison of 1957 and 1958 conviction rates with the average for the previous five-year periods in offenses included in the new crime index (excluding forcible rape, for which statistics are not available prior to 1958) and in four other classes of crimes (stolen property

PROPORTION OF PERSONS CHARGED WHO WERE CONVICTED, 1957 AND 1958
COMPARED WITH PREVIOUS 5-YEAR AVERAGES

| | Percentage of Convictions | | | | | |
|---|---|---|---|---|---|---|
| | 1952–56 Average | 1957 | Per Cent Change | 1953–57 Average | 1958 | Per Cent Change |
| Murder and nonnegligent manslaughter | 59.8 | 67.6 | +13.0 | 62.2 | 59.5 | −4.3 |
| Robbery | 76.7 | 62.3 | −18.8 | 74.0 | 60.8 | −17.8 |
| Aggravated Assault | 50.3 | 41.2 | −18.1 | 48.5 | 41.8 | −13.8 |
| Burglary—breaking and entering | 75.0 | 66.6 | −11.2 | 72.8 | 67.8 | −6.9 |
| Larceny—theft | 75.4 | 70.2 | −6.9 | 74.2 | 71.0 | −4.3 |
| Auto theft | 64.7 | 62.3 | −3.7 | 64.2 | 64.0 | −0.3 |
| Stolen property; buying, receiving | 54.2 | 47.8 | −11.8 | 53.5 | 45.6 | −14.8 |
| Weapons; carrying, possessing, etc. | 75.9 | 63.7 | −16.1 | 73.4 | 63.3 | −13.8 |
| Narcotic drug laws | 69.7 | 71.9 | +3.1 | 70.0 | 65.5 | −6.4 |
| Gambling | 65.2 | 45.4 | −30.4 | 63.1 | 45.1 | −28.5 |
| Total | 666.9 | 599.0 | −10.2 | 655.9 | 584.4 | −10.9 |

Note: Rape not included because statutory rape was excluded from this category in 1958.
Source: FEDERAL BUREAU OF INVESTIGATION, UNIFORM CRIME REPORTS (1952–1958).

offenses, weapons offenses, narcotic law violations, and gambling) reveal a startling trend, as is shown in the table reproduced here.

In each of these crime categories (except homicides and narcotic offenses in 1957), the 1957 and 1958 conviction rates are lower than the average for the preceding five years. In 1957 the conviction rate for robbery, compared to the previous five-year average, decreased 19%; for aggravated assault, 18%; for burglary, 11%; for stolen property offenses, 12%; for weapons offenses, 16%; for gambling, 30%. In 1958, the conviction rate for robbery, compared to the previous five-year average, decreased 18%; for aggravated assault, 14%; for burglary, 7%; for stolen property offenses, 14%; for gambling, 29%; for homicide, 4%; for narcotic offenses, 6%.

Decreases of such magnitude in conviction rates may be taken, with the persistent increase in crime, as a warning that the scales of justice are getting out of balance. Where lies the fault? There is no indication that police procedures used in marshaling evidence against the defendant are becoming less effective; indeed, the reverse seems more likely. Nor does it seem that prosecutors have grown less vigorous or that defense attorneys have suddenly discovered new and more successful techniques. May the explanation be found in the restrictions that have been imposed on the police by appellate decisions?

## THE PLIGHT OF THE POLICE

People on the whole want protection from criminal attack; they want to feel secure in their homes and on the streets from disturbances and molestations. To meet this need, local communities in our free society have created uniformed bodies of police to prevent crimes and to bring to court those who commit them. Responsibility for the prevention of crime rests principally on city police forces, sheriffs' departments, and local detachments of state police.

A crime occurs when a person who desires to commit it discovers the opportunity to do so. Such unwholesome desires spring from and are a measure of criminality. The police cannot prevent the development of criminality, except as their contacts with potential and actual offenders may have this wholesome effect; nor are the police charged with this responsibility. Their basic purpose is to remove or lessen by both physical and psychological means the opportunity to commit crimes.

To prevent crime, the police must either stand guard at every point of possible attack, which is a physical and economic impossibility, or intercept the person with criminal intent before he robs, rapes, or kills. It is better to have an alert police force that prevents the crime than one that devotes its time to seeking to identify the assailant after the life has been taken, the daughter ravished, or the pedestrian slugged and robbed.

The task of the police in preventing crime is quite different from that of identifying the perpetrator and marshaling evidence to prove his guilt. To prevent crime by intercepting the criminal while he seeks his prey is not unlike hunting a predatory animal; prompt and decisive action is called for at a critical moment not of the huntsman's choosing. The policeman who fails to act at the critical moment may nonetheless prevent an impending crime, but the criminal, who more times than not is wanted for previous unsolved crimes, remains at large to continue his depredations. Restrictions on arrest privileges hamper the police not only in preventing crime but also in clearing cases by the arrest of the perpetrator and in marshaling evidence to support prosecution.

The local police feel the restrictions imposed on arrest privileges more keenly than do the specialized police agencies whose principal responsibility is the gathering of evidence to identify and convict persons after they have committed a crime, rather than to prevent the act in the first instance. Frequently the criminal, whose act is within the jurisdiction of a specialized police agency, has already been arrested by local police who often apprehend him in the act or in flight from the crime scene. These are critical moments for police action. In cases where the culprit has not been arrested, the critical moment for arrest can often be set by the specialized police; it is planned after sufficient evidence is marshaled to justify the arrest which is often authorized by warrant. In contrast, most arrests by local police are made without warrant at a critical moment not of their choosing before they have had an opportunity to marshal evidence beyond what they personally observed at the time.

The typical citizen would feel that the police were remiss in their duty should they fail on their own initiative, or refuse on legal grounds, to investigate by questioning a person who was lurking in the neighborhood for no apparent reason. The disturbed citizen would expect the police to discover whether the suspect was armed and, if so, to disarm him and prosecute him should it be discovered that he was carrying the weapon illegally. Should the suspect refuse to explain what he was doing in the neighborhood, and the policeman apologized for questioning him and then went about his duties leaving the suspect to continue his lurking, the citizen would consider that he was not receiving adequate protection.

The typical citizen is surprised when he discovers that in many jurisdictions police arrest privileges are so carefully circumscribed by statutory and case law as to render the policeman virtually powerless to deal effectively and safely with situations that confront him almost hourly during his duty tour. The police action demanded by the citizen from his protector is illegal in many jurisdictions.

The police, under local control as in our form of government, are inclined to provide the protection their citizen-employers demand; otherwise the police fail to prevent crime and are subject to sharp criticism for their failure to protect the public. Also, since they usually act with courtesy, discretion, and good judgment, only infrequently is the legality of their acts questioned, and then by a citizen who fails to understand and appreciate the police motive or by a lawyer who uses the incident in the defense of his guilty client.

The discrepancy between what the people expect the police to do and what the police are privileged to do in protecting public peace and security results principally from a lack of understanding of the police purpose and of what the police must do to accomplish it.

The police must accept some blame for lack of public confidence in the means they use to achieve their purpose. Police abuse of their authority must be eliminated, not by withdrawing essential authority or by freeing the guilty criminal, but by raising police standards to a level of trustworthiness and by some action which will penalize the community that employs an officer who abuses his privileges.

Police leadership has been dilatory in raising service qualifications and ethical standards. However, the police now have an acceptable code of ethics and their qualification standards are being raised from coast to coast. Each local community should insist on improvement in the quality of its police service until all have achieved professional status. The community that is penalized for abuse of arrest privileges will be likely to demand both higher standards and disciplinary action against the offending officer.

Lack of public understanding of the police purpose and what the police must do to accomplish it is accentuated by two circumstances that tend to cast the police in the role of agents bent on unnecessarily oppressing freedom. The first grows out of police responsibility in the enforcement of traffic and other regulatory laws sometimes violated by the most conscientious citizen, an enforcement that aligns good citizens against the police. The other is ignorance of the facts involved in the war against crime in a free society. People are apt to fear and hate what they do not understand— and the hate is often stimulated by traffic violation experiences.

These misunderstandings continue unabated because the police are not a vocal, scholarly group that devotes much time to presenting in a favorable light the facts that bear on the problem. The literature in consequence is principally devoted to the case against the police; little has been written in their defense. The press, the literature, and even case law are all directed at incidents that discredit the police. Small wonder that those who read the papers or research the literature and case law conclude that the police are evil. Information on which a fairer judgment might be based is not generally circulated.

Highly intelligent people ponder the police role as a hypothetical abstraction, in ignorance of the true facts, and conceive the police to be a potential instrument of tyranny which will destroy the essential freedom of a free society. Since their reading and research are restricted to incidents that discredit the police, they conclude that all police are bad. These citizens, as protectors of liberty and freedom, then align themselves against the police without giving attention to the cost of criminal depredations.

There have been exceptions in which men whose integrity and judgment are respected have accompanied the police on their tours of duty in order to learn and report the true facts. Professors John Barker Waite of the University of Michigan Law School and Sam Bass Warner of the Harvard Law School are two examples. Their experiences gave them a sympathetic understanding of the problems confronted by the police in consequence of antiquated rules governing the questioning and detaining of suspects, searching them for weapons when police safety is jeopardized, arresting them when conditions warrant such action, and the right of the suspect under some conditions forcibly to resist arrest by a uniformed policeman. These men have championed in books and articles the liberalization of arrest privileges because through their experiences they have gained a sound understanding of the handicaps of the modern policeman in his legal war against crime. On the basis of his police experiences, Professor Warner played the principal role in drafting the Uniform Arrest Act.

## ESSENTIAL POLICE ARREST PRIVILEGES

Law enforcement may be strengthened by legalizing common police practices, already legal in some jurisdictions, which would have the effect of facilitating the discovery of criminals and evidence of their guilt and of lessening the exclusion of relevant evidence from their trials. The police should be authorized to question persons whose actions under the circumstances then existing are such as to arouse reasonable suspicion that the suspect may be seeking an opportunity to commit a crime. A police officer should be privileged to search such a suspect for weapons when the officer has reasonable grounds to believe that he is in danger if the person possesses a dangerous weapon, and, should the suspect be illegally armed, to arrest him for this offense. Should the suspect be unable or unwilling to explain satisfactorily the reasons for his presence and actions, the officer should be authorized to take him to a police station and hold him while the investigation is continued, for a period of two hours, without placing him under arrest.

The police should be privileged to release an arrested person without bringing him before a magistrate when their investigation reveals his innocence or when a drunk has become sober. The police should be authorized to hold an arrested person before bringing him before a magistrate for at least 24 hours, excluding days when courts are not in session. Magistrates should be authorized to order the defendant to be held for an additional period when good cause for such detention is shown.

A police officer should be authorized to arrest under a warrant when the warrant is not in his possession, to arrest without a warrant for any misdemeanor committed in his presence, and to arrest without a warrant for petty thefts and other misdemeanors not committed in his presence when he has reasonable grounds to believe that the defendant could not be found after the warrant was issued.

Suspects should be denied the right to resist illegal arrest by a person the suspect has reasonable grounds to believe to be a police officer. The police should be authorized and urged to use notices to appear in court in lieu of physical arrest in suitable misdemeanor cases when they believe the defendant will appear as agreed. Persons the police have reasonable grounds to believe to be witnesses to crimes should be legally required to identify themselves to the police.

These are essentially the provisions of the Uniform Arrest Act. To them should be added authority for the police to search any convicted narcotic offender for contraband, without a warrant, when his actions, under the circumstances then existing, are such as to arouse reasonable suspicion that the suspect may have contraband in his possession.

The reasonable arrest privileges mentioned above would facilitate the achievement of objectives in law enforcement desired by all persons except the criminals themselves. The privileges would enable the police to exercise such control over persons in public places as to enhance the peace and security of all citizens.

These privileges do not threaten the lives or health of the innocent; the inconvenience of two hours of detention short of arrest is experienced only by the innocent person who inadvertently or by poor judgment is found in a situation that arouses police suspicion and which the suspect is unable or unwilling to explain on the spot. In view of the present jeopardy to public security, such inconvenience seems a small price to pay for the privilege of living securely and peacefully.

## SAFEGUARDS AGAINST POLICE ABUSE OF AUTHORITY

Police abuse of authority with criminal intent resulting in serious offenses must always be dealt with by criminal prosecution and disciplinary action. Establishing safeguards against abuse of authority by the overzealous policeman in the day-to-day performance of his duty presents quite a different problem. Safeguards that weaken law enforcement or free the guilty are socially undesirable; if possible the problem should be solved in some other way.

Civil suits for damages filed against the individual officer have not proved adequately effective in preventing police abuse of authority. Were this procedure effective, however, it would emasculate vigorous police action and law enforcement would be weakened at a time when it needs to be strengthened.

Negating police overzealousness by freeing guilty defendants violates the principle that the guilty should be adjudged guilty, punishes society rather than the policeman, rewards the guilty, and

is a miscarriage of justice. Its effectiveness as a control of police abuse of authority has not been demonstrated.

The Committee on Criminal Law and Procedure of the California State Bar proposed that

" . . . the answer might lie in a new kind of civil action, or better, a summary type of proceeding, for a substantial money judgment in favor of the wronged individual, whether innocent or guilty, and against the political subdivision whose enforcement officers violated that person's rights. After not many outlays of public funds the taxpayers and administrative heads would insist upon curbing unlawful police action.[1]

Professor Edward L. Barrett, Jr., of the University of California Law School, in commenting on this proposal, stated:

"Legislative action along these general lines gives promise of providing a more adequate solution than the exclusionary rule at a smaller social cost. . . . The remedy would be available to the innocent as well as the guilty, for the illegal arrest as well as the illegal search. The courts would have frequent opportunities for ruling on the legality of police action, for enunciating and developing the governing law. If in any community a substantial number of such actions become successful, the financial pressure on the police to conform more closely to judicial standards would doubtless follow. Finally, if a careful line is drawn between those situations where increased personal liability should be placed upon the individual policeman (basically those involving serious and intentional violations of law) and those where he should be immunized and sole liability placed upon the governmental agency, interference with the efficient functioning of law enforcement would be minimized."[2]

## CONCLUSION

The modernization of arrest privileges is needed to make them consistent with the conditions under which the police today must protect the public from criminal attack. The following advantages

[1] 29 CAL. ST. BAR JOUR. 263–64 (1954).
[2] 43 CALIF. L. REV. 565, 595 (1955).

would be gained from liberalizing ancient rules of arrest based on conditions that no longer exist and from penalizing a political subdivision for abuse of authority by its police:

1) Public peace and security would be increased by enhancing the likelihood of discovering persons seeking an opportunity to attack.

2) The effectiveness of the administration of justice would be increased by facilitating the investigation of suspects, the arrest of criminals, and the collection of admissible evidence. By these means both clearance and conviction rates would be increased.

3) The security of the police would be increased by permitting them to discover weapons that may be used to attack them and by making it illegal to resist arrest by a known peace officer.

4) Higher standards of service and stricter adherence to the legal restrictions imposed on the police would result when a community or other political subdivision was penalized for abuse of authority by its police.

# The Fourth Amendment: Obstacle or Necessity in the Law of Arrest?

CALEB FOOTE

The assertion that conventional arrest law and constitutional limitations unduly restrict police activity is as old as our history. With the increases in crime rates which have accompanied the development of modern urban civilization, the demands to accord the police more flexibility for action have grown steadily more insistent.

Since the so-called Uniform Arrest Act was first proposed in 1942, much of this controversy has centered upon a provision of that act which would authorize a policeman to "stop any person abroad who he has reasonable ground to suspect is committing, has committed or is about to commit a crime, and may demand of him his name, address, business abroad and whither he is going."[1] Such a stopping would constitute not an "arrest" but a "detention," and the detention could be continued for two hours to permit further investigation. During that time the suspect could be searched for dangerous weapons.

The questions before us at this session of the conference are clearly based on this act. In an important aspect, however, one of the questions posed is more explicit than the act. This particular question asks whether the police should be permitted to search a detained person not only for weapons but also for other "incriminating evidence." In this discussion I intend to treat together the Uniform Act and the question framed for us.

The key question put for this session provides:
"In the absence of sufficient grounds for an arrest, should the police have a right to stop and question a person as to his identity and reason for being where he is, if the appearance or conduct of that person has reasonably aroused police suspicion?"

The fine hand of the advocate can be detected in the deceptively simple formulation of this proposal. It carefully sugar-coats a proposition which, if accepted, would severely curtail individual rights in rejecting one of our oldest legal traditions and which, at least in part, is almost certainly unconstitutional. Like any good advocate's question, it is so worded that it seems to compel the desired answer. The proposal purports to authorize only "reasonable" police action—the custody of one who has "reasonably aroused police suspicion." Thus one who answers "No" is placed in the position of throttling "reasonable" police activity. The catch, of course, is that the word "reasonable" as used in this proposal and in the Uniform Arrest Act has a meaning all its own.

In the law of arrest and by long constitutional history, "reasonable" has been interpreted as the equivalent of probable cause. An officer acts reasonably if, on the facts before him, it would appear that the suspect has probably committed a specific crime. This is the context in which the word is used in the fourth amendment and in most state arrest laws. Our cases sharply distinguish the reasonableness of an arrest on probable cause from unreasonable apprehension grounded on "mere" suspicion. It might appear, therefore, that the detention provision of the Uniform Arrest Act in the proposal before us is wholly innocuous—an officer can act on reasonable suspicion, *i.e.*, probable cause, which of course he can do anyway without any change in the law.

[1] Warner, *The Uniform Arrest Act*, 28 VA. L. REV. 315 (1942).

In a very recent case construing the Uniform Arrest Act's detention provision, the Delaware Supreme Court made such an equation. Apparently unaware of what it was doing to the act in the process, the court uttered the following dictum:

"We can find nothing in 11 Del.C., § 1902 [detention provision] which infringes on the rights of a citizen to be free from detention except, as appellant says, 'for probable cause'. Indeed, we think appellant's attempt to draw a distinction between an admittedly valid detention [conventional arrest] upon 'reasonable ground to believe' and the requirement of § 1902 of 'reasonable ground to suspect' is a semantic quibble. . . . In this context, the words 'suspect' and 'believe' are equivalents."[2]

Such a construction of the Uniform Arrest Act, of course, saves its constitutionality at the expense of negating its whole purpose. Clearly this is intended neither by the act, the objective of which was to increase and not just to restate police power, nor by the topic before us, which postulates "In the absence of sufficient grounds for arrest . . .", i.e., without probable cause. The word "reasonable" as a qualifier of suspicion in these proposals must be understood to include at least part of what would be unreasonable under present law. It is perhaps poetic justice that this little deception has backfired in its first court test. In any event, a more accurate posing of the question before us would be: "Should a policeman be allowed to stop and detain even if his action would be unreasonable under the fourth amendment or the common law of arrest?"

Along with this misleading use of the term "reasonable" is another semantic sleight of hand which tends to obscure the real nature of the proposed change. The chief draftsman of the Uniform Arrest Act has stipulated (and our topic implies) that this stopping for questioning and search "is not an arrest" but is merely a detention. One can certainly understand the wish which has fathered this attempted distinction, for "arrest" is a blunt word, implying stigma and dramatizing

the instant at which the liberty of the citizen is totally subjected to the power of the state. It has been our boast that under a democratic form of government such awesome power can be exercised only on reasonable belief, i.e., probable cause, and that this limitation constitutes a key link in the protection of the subject's liberty. It is no wonder, therefore, that the authors have attempted to soften the sharp image of their proposed change with a semantic curtain. They would have us believe that a taking into custody for questioning and search is not an arrest but something else, as if a change in the descriptive label of a concept effects a change in the nature of the concept itself. This is Madison Avenue at its best, but it is hard to see how it advances the cause of legal analysis of this proposal on its merits.

The most commonly accepted definition of an arrest, a definition which is incorporated even in the Uniform Arrest Act, is "the taking of a person into custody in order that he may be forthcoming to answer for the commission of an offense."[3] Custody is "an actual restraint of the person to be arrested," which occurs at the moment an individual is no longer a free agent to do as he pleases. The Constitution does not use the word "arrest" but expresses the same idea in its reference to "seizure," an even more unambiguous word. A seizure or arrest can be and often is of short duration, and of course the fact whether it is regarded or recorded by the police as an arrest is irrelevant. To determine whether an arrest has taken place we look at the facts to see if there has been "an actual restraint of the person." Often this is not easy to determine, as where an officer says to a pedestrian, "Just a minute, I want to ask you a few questions." Were a civilian to ask such a question there would certainly be no restraint, but what on their face are merely words of request take on color from the officer's uniform, badge, gun and demeanor. The Uniform Arrest Act, however, is unambiguous; the officer can enforce his request by forceably restraining for

[2] De Salvatore v. State, No. 68, 1959 Term, Delaware Supreme Court, June 3, 1960.

[3] ALI CODE OF CRIMINAL PROCEDURE §18 (1931). For the same definition in the Uniform Act, see Warner, supra note 1, at 344.

up to two hours the suspect against whom there is no probable cause.

Under the definition of arrest given above, the only way in which such a restraint of a criminal suspect can be viewed as a nonarrest is to quibble over the qualifying phrase, ". . . in order that he may be forthcoming to answer for the commission of an offense." The most reasonable interpretation of this language would be that it merely distinguishes a restraint the purpose of which is related to the enforcement of the criminal law from the seizure of a lost child in order to return it to its parents, the enforcement of quarantine measures, or the detention of a mentally ill person who requires care and treatment.

There is, however, another possible interpretation which can be found from the bare words alone, if one disregards obvious policy considerations, common sense and a voluminous case law. Hundreds of tort cases to the contrary notwithstanding, many police officers profess to believe that they have not "arrested" their prisoner until they have formally booked him on the police blotter. In the recent celebrated Apalachin case in New York, Judge Kaufman gives his judicial weight to this view:

> "It is clear that a technical arrest demands an intent on the part of the arresting officer to bring in a person so that he might be put through the steps preliminary to answering for a crime such as fingerprinting, booking, arraigning, etc."[4]

He then proceeds to try to square this belief with the fourth amendment by stating that "it cannot be contended that every detention of an individual" is a seizure in the constitutional sense. As the Apalachin case involved a roundup and detention of alleged Mafia conspirators, Judge Kaufman was presumably not referring to non-criminal child welfare or contagious disease detentions, as to which his statement would of course be true. Aside from a misrepresentation of British law,[5] he

cites no authority for these sweeping assertions. It is apparent, however, that such a construction is absurd, for inasmuch as it makes the officer's intent the controlling factor, it would substitute the policeman for court and law as a protector of liberty. Seizures or arrests without probable cause would be illegal only if the officer ultimately entered a formal charge of crime on insufficient evidence; he would be within the law if the suspect were released after imprisonment without having been booked, or if the period of detention turned up probable cause through search or detention and only then did the officer decide to book him. The short answer to such reasoning is that if Judge Kaufman is correct, then both our tort law of false imprisonment and the whole law of search and seizure developed by the United States Supreme Court in its construction of the fourth amendment are wrong. See, for example, Mr. Justice Jackson's opinion for a unanimous Court in *United States v. Di Re:*

> "The government's last resort in support of the arrest is to reason from the fruits of the search to the conclusion that the officer's knowledge at the time gave him grounds for it. We have had frequent occasion to point out that a search is not made legal by what it turns up. In law it is good or bad when it starts and does not change character from its success."[6]

In his recent book, THE CRIMINAL PROSECUTION IN ENGLAND, Lord Justice Devlin writes of the law from which both our common law of arrest and the fourth amendment were drawn, and he puts this matter very well indeed:

> "The police have no power to detain anyone unless they charge him with a specified crime and arrest him accordingly. Arrest and imprisonment are in law the same thing. Any form of physical restraint is an arrest and imprisonment is only a continuing arrest. If an arrest is un-

---

[4] United States v. Bonanno, 180 F.Supp. 71, 77 (S.D.N.Y. 1960).

[5] Judge Kaufman cites DEVLIN, THE CRIMINAL PROSECUTION IN ENGLAND 31–62 (1960), on the British practice of questioning suspects and the operation of the Judges' Rules. He uses this material in the context of

enforced detention for questioning but neglects to make reference to Lord Justice Devlin's important qualification that the English police cannot use detention or compulsion for such questioning and that "it is up to the police to make sure that a man comes to the station" for questioning "voluntarily." *Id.* at 68.

[6] 332 U.S. 581, 595 (1948).

justified, it is wrongful in law and is known as false imprisonment. The police have no power whatever to detain anyone on suspicion or for the purpose of questioning him. They cannot even compel anyone whom they do not arrest to come to the police station."[7]

I have stressed the falsity of this alleged distinction between arrest and detention because an awareness of it is essential to a complete understanding of the nature and complexity of the proposal before us. Probable cause as a standard to guide the police and against which to measure the legality of an arrest or seizure is to be abandonned in favor of some other as yet unformulated standard more favorable to the police. It is true that the detention-arrest permitted under the Uniform Arrest Act would be limited in duration, and that at the end of some time period such as two hours the arrest must be terminated unless by that time the police have acquired sufficient evidence to meet the conventional burden of probable cause. But such a time limitation does not make the detention any less an arrest for the period during which liberty is actually restrained in order to facilitate a criminal investigation. As the standard of probable cause is embodied in the federal and most state constitutions, it seems to me that we are talking about constitutional revision and not merely statutory enactment. That of course does not automatically condemn it, for I suppose not even the fourth amendment is sacrosanct if imperative policy considerations demand its revision. Reference to this constitutional issue, however, does point up the difficulty and gravity of the proposal.

Underlying this whole discussion is the premise that the police as presently constituted are less effective than they should be. I suppose this is probably true, although it is certainly not established by a high incidence of crime or low clearance rates or the number of instances in which known criminals escape justice. In a democracy police effectiveness is measured even more by what the police do *not* do than by their positive accomplishments:

[7] DEVLIN, THE CRIMINAL PROSECUTION IN ENGLAND 68 (1960).

"... the worth of a society will eventually be reckoned not in proportion to the number of criminals it crucifies, burns, hangs or imprisons, but rather by the degree of liberty experienced by the great body of its citizenry. There have never been more determined law enforcers than Nazi Germany or the Soviet."[8]

Accepting the premise of ineffectiveness as true, however, it does not follow that the proposed changes in the law of arrest are a prerequisite—or even the best way—to increased efficiency or that such changes will have any significant effect at all. There is a measure of cynicism in the typical advocacy of change, implying that present law handcuffs the police, and that essential, routine, everyday police tactics which are now illegal should receive the law's official sanction. The first argument assumes that the police are actually restrained from necessary action by the law, but the second assumes action and asks for the removal of a stigma of illegality, immunization from the presently nominal threat of false imprisonment actions and protection of police evidence against the onslaught of the exclusionary rule. No doubt in some instances the law actually has the effect of restraining action which would solve crimes, but to the extent that the police generally already stop, question, search and harass along the lines proposed in the queries to this conference, it is hard to see how change in the law is going to have much effect on clearance or conviction rates.

If the goal is improved law enforcement, there are obvious alternatives to change in the law. One would be to improve the caliber of policemen, and it is certainly significant that the federal police forces, which have to operate under the most restrictive legal "handcuffs" in the nation, also enjoy a relatively superior reputation for efficiency and respect for individual rights. This would suggest that when you are willing to pay enough to get a police force which is both adequately trained and reasonably dissociated from politics, you can obtain marked improvement in effectiveness. It would also suggest that the effect of restrictive law upon police activity may be just the opposite

[8] Schwartz, *On Current Proposals to Legalize Wiretapping*, 103 U.PA.L.REV. 157, 158 (1954).

of what is generally assumed. One reason that the F.B.I. has been able to recruit a higher caliber of personnel is the public confidence it has built for itself by operating within the law. The same has been said of British and Canadian police forces, where the seed of lawful operation has led to a harvest of public respect and cooperation.

A related alternative which is less satisfactory in the long run but may be politically more expedient is to concentrate upon an increase in the numerical strength and supervision of a police force instead of or in addition to efforts to improve overall personnel quality. During the last four months of 1954 the New York police conducted an experiment in their 25th precinct, an area of about one square mile with a population of 120,000 and an extremely high crime rate. The number of patrolmen on duty was increased from 188 to 440, and the number of supervising sergeants, from 15 to 33. Proportional increases were made also in personnel of higher rank. Foot posts were reduced in size to a point where the officer assigned could reasonably be expected to observe all incidents and conditions on his post, and the men were held closely accountable for what happened. While the statistics are incomplete and may have defects because of the department's self-interest in building a case for higher appropriations, the total number of felonies reported in the precinct declined 55.6% from the comparable period of the year before, while the clearance rate for felonies rose from 20.2% to 65.6%. No comparable changes were reported in the rest of the city.[9]

The chief disadvantages of these alternatives is that they cost money and require the exercise of political and administrative statesmanship, whereas enacting new arrest laws offers the illusion of doing something about crime without financial or political complications and has a natural appeal to political expediency. I suspect that in police work, as elsewhere, one generally gets no more than he pays for, and that legislation on police power is a wholly inadequate substitute for responsible police fiscal and personnel policy.

The importance of seeking alternatives within the present legal framework is emphasised when one examines the impact of police arrest practices upon our constitutional respect for privacy. The right to be let alone—to be able sit in one's house or drive one's car or walk the streets without unwarranted police intrusion—is surely one of the most important factors to be weighed in achieving a balance between individual liberty and public necessity. Ironically, it is this factor about which we know the least. Although they are often inadequate, we collect at least some data on the number of crimes reported, the number of crimes cleared by arrest, and the mortality between charge and conviction. We also have figures purporting to state the number of persons "arrested," but usually this only reflects cases where the police have booked, fingerprinted and charged the suspect. We cannot even guess at the true arrest rate because we have no data on the number of people whose liberty is restrained but who after investigation are released without charge. Under these circumstances to try to make an intelligent evaluation of how the right of privacy fares under present conditions and how proposed changes in the law would affect it is very much like trying to compute batting averages when one knows only the number of hits for each player but has no data on numbers of times at bat.

Only occasionally, and then usually in newspapers or other unofficial sources, do statistical tidbits appear which cast glimmers of light. Recently, for example, the Baltimore Sun gave its "Policeman of the Year" award to the inventor of the "Battaglia plan."[10] This hardly novel invention was to stop and "check" cars driven by teenagers at night. The Sun reported that during its first year of operation 157,000 cars were stopped in this operation, netting "more than 1,000 arrests" for non-traffic offenses. How many of these arrests proved to be well grounded is not stated. Assuming a figure of 1,000, and further assuming that the cars averaged two occupants each, the Baltimore police were making one hit for every 314 persons "checked." The nature of the checking process is not described; for some it was doubtless

[9] NEW YORK CITY POLICE DEP'T OPERATION 25 (undated, probably 1955).

[10] Baltimore Sun, Jan. 22, 1960. See especially lead editorial, "The Captain's Plan."

only a roadside detention, but for others additional restraint may have been involved. In Massachusetts, state police stopped 400 motorists in a drive to catch residents who were buying their holiday cheer at cut rate New Hampshire prices and bagged one violator, described as "an elderly, bewildered man."[11] A five hour roadblock on Chicago's south side is reported to have involved stopping 1,190 cars, with a net catch of seven persons arrested for narcotics investigation, five suspected drunken drivers and six drivers who did not have licenses in their possession.[12]

These are the minor surface manifestations of a very serious problem. Of much more importance are the spectacular round-ups of suspects after major crimes and the routine daily investigations of suspicious characters, loiterers, past offenders and others deemed suspect or undesirable by unarticulated police standards. The roadblock affects everyone indiscriminately and probably does not develop any focused public resentment, but these other activities are concentrated in poorer economic areas with high crime rates. The police batting average here may not be as low as in indiscriminate roadblocks, but it is probably not very high. What does the right of privacy mean for such people in such neighborhoods? What proportion of the total number of arrests is made up of persons abruptly arrested, investigated for minutes or hours or days, and as abruptly released without booking? What is the cumulative impact of a high ratio of mistaken "detentions" upon police public relations and the development of attitudes of active public cooperation with the police? These and many other related questions urgently need to be answered if we are to be able to evaluate and reassess the role the police should play in our society. In our present state of ignorance the hypothesis that the best interests of democratic law enforcement demand stricter compliance with the fourth amendment is at least as

[11] Boston Hearald, Dec. 22, 1959, p. 1, col. 1; *id.*, Dec. 23, 1959, p. 3, col. 1.
[12] See photostats of Chicago newspaper clippings dated Sept. 11 and 12, 1954, reproduced in CHICAGO MOTOR CLUB, THE CONSTITUTION—SHALL IT BE VIOLATED WHEN APPLIED TO MOTORISTS 8–9 (1954).

plausible as the view that the standard of the fourth amendment should be relaxed.

The last point I wish to make is that analysis of any proposal to increase police power is handicapped because of the imprecision of what is being proposed. After many years of discussion we are still left very much in the dark as to precisely what is desired by advocates of reform. I have already noted that the standard employed in the Uniform Arrest Act and in the queries for this session—reasonable suspicion—is meaningless if reasonable is not equated with probable cause. And obviously it is not; it suggests only that there should be some undefined limitation upon the police. If probable cause is no longer to be the test, at least at the initial point of arrest, where is the line to be drawn short of indiscriminate police detentions on hunch? No greater service could be rendered by advocates of change in the law than the formulation of specific standards illuminating the limits of the proposed buffer zone which would lie between arrest on probable cause and the protection of the individual from intrusion based on nothing more substantial than a policeman's hunch.

The factors suggested in this session's query are a disturbing illustration of the difficulties of such a formulation. An officer's impressions of a suspect's explanation of his "identity and reason for being where he is" are wholly subjective and seem to suggest almost unlimited discretion in the police. They are, moreover, reminiscent of the elements of common law vagrancy, an outmoded relic of feudal class distinctions which has been grossly abused by the police in dealing with socially and economically disadvantaged elements of our society, but without whatever protection is afforded from the fact that vagrancy is a status offense which in theory can be established only by repeated observation over a period of days or weeks.

Most of the limited judicial opinion which could be enlisted in support of a detention drafting project comes from automobile cases. As has been noted, the police today can question a pedestrian on the streets or go to a house to request an interview with a suspect. They can solicit a confession or statement, bluff the suspect by pretending that they already know he is carrying contraband, or take advantage of the mere opportunity to ask questions to induce the suspect to tip his hand. In England the police frequently invite a suspect to come to the police station for an interview, a practice of which American police apparently have not taken advantage. If such measures cause the suspect to make an incriminating admission or to try to dispose of incriminating evidence, an arrest on probable cause can follow. Most of the cases, incidentally, which are cited as purporting to authorize a power to "stop and question" a suspect involve an incriminating admission to an officer's first question. They are authority for the power to ask a question but not for a restraint of one who declines to stop and talk. The case upon which the so-called Maryland "accosting" rule is based, for example, qualifies the right to question upon lack of "coercion" by the police: "If he had been merely passive and silent, when confronted with the sergeant's implied accusation, he would have been immune from any police interference until a warrant had been procured."[13] In his discussion of the British practice, Lord Justice Devlin emphasizes: "But it is up to the police to make sure that a man comes to the station voluntarily. . . ."[14] No doubt many people feel compelled to stop and answer when questioned by an officer, and the unavoidable ambiguity in such a situation operates to the officer's advantage.

If the suspect is in a moving automobile, however, there is no ambiguity. The officers cannot ask a question as he drives past. They can follow the car until it is parked or perhaps stopped by a red light, and then approach the occupant as they would a pedestrian; or they can forego the opportunity to question; or they can stop the car. The last alternative is often the only practicable one, and because the restraint involved in hailing a car to the side of the road is much more direct than asking a question of a pedestrian it is here that a right of detention on something less than

probable cause would seem to be most likely to arise. In *Carroll v. United States*, however, the Court equated the stopping or interruption of a car with a search and proscribed either except upon probable cause:

"It would be intolerable and unreasonable if a prohibition agent were authorized to stop every automobile on the chance of finding liquor and thus subject all persons lawfully using the highways to the inconvenience and indignity of such a search. . . . [T]hose lawfully within the country, entitled to use the public highways, have a right to free passage *without interruption or search* unless there is [probable cause]." (Emphasis added.)[15]

The later cases of *Brinegar v. United States*[16] and *Henry v. United States*[17] have also been decided on the assumption that probable cause must exist before the car is stopped. No other justice joined Mr. Justice Burton's concurring opinion in *Brinegar* suggesting the existence of an intermediate zone which would warrant stopping a car for questioning on evidence insufficient to justify a search. Neither this opinion nor the few cases which have purported to apply it are helpful as explorations of the possible limits of such a rule, distinguishing it from roadblocks or other random interruptions.

Nor would the attempt to formulate standards for detention receive much useful guidance from discussions of hypothetical emergency situations such as the right of the police temporarily to detain one found near a fresh corpse, or Mr. Justice Jackson's reference to the kidnapping of a child after which "the officers throw a roadblock about the neighborhood and search every outgoing car. . . ."[18] Whatever the law may be in such situations, the reasonableness of the police action is conditioned by an immediate crisis and would have no general application. Mr. Justice Jackson proceeds to qualify his illustration by distinguish-

---

[13] Blager v. State, 162 Md. 664, 161 Atl. 1 (1932).
[14] Devlin, *supra* note 7, at 68.

[15] 267 U.S. 132, 153–4 (1925).
[16] 338 U.S. 160 (1949).
[17] 361 U.S. 98, 103 (1959).
[18] Brinegar v. United States, 338 U.S. 160, 183 (1949) (dissenting opinion)

ing a roadblock which is "the only way to save a threatened life and detect a vicious crime" from "a roadblock and universal search to salvage a few bottles of bourbon and catch a bootlegger." Narrowly drawn exceptions to the requirement of probable cause to cover such emergencies would have great merit but would have little bearing on the everyday police problems to which our topic invites attention.

Those of us who believe that the fourth amendment's resolution of a very difficult problem through the formula of probable cause is as good a compromise as we can find are not likely to be convinced otherwise unless we can see how a power of arrest without probable cause would be limited, how it would work in specific situations, and how its proponents propose to deal with the constitutional obstacles to its validity. In the meantime, I am afraid that the pressing problem which faces us in the law of arrest is not how to find ways to increase the power of the police. If illegality in police arrests is as widespread as present evidence would suggest, and existing sanctions against it as ineffective as I believe them to be, perhaps the appropriate queries for the next conference would be: Can we afford to enforce the fourth amendment and the law of arrest, and if so, how?

# Police Detention and Arrest Privileges
## Under Foreign Law

## Canada\*

G. ARTHUR MARTIN

### POWERS OF ARREST[1]

*In general*

The powers of a peace officer to arrest for suspected violations or suspected potential violations of the criminal law are to be found in the Criminal Code of Canada,[2] or in Provincial enactments creating Provincial offences. The common law distinction between felonies and misdemeanours has been abolished. Crimes are designated simply as indictable offences (i.e., offences which may be tried by indictment) and offences (i.e., less serious types of crimes which are triable by a Magistrate or Justice of the Peace under a special code of procedure set out in Part XXIV of the Code).[3]

The Criminal Code empowers both the peace officer and the ordinary citizen to arrest without warrant in certain circumstances, the powers of the peace officer being wider than those of the citizen. Section 434 of the Code relates to the powers of the citizen and reads as follows:

"Anyone may arrest without warrant a person whom he finds committing an indictable offence."

Section 435 deals with power of a peace officer to arrest without warrant and reads as follows:

"A peace officer may arrest without warrant

(a) A person who has committed or who, on reasonable and probable grounds he believes has committed or is about to commit an *indictable* offence, or

(b) A person whom he finds committing a *criminal* offence."

Criminal offence in subsection (b) means any offence punishable on indictment or upon summary conviction under the Criminal Code or any Dominion Statute but does not include a violation of a Provincial Statute.[4]

There are certain other sections dealing with the power of the citizen to arrest in certain circumstances. Section 30 authorizes *every person* who witnesses a breach to detain any person who commits or is about to join in or to renew the breach of the peace, for the purpose of giving him in custody to a police officer. Section 436 provides that *anyone* may arrest without warrant a person who on reasonable and probable grounds he believes has committed a *criminal* offence and is escaping therefrom and is freshly pursued by persons who have a lawful authority to arrest

---

\* A brief discussion of the Canadian federal system, which may be helpful in better understanding certain portions of this paper, appears in my report on the privilege against self-incrimination in Part IV of this volume.

[1] The subject of arrest under a warrant is not discussed in this report. Section 440 of the Criminal Code provides that the Justice, upon an Information under oath, may issue a warrant or a summons to compel the attendance of the accused before him.

[2] 1953–54 (CAN.) c.51; Frey v. Fedoruk, [1950] S.C.R. 517.

[3] Section 28 of The Interpretation Act, R.S.C., c.158 (1952), provides:

"(1) Every Act shall be read and construed as if any offence for which the offender may be

(a) prosecuted by indictment, howsoever such offence may be therein described or referred to, were described or referred to as an indictable offence;

(b) punishable on summary conviction, were described or referred to as an offence; and all provisions of the Criminal Code relating to indictable offences, or offences, as the case may be, shall apply to every such offence."

[4] CRANKSHAW'S CRIMINAL CODE OF CANADA 595 (7th ed.).

POLICE POWER AND INDIVIDUAL FREEDOM

that person. Section 437 empowers the owner or any person in lawful possession of any property or any person authorized by the owner or any person in lawful possession of property to arrest without warrant a person whom he finds committing a criminal offence on or in relation to that property.

*Powers of the Police Officer*

Section 435, in its present form, was first enacted in 1955 and was derived in part from the former Section 652,[5] which reads as follows:

"Any peace officer may, without a warrant, take into custody any person whom he finds lying or loitering in any highway, yard or other place during the night, and whom he has good cause to suspect of having committed or being about to commit, any indictable offence, and may detain such person until he can be brought before a justice to be dealt with according to law.

"(2) No person who has been so apprehended shall be detained after noon of the following day without being brought before a justice."

Section 435 in its present form gives the police officer much wider powers than were enjoyed by him at common law. The power to arrest one whom he on reasonable and probable grounds believes *to be about* to commit an indictable offence obviously enables the officer to intervene at a stage prior to the commission of an attempt. The attempt to commit an indictable offence is itself an indictable offence and an attempt to commit an offence punishable on summary conviction only is a summary conviction offence.[6] Since by Section 435 a peace officer has the power to arrest any person whom he finds committing a criminal offence, it is clear he could justify arresting a person attempting to commit any criminal offence by the power there conferred, and the power to arrest a person whom he believes "is about to commit an indictable offence" would be unnecessary if this power were construed as being limited

[5] R.S.C., c.36 (1927).
[6] CRIMINAL CODE OF CANADA, §406.

to situations where an attempt to commit an offence has already begun. It follows that a police officer may arrest under Section 435 where he believes the person arrested is about to commit an indictable offence although he has no basis for charging him with the commission of any offence. The peace officer is by virtue of Section 438(2) of the Code required to bring the arrested person before a Justice of the Peace within 24 hours, if one is available within that period, and if a Justice is not available within that period he must bring the prisoner before the Justice as soon as possible.[7]

If, during that period, as a result of his investigation or as a result of admissions made by the prisoner, the officer obtains sufficient evidence to warrant the laying of a charge, he may do so; otherwise, the prisoner must be discharged upon being brought before the justice as required by Section 438(2).

The wide powers conferred by Section 435 may be justified as a form of preventive justice, and no doubt the taking into custody of a person whom the police believe is about to commit a crime has some therapeutic value even though no charge is ultimately laid. A recent case decided by the Ontario Court of Appeal makes it clear, however, that in order to justify himself under this section

[7] "438(1). Any one who arrests a person without warrant shall forthwith deliver that person to a peace officer, and the peace officer may detain the person until he is dealt with in accordance with this section. (2) A peace officer who receives delivery of and detains a person who has been arrested without warrant or who arrests a person with or without warrant shall, in accordance with the following provisions, take or cause that person to be taken before a justice to be dealt with according to law, namely,
(a) where a justice is available within a period of twenty-four hours after the person has been delivered to or has been arrested by the peace officer, the person shall be taken before a justice before the expiration of that period; and
(b) where a justice is not available within a period of twenty-four hours after the person has been delivered to or has been arrested by the peace officer, the person shall be taken before a justice as soon as possible."
Since the provisions of §438 are for the benefit of the prisoner, it would seem that the officer might lawfully release the prisoner at any time before the expiration of the period without taking his prisoner before a Justice of the Peace.

38

the officer must have some objective grounds for believing that the person arrested was about to commit an indictable offence.

In *Koechlin v. Waugh & Hamilton*,[8] the plaintiff was awarded damages against two policemen for unlawful arrest. The plaintiff was walking home with a friend after having attended a picture show. There had been a number of crimes of breaking and entering in the area, and the attention of the defendant officers was attracted to the plaintiff and his companion by reason of the dress of the plaintiff's companion, who was wearing rubbersoled shoes and a windbreaker. The officers asked the plaintiff to identify himself and, when he refused, removed him forcibly to the police station. Laidlaw, J. A., in delivering the judgment of the court, said:

"A police officer has not in law an unlimited power to arrest a law-abiding citizen. The power given expressly to him by the Criminal Code to arrest without warrant is contained in s. 435, but we direct careful attention of the public to the fact that the law empowers a police officer in many cases and under certain circumstances to require a person to account for his presence and identify himself and to furnish other information, and any person who wrongfully fails to comply with such lawful requirements does so at the risk of arrest and imprisonment. None of these circumstances exist in this case. No unnecessary restriction on his power which results in increased difficulty to a police officer to perform his duties of office should be imposed by a Court. At the same time, the rights and freedom under law from unlawful arrest and imprisonment of an innocent citizen must be fully guarded by the Courts. In this case, the fact that the companion of the infant plaintiff was wearing rubber-soled shoes and a windbreaker and that his dress attracted the attention of the police officers, falls far short of reasonable and probable grounds for believing that the infant plaintiff had committed an indictable offence or was about to commit such an offence. We do not criticize the police officers in any

[8] [1957] O.W.N. 245, 118 Can. C.C. 24.

way for asking the infant plaintiff and his companion to identify themselves, but we are satisfied that when the infant plaintiff, who was entirely innocent of any wrong doing, refused to do so, the police officer had no right to use force to compel him to identify himself. It would have been wise and, indeed, a duty as a good citizen, for the infant plaintiff to have identified himself when asked to do so by the police officers. It is altogether likely that if the infant plaintiff had been courteous and co-operative, the incident giving rise to this action would not have occurred, but that does not in law excuse the defendants for acting as they did in the particular circumstances. . . ."[9]

The *Koechlin* case, *supra*, may be contrasted with that of *R. v. Beaudette*.[10] In the latter case, the accused appealed from his conviction on a charge of unlawfully resisting a peace officer in the execution of his duty in arresting the accused. The principal ground of appeal was that the officer was not authorized by law to arrest the accused in the circumstances and hence was not acting in the execution of his duty. The evidence disclosed that the accused had been in a beverage room and had become intoxicated. When he refused to leave at the closing hour, the police were summoned and they eventually persuaded the accused to leave. Outside the premises a man in a taxi, of which the accused was the owner, shouted to the accused to drive him home. It became evident to the police that the accused intended to drive the car while in an intoxicated condition. The court, in dismissing the appeal, held that there was substantial justification for the police officer entertaining the belief that accused was about to commit the indictable offence of driving a motor vehicle while intoxicated. These authorities make it abundantly clear that the peace officer is confined within the limits of the powers conferred on him by the statute, and when he interferes with the liberty

[9] See also *R. v. Carroll*, [1960] O.W.N. 9, holding that in the circumstances before the court the accused was under no duty to identify himself to the constable when requested so to do.
[10] 118 Can. C.C. 295 (1957).

of the citizen he does so with the knowledge that he may subsequently be called upon to justify his action in a court of law.

It is of course a truism that a police officer investigating a crime is entitled to question any person that he thinks may be able to throw light upon the subject whether or not he suspects the person to whom the questions are directed. However, there is no general right to *detain* a person for questioning unless that detention is specifically authorized by Section 435 or some other statutory provision. If the person sought to be questioned chooses to co-operate, well and good, but if he does not the peace officer must be prepared to make an arrest and subsequently justify his action or let the citizen continue on his way. Very frequently the police assert that a suspected person voluntarily accompanied them to a police station for questioning although he was not under arrest and hence free to refuse if he had desired to do so.

Under the vagrancy section of the Code a police officer has a certain limited right to call upon a person to justify his presence at a particular place. Section 164 of the Code in part defines a vagrant as one who,

"(a) not having any visible means of support is found wandering abroad or trespassing and does not when required justify his presence in the place where he is found."

### POWER TO SEARCH SUSPECTED PERSONS

Generally speaking, a police officer has no right to search a suspected person unless he is under arrest, and such unlawful interference with the person would render him liable in an action for damages for assault. A peace officer has the right to search a person under arrest for the purpose of discovering evidence of the crime for which he has been arrested or for weapons with which he might do harm to himself or others.[11]

In *R. v. Brezack*[12] the accused appealed against his conviction on a charge of assaulting a peace

officer in the execution of his duty. The peace officer arrested the accused in the reasonable belief that he way carrying narcotic drugs in his mouth; he seized the accused by the throat and thrust his fingers into the accused's mouth and was bitten by the accused. The court held that under the circumstances the officer was justified in thrusting his fingers into the accused's mouth and that accused was properly convicted.

The police may be assisted in the investigation of certain types of crimes by special statutory provisions. Section 19 of the Opium and Narcotic Drug Act[13] provides that a peace officer who has reasonable cause to suspect that any drug is kept concealed in any place may search such place for such drug without a warrant and, if necessary, by force *may search any person there found*. Under Section 76(1) of the Highway Traffic Act,[14] every operator of a motor vehicle is required to carry his license with him at all times while he is in charge of a motor vehicle and to produce it when demanded by a constable.

The Ontario Liquor Control Act[15] by Section 110 authorizes a police officer, if he believes that liquor is unlawfully kept or had for unlawful purposes, to search without warrant for such liquor wherever he may suspect it to be. Moreover, the officer may search by force, if need be, anyone who is suspected to have such liquor upon him.

### DUTY OF PEACE OFFICER TO GIVE NOTICE OF THE CAUSE OF ARREST

At common law a peace officer who arrested a person either with or without a warrant is, subject to certain exceptions, required to inform the person arrested of the cause of arrest.[16] If the citizen is not so informed the peace officer is liable for false imprisonment.

That duty is now statutory in Canada. Section 29 of the Criminal Code provides as follows:

"(1) It is the duty of every one who executes a

[11] CRANKSHAW'S CRIMINAL CODE OF CANADA 78 (7th ed.).
[12] [1949] O.R. 888, 96 Can. C.C. 97.

[13] R.S.C., c.201 (1952). The right to search premises without warrant probably does not extend to a dwelling house.
[14] R.S.O., c.167 (1950).
[15] R.S.O., c.210 (1950).
[16] Christie v. Leachinsky, [1947] A.C. 573.

process or warrant to have it with him, where it is feasible to do so, and to produce it when requested to do so.

(2) It is the duty of every one who arrests a person, whether with or without warrant, to give notice to that person, where it is feasible to do so, of

    (a) the process or warrant under which he makes the arrest, or

    (b) the reason for the arrest.

(3) Failure to comply with subsection (1) or (2) does not of itself deprive a person who executes a process or warrant, or a person who makes an arrest, or those who assist them, of protection from *criminal* responsibility."

It will be noted that subsection (3) provides that failure to comply with subsection (1) or (2) does not of itself deprive the person making the arrest of protection from *criminal* responsibility. The civil responsibility of the person making the arrest remains as it was at common law.

In *Garthus v. Van Caeseele*,[17] Lord, J., said: "It has been held that although police officers *bona*

[17] 122 Can. C.C. 369, 374 (1959).

*fide* and on reasonable grounds believed a person had committed an offence but failed to inform him as to why he was being arrested, they would be liable in damages for false imprisonment." In *Koechlin v. Waugh & Hamilton*, Laidlaw, J. A., speaking for the court said:[18]

"We direct attention to an important fact. The infant plaintiff was not told by either of the police officers any reason for his arrest. The infant plaintiff was entitled to know on what charge or on suspicion of what crime he was seized. He was not required in law to submit to restraint on his freedom unless he knew the reason why that restraint should be imposed."

The right of the accused to be informed of the cause of arrest is not absolute and does not exist if the circumstances are such that he must know the general nature of the alleged offence for which he is detained or if the menacing attitude of the accused and his associates renders it impractical for the officer to inform him of the cause of arrest.[19]

[18] [1957] O.W.N. 245, 247.
[19] R. v. Beaudette, *supra* note 10; R. v. Hurlen, 123 Can. C.C. 54 (1959); R. v. George, 63 Can. C.C. 225 (1934), *aff'd on app. to the Sup. Ct. of Can.*, 67 Can. C.C. 33 (1936); R. v. Bain, 111 Can. C.C. 281 (1955).

# *England*

GLANVILLE L. WILLIAMS

To apprehend a suspect as a step in charging him with crime is a serious matter. What can the police do short of this? Whether or not they have power to arrest in a particular instance, may they take some action against a suspect which does not amount to arrest?

## *The questioning of suspects*

A constable may, of course, invite the suspect's voluntary co-operation in the further investigation of the suspected offence. He may question him, either in the street or, with his consent, in the police station.

If the suspect is requested to remain where he is for questioning, he need not answer the questions put to him; but if he does submit to answer, he may give the constable sufficient material to justify an arrest, even though there were insufficient grounds of suspicion before. It seems that the suspect's refusal to stop and answer could not add anything to the constable's justification. This is because the exercise by the citizen of his constitutional right to keep silent cannot be regarded as a circumstance of suspicion.

## Detention for questioning

Can the officer, in the earliest stage of suspicion and without any arrest, use force to make the suspect stop and submit to questioning, or to make him go to the police station for questioning? Continental systems recognise a distinction between arrest proper and detention for questioning: the latter, unlike the former, does not require reasonable suspicion or a definite charge. It is quite common even in the most liberal and democratic of Continental countries for a suspect to lie in prison for many months, without a definite charge, while the police are building up the case against him. Even in England the police make a practice of "detention for questioning", though they limit it at most to three or four days. The suspect is not regarded as under arrest, yet he is not at liberty. Sir Archibald Bodkin, the Director of Public Prosecutions, described the procedure in his evidence before the Royal Commission on Police Powers. The suspect was put in the waiting room and given a bed there, not in a cell; he was questioned freely without caution or charge, but was fed and treated well, and not kept in this condition for more than three days.[1] Commenting on this, the Royal Commission pointed out that in the case of *Voisin*[2] the detention was for four days; and an admission made by Voisin while in this custody was held admissible against him. The Commission had no doubt that the practice of detention for questioning was illegal: any form of restraint is in law an imprisonment; nor is the alleged distinction material for the purpose of Rule 3 of the Judges' Rules, relating to questioning.[3] This, too, was the opinion of the Home Office, and it is abundantly clear on the authorities.[4] The decision in *Voisin* is not to

the contrary, for that merely shows that an admission may be allowed to be given in evidence although obtained contrary to the Judges' Rules.

Since *Christie* v. *Leachinsky*[5] it has become clear that detention for questioning cannot be justified as an arrest, even in circumstances where the police would have power to arrest. A suspect detained for questioning is not informed that any charge is made against him; consequently his imprisonment cannot be supported by common-law or statutory powers of arrest. It seems that this is so even though the particular statute uses some word other than "arrest." Parliament has no fixed language in relation to arrest; instead of using the expression "arrest" it may allow a constable to "apprehend," "detain," "seize and detain," or "take into custody." Pretty evidently, all these are synonyms for "arrest." Even a statute using the word "detain" would not authorise an indefinite detention without bringing the prisoner before a magistrate. Nor would it authorise a detention without stating the reason for the arrest. Exceptionally, there is a group of statutes authorising the police to search for goods unlawfully possessed.[6] Apart from these statutes, and a few other statutes of limited scope, every detention for questioning is a false imprisonment, unless it satisfies the rules for a valid arrest.

Although the law on this subject is reasonably clear, there is much evidence that the practice of detention for questioning continues. On some occasions the police protect themselves by using the language of request, but there can be no doubt that on other occasions, when compulsion is evidently intended, the action of the police is illegal.

The objection to "detention for questioning"

---

[1] ROYAL COMM'N ON POLICE POWERS, MINUTES OF EVIDENCE 1385 *et seq.* (1928).
[2] [1918] 1 K.B. 531 (C.C.A.).
[3] CMD. No. 3297, at 55 (1929).
[4] Dunne v. Clinton, [1930] Ir. R. 366, is directly in point. But the rule is also evident from the cases

requiring arrested persons to be taken before a magistrate as soon as reasonably possible (*e.g.*, John Lewis & Co. v. Tims, [1952] A.C. 676). It is clear that this rule cannot be circumvented by claiming that the accused is not arrested but only detained. The judges set their faces against detention in custody for the purpose of collecting evidence without bringing the subject before a magistrate: Wright v. Court, 4 B.&C. 596 (1825).
[5] [1947] A.C. 573.
[6] See the last section of this article.

is that it deprives the accused of the safeguards that have been thought necessary to be included in the law of arrest. The argument in its favour is that the man may be innocent, and then detention without charge gives him a good prospect of being released without any publicity or stigma. The importance of avoiding publicity where guilt is not fairly clear was recognized by the Royal Commission which referred in its Report to Section 19 of the Indictable Offences Act of 1848 (now Section 4 of the Magistrates' Courts Act of 1952), which allows the preliminary examination to be conducted behind closed doors. "In cases where the police find that a mistake has been made, although a charge has been preferred, and wish merely to ask for the prisoner's discharge, or where they propose to ask for a remand on evidence so slight as still to admit of the possibility that they have got the wrong man, we think that, in the words of the section, 'the ends of justice will be best answered' by conducting the proceedings *in camera*." For some reason this valuable suggestion seems never to have been acted on, and indeed the statutory power of proceeding *in camera* has rarely been used.

In the type of case first mentioned in the above-quoted passage from the Commission's Report, namely where a charge has been made and the police now wish to discontinue the case, it may be suggested that no appearance before a magistrate is necessary.

### Defects in the law

The extent to which the police are hindered by not possessing a power of detention for questioning stands in inverse relation to the extent of their powers of arrest. The English law of arrest is extremely complex, and little purpose would be served in reproducing the multifarious statutes which give special powers. However, it is worth mentioning the power of arrest of those "found" in certain private premises for an unlawful purpose, and the power of arrest of suspected persons who loiter with intent to commit felony. These powers

are indulgently construed;[7] but still they would not justify an arrest if the court took the view that the suspicion felt by the officer was unreasonable.

The real reason why the police wish to detain for questioning is because they feel that they have not sufficient evidence to make a positive charge, and yet they have enough to put them on enquiry. Under the present law, there is no power to detain for questioning without arrest even for a few minutes, and even though the suspect's name and address are unknown. Nor is there a general power to arrest on refusal of name and address. This is an inadequacy in the police powers of law enforcement, or would be so if actions against the police were commoner than they now are.

### The distinction between command and request

The foregoing remarks do not mean that every request by a police constable to a suspect to accompany him to the police station, followed by acquiescence, amounts to an arrest. One has to face the very difficult distinction between a command and a request.

It is submitted that if the officer merely makes a request to the suspect, giving him to understand that he is at liberty to come or refuse, there is no imprisonment and no arrest. If, however, the impression is conveyed that there is no such option and that the suspect is compelled to come, it is an imprisonment. The distinction does not turn merely on the words used but on the way in which they are spoken and on all the circumstances. All manner of ambiguous expressions may be used by the officer, as if he says: "I must ask you to come with me"; or "I think it would be better if you came with me"; or, weaker, "I suggest that we both go to the police station where you can tell your story to the superintendent." The question "Will you come with me?" may look in print like a request; but it is capable of being intoned as an imperative instead of as a question, and will then be a command.

This view of the law, that a person who goes voluntarily is not imprisoned, runs counter to the

[7] See [1955] CRIM. L.R. 66, 136.

charge to the jury of Alderson, B., in *Peters v. Stanway*.[8] He said:

"The question as to the verdict will depend, not on whether the plaintiff went voluntarily from the defendant's house to the stationhouse, but whether she volunteered to go in the first instance. There is a great difference between the case of a person who volunteers to go in the first instance, and that of a person who, having a charge made against him, goes voluntarily to meet it. The question, therefore, is, whether you think the going to the stationhouse proceeded originally from the plaintiff's own willingness, or from the defendant's making a charge against her; for, if it proceeded from the defendant's making a charge, the plaintiff will not be deprived of her right of action by her having willingly gone to meet the charge."

The ruling of Alderson, B., even if accepted, might not invalidate the practice of the police in inviting a suspect to go to the police station to help them with their enquiries into a specified crime, because this form of words does not involve the making of a charge. However, it is possible that the learned Baron would have regarded the formula as equivalent to the making of a charge. It is submitted that in any event his ruling is unacceptable, because it gives too great an ambit to the concept of false imprisonment.

The ruling of Alderson, B., was quoted with approval in the Canadian case of *Conn v. David Spencer Ltd.*[9] The plaintiff was making some purchases in a self-service store, when he was mistakenly accused by the house detective of stealing soap. The detective requested him to go upstairs, which after some demur he did, thinking it advisable to give way in view of the crowded state of the store. In the upstairs room, the plaintiff consented to be searched, and, no soap being found, he was allowed to leave. In an action for false imprisonment, the store detective (who was a woman) admitted that she maintained control over the plaintiff, and that if he had tried to escape she might not have been able to hold him but would

have done her best to prevent it. On these facts the Supreme Court of British Columbia held that there was a false imprisonment. The decision was justifiable on the facts of the case, but it may be perhaps respectfully doubted whether those facts necessitated approval being given to the ruling of Alderson, B.

At first sight it may seem attractive to argue that a request to visit the police station should always be taken as a command in law unless the police make it clear that the request can be declined. To the ordinary citizen, a request of the police is a command—particularly if he feels himself implicated in suspicion. On the other hand, there are certainly some cases where a request cannot be taken as a command. For example, it sometimes happens that the police leave a note at the house of a suspect, asking him to attend at the police station because it is thought that he may be able to help them with their enquiries into a specified matter. Such a written request cannot be construed as carrying an implied threat of immediate force if the request be not complied with. Even where the request is conveyed by word of mouth, it would be a strong thing in many circumstances to regard it as equivalent to a command. An ordinary witness may sometimes be invited to attend at the police station to give evidence, and it would be absurd to hold that this invitation when accepted amounts to a false imprisonment by the police. The argument that there is an imprisonment is stronger when the request is addressed to the suspect. Yet the suspect may not know at that moment how strong the suspicion is against him; and the police may not have made up their minds to arrest him. To interrogate a suspect by arrangement at the police station is often kinder than an official visit to his home, because the latter may be harmful to his reputation. The suspect may well feel that, if he has to visit the police station, he would rather go there "voluntarily" to assist the police in their enquiries than under technical arrest. A newspaper report of the suspect's being arrested is more damaging to him than a report that he has visited the police station. Also, the law creating the offence of escape comes into operation only if there

[8] 6 C.&P. 737, 172 E.R. 1442 (1835).
[9] 42 B.C.R. 128, [1930] 1 D.L.R. 805, 1 W.W.R. 26.

has been a technical arrest; and for this reason, if for no other, the courts should be slow to find that there is an arrest unless the suspect has clearly been told that he is under arrest.

On all these accounts, it seems clearly necessary to maintain the distinction between a command which results in an imprisonment and a request which does not, and to hold that there can be no imprisonment in the absence of words or conduct by the arrester intimating that the suspect is under arrest or that force will be used if he fails to comply with the invitation.

The best course for the suspect, if he is "invited" to accompany the officer to the police station and if he wishes to decline the invitation, is to ask point-blank: "Is this an arrest?" If the answer is in the affirmative, he will then have his action for false imprisonment if he complies and the arrest is illegal. If the answer is in the negative, he can refuse the invitation and will not be guilty of obstructing the police.

The interpretation of words as amounting to command or request is somewhat affected by the proceedings in which it has to be determined. If the suspect is being charged with escape, or with obstructing the officer in the execution of his duty, the question is: did the suspect realise that he was under arrest? If the suspect is suing for the tort of false imprisonment, the question is: did the officer intentionally or negligently cause the suspect to believe that he was under arrest or otherwise detained? If the officer is being prosecuted for the crime of false imprisonment, the question is: did he intentionally or recklessly cause the suspect to believe that he was under arrest or otherwise detained? The distinction between the tort and the crime arises from the fact that on a charge of crime, *mens rea* must be shown. In each case the question is what was conveyed to the mind of the suspect, except that in a legal proceeding against the officer fault or *mens rea* has to be considered.

### The effect of a secret intention to detain

In English law a person can be falsely imprisoned without his knowledge. This follows from *Meering*

v. *Grahame-White Aviation Co.* [10] where the Court of Appeal held that a man was falsely imprisoned when he was kept in an office under pretence of his evidence being needed, there being men stationed outside the door to prevent his escape, even though he did not realise that he had been deprived of his liberty. Atkin, L. J., said that "a person can be imprisoned while he is asleep, while he is in a state of drunkenness, while he is unconscious, and while he is a lunatic." The concluding reference to the lunatic may be thought to be beside the point, because even a lunatic is physically able to move about, so that the question of imprisonment is in his case a realistic one. The case of the unconscious man is different; he cannot move, and it may seem somewhat pedantic to assert that if his door is locked and then unlocked during the state of unconsciousness, he can, when he gets to know of it, sue for nominal charges for false imprisonment. It is true that false imprisonment, being an application of trespass *vi et armis*, is actionable *per se*; but this assumes that there has been an imprisonment. Although the decision of the Court of Appeal settles the law for all English courts short of the House of Lords, it will not necessarily be followed in other jurisdictions. Section 42 of the Restatement of the Law of Torts adopts the opposite rule and rejects the opinion of the English Court of Appeal.

An analogy with battery may bring out the difficulty in the English view. Suppose that D points a loaded pistol at P from behind, and is about to pull the trigger when he is stopped by the intervention of a third party. P is unaware of the whole incident until he gets to hear of it afterwards. No tort has been committed against P. It is not an assault because he suffered no apprehension. D is guilty of the crime of attempted battery, and also of other graver crimes; he is punishable in the criminal law for his wicked intent; but he is not liable in tort, because his intended victim did not suffer any damage—not even the momentary damage of apprehension. Returning now to the person who is imprisoned without knowing it, it is submitted that he should not be able to

[10] 122 L.T. 44 (1919).

recover in tort, because he has sustained no damage of any kind—he suffers no anxiety or humiliation, except possibly in retrospect, and there is not even a momentary contact with his person or property.

The decision in *Meering's* case is of doubtful policy because it seems to penalise a person who acts with caution and consideration. If P is reasonably suspected of a felony like shoplifting (larceny), and if the felony has been committed by someone, it is generally lawful for D to say to him: "I arrest you on a charge of stealing goods from the counter." But if D, wishing to give P every chance to explain himself, and trying to avoid an accusation unless it becomes absolutely necessary, says to P: "Please step this way because the manager would like to see you," and then stands outside the door in case P decides to run away while he is being questioned, this is an actionable tort. *Meering's* case decides that it is an imprisonment, and if so, it cannot be justified as an arrest, because there has been no proper communication of the cause of arrest to the person arrested. There seems to be no social policy in penalising such conduct when an outright arrest would be lawful.

Another argument may be developed against *Meering's* case by supposing the following pair of hypothetical cases. (1) D is a policeman sitting next to P. He suddenly suspects P of a minor crime (for which he has no power to arrest) and makes up his mind that if P attempts flight, he will apprehend him. Shortly afterwards the circumstances of suspicion are explained, and D changes his mind. He is not liable in trespass for false imprisonment, because there has been no act on D's part, but only a mental resolution. (2) As before, except that D moved to P's side after forming the intention to detain P. Here there is an act, namely of moving, so that this particular requirement of the action of trespass is satisfied. But is it not excessively technical to say that there is a false imprisonment, in the absence of any actual restraint and of any constraint upon the mind of the person supposed to be imprisoned? Let us suppose that D communicated his intention to P, but P refused to submit to the arrest, and

walked away unmolested. The law is that there is then no arrest because there is no actual restraint and no touching of the body.[11] If this is so, there can surely be no arrest before the intention to arrest has even been communicated.

The practical effect of *Meering's* case seems to be that, where the police have requested a suspect to attend to help them with their enquiries and the suspect complies but afterwards sues for false imprisonment, the outcome of the action will depend upon the answer to a hypothetical question addressed to the police officer on cross-examination. The officer may be asked what he would have done if the plaintiff had attempted to escape. If the officer replies that he would have let him go, and is believed, there is no imprisonment. If the officer replies that he would have tried to stop him,[12] there is an imprisonment.

This assumes that the officer's secret intent is accompanied by a course of conduct on the officer's part, as where the officer walks to the station with the suspect. Such a course of conduct constitutes the "act" which makes the officer liable in trespass. But now suppose that the officer's secret intent is unaccompanied by an act on his part. This may happen if the intent is formed only after the suspect is in the police station. The police have been interrogating him and at a certain point in their interrogation become convinced that they are on the right track. In that event, as the Royal Commission on Police Powers pointed out,[13] either of two courses may properly be pursued. The police may ask the suspect whether he is willing to stay voluntarily at the station until his statements have been verified. But as soon as he expresses a wish to leave, the police should either let him go or else arrest him and adopt the procedure of the formal charge. If they do not do this, but continue to keep him at the police station (perhaps for further questioning), secretly intending not to let him go, can there be said to be an imprisonment? The question is a difficult one, on which there is no direct judicial authority. If there

[11] [1954] CRIM. L.R. 11–14.
[12] This was the fatal reply given in Conn v. David Spencer Ltd., *op. cit. supra* note 9.
[13] CMD. No. 3297, at 59 (1929).

is an imprisonment, it is certainly illegal; it cannot be justified as an arrest, because the grounds of the arrest have not been communicated, so that the rule in *Christie* v. *Leachinsky*[14] is violated. It may be argued that there is an imprisonment, under the doctrine of *Meering's* case. But in *Meering's* case there was a positive act of imprisonment by the servants of the defendant, who stationed themselves near the room in which the plaintiff was in order to prevent the plaintiff escaping from the room should he try to do so. In the case we are considering, there is no positive act, but merely a mental resolution on the part of a policeman not to let the suspect go. Can the formation of a mental state mark the transition from a state of affairs that is not an imprisonment to one that is? Surprising as it may at first appear, the answer seems to be in the affirmative. For example, suppose that an employer locks the factory gates in order to prevent the ingress of unauthorised persons. An employee demands to be allowed to leave before the end of his work period, and the employer then for the first time decides to keep the gates locked to prevent the egress of the employee. It would seem that, were it not for the defence of consent on the part of the employee,[15] the employer would be guilty of a false imprisonment, notwithstanding that his wrong consists of a mental resolution resulting in an omission to act.

## The "frisking" of criminals

Where a suspected criminal is also suspected of being offensively armed, can the police search him for arms, by tapping his pockets, before making up their minds whether to arrest him? There is no English authority, but the power is so obviously necessary for the protection of the police that it is difficult to believe that it can be condemned by the courts. It might be regarded as a reasonable extension of the existing law of self-defence, or as an application of the doctrine of necessity, or as an essential power of the police in the performance of their duty of preserving the peace.

## Motor vehicles

The police have an important power of controlling motor vehicles, without being put to the embarrassment of arresting the driver. By Section 20(3) of the Road Traffic Act of 1930 a police constable *in uniform* can require any vehicle to stop; and he can then exercise his statutory powers of demanding to see the driving licence or insurance certificate.[16] It is not stated in the Act for what other purpose the officer may require the vehicle to remain stationary, and one is safe in saying that the power to stop a vehicle does not give the power to detain it indefinitely. Probably the vehicle can be detained only for a reasonable time as a mode of controlling traffic. There is certainly no power under the Act to search the vehicle or to require its occupants to alight. At the same time, the power to stop gives a useful means of delaying a suspected criminal and ascertaining his identity. Also, it seems safe to say that comparatively small circumstances of suspicion would suffice to justify an arrest under Section 28(3) of the Act, which empowers a police constable to arrest a person whom he reasonably suspects of driving a vehicle without the owner's consent. When the arrest has been made under this section, it may well be found that a big fish has been netted, since fleeing criminals often drive purloined vehicles.

Goods vehicles are subject to a special regime. Section 16 of the Road and Rail Traffic Act of 1933 requires the holder of a licence for the carriage of goods to cause work records to be kept showing particulars of each journey, etc.; and regulations made under this Act require the work records to be carried on the vehicle.[17] By Section 8, examiners appointed under the Act, and also police constables, may require the driver to produce his work records, and may inspect and copy them. The same statutory powers are applied to the provisions of the Transport Act of 1947, by Section 60(4) of that Act.

Whether acting under the Road Traffic Acts

---

[14] [1947] A.C. 573.
[15] See Burns v. Johnston, [1916] 2 Ir.R. 444, *aff'd*, [1917] 2 Ir.R. 137 (C.A.).

[16] ROAD TRAFFIC ACT, §§ 4(5), 40(1) (1930).
[17] GOODS VEHICLES (KEEPING OF RECORDS) REGULATIONS, [1935] STAT. RULES & ORDERS (No. 314).

or not, the police do in fact stop vehicles and question drivers as a means of controlling crime. Their activities are sometimes strikingly rewarded. On August 13, 1955, at 2 a.m. a band of armed men broke into a military training centre at Arborfield and stole arms and ammunition which they carried off in vans. Before the theft had been reported, two policemen in a radio car, carrying out a routine check on the Reading-Ascot road, stopped and searched a two-ton motorvan. Two men inside offered no resistance. In the back were 15,000 rounds of the missing ammunition.[18] It is not clear whether the search of the van was lawful, but the police certainly had a right to see the driver's work records, and possibly some circumstance connected with these records or the demeanour of the men aroused a reasonable suspicion of felony.

### Statutory powers of search and arrest on the ground of unlawful possession

It remains to be mentioned that there are certain

[18] *News Chronicle*, August 15, 1955.

local statutes giving the police power to search vessels and carriages on reasonable suspicion that they are being used to convey stolen goods, and also to search persons who may be reasonably suspected of such conveyance. The first of these statutes was the metropolitan Police Act of 1839, Section 66. It is still extensively used in London, the police stopping several hundred thousand people a year in the streets and asking to see the contents of a bag they are carrying, or enquiring as to any other thing they may have which may possibly have been stolen. Litigation rarely arises and the police report that they have few complaints; yet their exercise of the statutory powers does not seem to be legal. The statute is plainly limited to cases where the police have reason to suppose that a stolen article is being conveyed; yet they use it to make a random check in the hope of netting a thief or receiver. In any case, most large cities are without these special powers, and Parliament is no longer willing to extend them to areas where they do not now exist.

# France

ROBERT VOUIN

(a) Generally, according to the new Code of Penal Procedure, applicable in France since March 2, 1959, a person can be taken into custody only if the examining magistrate (Juge d'Instruction) has delivered a warrant of arrest against him.[1] However, the Code provides otherwise in the case of an obvious crime (or of offences of moderate gravity punished by a sentence of imprisonment where such offences are obvious), that is to say, in the case of the crime which is being committed or has just been committed, or in the case where,

[1] CODE OF PENAL PROCEDURE (hereinafter C.P.P.), art. 122.

shortly after a crime, a person is either prosecuted by public outcry or in possession of objects or presenting signs leading to a suspicion he participated in the crime.[2] In such a case, in fact, any person is qualified to arrest the author of a flagrant offence and to take him before the nearest judicial police officer; in this instance, no warrant of justice is necessary.[3]

In addition to the right to arrest, the French law grants also to the Police (that is to say to the Gendarmerie Nationale, to the Surete Nationale, and in Paris to the Prefecture de Police) the right of keeping a close watch on someone, or checking his identity, or searching him.

[2] C.P.P., arts. 53, 57.
[3] C.P.P., art. 73.

48

*1.—Keeping a close watch on somebody—*

In the case of a crime or a flagrant delict, the judicial police officer in charge of the investigation may keep in his power, for 24 hours at the most, three categories of persons:

(1) Those who happen to be at the place of the breach of the law.

(2) Those for whom it seems necessary to establish or verify identity.

(3) Those who seem able to give information on the facts. This keeping on a close watch may be extended for another period of 24 hours, with written permission from the "Procureur of the Republique," but only in the case of persons against whom serious and concordant incriminating evidence exists.[4] Persons kept on a close watch may be interrogated by the judicial police officers, provided they observe a certain number of rules which tend to guarantee the correctness of the close watch and of the interrogation.[5]

On another hand, even outside the case of crime and flagrant delict, the judicial police officer may carry out enquiries called "preliminary enquiries," either on the Procureur de la Republique's request or of his own accord.[6] In this case, house-searches and seizures of material evidence may be carried out only with the written permission of the persons whose houses are thus visited. However, the judicial police officer may then legally retain at his disposal certain persons for 24 hours at the most "for the necessities of preliminary enquiry," and this delay may be extended for another 24 hours by decision of the Procureur de la Republique, even if there is no serious and concordant incriminating evidence.[7]

*2.—Checking of Identity—*In case of a crime or a flagrant delict (in addition to the possibility of keeping a close watch on a person as just mentioned), "every person whose identity it seems necessary to establish or check, must lend himself to the operations requested by this measure," otherwise he might be liable to imprisonment, and to a fine of 10 days maximum and 360 NF.[8]

It should be noticed that this obligation of lending oneself to this proof and checking of identity was provided for previously by Article 8, paragraph 1, of the law of Nov. 27, 1943, which created a service of technical police. Moreover, this text, which was not abrogated at the time of the coming into force of the Penal Procedure Code, may be applied even outside the hypothesis of a crime or a flagrant delict.

On another hand, one should also take into account the authority given to the military of the "Gendarmerie Nationale" as it is stated in the decree of May 20, 1903 (modified by the decree of August 22, 1958), dealing with the organization and service of the "Gendarmerie". The latter. for instance, is bound to secure bodily any person circulating in France without any card stating his identity (ou bien: without his identity duly authenticated by documents). To this end, any policeman in uniform is entitled to ask to be shown documents of identity and cannot suffer a refusal. The checking of these documents should be done in one of the community rooms of the hotel, never in the traveller's own room, and generally speaking, "the gendarmerie is directed to behave with courteousness in performing this duty, and not to feel entitled to any action which might be qualified as a vexatious measure or misuse of authority."[9]

The military personnel of the Gendarmerie may even use their fire arms if there is no other possibility to arrest persons who, in spite of repeated calls of "Halte, Gendarmerie," uttered in a loud voice, try to escape their investigation or custody or "when it is impossible for them to stop vehicles, boats or other means of transportation whose conductors do not obey the order to stop."[10]

Actually, the Gendarmerie, which alone is granted the right of using fire arms, very seldom takes advantage of it, for the ordinary "Gendarme", who is always a regular soldier with the grade of sergeant, is a wise man, disciplined and self-controlled. In the ordinary course of things,

---

[4] C.P.P., art. 63.
[5] C.P.P., art. 64.
[6] C.P.P., art. 75.

[7] C.P.P., art. 77.
[8] C.P.P., art. 61.

[9] DECREE OF MAY 20, 1903 (as modified), arts. 165, 166.
[10] *Id.*, art. 174.

the only penalty inflicted for the "refusal to comply" of the driver who refuses to stop is the one provided by Article L. 4 of the highway code (ordonnance of December 15, 1958), according to which "any conductor of a vehicle who has knowingly omitted to obey the summons to stop given by an official person or policeman whose duty is to state breaches of the law, and who carries the exterior and apparent badges of his quality, or, who will refuse to submit to all prescribed checkings concerning the vehicle or the person, will be punished with imprisonment which can last from ten days to 3 months, and will be fined from 500 to 3,000 frs, or with one of these two penalties only."

3.—*Searching of a Person*—According to the French Law, one may still wonder to what extent the police are permitted to practice the searching of a person, or "fouille a corps," with someone whose appearance or behaviour aroused police suspicion.

(b) The fundamental principle according to the French jurisprudence is that the searching of a person must be assimilated to the house-search or domiciliary visit, and that it is legally impossible whenever the searching of the person's house itself would be impossible.[11] On the other hand, the searching of the person may be undertaken by the judicial police officer when he would be entitled to carry out a search of the man's house. Mere suspicions cannot justify the arrest and search of a person, because they do not make the delict flagrant. Thus, a judicial police officer cannot—without a warrant from an examining magistrate—arrest in the street and search a person who is merely suspected either of collecting illicit bettings on horse-races or carrying weapons illegally.[12] On the other hand, the searching of such a person is proper if the delict is flagrant, i.e., if the weapon is conspicuous or if it can be seen in the person's hands.[13] In the same way, the arrest and searching of a person are also possible when a judicial police officer knows for certain that a person carries with him a certain quantity of a drug, such as cocain.[14]

Also, the French jurisprudence admits of searching a person who is legally under arrest as a "mere police measure, the application of which is general and necessary, taken as well for the public interest as for the arrested person's interest." And, in this case, a penal sentence may be built upon the facts established in the process of the searching. If, for instance, a person is searched after having been arrested because, drunk and disorderly, he has been a cause of disturbances, the discovery of a gun on this person justifies his being sentenced for "port d'arme prohibé" (carrying unlawful weapons).[15]

If these solutions are quite certain, there is still a question, in France, whether the "garde a vue" (keeping a close watch on somebody), now admitted and under the regulation of the Code of Penal Procedure, must be assimilated to a real arrest—in a word, to know whether the person on whom the police keep a close watch may be subjected to a search as in the case of a person legally arrested. Until the question is solved by the jurisprudence, it is propounded to admit that the searching of a person merely kept on watch is possible, as a "mere police measure," if the person is kept for serious and concordant incriminating evidence.[16] According to the decree of May 20, 1903, Article 307, the persons arrested by the constabulary in the case of a crime or a flagrant delict, and kept on a close watch before being brought before the Public Prosecutor, "must be searched, in order to insure as well their own security ... or for the discovery of things which might help to the revelation of the truth."

(c) As we just saw, the French Law gives to the police a certain number of rights which, outside all properly so-called arrests, allow them to summon persons, to keep them, to hear them and even to interrogate and possibly to search them. These powers, of course, are not granted without restrictions and conditions. Related to the close

---

[11] Cass. Crim., Rec. Dalloz 1953.533 (1953).
[12] Nimes, Rec. Dalloz 1929.2.46 (1928).
[13] *Ibid.*

[14] Nimes, Rec. Sirey 1930.2.80 (1930).
[15] Nimes, Rec. Dalloz 1928.2.64 (1926).
[16] *Cf.* BESSON, VOUIN & ARPAILLANGE, CODE ANOTÉ DE PROCÉDURE, art. 76, al.1.

watch of persons in the enquiry for flagrant delict, particularly, Article 64 of the Penal Code embodies some important dispositions.

First of all, the judicial police officer must mention on the report of the hearing of the person who is kept on a close watch how long the interrogatories and the breaks that divided them lasted, the exact day and time when the person started being kept on a close watch, and the exact day and time when he or she was either discharged or brought before the competent magistrate. The report must mention also the reasons for the close watch.

Secondly, these mentions must be specially initialled by the persons concerned (or, in the case of a refusal of signature, the report must be made complete by exposing the reasons of the refusal). In addition, they must appear on a special register, maintained for this purpose in every police quarter liable to receive persons kept a close watch.

Finally, of his own accord, or on the request of one of the person's relatives, the public prosecutor may have the person kept on a close watch checked by a doctor at any time during the watch. After 24 hours, this medical examination cannot be refused if the person who is kept on a close watch asks for it.

All these precisions are not unimportant. But, there are still more important guarantees for individual liberites, such as those which result either from the fact that keeping a close watch on a person, according to the Code, can never be decided but by a magistrate or a judicial police officer (and never by an ordinary police constable), or from the conditions to which the jurisprudence subordinates the possibility of compelling a person to be searched.

(d) In France the juridical system explained above seems to be accepted by the public and the police do not actually ask for other powers than the ones which are granted by the legislation. Concerns expressed at the time of the promulgation of the Code of Penal Procedure concerning the shortness of time allowed by the Code for keeping a close watch of a person seem already to have died away, except perhaps when it comes to dealing with attempts against the State safety, or struggles against criminal gangs, such as the ones which practise the drug-traffic or coinage offence.

However, it is not true that the police, according to the French law, are permitted to summon anybody in the street, and to ask this person what he or she is doing, only because the person's appearance or behaviour might have aroused suspicion. But one must notice that the policeman may always speak politely to another person, like any citizen, and collect his statements, if he gets any. This possibility, carried on by policemen who know their jobs, seems to be sufficient, and there is no need in this matter to change or add anything to the French Law.

# *Germany*

WALTER R. CLEMENS

In the field of fighting delinquency the police in Germany have to perform a twofold task: first, the preventive one of avoiding crimes, and, secondly, the repressive one of taking part in the detection and prosecution of crimes. The repressive function of the police will be outlined first. Their preventive function will be discussed later.

## POLICE RIGHTS AND DUTIES IN THE PROSECUTION OF CRIME

### *General duties*

Pursuant to Section 152 of the German Code of Criminal Procedure (hereinafter called CCP), neither the police nor any other administrative authority has, in principle, the right to prosecute in court. This right is exercised exclusively by the Staatsanwalt (public prosecutor, district attorney), a fully qualified lawyer who has a career position with permanent tenure. He *must* take action as soon as he is notified of any offense punishable in a criminal court, provided he has reasonable cause for believing such act to have in fact been committed. He has no discretion.

In his work he will be supported by the police who act as the district attorney's "auxiliary organs." The police, pursuant to Section 161, CCP, have to comply with all orders and instructions of the district attorney. Further, on their own initiative they prepare the prosecution for the district attorney and assist him in his work; their duties in this regard are laid down in Section 163, CCP, which provides:

"(i) The offices and officers of the police shall investigate criminal offenses and take all measures that permit of no delay, with a view to preventing collusion in the case.

"(ii) The provisions of sec. 136a and sec. 69(iii)[1] will apply.

"(iii) The offices and officers of the police will submit their reports to the district attorney without delay. If the speedy grant of judicial rulings appears necessary during the course of the investigation, the reports may be summitted directly to the County Court Judge."

According to Section 163, CCP, the police, when faced with lawbreakers, have the so-called "right to make the first move" ("Recht des ersten Zugriffs"). Their concrete measures are subject to the same restrictions as those of the district attorney. Just like the district attorney, the police must respect the rights of the individual, guaranteed by the Basic Law and the provisions of the CCP.

### *In detail*

#### (a) *Preliminary arrest of suspects*

The liberty of the person is guaranteed in Germany through Article 2(ii) and Article 104(i) of the Basic Law for the Federal Republic of Germany dated May 23, 1949.[2]

In implementation of these Basic Law provisions, the right of preliminary arrest is governed by Section 127, CCP, as follows:

"(i) If a person is caught in the act or on pursuit, anybody is authorized to apprehend him even in the absence of a judicial warrant, if he is sus-

---

[1] These two provisions outlaw the use of dubious methods in connection with the interrogation of the defendant and of a witness.

[2] These provisions, as far as of interest here, read:

"*Article 2(ii)*. Everyone shall have the right to life and to physical inviolability. The freedom of the individual shall be inviolable. These rights may be interfered with only on the basis of a law.

"*Article 104*. (i) The freedom of the individual may be restricted only on the basis of a formal law and only with due regard to the forms prescribed therein. Detained persons may be subjected neither to mental nor physical ill-treatment."

pected of escape, or his identity cannot be established on the spot.

"(ii) In the event of imminent danger the district attorney and the police are authorized to make a preliminary arrest, if the legal requirements of a warrant of arrest are complied with."

While within the limits of subparagraph (i), *supra*, everybody—not just the district attorney and the police—is authorized to make a preliminary arrest, the rights established in Section 127, CCP, subparagraph (ii), *supra*, are vested exclusively in the district attorney and all members of the police.

The use of these rights presupposes that the facts of the case warrant judicial arrest, and further that imminent danger prevails. The requirements established in Section 112, CCP,[3] for the issuance of a warrant of arrest, which can only be granted by a judge, are strong suspicion of an offense *and* danger of escape or collusion.

The first requirement of a preliminary arrest by the police is therefore that the facts warrant strong suspicion (that is, a high degree of probability) of the commission of an offense by the suspect. A faint or remote or even reasonable suspicion is not sufficient.

In addition to a strong suspicion, either the danger of escape (Section 112(i)(1), CCP) or the

---

[3] Section 112, CCP, reads:
"(i) Custody awaiting trial can only be ordered against the suspect if there is strong suspicion against the suspect and if
(1) he has escaped or is in hiding or if, in recognition of the merits of the case, especially the circumstances of the suspect and the opportunities of an escape, there is cause for concern that he will evade trial or
(2) if specific facts exist giving rise to the concern that the suspect by means of destroying traces of the act or other evidence or by influencing witnesses or accomplices might impede the finding of the truth.
(ii) The facts evidencing the suspicion of escape or danger of collusion must be entered on the record. The danger of escape requires no further proof if
(1) a major crime is the subject matter of the investigation or
(2) within the area of jurisdiction of this Federal Law the suspect has no fixed residence or address, especially if he is a vagrant or fails to prove his identity."

---

danger of collusion (Section 112(i)(2), CCP) must be present. The suspicion of escape will arise if the offender intends to evade prosecution. Whether there is suspicion of escape will be decided on the facts of the case. The police will be safe in assuming danger of escape if the offender is taking measures to prepare his escape, e.g., abandoning his regular work or inquiring about travel facilities. In the cases of Section 112(ii)(1) and (2) the danger of escape appears patent and therefore needs no further proof.

The last requirement of a preliminary police arrest is "imminent danger." It exists if obtaining a judicial warrant entails a loss of time which would give rise to concern that the arrest of the suspected person might thereby become impossible.

The police officer who wants to effect a preliminary arrest pursuant to Section 127, CCP, has to use his discretion in deciding whether the mentioned legal requirements are complied with. A bona fide error in the use of such discretion will not affect the legality of the arrest made by him.[4]

Under German Law the preliminarily arrested person must be taken before a judge who shall decide whether or not to issue a warrant of arrest.[5]

The preliminary arrest of a suspected person by the police is often hampered by the latter's escape or forcible resistance. The statute does not answer the question as to what means may be used to enforce arrest. It is, however, common ground in the practice of the courts as well as in the opinion of the law professors that for the enforcement of arrest, preliminary or judicial, adequate means, including necessary force, may be used. The Supreme Court of the former Deutsche Reich (Reichsgericht) holds that the extent and limit of an arrest has to be confined to the purpose of neutralizing the freedom of movement of the person to be arrested, and that every force in excess of actual apprehension shall only be permissible in the event of resistance being offered

---

[4] 37 Entscheidungen des Reichsgerichts in Strafsachen 37 (Decisions of the Reichsgericht in Criminal Matters) and 55 *id.* 166.
[5] This question is dealt with in my report concerning "Police Interrogation Privileges and Limitations" which appears in Part III of this volume.

to the arrest.[6] The chaining or tying of the suspect is therefore allowed only in an exceptional case.[7] The right to make an arrest does not include the authority to inflict injuries to life or limb.[8] Resistance against a legitimate arrest (e.g., the person seized by a police officer hits him in the face or points a pistol at him or a bank-robber shoots at the police) will justify self-defense by means of a weapon.[9] The use of arms by police officers is governed in the various German Länder by Service Regulations which—in appreciation of the especially dangerous nature of fire-arms—limit the use of weapons to a narrow scope.

The requirements which must be complied with by the police if a suspect is intended to be deprived of his liberty for prosecution purposes are governed exhaustively by Section 127, CCP. If they are not complied with, if, in particular, the "strong" suspicion is missing (a mere "police suspicion" will not be sufficient), the police are not entitled, according to the consistent practice of the Reichsgericht[10] which still today is acknowledged without reserve, to arrest the suspect against his will, to march him to the police station, or otherwise make any restraint on his liberty, be it only by holding him on the street.

### (b) Questioning of suspects

The police—in pursuit of their duty established in Section 163, CCP, to investigate criminal offenses—may question suspects who are at large, or volunteer to an interrogation, or are in legal custody. But in the absence of a legal basis, they cannot force a suspect at large into appearing before them for an interrogation, or into being interrogated on the street or elsewhere, unless the qualifications of Section 127, CCP, which justify his preliminary arrest, are fulfilled. Apart from this, the suspect can always obstruct his

[6] 17 Entscheidungen des Reichsgerichts in Strafsachen 28.
[7] See 17 Entscheidungen des Reichsgerichts in Strafsachen 28.
[8] See 34 Entscheidungen des Reichsgerichts in Strafsachen 446; 65 id. 392; 69 id. 312.
[9] See 34 Entscheidungen des Reichsgerichts in Strafsachen 446.
[10] 27 Entscheidungen des Reichsgerichts in Strafsachen 155; 32 id. 271; 38 id. 374; and 59 id. 114.

interrogation by using his privilege of silence.[11]

### (c) Physical examination of suspects

Section 81a, CCP, provides for the physical examination or blood-testing of suspects. A mere, that is, "reasonable", suspicion of an offense is sufficient for the ascertainment of facts relevant to the issue. Bodily interferences by a doctor as well as the taking of blood-tests without the consent of the suspect are permissible only if there are no grounds for an apprehension that they might result in detriments to his health.

Further, Section 81d, CCP, provides for the physical examination of a woman, irrespective of her consent, to be made by a woman or a doctor, and for the calling in, on request, of a woman or next-of-kin, if the examination might hurt the sense of shame of the woman to be examined.

Orders of such nature are in principle reserved to the judge. Only in cases where the success of the investigation is endangered through delay, the district attorney and especially qualified police officers (namely members of the Criminal Police) are entitled to take appropriate action in their own right. This will always apply in a traffic accident, if an alcohol-test is required from a suspect, because the alcohol will soon be eliminated from the body and hence cease to serve as evidence for the suspected offenses.

### (d) Taking of fingerprints, photos, etc., from suspects

Section 81b, CCP, authorizes the police—as well as the judge and the district attorney—to take photos, fingerprints, measurements and similar evidence from a suspect even against his will to the extent that this will serve the purpose of furthering the prosecution or establishing his identity.

### (e) Searches against the suspect

Searches against the suspect (which include his

[11] As regards the interrogation of the suspect by the police, see my report on self-incrimination which appears in Part IV of this volume. This question is also dealt with in my report concerning "Police Interrogation Privileges and Limitations" in Part III.

frisking) can only be ordered by a judge; in the case of imminent danger, however, the district attorney and specially qualified police officers (namely members of the Criminal Police) can also effect them (see Article 13(i) of the Basic Law, as well as Section 105(i), CCP). The details of searches against suspects are laid down in Sections 102 *et. seq.*, CCP. The most important provisions are Sections 102 and 104, CCP.[12] Section 102 provides for the permissibility of a search against a suspect in general, while Section 104 imposes restrictions on the search in regard to the time during which the search of rooms and fenced-in property, the so-called house-search, is permissible.

It appears noteworthy that a search is permitted where there is mere suspicion—that means "reasonable suspicion"—whereas arrest presupposes "strong suspicion."

### (f) Impounding against suspects

The permissibility of impoundings which constitute a restraint of property and therefore, under Article 14(ii) of the Basic Law, are permissible only on the strength of a law, is governed by Sections 94 to 101, CCP. The most important provision is Section 94, which says that objects

---

[12] They read:

"*Section 102.* A search of the abode and of other rooms as well as of the person, and of the personal belongings can be effected against anybody who is under suspicion as perpetrator of the crime or accomplice thereto before or after the fact or as a receiver. The search can be made for the purpose of his apprehension or in the event that there are reasonable grounds to assume that it will result in the discovery of evidence.

"*Section 104.* (i) During night-time the dwellings, the business premises and the fenced-in property must be entered only in hot pursuit or in case of danger or in case of the capture of an escaped person.

(ii) This restriction will not apply to dwellings of persons who are under police supervision or to rooms which during night-time are accessible to everybody or which are known to the police as shelters or meeting-places of persons with previous convictions, as a deposit for objects received by means of criminal acts or as hiding-places for gambling or prostitution.

(iii) Within the period from April 1st to September 30th the night-time covers the hours beginning 9 o'clock p.m. and ending 4 o'clock a.m., and within the period from October 1st to March 31st the hours beginning 9 o'clock p.m. and ending 6 o'clock a.m."

which may be of importance as exhibits for the investigation will be taken into custody or otherwise safeguarded, and that impounding is necessary if the objects are in the custody of another person and are not surrendered voluntarily. To order impoundings against the suspect is principally reserved to the judge; only in the case of imminent danger are the district attorney and the members of the Criminal Police allowed to effect them (see Section 98(i), CCP). Sections 95 to 97, CCP, are not applicable to impoundings against the suspect. Sections 99 to 101 provide for the impounding of mails coming from, or addressed to, the suspect; they are without importance for the purposes of this report, as such actions can be effected by the judge or district attorney only, and never by the police.

It must be pointed out also that an impounding against the suspect requires only "reasonable" rather than "strong" suspicion.

## POLICE RIGHTS AND DUTIES IN THE PREVENTION OF CRIME

The preventive function of the police is dealt with in the police statutes of the Länder rather than in the CCP, which covers only repressive police measures. Their legal ground is afforded by Sections 14 and 15 of the former Prussian Police Administration Act, dated June 1, 1931, which enable the police to take action to ward off dangers threatening public security and order.[13]

These provisions are in force in all Länder of the Federal Republic of Germany, partly on the strength of statutes of the same or similar tenor enacted subsequent to 1945, partly as common law which was valid long before 1931. Naturally, the

---

[13] These provisions read:

"*Section 14.* (i) The police authorities shall, within the limits of the existing laws, take the necessary action to ward off, from the public or the individual, dangers threatening public security and order.

(ii) Moreover the police authorities will perform such duties as have been especially assigned to them by law.

"*Section 15.* (i) The police are authorized to take persons into police custody only if such measure is necessary

(a) for the protection of such persons

(b) to remove a disturbance of public safety or

dividing line between a preventive action of the police on the strength of the said provisions, and a repressive action under the provisions of the CCP is blurred. This becomes obvious especially in the cases of raids. Provided all the persons who are arrested and frisked on this occasion are under strong suspicion, their arrest and their frisking is covered by the provision of the CCP. However, the problem of such raids lies in the very fact that not only strongly suspected persons but also law-abiding and unsuspected individuals, who under the CCP are not subject to arrest and searching, are subjected to arrest and frisking. Nevertheless, it is the common belief in Germany that on the strength of the above-quoted provisions such round-ups are permitted as a preventive police measure.

Hence, the Reichsgericht held in a decision rendered in 1906 that the police were authorized to frisk some coal miners for weapons.[14] A few in fact carried weapons and had already shot at and wounded other people. In the opinion of the Reichsgericht, the frisking was necessary to prevent further illegal use of fire-arms and thus remove a public menace.

Similar considerations played their part in German courts in the years following the Second World War. At that time the police—often by order of the Military Government—were searching the baggage of railway and motor-car travelers with a view to detecting and impounding victuals that had been acquired contrary to the rationing regulations. Undoubtedly in such cases the statutory prerequisites of Section 102, CCP, and following, do not apply in regard to all searched

travelers, because there were no reasonable grounds to assume that all of them were under the suspicion of rationing offenses.

Even so, the courts ruled such measures to be legal because they were necessary to prevent the food supply of the population from being jeopardized. However, in areas where no "black market" existed such searching was held to be illegal.[15]

This broad interpretation of the preventive functions of the police will certainly give rise to objections on the part of liberal observers, because it tends to further a far-reaching undermining of well-considered safeguards embodied in the CCP in connection with the repressive activities of the police.

### CONCLUSION

In the light of the foregoing observations on the rights of the police in the prosecution and prevention of crimes, the four questions posed for discussion in connection with this topic[16] can under German Law be answered as follows:

(1) In the absence of a legal basis, police suspicion alone does not entitle the police to stop a person on the street and question him as to his identity and reason for being where he is, unless he consents to his being questioned. On the contrary, such repressive measures are permitted only in the event of a preliminary arrest based upon "strong suspicion," as that term is used in the CCP. As preventive measures they are justified, though, if they are necessary to ward off from the public such dangers as are threatening public security and order. This however, will occur only on rare occasions.

(2) "On the street" searches for weapons or incriminating evidence can only be made by the police upon "reasonable" suspicion, which, as mentioned before, is less than "strong" suspicion, the requisite to an arrest.

As a preventive police measure, however, searches are confined to the rare occasions where

---

order which has already occurred, or to avoid an imminent danger subject to public action if the removal of such disturbance or the avoidability of such danger is not otherwise possible.

(ii) The persons taken into police custody must, except in cases of publicly dangerous mentally disordered individuals, be released from police custody during the course of the following day at the latest.

(iii) The above provisions will not apply in extradition and expulsion cases."

[14] See 39 Entscheidungen des Reichsgerichts in Strafsachen 192.

[15] As far as can be traced here, the decisions bearing on the matter have not been published.

[16] The four questions are set forth in the introduction at the beginning of Part I of this volume.

they appear necessary to avoid a public danger.

(3) There is no need of curtailing the powers of the police in the execution of their repressive activities. The regulation so far has proved a success. Curtailing the powers vested in the police under the present law would intolerably paralyze their striking power.

However, a more precise regulation of the preventive powers of the police, in particular the permissibility of raids, would be a matter worth considering. Under normal conditions they should be permitted only for clearing out hiding places of criminals and, in politically turbulent times, for the prevention of riots and other disturbances. It would appear advisable to enact a law which reserves the order for a raid to the judge only and subjects the judge to the above requirements.

(4) There is also no need of broadening the statutory powers justifying a police arrest, repressive or preventive, all the less as this would mean a relapse into the foul practices of the Nazi police state which thought nothing of personal freedom. That state had expanded by a law enacted in 1935[17]

[17] Article 5 des Gesetzes zur Änderung der Vorschriften des Strafverfahrens und des Gerichtsverfas-

the requisites for an arrest and therewith also of a preliminary arrest on the part of the police.

Under that law a suspect could also be arrested for fear he might abuse his liberty to commit new criminal acts, and further, if in consideration of the serious nature of his crime and the public resentment aroused thereby, leaving him at liberty appeared intolerable. The second requirement for an arrest obviously originated in typical Nazi-trains of thought and was repealed as early as 1945. The first requirement was abolished in 1950 in the course of an amendment of the CCP,[18] because it was justly felt that this requirement of an arrest could not be reconciled with the principles of a constitutional system and with the basic right of the freedom of the person.

---

sungsgesetzes (Law for the Amendment of the Provisions respecting Criminal Procedure and the Court Constitution Law, dated June 28, 1935).

[18] Article 3, No. 44, des Gesetzes zur Wiederherstellung der Rechtseinheit auf dem Gebiete der Gerichtsverfassung, der bürgerlichen Rechtspflege, des Strafverfahrens und des Kostenrechts vom 12.9.50 (Law dated September 12, 1950 on the Restoration of Legal Unity in the Field of Court Constitution, Administration of Civil and Criminal Justice and Law Costs).

# *Israel*

## HAIM H. COHN

Under Israel law, a police officer may arrest any person without warrant when he has reasonable grounds for believing that that person has committed a felony;[1] or when that person has in his presence, or has recently,[2] committed an offence

[1] A felony is an offence punishable with imprisonment exceeding three years: CRIMINAL CODE ORDINANCE §5 (Palestine 1936), and Interpretation Ordinance §1.

[2] "Recently" has been held to mean immediately after the commission of the offence: 11 Pesakim Mekhouziyim (District Court Judgments) 253.

punishable with imprisonment for a period exceeding six months; or when that person commits, or is accused before him of having committed, an offence, or when he believes on reasonable grounds that that person has committed an offence, and that person refuses to give his name and address or has no known or fixed abode. Likewise, he may arrest without warrant a person obstructing him while in the execution of his duty, or who has escaped, or attempts to escape, from lawful custody, or who is pursued by hue and cry. Finally, a police officer may arrest without warrant a person found in suspicious circumstances, taking

57

precautions to conceal himself or having no ostensible means of subsistence and unable to give a satisfactory account of himself.[3]

The powers vested in police officers may be conferred on any public officer designated by the Minister of Justice[4] and have been so conferred on port inspectors, road traffic inspectors, and officers in charge of investigations into black-marketeering offences.

Special powers to arrest without a warrant are given to customs officers and police officers where they have reasonable ground to believe that a person is committing, or attempting to commit, or being concerned in the commission of, any smuggling offences;[5] and to police officers where the driver of a vehicle commits a driving offence within his view and fails to give his name and address or to produce his driving licence on demand.[6]

As to a person who is about to commit an offence but has not yet committed it, it is a misdemeanour punishable with two years' imprisonment to fail to use all reasonable means to prevent the commission or completion of a felony, where it is known that a felony is designed to be committed.[7] The reasonable means to prevent the felonious act may include, or consist of, the arrest of the would-be offender without a warrant. But the Supreme Court has ruled that this provision "imposes a duty on every person to act only where that persons *knows* that another designs to commit a felony. 'Knows' means what it says: you do not know that which you only conclude, however reasonably, from the circumstances. . . ."[8]

In many cases arrests by police officers were held unlawful where the statutory powers of arrest had been exceeded. Thus, an inferior court

is reported to have held that where a police officer in whose presence the offence of soliciting for immoral purposes[9] had been committed notified the offender that he was arresting her, and only afterwards asked her for her name and address and, when she refused, asked her to accompany him to the police station—the arrest and all subsequent proceedings were unlawful.[10] And where a police officer would have been justified in arresting a person for a felony he actually had committed, but on arresting him told him by mistake that he was being arrested on a charge involving a misdemeanour only (as distinguished from a felony), the arrest was held unlawful by the Supreme Count, as the offence had not been committed in the officer's presence, and in respect of the misdemeanour he had no power of arrest unless it was committed in his presence.[11]

A police officer effecting an arrest may search the arrested person, or cause him to be searched, and may take from him any offensive weapons which he has about his person.[12] Where the police officer is not empowered to arrest without a warrant, he is not entitled to search any person except on a warrant of search (or, of course, a warrant of arrest).[13]

It is an offence punishable with one month's imprisonment (or, in the case of subsequent offences after previous convictions of the same offence, with one year's imprisonment) for any person to behave in a disorderly or indecent manner in any public place; or to conduct himself in any public place in a manner likely to cause a breach of the peace; or to be found wandering in any public place at such time and under such circumstances as to lead to the conclusion that he is there for an illegal or disorderly purpose.[14] As subsequent offences are punishable with imprison-

---

[3] Section 3(1), CRIMINAL PROCEDURE (ARREST AND SEARCHES) ORDINANCE §3(1), LAWS OF PALESTINE cap. 33.
[4] *Id.* §3(3).
[5] CUSTOMS ORDINANCE §193, LAWS OF PALESTINE cap. 42.
[6] ROAD TRANSPORT ORDINANCE §19, LAWS OF PALESTINE cap. 128.
[7] CRIMINAL CODE ORDINANCE §33 (Palestine 1936).
[8] Frenkel v. Attorney-General, 5 Piskei Din 1602, 1606 (1951).

[9] Punishable with one month's imprisonment only: CRIMINAL CODE ORDINANCE §167 (Palestine 1936).
[10] Reported in 1 ISRAEL POLICE QUARTERLY 56 (in Hebrew).
[11] Attorney-General v. Kedoshim, 10 Piskei Din 972, 976 (1956).
[12] CRIMINAL PROCEDURE (ARREST AND SEARCHES) ORDINANCE §11(1), LAWS OF PALESTINE cap. 33.
[13] *Id.*, §§13, 16.
[14] CRIMINAL CODE ORDINANCE §193 (Palestine 1936)

ment exceeding six months, a police officer may arrest without a warrant a recidivist offender of this kind, and police have tried to exercise their power of arrest under this provision in respect of known prostitutes found in the streets. It has, however, been held by the Supreme Court that it is not sufficient that circumstances are such as to lead to the conclusion that the person arrested was there for an illegal or disorderly purpose; but under the statute both the "circumstances" and the "time" of his being found wandering must lead to that conclusion; and where the time is a time of day or evening where streets are normally and generally frequented, no such conclusion may be drawn.[15]

Apart from the power to arrest without warrant, every police officer has the power "to require any person whom he has reasonable grounds for believing to have committed any offence, to furnish him with his name and address, and may require such person to accompany him to the police station, and, if the person refuses to accompany him, he may arrest him."[16] Even this right to stop and question a person as to his identity and abode is thus confined to criminal offenders or persons reasonably believed to have committed an offence, and in the absence of such belief or of reason for such belief, a person may not be stopped and questioned by a police officer except to give "a satisfactory account of himself" where he was found in suspicious circumstances, taking precautions to conceal himself, or has no ostensible means of subsistence. As a matter of practice, no person is stopped and questioned by police in Israel except in the small hours of the night where the behaviour of the person in the street arouses suspicion; and no case is reported in which the conduct of the police in stopping and questioning such persons, or in arresting persons who could not give a satisfactory account of themselves, has given rise to any complaints.

The opinion generally prevailing in Israel is that the law as it stands (although of British origin and enacted by the Mandatory Government of Palestine[17]), and as interpreted by the Israel judiciary, is not in need of revision or reform. The police do not claim that the powers of arrest and questioning vested in them, however restricted they are and however restrictively they are interpreted, are not sufficient to enable them to provide the public with adequate police protection. Hence the question has not arisen, and is not in the near future likely to arise, in this country, whether police should be permitted to arrest, search or question people in the streets in circumstances which are not covered by existing legislation.

It appears arguable, however, that the existing law stands in need of simplification. While the commission of an offence, or the loitering in suspicious circumstances, coupled with either precautions to conceal himself or lack of ostensible means of subsistence, might be retained as minimum conditions precedent to a police officer stopping a person in the street and requiring his identification, it is submitted that whether the offence committed was a felony or a misdemeanour, or whether it was punishable with imprisonment up to or exceeding six months, should be irrelevant for the determination of the question whether it should be permissible for a police officer to effect an arrest without warrant. Moreover, this existing test presupposes that every police officer knows by heart the measures of punishment prescribed for each and every offence—an erudition which, even if it exists in a police officer, appears to be quite unnecessary. It is suggested that the law should be that a police officer may arrest without warrant any person committing an offence in his presence, where the officer has reasonable grounds to believe that failing such arrest the person could not be brought to justice or would endanger public safety or cause a breach of peace. Where the identity of the offender is known and there is no immediate danger

---

[15] FRENKEL v. Attorney-General, *op. cit. supra* note 8 at 1611.

[16] CRIMINAL PROCEDURE (ARREST AND SEARCHES) ORDINANCE §3(2), LAWS OF PALESTINE cap. 33.

[17] The police powers in Palestine and Israel in this respect are, however, much more limited than the powers conferred on police officers by the law of England: See ARCHBOLD'S PLEADING, EVIDENCE AND PRACTICE IN CRIMINAL CASES 1076 (34th ed. 1959).

from him if he is left at large, there is no reason why a warrant for his arrest should not first be obtained, however long the term of imprisonment to which he may ultimately be liable; and, on the other hand, where the offence was of a light nature (e.g., conducting himself in a manner likely to cause a breach of the peace), but in all the circumstances the officer reasonably concludes that violence is likely to ensue unless he arrests forthwith, there is no valid reason why he should not have the power to arrest without a warrant. In many—if not in most—cases, the nature of the offence committed will afford *prima facie* indication as to whether the apprehension of immediate danger is justified; in the same way, the nature and gravity of the offence will in most cases indicate whether the offender is likely to escape from justice. But the considerations prompting—and justifying—a police officer to effect an arrest should be police considerations, properly within his province, and whether he acts rightly or wrongly will depend upon the exercise of a discretion which, as a police officer, he is qualified and trained to exercise, and not upon his knowledge, or lack of knowledge, of detailed and complicated provisions of hundreds of criminal statutes.

To sum up *de lege ferenda:*

1) The police may not stop and ask any person in any public place to identify, or give an account of, himself, except—
   a) where that person has committed an offence in the presence of the officer or is reasonably believed by the officer to have committed an offence; or
   b) where that person was found in circumstances which reasonably caused suspicion that he was there for an illegal or disorderly purpose, and either took precautions to conceal himself or had no ostensible means of subsistence;

and in any such case the officer may require such person to accompany him to the nearest police station.

2) The police may not arrest any person without warrant of a competent judicial officer, except—
   a) where an offence was committed, and there are reasonable grounds to apprehend that unless arrested forthwith, the person suspected of the offence may commit a further offence or otherwise endanger public order, or that he may attempt to prevent his being brought to justice; or
   b) where a police officer is obstructed while in the execution of a duty; or
   c) where the person to be arrested has escaped, or attempts to escape, from lawful custody, or is pursued by hue and cry; or
   d) where a police officer has, in lawful exercise of his powers under subparagraph 1, above, required the person to be arrested to accompany him to the police station, and that person refused to do so.

# Japan*

HARUO ABE

## POLICE ARREST STATUTES IN GENERAL

The Japanese Code of Criminal Procedure of 1948[1] is the general source of law controlling the police arrest procedure. Under the general law a warrant issued by a judge is necessary for an arrest.[2] This is an application of the basic principle of Japanese criminal procedure that the exercise of investigative power upon persons or things having evidentiary value shall be generally subject to judicial control in the form of warrants for arrest or search and seizure. This "warrant principle" is a basic requirement of the pertinent provisions of the Constitution.[3]

However, it should be noted here that there are two important exceptions to the principle of "arrest with warrant."

One of them is the rule that any person may arrest, without warrant, an offender who is committing or has just committed a crime in his presence.[4] This exceptional rule is basically declared by Article 33 of the Japanese Constitution, which indicates that the offender may be exceptionally arrested without warrant, if he is arrested for *genko-han* (offense being committed or flagrant délit).[5] The concept of *genko-han* as used in the Constitution has been interpreted as comprising the offense which has just been committed[6] and the "*quasi genko-han.*"[7]

The second of the exceptions is the rule that an

---

* A brief historical note concerning the Japanese legal system, which may be helpful in better understanding certain portions of this paper, appears in my report on the privilege against self-incrimination which appears in Part IV of this volume.

The author gratefully acknowledges the encouragement and advice of Professors Fred E. Inbau and Claude R. Sowle in preparing the four reports which appear in this volume. The author also wishes to express his appreciation to Miss Ruth E. McKee of the American Embassy, Tokyo, who has been kind enough to refine the English and give him valuable advice on linguistic matters.

[1] THE CODE OF CRIMINAL PROCEDURE (Law No. 131 of 1948, with the latest amendment by Law No. 108 of 1958).

[2] THE CODE OF CRIMINAL PROCEDURE, art. 199, par. 1: "Where there exists any reasonable ground sufficient to suspect that an offense has been committed by the suspect, a public prosecutor, public prosecutor's assistant officer or judicial police official may arrest him upon a warrant of arrest issued in advance by a judge; provided, however, that for the offenses punishable with a fine not exceeding 500 yen [which in most cases should read as 25,000 yen—*author*], penal detention or minor fine, such arrest may be effected only in cases where the suspect has no fixed dwelling or where he fails, without good reason, to comply with the request for appearance which has been made in accordance with the preceding Article."

[3] THE CONSTITUTION OF JAPAN, art. 31: "No person shall be deprived of life or liberty, nor shall any criminal penalty be imposed, except according to procedure established by law."

*Ibid.*, art. 33: "No person shall be apprehended except upon warrant issued by a competent judicial officer which specifies the offense with which the person is charged, unless he is apprehended, the offense being committed." ["... unless he is apprehended, the offense being committed" means "... unless he is apprehended in the act of committing the offense."—*author*].

*Ibid.*, art. 35: "The right of all persons to be secure in their homes, papers and effects against entries, searches and seizures shall not be impaired except upon warrant issued for adequate cause and particularly describing the place to be searched and things to be seized, or except as provided by Art. 33.

"Each search or seizure shall be made upon separate warrant issued by a competent judicial officer."

[4] THE CODE OF CRIMINAL PROCEDURE, art. 213: "Any person whosoever may arrest a *genko-hannin* without warrant."

[5] For the English translation of art. 33 of the Constitution see note 3, *supra.*

[6] THE CODE OF CRIMINAL PROCEDURE, art. 212, par. 1: "*genko-hannin* [i.e., l'agent du flagrant délit—*author*] shall be defined as a person who is committing or has just committed an offense."

[7] *Ibid.*, art. 212, par. 2: "If any person who falls under one of the following items is found under circumstances which indicate clearly that an offense has just been committed, he shall be deemed a *genko-hannin*: (1) A person being pursued with hue and cry; (2) a person carrying with him illgotten goods, or weapons or other objects apparently used in connection with the offense; (3) a person bearing on his body or clothes visible traces of the offense; and, (4) a person who attempts to run away when asked to identify himself."

investigating official may arrest the suspect without warrant if he has sufficient grounds for believing that the latter has committed any of certain types of serious crimes and if, in addition, there is no time to procure a warrant.[8] This is so-called the system of "urgent arrest." In the case of urgent arrest, however, a warrant must be procured soon afterwards.[9] There have been a few cases where the constitutionality of this exceptional rule has been challenged, but the majority of theories and the judicial precedents have supported the constitutionality of the system of urgent arrest.[10] I do not entirely agree with the reasons for which the Supreme Court justified the system of urgent arrest,[11] but I am of the opinion that the system is constitutional, because Article 33 of the Constitution, whose basic idea was adopted from the Anglo-American legal system, should be interpreted to presuppose such traditional exceptions to the warrant principle as have been historically justified in Anglo-American common law.[12]

It has frequently been suggested that in the United States the percentage of arrests without warrant or of illegal arrests is quite high.[13] Fortunately, however, the rate of arrests without warrant has not been very high in Japan according to statistics.[14] This may be one of the psychological reasons why the argument against the constitutionality of the "urgent arrest" has not become very popular among Japanese lawyers.

## THE POLICE PRIVILEGES TO STOP AND QUESTION A SUSPICIOUS PERSON

In the absence of sufficient grounds for an arrest, should the police have a right to stop and question a person on the street as to his identity and reason for being where he is, if the appearance or conduct of that person has reasonably aroused police suspicion? Under the Japanese law, this question is answered in the affirmative with some statutory restrictions. The Police Duty Law,[15] which is the sole statute controlling this aspect of police practice, authorizes a police officer "to stop and

---

[8] *Ibid.*, art. 210, par. 1: "When there are sufficient grounds to suspect the commission of an offense punishable by the death penalty, or imprisonment with or without forced labor for life or for a maximum period of three years or more, and if, in addition, because of great urgency a warrant of arrest cannot be obtained beforehand from a judge, a public prosecutor, a public prosecutor's assistant officer or a judicial police official may, upon statement of the reasons therefor, apprehend the suspect; in such cases, measures for obtaining a warrant of arrest from a judge shall be immediately taken. If a warrant of arrest is not issued the suspect must be released immediately."

[9] *Ibid.* This is a system of judicial control *post facto.*

[10] For the leading case, see Vol. 9, No. 13 Sup. Ct. Crim Rep. 2760 (Grand Bench 1955).

[11] In the Supreme Court decision cited in note 10, *supra,* the opinion of the Court stated in substance that the system of arrest without warrant in such a limited form was not repugnant to the spirit of the Constitution. This is nothing but replacing one question with another. One of the two supplementary opinions maintained that art. 33 of the Constitution, as well as the Fourth Amendment of the United States Constitution, excluded reasonable arrest or search and seizure from the cases where warrants were required. The other made practical necessity the grounds for justification. Neither is satisfactory. For further discussion, see ARREST, DETENTION AND RELEASE ON BAIL 52–58 (Yokogawa ed., Tokyo, 1958) (in Japanese).

[12] It should be noted here that in the majority of

American jurisdictions the system of arrest without a warrant prevails to a great extent.

[13] See, *e.g.*, Foote, *Tort Remedies for Police Violations of Individual Rights*, 39 MINN. L. REV. 493 n.1 (1955); Note, *Philadelphia Police Practice and the Law of Arrest*, 100 U. PA. L. REV. 1182, 1183 n. 13 (1952).

[14] See, *e.g.*, the following table extracted from ARREST, DETENTION AND RELEASE ON BAIL 4 (Yokogawa ed., Tokyo, 1958) (in Japanese):

Number of Suspects Arrested by Police in 1956

| | Total Suspects | Not Arrested | Arrest with Warrant | Urgent Arrests* | Arrests in the act of Committing the Offense |
|---|---|---|---|---|---|
| Offense against Penal Code | 565,517 (100%) | 295,613 (52.°%) | 123,851 (21.9%) | 33,960 (6.0%) | 112,093 (19.8%) |
| Offense against Special laws | 2,419,042 (100%) | 2,373,059 (98.1%) | 12,268 (0.5%) | 660 (0.03%) | 33,055 (1.4%) |
| Total | 2,984,559 (100%) | 2 668,672 (89.3%) | 136,119 (4.6%) | 34,620 (1.2%) | 145,148 (4.9%) |

* It should also be noted that almost 100% of urgent arrests have been justified by the subsequent issuance of arrest warrants.

[15] POLICE DUTY LAW (Law No. 136, 1948, with the latest amendment by Law No. 163, 1954).

question a person whom the officer, judging reasonably from his unusual conduct and/or other circumstances, has sufficient ground for suspecting to have committed or to be about to commit a crime."[16] In consideration of possible embarrassment of the subject person or the possible disturbance to the traffic, the officer may ask the subject person to come to a nearby police station or police box for further questioning.[17] This, of course, does not mean that compulsion may be used for detention or questioning.[18]

Statistics indicate that the "on the street" questioning is contributing considerably toward the successful detection of crime.[19] It would be wise

[16] *Ibid.*, art. 2, par. 1: "A police officer is authorized to stop and question any person whom the officer, judging reasonably from his unusual conduct and/or other circumstances, has sufficient ground for suspecting to have committed or to be about to commit a crime, or who appears to have knowledge about a crime which has been committed or is about to be committed."

[17] *Ibid.*, art. 2, par. 2: "When the police officer considers that questioning the subject person on the spot as prescribed in the preceding paragraph may be to the disadvantage of the subject person or disturb the traffic, the officer may ask the person to come to a nearby police station, police box or residential police box for questioning."

[18] *Ibid.*, art. 2, par. 3: "No person mentioned in the preceding two paragraphs shall be detained or forced to come to the police box or residential police box or compelled to answer questions against his will, except in accordance with the provisions of laws concerning criminal procedure."

[19] The following table was constructed upon the data obtained from NATIONAL POLICE AGENCY, CRIMINAL STATISTICS FOR 1958, 174–175 (1959).

Penal Code Offenses Investigated by the Police as Classified by Causes Leading to Investigation (1958)

| | |
|---|---|
| Total Cases | 902,316 |
| Criminal Interrogation | 383,981 |
| Information Obtained by Detectives | 149,255 |
| Private Information | 152,795 |
| Offense Committed in the Presence of Other Persons | 69,343 |
| "*Duty Law*" *Questioning* | *33,517* |
| Stolen Goods | 33,334 |
| Complaint by Victim | 26,096 |
| Arrest by Private Person | 9,213 |
| Self-Surrender | 7,744 |
| Third Person Accusation | 3,219 |
| Modus Operandi | 3,214 |
| Personal Identification | 2,825 |
| Finger Print | 1,612 |
| Other Cases | 26,168 |

to keep the efficiency of this practice at the present level rather than revert to the pre-war practice of "on the street" questioning which was efficient enough to infringe upon the privacy of citizens. There have been no adequate data available regarding the post-war practice of "on the street" questioning except for the very limited data obtained by a pilot investigation into this matter.[20]

In principle, no physical power or compulsion shall be used in stopping and questioning under the Police Duty Law. However, there may be some cases where reasonable physical force must be used to stop a subject person who tries to avoid the questioning in an unreasonable manner. For example, a suspicious person may intentionally disregard the request of a police officer who wants to stop him in a lawful manner; or a suspicious person walking along a back street with a suspicious package may take flight when he is asked to stop. In such unusual cases it shall be lawful for the police to exercise the minimum amount of physical power needed to stop the person, such as following the person and crying out, "Stop a moment, please," or stopping him by standing in his way, touching him on the shoulder or grasping him by the arm.[21] This position has been substantially supported by High Court decisions.[22] The

[20] From Nov. 18 to 23, 1959, a survey of "on the street" questioning was made by a police station having jurisdiction over a police ward located in the heart of Tokyo. The day and night population of the area was 300,000 and 40,000 respectively; 9 police boxes with 30 policemen guarded and patrolled the area. The survey revealed among others the following facts: 98 were questioned; more than half of them were questioned from 10 p.m. to 2 a.m.; in most cases 10 minutes were used for each questioning; with regard to attitudes, 10 of the questioned persons were "uncooperative"; in majority of cases other measures in addition to questioning (*e.g.,* touching a package from outside) were taken; in 3 cases the questioning led to obtaining incriminating evidence (physical or testimonial); in 94 cases suspicion was cleared; dispositions made were as follows: 95 released (including 6 taken to police boxes for questioning), 2 taken to the police station, and 1 arrested.

[21] *Cf.* NATIONAL POLICE AGENCY, POLICE MANUAL FOR FIELD WORK 128 (3d ed. 1957) (in Japanese); NATIONAL POLICE AGENCY, PRACTICE IN QUESTIONING UNDER THE POLICE DUTY LAW 17 (1958) (in Japanese).

[22] Vol. 5, No. 12 High Courts Crim. Rep. 2294 (Sapporo High Court 1952). Prosecution for beating

over the face of a police officer who allegedly was engaging in official duty. The issue was on the legality of the act of the officer who grasped the defendant by the shoulder to stop him for further questioning when he tried to take flight under suspicious circumstances. The defendant appealed from the judgment of the district court which held against him. The high Court held that the officer's act of grasping the suspicious person by the shoulder when he tried to escape without answering the question was within the scope of lawful performance of official duty under the Police Duty Law.

Supp. No. 33 High Courts Crim. Rep. 47 (Nagoya High Court 1953). Prosecution for kicking and injuring a police officer who allegedly was engaging in official duty under the Police Duty Law. The police officer noticed four suspicious persons, one of whom was the defendant, conferring at a dark corner of a park at about 9:00 p.m. Three of them stated their names when asked. But the defendant refused to state his name and to open a suspicious package he carried. The officer touched the package from outside and felt something like a lady's handbag. When the defendant was asked to open the package, he refused to do so and started to run away with the package. The officer pursued him and reached him when he stumbled and fell down. Then, the defendant, lying on the ground kicked and hurt the officer when the latter tried to approach the former. The District Court held that the officer had no right to pursue the defendant when he ran. The prosecution appealed from the judgment for the defendant. The High Court held that an officer should have the right as well as duty to pursue a suspected person if he took flight when questioned and, therefore, the officer was engaging in official duty in a lawful manner. The judgment below was reversed and a new judgment was rendered against the defendant.

Supp. No. 33 High Courts Crim. Rep. 58–64 (Nagoya High Court 1953). Prosecution for beating, kicking and injuring a police officer who allegedly was engaging in official duty under the Police Duty Law. At about a quarter past 12 o'clock midnight, two officers noticed a suspicious person, the defendant, approaching on a bicycle. They stopped the defendant and took him with his consent to the nearby police box for questioning. After being questioned a short while, the defendant took sudden flight. Another officer who was there by chance pursued him about 130 meters, reached him from behind and caught him by the arm, crying "Why are you running away?" At that moment the defendant turned around and started to beat him over the head and to kick him. The District Court held that the act of the Officer was "arresting" and beyond the limit of lawful performance of duty under the Police Duty Law, and that the defendant was not guilty, having made a lawful counter-attack in self-defense against the unlawful attack by the officer. (Nagoya District Court, May 6, 1953; 1 HANREI JIHO (Law Reports Times) 19 (1953).) The prosecution appealed from the judgment of the District Court for the defendant. The High Court held that under such circumstances it was lawful for the officer to pursue and stop the defendant by reasonable use of physical power, such as catching

view of Professor Dando of Tokyo University also appears to be compatible with these decisions.[23]

## THE POLICE PRIVILEGE TO SEARCH A SUSPECTED PERSON FOR WEAPONS OR FOR INCRIMINATING EVIDENCE

If, in the absence of sufficient grounds for an arrest, the police have a right to stop and question a suspected person under certain suspicious circumstances, should the police be permitted to search such a person for weapons or for incriminating evidence? Under the Japanese law this question has been answered in the negative.

As stated above, under the Japanese system the warrant is one of the indispensable conditions for compulsory search and seizure made on a person by the police.[24] The sole exception to this rule is found in Article 220[25] of the Code of Criminal Procedure, which provides in substance that a person suspected by the police may, on the spot of arrest and without a warrant, be searched and subjected to seizure of dubious articles carried on

---

the defendant by the arm while calling upon him to stop. The judgment below was reversed and a new judgment was rendered against the defendant.

[23] Dando, *The Limitations of Lawfulness of Police Questioning under the Police Duty Law*, 3 HANREI JIHO (Law Reports Times) 2 (1953). In this article Professor Dando criticized the Nagoya District Court decision, *supra* note 22, and suggested that at least it would be lawful for a police officer to touch the body of the subject person to draw his attention or to ask his reconsideration.

[24] THE CONSTITUTION OF JAPAN, art. 35 (for English translation see note 3, *supra*); THE CODE OF CRIMINAL PROCEDURE, arts. 218, 219.

[25] Art. 220:1. "When a public prosecutor, a public prosecutor's assistant officer or a judicial police official arrests a suspect in accordance with Art. 199 or he arrests a *genko-hannin* [a person who is committing or has just committed a crime], he may, if necessary, take the following measures; the same shall apply, if necessary, to the case where a suspect is arrested in accordance with Art. 210:(1) To enter the dwelling of a person, or the premises, building or vessels guarded by persons to search for the suspect; (2) To seize, search or inspect on the spot of the arrest. 2. The things seized shall be returned immediately if a warrant of arrest is not obtained in the case mentioned in the latter part of the preceding paragraph. 3. For the measures mentioned in the first paragraph, a warrant need not be obtained. 4. [Omitted]."

his person. This implies that, except on the occasion of a lawful arrest, it is unlawful for the police to search the suspected person who is stopped and questioned under the Police Duty Law and seize dubious articles carried on his person. Article 2, paragraph 4, of the Police Duty Law specifically provides that "If a person is under arrest in accordance with laws concerning criminal procedure, a police officer is authorized to search the person for a dangerous weapon." This is a restatement of the logical consequence of the established rule of criminal procedure with specific regard to dangerous weapons.

Under such a general prohibition of search and seizure of the suspect, the police may not even "frisk" him. This means that the police may not even search the person by passing a hand over his clothes or through his pockets. This, however, does not necessarily mean that touching should be absolutely prohibited. It should be permitted for the police to touch the person or package, to a reasonable extent, to fulfill the purpose of questioning. For example, he may pass his hand lightly over the person's clothes or touch the outside of the package he is carrying while asking such questions as "What is this?" or "You appear to have something like a knife; will you let me have a look at it?"[26] But no further search without consent should be made.

### Legitimate Limitations to be Imposed on Police Practices Regarding "On the Street" Detention, Questioning and Frisking of Suspected Persons

Most Japanese lawyers appear to be satisfied with the present status of limitations imposed upon police practices by the provisions of the Police Duty Law. However, a strong feeling of dissatisfaction with these limitations has been growing among the police and investigators. In response to a growing demand for changing the present situation, the National Police Agency tried to add a new paragraph to Article 2 of the

[26] *Cf.*, National Police Agency, Practice in Questioning under the Police Duty Law 20 (1958) (in Japanese).

Police Duty Law intended to safeguard the police against dangerous weapons, proposing a bill for partial amendment[27] of the Police Duty Law in the 30th Diet Session in October, 1958. In the Diet debate the National Police Agency pointed out many cases where the lack of authority to search for weapons had endangered the police or private citizens and emphasized the necessity of such an amendment.[28]

The pertinent provisions of what was intended to be the new paragraph 3 of Article 2 read as follows:

"3. If, on the occasion of questioning by a police officer under Paragraph 1 of this Article, the person, by unusual conduct or other circumstances, provides reasonable cause for being suspected of having committed or being about to commit a crime, or if he carries a dangerous weapon or any other object that might endanger the life or body of other persons, the police officer may cause the person to submit the article for temporary custody; or if the officer recognizes that there is a reasonable ground for suspecting that the person is carrying such an article, the officer may cause the person to submit the personal effects carried by him for inspection."

Of course this proposal did not mean that the police should have the right to compel the subject person to submit things he carries. It is obvious that the person has the right to refuse to comply with the officer's request even under this proposed provision. Since even under the present law it is lawful for the police reasonably to persuade the

[27] The proposed bill contained several other points of amendment which are designed to facilitate police activities in many respects.

[28] One of the mimeographed materials prepared by the National Police Agency contained many cases, among which only two remarkable ones shall be mentioned here. *Case A*: A police officer questioning a suspected person on the street was stabbed by the person with a concealed knife and died shortly afterwards. *Case B*: A police officer questioning a suspected person had good reason to suspect that the person had a dangerous weapon but could not request him to submit it because of lack of authority to do so; while the officer continued questioning, he was stabbed in the abdomen by the person with a concealed spring knife.

suspected person to submit things he is carrying, this proposal theoretically provides very little enlargement of police authority. However, this proposal of amendment was not very popular among those people who are seriously concerned with the protection of human rights. In theory the proposal did not mean much; but in practice it would allow the possibility of abusive exercise of psychological compulsion on innocent citizens. Among the opponents of the amendment there seems to have been this feeling: Allow the police seven miles and they will go nine miles; therefore, if we want to keep them at seven miles, better give them six miles. In any event, the Police Bill as a whole—and it contained many points of amendment—was very unpopular except among certain conservative groups. The bill was vigorously counter-attacked[29] and automatically quashed when the period of the Diet session expired with the bill still pending in the House of Representatives. The basis for the opposition to the bill was emotional fear of the probable misuse of enlarged authority, rather than a calculated possibility of mispractice; but there was some wisdom in such distrust of the police. The bitter memory of police brutality in pre-war Japan makes people hesitant to enlarge police authority.

However, practical-minded persons who are seeking for a realistic solution of the matter are dissatisfied with the unrealistic and excessive control of police practices. It is feared that excessive control may give rise to some undesirable by-products, such as (1) excessive timidity on the part of the police in fighting crimes for the protection of society[30] and (2) a good excuse for the clandestine practices of the police who try to justify the evasion of legal restrictions on the

grounds that it is necessary for attaining a righteous purpose. The well-known police practice of so-called "Youth Guidance" appears to be an example of the latter phenomenon. Annually more than 700,000 problem youths are "guided" by the police with allegedly "free" consent on the part of the youths. It is obvious that a great number of problem youths who are not actually delinquent are often stopped and questioned on the street and sometimes are, as a matter of fact, psychologically compelled to come to police boxes, notwithstanding the fact that they do not actually fall under the category of suspicious persons as prescribed by paragraph 1 of Article 1 or fall under the category of persons who shall be protected under Article 3 of the Police Duty Law.[31] It is desirable that a procedure for youth guidance should be clearly prescribed and be subject to proper legal control.

## FREEDOM OF THE POLICE AND FREEDOM OF CITIZENS

It is said that under Anglo-American law arrest is not the beginning but the end of criminal investigation. For a more exact statement, however, the phase "is not" should be changed into "should not be." Even under Anglo-American law most criminal investigators and practical-minded lawyers will admit that usually the most important evidence is obtained by questioning the suspect after the arrest.[32] The problem is how to harmonize the freedom of the police with the freedom of citizens.

With respect to police arrest statutes, should more freedom be granted to the police in recognition of the fact that existing laws hamper police attempts to meet the public demand for adequate police protection?

[29] Almost the entire press was against the bill. It is reported that about 66 liberal or "democratic" organizations throughout Japan declared their opposition to the bill. For pros and cons concerning the bill, see, e.g., Tsuchiya, *Criticism of the Bill for the Partial Amendment to the Police Duty Law,* 30 KEISATSU KENKYU (The Police Studies) 3, 22 (1959) (in Japanese); Miyazawa, *et al., Symposium on the Amendment to the Police Duty Law,* 166 JURIST 2 (1958) (in Japanese).

[30] Similar apprehension is seen in Vol. 33 (supp.) High Courts Crim. Rep. 59 (Nagoya High Court 1953) which stated: "It is obvious that the police should

make efforts to avoid the abuse of the provisions . . . however, on the other hand it is likely that the police are prone to be too timid with excessive fear of the voice of protection of human rights . . . such will lead to endangering the public welfare and the basis of democracy. . . ."

[31] Persons who need police protection, such as insane or drunken persons, lost children, or sick or wounded persons.

[32] See Inbau, *Restrictions in the Law of Investigation and Confessions,* 52 Nw. U. L. R. 80, 81 (1957).

The key to the realistic solution of this problem is the discipline of the police. In Japan it would be useless or even dangerous to relax the present restrictions on arrest. Such a step would not only infringe upon human rights but also hamper the progress of police discipline. Despite the complaints made by the police about the strictness of the present arrest statutes, most Japanese lawyers appear to be content with the present status of the law of arrest. Statistics show that 99.5% of applications for arrest warrants are granted by the judge.[33] This seems to indicate that the judicial control over arrest is not so strict as to hamper police attempts to meet the public demand for adequate police protection.

It was reported that in 1956 in Japan 136,488 suspects were prosecuted in formal proceedings. 91,699 or 67% of those accused had been arrested for investigation, while only 44,789 or 33% of them had not been arrested.[34] This statistical fact seems to indicate that the arrest is still the beginning of criminal investigation in Japan. However, this phenomenon may be partially attributed to the fact that in Japan there is no such system as summons for the suspect. Because of the lack of a summons system the police or prosecutors must sometimes arrest those suspects who have committed minor offenses and have refused to report at the investigators' office for questioning. This practice apparently is one of the factors contributing to the increase in the arrest rate in Japan. Introduction of a summons system is a measure that should be seriously considered.

## Some Measures Against Illegal Arrest by the Police with Specific Reference to the Compensation for the Suspected Person

### Penal Sanctions Against Illegal Arrest

In Japan, what penal deterrents to illegal arrest practices by the police are used? In the first place, attention should be drawn to the provisions of the Penal Code[35] which are specifically designed to deter government officials from engaging in uncivilized practices.[36] Under these provisions a police officer who illegally arrests or imprisons a person is punished by imprisonment with or without forced labor for not more than ten years and not less than six months.[37]

One might doubt the practicability of the enforcement of these provisions, because public prosecutors may be reluctant to prosecute their fellow investigators or may be influenced by political pressure. Such apprehension, however, is unfounded. The legislature has wisely set up a safeguard against the possibility of unfair or arbitrary dropping of cases. Under the Code of Criminal Procedure a citizen who believes that his accusation against a public officer for certain crimes involving uncivilized practices has been unreasonably turned down may have prompt recourse to the judicial court which, in turn, may order the public prosecutor to institute a prosecution against the public officer who allegedly exercised his authority in an illegal manner.[38] In this case the court must appoint an *ad hoc* public prosecutor from among private practicing lawyers, so that a fair and sincere prosecution may be secured by this impartial prosecuting agency. This special recourse is called "quasi public prosecution" and has been taken rather frequently. It is reported that for the last decade (1949–1958) 624 persons including 132 police officers, 65 public prosecutors, 36 judges and 391 others have been brought before judicial courts pursuant to this procedure for consideration as to whether they should actually be prosecuted.[39]

---

[33] ARREST, DETENTION AND RELEASE ON BAIL 47 (Yokogawa Ed., Tokyo, 1958) (in Japanese).

[34] Id. at 99.

[35] THE PENAL CODE OF JAPAN, arts. 193–196.

[36] It should be noted that beside these specific provisions there are general ones under which malfeasant officers are punished as ordinary persons. For example, an illegal arrest or imprisonment is punished by arts. 200 and 221; an officer who makes illegal search and seizure is also liable for robbery (art. 236) or larceny (art. 235).

[37] THE PENAL CODE OF JAPAN, art. 194.

[38] THE CODE OF CRIMINAL PROCEDURE, arts. 262–267.

[39] These figures were taken from the records kept at the Criminal Affairs Bureau of the Ministry of Justice. Of these 624 persons, only 5 persons were actually prosecuted and tried on the grounds of their brutality. In the five cases tried, four defendants were found guilty and one case is still pending. The extremely

## Civil Actions for Damages Caused by the Police

A citizen who has suffered from illegal arrest by public officers has recourse to either of two types of judicial remedy. First, he may bring an ordinary civil suit against the public officers for damages caused by the illegal arrest. Secondly, he may institute a civil action against the State for damages wrongfully caused by the arrest performed by an investigating officer working within the scope of his official duty.[40] The system of legal aids in civil litigation applies equally to these cases, so that even poor citizens may bring such suits against investigating officers. Data taken from materials kept at the Ministry of Justice show that for seven years, from October, 1947, to April, 1954, 69 civil suits were brought against the Government for damages wrongfully caused by police officers and prosecuting officials.[41]

## Insufficiency of the Traditional Remedies

What has been explained might have created the impression that Japanese citizens are well protected from illegal exercises of investigating authority. But such an impression is rather delusive.

Unfortunately, many over-zealous investigators pay little attention to civil rights of citizens. It appears that even the penal sanction has very limited value as a deterrent to investigating officers. The fact that very few investigating officials have been punished for abusing their authority suggests the inefficacy of the penal sanction.[42] Moreover, Japan, where the level of "legal consciousness" is not very high, has very few citizens as brave as "Michael Kohlhaas" who declared war on his Government in pursuit of his personal rights. Even if a citizen be brave enough to bring a civil suit against the Government, he faces the difficult task of *proving* his case against the Government. Everyone knows how hard it is to collect sufficient pieces of evidence from the stronghold of the Government to make a strong case against it. It is also very difficult to prove such mental elements as "malicious intent" or "negligence" on the part of a government official. What, then, is the remedy?

## A Suggested Remedy—State's Strict or Absolute Liability

One possible suggestion for remedying this situation would be to proceed a few steps toward the system of State's strict or absolute liability. If a highly organized modern State, a veritable "Leviathan," happens to infringe upon individual rights in exercising its investigating authority, it should be only fair for the State to pay the damages under certain conditions, whether or not the officials, as the agents of the State, have caused the damages intentionally or negligently. Theoretically, strict or absolute liability or "risk" liability has little to do with illegal exercise of public authority. However, we can hardly say that the official exercised the public authority illegally until or unless we succeed in proving that he did so intentionally or negligently. Therefore, substantially the system of State's strict or absolute liability is a substitute for ordinary litigation

---

low percentage of cases actually prosecuted may mean that this procedure is not used by those who need its merit. The procedure has frequently been misused as a political challenge. Those who are actually suffering from the abuse of investigating authority are often too ignorant or timid to take recourse to this procedure.

[40] The system of governmental liability is established by THE CONSTITUTION OF JAPAN, art. 17, which provides that "Every person may sue for redress as provided by law from the State or a public entity, in case he has suffered damage through illegal act of any public official." Pursuant to this provision the STATE LIABILITY LAW (Law No. 125; Oct. 27, 1947) provides that the State or public entity is primarily liable for damages when a person's rights have been violated by illegal governmental activity. However, the law further provides that such liability exists only in the event that the illegal act of the public official is due to his intent or negligence. This means that fault, not risk, is the basis of state liability in Japan.

[41] This figure does not necessarily include the number of cases involving illegal arrests by the police. On the contrary, most of them are those involving brutality allegedly inflicted by police officers or prosecuting officials.

[42] See Hirano, *Control of Investigation by Exclusion of Evidence,* 7 KEIHO ZASSHI (Jour. of Crim. Law) 165, 168, 172 n.2 (1957).

for State's liability based upon intent or negligence of public officials, because it allows the citizen to dispense with proof of intent or negligence which is otherwise indispensable to the recovery of damages from the State. This system would be particularly useful in the field of criminal investigation where investigating officials are required to make speedy and vigorous moves with high probability of infringing upon citizens' rights.

### An Experience in Japan—Criminal Compensation Law

It would be of some interest to review the progress which Japan has made in this direction in recent years.

Under the "Criminal Compensation Law," which was originally enacted in 1933 and repealed by the new law of the same title in 1950,[43] an accused who has been arrested or detained and has been finally adjudged "not guilty" by the court is entitled, under certain conditions, to be awarded some flat compensation by the court. The maximum amount of compensation is fixed at 400 yen per diem for the period of illegal restraint of freedom. Although the amount of flat compensation is not sufficient for recovering damages actually caused, the significance of this system should not be underestimated.[44]

One of the defects of this system, however, is the point that the Criminal Compensation Law does not cover the case involving a criminal suspect who is arrested for investigation but eventually discharged by the investigating officials.

Let us suppose, for example, that Mr. John Doe was arrested while he was walking along Ginza Street in Tokyo. His conscience was clear, but the police had good reason for believing that he might be the criminal being sought. After 24 hours of investigation at the police station, he turned out to be innocent and was released. In such a case, is he entitled to compensation under the Criminal

Compensation Law? This answer is "No." He can not sue for damages against the police because there was no irregularity or fault on the part of the police; nor is he entitled to compensation under the Criminal Compensation Law because he was not formally prosecuted as a criminal defendant.

### The Birth of the Regulation for Suspect's Compensation

Increasing criticism of such an unsatisfactory situation stimulated the issuance of "the Regulation for Suspect's Compensation."[45] Under this Regulation an amount not exceeding 400 yen per diem may be paid to the suspect, under certain

recent years. According to these statistics amount of compensation *per capita* is 28,445 yen.

Table I. Criminal Compensation Cases
Finally Disposed Of
(1956–1958)

| Year | Total Cases Considered | Compensation Granted | | | Dismissed, etc. |
|---|---|---|---|---|---|
| | | Grantees | Days | Amount (yen) | |
| 1956 | 279 | 271 | 26,093 | 6,622,670 | 8 |
| 1957 | 184 | 161 | 15,514 | 3,838,367 | 23 |
| 1958 | 133 | 126 | 18,326 | 5,411,550 | 7 |
| Total | 596 | 558 | 59,933 | 15,872,587 | 38 |

(Source: The Secretariat General, The Supreme Court of Japan, Annual Report of Judicial Statistics, 2. Criminal Cases, Part II for 1956, '57 and '58)

Table II. Number of Persons Compensated as Classified by Amount Granted *Per Diem*

| Year | 400 yen | 399–300 yen | 299–200 yen | Other | Total |
|---|---|---|---|---|---|
| 1956 | 41 (15.1%) | 75 (27.7%) | 154 (56.8%) | 1 (0.4%) | 271 (100%) |
| 1957 | 33 (20.5%) | 46 (28.6%) | 80 (49.7%) | 2 (1.2%) | 161 (100%) |

(Source: Secretariat General, the Supreme Court of Japan)

[43] Law No. 1, Jan. 1, 1950, repealing Law No. 60, April 1, 1933.

[44] The following tables constructed from the data provided by judicial statistics show how the Criminal Compensation Law has been actually administered in

[45] MINISTRY OF JUSTICE, INSTRUCTION NO. 1 (1957).

conditions, in compensation for the mental pains and property damage which he has suffered from physical restraint pending criminal investigation, in the event the real offender has been discovered or the suspect has been finally found innocent after a certain period of arrest or detention. In this procedure the public prosecutor decides to make such compensation upon the request of the discharged suspect, but the request is not the prerequisite for the compensation. In addition, if the person compensated requests a public notification that he was compensated, an account to that effect must be published in the *Official Gazette* or a newspaper for the rehabilitation of his honor.

Theoretically, this compensation is of a gratuitous nature and the suspect is not entitled to take recourse to the judicial court from the public prosecutor's discretionary decision of not awarding compensation. But, as a matter of practice, prosecutors have been rather generous in awarding compensation pursuant to Article 1 of the Regula-

tion providing that "this Regulation shall be reasonably administered in the spirit of respecting human rights and in accordance with individual circumstances." Moreover, it is generally agreed that the discharged suspect who is not content with the decision made by a public prosecutor with regard to the compensation may take a special administrative appeal from this decision to the hierarchical superior of the public prosecutor.

Thus far only a few persons have been compensated under this Regulation.[46] However, it appears to be too early to decide whether this is due to the fact that the system has not yet become familiar to the people or to the fact that the arrest privilege of the police has been exercised moderately.

[46] From June, 1957, to February, 1960, fifteen cases involving fifteen suspects arrested and detained were considered for compensation under the Regulation. Of the fifteen cases, thirteen were disposed of and seven suspects were granted compensation. This data was taken from the records kept at the Criminal Affairs Bureau, Ministry of Justice.

# *Norway*

ANDERS BRATHOLM

The power of the police in Norway to arrest suspected persons is regulated by the Norwegian Criminal Procedure Act of 1887.

The chief provisions are found in Chapter 19 of the act. They may be divided into *material* and *formal* prerequisites. The material prerequisites deal with the requirements to be met as regards the punishable act. The formal prerequisites refer to the procedure to be followed when arrest is ordered.

The material prerequisites may be divided into *general* and *special* prerequisites. Arrest may take place only when the general and at least one of the special conditions are present.

The chief general provision is found in Section 228(1). According to this provision the police can arrest a person who, on reasonable grounds, is suspected of a punishable action for which the maximum statutory penalty is a term of imprisonment longer than six months.

If the general conditions are satisfied, arrest may take place when at least one of the following special conditions is met:

(1) The suspected person is seized *in flagrante delicto*, or the traces of his action are fresh.
(2) There is reason to fear that he will flee to avoid punishment.
(3) His conduct gives special reason to fear that he will tamper with evidence.

(4) There is special reason to fear that he will repeat the punishable offence.

(5) The question will arise of application of security measures (that is, generally speaking, relatively indefinite measures in the case of recidivists).[1]

The police can, in certain cases, arrest a suspect even if the maximum statutory penalty cannot exceed six months of imprisonment.

The most important of the provisions in this regard is Section 229 of the Criminal Procedure Act. In this section it is laid down that arrest may be made regardless of the weight of penalty when at least one of these three special conditions is present:

(1) The suspected person is taken *in flagrante delicto* and does not desist from his punishable activity.

(2) He is found in the act of absconding or evidently preparing to abscond.

(3) He has no fixed address in the country, and there is reason to fear that he will attempt to avoid punishment.

The most important *formal* requirement is that the police shall procure a warrant—that is, the consent of a Magistrate—before the arrest is made. But if the purpose of the arrest might be thwarted by waiting, the arrest may be made without a warrant. In practice, however, it is very seldom that the police do procure the consent of the court, even in cases where there is ample time to do so. This police practice was strongly criticised by the Supreme Court in a ruling of 1936;[2] however, this did not have the effect of changing matters to any significant degree.

It may be mentioned that the arrested persons in the 1936 case were two well known Norwegian lawyers who were suspected of financial crimes. The charges were dropped on lack of evidence, and the lawyers claimed and were awarded high damages under Section 469 of the Criminal Procedure Act. According to this section, the State is responsible for the economic loss detention in custody

has caused the detained person, where there are grounds for believing that he is innocent. This rule applies even if nobody can be blamed for the detention of the innocent.[3]

It is interesting to note that, after the Supreme Court ruling in 1936, the police in Norway, as far as possible, have avoided arresting a lawyer without having obtained a warrant in advance.

If the arrested person is not released the day after his arrest, the police must bring him before an examining judge with an application for commitment to custody.[4] If the judge finds that the general material conditions, and at least one of the special conditions mentioned in Section 228(2)–(5), or Section 229(2)–(3), exist (Sections 228(1) and 229(1) only grant the power to *arrest*), he can pronounce judgement that the arrested person shall be detained in custody for a certain time.[5]

We thus see that the conditions of arrest, as well as of detention in custody, are carefully regulated by the Criminal Procedure Act. This is taken to be a necessary consequence of Section 99 of the Norwegian Constitution of 1814, which, *inter alia*, lays down that arrest and imprisonment can only take place as determined by the law and in the manner prescribed by the law. This is one aspect of the general principle of legality on which the Norwegion Constitution is built and which demands that regulations that invade the sphere of the rights of an individual shall in general have the form of *written law*.

While this principle applies unimpaired as regards imprisonment as penalty, it is to a certain extent neglected as far as arrest (and detention) is concerned.[6] Thus it is quite common for the police to halt and examine persons who are found in the neighborhood of the place where a crime has just been committed and who could be suspected of

---

[1] A more detailed statement of the prerequisites to arrest and detention will be found in Bratholm, *Arrest and Detention in Norway*, 108 U.PA.L.REV. 336 (1960).

[2] Norsk Retstidende (Nor. Law Rep.) 567 (1936).

[3] Section 469 has also a rule according to which damages can be awarded an accused person who has not been arrested or remanded in custody. However, in these cases the court has a discretionary power to refuse damages.

[4] CRIMINAL PROCEDURE ACT (hereinafter called CPA), §§235, 236.

[5] CPA, §§240, 239.

[6] For more detailed information than given in this article, see Bratholm, *op.cit.supra* note 1, at 343–47.

being implicated in the crime or who could have been witnesses of it.[7]

It may be said that the right to halt and detain for a short time can be justified by Section 333 of the Norwegian Penal Code of 1902, which declares it the duty of every person to give his name, position and address to a policeman who requests this information in the public interest.[8] The police practice does not, however, involve merely halting a person and requesting his name and address. He may also be examined with respect to the crime or searched without the full authority of the law. It may be added that Norwegian criminals, as well as the police, very seldom are armed, and frisking for weapons does not often occur.

If the person who was questioned cannot give a fully satisfactory account of himself, or if compromising articles are found on him, he generally will be taken to the police station for closer examination.

Especially in cases where a serious crime has been committed (for example, murder) can the police go to considerable lengths when it comes to taking to the police station persons who might be suspected of having had something to do with the offence. Most of these are set free after a short time—if, for example, their alibi is in order—but in some cases they may be detained in police arrest overnight. In such cases, where several persons are detained as suspected of a crime which only one single person can be imagined to have committed, the terms of the Criminal Procedure Act, which demand that there shall exist *reasonable* grounds for suspicion, will not be complied with, and the police will therefore make no attempt to obtain the court's ruling for detention. Only if special reasons should be present for the belief that one single individual among the suspects is guilty will the person concerned be brought before the court with application for remand in custody.

Such a check-up of a number of persons who can be suspected of having had something to do with

the crime often permits the police to lay their hands on the guilty party. The trial and error method is fairly effective in Norway, where the conditions are so uncomplicated that the police can often point with considerable confidence to the milieu within which the offender is to be found.

Furthermore, it is not only when it is known that a crime has already been committed that the police sometimes arrest persons on a vague suspicion. Under other circumstances the police detain and examine and, if necessary, take to the police station, persons whose conduct arouses suspicion. Thus, some time ago, the police took a young man to the police station who at a late hour of the night was unable to give a satisfactory account of himself. The police had a strong impression that he had stolen the bicycle which he had with him, but this proved not to be the case. However, before they had given the young man his liberty, a report came in of a brutal sex murder that had been committed in the neighborhood in which he had been arrested, and further examination showed that the arrested man was the criminal.

In this case it may well be said that a legally most doubtful arrest led to the solution of one of the most brutal murders committed in Norway since the second world war. (It may be added that a confession or other evidence obtained in connection with an illegal arrest will not be excluded during the trial.)

In such routine check-ups of suspected persons, it is seldom necessary for the police to use force. Those who have come under scrutiny nearly always go willingly to the police station, because they know that otherwise force will be used and that a refusal will only aggravate suspicion against them.

The police seldom designate persons who are arrested on a vague suspicion as "suspected" persons or "arrested" persons, but they are referred to as "taken" or "brought in"—designations which the law does not use.[9] The same procedure is used to some extent in Denmark.[10]

In spite of the terminology of the police, the sus-

[7] See BRATHOLM, PAAGRIPELSE OG VARETEKTSFENG-SEL (Arrest and Detention Before Trial) 9–10 (Oslo 1957).
[8] Offences against §333 are punishable by a fine or imprisonment for a term not exceeding three months.

[9] See BRATHOLM, *op. cit. supra* note 7, at 10.
[10] See HURWITZ, DEN DANSKE STRAFFERETSPLEJE 648 (2d ed. Copenhagen 1949).

pected person in such cases must be considered as arrested, and therefore he must also have the rights of an arrested person. This means, among other things, that he, like other accused persons, cannot be punished for giving a false statement (as can a witness). In a decision of the Supreme Court in 1940 this was expressly laid down.[11] The court concluded that when a suspected person is more or less expressly faced with the choice between voluntarily accompanying an officer to the police station and arrest, then from a legal point of view, he must be considered as arrested.

The police practice which I have described here, and which in certain cases undoubtedly lacks the authority of the present law, and in other cases must be said to lie on the borderline of legality, has not to any great extent led to complaints from arrested persons or from other quarters. This is due partly to the fact that the suspected persons as a rule are not aware that the police are acting on the borderline of their authority or even beyond it.

In this connection, it can be mentioned that persons who are arrested and detained at the police station for a short period of time seldom acquire counsel, although they are entitled by the law to to so on their own expense.[12] The deprivation of liberty is so short in most cases that there is no time to obtain legal assistance. Most of them, therefore, do not know that the action of the police can give rise to criticism.

Another reason why the doubtful police practice has not led to complaint or public criticism to any great extent is that most people realize that the present police practice seldom goes beyond the bounds of what may be called reasonable action. It seems to be generally agreed that the current provisions of law, which regulate the power of the police to arrest suspected persons and which were passed in a society quite different from the present society, are somewhat too restricted and that they should be revised so that the prevailing practice would be to some degree legalized.[13]

In this connection it can be mentioned that the new Swedish law of procedure (1942) has legalized the former Swedish police practice of bringing persons to the police station for questioning, check-up, etc. Thus a person who has been on the spot where a crime has been committed has a duty, if requested by an officer, to accompany him to the police station for questioning. If the person refuses without good reason, he can be compelled to go with the officer.[14]

Furthermore, the Swedish police can arrest a suspected person, even if the suspicion is not founded on reasonable grounds, as it must be in the case of detention in custody.[15] The strength of suspicion consequently need not be so great in the case of arrest as in case of detention. The same applies in the case of Danish law.[16]

The Norwegian Criminal Procedure Act is now under revision, and there is much to be said for Norwegian adoption of arrest provisions corresponding to those now existing in Sweden. The objections against introducing such regulations need hardly be very great, since the Norwegian police, practically speaking, never behave brutally towards suspected persons, and since the arrangement does not seem to be attended by serious handicaps in any other way. It should, however, be considered as a safeguard to introduce rules which make it mandatory that the accused shall be provided with counsel at public expense if he is not released within a reasonable period (e.g., 24 hours) after his arrest.[17]

[11] Norsk Retstidende (Nor. Law Rep.) 343 (1940); PENAL CODE, §167. The terminology of the police may in certain respects be of advantage to the suspect. Thus, when he is considered as "taken in", he is not recorded as arrested in the police-register.

[12] CPA, §99. In rare cases, counsel may be appointed for the accused at public expense just after his arrest. See CPA, §102, which prescribes that counsel shall be appointed if it is considered necessary in view of the nature of the case, provided that the accused has applied for appointment of counsel. If the defendant is going to be tried, then he, as a rule, is entitled to counsel at public expense. See CPA, §§100, 101.

[13] For some suggestions for reform, see Bratholm, *op. cit. supra* note 1, at 349–53.

[14] THE SWEDISH PROCEDURE ACT OF 1942, c. 23, §8. The person can be kept at the police station for questioning for a period up to six hours, but if there is reason to suspect him of a crime, up to twelve hours. If then the suspicion does not appear strong enough to justify his imprisonment, the police must set him free.

[15] THE SWEDISH PROCEDURE ACT OF 1942, c.24, §§5, 1.

[16] THE DANISH PROCEDURE ACT OF 1916, §§771, 780.

[17] See Bratholm, *op. cit. supra* note 1, at 353.

PART TWO

# The
# Exclusionary Rule
# Regarding
# Illegally Seized
# Evidence

In the preparation of their papers dealing with the exclusionary rule, the Conference participants were asked to consider the following matters:

The usually stated purpose of the exclusionary rule is to protect constitutional rights by indirectly penalizing police failure to comply with prescribed search and seizure procedures.

(1) Does the rule accomplish that objective?

(2) If the rule does not accomplish that objective, can it nonetheless be supported on the ethical ground that any evidence obtained in violation of the Constitution should not be used to convict an accused person?

(3) In countries which have no such rule, are citizen rights adequately protected by other prevailing rules or practices?

The papers dealing with these and related problems are reproduced in the following pages. At the outset appears a summary of the American law with respect to the exclusionary rule prepared by Professor Francis A. Allen of the University of Chicago Law School. Next appear the policy-oriented papers of the two American participants who dealt with this subject, Professor Monrad G. Paulsen of the Law School of Columbia University and Frank J. McGarr of the Chicago Bar. Part II concludes with the reports of the seven foreign authorities with respect to the admissibility of illegally seized evidence in their countries.

# The Exclusionary Rule in the American Law of Search and Seizure

FRANCIS A. ALLEN

The American law of search and seizure and the enforcement of constitutional rights of privacy constitute a prime instance of law under stress. If, as we are told, hard cases make bad law, one would expect much bad law in the search and seizure area; for the cases are often hard, indeed. They are hard both because they place in sharp conflict interests of great and of the most obvious importance and because of confusion and inadequacy in the theory of the "right of privacy." In looking into the law of search and seizure our expectations are realized: it is an area in which bad law abounds. Where else does one find quite such enthusiastic efforts on the part of courts, legislatures, and even commentators, to have their cake and eat it, too? Where else do we find such fervant attempts to obtain advantage from the simultaneous acceptance of mutually inconsistent alternatives? One should not expect that all the tough and intractable problems in this area will be resolved by this series of papers. But, one may properly hope and expect that the following discussion gives due recognition to one fundamental proposition. That proposition is this: Any decision with reference to the exclusionary rule in the search and seizure cases involves costs. Any discussion of these issues, if it is to be responsible, must clearly identify these costs. Any proposals for legislative or judicial action, if they are to deserve attention, must be founded on conscientious effort to take these costs into account.

First, what is the exclusionary rule in the search and seizure cases? There are, of course, many rules and doctrines, dealing with particular problems,

that result in exclusion of evidence from criminal trials. The rules relating to the inadmissibility of "involuntary" confessions provide one example.[1] Sometimes a legislature in its wisdom will construct a special rule of exclusion such as the remarkable and little-noticed provision of the Illinois statutes that declares inadmissible any evidence obtained by a private detective in the employ of a governmental official, when the compensation paid the detective is calculated on any basis other than the time spent by him in the investigation.[2] We are concerned here, however, with the special rule of exclusion recognized in some American jurisdictions relating to evidence illegally seized. The rule in its broadest form can be described rather simply. Upon appropriate motion by the defendant in a criminal prosecution, evidence obtained from the defendant in violation of his constitutional rights to be free from unreasonable searches and seizures will be suppressed by order of court. In some jurisdictions the evidence subject to suppression need not be physical or tangible evidence. Thus, the Illinois case, *People v. Albea*,[3] held that the testimony of a prosecution witness, a person discovered by the police in the course of an unlawful search, should have been excluded at the criminal trial.[4] Moreover, in some circumstances, evidence other than that

---

[1] The basic confession rule may be supplemented by special statutory rules of exclusion. Thus in Illinois the prosecutor is under obligation to furnish the defendant with a copy of his confession before arraignment. The provision is mandatory. Failure of the prosecution to comply renders the confession inadmissible. ILL. REV. STAT. c. 38, §729 (1959).

[2] ILL. REV. STAT. c. 38, §608a (1959).

[3] 2 Ill.2d 317, 118 N.E.2d 277 (1954).

[4] And see Nueslein v. District of Columbia, 115 F.2d 690 (D.C. Cir. 1940). The cases on this and related

directly obtained through unreasonable search and seizure may be suppressed. Ever since the decision of the *Silverthorne* case[5] by the United States Supreme Court it has been understood in the federal courts, and in at least some of the state courts recognizing the exclusionary rule,[6] that the so-called "derivative use" of illegally seized evidence may be denied. Thus, evidence obtained legitimately but brought to the prosecutor's attention by clues or leads supplied by illegally seized evidence may, upon proper showing, also be suppressed.

The exclusionary rule, as just described, is subject to certain implicit limitations. These limitations are important, not only because a statement of them is necessary to the precise definition of the rule, but because some commentators regard these limitations as imperiling the effectiveness of the exclusionary rule as a deterrent to police misconduct.[7] There are at least four such limitations. First, it has been clearly held in the federal cases that evidence obtained unlawfully from the defendant by a private person is not subject to suppression. The theory here is that the exclusionary rule is designed to enforce constitutional rights of privacy. The Fourth Amendment provides an immunity from official or governmental misconduct, not a protection against private action, however illegal or even criminal it may be.[8]

Second, it is generally understood that one moving to suppress evidence has standing to complain only of illegal searches which violated his own constitutional rights.[9] Thus, a defendant may not obtain the exclusion of incriminating evidence illegally seized by the police solely in violation of a third party's rights of privacy. Nevertheless, the determination of when a petitioner's rights have been sufficiently affected by a search or seizure to give him standing to suppress the evidence so obtained is one of some difficulty. The 1951 decision in *United States v. Jeffers* indicated that the Supreme Court, at least, was disposed toward a rather liberal view of the standing requirements.[10] This impression is strongly confirmed by the recent decision in *Jones v. United States*.[11] The opinion recognizes the general formula that one having standing to invoke the exclusionary rule "must have been a *victim* of a search or seizure, one against whom the search was directed."[12] In *Jones* the defendant was accused of a narcotics offense. The apartment searched and in which the drugs were seized was leased by a friend who had merely given defendant permission to make temporary use of the premises. The Court recognized defendant's substantial dilemma. If his interest in the apartment was not sufficient to support a motion to suppress, standing

---

points, however, have not often gone so far. For a recent discussion, see Kamisar, *Illegal Searches and Seizures and Contemporaneous Incriminating Statements*, 1961 U. ILL. L. FORUM 78.

[5] 251 U.S. 385 (1920). See also Nardone v. United States, 308 U.S. 338 (1939).

[6] *E.g.*, People v. Martin, 382 Ill. 192, 46 N.E.2d 997 (1943).

[7] This position has been frequently taken. Typical expressions may be found in Grant, *Circumventing the Fourth Amendment*, 14 So. CALIF. L. REV. 359 (1941); Comment, *Judicial Control of Illegal Search and Seizure*, 58 YALE L. J. 144 (1948).

[8] The leading case is Burdeau v. McDowell, 256 U.S. 465 (1921). See also Gindrat v. People, 138 Ill. 103, 27 N.E. 1085 (1891); Siebert v. People, 143 Ill. 571, 32 N.E. 431 (1892); State v. Owens, 302 Mo. 348, 377, 259 S.W. 100, 108-09 (1924). *But cf.* Black, *Burdeau v. McDowell; A Judicial Milepost on the Road to Absolutism*, 12 B.U.L. REV. 32 (1932); Chafee, *The Progress of the Law, 1919-1922*, 35 HARV. L. REV. 673, 700-703 (1922).

[9] Edwards, *Standing to Suppress Unreasonably Seized Evidence*, 47 Nw. U.L. REV. 471 (1952). And see Cantrell v. United States, 15 F.2d 955 (5th Cir. 1926); Walker v. State, 194 Ind. 402, 142 N.E. 16 (1924); Tongut v. State, 197 Ind. 539, 151 N.E. 427 (1926). Corporate officers are usually held to lack standing to complain of an unreasonable search and seizure directed against the corporation: Guckenheimer and Bros. Co. v. United States, 3 F.2d 786 (3d Cir. 1925); Bilodeau v. United States, 14 F.2d 582 (9th Cir. 1926); People v. Perry, 1 Ill.2d 482, 116 N.E.2d 360 (1954). *Cf.* Haywood v. United States, 268 Fed. 795 (7th Cir. 1920) (same result as to officer of an unincorporated association).

[10] 342 U.S. 48 (1951). Narcotics were unlawfully seized from hotel rooms rented, not by defendant, but by his aunts. The latter had given him free access to the rooms. The Court held that defendant had standing primarily by reason of his "property" interest in the drugs. Although the drugs were "contraband" they were to be treated as defendant's property for purposes of invoking the exclusionary rule.

[11] 362 U.S. 257 (1960).

[12] *Id.* at 261. (Emphasis added.)

could only be predicated on his "ownership" of the drugs seized. But the latter allegation would go far to establish defendant's guilt of the offense charged. The Court resolves the dilemma by finding the defendant's "interest" in the premises sufficient. The holding is that "anyone legitimately on the premises where a search occurs may challenge its legality by way of motion to suppress, when its fruits are proposed to be used against him."[13]

A third and much less significant limitation on the exclusionary rule was delineated by the Supreme Court in *Walder v. United States*.[14] In 1950 defendant successfully moved to suppress the use of a narcotic capsule as evidence which had been illegally seized from him by federal officers. Two years later, when defendant was again on trial on a different narcotics charge, defendant testified on direct examination that he had never had narcotics in his possession. The trial judge permitted the government to impeach defendant's testimony by bringing to the stand one of the officers who had participated in the earlier illegal seizure and allowing him to testify that drugs at that time had been taken from defendant's person. In affirming the conviction, the Court said: "It is one thing to say that the Government cannot make use of evidence unlawfully obtained. It is quite another to say that defendant can turn the illegal method by which the Government's possession was obtained to his own advantage, and provide himself with a shield against contradiction of his untruths."[15]

A fourth limitation on the exclusionary rule is the so-called "silver-platter" doctrine. The phrase is that of Mr. Justice Frankfurter[16] and is descriptive of the holdings in many federal cases, prior to *Elkins v. United States*,[17] that evidence illegally seized by state officers may be handed over—on a silver platter—to federal officers and be admitted in a federal trial, so long as there was no federal

participation in the illegal activities of the state police.[18] But in the 1960 decision of *Elkins* a majority of the Supreme Court concluded that "this doctrine can no longer be accepted."[19] The result, according to the Court's opinion, was induced by the "logic" of the holding in *Wolf v. Colorado*, decided eleven years earlier.[20] The *Wolf* case established the proposition that rights against unreasonable searches and seizures by state officers are included among the protections of the Fourteenth Amendment. Nevertheless, the holding in *Elkins* appears directly predicated, not on a constitutional ground, but on the Court's supervisory powers over federal criminal justice. The test to determine whether evidence illegally seized by state authority is to be suppressed in a federal trial is stated as follows: ". . . evidence obtained by state officers during a search which, if conducted by federal officers, would have violated the defendant's immunity from unreasonable searches and seizures under the *Fourth* Amendment is inadmissible over the defendant's timely objection in a federal criminal trial."[21] The complexities inherent in the *Elkins* rule cannot adequately be canvassed in a single paragraph; but that there are unanswered questions seems apparent. Thus the majority opinion seems tacitly to assume that the rights protected by the Fourth Amendment against federal action are in all respects the same as those against unreasonable search and seizure by state officials implicit in the Fourteenth. If, as one might have supposed,[22] the protections of the Fourth Amendment are *broader*, then the

---

[13] *Id.* at 267.

[14] 347 U.S. 62 (1954).

[15] *Id.* at 65.

[16] See Lustig v. United States, 338 U.S. 74, 78–79 (1949).

[17] 364 U.S. 206 (1960).

[18] The leading case in this series is Byars v. United States, 273 U.S. 28 (1927). For a state case dealing with the same problem, see People v. Touhy, 361 Ill. 332, 197 N.E. 849 (1935). Consult the interesting and important discussion, Kamisar, *Wolf and Lustig Ten Years Later: Illegal State Evidence in State and Federal Courts*, 43 MINN. L. REV. 1083 (1959). As might be expected, the questions of what constituted federal "participation" and what quantum of evidence is necessary to establish it proved difficult and vexing.

[19] 364 U.S. 206, 208 (1960).

[20] 338 U.S. 25 (1949). Consult, Allen, *The Wolf Case: Search and Seizure, Federalism, and the Civil Liberties*, 45 ILL. L. REV. 1 (1950).

[21] 364 U.S. 206, 223–24 (1960). (Emphasis added.)

[22] See the dissenting opinion of Mr. Justice Frankfurter in the *Elkins* case, *id.* at 237 *et seq.* Cf. Kamisar, *op. cit. supra* note 18.

federal courts may be required to exclude evidence from the federal trial which was obtained by state officers without violation of defendant's federal constitutional rights. On the other hand, if the Fourth Amendment rights are defined more *narrowly* than those recognized under state constitutional or statutory provisions, the federal court may be authorized to admit evidence which would have been barred by a state court recognizing the exclusionary rule. Moreover, there is another side to the platter: What about the obligations of state courts with reference to evidence seized unlawfully by federal officials? Given the conclusion in *Wolf* that states are not required to adopt the exclusionary rule, it must surely follow that a state need not suppress evidence illegally seized by federal officials when it is free to admit evidence illegally seized by its own officers. Nevertheless, a number of states prior to *Elkins* had already ruled as a matter of local law that evidence illegally seized by federal officers should be barred from state proceedings.[23] The *Elkins* ruling may induce other state courts to adopt a similar position. It should also be recalled that in *Rea v. United States* the Court approved an injunction restraining a federal officer from testifying in a state proceeding as to matters discovered in the course of executing an invalid federal search warrant.[24] For the purposes at hand it must suffice to say that many problems in this area are yet to be resolved and much remains to be considered in the years ahead.

These, then, are the major limitations on the scope of the exclusionary rule in the search and seizure cases. They do not, however, exhaust the list, for various local doctrines constricting the application of the rule have emerged. Some of these will be noted in connection with the discussion of other matters to which I now must turn.

A word needs to be said about what might be called the procedure of the exclusionary rule. There

[23] The authorities are collected in Grant, *The Tarnished Silver Platter: Federalism and Admissibility of Illegally Seized Evidence*, 8 UCLA L. REV. 1, 28, n. 144 (1961).
[24] 350 U.S. 214 (1956). And see Wilson v. Schnettler, 365 U.S. 381 (1961).

are variations from one jurisdiction to another in these matters. But the situation in general can be simply stated. In most jurisdictions recognizing the rule, the issue of illegal search must be raised in a pre-trial motion to suppress, unless the facts supporting the motion did not come to the attention of the defendant or could not reasonably have been discovered by him until after commencement of the trial.[25] Many cases hold that if the motion to suppress is denied, the issue of unreasonable search can be preserved for appeal only by defense counsel's making appropriate objection at the trial when the contested evidence is offered by the prosecution.[26] One further procedural matter deserves attention. In many jurisdictions, if a motion to suppress is granted, there may often be no way for the prosecution to challenge the trial judge's ruling that the evidence was obtained by or derived from an unconstitutional search and seizure. Quite generally, a ruling on the motion to suppress is not itself appealable because it is not regarded as a "final order" or

[25] See, *e.g.*, People v. Anderson, 337 Ill. 310, 328, 169 N.E. 243 (1929) ("Where it is claimed that evidence against one accused of crime has been obtained by an unlawful search of his house and seizure of his effects, the question of such unlawful search and seizure must be presented to the court before the trial, if possible. If the accused has not raised the question before the trial he cannot avail himself of it when the evidence is offered on the trial."); State v. Gillam, 230 Iowa 1287, 300 N.W. 567 (1942); Robertson v. State, 94 Fla. 770, 114 So. 534 (1927). And see FED. R. CRIM. P. 41(e): "The motion shall be made before trial or hearing unless opportunity therefore did not exist or the defendant was not aware of the grounds for the motion at the trial or hearing." But some courts have ruled to the contrary: Youman v. Commonwealth, 189 Ky. 152, 169, 224 S.W. 860 (1920) ("In our practice the proper time, and the only time, in which objection can be made to the introduction of evidence by the mouth of witnesses is when it is offered during the trial. . . ."); Shuck v. State, 223 Ind. 155, 59 N.E.2d 124 (1945). The burden of proof in the hearing to suppress is ordinarily held to be on the moving party, Mata v. State, 203 Ind. 291, 179 N.E. 916 (1932). In one case in which the motion to suppress was made at the trial, the appellate court ruled that the hearing conducted in the presence of the jury did not constitute reversible error but was a matter within the trial judge's discretion. Italiano v. State, 141 Fla. 249, 193 So. 48 (1940).
[26] People v. Reid, 336 Ill. 421, 168 N.E. 344 (1929); Robertson v. State, 94 Fla. 770, 114 So. 534 (1927); Wishmire v. State, 196 Ind. 104, 147 N.E. 278 (1925).

for some other reason.[27] On the other hand, if the motion is granted and the evidence suppressed, the prosecution may have no case, with the result that the charge must be dismissed or the defendant acquitted. If the defendant is acquitted, the prosecution, of course, is barred from access to the appellate court by appeal. The serious consequence of this situation is that, particularly in areas of criminal litigation such as gambling, where motions to suppress are frequently filed and frequently granted,[28] the decisions of trial judges are substantially immune from effective appellate supervision. There is reason to believe that the search and seizure law being applied in inferior trial courts sometimes bears only coincidental relation to the principles announced in decisions of the highest court of the jurisdiction.

If the foregoing will suffice as a brief sketch of the nature of the exclusionary rule and its mode of application, we may now direct our attention to other questions. What is the historical and legal basis of the exclusionary rule?

There is a notion—I am almost tempted to call it a myth—that the exclusionary rule in the search and seizure cases is merely the illegitimate progeny of the American prohibition experiment. The rule, according to this version of its history, was conceived in sin, for it represented little more than an elaborate effort at judicial nullification by judges hostile to the enforcement of the Eighteenth Amendment. This explanation of the exclusionary rule is vulnerable on two scores. First, it is probably not true or, at least, it contains only a partial truth. Second, acceptance of any such notion as the sole or primary explanation for the creation and survival of the exclusionary rule requires one to ignore or trivialize persisting and pressing issues in the current administration of criminal justice.

Certainly, in the federal courts, the origins of the exclusionary rule long antedated national prohibi-

tion. *Boyd v. United States*[29] and *Weeks v. United States*[30] were decided by the Supreme Court of the United States in 1886 and 1914, respectively. Neither involved the enforcement of liquor laws. As late as 1955, long after the Noble Experiment had become only a quaint historical memory, the California court in *People v. Cahan*[31] overturned its long-established law and adopted the exclusionary rule. To be sure, most of the states that accepted the "Weeks Rule" did so in the period of national prohibition. No doubt, in some cases, the adoption or rejection of the exclusionary rule reflected the attitude of particular judges toward the whole prohibition enterprise. But it should also be noticed that the prohibition laws provided many state courts with their first occasions to give serious consideration to the problem of enforcement of individual rights against unreasonable search and seizure. When national prohibition suddenly burst upon the country the jurisprudence of many states was almost completely innocent of authoritative precedents, not only as to ways and means of enforcement, but as to substance of these rights in the multitude of situations then being presented for the first time to the courts for adjudication.[32] The Volstead Act and supporting state legislation represented the first important nation-wide effort to enforce criminal sanctions against conduct which involves no victims or, at least those who may be called willing victims. Such areas of penal regulation present peculiar problems of enforcement; in such areas the likelihood of violations of constitutional rights of privacy is greatest.[33] The prohibition experiment

---

[27] Cogen v. United States, 278 U.S. 221 (1929). *But cf*. United States v. Sineiro, 190 F.2d 397 (3d Cir. 1951).

[28] See the instructive data presented in Comment, *Search and Seizure in Illinois: Enforcement of the Constitutional Right of Privacy*, 47 Nw. U.L. Rev. 493 (1952).

[29] 116 U.S. 616 (1886).

[30] 232 U.S. 383 (1914).

[31] 44 Cal.2d 434, 282 P.2d 905 (1955).

[32] The difficulties associated with the paucity of settled law are graphically illustrated in an article written in this period by a Wisconsin prosecutor, Roberts, *Does the Search and Seizure Clause Hinder the Proper Administration of the Criminal Justice?*, 5 Wis. L. Rev. 195 (1929). At one point he asserts: "It can probably be safely said that the decisions passing squarely upon the search and seizure clause of the Constitutions of the states prior to prohibition would not average one for each state." *Id*. at 200.

[33] See Allen, *The Borderland of the Criminal Law: Problems of "Socializing" Criminal Justice*, 32 Soc. Ser. Rev. 107, 112 (1958).

has, by and large, been abandoned. But efforts at law enforcement in other areas, presenting comparable problems, persist and have become more important with the passing of the years. Insofar as the problems we are discussing today are concerned, those associated with the gambling laws and narcotics enforcement are, after all, not so very different from those of thirty years ago. It will not do, therefore, to brush aside the exclusionary rule in the search and seizure cases as an historical aberration arising out of an effort at penal regulation fortunately long since abandoned. Whatever one's conclusion as to the propriety of the exclusionary rule, the problems it attempts to confront are clear and present.

So much for the historical background of the exclusionary rule. What can be said of its legal or constitutional basis? It is strange that after the decision of hundreds of cases by state and federal courts in which the exclusionary rule has been applied these questions are still in doubt. From the decision of the first important case, *Boyd v. United States*,[34] the privilege against self-incrimination has played some role in efforts to articulate the legal basis of the rule. But its role has been confusing and ill-defined. In *Agnello v. United States* the Supreme Court announced the stark proposition: "It is well settled that when properly invoked, the Fifth Amendment protects every person from incrimination by the use of evidence obtained through a search or seizure made in violation of his rights under the Fourth Amendment."[35] But by 1949 and the decision of *Wolf v. Colorado*,[36] a case surely requiring the most precise articulation of the constitutional basis for the exclusionary rule, the privilege against self-incrimination is almost totally ignored. Mr. Justice Black describes the rule simply as a rule of evidence applied by the federal courts. Mr. Justice Frankfurter sees it as deriving from the Fourth Amendment by "judicial implication." The dissenting justices treat it as a necessary and inherent part of the Fourth Amendment's protections.

[34] 116 U.S. 616 (1886).
[35] 269 U.S. 20, 33–34 (1925).
[36] 338 U.S. 26 (1949).

The reliance on the privilege against self-incrimination in these cases, it seems to me, has contributed neither to clarity nor sense. Certainly, the reliance on the privilege has not been consistent. Thus, it is generally held that a corporation may move to suppress evidence illegally seized from it, despite the fact that corporate bodies are said to lack capacity to invoke the privilege against self-incrimination.[37] Reliance on the privilege as the rationale of the exclusionary rule is also probably responsible for some egregious decisions denying the exclusion of evidence in cases in which the defendant, although the victim of illegal search, disclaims ownership of the property seized.[38]

It is clear, as opponents of the rule have frequently pointed out, that the exclusionary rule in the search and seizure cases is in opposition to the ordinary assumptions of the Anglo-American law of evidence which generally, though not universally, postulates that competent evidence is not rendered incompetent by virtue of the fact that the evidence was obtained in an improper or illegal fashion. How has this deviation from normal assumptions been justified by courts accepting the exclusionary rule? Apart from reliance on the privilege against self-incrimination, I find two principal grounds being relied on in the cases. First, it is said, the exclusion of unlawfully

[37] Silverthorne Lumber Co. v. United States, 251 U.S. 385 (1920). *Cf.* Oklahoma Press Publishing Co. v. Wattling, 327 U.S. 186 (1946).
[38] *Compare* People v. Exum, 382 Ill. 204, 209, 47 N.E.2d 56 (1943) ("Nowhere in his motion is it alleged that any of the property seized is claimed to be the property of the defendant, nor does he claim any interest in it or ask for its return. . . . The property admittedly not belonging to him or being property in which he has an interest or right of possession, we are at a loss to see how he can complain whether of its seizure or its use as being a violation of his constitutional rights. Clearly, if the property is not his and he has no interest in it, and no right to its possession, he is not in the position of giving evidence against himself when it is introduced as exhibits upon the trial.") *with* People v. Grod, 385 Ill. 584, 591–92, 53 N.E.2d 591 (1944) ("If, in order to have them suppressed he must allege that he owned them, then he has in effect been compelled to admit the possession of stolen property recently following a crime, which is sufficient in itself, unless explained, to authorize conviction."). See Note, 96 L. ED. 66 (1951).

seized evidence is necessary to deter police misconduct and provides an indispensable device for enforcement of constitutional rights of privacy. Mr. Justice Douglas, in his dissenting opinion in the *Wolf* case, gives succinct expression to this view, when he says: "[E]vidence obtained [by unreasonable search and seizure] *must* be excluded . . . , since in the absence of that rule of evidence the Amendment would have no effective sanction."[39] The second basis of the exclusionary rule, frequently articulated in state as well as federal opinions, is essentially an ethical ground. A typical expression is that of the Florida court in a case decided almost forty years ago: "To permit an officer of the State to *acquire evidence illegally* and in *violation of sacred constitutional guaranties*, and to use the *illegally acquired* evidence in the prosecution of the person who illegally acquired the intoxicants strikes at the very foundation of the administration of justice, and where such practices prevail makes law enforcement a mockery."[40] Needless to say, the critics of the exclusionary rule find neither of these grounds persuasive or sufficient.

Not all of the American states have adopted the exclusionary rule; indeed, only about half of them have done so.[41] Twenty of the states appear to have adopted the rule without substantial qualification. These include[42] such populous jurisdictions

as California,[43] Illinois,[44] Indiana,[45] Missouri,[46] Texas,[47] and Wisconsin.[48] In Michigan, although the exclusionary rule was adopted early by the courts,[49] certain categories of evidence are now placed outside the operation of the rule by constitutional amendment, including narcotics, firearms and other dangerous weapons seized in places other than a dwelling house.[50] Alabama,[51] Maryland,[52] and South Dakota[53] have by legislation adopted the rule only as to the situations stipulated in their statutes. Hawaii and Alaska have apparently not spoken to the question since becoming states.[54] The federal rule of exclusion operates in the District of Columbia.[55]

The division of the American states into exclusion and non-exclusion jurisdictions suggests one final cluster of problems. These problems can hardly be more than noted, for they are extremely complex, involving basic constitutional issues

---

[39] 338 U.S. 25, 40 (1949). (Italics in the original.)

[40] Atz v. Andrews, 84 Fla. 43, 52, 94 So. 329, 332 (1922). (Italics in the original.)

[41] Note, 50 A.L.R.2d 533 (1956). See also the appendix to the opinion of the Court in Elkins v. United States, 364 U.S. 206, 224–32 (1960).

[42] The jurisdictions not specifically mentioned in the text include the following: *Delaware* (Rickards v. State, 45 Del. 573, 77 A.2d 199 (1950)); *Florida* (Atz v. Andrews, 84 Fla. 43, 94 So. 329 (1922)); *Idaho* (State v. Arregui, 44 Idaho 43, 254 Pac. 788 (1927)); *Kentucky* (Youman v. Commonwealth, 189 Ky. 152, 224 S.W. 860 (1920)); *Mississippi* (Tucker v. State, 128 Miss. 211, 90 So. 845 (1922)); *Montana* (State *ex rel.* King v. District Court, 70 Mont. 191, 224 Pac. 862 (1924)); *North Carolina* (apparently full adoption of the exclusionary rule by statutory amendment, N.C. GEN. STAT. §15–27 (Supp. 1951); *Oklahoma* (Gore v. State, 24 Okla. Crim. 394, 218 Pac. 545 (1923)); *Oregon* (State v. Laundy, 103 Or. 443, 204 Pac. 958, 206 Pac. 290 (1922), and see comment in Kamisar, *op. cit. supra* note 18 at 1160, n.259); *Rhode Island* (R. I. GEN. LAWS

§§9–19–25 (1956). See State v. Hillman, 84 R.I. 396, 125 A.2d 94 (1956)); *Tennessee* (Hughes v. State, 145 Tenn. 544, 238 S.W. 588 (1921)); *Washington* (State v. Gibbons, 118 Wash. 171, 203 Pac. 390 (1922)); *West Virginia* (State v. Wills, 91 W. Va. 659, 114 S.E. 261 (1922)); *Wyoming* (State v. George, 32 Wyo. 223, 231 Pac. 683 (1924)).

[43] People v. Cahan, 44 Cal.2d 434, 282 P.2d 905 (1955).

[44] People v. Castree, 311 Ill. 392, 143 N.E. 112 (1924).

[45] Callender v. State, 193 Ind. 91, 138 N.E. 817 (1922).

[46] State v. Owens, 302 Mo. 348, 259 S.W. 100 (1924).

[47] TEX. CODE CRIM. PROC. art. 727a (Vernon, 1941). See Williamson v. State, 156 Tex. Crim. 520, 244 S.W.2d 202 (1951).

[48] Hoyer v. State, 180 Wis. 407, 193 N.W. 89 (1923).

[49] People v. Marxhausen, 204 Mich. 559, 171 N.W. 557 (1919).

[50] MICH. CONST. 1908, art. II, §10 (as amended in 1934 and 1952).

[51] Act of September 12, 1951 (ALA. CODE tit. 29, §210 (1940)).

[52] MD. LAWS 1929, c. 194. See Sugarman v. State, 173 Md. 52, 195 Atl. 324 (1937). See also Salsburg v. Maryland, 346 U.S. 545 (1954).

[53] S. D. CODE §34.1102 (1935) (evidence seized under color of an invalid search warrant admissible). See State v. Land, 76 S.D. 544, 82 N.W.2d 286 (1957).

[54] Prior to statehood courts of both jurisdictions followed the federal rule. See United States v. Doumain, 7 Alaska 31 (1923), and Territory v. Ho Me, 26 Hawaii 331 (1922), cited in Kamisar, *op. cit. supra* note 18 at 1160, n. 259.

[55] Darnall v. United States, 33 A.2d 734 (Mun. Ct. App., D.C., 1943).

implicit in a system of federalism. The most important question can be put in this fashion: By virtue of the Fourteenth Amendment or other provision of the United States constitution, can federal power be employed to force upon an unwilling state court the exclusion of illegally-seized evidence in a state proceeding? This question could scarcely have been seriously asked as recently as a generation ago. But in 1949 the Supreme Court of the United States decided the case of *Wolf v. Colorado*.[56] The opinion of the Court, written by Mr. Justice Frankfurter, appears to announce two propositions. First, individual immunities from unreasonable search and seizure by state officials are to be regarded, in the language of the traditional due process formula, as rights "basic to a free society" and, hence, fall within the due process clause of the Fourteenth Amendment. But second, the exclusion of evidence illegally seized is merely one method of enforcement among many, and the states are free to accept or reject the exclusionary rule according to local conceptions of policy. Two years later, the Court, again through Mr. Justice Frankfurter, emphasized its unwillingness to enforce the exclusion of illegally-seized evidence against the states when it denied federal injunctive relief to the defendant in a state proceeding who alleged that evidence against him had been illegally seized by state officials and that this evidence was to be introduced in the state trial.[57]

What has been the practical impact of the *Wolf* case on state criminal procedure? To date it has not been great. True enough, in *Rochin v. California*, the stomach-pump case, a state conviction was reversed; but this result was reached with almost scrupulous avoidance of all talk of search and seizure and of reliance on the authority of the *Wolf* case.[58] Later, in *Irvine v. California*, the case in which state police planted a microphone in defendant's home, the Court affirmed the conviction on the authority of *Wolf*, although the majority expressed shock and dismay at the police

practices involved.[59] Interestingly enough, Mr. Justice Frankfurter dissented vigorously, insisting that the *Wolf* precedent required no such result. However one may feel about the result contended for in the dissent, it seems fair to suggest, with all gentleness, that Mr. Justice Frankfurter had become entoiled in a semantic mesh of his own making. To label a right as one "basic to a free society" is to say about as much as one can say of a constitutional protection. The right of petitioner Wolf had been so labelled; and yet, Mr. Justice Frankfurter for the Court had ruled in *Wolf v. Colorado* that the state need not exclude the evidence from the criminal trial. But if in *Irvine*, as Mr. Justice Frankfurter insists, exclusion of the illegally obtained evidence should be enforced by federal power, how is defendant's violated right to be characterized? Is Irvine's right one "very, very" basic to a free society?[60] The position seems almost to involve a comparison of superlatives, which, whatever may be said for its logic, presents some difficulties of grammar.

The problems of the exclusionary rule in the area of federal-state relations are many. It is not possible in the brief compass of this paper to embark on a full analysis of all of them. For purposes of illustration, however, one further issue may be noted. Assume a case arising from a state that has *accepted* the exclusionary rule but has permitted evidence to be admitted on what defendant claims to be an erroneous interpretation of his constitutional rights of privacy. Under the *Wolf* case, may the Supreme Court intervene and reverse the state conviction? It would certainly seem that such a result might and, in an appropriate case, should follow. Yet one of the Courts of Appeal has reached a contrary decision.[61]

This, then, must serve as the background for our discussion of the exclusionary rule in the search and seizure cases. What does forty years of widespread experience with the rule teach us? In previous efforts to evaluate this experience have the right questions been asked? These and

---

[56] 338 U.S. 25 (1949).
[57] Stefanelli v. Menard, 342 U.S. 117 (1951).
[58] 342 U.S. 165 (1952).

[59] 347 U.S. 128 (1954).
[60] These matters have been recently discussed in Kamisar, *op. cit. supra* note 18.
[61] Sisk v. Overlade, 220 F.2d 68 (7th Cir. 1955).

many more difficult problems I happily surrender to bolder and more competent hands.

\* \* \*

ADDENDUM

One of the hazards of the legal commentator, especially one who concerns himself with the work of the United States Supreme Court, is that events sometimes outrun publishing schedules. Thus the decision of the Court in *Mapp v. Ohio*,[62] announced on the last day of the 1960 term, requires fundamental modifications in the description, given above, of the American law as it relates to the exclusionary rule in search and seizure cases. *Mapp* holds that the states are now required, by reason of the due process clause of the Fourteenth Amendment, to exclude from state criminal trials evidence seized in violation of the accused's constitutional rights by state officers. In so doing the Court specifically overruled its 1949 decision in *Wolf v.*

*Colorado*, insofar as that case held the states free to accept or reject the exclusionary rule as a means to enforce rights against unreasonable search.[53]

That the Court might one day overturn, or at least substantially modify, its holding in *Wolf* was undoubtedly recognized by many who follow the Court's work. There were several straws in the wind, such as the tenor of the opinion of the Court in *Elkins v. United States*,[64] which suggested that this might occur sooner rather than later. Nevertheless, that the Court should act when it did and that it should employ the *Mapp* case as the vehicle to effect this change in due process doctrine probably came as a surprise to most.[65]

The brief compass of these remarks does not make possible a full evaluation of the Court's action. It must suffice to say that an appraisal of the *Mapp* case involves more than a canvassing of opinions relating to the desirability and effectiveness of the exclusionary rule as a device to enforce constitutional rights against unreasonable search and seizure. It involves questions of the proper exercise of judicial power in a federal system. There will undoubtedly be many who will contend that the Court has invaded areas of discretion and self-determination reserved to the states. The controversies on this and other issues are likely to persist in the years ahead.

It is not possible to anticipate all of the consequences of the *Mapp* decision, but some can be stated with reasonable assurance. The immediate impact of the holding will, of course, be felt most strongly in those states which have consistently rejected the exclusionary rule as a matter of local law.[66] Rights to suppress illegally seized evidence must now be recognized in these jurisdictions. *Mapp* also presumably sweeps aside provisions of

[62] 81 S.Ct. 1684 (1961), decided on June 19, 1961. City police acting pursuant to information that a person involved in a bombing was hiding in petitioner's apartment and that policy paraphernalia was hidden in the home, requested admission for purposes of search. After calling her lawyer, petitioner refused admission except under the authority of a search warrant. Later the police returned, broke open the outside door, and gained admission to the apartment armed with a document said to be a search warrant. There is reason to believe that no warrant had in fact issued or that the police had adequate grounds for issuance of a valid warrant. Petitioner's request to see the warrant was refused, and when she snatched the paper from the officer's hands, a scuffle ensued and the paper was retrieved. Petitioner was handcuffed and her apartment and the basement of the building were thoroughly searched. Petitioner's counsel, who arrived on the scene when the search was in progress, was denied admission. In the course of the search obscene books and pictures were seized. Petitioner, who explained that the objects seized were owned by a roomer who had vacated the apartment, was convicted of possession of the obscene materials. The conviction was affirmed by the Ohio supreme court. State v. Mapp, 170 Ohio St. 427, 166 N.E.2d 387 (1960). Due to a rule limiting the power of the Ohio court to invalidate state legislation, the affirmance occurred despite the fact that a majority of the state supreme court felt that the statute under which petitioner was convicted was unconstitutional. Ohio has refused to adopt the exclusionary rule as a matter of local law; hence the admission of the fruits of the unlawful search did not provide grounds for reversal.

[63] See discussion in the text at note 56, *supra.*

[64] 364 U. S. 206 (1960). An interesting contrast is provided by comparing the remarks relating to the exclusionary rule in the opinion of the Court in the *Elkins* case with those of Mr. Justice Jackson in Irvine v. California, 347 U.S. 128, 135, 136–37 (1954).

[65] Including, presumably, Mapp's counsel. The decision of Wolf v. California is not cited in appellant's brief. See Brief of Appellant on the Merits, No. 236, October Term, 1960.

[66] See discussion in the text at note 41, *supra.*

state constitutions[67] and statutes[68] which give only a partial recognition to the exclusionary rule. The statement of certain procedural requirements relating to the motion to suppress, such as the rule that the motion must be made before trial,[69] will undoubtedly be left to the law of the states. On the other hand, one may anticipate that issues of standing to object to an illegal search and the right to object to the derivative use of unlawfully obtained evidence will in the main be resolved by federal law.[70] It seems likely, also, that the Supreme Court will be called upon to review state court decisions relating to the validity of searches and seizures by state officers much more frequently than in the past. The implicit assumption of the *Elkins* case, that the rights against unreasonable search and seizure protected by the Fourteenth Amendment are in all respects the same as those protected by the Fourth, may thereby be put to the test.[71] Both state and federal courts will inevitably be confronted by petitions from state prisoners alleging that their convictions, prior to *Mapp*, are void because based on illegally seized evidence.

The ramifications of the *Mapp* decision in other areas of constitutional adjudication are obviously more speculative. It is possible, for example, that the Court may be induced to apply the *Elkins* doctrine to the state courts and require the latter to suppress evidence illegally seized by federal officers when there has been no participation in the illegal behavior by state police.[72] *Mapp* may also induce reconsideration of the Court's interpretation of Section 605 of the Federal Communications Act,[73] insofar as it involves the admission of wiretap evidence in state proceedings. The problem of wiretapping, to be sure, involves a federal statute rather than a constitutional provision and may in other respects differ from the problem of unreasonable searches and seizures. Nevertheless, the holding in *Schwartz v. Texas*[74] which permitted the states to admit wiretap evidence in state proceedings, was based in significant part on the analogous authority of *Wolf v. Colorado*. That authority has now been overturned.

Perhaps enough has been said to indicate that by its decision in *Mapp v. Ohio* the Court has effected far-reaching modifications in the American law of search and seizure. The reverberations of that decision have only just begun.

---

[67] See note 50, *supra*.
[68] See notes 51–53, *supra*.
[69] See discussion in the text at note 25, *supra*.
[70] See discussion in the text at note 9, *supra*.
[71] See discussion in the text at note 22, *supra*.

[72] See discussion in the text at note 23, *supra*.
[73] 48 Stat. 1064, 1103 (1934), 47 U.S.C. §605 (1958).
[74] 344 U.S. 199 (1952).

# The Exclusionary Rule and Misconduct by the Police

MONRAD G. PAULSEN

In the federal courts and in the courts of over twenty American states, evidence illegally obtained by law-enforcement officers cannot be received in a criminal prosecution, provided the accused objects to its admission.[1] Under the exclusionary rule if the residence quarters of a kidnapper are illegally searched by the police, the most incriminating evidence found therein, including such items as copies of ransom notes actually sent or the clothing of the victim, could not be used in a criminal proceeding against the kidnapper.[2] Whether such a rule can be defended in principle and whether it operates to discourage illegal police practices are the questions posed by this discussion.

[1] The jurisdictions are listed in MORGAN, MAGUIRE & WEINSTEIN, CASES AND MATERIALS ON EVIDENCE 745 (1957).

[2] Some states apply the exclusionary rule only in certain classes of cases. In Alabama, evidence illegally obtained from a dwelling house is excluded in the trial of certain alcohol control cases. ALA. CODE tit. 29, §210 (Supp. 1959). In Maryland, illegally obtained evidence is inadmissible in misdemeanor cases except that such evidence is admissible in prosecutions for carrying a concealed weapon. Also, in certain counties of Maryland, the exclusionary rule is inapplicable in gambling cases and, in a slightly different list of counties, the rule is inapplicable in lottery cases. MD. CODE ANN. art. 35, §5. See Salsburg v. Maryland, 346 U.S. 545 (1954). In Michigan, article 2, §10, of the state constitution provides that the exclusionary rule, otherwise applicable, shall not bar from evidence certain items listed therein.

If there is merit in the arguments of this paper, i.e., that the exclusionary rule does work to deter police misconduct, these compromises must be based upon a judgment that the deterrent effect of the exclusionary rule is a value outweighed by the value of securing convictions in some kinds of cases.

At the outset it should be recognized that the evidence which may not be introduced is as trustworthy and reliable as any which may be considered in court. The evidence is kept out of the trial not because it is unworthy of belief, but because it is the product of police methods which violate the law.

The exclusionary evidence rule says nothing about the content of the law governing the police. It takes no position with respect to which arrests, searches and seizures, or other enforcement actions are legal or illegal. To defend the rule is not to defend any particular formulation regulating the activities of law enforcement. One can support the rule and still support the proposition that wiretapping ought to be permitted in certain circumstances under certain safeguards. One can support the rule and still hold that the present law of arrest, formed as it was before the appearance of modern professional police forces, is outmoded and requires drastic reformulation. The rule merely states the consequences of a breach of whatever principles might be adopted to control law enforcement officers.

Police officers are not controlled more rigorously by the exclusionary evidence rule than they are by force of their own respect for the law. If police obey the rules set by the community to govern police practice, they obviously will not obtain evidence illegally. The point is often missed. The chief of police of Los Angeles, writing after California adopted the exclusionary rule, stated that the "ability to prevent the commission of crimes has been greatly diminished."[3] He meant to suggest that the diminution occurred because he would have to comply with the California decision.

[3] PARKER, POLICE 117 (Wilson ed. 1957).

Yet, that decision merely adopted the exclusionary rule in California; it did not change the substantive law of arrest or search at all. If the decision diminished the effectiveness of law enforcement in California, it did so by securing obedience to the law in a manner which influenced the police.

Nor are the police alone in falling into the error. Professor Edward Barrett has recently written:

"The interplay between the exclusionary rule and the rule that searches must be justified as incidental to valid arrests presents the danger of two undesirable side effects. Pressure may be placed on the police to make arrests too early in the investigative process. Pressure may be placed on the courts to water down the standards for probable cause to make formal arrests in order to avoid freeing obviously guilty defendants because of relatively minor invasions of their privacy."[4]

The pressure to arrest in order to search exists not because of the exclusionary rule, but because the law governing police conduct prohibits a search without a warrant, unless the search is incident to a valid arrest. The "side effects" referred to by Professor Barrett would, I submit, be observed in the operation of any sanction severe enough to deter the police. If courts were called upon to impose mandatory jail sentences or large fines upon officers guilty of minor violations of the rules, these side effects would be present. One can imagine judges who would place heavy burdens on the "technical" violator but who would not free the accused because of the violation, but I doubt that such judges exist in reality. Whenever the rules are enforced by meaningful sanctions, our attention is drawn to their content. The comfort of Freedom's words spoken in the abstract is always disturbed by their application to a contested instance. Any rule of police regulation enforced in fact will generate pressures to weaken the rule.

One further preliminary observation: The point is often made that the exclusionary rule should be rejected because the law of search and seizure and the law of arrest are filled with technicalities

[4] Barrett, *Personal Rights, Property Rights and the Fourth Amendment*, 1960 SUP. CT. REV. 46, 65.

and inconsistencies. This point, too, goes to the content of the rules rather than to the remedy. If the rules are unrealistic or unprincipled they ought to be changed. One may note that the California Supreme Court, in cases applying the exclusionary rule after its adoption, has greatly broadened the power of the police to search and to make arrests.[5]

Any fair-minded observer will find the case against excluding illegal evidence an impressive one.

Under the rule, a great many obviously guilty people must be acquitted. If the tainted evidence is barred from trial, the prosecution will frequently fail to carry its considerable burden of proof. The aim is to deter law enforcement officers from violating individual rights; however, the rule does not impose money damages or loss of liberty upon the offending officers, nor does it provide compensation for persons injured by official overreaching. Opponents have often emphasized the startling result achieved under the rule: to deter the police both the guilty defendant and the law-breaking officer go unpunished. As Judge Cardozo once put it, "The criminal is to go free because the constable blundered."[6] By freeing the criminal to return to his trade, the argument goes, the rule punishes not the official law-breaker, but rather the law-abiding citizen.[7]

The rule gives an ordinary policeman the power to confer immunity upon an offender. By over-

[5] Comment, *The Cahan Case: The Interpretation and Operation of the Exclusionary Rule in California*, 4 U.C.L.A. L. REV. 252 (1957); Comment, *Two Years with the Cahan Rule*, 9 STAN. L. REV. 515 (1957); Comment, *Search and Seizure: A Review of the Cases since People v. Cahan*, 45 CALIF. L. REV. 50 (1957).

[6] People v. Defore, 242 N.Y. 13, 21, 150 N.E. 585, 587 (1926).

[7] The proposed indirect and unnatural method is as follows: "Titus, you have been found guilty of conducting a lottery; Flavius, you have confessedly violated the constitution. Titus ought to suffer imprisonment for crime, and Flavius for contempt. But no! We shall let you *both* go free. We shall not punish Flavius directly, but shall do so by reversing Titus' conviction. This is our way of teaching people like Flavius to behave, and incidentally of securing respect for the Constitution. Our way of upholding the Constitution is not to strike at the man who breaks it, but to let off somebody else who broke something else." 8 WIGMORE, EVIDENCE §2184, at 40 (3d ed. 1940).

stepping the bounds of the law, a policeman's action can place vital evidence beyond the reach of the prosecution.[8]

The opponents of the rule urge that the exclusion of illegally obtained evidence is appropriate only to a tidy "fox-hunting" theory of criminal justice. The community will permit the game only so long as gamblers and other petty crooks are involved. "If a murderer, bank robber or kidnapper should go free in the face of his guilt," writes one critic, "the public would surely arise and condemn the helplessness of the courts against the depradations of the outlaws."[9] The rule destroys respect for law because it provides the spectacle of the courts letting the guilty go free.

The rule attempts to redress a violation of law without the time-honored method of direct complaint and trial on a carefully defined issue.[10] The procedure looking toward exclusion of evidence interrupts, delays, and confuses the main issue at hand—the trial of the accused. The principal proceeding may be turned into a trial of the police rather than of the defendant.

Furthermore, it is argued that the social danger of police excesses is greatly exaggerated.[11] The police are restrained by their own discipline and by the political power in the community. They will take pains not to go beyond the limits of social tolerance. Only the guilty suffer or profit by admission or exclusion of evidence, the innocent have little to fear.[12] The guilty whose privacy is invaded do not suffer harm as do the innocent in a similar circumstance.[13] "He who has made his home a den of thieves, a distillery for the manufacture of contraband liquor, a warehouse for infernal machines, or a safety deposit box for forged documents . . . has not sustained the damages when its sanctity is invaded, as has the citizen who has maintained that sanctity."[14]

Finally, the case against the rule makes the most serious assertion of all: The rule does not succeed in its principal aim: to discourage illegal police action. The police, it is said, are not concerned with convictions in an important degree. A failure to convict does not touch the officer in his person or his pocketbook.[15] Professional law enforcement training is not affected by the exclusionary rule.[16] Many states which employ it are most backward in providing for police education. Without instruction most well-meaning policemen remain unaware of the law. Abusive police, of course, will be deterred by nothing. Officers will find illegal practices useful because of the clues which they reveal, although the item actually taken may not be used in court.[17] Illegal searches are not less frequent than illegal arrests in the jurisdictions which embrace the rule, yet an illegal search does forbid the use of evidence, but the illegal arrest does not affect the courts' power to try the defendant.[18]

Most disturbing is the argument that if the police are subject to the restrictions of the exclusionary rule they cannot obtain the convictions necessary to carry out their law enforcement function, and if they cannot obtain such convictions they will be tempted to harass suspects, to inflict extra-legal punishments. "The exclusionary rule," wrote Professor Waite, "has driven the police to methods less desirable than those for which the judges shut truth from the jury's ears."[19]

The case against the rule is an impressive one.

In spite of the force of argument, I submit that the rule should be retained where it is in force and should be adopted where it is not now respected. Some of the arguments against the rule are unsound. Some can be met by measures other

---

[8] People v. Defore, 242 N.Y. 13, 23, 150 N.E. 585, 588 (1926).

[9] Plumb, *Illegal Enforcement of the Law*, 24 CORNELL L.Q. 337, 379 (1939). This article presents a well argued case against the exclusionary rule. Another very good statement in the same vein is Waite, *Judges and the Crime Burden*, 54 MICH. L. REV. 169 (1955).

[10] On Lee v. United States, 343 U.S. 747, 755 (1951) (Jackson, J.); Wigmore, *Using Evidence Obtained by Illegal Search and Seizure*, 8 A.B.A.J. 479 (1922).

[11] 8 WIGMORE, EVIDENCE §2184 (3d ed. 1940).

[12] Plumb, *op. cit. supra* note 9 at 371.

[13] *Id.* at 386.

[14] Massantonio v. People, 77 Colo. 392, 398, 236 Pac. 1019, 1021 (1925).

[15] Waite, *op. cit. supra* note 9, at 194.

[16] *Ibid.*

[17] Plumb, *op. cit. supra* note 9, at 380.

[18] Waite, *op. cit. supra* note 9, at 193.

[19] *Id.* at 196.

than abandoning the rule. The disadvantages which the rule does entail are worth the price which must be paid. The exclusionary evidence rule is morally correct and appropriate to a free society. It is a rule naturally suggested by the Constitution itself. It insures that the issues respecting defendants' rights are raised and litigated frequently, without great inconvenience. It is the most effective remedy we possess to deter police lawlessness.

A moral position of a high order gives support to the rule. It is unseemly that the government should with one hand forbid certain police conduct and yet, at the same time, attempt to convict accused persons through use of the fruits of the very conduct which is forbidden. As Mr. Justice Holmes put it in his *Olmstead* dissent:

> "It is also desirable that the Government should not itself foster and pay for other crimes, when they are the means by which the evidence is to be obtained. . . . I can attach no importance to protestations of disapproval if it knowingly accepts and pays and announces that in the future it will pay for the fruits. We have to choose, and for my part I think it a less evil, that some criminal should escape than the Government should play an ignoble part."[20]

And Mr. Justice Brandeis, also dissenting in *Olmstead*, insisted that the use of illegal evidence "is denied in order to maintain respect for law; in order to promote confidence in the administration of justice; in order to preserve the judicial process from contamination."[21]

[20] Olmstead v. United States, 277 U.S. 438, 470 (1928).

[21] *Id.* at 484.

The Director of the Federal Bureau of Investigation has written as follows:

> "One of the quickest ways for any law enforcement officer to bring public disrepute upon himself, his organization and the entire profession is to be found guilty of a violation of civil rights. Our people may tolerate many mistakes of both intent and performance, but, with unerring instinct, they know that when any person is intentionally deprived of his constitutional rights those responsible have committed no ordinary offense. A crime of this nature, if subtly encouraged by failure to condemn and punish, certainly leads down the road to totalitarianism." FBI Law Enforcement Bulletin 1-2 (September 1952).

The moral point not only rests upon an ethical judgment that governmental hypocrisy is an evil to be avoided for its own sake, but also it takes into account the serious undermining of trust in government which is an unavoidable consequence of any scheme permitting the state to benefit from unlawful conduct. Surely the government is a teacher, particularly in a society which leaves large areas of life for private planning and action. Public conduct becomes the model for private behavior. Few things are more subversive of free institutions than a mistrust of official integrity. When the police themselves break the law and other agencies of government eagerly reach for the benefits which flow from the breach, it is difficult for the citizenry to believe that the government truly meant to forbid the conduct in the first place. In our common speech we often refer to our officials with words of "otherness." How often do we say, "they" will tax us, "they" will appoint the police chief, or "they" will pass a law. It is corrosive of the vitally necessary trust in government if we all understand that "they" do not abide by the law which "they" assert. The conviction that all government is staffed by self-seeking hypocrites is easy to instill and difficult to erase.

No one has insisted on this point more eloquently than Justices Brandeis and Frankfurter. "Our Government is the potent, the omnipresent teacher," wrote Mr. Justice Brandeis.

> "For good or for ill, it teaches the whole people by its example. Crime is contagious. If the Government becomes a lawbreaker, it breeds contempt for law; . . . it invites anarchy. To declare that in the administration of the criminal law the end justifies the means—to declare that the Government may commit crimes in order to secure the conviction of a private criminal—would bring terrible retribution. Against that pernicious doctrine this Court should resolutely set its face."[22]

Mr. Justice Frankfurter put it in these words:

> "The contrast between morality professed by society and immorality practiced on its behalf

[22] Olmstead v. United States, 277 U.S. 438, 485 (1928) (dissenting opinion).

makes for contempt of law. Respect for law cannot be turned off and on as though it were a hot-water faucet."[23]

The use of illegal evidence involves the courts, the branch of government most dependent upon popular respect, in a kind of ratification of illegal conduct. Judge Traynor of the Supreme Court of California has observed, "The success of the lawless venture depends entirely on the court's lending its aid by allowing the evidence to be introduced."[24] When the prosecutor takes evidence gained by the lawless enforcement of the law and places it before a court, that court by accepting the offer of proof becomes inevitably drawn into the lawlessness. At least, many of the community's most scrupulous and noble will see it so. Judge Condon of Rhode Island has made the point in these words: "If courts receive evidence knowing that it has been unconstitutionally obtained, they . . . give judicial countenance to the government's violation of the Constitution."[25] Listen once more to a sentence from Holmes: "If the existing code does not permit district attorneys to have a hand in such dirty business it does not permit the judge to allow such iniquities to succeed."[26] The exclusionary rule dissociates the court from any police policy of systematic violation of law.

In the federal courts the exclusionary rule is grounded in the provisions of the Fourth Amendment. In part, this constitutional position was taken because the justices in *Weeks v. United States* embraced the view that the courts, by permitting the use of illegally obtained evidence, came to participate in the violation of the offending federal police officer and hence to violate the Constitution themselves. Mr. Justice Day, speaking for a unanimous court, wrote concerning the Fourth Amendment:

"This protection is equally extended to the action of the Government and officers of the law acting under it. To sanction such proceedings would be to affirm by judicial decision a manifest neglect if not an open defiance of the prohibitions of the Constitution, intended for the protection of the people against such unauthorized action."[27]

The point about ratification becomes even more persuasive if we take a look at the facts of the 1955 case, *People v. Cahan*, in which the Supreme Court of California overturned a practice of many years standing and adopted the exclusionary rule:

"Gerald Wooters, an officer attached to the intelligence unit of that department, testified that after securing the permission of the chief of police to make microphone installations at two places occupied by defendants, he, Sergeant Keeler, and Officer Phillips one night at about 8:45, entered one 'house through the side window of the first floor,' and that he 'directed the officers to place a listening device under a chest of drawers.' Another officer made recordings and transcriptions of the conversations that came over in a nearby garage. About a month later, at Officer Wooters' direction, a similar device was surreptitiously installed in another house and receiving equipment was also set up in a nearby garage."[28]

---

[23] On Lee v. United States, 343 U.S. 747, 759 (1959) (dissenting opinion).

[24] People v. Cahan, 44 Cal.2d 434, 445, 282 P.2d 905, 912 (1955).

[25] State v. Olynick, 113 A.2d 123, 131 (R.I. 1955) (dissenting opinion).

[26] Olmstead v. United States, 277 U.S. 438, 470 (1928) (dissenting opinion).

[27] Weeks v. United States, 232 U.S. 383, 394 (1914). See also the statement of the Delaware Supreme Court in Rickards v. State, 45 Del. 573, 585, 77 A.2d 199, 205 (1950), to the effect that as long as constitutional guarantees exist "we have no choice but to use every means at our disposal to preserve those guarantees."

Another constitutional point has been made. "To protect that right, every unjustifiable intrusion by the Government upon the privacy of the individual, whatever the means employed, must be deemed a violation of the Fourth Amendment. And the use, as evidence in a criminal proceeding, of facts ascertained by such intrusion must be deemed a violation of the Fifth." Brandeis, J., dissenting in Olmstead v. United States, 277 U.S. 438, 472 (1928). This point has not fared well with scholars. See 8 WIGMORE, EVIDENCE §2184, at 31 (3d ed. 1940) and Allen, *The Exclusionary Rule in the American Law of Search and Seizure*, 52 J. CRIM. L., C. & P.S. 246, 250 (1961).

[28] People v. Cahan, 44 Cal.2d 434, 445, 282 P.2d 905, 911–12 (1955).

When I first considered the *Cahan* case three years ago I was moved to write:

"This police conduct is not only an example of illegality, it is illegality elaborately planned with the connivance of the Los Angeles Chief of Police. It is not the case of the over-eager rookie misjudging the fine lines of the law of arrest. It is constitutional violation as a matter of police policy."[29]

So it still seems to me. The violation of constitutional rights in the case took place because the chief of police thought the evidence would be used in court. Otherwise there would have been little point to the planning of the trespass. Had it permitted the use of the evidence, the court would not only have sanctioned the infraction at hand but also encouraged other violations.

California is not alone in moving to adopt the rule because police officers were tempted to unconstitutional action by the availability of the evidence in court. The 1950 opinion of the Supreme Court of Delaware which recognized the rule in that state speaks of safeguarding against "deliberate invasion."[30]

Most constitutional or statutory restrictions on police conduct are decisions by legislators or constitution-makers that it is better for some guilty persons to go free than for the police to behave in forbidden fashion. They are, however, decisions in the abstract. The exclusionary rule has the advantage of applying the constitutional or statutory decision to a particular case. The second argument for the rule is thus that the use of the rule is a natural consequence of the restrictive principle. The rule is needed to make the constitutional or statutory safeguards something real. At the New York State Constitutional Convention of 1938, United States Senator Robert F. Wagner spoke about this point:

"Mr. Chairman, I profoundly believe that a search and seizure guarantee which does not carry with it the exclusion of evidence obtained by its violation is an empty gesture; it is an amendment which will be wholly ineffective in protecting the constitutional right of privacy which we seek to confer. If I may borrow a phrase of Justice Cardozo's which has not been quoted before, it speaks the word of promise to the ear and it breaks it to the hope. I profoundly believe that an amendment which does not provide for the exclusion of evidence is not only ineffective but it is dangerous; it is dangerous because it will promote the spectacle, unfortunately not unknown in our time, of constitutional rights which have their meaning on paper and on paper alone. Let no one who cares for civil liberty discount this danger. To guarantee civil rights in theory and permit constituted authority to deny them in practice, no matter how justifiable the ends may be or may seem, is to imperil the very foundation on which our Democracy rests."[31]

Thirdly, the exclusionary rule gives every prosecuted person an opportunity to vindicate search and seizure principles for the benefit of all, insofar as violations of these principles have resulted in the production of evidence against the accused. The accused has a motive to challenge the police overreaching. He need not resort to another proceeding or hire another lawyer. The rule assures a great deal of judicial attention to these questions.

The law of arrest and illegal searches is undeveloped in states without the rule. Many legal questions about proper police conduct cannot be answered in New York because the New York courts admit illegally obtained evidence and hence have little chance to pass on questions of police behavior. The questions have not been resolved by legislation. As a by-product of California's recent acceptance of the rule, great clarification and modification of the law of arrest and search and seizure has taken place. The task is not done unless there is an easy opportunity for litigation.

The fourth principal reason supporting the exclusionary evidence rule is a kind of counsel of despair. The other remedies are totally unsatis-

[29] Paulsen, *Safeguards in the Law of Search and Seizure*, 52 Nw. U.L. Rev. 65, 75–76 (1957).

[30] Rickards v. State, 45 Del. 573, 77 A.2d 199, 205 (1950).

[31] N.Y. State Const. Conv., Revised Record 559 (1938).

factory.[32] On the other hand there are reasons to believe that the exclusionary rule has an important practical influence.

An illegal arrest or search may violate the criminal law. Yet, very few criminal prosecutions of those engaging in such conduct can be found in the reported cases—a startling fact when one considers the great number of reported instances of police misconduct. Prosecutions must be brought by district attorneys, who are not likely to take a position opposed to the front line law enforcement personnel. Prosecutors are judged in terms of their record of successful prosecutions. They cannot afford the hostility of the police. Even if a willing district attorney were to be found, he would probably have a pessimistic view of his chances to succeed in a prosecution. In the overwhelming number of cases, the jury box will hold more who sympathize with the officer than with his victim.

Such evidence as we have suggests that tort suits for trespass or false arrest are ineffective either as deterrents against the police or as instruments for compensating the injured persons. Again, juries in such cases are not apt to be very sympathetic to the run-of-the-mill dope peddler, petty thief, or gambler against whom the overwhelming number of police infractions are committed. The typical plaintiff in such actions has some disadvantages which flow from the rules surrounding an action for false imprisonment or false arrest. Proof of prior reputation may be admitted to impeach credibility, to mitigate damages by demonstrating that a criminal record has already destroyed the plaintiff's reputation, and to show that a proper cause existed to support the arrest. In a good many cases, the potential plaintiff will have been convicted and imprisoned before the tort action can be started. The conviction itself may establish conclusively the presumption of proper cause for the arrest. This plaintiff will find it difficult to leave prison in order to testify

and, in some jurisdictions, the civil death statutes suspend the right to sue after a conviction.

Even if he should succeed, the plaintiff in a tort action may find himself possessed of a judgment against a person unable to pay. Police are neither wealthy nor bonded. Inability to collect damages may not present the biggest problem. Actual damages may be quite small—inadequate to deter any officer or to encourage the victim to bring suit. Compensatory damages in the case of an illegal search or arrest of short duration will be an insignificant amount. Punitive damages may not be available. Infractions will seem to cause a very slight harm, hardly worth the payment of money. In short, the guilty cannot sue and the innocent will not find it profitable. Thus, injury to the "peace of mind" of the individual and the harm done to the community—the truly serious consequences of police misconduct—escape redress.

Tort recovery from the individual officer and criminal sanctions against him are disadvantageous from another point of view. If the criminal and tort law operate too efficiently against individual officers, the officers may become overcautious. Because tort damages are proportioned to harm rather than fault, tort suits may end in a great injustice to the policeman. A relatively slight infraction of the rules could result in very great harm to the victim.

The inadequacy of the conventional remedies has led to a series of suggestions to supplement or replace them. Two leading commentators have urged that the tort law be changed to provide for minimum liquidated damages and for governmental liability. They also urge that the position of the plaintiff in the tort action be improved by restricting the use of character information against him and permitting him to bring suit while in custody.[33] These changes would enhance the usefulness of the tort action in controlling official overreaching by the police department. Governmental liability would assure compensation to

[32] Foote, *Tort Remedies for Police Violations of Individual Rights*, 39 MINN. L. REV. 493 (1955); Note, *Search and Seizure in Illinois: Enforcement of the Constitutional Right to Privacy*, 47 NW. U.L. REV. 493 (1952).

[33] Foote, *op. cit. supra* note 32; Barrett, *Exclusion of Evidence Obtained by Illegal Searches and Seizures, A Comment on People v. Cahan*, 43 CALIF. L. REV. 565 (1955).

the victim. It would not too harshly penalize the offending officer. It is assumed that the governmental unit would take steps to eliminate police guilty of serious infractions or of continued minor ones. The provision for minimum liquidated damages would ensure payment to persons of damaged reputations. It would also provide recovery in cases involving little actual damage and in cases where the harm caused by police misconduct is difficult to translate into money. Such proposals are very attractive. Were they a reality, the case in favor of the exclusionary rule would be much weakened.

Our aim should be to provide a system which could tolerate isolated instances of over-zealousness, if they were promptly and justly corrected by sanctions proportioned to the fault of the officer, and which would provide compensation for injury to the victim. These objectives are consistent with the proposals to put financial responsibility upon the units of government rather than the individual officer. Yet I cannot believe that governmental units will bear any substantial expenditure to compensate the most probable victims of illegal police misconduct—the bums, drifters, petty crooks, or big-time operators—in the face of the pressing public need for schools, hospitals, roads, and yes, prisons. Until some governmental unit somewhere is in fact giving adequate civil recovery for unconstitutional law enforcement, I retain my stubborn doubt whether the idea can be made to work.

Imposing liability on government units, moreover, will not completely deter the state from engaging in unconstitutional practices. It may be very attractive for state officials, acting according to a calculus of police values, to violate now and pay later.

The proposal for a civil rights office, independent of the regular prosecutor, for prosecution of offenses committed by police officers, has several disadvantages.[34] First, it does not provide for compensation to the injured party. In this respect it is no better than the exclusionary rule. Secondly, it either puts the sanction directly on the police officer, by making him liable to prosecution for each instance of misconduct, or leaves prosecution so haphazard that it will fail as a deterrent. Administrative elimination of the unfit for repeated disregard of civil rights is to be preferred to the caution which might result from harsh punishment of the individual officer for a single misdeed. Thirdly, even if direct punishment is thought useful, I doubt whether many juries will convict a policeman who has violated the civil rights of a gangster.

Systematic discipline within the police department itself would be a splendid sanction if it were practiced. We just do not have examples of cities or other governmental units which have insisted that departments get rid of police officers who refuse to obey the search and seizure rules.[35]

The remedies which we have neither deter nor compensate. The exclusionary principle does not make the injured person whole; does it, in fact, act as a deterrent?

We cannot make an answer irrefutably supported by the facts. The kind of social investigation necessary to convince the already committed has not been made. The pilot studies of the American Bar Foundation are reported to be inconclusive on this issue.[36] The student editors of the *Northwestern University Law Review* made a statistical study in 1952 of the operation of the rule in a branch of the Municipal Court of Chicago.[37] The statistics demonstrated that in from seventy to eighty-five per cent of the gambling cases motions to suppress evidence on the ground of illegal search were granted. Motions succeeded in about twenty-five per cent of the narcotics cases, and

---

[34] Peterson, *Restrictions in the Law of Search and Seizure*, 52 Nw. U.L. Rev. 46, 62 (1957); Note, *Judicial Control of Illegal Search and Seizure*, 58 Yale L. J. 144, 163 (1948).

[35] The internal disciplinary machinery in Philadelphia "has not yet been used in the case of an illegal search or arrest." Note, *Philadelphia Police Practice and the Law of Arrest*, 100 U. Pa. L. Rev. 1182, 1211 (1952). This note also contains a useful estimate of the available remedies for illegal arrest. *Id.* at 1206–12.

[36] Kamisar, *Wolf and Lustig Ten Years Later: Illegal State Evidence in State and Federal Courts*, 43 Minn. L. Rev. 1083, 1145 n.226 (1959).

[37] Note, *Search and Seizure in Illinois: Enforcement of the Constitutional Right to Privacy*, 47 Nw. U.L. Rev. 493, 497–99 (1952).

in about nineteen per cent of the prosecutions for carrying concealed weapons. The data, partial and inconclusive as it is, suggests that the Chicago police engaged in a great deal of harassment of gamblers by bringing cases which they knew they could not win. In these cases they paid little attention to the rules of law. The lower percentage of successful motions to suppress made with respect to the more serious crimes, narcotics and carrying concealed weapons, suggests, however, that the police comply with the law in more instances when they intend to get a conviction. Perhaps the exclusionary rule has an influence here. At any rate, any study of the Chicago police must take into account the fact that one is, indeed, studying the Chicago police department, a department which has stood in need of a reformation which cannot be accomplished by legal rules alone.

Any attempt to assess the impact of the exclusionary rule is vexed by troublesome questions of cause and effect.[38] Many states with the rule of admissibility enjoy police compliance with the law, but the very infrequency of police excesses may be a reason why the rule of admissibility is tolerated. The police may control their behavior for fear the exclusionary rule might tempt the local Supreme Court if unconstitutional police conduct were to become a serious problem. In California the exclusionary rule was adopted for the very reason that outrageous police work has become common under the rule of admissibility. In some states which embrace the exclusionary principle, police behavior is of the worst sort. Yet we know that bad law enforcement depends on a great many things in addition to a rule of evidence. If the situation is bad in a state having the rule, abolition may make things a great deal worse.

If statistical proof is lacking that the rule modifies police conduct, what evidence do we have that the rule has an effect on police?

In the first place, the arguments of police spokesmen against the exclusionary evidence rule give an indication of reluctance to change police practice. For example, Chief Parker of Los Angeles

said after the *Cahan* case that now the police could arrest only if they had sufficient information to constitute "probable cause" that the suspect was guilty.[39] The law to which the Chief adverted had been in force in California for a long time but, with the new rule of exclusion, the police would apparently have to take it into account. There would be little reason to complain of the substantive rules unless the exclusionary rule made them relevant to police action.

In the second place, it seems reasonable that the rule will generate pressure upon enforcement officers to improve the quality of their work. I believe that the police officers themselves are interested in obtaining convictions. Men have an interest in the final product of their work. However that may be, prosecuting attorneys are certainly interested in convictions. They can be counted upon to exercise an influence toward obedience of the law. Public opinion may join the prosecutors in a demand for more careful enforcement if citizens witness many persons released because of official infractions.[40]

Thirdly, we can look at police training schools and discover that a great deal of emphasis is placed on the rules of arrest and search and seizure in the schools of the exclusionary jurisdictions. Mr. Justice Murphy's inquiry, described in his dissent in *Wolf v. Colorado*, has often been cited.[41] The Metropolitan Police Department of the District of Columbia received a series of lectures on how to operate under the law after the decision in *Mallory v. United States*, a United States Supreme Court decision excluding from evidence in federal courts any confession made during a period of illegal detention.[42] In a speech to the International Association of Chiefs of Police in September, 1959, Mr. Quinn Tamm, Assistant Director of the F.B.I., said:

"We must present in our schools thoughts such as these for the cogitation of our trainees:

[38] See the estimate of the effect of the exclusionary rule, especially in California after the *Cahan* case, in Kamisar, *op. cit. supra* note 36, at 1145–58.

[39] *Id.* at 1158.
[40] Allen, *The Wolf Case: Search and Seizure, Federalism, and the Civil Liberties,* 45 ILL. L. REV. 1 (1950).
[41] 338 U.S. 25, 41 (1949).
[42] THOMAS, THE MALLORY RULE: PRESENT STATUS AND EFFECT 20 (unpublished paper on file in the Columbia University Law School Library, 1960).

"What does it profit a police officer to discover and apprehend a person responsible for a crime if he does so in a manner so reprehensible to the rule of law that the evidence is inadmissible in court and consequently worthless in bringing him to justice? What good is a confession, even one which conclusively is shown to be true by after-discovered evidence, if it is declared inadmissible in evidence because the court deems that it was involuntarily obtained? We must emphasize the fact that the short-cut of an involuntary confession becomes a boomerang which flies back and hits not only the officer himself but his entire department and the community as a whole. . . ."[43]

Finally, we sometimes find statements, worthy of our attention, which assert that the rule has a corrective effect. Recently, Mr. Justice Stewart of the United States Supreme Court stated that the weight of the available evidence supports the proposition that the exclusionary rule is useful.

"But pragmatic evidence of a sort is not wanting. The federal courts themselves have operated under the exclusionary rule of *Weeks* for almost half a century; yet it has not been suggested either that the Federal Bureau of Investigation has thereby been rendered ineffective, or that the administration of criminal justice in the federal courts has thereby been disrupted."[44]

Mr. Myron G. Ehrlich, a Washington, D. C., lawyer, has reported that since the *Mallory* case magistrates are available for preliminary examination twenty-four hours a day in the District.[45] The *Washington Post* has reported its opinion that the Washington police have exhibited more diligence in complying with the law since *Mallory*.[46] Governor Brown, while he was still Attorney General of California, expressed his conviction that the exclusionary rule had improved police practice in California.[47] Further, a reading of the lower court opinions in the District of Columbia leaves the writer with the impression that police practices there have changed after *Mallory*.[48]

Let me take just a few more moments to make very brief responses to propositions advanced by opponents of the rule.

Opponents say that the police will act illegally to obtain clues although, under the rule, any evidence taken by the illegality could not be used. The point raises a problem under the rule but not an argument against it. The exclusionary principle applies to the "fruit of the poisonous tree" as well as to the tree itself.[49] The problem is how to discover what evidence is the "fruit" of illegality in order to suppress it. The answer lies in requiring the police to disclose the source of offered proof if it is requested.[50]

Opponents say that the police will, themselves, impose extra-judicial punishments, such as beatings, if they are prevented from convicting the most dangerous. Surely no community ought to permit continual assaults by officers, no matter how lofty the motive with which the blows are struck. I cannot believe such conduct would long be tolerated.

Opponents say that the exclusionary rule is itself overly technical and arbitrary. They are right. That the rule is somewhat capricious is an argument for improvement, not abolition. The United States Supreme Court only recently swept away a lot of technical law concerning who has

---

[43] Reported in 8 Civil Liberties in New York, No. 2, p. 4, col. 5 (November 1959). This paper is the official organ of the New York Civil Liberties Union.

[44] Elkins v. United States, 364 U.S. 206, 218 (1960).

[45] THOMAS, *op. cit. supra* note 42, at 23. Thomas also reports that Senator Hennings of Missouri held the opinion that the *Mallory* rule has changed police practice in the District of Columbia; that the United States Park Police claim to have made changes in their mode of operation. *Id.* at 24. A lawyer in the criminal practice, Mr. James R. Scullen, disagreed and asserted that police methods in the District are unchanged by *Mallory*. *Id.* at 23.

[46] Washington Post and Times Herald, June 14, 1959, p. E1, col. 1–6.

[47] Letter republished in Kamisar, *op. cit. supra* note 36, at 1158.

[48] THOMAS, *op. cit. supra* note 42, at 3.

[49] Silverthorne Lumber Co. v. United States, 251 U.S. 385 (1920).

[50] United States v. Frankfeld, 100 F. Supp. 934 (D. Md. 1951), shows how difficult it is to get a hearing on wiretapping allegations. The problem is discussed in Note, *Exclusion of Evidence Obtained by Wiretapping: An Illusory Safeguard*, 61 YALE L. J. 1221 (1952).

standing to challenge illegal evidence.[51] The deterrent effect of the rule will be increased because of this development.

Opponents say that the rule is disruptive of the main business of a trial. I am not persuaded. The motion to suppress is properly made in advance. Where a later determination is necessary or proper, there is little in actual experience to suggest that proceedings are unduly disturbed by the administration of the rule.

Opponents say that the exclusionary rule interferes with the process of getting at the truth at a trial. They are right. Some evidence may be excluded which could have helped to establish the facts. Yet, surely, a trial has purposes other than to lay reality bare. A trial is a part of government's teaching apparatus. Social values of the greatest importance receive expression in the court room. To reach a decision in accordance with the truth is only one value which, in some circumstances, may have to bow before others.

A recently formulated criticism suggests that the rule is deficient in that it gives a remedy for invasions of privacy which are not as important as other outrages which the exclusionary rule cannot reach.

"An inherent characteristic of the exclusionary rule is that it puts the greatest pressure to conform to the rules regarding arrest and detention. In its direct application, of course, the rule comes into play only when a successful police search has turned up evidence which is to be offered at the trial. But even as a deterrent it affects only those aspects of police illegality which are likely to result in the acquisition of physical evidence of guilt and are undertaken for the purpose of securing the prosecution and conviction of a suspected offender. Illegal arrests which are designed to harass rather than to prosecute, physical abuse of suspects or persons in custody, unnecessary destruction of property, illegal detentions which are not motivated by a desire to secure confessions, and similar serious forms of police illegality

are not affected by the rule or by the cognate rule excluding coerced or illegally obtained confessions. In short, the rule has a deterrent impact only on illegal searches and those illegal arrests to which searches are incident. And it has impact on those procedures only in those situations in which the police are proceeding with the conscious purpose of securing evidence to use in prosecuting the defendant."[52]

This passage contributes an important idea to the discussion, but the argument does not speak to the worth of the exclusionary rule. The passage ought to be followed by a call to create better remedies *in addition* to the rule. To say that the exclusionary rule cannot operate to deter all police misconduct is not to say that the rule should be abandoned. It should be supplemented.

The basic political problem of a free society is the problem of controlling the public monopoly of force. All the other freedoms, freedom of speech, of assembly, of religion, of political action, presuppose that arbitrary and capricious police action has been restrained. Security in one's home and person is the fundamental without which there can be no liberty. The exclusionary rule is the best and the most practical way for the law to deter those officials who would make inroads upon that security. It is morally right. It provides frequent opportunities for litigation of the issues. It is the best tool we have to give life to the constitutional safeguards against unreasonable interferences by the professional agencies of law enforcement.

\* \* \*

### ADDENDUM

Since the preceding pages were written the Supreme Court of the United States has held that the states are bound to exclude illegally obtained evidence in state criminal trials.[53] The reasons given for that decision are, of course, directly relevant to the thesis of the present paper. First, the majority of the Court affirmed that the exclusionary rule is required by the Constitution itself. The rule was

[51] Jones v. United States, 362 U.S. 257 (1960).

[52] Barrett, *op. cit. supra* note 4, at 54–55.
[53] Mapp v. Ohio, 81 S. Ct. 1684 (1961).

said to be "a clear, specific, and constitutionally required—even if judicially implied—deterrent safeguard without insistence upon which the Fourth Amendment would have been 'reduced to a form of words'."[54] An interesting point about this formulation is the fact that it does assert that the exclusionary rule is a *"deterrent* safeguard." The point is not simply that the Constitution requires the rule without respect to its aspect as a deterrent to police misconduct. Secondly, the opinion points out, "If the government becomes a lawbreaker, it breeds contempt for law." Thirdly, the opinion states, quoting from *Elkins v. United States,*[55] there is "pragmatic evidence of a sort" to warrant a belief that the exclusionary rule does deter. Fourthly, "Our decision, founded on reason and truth, gives to the individual no more than that which the Constitution guarantees him, to the police officer no less than that to which honest law enforcement is entitled, and, to the courts, that judicial integrity so necessary in the true administration of justice."[56]

One final reason was given by the Court. Because the states, before Mapp, could use illegally seized evidence and the federal prosecutors could not, an unhappy temptation existed in some states. "In non-exclusionary States, federal officers, being human, were by it invited to and did, as our cases indicate, step across the street to the State's attorney with their unconstitutionally seized evidence. Prosecution on the basis of that evidence was then had in a state court in utter disregard of the enforceable Fourth Amendment. If the fruits of an unconstitutional search had been inadmissible in both state and federal courts, this inducement to evasion would have been sooner eliminated."[57]

Mr. Justice Black joined in the Court's opinion but based his decision on the ground that the interrelationship between the Fourth and the Fifth Amendments requires the application of the exclusionary rule.

The battle for the exclusionary evidence rule as a principal weapon against police misconduct has been won—for the moment, at least. In my view the reasons in support of the rule clearly justify the outcome. Whether the view is correct is now a question to be put to experience. We have a chance to determine whether we can operate law enforcement agencies within the bounds of the constitutional rights to privacy.

[54] *Id.* at 1688.
[55] 364 U.S. 206 (1960).
[56] 81 S. Ct. at 1694.

[57] *Id.* at 1693.

# The Exclusionary Rule: An Ill Conceived and Ineffective Remedy

FRANK J. McGARR

I am very impressed by the presentation of Professor Paulsen who, with very commendable objectivity, presented my side of the story as ably as he did his own. In a sense, he stole my thunder because I think he did an excellent job of indicating the arguments against the exclusionary rule as well as those for it.

In arguing against this rule, I realize that I take a somewhat lonely position. After forty or fifty years of its general acceptance as part of the body of American law and with the lip service that is almost habitually done it, it is hard to find people who are willing to stand against the rule. I am willing to do so, perhaps, because in my experience as a prosecutor I frequently saw guilty persons released to prey again upon society because of the operation of the rule, and I could not help but be disturbed by the experience. And I think, too, that most of us will recognize that there is a very nasty situation involving the exclusionary rule whereby corrupt law enforcement agents will make deliberate illegal searches for the express purpose, in cooperation with criminals, of forever tainting and rendering inadmissible the evidence they seize. These two circumstances give me the courage to stand against the world as far as the exclusionary rule is concerned. I have one more circumstance and that is my delight that Dean Wigmore takes my side. Where better than at Northwestern could I cite such hallowed authority for my position as Dean Wigmore?

By way of background for what I think is the approach that must be taken to the exclusionary rule, I'd like to observe that one of the major problems currently besetting our society is the rising incidence of crime. Now, we are not facing up to this problem today because it is not so intriguing and emotionally charged as integration or the missile lag or something of this sort, but it is a very real problem. Without spending a lot of time on statistics or statistical argument, it could be demonstrated, if I devoted the time to it, that in the years since the war the incidence of crime has steadily increased in the United States at a rate more rapid than the increase in population and that, in the categories of crimes committed, there has been a gradual but perceptible shift from the less serious to the more serious offenses. Another equally disturbing fact, which I cannot statistically support but which I base on personal observation in the field, is that there is an increasing success enjoyed by defense counsel with, of course, the cooperation of the courts, and particularly the United States Supreme Court, in hiding their clients from justice and retribution in the nooks and crannies of Constitutional law, leaving them free to return to their antisocial careers. I don't pretend to be able to analyze all the causes for what I regard as this fairly sad state of affairs, but it is my thesis that one of these causes, to a greater or lesser degree, is the exclusionary rule.

With this in mind, I would like to take a fresh look at this rule, to try to strip away from it forty or fifty years of acceptance and lip service, and to try a new approach.

We are living in an era of great emphasis upon civil liberties. We sometimes act as though this generation wrote the Bill of Rights or had just recently discovered it. In our time, the Bill of Rights has been extensively rewritten by the

Supreme Court and considerably broadened and expanded in the process. In our general satisfaction with this development, we sometimes tend to forget that every extension of the rights of the individual in the criminal field must necessarily and proportionately diminish the ability of society as a whole to protect itself against the criminal. The very delicate balance between the rights of the individual and the rights of society is not easily arrived at. It was the object of very considerable concern on the part of the architects of the Constitution, who built upon the experience and accumulated wisdom of Western civilization. I think they achieved a very nice balance, and I think we tinker with it somewhat at our peril. I digress to point this out because there seems to be a current assumption that Justice Holmes invented human rights and that Justices Frankfurter, Douglas, and Black stand alone bearing the torch of human freedom.

Before 1900 there was as genuine a concern for human rights and civil liberties as there is today, but before 1900 illegally seized evidence was generally admissible in criminal proceedings in both state and federal courts without question and without qualification. We have a tendency to look back upon this as a somewhat uncivilized era. They didn't enjoy the blessings we now have such as inside plumbing, atom bombs, and automatic elevators. But they were quite a civilized society with a really genuine concern for civil rights. I think it might safely be said that in the overall view, the citizen of the nineteenth century was far freer from government regimentation and restraint than any of us in our lifetime may hope to be. The best legal minds of that era believed that we should admit all relevant evidence in a criminal proceeding, and my thesis is that we should not take their opinion lightly nor turn our back on it simply because it has become fashionable to do so over the last forty or fifty years. It was the belief of that time that the only proper criminal trial was one wherein all relevant evidence, however obtained, was produced so that justice would be done. It is at this point I take my first step in opposition to Professor Paulsen.

I disagree that the criminal trial has any other function except to determine the applicability of the criminal law to the particular fact situation then before the court; in other words, to determine the guilt or innocence of the individual then standing before the bar of justice. That is not only its most important function; it is its only function.

The obligation to see that justice is done has a dual aspect. It was as important in 1900 as it is today, and as generally recognized in 1900 as it is today, that the innocent be acquitted for the sake of the rights of the individual. But, in 1900 it was equally important in the minds of the Court and legal thinkers generally that the guilty be convicted for the sake of the rights of society—the rights of society to live secure in their persons and in their property. Under the view in that time, it was as unthinkable as it is today that the innocent be convicted. But we seem to have digressed completely from the second point of view because it was very unthinkable then that a guilty man be turned loose to prey again on society as an object lesson to an over zealous policeman. Today this is considered the enlightened and prudent view. I emphasize this because I think the sharp difference of opinion between our modern attitude on this problem and the attitude of a generation or two ago should cause us to stop, pause, and reflect as to whether our view today is as enlightened as we think it is.

To turn to Wigmore for moral support, I point to a comment of his on *Weeks v. United States*,[1] which is the foundation stone for the federal exclusionary rule. Wigmore says,

"But the essential fallacy of *Weeks v. United States* and its successors is that it virtually creates a novel exception where the Fourth Amendment is involved, to the fundamental principal that *an illegality in the mode of procuring evidence is no ground for excluding it.* The doctrine of such an exception rests upon a reverance for the Fourth Amendment so deep and cogent that its violation will be taken notice

[1] 232 U.S. 383 (1914).

of, at any cost of other justice, and even in the most indirect way."[2]

After citing some cases, Wigmore goes on,

"All this is misguided sentimentality. For the sake of indirectly and contingently protecting the Fourth Amendment, this view appears indifferent to the direct and immediate result, viz., of making Justice inefficient, and of coddling the law-evading classes of the population. It puts Supreme Courts in the position of assisting to undermine the foundations of the very institutions they are set there to protect. It regards the over-zealous officer of the law as a greater danger to the community than the unpunished murderer, or embezzler, or panderer."[3]

Wigmore was given to strong words, and those are about as strong as his usually are, but I think they emphasize his point and mine.

Now, I am as aware, I think, as most, of the abuses of law enforcement, and I am as concerned as the next man for their correction. But, I cannot accept the proposition that turning criminals loose on society by suppressing illegally seized evidence does adequately solve the problem of punishing the over zealous and misbehaving officer. It punishes, in fact, the innocent citizenry. The officer is not disciplined for the failure to obtain a conviction. The officer is not disciplined in our modern society for his illegal search. The federal exclusionary rule in effect now for nearly fifty years has not noticeably deterred illegal searches and seizures which, if the civil liberties groups are to be believed, are as pressing a problem today as they ever were. This federal exclusionary rule has been adopted over the years by about half of the states. There is no indication that law enforcement in these states has been imbued with any greater respect for civil liberties than in the less enlightened half of the Union not following the rule. There is not the slightest indication that the Chicago Police Department, operating under the exclusionary rule adopted by the State of Illinois, is any more zealous to protect

civil liberties than the New York City Police Department which does not have such a sanction or censure hanging over it. It can be debated endlessly whether in areas where the exclusionary rule has been adopted by the state you do have better law enforcement or better regard by law enforcement agencies for the rights of individuals, but, as Professor Paulsen pointed out, so many other factors are involved that it can never be definitely stated that the exclusionary rule has had any bearing on this.

It should be remembered also that there are means other than the exclusionary rule for protecting the Fourth Amendment rights of our citizens. Admittedly, these do not seem adequate at the moment. I would suggest, however, that much of the energy now being given to supporting the federal exclusionary rule might be directed to an exploration of the possibilities of strengthening the remedy of the citizen against the officer violating the rights. I know of no serious studies currently going on to consider the problem, and it is an area which should be explored. I recognize the futility of giving the individual, the injured citizen, a civil remedy against an impoverished policeman where his only remedy must be in damages. But, I agree with the comment of Professor Paulsen that one of the considerations most deserving of attention in this field is that of shifting the financial responsibility for improper conduct of policemen, on a *respondeat superior* basis, to the municipality or sovereign which employs them. This would be difficult to achieve, but it certainly would be worth the effort. Proper administration of such a system might not be easy to come by, but again it certainly would be worth the effort.

If the remedy were against the municipality and if it were fairly applied by a court, I think the city might very quickly take steps to educate, restrain, and deter its police force from illegal conduct, and I cannot accept the proposition that this could not be worked out. The redressing of the rights of an individual by awarding him damages in a court of law is something so fundamental to our system that I don't think it can

[2] 8 Wigmore, Evidence §2184, at 36 (1940). (Italics in the original.)
[3] *Id.* at 36–37.

101

be lightly said that in this area or in any other it cannot be applied to any current problem we have.

My conclusion then is that *Weeks v. United States* is a piece of pure judicial legislation and an attempt to achieve a social goal. I hate to see the Court legislating to achieve social goals, but it seems to have become a Supreme Court hobby in recent years. The Court created an evidentiary rule to achieve a stated social purpose. I think the rule was ill conceived, and the purpose is not being achieved by it. Another deterrent for illegal searches and seizures must be found which does not punish society as a whole for the misconduct of the individual law enforcement agent.

As I mentioned earlier, the federal exclusionary rule in the forty to fifty years of its existence has been adopted by only about half of the states. Apparently it has not been found to be so completely impressive and overwhelmingly logical that the forty-eight (or now fifty) states rushed to accept it. I think it should be abandoned by those states that now follow it and dropped by the federal courts as well. The decisions applying it demonstrate its lack of logic, and I think history demonstrates its failure. Better ways to enforce the strictures of the Fourth Amendment against law enforcement agents can certainly be found, and I don't think any genuine effort has been made to develop them. But, far from abandoning the exclusionary rule, the federal courts and the United States Supreme Court are now moving swiftly in the opposite direction.

In recognition of the inherent limitations of the rule, its application has been traditionally hedged about with some very broad exceptions which Professor Paulsen has described for you. The chief of these is the generally recognized and long standing rule that evidence illegally seized by state officers may be used in the federal courts if federal agents have not cooperated in the seizure. This major exception to the exclusionary rule, which drastically reduced its potential for public mischief, is apparently about to disappear. Despite clear-cut and long standing precedent, the United States Court of Appeals for the District of Colum-

bia in October, 1958, in *Hanna v. United States*,[4] reversed a federal conviction based upon evidence illegally seized by state officers in Maryland. This state seizure was not a brazen violation of individual rights but a rather close question of whether the officers had acted properly. (I'd agree with the court in deciding that the officers did not act properly, but I merely point out that it was not an outrageous abuse of the officers' discretion.) The court based its decision on a study of a progressive series of Supreme Court opinions, and the conclusion it drew from these opinions was that the trend of the Supreme Court thinking was toward eliminating the so-called "silver platter doctrine." So Judge Hastie hurried to be the first on the band wagon and beat the Supreme Court to it. The Seventh Circuit subsequently considered the same question in *United States v. Camara*[5] and, unlike the District of Columbia and in the face of the *Hanna* decision, they thought it appropriate to wait for the Supreme Court rather than to lead the way, so they followed the traditional rule. But, Judge Hastie's prediction is probably right, and I think the federal "silver platter doctrine" is on its way out.[6]

One final comment, however, on an even more far reaching decision which received far less attention than the Hanna decision, *Rea v. United States*.[7] In *Rea*, a federal officer seized narcotic evidence, some marijuana, in a search which was later held to have been improper, and the evidence was ordered suppressed. A prosecution of the same individual was undertaken by the state for the same narcotics violation, and the federal narcotics agent was subpoenaed to testify for the state and to produce the evidence he had seized. In a very extraordinary and to my mind unprecedented move, the defense went into federal court and moved for an order enjoining the federal narcotics officer from testifying in the state pro-

[4] 260 F.2d 723 (D.C. Cir. 1958).
[5] 271 F. 2d 787 (7th Cir. 1959).
[6] Several months after the completion of the Conference at which this paper was delivered, the Supreme Court lived up to the advance billing in the *Hanna* case and overruled the "silver platter doctrine." See Elkins v. United States, 364 U.S. 206 (1960).
[7] 350 U.S. 214 (1956).

ceeding or producing his evidence there. His motion was denied. On appeal, the Supreme Court enthusiastically embraced the notion that this federal officer certainly should be enjoined from playing his ignoble role as a person appearing for the state to produce the ill-gotten evidence which he had in his possession. No constitutional question was involved in this case, the Court said. It was acting under its general supervisory authority over federal law enforcement agents. Now, that concept lies in the case like a time bomb. If the Supreme Court has had a general supervisory authority over federal law enforcement agents, it has never occurred to me to suspect its existence prior to now. And the Court was so confident that it had it, it did not bother to explain, give precedent, or indicate where it got it. This ignoring of the concept of the division of our government into three separate branches wherein authority of a supervisory nature over law enforcement agents rests, as I thought, with the executive branch, leads me to wonder where the Court is going to go next in following up this so called supervisory authority that it has invented for itself. With this simple phrase and explanation, the Court said that it would prevent a federal law enforcement agent from testifying in the state criminal proceedings. I think that case is probably more startling than *Hanna* and will have, in the course of the next generation, far-reaching consequences. I do not rejoice that the Court has adopted this supervisory role, because I do not agree with the philosophy of the Court with regard to federal law enforcement agencies and their tactics.

I think we are living in an era where in the course of emphasis upon individual civil liberties the Court has come dangerously close to upsetting the balance which it is necessary to preserve between the rights of the individual and the rights of society as a whole. In tying the hands of our law enforcement agencies under the philosophy that a criminal prosecution is sort of a sporting contest where the odds must be even, we may be submitting our society to the inroads of a criminal element which ultimately we will not be able to control. I am not suggesting as a blood-thirsty prosecutor that everybody is guilty and they should be marched to jail without a trial. But, I do suggest to you that we consider how far we have strayed from the proposition that the function of a trial is to send a guilty man to jail and to acquit an innocent man. If we disturb that function or envision the function of a trial to be anything else, we are stripping the government of the power to protect us against criminals and crime.

The views I have expressed, I gather, have been very rarely heard lately, but I commend them for your serious consideration.

\* \* \*

### Addendum

In the case of *Mapp v. Ohio*,[8] the United States Supreme Court had before it a search by local police officers, clearly illegal by federal standards but not so in the mind of the Ohio Supreme Court. The Court decided to take a new look at the rule of *Wolf v. Colorado*,[9] "that in a prosecution in a State Court for a State crime, the Fourteenth Amendment does not forbid the admission of evidence obtained by an unreasonable search and seizure."

In lengthy opinions, the Justices impatiently note that the progress of the states in embracing the exclusionary rule while "inexorable" is also "halting." Unable to wait, the Court convinces itself at length that the exclusionary rule is inherent in the Due Process Clause where *Wolf* had specifically found it not to be. Thus the last exception falls. Illegally seized evidence is inadmissible in all courts, no matter by whom seized.

[8] 81 S. Ct. 1684 (1961).
[9] 338 U. S. 25 (1949).

103

# The Exclusionary Rule Under Foreign Law

## Canada

G. ARTHUR MARTIN

In Canada, the general rule is that evidence otherwise admissible is not rendered inadmissible by the fact that it was illegally obtained. This statement is, however, subject to the rules respecting the admissibility of confessions. Articles seized under an illegal search warrant or obtained by a trespass are admissible,[1] and evidence obtained by an illegal search of the person is also admissible.

In *Kuruma v. The Queen*, Lord Goddard, speaking for the Judicial Committee of the Privy Council, said:

"In their Lordships' opinion the test to be applied in considering whether evidence is admissible is whether it is relevant to the matters in issue. If it is, it is admissible and the court is not concerned with how the evidence was obtained."[2]

In *A.G. of Quebec v. Begin*,[3] the accused was convicted of motor manslaughter. Section 285 (4d) of the Code (now sec. 224 (3)) provided that, on charges of driving a motor vehicle while intoxicated or while impaired by alcohol or a drug, the result of a chemical analysis of the blood, urine, breath or other bodily substance of a person may be admitted in evidence on the issue of whether that person was intoxicated or under the influence of a narcotic drug or whether his ability to drive was impaired by alcohol or a drug, notwithstanding that he was not, before he gave the sample,

warned that he need not give the sample or that the results of the sample might be used in evidence. No warning was given to the accused, and it was argued that since the charge was not one of those referred to in the section, but one of manslaughter, a warning was required to render the result of the analysis of the accused's blood admissible. The Supreme Court held that no warning was necessary. The accused had in fact consented to the giving of the blood sample; the court stated, however, that the evidence of the analysis would have been admissible even if the sample had been taken without his consent, although section 285 (4e) (now sec. 224(4)) provided that no person was required to give such a sample.

In a subsequent case[4] the court clearly limited the confession rule to *self-criminating statements* and held that it did not embrace "the *incriminating conditions* of the body, features, fingerprints, clothing, or behaviour of the accused, that persons, other than himself, observe or detect and ultimately report as witnesses in judicial proceedings."[5]

In *Kuruma v. The Queen*, the Judicial Committee of the Privy Council indicated that the court had a discretion to exclude evidence which had been obtained by improper means if its admission would operate unfairly against the accused. Lord Goddard, speaking for the Judicial Committee of the Privy Council, said:

[1] R. v. Lee Hai, 64 Can. C.C. 49 (1935); R. v. Honan, 20 Can. C.C. 10 (1912); R. v. Doyle, 12 O.R. 347 (1886).

[2] [1955] 2 W.L.R. 223, 226–27.

[3] 112 Can. C.C. 209 (1955).

[4] Reference under the Constitutional Questions Act re section 92(4) of The Vehicles Act, 1957 (Sask.) c. 93, 121 Can. C.C. 321 (1958).

[5] Per Fauteux, J., *id.* at 331. *Cf.* R. v. Barker, [1941] 2 K.B. 381, 28 C.A.R. 52, where the English Court of Criminal Appeal held that books and records produced by the accused to government investigators under a promise of immunity from prosecution stood on the same footing as any oral or written confession.

"No doubt in a criminal case the judge always has a discretion to disallow evidence if the strict rules of admissibility would operate unfairly against an accused. This was emphasized in the case before this Board of *Noor Mohamed v. The King*, [1949] A.C. 182, and in the recent case in the House of Lords, *Harris v. Director of Public Prosecutions*, [1952] A.C. 694. If, for instance, some admission of some piece of paper, e.g. a document, had been obtained from a defendant by a trick, no doubt the judge might properly rule it out."[6]

It is to be noted that the principle laid down in *Noor Mohamed v. The King*[7] and *Harris v. Director of Public Prosecutions*[8] was an entirely different one, namely, that the trial judge has a discretion to exclude evidence of trifling weight having regard to the purpose for which it is professedly offered if its admission would unfairly prejudice the prisoner. The suggestion in the case of *Kuruma v. The Queen* that a court may in the exercise of its discretion exclude evidence of physical things discovered by unfair means is somewhat novel and runs counter to the long line of authorities holding that facts discovered as a result of a confession

---

[6] [1955] 2 W.L.R. 223, 227.
[7] [1949] A.C. 182.
[8] [1952] A.C. 694.

obtained by improper means are admissible.[9] Indeed it was recently held in Ontario that as much of an illegally obtained confession as is confirmed by facts discovered as a result of the confession may be admitted.[10] It is true that Lord Goddard did not purport to be dealing with material things obtained by illegal seizure, but instead with things obtained by a trick; still, it is difficult to see why the same principle should not apply in both cases.

If the courts consider that they have a discretion to exclude illegally obtained evidence, they do not appear to have exercised that discretion in favour of the accused. The problem of deliberate violation of the rights of the citizen by the police in their efforts to obtain evidence has not been as pressing in Canada as in some other countries. In the absence of constitutional restrictions, the powers of the police can be enlarged by legislation when required to cope with some particularly serious problem of law enforcement. In addition, the remedy in tort has proved reasonably effective; Canadian juries are quick to resent illegal activity on the part of the police and to express that resentment by a proportionate judgment for damages.

---

[9] R. v. Warickshall, 1 Leach 263 (1783); R. v. Gould, 9 C. & P. 364 (1840); R. v. White, 15 Can. C.C. 30 (1908).
[10] R. v. St. Lawrence, 93 Can. C.C. 376 (1949).

---

# England

GLANVILLE L. WILLIAMS

### THE ENGLISH VIEW: REJECTION OF THE EXCLUSIONARY RULE

Under the prevailing English rule, the fact that evidence is obtained through a trespass or other illegal search or seizure does not exclude it

from evidence. This rule was accepted during the nineteenth century in two cases of a somewhat low order of authority. In *Derrington*,[1] the prisoner gave a letter to the turnkey, who promised to post it, but who instead gave it to the prosecutor. The letter was received in evidence. In *Jones v. Owens*,[2] a constable illegally searched the defendant and

---

[1] 2 C.&P. 418, 172 E.R. 189 (1826).
[2] 34 J.P. 759 (1870).

found twenty-five young salmon in his pocket; it was held that the evidence was admissible on a charge of illegal fishing. Mellor, J., said: "I think it would be a dangerous obstacle to the administration of justice if we were to hold, because evidence was obtained by illegal means, it could not be used against a party charged with an offence."

The issue lay dormant in the criminal courts until it was revived before the Privy Council in *Kuruma* in 1955.[3] The defendant had been convicted of being in unlawful possession of ammunition, evidence having been given by police officers that they had searched him and found the ammunition on him. It was alleged for the defence that this search was unlawful. The Privy Council refused to allow an appeal against conviction, holding that even if the search was illegal, the evidence obtained by it did not become inadmissible. The judgment was delivered by Lord Goddard, C. J., who laid it down that the test to be applied in considering whether evidence is admissible is whether it is relevant to matters in issue. If it is, it is admissible, and the court is not concerned with how the evidence was obtained. However, the learned Chief Justice qualified this by saying: "No doubt in a criminal case the judge always has a discretion to disallow evidence if the strict rules of admissibility would operate unfairly against the accused. . . . If, for instance, some admission of some piece of evidence, *e.g.* a document, had been obtained from a defendant by a trick, no doubt the judge might properly rule it out." It is not easy to see why evidence obtained by trickery should be ruled out, when evidence obtained by unlawful force is not; the latter would seem to be a more flagrant breach of the law than the former.

Lord Goddard went on to say: "It should be stated that the rule with regard to the admission of confessions [*i.e.*, the rule excluding induced confessions], whether it be regarded as an exception to the general rule [*i.e.*, the rule that relevant evidence is admissible] or not, is a rule of law which their Lordships are not qualifying in any degree whatsoever." This statement is satisfactory as

far as it goes, but one would like to know the reason for not applying the general rule of admissibility to the special case of induced confessions. There must be some reason why an induced confession is excluded, though relevant, while evidence obtained by an illegal search is admitted. Some consideration other than that of relevancy must create this distinction. It would have been more satisfactory if we had been told what the consideration is. In the absence of an explanation, one does not know whether English law is fundamentally consistent with itself. For example, one possible reason for excluding induced confessions is that this is necessary in order to hold the police and prosecution to proper behaviour. But this reason would equally suggest the exclusion of evidence obtained by an illegal search.

There are other grounds for dissatisfaction with the decision in *Kuruma*. The American decisions which hold the contrary were not properly considered, and their basis was quite possibly misunderstood. Similarly the Scottish decisions, which are also to the contrary, were misinterpreted and misstated.[4] Since decisions of the Privy Council are not absolutely binding in future cases, even upon the Privy Council itself, this important question of public policy cannot be regarded as finally settled.

There are a few civil cases bearing on the issue. In *Calcraft v. Guest*,[5] the defendant came into posssession of certain of the plaintiff's documents which the defendant could not produce in evidence because they were privileged. The defendant returned the documents to the plaintiff, but not before he had made copies of them. It was held that the defendant could give secondary evidence of the contents of the documents. The court assumed that the way in which the defendant got his evidence was of no interest to justice, and it seems to have assumed that the evidence would

[3] [1955] A.C. 197.

[4] See the powerful criticism of *Kuruma* by Prof. Franck in 33 CAN. B. REV. 721, and subsequent correspondence in *id.* at 984, 1111. See also COWEN & CARTER, ESSAYS ON THE LAW OF EVIDENCE c. 2 (Oxford 1956).

[5] [1898] 1 Q.B. 759 (C.A.). Compare Lloyd v. Mostyn, 10 M. & W. 478, 152 E.R. 558 (1842).

have been admissible even if it had been stolen from the other side. The decision is an extraordinary one, for there can be little point in conferring privilege upon original documents if pirated copies of them are admissible.

In *Lord Ashburton v. Pape*,[6] a way was found to avoid this consequence. Pape was a bankrupt, whose discharge was opposed by the plaintiff. Pape, by a trick, obtained privileged letters written by the plaintiff to his solicitor. Pape had these letters copied and proposed to use them in the bankruptcy proceedings as secondary evidence of their contents. The plaintiff sought an injunction against Pape to restrain him from disclosing the letters or their copies. The injunction was granted. This outcome is satisfactory; however, it is vexatious to require separate proceedings to be brought in such circumstances, particularly against an undischarged bankrupt who will be unable to contribute to the costs. If a court of equity will enjoin the use of such documents, it would seem to follow under the Judicature Act that the view of equity should prevail in all courts; separate proceedings should not be required to give effect to it.

Yet even if this is so, there are difficulties in applying the rule in *Lord Ashburton v. Pape* to criminal proceedings. If the defendant to a criminal charge appealed to equity to suppress illegally obtained documentary evidence of his guilt, equity would quite possibly refuse to assist him. In any case, the rule in *Lord Ashburton v. Pape* can apply only to documentary evidence the use of which would be a breach of what may be called the accused's equitable copyright; the rule would not suppress evidence concerning other types of incriminating articles.

### RULES OF OTHER COMMON LAW JURISDICTIONS

Other common law jurisdictions have almost invariably followed the traditional view and admitted evidence illegally obtained. Canada, as indicated by Mr. Martin in the preceding article,

[6] [1913] 2 Ch. 469 (C.A.).

follows this approach. Another example is Ceylon.[7]

Irish courts seem to have undergone a change of attitude. In an 1887 case, evidence was admitted although illegally obtained;[8] but in 1955 a judge refused to admit evidence of fingerprints that had been taken with the consent of the accused when he was in custody on a different charge, since he had not been told of his right to refuse consent.[9]

The Scottish courts recognise that there are two important interests that are liable to come into conflict, (a) the interest of the citizen to be protected from illegal invasions of his liberty by the authorities, and (b) the interest of the state to ensure that evidence bearing upon the commission of crime and necessary to enable justice to be done shall not be withheld from courts of law on any merely formal or technical ground. Neither of these objects, said Lord Justice-General Cooper in *Lawrie v. Muir*,[10] can be insisted upon to the uttermost, and the judge has a discretion to admit or exclude the evidence. "Irregularities require to be excused, and infringements of the formalities of the law are not lightly to be condoned." One question to ask is whether the departure from strict procedure has been adopted deliberately and by way of trick. Another is whether Parliament has prescribed a special procedure, departure from which is likely to be regarded as fatal.

The facts of *Lawrie v. Muir* were that the keeper of a dairy was convicted of violating a statutory order by selling her milk in bottles belonging to other persons. The evidence against her consisted of testimony by two inspectors of a limited company formed for the purpose of restoring milk bottles to their rightful owners. The inspectors had no right to enter the defendant's premises, because she had not contracted with the Milk Marketing Board; it was only the Board's contracts that gave the inspectors a right of entry. However, the defendant permitted the inspectors, who produced their warrants, to make a full in-

[7] Rajapakse v. Fernando, 52 N.R.L. 361 (1951); see [1955] CRIM. L. REV. 328.
[8] Dillon v. O'Brien, L. R. Ir. 300, 16 Cox C. C. 245 (1887).
[9] People v. Lawlor, [1955–6] Ir. Jur. Rep. 38, 21 J. CRIM. L. (Eng.) 263 (1957).
[10] [1950] Just. Cas. 19.

107

spection. It was held by a Full Bench of the High Court of Justiciary that the inspectors, though acting in good faith, had illegally entered the premises by misrepresentation, and that their evidence was inadmissible; a conviction was accordingly quashed. The reason why the court exercised its discretion to rule out the evidence was that the inspectors had only narrow powers, the limits of which they ought to know. The decision is all the more striking to an English lawyer because he would not regard the inspectors' entry, made with the defendant's consent, as wrongful. The misrepresentation as to the right to enter would not vitiate the consent in English law. However, it is an intelligible view that the entry, though not tortious, was sufficiently wrongful to exclude the evidence that came to light as a result of it.

In a later case, *Fairley v. Fishmongers of London*,[11] the inspector's departure from the strict procedure was a very narrow one. He was authorised to search for evidence relating to the contravention of food regulations and of an order dealing with salmon, but not concerning the Salmon Fisheries Act, under which the prosecution was taken. In the circumstances the court allowed the evidence to be given.

In *Turnbull*[12] a search was made upon the defendant's premises under warrant, but documents were taken which were not within the scope of the warrant. Lord Guthrie refused to admit the documents in evidence, because in the circumstances a contrary ruling would tend not only to nullify the protection afforded to a citizen by the requirement of a magistrate's warrant, but also to offer a positive inducement to the authorities to proceed by irregular methods. Lord Guthrie

pointed out that there were no circumstances of urgency at the time of the seizure; nor were the documents taken plainly incriminating on their face. In *Kuruma*, Lord Goddard referred to this ruling with apparent approval;[13] but he did not explain why evidence obtained by trespass to property is more objectionable, or more unfair to the accused, than evidence obtained by an assault upon the person.

Perhaps the most important of these Scottish cases is *McGovern*.[14] Here the police illegally took scrapings from the fingernails of a person who was at the police station under suspicion. Since this action was taken without his consent, it amounted to an assault. The court excluded the evidence of the scrapings. Lord Justice-General Cooper again laid down the principle upon which the Scottish courts act: "Irregularities of this kind always need to be 'excused' or condoned, if they can be excused or condoned, whether by the existence of urgency, the relative triviality of the irregularity, or other circumstances. This is not a case where I feel disposed to 'excuse' the conduct of the police." This important decision was directly in point on the facts of *Kuruma*, because it involved a trespass to the person; it was not cited, however, in the judgment in *Kuruma*, which is misleading on the Scottish doctrine.

The latest in the series of Scottish cases is *Marsh v. Johnston*,[15] where policemen bought liquor out of hours in order to obtain evidence of an illegal sale. It was held that their evidence was admissible. The purchase, although technically an offence by the police themselves, was not a wrong as to the defendants.

[11] [1951] Just. Cas. 14.
[12] [1951] Just. Cas. 96.

[13] [1955] A.C. 197, 204.
[14] [1950] Just. Cas. 33.
[15] [1959] CRIM. L. REV. 444 (H.C. of Justiciary).

# *France*

ROBERT VOUIN

In French criminal law, the fundamental rule concerning the burden of proof is the principle of presumption of innocence: it rests with the prosecution to present the proof, and any accused person is deemed innocent as long as his culpability has not been proved by the prosecution.

The second rule, concerning the administration of the proof, is what we call the principle of the deep-seated conviction. As the instruction used for the jury of the Assize Court says:

"The law does not call upon the jurymen to account for the means through which they let themselves be persuaded, it does not lay down rules upon which they must particularly make the completeness and adequacy of a proof depend; it prescribes to them to interrogate themselves in silence and meditation, and to try to find, in the sincerity of their own conscience, what impression was made on their reason by the proofs reported against the accused and the means of his defence. This is the only question stated by the law, a question which encloses the whole measure of their duties: Do you have a deep-seated conviction?"[1]

Two consequences proceed from this principle of the deep-seated conviction. On the one hand, with certain exceptions stated by law, the proof may be made by any means. But on the other hand any proof, with certain exceptions, is dependent upon the judge's deep-seated conviction. All proofs can be received in France in a criminal trial, because any proof appreciated by the judge according to his deep-seated conviction is never conclusive in itself. So it is, for example, that the admissibility of hearsay evidence can be explained, this evidence which is so disgraceful in the eyes of the common law jurist.

Another rule, however, restricts the ability to

[1] CODE OF PENAL PROCEDURE, art. 353.

prove by any means. Proofs are admissible in the criminal trial only if they have been legally secured and legally adduced. If the French law accepts all modes of proofs, it emphasizes, nevertheless, the way to proceed to get the proof, with the result that any proof illegally obtained must be dismissed from the judiciary proceedings. The principle of the legality of the proof should be comprehended not in view of the nature of the proof, but of the means used to obtain it. The proof must be legal, in France, in the sense that the judge can build his deep-seated conviction only on proofs obtained and introduced according to the law.

It is from this principle that the rules proceed concerning house searches, illegal seizures, and confessions obtained through illegal means or following an illegal search.

The invalidity of a house-search made without a search warrant from a judge does not annul the sentence which has followed, if the judgment of sentence makes it explicit that the illegal house-search has not been taken into account.[2] However, a sentence must be annuled if it has been delivered exclusively on the basis of an official report which is null and void for having resulted from an illegal house search.[3]

It is clear though that a search carried out without a warrant is legal if it is carried out with the consent of the master of the house. In this case, as a matter of fact, there is no violation of the privacy of a person's house. The principle of the inviolacy of a person's house, described by art. 76, still in force, of the constitution of 22 Frimaire VIIIth year, must be then considered as respected.

But the concerned person's consent can validate the search carried out without a warrant only if the consent is given "with full knowledge of the facts, that is to say with the knowledge that the proceeding is illegal." The consent can validate

[2] Cass. Crim., Bull. Crim. No. 394 (1924).
[3] Cass. Crim., Rec. de Dr. Pénal 231 (1948).

the search only if it is given by a person who knows he has a right to refuse the search. The Supreme Court of Appeal rescinds all sentences based upon searches carried out without a warrant, if the sentences do not include the acknowledgement of a consent given "with full knowledge of the facts."[4]

The man on the street, the average Frenchman, is not always fully aware of the exact measure of his rights, and if he is guilty is apt to confess his culpability as the result of a search, even if the search is illegal.

The invalidity of a search does not necessarily lead to the invalidity of a procedure started or carried on thereafter.[5] The judge, as a general rule, must estimate the probative value of the preliminary investigation writs which will have followed. But what about a confession resulting from an illegal procedure?

In 1935, in the *Boutros* case, the "Chambre Criminelle" quashed a verdict of not guilty, judging that the nullity of search or seizure procedures "did not forbid the judge to take into consideration all the factors of the proof independently of illegal deeds; and particularly the accused's later confessions, if they could be regarded as made without restraint, could not be considered as non-existent, on the sole ground they had followed an illegal house search."[6]

However, in 1953, in the *Isnard* case, the same jurisdiction quashed a verdict of conviction for the reason that the "proceeding concerning Isnard . . . reported altogether his arrest, his search and his statements; that the operations the police had carried out made a whole; that the confessions the judges of the Court of Appeal took into account could have been valid only if they had been made freely; that in the case in point, it was not so, considering the circumstances in which they had been obtained."[7]

These two judgments dealt with the same problem; the second one was careful to equate the "search of a person" with a house-search. But though one quashed a verdict of conviction and the other a verdict of not guilty, there is no contradiction between them. The *Boutros* judgment had laid upon the judges the obligation to find whether the confession consequent upon the illegal house-search might still have been free, and consequently admittable as proof. The *Isnard* judgment only added the affirmation of the right of supervision that the Supreme Court of Appeal grants itself upon the judges' official investigations, and from which it would proceed that a confession resulting from an illegal search might or might not have been free.

It may happen that confessions obtained by trickery or guile cannot be accepted in the preliminary judicial inquiry. The Supreme Court of Appeal declares, in the same way, that confessions which have been illegally obtained cannot be used as proofs.

In 1888, the examining magistrate in charge of the *Wilson* case ventured to call on the phone a person whom he suspected of complicity, passing himself off as another person also suspected. This magistrate was censured by the Supreme Court of the Magistrature on January 31, 1888.[8]

In 1949 in the *Imbert* case, a police superintendent arranged a telephone conversation between two suspected persons and overheard it from another receiver. The sentence later pronounced was quashed by the "Chambre Criminelle" of the Supreme Court of Appeal on the ground that the police officer's intervention "had as an aim and a result to elude the legal dispositions and the general rules of procedure that the examining magistrate or his delegate should not fail to recognize without jeopardizing the rights of the Defence." This judgment is very important, because it states that the violation of the rights of the defence, even

[4] Cass. Crim., Rec. Dalloz 1924.1.174 (1923); *id.*, Rec. Dalloz 1936.1.46 (1936); *id.* Rec. Dalloz 1954.110 (1953).

[5] Cass. Crim., Rec. Sirey 1937.1.73, note L. Hugueney (1936).

[6] Cass. Crim., Rec. Dalloz 1936.1.20, not minin. (1935).

[7] Cass. Crim., Rec. Dalloz 1953.533, note Lapp

(1953); *cf.*, Vouin, *Illegally Obtained Evidence*, INTL. CRIM. POLICE REV. 241 (No. 91 1955).

[8] Rec. Sirey 1889.1.242; *cf.*, Rousselet, REV. DE SCIENCE CRIMINELLE 50 (1946).

outside any violation of a written law, may lead to the annulment of the procedure.[9]

A short time later, another police superintendent, in the *Jolivot* case,[10] in order to identify the guilty person, had a recorder plugged into the receiver of the telephone of a couple who had complained of being insulted regularly over the telephone. The "Chambre Civile" of the Supreme Court of Appeal decided that the plaintiff's civil rights were violated by the installing of this recorder set, with the couple's consent, to detect the telephone call.

[9] Cass. Crim., Sem. Jurid. 1952.11.7241, note J. Brouchot (1952); *cf.*, Vouin, CRIM. L. REV. 10 (1955).

[10] Cass. Civ., Gaz. Palais 1955.1.249 (2d sec. 1955).

This decision has not been approved by everybody and is questionable law. But it clearly demonstrates the will of the Supreme Court of Appeal to disapprove, in the civil as well as penal law, police methods which might allow some persons to come upon confessions dishonestly.

As a conclusion, it is well established in the French penal law, without reference to the constitutional law or public liberties, that the conviction of a suspected or accused person cannot be based upon an illegal proof, because any proof illegally or irregularly obtained must be dismissed from the proceedings in court.

This solution guarantees the rights of the defence and the protection of all citizens.

# Germany

## WALTER R. CLEMENS

In the German law of procedure, the "rule of free evaluation of evidence" as laid down in section 261 of the Code of Criminal Procedure (hereinafter called CCP) prevails. This provision reads: "The Court shall evaluate the evidence according to its unlimited estimation and with due regard to the general course of the trial." Section 261 is closely related to Section 244(ii), CCP, which reads: "The Court shall ex officio expand the taking of the evidence to all facts and evidence relevant to the exploration of the truth." Such evidence includes that which has been obtained by the police.

Hence the principle of free evaluation of evidence permits the judge, and binds him at the same time, freely to weigh the evidence without any ties to strict rules. Thus, for instance, he may not be satisfied with the sworn statements of one or more

police officers and instead credit the conflicting statement of the defendant. He may, on the other hand, disbelieve the defendant's confession if he has reasonable grounds to assume the defendant made it only to protect another person. He may also refrain from using evidence which appears dubious for other reasons, or which was obtained in a dubious way.

To some extent, however, the judge's right to an unlimited evaluation of evidence is curtailed by the law. In certain cases it prohibits the judge, expressly or by interpretation, from using certain evidence, especially evidence obtained in violation of legal commands or bans. But in the vast majority of cases the use of such evidence is admissible in principle.

Although it is the primary objective of this report to discuss the exclusion of illegally seized *physical* evidence, it appears advisable to extend the discussion to evidence other than physical, since only thus can the German system of the exclusionary rule be clearly represented.

## Illegally Obtained Evidence The Use of Which Is Prohibited

(1) The most unambiguous prohibition against the use of illegally obtained evidence is laid down in Section 136a, CCP.[1] It prohibits certain immoral methods of interrogation and says that statements of the defendant obtained in violation of this provision shall not be used in evidence, regardless of his consent.

(2) Section 69(iii), CCP, provides that Section 136a, CCP, is applicable to the hearing of witnesses. Therefore, the judge is prohibited from using a witness's testimony obtained in violation of Section 136a, CCP.

(3) Section 252, CCP, says: "The statement of a witness heard prior to the trial who only in court takes advantage of his right to refuse to give evidence, shall not be read out." This provision has been extensively interpreted by the courts and law professors to go far beyond its wording. It is regarded as a far-reaching ban on the use of evidence. The extent of this ban is a matter of argument.

Following the generally accepted opinion of the courts[2] and law teachers,[3] Section 252, which is considered to be supplementary to the provisions of the CCP regarding the privilege of the witness to refuse his testimony, prohibits the judge from using statements made by such witnesses as have taken advantage of their privilege only subsequent to their interrogation.

The privilege of silence is granted by the CCP to the near relations of the defendant;[4] to certain persons who are under an obligation of secrecy, *e.g.*, parsons, defense counsel, lawyers, doctors, members of the Bundestag and the Landtage, editors, etc., and their assistants (with the restriction that they have no right to refuse their testimony if they were already released from their obligation of secrecy);[5] and to every witness in regard to all questions an answer to which would expose him or his near relations to the danger of a criminal prosecution.[6]

Further, Section 252 bans the use of a statement made by a witness who, contrary to a command of the CCP, was not advised on his privilege of silence prior to his interrogation. This is generally accepted as far as regards the command to advise the near relations of the defendant.[7] There is controversy, however, with respect to the command to advise witnesses who by making a statement expose themselves or near relations to the risk of a criminal prosecution. While the Federal Supreme Court[8] denies a ban on the use of a statement taken in violation of this command, prominent law theorists[9] are right in affirming such ban.

Finally, Section 252, which speaks only of the case of a genuine privilege of silence, is deemed applicable in cases where the CCP affords a protection which is rooted in such privilege. Section 81c, CCP, provides that persons other than the defendant may refuse a bodily examination or the taking of a blood test for the same reasons as they may refuse their testimony. According to the relevant court decisions[10] and law teachers[11] the result of such examination or blood test as was made in spite of a refusal shall not be used in evidence, in analogous application of Section 252, because "the duty to tolerate the bodily examina-

---

[1] Regarding the text of this provision and further details, see my paper on police interrogation privileges and limitations in Part III of this volume.

[2] 2 Entscheidungen des Bundesgerichtshofs in Strafsachen 105 (Decisions of the Federal Supreme Court in Criminal Matters); 7 *id.* 195.

[3] Kleinknecht-Müller, Kommentar zur Strafprozessordnung (Commentary on the CCP) §48, preliminary note 2e I (4th ed.); Eberhard Schmidt, Lehrkommentar zur Strafprozessordnung (Instructional Commentary of Criminal Procedure) pt. II, §252, n.1 (1957).

[4] CCP, §52, para. (i).

[5] CCP, §§52, 53(a).

[6] CCP, §55, para. (i).

[7] See, *e.g.*, Kleinknecht-Müller, *op. cit. supra* note 3, at §52, n.3f.

[8] 1 Entscheidungen des Bundesgerichtshofs in Strafsachen 40 (Decisions of the Federal Supreme Court in Criminal Matters).

[9] Kleinknecht-Müller, *op. cit. supra* note 3, at §55, n.4; Eberhard Schmidt, *op. cit. supra* note 3, at §55, n.9.

[10] 1 Entscheidungen des Bundesgerichtshofs in Strafsachen 135 (Decisions of the Federal Supreme Court in Criminal Matters).

[11] Kleinknecht-Müller, *op. cit. supra* note 3, at §81c, n.5b.

tion or the blood test is kind of an extended duty to give evidence."[12] Section 95, CCP, provides that everybody (with the exception of the defendant) who has in his custody objects which may be of importance as evidence or are subject to confiscation is under the obligation to produce and surrender them by request, but that the action which is provided by law for the enforcement of such obligation shall not be taken against persons who have the privilege of silence. The question is whether any objects which were obtained through the illegal use of force against a person thus privileged can be used in evidence. An explicit regulation to this effect is missing in the German law. Whether a ban on the use can be derived from the fact that the banning provision of Section 95, CCP, is in close connection with the provisions of Sections 52, 53, and 55, CCP,[13] should be answered in the affirmative.[14] Section 97 provides that written communications between the defendant and certain persons who are under the privilege of silence, or written material which is in the possession of such privileged persons, is not subject to impounding, unless these persons are suspected of being parties in the crime, accessories after the fact, or receivers. In the event that such documents are impounded contrary to the ban of Section 97, CCP, it is commonly held[15] that they shall not be used in evidence, because they represent a kind of written memory of the privileged person and hence are barred from any use, exactly as would be his oral evidence pursuant to Section 252 in conjunction with the relevant provision of the CCP regarding the privilege of silence.

(4) Section 96, CCP, reads:

"The submission or surrender of file-records or other documents in official custody by authori-

ties or civil servants shall not be demanded if their supreme office declares that the divulgement of the contents of such files or documents would be detrimental to the weal of the Federal Republic or a German Land."

Whether this provision contains a prohibition against the use of evidence becomes acute in a case where such documents are submitted to the judge in spite of the above declaration of the supreme office, or where the supreme office makes out the declaration only subsequent to the receipt by the judge of the files and records. The prevailing opinion of the courts,[16] and the better legal theory,[17] is that in such case the judge is denied the use of the documents, although Section 96 does not provide for such consequence *expressis verbis*. It would appear intolerable that the judge by using such documents would contribute to the harming of the weal of the Federal Republic or a German Land.

The above prohibitions mainly exclude the use of evidence obtained in violation of statutory provisions, and this in principle both in favor and to the detriment of the accused.[18] An appeal on law lies in the event of their violation.

Another question is whether the above prohibitions cease to be effective if he whose protection the law has in view (mostly the defendant or a witness) gives his consent to the use of such evidence. Doubtless the answer is no, if the law forbids the use notwithstanding the consent of the protected person. This applies for instance to Section 136a, paragraph (iii), CCP, with regard to a statement of the defendant which came about through the application of immoral means. The question whether, in the absence of an explicit rule, the use is admissible with the consent of the protected person should as a rule be answered in the affirmative. Hence, for example, there should be no objection to the use of the statement of a witness who made it without being advised under

---

[12] 5 Entscheidungen des Bundesgerichtshofs in Strafsachen 133 (Decisions of the Federal Supreme Court in Criminal Matters).

[13] See text accompanying notes 4, 5, and 6 *supra*.

[14] Assenting, EBERHARD SCHMIDT, *op. cit. supra* note 3, at §95, n.10; dissenting, KLEINKNECHT-MÜLLER, *op. cit. supra* note 3, at §94, preliminary note 7b.

[15] KLEINKNECHT-MÜLLER, *op. cit. supra* note 3, at §94, preliminary note 7d; EBERHARD SCHMIDT, *op. cit. supra* note, 3 at §97, n.9.

[16] 72 Entscheidungen des Reichsgerichts in Strafsachen 271 (Decisions of the Reichsgericht in Criminal Matters).

[17] KLEINKNECHT-MÜLLER, *op. cit. supra* note 3, at §96, nn.4b & c, and §94, preliminary note 7c.

[18] See KLEINKNECHT-MÜLLER, *op. cit. supra* note 3, at §48, preliminary note 2b.

Section 52(ii), CCP, on his privilege of silence, if he, on being advised subsequently, consents to the use of his former statement.

Some law theorists[19] hold that the statutory prohibitions against the use of evidence do not oppose its use in cases where such use will benefit predominant, legitimate interests. This opinion cannot be favored, because it has no sufficient foundation in the statute and might result in a dangerous undermining of the statutory prohibitions.

### Illegally Obtained Evidence the Use Of Which Is Permitted

In two decisions[20] the Reichsgericht held unrestrictedly, without adducing reasons for its view, that the ban on a seizure in violation of the CCP excludes the use in evidence of the illegally seized object. Today the courts no longer adhere to this view, which is patently the application of the general principle that the use of each and every item of illegally seized evidence is prohibited. Rather it is the opinion of the Federal Supreme Court—the pertinent decision was rendered on November 13th, 1952[21]—and the apparently generally accepted opinion of the law teachers[22] that evidence which in itself is admissible may in principle be used although it was obtained in violation of legal provisions.

According to this opinion illegally obtained evidence may be used—in default of a legal provision to the contrary—in the following examples (which could be increased at choice):

(a) A weapon which contained the finger-prints of the defendant had been impounded by the police. The impounding proved to be faulty because the police officer effecting it was not a member of the Criminal Police and therefore not authorized to impound.[23]

(b) An important exhibit, impounded by a Criminal Police officer as the result of a search, was produced before the court. The search was defective, because in the absence of imminent danger prevailing it should have been made only by order of the judge.[24]

(c) The weapon which the defendant had allegedly used in committing a murder had been seized during a search effected during the nighttime, in violation of Section 104, CCP.[25]

(d) The bodily examination of a witness had been effected upon orders received by the police, in spite of the fact that contrary to Section 81c, CCP, the examination had failed to serve the purpose of ascertaining a certain trail or a consequence of the criminal act, the examination could not be expected to be tolerated, detrimental effects on the health of the witness had been envisaged or taken place, or the police—in bad or good faith—had erroneously taken the view that imminent danger was prevailing.[26]

(e) A suspect had justly been preliminarily arrested, but contrary to Section 128, CCP, and Article 104(iii), Basic Law,[27] had not been brought before the judge during the day following his preliminary arrest. He made a confession before the police on the second day following his arrest. This confession may be used unless the interrogation took place in violation of Section 136a, paragraphs (i) and (ii), CCP.

Although, as mentioned, the use of illegally obtained evidence is *in principle* admissible in the absence of a statutory ban, yet there is an exception to the rule which has been ably elaborated by the notable CCP commentators Kleinknecht-Müller:[28]

---

[19] *Id.* at §48, preliminary note 2h III.

[20] 20 Entscheidungen des Reichsgerichts in Strafsachen 92 (Decisions of the Reichsgericht in Criminal Matters); 47 *id.* 196.

[21] Not published, but quoted in MONATSSCHRIFT FÜR DEUTSCHES RECHT (German Law Monthly) 148 (1953).

[22] KLEINKNECHT-MÜLLER, *op. cit. supra* note 3, at §48, preliminary note 2c; EBERHARD SCHMIDT, *op. cit. supra* note 3, at §94, n.14; NIESE, DOPPELFUNKTIONELLE PROZESSHANDLUNGEN (Bifunctional Procedural Acts) 139 (1950).

[23] See CCP, §98.

[24] See CCP, §105(i).

[25] For the wording of this section, see my paper on police interrogation privileges and limitations in Part III of this volume.

[26] KLEINKNECHT-MÜLLER, *op. cit. supra* note 3, at §81c, n.7, justly holds that in these cases the result of the examination may be used.

[27] For the wording of these provisions, see my paper on police interrogation privileges and limitations in Part III of this volume.

[28] See KLEINKNECHT-MÜLLER, *op. cit. supra* note 3, at §94, preliminary note 7.

"The statutory provisions governing procedure are based on a balance of the public interest in the enforcement of the State's prosecuting claims and the public interest in ensuring that the State's measures which appear necessary to accomplish this objective encroach only to a tolerable extent upon the individual. The numerous reservations as regards the admissibility of public constraint are the result of such compromise between either interest. No Code of Procedure will be able, though, to cram this counterbalance into rules fitting the thousandfold phenomena of life. While as a guarantee for the necessary continuity some rigor must be endured, yet in an individual case the rigor can reach such unbearable dimensions that a deviation from the statutory law appears adequate. This tacit general clause of the law justifies the judge to found the inadmissibility of the evidence upon a heavy procedural infringement, even though such consequence is not expressly laid down by the law. The judge in arriving at his decision will consider the public interest in the prosecution. An irreparable procedural blunder which might be ignored in the interest of the public claim to a prosecution for murder, can in petty larceny cases ensue the inadmissibility of the evidence."

The legal basis of the right of the judge thus established to refrain in a single case from using evidence the use of which is not prohibited by the statute and therefore permitted *in principle* is to be found in Section 261, CCP, quoted at the beginning of this report.

### EVALUATION

In accordance with most constitutions of the western civilized countries, the Basic Law for the German Federal Republic, dated May 23, 1949, establishes certain basic rights. To these belong in particular the inviolability of human dignity (Article 1), the right to free personal development, the right to life and bodily integrity, and further the inviolability of the freedom of the person (Articles 2 and 104), the inviolability of the abode (Article 13), and the safeguarding of property (Article 14). These rights, however, are subject to certain restrictions; otherwise public order could not be maintained. The Basic Law pays regard to that by providing, for instance, in Article 2 that infringements upon the right to life and bodily integrity and upon the inviolability of the freedom of a person can be made only on the basis of a statute. Further, Article 13 provides that searches can in principle be ordered only by the judge and can be effected only in the forms prescribed by statute. And Article 14 says that the limits of property are drawn only by statute.

Such legal restrictions of the basic rights are to be found in the CCP in great number: the blood-test confines the right to bodily integrity, the duty of a witness to appear before the court and to make a statement infringes upon his liberty, the search of an abode violates its inviolability, the confiscation of an object entrenches upon property, etc. The CCP makes these infringements with as much consideration as is possible by providing, for instance, that certain witnesses shall be advised of their privilege of silence, that the taking of a blood-test can be effected only by a doctor, that the order for especially serious encroachments is reserved to the judge, that normally the search of an abode during the hours of night is prohibited, and that the detention by the police of a preliminarily arrested suspect is temporary. Infractions of these commands and prohibitions will as a rule also constitute infractions of a basic right, because the Basic Law prescribes that an encroachment upon a basic right shall be allowed *only* on the basis of a statute, and therefore only with due regard to the precautions contained therein. Such infractions could, of course, easily be counteracted, in that the statute could prohibit the use of all evidence obtained in violation of constitutionally protected basic rights.

The German law has not laid down such rule, obviously because this was deemed incompatible with the "principle of the exploration of the truth which for the sake of the public weal demands the investigation, prosecution and just punishment of crimes through the use of all evidence available."[29]

[29] 2 Entscheidungen des Bundesgerichtshofs in Straf-

On behalf of this principle the German law has rather refrained from a general ban on the use of such evidence as was obtained in violation of basic rights. The CCP has laid down bans on the use of evidence only in respect of such evidence as was obtained in violation of human dignity or of the privilege of silence in its broadest meaning, and where the use would result in detriments to the weal of the Federal Republic or a German Land. By doing this, the law indicates that it gives priority to these rights and interests alone over the principle of the free exploration of the truth.

## Conclusion

In light of the foregoing observations, the three questions posed for discussion in connection with this topic[30] can be answered as follows:

(1 & 2) A statutory ban on the use, in criminal proceedings, of evidence obtained in violation of basic rights could aim at (a) the "punishment" of the individual responsible for such violation, (b) the protection of the basic rights, or (c) the protection of the suspect.

The "punishment" of the responsible individual—usually an official—cannot be achieved with the help of such ban, because the ban would have no consequences to his disadvantage. The disadvantages would be on the side of the state or the public alone, because the ban would place restrictions on the evidence available for the exploration of the truth and thus hamper or defeat the revenge on crimes which is in the state or public interest.

An effective punishment of the responsible person can be achieved only by holding him responsible under the Criminal Code,[31] by suing him for

damages under the Civil Code, or by taking disciplinary action against him under the appropriate disciplinary statutes.[32]

Doubtless, the ban in question affords a far-reaching protection of the basic rights. But in view of its hampering effect on the exploration of the truth, the question remains if this protection is proper and worth being advocated in *every* case of violation of basic rights. An injury to human dignity—the interrogation of the suspect or a witness in violation of Section 136a paragraphs (i) and (ii), CCP—will by all means be worthy of protection, particularly since a statement thus effected fails to have the slightest evidential value in trial anyway. On the other hand, if only a small violation of basic rights occurs—a search was ordered by a police officer contrary to Section 105, CCP, although there was no imminent danger prevailing—the protection of the basic rights will have to make way for the higher-valued interest in the exploration of the truth.

Whether the protection of the suspect calls for a statutory ban on the use of evidence obtained in violation of basic rights should be considered from a similar angle. Certainly, he has in principle the right of seeing the proceedings against him performed lawfully. But this right will have to stand back if only a negligible violation of a basic right has occurred.

(3) As was mentioned above, the use of evidence obtained in violation of basic rights is not generally prohibited under German law. Rather, the law has decided on a compromise. It lays a ban on the use of such evidence only in the few cases where it deems the violation of basic rights or state interests to be an especially serious one; in all other cases it permits the use of illegally or even unconstitutionally obtained evidence, only reserving to the judge a dissenting ruling in the scope of his free evaluation of evidence.

Naturally, it is open to argument whether the German law has drawn a just border-line between admissible and inadmissible evidence. In principle,

---

sachen 105 (Decisions of the Federal Supreme Court in Criminal Matters).

[30] The three questions are set forth in the introduction to Part II of this volume.

[31] In the case of an official, §341, Criminal Code, comes into question, which penalizes the official who wilfully and without being entitled to do so effects, or causes or allows to be effected, an arrest or a preliminary apprehension and detention; also applicable is §343, which penalizes an official who during an investigation uses or causes or allows to be used means of coercion to extort confessions or statements.

[32] This is possible under German Law.

the regulation of the law appears satisfactory and convincing. Technically, however, it is not satisfactory. It would be desirable that in all cases where the CCP wants to prohibit the use of illegally obtained evidence, such prohibitions were enunciated *expressis verbis* and just as clearly as was done in Section 136a, paragraph (iii). And it would further be desirable that the law said with all distinction that in the absence of an explicit ban any evidence obtained in violation of statutory provisions may be used unless the judge rules otherwise under Section 261, CCP. This would considerably decrease the differences of opinion in the interpretation of the law.

# Israel

## HAIM H. COHN

The rule prevailing in Israel is the common law rule that, for the purpose of deciding whether certain evidence is or is not admissible, the court will not enquire into the methods by which that evidence was obtained.[1] The only exception to the rule is that the court will enquire into the circumstances under which a confession was made, so as to ascertain whether it was made freely and voluntarily.

It is submitted that both the rule and the exception stand in need of revision.

The sound principle underlying the rule is that direct evidence which is relevant to the issue and not privileged from disclosure should be available to the trier of fact; the sanction for any criminal offence and the remedy for any civil wrong which may have been committed in obtaining that evidence are matters not for the law of evidence, but for the criminal law or the law of torts, as the case may be. Cases are known in which persons have been restrained by injunction from producing evidence wrongfully obtained[2]; such an injunction is, of course, a remedy in tort, and implies no ruling one way or the other on the evidential issue.

In defence of the exclusion of illegally obtained evidence, it might—apart from purely ethical grounds—be argued that there is another instance in which the law of evidence is made subservient to extraneous considerations of public policy, namely, the privilege attaching to state secrets. In the one case the public interest is to discourage illegal practices on the part of the police and other evidence-collecting agencies; in the other case the public interest is to encourage and safeguard the proper and efficient administration of government. But the common law privilege in favour of state secrets has remained in full force and vigour only in England, and even there it time and again arouses vehement public and professional reactions. It has never, in its absolute form, been part of the law of Scotland, nor is it recognized as an absolute privilege by "what some commentators regard as the better decisions in the United States."[3] The Supreme Court of Israel, following Scots, Canadian, and the "better" American precedents, has recently laid down that there is no absolute privilege from the disclosure of state secrets in Israel, but that the trial judge has to satisfy himself, each time such privilege is claimed, that the harm which is likely to be caused to the state by the production of the evidence outweighs the public interest in a full disclosure to the court of all evidentiary material relevant to the issue.[4]

It thus appears that where the common law

[1] 8 WIGMORE, EVIDENCE §2183 (3d ed. 1940).
[2] *E.g.*, Ashburton v. Pape, [1913] 2 Ch. 469 (C.A.).

[3] MODEL CODE OF EVIDENCE, comment to rule 228, at 167.
[4] Ha'etzni v. Ben Gurion, 11 Piskei Din 403 (1947).

has provided an exclusionary rule of evidence in the public interest and for reasons of public policy, the modern tendency is to divest that rule of general and unrestricted application, and to vest in the trial judge a discretion as to whether or not, and to what extent, to apply the rule in the particular case before him. And there seems to be no valid reason why the development which has marked the exclusionary rule in respect of state secrets should not be brought to bear, *mutatis mutandis*, on an exclusionary rule in respect of illegally seized evidence. In both cases, there is a conflict of public interests and that conflict cannot justly and equitably be solved by an inflexible rule of general application, but rather should be solved in each individual case according to the best judgment of the trial judge.

These considerations apply no less to the rule that all illegally seized evidence is admissible than to the rule that all such evidence is inadmissible. There might well be instances in which it would be unconscionable to allow a party to establish his claim by unlawful means. Actions in equity, for instance, have always been defeated where the claimant has come to court with "unclean hands," and in any civil or criminal case there may be circumstances which require or justify the exclusion of illegally obtained evidence which, in other circumstances, might be held admissible in the interest of justice or in the general public interest.

Moreover, while it might in many cases be eminently just and legitimate to penalize a person for illegally seizing evidence by excluding that evidence in a suit to which he himself is a party or in the outcome of which he is beneficially interested, it is not by any means just or legitimate to penalize the state for the illegal seizure of evidence by one of its officers. That officer is not a party to the suit, nor has he normally any personal interest in its outcome. The exclusion of such evidence amounts to a penalization of the general public for the wrong of one individual—surely a violation of fundamental principles. While it may be maintained that a sanction should cause a wrongdoer to suffer, it can hardly be maintained that a sanction should not only fail to affect the wrongdoer, but also permit a different wrongdoer

to escape punishment for a totally unrelated transgression.

The Israeli Draft Code of Evidence[5] provides that the court may refuse to admit in evidence any document (including any form of record of anything said, written, printed, or photographed) which the party producing it has stolen or obtained by any other illegal means, or in making or circulating which the party producing it committed a criminal offence.[6] A provision to this effect enables the trial judge, in his discretion, to exclude illegally seized evidence, where such evidence is sought to be produced by a party to the litigation before him; it does not enable him in a criminal case to exclude evidence obtained by the illegal act of some police officer who is, of course, a stranger to the action (unless it is a private prosecution for an offence by which the private prosecutor himself was personally injured[7]).

It is submitted that there is no difference in principle between a confession wrongfully extorted and other evidence illegally seized; the misconduct of the police is as reprehensible in wrongfully extorting the one as in illegally seizing the other. With regard to confessions, the law as it stands is that, however wrongful the manner in which they were obtained, they are admissible in evidence if (notwithstanding the manner of their extortion) they were in fact free and voluntary; the reason is that if they were free and voluntary, they may be taken to be true. The *ratio excludendi*, then, is not that they were wrongfully obtained, but that they may be false. This *ratio* cannot apply to evidence the contents of which is normally unaffected by the manner in which it was obtained, and as to which such attributes as free and voluntary can have no meaning. If the reprehensibility of police misconduct in wrongfully extorting a confession does not, of itself, warrant the exclusion of the confession, there is no valid reason why the repre-

[5] DRAFT CODE OF EVIDENCE (1952) (English translation by Harvard Law School—Israel Cooperative Research, 1953).

[6] *Id.*, §75.

[7] Private prosecutions are permissible in Israel for assault, defamation, trespass, and the violation of trademarks and copyrights. MAGISTRATES' COURT JURISDICTION (AMENDMENT) ACT 5714-1954.

hensibility of police misconduct in illegally seizing other evidence should, of itself, warrant the exclusion of that evidence.

From the point of view of the law of evidence, exclusionary rules appear to be justified only where the evidence sought to be adduced is either irrelevant or inherently unreliable. (The various recognized privileges from disclosure do not really affect the admissibility of the privileged evidence and are, therefore, not to be classified as exclusionary rules.) Where available evidence is both relevant and manifestly true, the requirement of justice that it should be produced and admitted is paramount, and no desire to penalize any individual wrongdoer should be allowed to stand in the way.

The same result is reached when the problem is looked at from the point of view of practical efficiency. In the United States where the exclusionary rule in respect of illegally seized evidence has for many years and by many courts been rigorously applied, abuses by the police always were and still are notoriously widespread; the best experts have expressed doubts whether these exclusionary rules even tend to remedy the abuses.[8] The fact is, the exclusion of such evidence has failed so far, both in the United States and elsewhere, to deter the police from resorting to illegal means to procure evidence. Maybe the reason for this deprecable state of affairs lies in the knowledge of police officers that the only sanction likely to follow upon the illegal procuration of evidence is its exclusion and rejection, a sanction which may lead to acquittal of the accused, but which does not entail any punishment of the police officer.

There may be police forces in which an officer using illegal means to procure evidence is disciplined; there may be others in which such an officer is looked upon with approval and gratitude, having spared no effort and shown no qualms in executing his assignment. In the former, instances of illegal seizure of evidence will be rare; in the latter, they will be frequent. But in neither does it matter much whether the illegally seized evidence is eventually admitted or excluded.

The use by police of illegal means to procure evidence is not, however, a matter which may be left to the domestic disciplinary jurisdiction of the police force itself. It directly and vitally affects not only the fundamental (or constitutional) liberties of the citizen but also the administration of justice by the courts. It is an eminently criminal matter, calling for criminal sanctions to be administered in as effective and deterrent a manner as is compatible with the rule of law.

The Israeli legislature now has before it a bill[9] which provides that where a court is satisfied that a confession sought to be produced in evidence was unlawfully obtained—whether or not it was admitted in evidence—the court may commit the person who has so obtained it to trial in the competent court, or, with his consent, may try him summarily then and there for the offence he has committed in extorting the confession.[10] Where a committal order is made to another court, the finding of the committing court that the confession was unlawfully extorted is *prima facie* evidence against the extorter in the other court.

The same provision can and should be made in respect of any illegally seized evidence other than confessions. Such procedural provisions coupled with substantial increases in the punishment for criminal trespass and other abuses of office when committed by a police officer, should be all that is needed, and at any rate appears to be all that is possible, to curb illegal practices on the part of the police. Exclusionary rules in the law of evidence are neither useful nor justified.

[8] MODEL CODE OF EVIDENCE, comment to rule 505, at 243.

[9] Law of Evidence Revision (Privileged Evidence) Bill 5718-1958.
[10] The offence is punishable with three years' imprisonment. CRIMINAL CODE ORDINANCE §109B (Palestine 1936).

# *Japan*

HARUO ABE

### THE TRADITIONAL VIEW

Should illegally seized evidence be admissible to convict an accused? In Japan this question has been answered in the affirmative for many years.

Back in 1899 the Supreme Court of Japan held, in a case under the Code of Criminal Procedure of 1890, that the defendant's pocket notebook, illegally seized by a policeman, was lawfully received in evidence.[1] In 1949 the Supreme Court held, in a case under the Code of Criminal Procedure of 1922, that it was lawful for the trial court to convict the accused by receiving a piece of physical evidence which had been seized with illegal procedure.[2] In this case the Court amplified the justifications for the traditional rule concerning the admissibility of illegally seized evidence. It clarified among others the following two points: (1) The illegality of search and seizure procedure does not change the nature, condition, or shape, and therefore the evidential value, of the thing which has been illegally seized; (2) The problem concerning the admissibility of a statement obtained by illegal interrogation procedure should be distinguished from the problem of the admissibility of illegally seized evidence; in the former the illegality of the procedure may affect the substantive probative value of the statement, whereas in the latter the illegality of the procedure has nothing to do with the evidential value of the thing seized.

### PRESENT LAW AND PRACTICE

Under the new Code of Criminal Procedure of 1948 there have been no Supreme Court decisions precisely on point, but there are some high court decisions which follow the traditional rule.[3]

Majority opinion among judges and realistic-minded lawyers appears to favor the traditional position as established by judicial precedents.[4] The most important arguments supporting the traditional rule are those pointed out by the Supreme Court decision of December 13, 1949.[5] Beside those, however, the following two reasons have been maintained by the followers of the traditional rule: (1) It would be useless to deny admission to illegally seized evidence, because the prosecution may easily evade the strict rule by repeating the seizure in compliance with law; (2) It would be better to remedy the unfairness of an illegal seizure of evidence by punishing the officer who made the illegal seizure or by giving the accused some recourse such as the right to compensation by the state.

### PROGRESSIVE VIEWS

Most scholars and progressive lawyers,[6] influenced or encouraged by such American expe-

---

[1] Vol. 5, No. 1. Sup. Ct. Crim. Rep. 38 (1899).

[2] Decision of the Supreme Court (3rd Petty Bench, Dec. 31, 1949) (unpublished).

[3] *E.g.*, Supp. No. 16 High Courts Crim. Rep. 41 (Tokyo High Court 1950), holding an illegally seized receipt admissible.

[4] *E.g.*, THE SUPREME COURT, SECRETARIAT GENERAL, SUMMARY RECORD OF THE NATIONAL CONFERENCE OF CRIMINAL JUDGES ON CRIMINAL PROCEDURE (Materials on Criminal Justice, No. 66) 110 (1952) (in Japanese).

[5] See note 2, *supra*.

[6] *E.g.*, Dando, *Comments*, 3 COLLECTED CRIMINAL CASE COMMENTS 150 (1943) (in Japanese); Koke, *Admissibility of Illegally Obtained Evidence*, 2 KEIHO ZASSHI (J. of Crim. Law) (No. 3) 71 (1951) (in Japanese); Hirano, *Criminal Procedure*, in LAW LECTURE SERIES 119 (4th ed. 1956) (in Japanese); Hirano, *Control of Investigation by Exclusion of Evidence*, 7 KEIHO ZASSHI (J. of Crim. Law) (Nos. 2, 3, and 4, consolidated) 243 (1957) (in Japanese); HIRABA, LECTURE ON CRIMINAL LAW 177, 178 (1955) (in Japanese); Adachi, *Seizure, Search, and Inspection*, in 2 COURSE ON LEGAL PRACTICE 342–44 (1953) (in Japanese); YOKOGAWA, A STUDY ON CRIMINAL TRIAL 163 (1953) (in Japanese); Saito, *Relations Between the Illegality in Procedure of Obtaining Evidence and the Admissibility of Evidence*, 6 HOSO JIHO (Lawyers Ass'n J.) (No. 9) 1 (1954) (in Japanese).

rience as the development of the "federal exclu-sionary rule,"[7] have expressed various views counter to the traditional.[8]

The grounds for their contentions are not exactly the same, but their views are unanimous on the point that it will be impossible to stop police practices of collecting evidence with filthy hands without squashing the very object (*i.e.*, the con-viction of the accused) toward which the over-zealous police are desperately struggling.[9] The threat of punishment is not effective enough to intimidate a police officer who attempts to be a "hero" by sacrificing himself for illegally seized evidence.[10] It has been suggested that it is not the voluntary will of each individual officer but the blind will of the whole police organization which compels the individual to engage in the underhanded investigation.[11]

[7] *E.g.*, see articles by Hirano, Koke, and Seito, cited in note 6, *supra*.
[8] Some maintain that illegally seized evidence should be simply inadmissible; some contend that illegally seized evidence should be inadmissible unless illegality is due to minor technical errors; some contend that il-legally seized evidence should be inadmissible if the illegality constitutes a crime.
[9] See Hirano, *op. cit. supra* note 6, at 247: "If the cause of such illegal activities are eagerness or desire to succeed in official business one may squash these objec-tives in preventing the illegal activities. Obstructing the conviction of the accused by excluding evidence will be the most effective remedy for over-zealous investigating officers; criminal penalty will only invite their dissatis-faction and resistance. On the contrary, if the causes of such illegal activities are feelings of superiority, arro-gance, or indifference toward citizens, exclusion of evi-dence will not be very effective; direct discipline by punishment will be more effective.
"Which is the greater cause? This will not be simply decided. However, at least it may be said that there is a considerable tendency toward lawlessness owing to ex-cessive eagerness; and it can be foreseen that this tend-ency will be growing in the future."
[10] In the *Sugo* case (a case of "agent provocateur"; not guilty, the Oita District Court, Aug. 4, 1958; guilty but excused from punishment, the Fukuoka High Court, Sept. 12, 1959), a police officer was found guilty but excused from punishment for having supplied a radical group with dynamite for blasting a police box; but later he obtained a good position in a publishing company having connection with the police organiza-tion. It seems to be the general feeling among the police that a wounded "hero" must be warmly taken care of.
[11] Hirano, *op. cit. supra* note 6, at 247.

## CONCLUSION[12]

Fairness and quick detection are two essential components of criminal justice. The harmonization of these competing values has been and will be the eternal objective of law. It is remarkable that thousands of years ago the ingenious inventors of Chinese characters already perceived this func-tional structure of criminal justice and succeeded in symbolizing it in an archaic style of the Chinese ideograph signifying "law" or "justice."[13]

In the latter part of the twentieth century we are still suffering from the age-old problem of achieving quick and strict justice together with fair and humanitarian justice. Unquestionably the maxim *"in dubio pro reo"* has been an effective amulet to protect human rights of the suspect and accused from uncivilized practice on the part of criminal investigators. So long as instances remain of uncivilized police practices,[14] any device that safeguards human rights against abusive investigating authority is worthy of retention.

[12] This conclusion is purported to be a conclusive statement not only for the present report but also for my other papers which appear in this volume.
[13] *Cf*. HSÜ SHEN (2nd Century, A.D.), SHUO WEN CHIEH TZU 4352 (Ku lin edition, I-hsüen shu-chü, Shanghai, 1928). Etymologically the rather complicated symbol consists of two parts. The left hand component means water, which in ancient times symbolized the even-handed justice. The right hand component, which again can be broken down into an upper part and a lower part, signifies an imaginary animal resembling a unicorn which was supposed to have the supernatural power of tossing the guilty party to one side, out of the forum—a mystic living lie-detector! Our oriental ancestors who invented this ingenious device for symbolizing the pro-found abstract concepts seem to have perceived the two essential functions of criminal justice, *i.e.*, (a) quick and accurate identification of the guilty from the innocent and (b) fair and even treatment of the people. For the ancient ideograph for "Law" see the cover of CRIMINAL JUSTICE IN JAPAN (Ministry of Justice, Tokyo, 1957, 2d ed. 1960).
[14] Among the recent cases in which judgments of "guilty" were reversed by the high courts and the Su-preme Court for the reason that confessions were un-lawfully coerced, the following four cases were most shocking and sensational: the *Matsukawa* case, the *Futamata* case, the *Sachiura* case and the *Yakai* case. In these cases, in which most defendants had been sen-tenced to death in the district courts, police brutality was ascertained by the high courts and the Supreme Court.

On the other hand, it should not be overlooked that emphasis on the rights of suspects has led some judges to discharge suspicious defendants in difficult cases, particularly when there has been no confession to corroborate circumstantial evidence.[15]

[15] Among several recent cases of this nature, the *Crowley* case was most typical. In this case an American millionaire allegedly, while intoxicated, killed his brother-in-law in the Imperial Hotel in Tokyo, and he was prosecuted for the crime of "inflicting a bodily injury resulting in death" (PENAL CODE, art. 205, par. 1). The Tokyo District Court acquitted the accused because of insufficient proof. The records show that there were many pieces of circumstantial evidence tending to prove his guilt, but the judges appeared to hesitate to convict him on circumstantial evidence. In this case the police did not press a confession, and naturally there was no confession or admission volunteered by the accused. It is reported that when the police asked him to be tested on the polygraph he refused the request in a highly emotional manner.

It is my belief that the way of bridging the gap between idealism and realism is not to be found in elaborating the existing system into one of logical complexity or exquisite technicality, but in reconstructing the system practicably, giving consideration to human weakness as well as to human wisdom. The first step will be the establishment of a criminal justice with less reliance on confession or admission and more on the development of scientific investigation. The efforts to attain this objective should be accompanied by the painful activity of educating and enlightening both the general public and criminal investigators. It should be borne in mind that only by way of this thorny path can we hope to solve those difficult problems centered around the privilege against self-incrimination, the law of arrest and interrogation, the law of confession, and the rule relating to illegally seized evidence.

# Norway[*]

ANDERS BRATHOLM

## I.

Before we examine the question of excluding unlawfully acquired evidence, it is well to mention briefly the rules which apply to the right of the police to obtain evidence against an accused person.

The right of the police *to search* is strictly regulated by the Norwegian Criminal Procedure Act of 1887. When a person is suspected on reasonable grounds of a punishable offence for which the maximum statutory penalty can exceed a fine, the police may search the person or his dwelling, provided that there is reason to believe that the search will lead to his arrest, or to discovery of evidence of the punishable offence, or to seizure of objects involved.[1]

Search of another party's dwelling can also be undertaken under certain circumstances, for instance when there is strong reason to believe that a wanted person, stolen property, or traces of a punishable act can be found in the dwelling.[2]

Whether the above-mentioned conditions are present or not, the police can institute a search of a place of business which can be operated only with police permission or which is available to the public.[3]

If the person concerned does not consent to the

* This paper is mainly an abbreviated form of an article written by the author on the exclusion of illegally seized evidence. The article was published in NORDISK TIDSKRIFT FOR RETTSVITENSKAP (The Northern Journal of Law) 109–32 (1959).

[1] CRIMINAL PROCEDURE ACT (hereinafter called CPA) of 1887, §221.
[2] *Ibid.*
[3] CPA, §222.

search, it can be undertaken only on a court order. But if the purpose of the search is likely to be thwarted by the delay involved in awaiting the court order, the prosecuting authority can issue an order to proceed with the search. If there is not even time for this, the search may be undertaken by the police without an order, provided there is strong suspicion of an offence for which the maximum statutory penalty is a term of imprisonment longer than six months.[4]

A police officer who, by order of the court or the prosecuting authority, is empowered to arrest an accused person may search the latter's dwelling without special permission.[5]

The Act contains different regulations for the carrying out of the search.[6]

In practice the accused generally consents to the search, thus making it unnecessary for the police to obtain an order from the court or the prosecuting authority.

The Criminal Procedure Act also contains regulations on when *seizure* can take place. The main provision is that seizure may be made of objects which can be considered of importance as evidence, or that ought to be regarded as confiscable.[7]

If the person concerned does not consent to the seizure, a court order must be sought, or if time does not allow this, an order from the prosecuting authority. If even then the delay would be too long, the police may act on their own authority.[8]

If there has been no time to obtain a court order, the question whether the seizure shall be upheld must be laid before the court at the earliest possible opportunity.[9]

A person in possession of an object considered important as evidence can, if he is obliged to offer testimony in the case, be ordered by the court to produce the object.[10] Those exempt from the

obligation to give evidence are chiefly the family of the accused and persons bound by professional secrecy to whom the accused has given confidential information (defending counsel, doctors, ministers, etc.).[11]

There are detailed provisions in the act regarding the method of carrying out seizure and returning objects seized to the owner, etc.[12]

Evidence against an accused person may also be obtained by interrogation, blood tests, confrontation and the like. The question of the extent to which the police can question the accused, submit him to various tests, etc., is dealt with more thoroughly in earlier articles by the author in this series.[13]

## II.

The Norwegian Criminal Procedure Act has no provision concerning the admissibility of evidence seized in contravention of the Act. Nor is much guidance to be found in literature on Norwegian criminal procedure. The only declaration of principles I can find is given by the Norwegian Professor of Criminal law, Johs. Andenaes, who declares that if a confession is extracted under conditions at variance with those required at police questioning, there is much to be said for excluding the confession on the principle that the police should not be allowed to offer evidence acquired in an illegål manner. But, it is added, it is doubtful if our courts, generally speaking, would accept such a principle.[14]

So far as I can see the question of the steps that should be taken with regard to illegally seized evidence has not been comprehensively dealt with in any Scandinavian country.

## III.

Before we go further into the question of how the problem should be solved in Norway, it might

---

[4] CPA, §223.
[5] *Ibid.*
[6] CPA, §§224–26.
[7] CPA, §212.
[8] CPA, §215.
[9] *Ibid.*
[10] CPA, §216.

[11] CPA, §§176–78.
[12] CPA, §§218–20.
[13] See my report on self-incrimination which appears in Part IV of this volume, and my paper on police interrogation privileges and limitations which appears in Part III of this volume.
[14] ANDENAES, POLITIEMBEDSMENNENES BLAD (The Journal of Police Officials) 154 (Oslo 1958).

be profitable first to consider the most important reasons for and against excluding illegally seized evidence.

*In favour* of the acceptance of illegally seized evidence, it may be put forward that the task of the court is to come to a materially correct decision, and that all information, apart from that positively excluded by the law, should therefore be taken into consideration. There might be unhappy results, both in respect of the security of society and general deterrence, if persons who are blatantly guilty escape punishment simply because the evidence was obtained in an unlawful manner. This is especially important in the case of criminals who might commit grave punishable offences if not deprived of their liberty. If there is reason to reproach the police or others on account of the method in which the evidence was obtained, liability should be met in the form of punishment or other measures. If the measures which can now be applied are not considered stringent enough, stronger remedies should be considered.

*Against* the admission of illegally seized evidence, the objection can be raised that this would encourage the use of unjustified methods of investigation. For even if the guilty officer runs the risk of punishment or other sanctions, it would in practice be difficult to insure that the sanctions in fact are applied. It is clear that it is necessary to have a policeman investigate the case against another policeman, and this position, taken together with the circumstance that the illegal act was committed in the course of the fight against criminality, might easily lead to weakness in elucidation of the case and any possible penal consequences. Only if broad rules are laid down forbidding the admission of illegally acquired evidence can one hope to be able to put a stop to illegalities of this kind.

Another objection against the admission of illegally acquired evidence is that it could cause difficulties in respect of the rehabilitation of the individual offender, and besides it might reduce the general respect for the law. Experience indicates that criminals are especially sensitive to encroachment on the part of the authorities and that the feeling of having been unjustly treated

can have the effect of inducing criminality. These handicaps will, in the long run, more than counterbalance the advantage of convicting one or another criminal as a consequence of the illegal methods.

Besides, it can be claimed that it will be of little practical significance if an offender now and then should escape punishment. This is especially the case today when the suspension of prosecution or sentence has so wide an application.[15] The purpose of the prosecution often seems to be fulfilled when the case is cleared up and the offender identified, and this he generally will be, even if the evidence against him is excluded with the result that he escapes a formal sanction.

There seem to be weighty reasons in favour of both solutions, and this may well indicate that it is impractical to lay down any definite regulations in favour of one solution or the other. As far as I know, a definite choice between solutions has not been made in any country, but to a greater or lesser extent the decision has depended upon the circumstances in each particular case. In some countries, however, an attempt has been made to lay down definite solutions in certain types of cases; however, it seems to have proved difficult, even in such limited fields, to follow definite rules,[16] in the absence of compulsory legal provisions such as those in the West-German Criminal Procedure Act of 1950. This includes a provision, Section 136a, which forbids various closely defined methods of improper questioning. Evidence obtained by use of the forbidden methods cannot be admitted, even if the accused himself consents to the admission. Certainly no other country has such extensive provisions for the protection of the

[15] According to the Norwegian criminal statistics of 1958, about three out of four persons guilty of a felony (felonies may be generally defined as offenses punishable by more than three months' imprisonment) got suspended sentence or suspended prosecution. In Norway the Public Prosecution Authority may suspend prosecution though the guilt of the accused appears beyond doubt. For further information, see Bratholm, *Arrest and Detention in Norway*, 108 U. PA. L. REV. 336, 341, nn.24. 25, & 26 (1960).

[16] See COWEN & CARVER, ESSAYS ON THE LAW OF EVIDENCE 77 (Oxford 1956); Williams, *Evidence Obtained by Illegal Means*, CRIM. L. REV. (Eng.) 342 (1955); Comment, 49 J. CRIM. L., C. & P.S. 59, 63 (1958)

accused against illegal methods of questioning. These rules must be seen against the background of experiences gained by the German people under the National Socialist regime.

### IV.

When deciding whether unlawfully acquired evidence should be excluded, there are a number of points which may be taken into account.

(1) Attention should first be paid to the gravity of the unlawful procedure, whether it was wilful or inadvertent, or whether, perhaps, it was the result of completely innocent misconception of competence. In the latter case it does not seem likely that there would be any reason to exclude the evidence.

Generally speaking, a course of procedure which is punishable must be considered more grave than one to which no penalty is attached, in so far as criminal legislation gives special protection to essential interests. But there are important interests which do not lend themselves to protection by criminal law, or which have not yet attained such protection, and therefore decisive weight should not be laid on whether the course of action is a crime in law. In Anglo-Saxon law, for example, evidence has been excluded on the grounds that the method of obtaining it involved an "unfair trick" against the accused.[17]

Another important point to consider is whether material encroachment has taken place or whether there has only been a breach of the form prescribed by law. There is, for example, an essential difference between the seizure of evidence when the law positively forbids it (for example a medical case history) and the seizure of evidence when the police have failed to obtain consent of the court in a case where they could have obtained consent had they requested it. In the last mentioned case there is little to be said in favour of excluding the evidence, since the police have not acquired evidence unobtainable under the strict provisions of the law.

Generally, unlawful methods of procedure directed against the person, in the form of com-

[17] COWEN & CARTER, *op. cit. supra* note 16, at 88, 102.

pulsion, threats, and the like, must be considered more serious than unlawful acts performed in obtaining material evidence. A method of procedure is considered especially serious if it involves a breach of Section 96 of the Norwegian Constitution, which forbids questioning with torture.

(2) It must also be considered important whether the unlawful action constitutes a direct injury to the accused or whether it is harmful first and foremost to the interests of others. One can, for example, imagine that the police have acquired decisive evidence against the accused by an unlawful examination of a witness or by an unlawful search of the house of a third party. In these cases the *accused* hardly has a justifiable claim that the evidence should be excluded, since he had no control over the object produced in evidence and therefore should have been prepared for the fact that the witness or the third party might consent to the searching. On the other hand, in certain of these cases *the witness or the third party* must have the right to oppose the admission of evidence. The decision probably depends on a weighing on the one hand of the importance to justice of the admission of the evidence, and on the other hand of the extent of injury the admission could cause to the offended party.

(3) Who obtained the illegal evidence is also a significant question; it seems, generally speaking, less harsh to admit evidence unlawfully obtained by a private person than by the police, since there is no question of encroachment on the part of the authorities.

(4) Further, the type of accusation is important. The more serious the accusation, the more hesitancy must there be in excluding evidence. This is especially the case when there is a danger that the offender will commit more serious crimes if he is not imprisoned.

(5) The strength of the evidence is also probably important (if there is a basis for judging its strength). There will be little hesitancy in rejecting unlawfully obtained evidence considered to have little importance to the outcome of the case. However, in many cases, the fact that evidence was obtained unlawfully will itself lead to a serious weakening of its importance; if, for example, a

confession is obtained by force, there is little reason to pay attention to it.

(6) Lastly, an important point may arise concerning *when* an objection is raised against the unlawfully acquired evidence. The longer an accused person or his counsel waits before putting forward an objection, the weaker must that objection become, since the public prosecutor may have omitted to introduce other evidence, relying on the evidence already before the court. Moreover, difficult problems of procedure will easily arise if the accused postpones the raising of his objection, especially if he raises it for the first time after the evidence has been laid before the trial court. If evidence is to be excluded in such a case, either the court must disregard it—no easy matter when it is already known—or a new trial must be instituted, with other judges. These practical difficulties could justify the admission of evidence that ought to have been excluded had the objection been raised in time, especially when the accused is to blame for failing to object at an earlier stage.

## V.

It may be asked how the points of view given in the paragraphs above tally with court practice in Norway in respect of the admission of unlawfully obtained evidence. In reply it must be noted that it is difficult to form a reliable picture of this practice since there are so few published court decisions in Norway.

The dearth of court decisions could be taken as indicating that evidence is seldom obtained in Norway in an unlawful manner, but this would be a hasty conclusion. In this field one must assume the existence of a certain number of unknown instances of illegal seizures of evidence.

First, unlawfully obtained evidence can aid in clearing up a case without being known to anyone but the investigator concerned. For example, the investigator might come upon a trace of the guilty party's actions by unlawfully opening letters or tapping telephones. By means of such information the investigator finds a lead to other evidence, and neither during the investigation nor

later is it disclosed that the case was cleared up on the basis of unlawful means.

It must also be assumed that a certain number of accused persons who have been victims of unlawful methods of investigation omit to make a complaint on this point, either because they are not aware that the method is unlawful, or because they cannot prove that any unlawful act has been committed, or—if they can prove such an act—that there is any causal connection between the unlawful method of procedure and the evidence.

It is also possible that many accused persons and counsel in Norway doubt the possibility of excluding unlawfully obtained evidence. This too can help explain the paucity of cases in practice.

The scarcity of court decisions can also be attributed to the fact that the public prosecutor is somewhat reserved in using illegally obtained evidence, especially if the case turns on a serious illegality, both because he desires to conceal the illegality and because he considers it unfair to the accused to make use of the evidence. It may be that a fully solved criminal case is shelved where it would have been tried if the evidence had been obtained in a regular manner.

## VI.

I shall describe some cases of unlawful obtaining of evidence which have been recorded.

The first case concerned evidence obtained by means of unlawful arrest and seizure. The case concerned two Swedish citizens who had unlawfully transported a consignment of coffee from Norway over the border to Sweden, where they were arrested by Norwegian customs officials. They both accepted a fine, but later withdrew their acceptance and claimed that the decision must be quashed and the impounded coffee handed over to them because the arrest and seizure had taken place unlawfully on Swedish territory.

The judge of the Supreme Court delivering the court's opinion[18] declared that even if the customs officials had acted illegally in arresting the accused on the Swedish side of the border, this could be of no decisive importance in judging the criminal

---

[18] Norsk Retstidende (Nor. Law Rep.) 684 (1918 I).

nature of their conduct or the validity of their acceptance of the fine; the complaint was thereupon dismissed.

The second case concerned the use of unlawful methods of questioning. It involved three traitors who lay in prison in 1945 suspected of various punishable actions during the war, including the liquidation of a member of the Norwegian Resistance Movement. The accused declared themselves not guilty of the liquidation. Two constables on temporary service in the police decided they should attempt to extract a confession by taking the suspects by night to the place where the liquidation had taken place, under conditions as similar as possible to those which obtained on the night of the liquidation. The first man broke down and confessed before they had reached the spot; the second was taken there and then confessed; thereupon the third man admitted his guilt, before it was necessary to subject him to the same treatment.

The judge of the Supreme Court delivering the court's opinion[19] declared that on the occasion referred to the police had openly violated a number of procedural provisions designed for the protection of the accused, and that their action bore the stamp of a disrespect for law which was foreign to Norwegian justice and which must not be tolerated. But the court did not conclude that the confessions must therefore be excluded. The question of the admissibility of the evidence was not discussed clearly, and as far as I can see from the judgment, it was not clearly maintained by the defence that the manner in which the evidence was obtained should cause the court to disregard it completely.

There are some decisions concerning the admissibility of a statement given to the police by one closely related to the accused, when the witness was not informed by the police (as is required) of his right to refuse to make a statement, but later pleads exemption from court proceedings. The evidence can be used either by introducing the police report containing the witness's declaration or by testimony of the police officer concerning what the person questioned told him. Opinions

[19] Norsk Retstidende (Nor. Law Rep.) 46 (1948).

on the admissibility of such evidence are divided. There is no solution offered in the law, and consistent precedents are not available. In some cases evidence is admitted, but in others it is excluded.

## VII.

On the basis of the meagre precedent referred to here, we must conclude that apparently no extensive powers exist under Norwegian law to exclude unlawfully obtained evidence; nevertheless, we may not conclude that *no* such powers exist, since in the cases where such evidence has been admitted no especially strong reasons for excluding it have been present.

Little can be said in favour of quashing the conviction in the coffee smuggling case. The unlawful action of the customs officials hardly seems grave according to the information at hand. That the accused persons accepted the fine and waited to object until the time of their appeal may well have contributed to the result, even though the Supreme Court did not deal with this question.

Nor does the sentence of the Supreme Court in the case of the traitors seem open to criticism. The accusation related to the most serious crime known to criminal law, premeditated murder; moreover, even if the method of investigation was highly irregular, it can hardly be described as grave under the conditions which prevailed just after the war.

Another important point concerns the practical difficulties which probably would have arisen had the court decided to exclude the unlawfully obtained evidence in this case. It is not positively stated, but there is a strong probability that the suspects' confessions and their detailed statements on the liquidation led to the revelation of other evidence.

Had the court quashed the conviction because of the confessions, it would then have had to pass on the admissibility of the evidence brought to light as a consequence of the confessions. Much could be said in favour of excluding this evidence too, for the police would not have been able to obtain it if they had proceeded in a strictly lawful manner.

In practice it is at times difficult to distinguish between evidence directly obtained by unlawful methods, and other evidence; it may be asked how this doubt can be eliminated. Should all evidence be excluded which is a consequence of evidence obtained in an unlawful manner, or should discretion be the keynote of admission? The decision should probably be made along the lines I have mentioned earlier, that is, on the basis of such circumstances as the degree of illegality of the method of procedure, the type of crime, and so on.

In the case involving the traitors, if the charge had concerned a less serious crime, or the method of the investigation had been more reprehensible, then much could be said in favour of disregarding the evidence which was a probable consequence of the illegal proceeding. The likely result would then have been to disregard all evidence obtained after the unlawful behaviour of the police, because in practice it was not possible to make a distinction.

I also believe that elastic rules should be applicable to the taking of a deposition where the police have failed to clarify the witness's right of exemption. It is hardly practical to lay down an either-or regulation.

## VIII.

To sum up, in Norway it does not seem practicable to lay down an absolute rule in one direction or the other concerning evidence obtained in an unlawful manner, but the problem must be solved according to the circumstances in each separate case. Certain guiding principles for the decision can be put forward:

The exclusion of evidence would be difficult to support in the more excusable forms of illegality, for instance, when there is an inadvertent breach of rules or an overstepping of the bounds of legal forms prescribed for obtaining evidence.

The exclusion of evidence would also be difficult to support where there is a danger that the accused would be likely to commit dangerous crimes if allowed to go free. Generally speaking, there also seems to be little reason to exclude evidence obtained through the unlawful action of a private individual. The same applies to evidence acquired through an offence against a third party (and not directly against the accused); however, in exceptional cases consideration for the third party may require the exclusion of evidence.

There are strong reasons for excluding evidence obtained through gross, deliberate, illegal action against the accused, especially if this action has been directed against his person in the form of cruelty or other especially improper treatment. But it may be assumed that in Norway such cases will seldom occur in practice. One reason for this is that the public prosecutor will be most hesitant to offer evidence obtained by such a procedure. One may conceive of an exception where the dangerous character of the defendant speaks in favour of conviction, but in such cases the arguments for admission of the evidence would be very strong.

# Police Interrogation Privileges and Limitations

The Conference participants were asked to consider three general questions in their papers dealing with police interrogation privileges and limitations:

(1) Should the police be permitted an opportunity to interrogate an arrested person prior to taking him before a magistrate for a preliminary hearing? If so, should the provision for such delay be general (e.g., a "reasonable time" or "without unnecessary delay") or specific (e.g., four hours, twelve hours, or twenty-four hours)?

(2) Should an arrestee be entitled to counsel prior to his preliminary hearing? If so, what legal or ethical concepts should govern the prosecutor and defense counsel in their dealings with the arrestee during this pre-hearing period?

(3) What legal remedies should be available to an accused person who confessed to a crime during a period of police detention which extended beyond prescribed limits? Should he be entitled to have the confession suppressed?

The following papers deal with these questions and related problems. A summary of the American law concerning police interrogation by Professor Gerhard O. W. Mueller of New York University appears at the outset. Next appear two papers considering the problems of policy in this area by the two American participants who discussed this question, Professor Fred E. Inbau of Northwestern University and Bernard Weisberg, General Counsel for the Illinois Division of the American Civil Liberties Union. The concluding portion of Part III contains the reports of the seven foreign participants concerning the law of police interrogation in their countries.

# The Law Relating to Police Interrogation Privileges and Limitations*

GERHARD O. W. MUELLER

## DELIMITATION OF THE PROBLEM

### The Procedural Stage and Situation Type of Police Questioning

The papers in this symposium will focus on that phase of Criminal Law Administration which chronologically precedes the suspect's first contact with a judicial officer: the phase of police action against or upon a suspect. This is the most important phase of criminal procedure, for here, much more so than during trial, the case is to be won—or lost.

We shall assume that there has been contact by a police officer with one suspected of having committed a crime or at least with someone believed to know something about a crime believed to have been committed. A police officer may now enter the picture under any one of three different circumstances. He may

(1) be armed with a warrant of arrest, or

(2) have the right to make an arrest without a warrant, or

(3) he may not yet have reached the stage at which he has the right and duty to effect an arrest and thus may merely intend to elicit information from the suspect or source of information so as to lay the basis for a subsequent arrest and/or preliminary hearing, or to satisfy himself that his suspicion was unfounded and, thus, to clear the suspect.

In situations (1) and (2) the problem of questioning is not very acute. The evidence which sufficed for issuance of the warrant or for an arrest without a warrant, e.g., testimony of witnesses, real evidence, etc., will be available at a preliminary judicial hearing, just as it was available when the duty to effect the arrest arose. Further evidence, produced by lawful routine police work, is likely to be added after arrest and certainly before the case reaches the grand jury stage and, in the ordinary course of events, the case is "sewed up tight" when it goes to trial—granting, of course, that troublesome cases do arise to disturb the cozy sequence of our "ordinary course of events," especially when the evidence on which the arrest was made proves to be worthless or wrong. But the significant point is this: by demanding a relatively high degree of *provable* suspicion for arrest, the gap in the evidence requirements for arrest on the one hand,[1] and for magisterial commitment on the other,[2] is not so large as to necessitate an elaborate intermediate investigation or even insistence on confessions.[3]

[1] E.g., "reasonable ground to believe that an offense was committed and that the person against whom the complaint was made committed it." A.L.I., CODE OF CRIMINAL PROCEDURE §2, comment at 180 (1931), listing the state by state variations. For arrest without a warrant see *id.*, §21, comment at 231.

[2] "If it appears that any offense has been committed and that there is probable cause to believe the defendant guilty thereof, . . ." ALI, CODE OF CRIMINAL PROCEDURE §55, comment at 311 (1931); compare *id.*, §40.

[3] E.g., in comparison with the low degree of suspicion sufficient for arrest under the 17th and 18th century European penal codes, which, to bridge the gap, relied strongly on the extraction of confessions after arrest. Reliance on the method of torture was

* For relevant views on this topic published after oral delivery of this paper, see *Symposium, Police Questioning*, [1960] CRIM. L. REV. 298–356, with papers by Ian Brownlie, Glanville Williams, T. C. Smith and Christopher Williams. See also Stevens, *Confessions and Criminal Procedure—A Proposal*, 34 WASH. L. REV. 542 (1959); Note, 36 N.D.L. REV. 133 (1960).

The difficult cases are those under (3), where no legally sufficient evidence is available to warrant the arrest of one or several suspects, but where a crime certainly has been committed. It is under these circumstances that the police, not only driven by their own sense of urgent duty but also whipped into action by public opinion (the press), are most frequently tempted to resort to means and methods through which they expect a swift solution of the case, although the law may not approve of these means and methods. We shall have to concentrate, therefore, on this third situation type without, however, neglecting the other two.

In further delimiting and defining the subject of our inquiry it is worth pointing out that American law grants every citizen, even the worst ex-convict, a rather extensive right to speak or to keep silent when he pleases, subject, of course, to the limitation of practical wisdom that a person found under very incriminating circumstances who fails to give a reasonable explanation can blame only himself if an officer of the law takes permissible steps to determine the lawfulness or unlawfulness of his activity.[4] By the same token, the police have a virtually unlimited right to ask questions. They are not entitled to any answers, and whether or not they will receive any answers depends very much on their skill, their reputation and the time and circumstances of the questioning. In my own police experience I have learned that it is much easier to get answers from a suspect whom one engages in a friendly interview (chat) at his home, before sufficient evidence for an arrest has been accumulated, than from an arrestee at the station house. Somehow the suspect clams up at the station house and the chance for easy response is lost once and for all. True, the suspect's answers given at his home prior to arrest are quite likely false. So much the better! False answers are the wedge which will ultimately split the block. Involvement in contradictions, false alibis, etc., will render the ultimate conviction of the suspect *without his further personal participation* relatively easy. (At the same time, the innocent suspect is much more at ease in his own home and is saved the embarrassment of an appearance at the station house.) I therefore view with distrust and disfavor any argument to advance the arrest stage so as to acquire earlier custody of a suspect for the purpose of questioning him at the station house. It is my considered opinion that such would not tend toward greater efficiency in detection. There is, of course, no scientifically acceptable, empirical evidence available to substantiate the point, although comparative studies between American jurisdictions are possible since some American states know something like an arrest on mere suspicion,[5] while the American majority view is otherwise, at least theoretically.

## The Types of Questioning: Interview-Interrogation-Inquisition

Having determined the procedural stage and

---

believed necessary in view of the investigator's difficulties which lack of facilities for swift long-range communication posed, a difficulty with which the modern investigator is no longer faced. In general see SCHMIDT, EINFÜHRUNG IN DIE GESCHICHTE DER DEUTSCHEN STARFRECHTSPFLEGE §§7–76 (1951).

[4] The extent to which the statutes granting arrest rights for failure to give a good account of oneself are merely codifications of this common sense notion or exceed the bounds of legality, is of no interest in this connection. See, e.g., N.J. REV. STAT. §2:2002–16 (1937); 2 O'REGAN & SCHLOSSER, CRIMINAL LAWS OF NEW JERSEY §1814 (1942), see also *id.*, §1799, and cases cited there.

[5] For earlier efforts to legalize arrest on suspicion for the purpose of questioning, especially under the Uniform Arrest Act, see Warner, *The Uniform Arrest Act*, 28 VA. L. REV. 315, 320–21 (1942), patterned after some state statutes, especially Massachusetts, GEN. LAWS c. 41, §98 (1932). For an account of police practice in the thirties, see WAITE, CRIMINAL LAW IN ACTION cc. VII–IX (1934). For more recent accounts see MORELAND, MODERN CRIMINAL PROCEDURE c. 4 (1959). The practice is still with us and perhaps even increasing! For statutory sanction in Missouri see State v. Cantrell, 310 S.W.2d 866 (Mo. 1958). On arrest for refusal to identify and account for oneself under suspicious circumstances, see note 4, *supra*.

An aura of doubt surrounds the car-stop cases in which the officer "arrests" the progress of the occupants, for the purpose of questioning, but not (yet) for the purpose of an arrest. For more detailed discussion see Mueller, *Criminal Law and Administration—1960 Annual Survey of American Law*, 36 N.Y.U.L. REV. 111, 130 (1961).

situation type at which police questioning occurs, we must now identify the types of questioning which are employed. The type of questioning which operates without restraint of the suspect is frequently called interviewing. Even judges violently opposed to sharp questioning methods are willing to grant the police the right to interview sources of information, or, indeed, suspects, prior to arrest.[6] The interview, highly important for successful criminal investigation, should be distinguished from two other forms of questioning with which we are much more concerned. The *Army Field Manual on Criminal Investigation*, for example, makes the distinction between

> "*interviews*, which are conducted to learn facts from persons who may have knowledge of a wrongful act but who are not themselves implicated; and interrogations, which are conducted to learn facts and to obtain admissions or confessions of wrongful acts from persons who are implicated in a wrongful act. Persons who have been interviewed may later be interrogated."[7]

The third type of questioning is sometimes called "inquisition,"[8] and it differs from interrogation mainly in intensity and a higher degree of concomitant restraint.

We may proceed henceforth under the assumption that police officers do conduct interviews and interrogations, and perhaps even inquisitions, with the aim of gathering information leading to the solution of unsolved crime, that they do hope to obtain admissions and confessions, that they like confessions very much, regarding them as virtually tantamount to a conviction.

## THE MARK OF UNLAWFULNESS OF QUESTIONING

Although, as we shall see, determination of the unlawfulness of a given type of questioning by direct criteria is neither impossible nor unknown,

the determination is commonly made in terms of the procedural-evidentiary consequences. It is the answer to the question whether a confession will be sanctioned as evidence in court which ultimately permits us to draw a conclusion about the lawfulness of the type of questioning from which the confession resulted.

Some confessions, and thus some types of questioning, are regarded as quite proper and approvable by the courts, while others are regarded as obnoxious, improper, objectionable and unlawful. We must, therefore, seek to ascertain the mark of unlawfulness of a confession in terms of its evidentiary fate.

### Exclusion of Confessions

The only really significant mark of unlawfulness of a confession under federal law is its exclusion from evidence.[9] The rule in the states is no different on principle, although only in a minority of states is there full identity of unlawfulness of the mode of obtaining the confession and its exclusion from evidence, while in a majority unlawfulness of the questioning does not necessarily lead to exclusion from evidence. The point is too well known to require any annotation. In this majority of the states, therefore, not even exclusion from evidence can serve us as a safe criterion. In those states our test of unlawfulness is, in essence, a symptomatic one derived from those factual criteria which make for unlawfulness and exclusion in the exclusionary jurisdictions.

There may be other or additional consequences of procuring a confession in an unlawful manner, and it might be contended that those other consequences could serve us as a mark, e.g., cause of action for damages against the police officer, the department, the municipality or state,[10] causes of action on the delinquent officer's bond,[11] disciplinary proceedings, or even criminal punish-

[6] E.g., Bazelon, J., dissenting in Heideman v. United States, 259 F.2d 943, 947 (D.C. Cir. 1958), *cert. denied*, 359 U.S. 959 (1959).

[7] DEPARTMENT OF THE ARMY, CRIMINAL INVESTIGATION 36 (Field Manual 19–20, 1951).

[8] Watts v. Indiana, 338 U.S. 49 (1949); see also Ashcraft v. Tennessee, 322 U.S. 143, 152 n.6 (1943).

[9] Weeks v. United States, 232 U.S. 383 (1914), applicable to all illegally obtained evidence.

[10] E.g., see Wakat v. Harlib, 253 F.2d 59 (7th Cir. 1958); Hargrove v. Town of Cocoa Beach, 96 So.2d 130 (Fla. 1958), not a confession case; Houghtaling v. State, 175 N.Y.S.2d 659 (Ct. Cl. 1958).

[11] In general, see Branton, *Financial Responsibility of Police Officers*, 19 LAW. GUILD REV. 52 (1959).

ment of those who procure what ad hoc is determined to have been an unlawful questioning. But all these consequences are collateral and quite clearly of secondary significance. In fact, they are unreal, since rarely employed and rarely successful.

Whether exclusion from evidence is the proper and preferable method for achieving what society wants to achieve remains to be discussed after we decide what it really is that we want to achieve.

### The Purpose of Exclusion of Confessions

Ultimately all rules of criminal procedure and evidence serve two goals: conviction of those guilty under law and acquittal of those innocent under law. For this purpose we need, first of all, trustworthy and reliable evidence. We cannot do better than to convict or to acquit on the basis of reliable evidence. This and no more was postulated by all the older confession cases. But another line of cases soon began to test the lawfulness of a confession—and thus of the questioning which produced it—in terms of the degree of voluntariness with which it had been made. But the voluntariness cases pursued no other goal than the trustworthiness cases, as Inbau rightly pointed out,[12] the theory simply being that compulsion renders what would otherwise be a trustworthy confession completely unreliable. But many judges made it quite clear that they also meant to apply that old stimulus-response theory on which all law rests: the exclusionary rule was to serve as stimulus on law enforcement officers to cause them to abstain from undesirable practices in the eliciting of confessions.[13] This reasoning supposed that the police and prosecutors would like to maintain a relatively unblemished record of convictions and so would refrain from objectionable practices which might lead a court to tarnish this record by a directed acquittal or reversal of conviction. Thus, the second purpose of the exclusionary rule was a disciplinary one, and few have doubted that it is proper for courts to thus discipline the subalterns of an arm of the court, the prosecution.[14]

There is much speculation on whether or not the stimulus-response hypothesis is borne out by practical experience. Empirical research has not been done, so that we must simply continue to guess. Professor Inbau, our country's leading expert in the matter, believes that practice does not support the supposition.[15] From my personal practical experience as a police officer, working under the English Judges' Rules, I am inclined to think otherwise, namely that members of a professional police force will do what is necessary to obtain a conviction record to which they can point with pride, and they will abstain from practices which might jeopardize such a record, whether they agree with the courts' reasoning or not.

### The General Legal Framework of Unlawfulness

(a) *Constitutional and Evidentiary Limitations*

In the *good old days*, state and federal courts employed largely their own limitations in determining the unlawfulness of a confession. A fair body of common law precedents as to what constituted voluntariness and trustworthiness[16] formed the background for later decisions under state constitutional due process provisions and under the federal Fifth Amendment due process provision,[17] as well as under the general supervisory power of the United States Supreme Court over the federal judiciary.[18]

[12] INBAU, LIE DETECTION AND CRIMINAL INTERROGATION 150 (2d ed. 1948).

[13] McCormick, *The Scope of Privilege in the Law of Evidence*, 16 TEX. L. REV. 447 (1938); Allen, *The Supreme Court, Federalism and State Systems of Criminal Justice*, 8(1) U. of Chi. L.S. Rec. 3, 11 (1958), citing cases.

[14] Inbau argued that "the fundamental concept of a three-fold division of power seems to indicate that there is no authority for any court to exercise disciplinary control over the police." Inbau, *Law and Police Practice: Restrictions in the Law of Interrogation and Confessions*, 52 Nw. U.L. REV. 77 (1957).

[15] Inbau, *The Confession Dilemma in the United States Supreme Court*, 43 ILL. L. REV. 442, 460 (1948).

[16] For the then prevailing line of authority, see Wilson v. United States, 162 U.S. 613 (1895); Hopt v. Utah, 110 U.S. 574 (1884). The earliest American case in point I have been able to locate is State v. Hobbs, 2 Vt. 380 (1803).

[17] In general, see Allen, *op. cit. supra* note 13, and the works by Inbau, cited herein.

[18] In McNabb v. United States, 318 U.S. 332, 341 (1942), Justice Frankfurter supports the point by authority. But apart from Rule 5, Federal Rules of Criminal Procedure, and Fifth Amendment cases, the

But by 1936 local police forces all over the United States had so irritated and antagonized the public and the Supreme Court with *Gestapo* and *K.P.U.* methods,[19] that the Court felt compelled to begin its supervision of state practice under the authority of the Fourteenth Amendment, with both mentioned goals in mind.[20] Regardless of the admissibility of a confession in a state court, federal due process would now invalidate a conviction based on a confession obtained through questioning in violation of the federal standard. For a while, therefore, the practice as to the unlawfulness of confessions and questionings was identical for both federal (Fifth Amendment) and state (Fourteenth Amendment) courts, at least as far as the *strictly constitutional minimum* limit is concerned. And with this proviso, such is still the state of the law today.

(b) *The Federal Rules: Delay*

But *federal* practice was to change less than a decade after the usefulness of the Fourteenth Amendment as an anti-coerced-state-confession weapon had been discovered by the Supreme Court. The Federal Rules of Criminal Procedure just being under consideration, the Court found a new weapon against non-conforming federal officers and prosecutors in a statute which was just standing model for the creation of Federal Rule 5(a), requiring production of an arrestee before a U. S. Commissioner *forthwith* (in case of arrest with warrant) or *without unnecessary delay* (in case of arrest without a warrant). Inbau traced

the origin of this rule and found that it had been created to prevent federal marshals from cheating the government on mileage fees in delivering prisoners.[21] This original purpose, of course, did not prevent the Court from seizing upon the rule to make it serve any other purpose which the language of the statute permits.

Although the Court had previously talked about holding federal officers to decent standards of law enforcement, it was not until *McNabb* v. *United States* that the Court for the first time talked freely of its supervisory functions,[22] civilized police practices, and the dangers inherent in delaying the production of an arrestee before a judicial officer (incommunicado detention), all adding up to the rule that, trustworthy or not, a confession is tainted when procured by uncivilized practices, and unnecessary delay, in violation of Federal Rule 5, may well furnish the proof of uncivilized practices.[23]

Since that decision the Court has adhered to its rule,[24] slowly overcoming the reluctance of federal trial courts to direct an occasional acquittal. *Upshaw* and *Mallory* are the milestones on the road from *McNabb*.[25] Under these cases the test of unlawfulness is not one measurable by the length of detention, in minutes and hours, preceding the production of an arrestee before the commisioner or judge but, essentially, it is a test of reasonableness of effort to produce the arrestee promptly,

---

Court has not really *made* any evidence rules on confessions. Wan v. United States, 266 U.S. 14 (1924), cited by Justice Frankfurter in *McNabb*, as supporting the Court's power to create rules of evidence, had not actually *made* any such rule. While in laying down the standard it did not refer to the Fifth Amendment, it relied on cases decided under the Fifth Amendment, at 14, n. 5.

[19] Especially as revealed by the Wickersham Commission Report, IV REPORTS OF NATIONAL COMMISSION ON LAW OBSERVANCE AND ENFORCEMENT (1931).

[20] Brown v. Mississippi, 297 U.S. 278 (1936); followed by Ashcraft v. Tennessee, 322 U.S. 143 (1944), originating the "inherently coercive" doctrine; Malinsky v. New York, 324 U.S. 401 (1944); Haley v. Ohio, 332 U.S. 596 (1947); and see Brown v. Allen, 344 U.S. 443 (1953), as to the scope of supervision and review.

[21] Inbau, *op. cit. supra* note 15.

[22] McNabb v. United States, 318 U.S. 332 (1943); Anderson v. United States, 318 U.S. 350 (1943), a case of collaboration with state officers.

[23] This is not a constitutional but only a rule-interpreting decision. Note that in *McNabb* there was both delay and subtle psychological pressure.

[24] United States v. Mitchell, 322 U.S. 65 (1944), is sometimes cited as inconsonant with the mainstream of cases. Strictly speaking this is incorrect. Mitchell was a confession-delay case, the others are delay-confession cases, so that the inducement factor is the distinguishing criterion. The only surprising aspect of *Mitchell* is Justice Frankfurter's statement that the Supreme Court's power to shape rules of evidence "is not to be used as an indirect mode of disciplining misconduct," *id*. at 17, which appears inconsistent with the rationale of *McNabb, Upshaw, supra* note 18, and *Mallory, infra* note 25.

[25] Upshaw v. United States, 335 U.S. 410 (1948); Mallory v. United States, 354 U.S. 449 (1957).

leaving unaffected civilized standard inquiries under the Fifth Amendment.[26]

All this leaves federal officers somewhat in doubt in the execution of their sworn duties. Theoretically they must forthwith, or without unnecessary delay,—note the difference in terminology, depending on the nature of the arrest—take each arrestee before a judicial officer. Obviously, if no judge is available, they cannot do so but must, I suppose, stand ready to prove effort, good faith and unavailability of a judge.[27] The police may, *of course*, properly discharge their administrative duties connected with arrest, and such is not violative of the anti-delay rule.[28] Perhaps, since the rule governing delay after arrest without a warrant is phrased in terms of necessity, the officer may even question the arrestee

> "immediately after an arrest, provided the interrogation is not prolonged. . . . The rule of the Mallory case is that a seven and one-half hour delay is too long. Where the line is to be drawn must be determined according to the usual process of the common law by judicial decisions as cases arise. A graph must be gradually plotted by a series of rulings on specific states of facts. . . ."[29]

[26] Note that, of course, prompt arraignment provisions are to be found in the constitutions or statutes of most states as well. For citations see McNabb v. United States, 318 U.S. 332, 343–44, n.7 (1942).

[27] E.g., Porter v. United States, 258 F.2d 685 (D.C. Cir. 1958).

[28] In a recent case this took less than one hour. Heideman v. United States, 259 F.2d 943 (D.C. Cir. 1958). Compare an older state decision in which a one hour delay was held to be unlawful, Harness v. State, 159 Ind. 286, 64 N.E. 875 (1902).
How many hours does discharge of the administrative routine duties actually consume? In New York City, for example, "it may mean eight or ten more hours beyond the regular working schedule to take the prisoner through the involved procedures of *booking, identification* and *arraignment in court*." Phillips, *New York's Finest—Again under Fire*, N.Y. Times Mag., March 1, 1959, p. 14, at 31. Note that Puttkammer speaks of possible overnight detention *prior to booking*. (Does this imply idle detention or a night of questioning?) PUTTKAMMER, MANUAL ON CRIMINAL LAW AND PROCEDURE §127 (Chicago Crime Commission, 1946). " 'Every time I make an arrest,' said a New York Officer, 'I know it is more than just another notch for my record—it's a cold supper and an unhappy wife.' " Phillips, *supra*, at 34.

[29] Holtzoff, J., in Heideman v. United States, 21 F.R.D.

At least, such is the opinion of an informed District Court Judge who helped draft Rule 5. While I cannot agree with the judge that the ultimate test is one which measures necessity of the delay, or unlawfulness of the delay, with a stop watch,—there is no indication that the Supreme Court is willing to sanction such a test—I certainly concur with the learned judge that officers may indeed question the arrestee under the law as it stands now. Any rule forbidding a police officer from talking to his suspect might be applicable on the Moon, but even there it would have to be changed after arrival of the first rocket load of earthlings.

Judge Bazelon, the vigorous and libertarian District dissenter, opposes the District Court interpretation of Mallory,[30] but even he would grant the police the right to question a suspect prior to arrest, as noted. But this itself is a dangerous rule unless we make certain that the privilege extends to interviews only, not to interrogations or inquisitions,—all to be further defined. But once arrested, it is Judge Bazelon's belief that the suspect ought to be immediately arraigned before a magistrate, so that he may be advised of his rights. Speaking about the majority's position contra, Judge Bazelon thundered:

> "They say such a procedure is actually for the benefit of the arrested person because it gives him a chance to avoid being formally charged before a magistrate. I think it is the height of irony that the arrested person's greatest protection—his right to be brought before a magistrate under Rule 5—should be treated as an evil to be avoided."[31]

This exemplifies the presently raging controversy over the Supreme Court's anti-delay ruling. Which way the Court will now turn is anybody's

335, 339 (D.D.C. 1958), *aff'd*, 259 F.2d 943 (D.C. Cir.) *cert. denied*, 359 U.S. 959 (1959).

[30] Heideman v. United States, 259 F.2d 943, 947–50 (D.C. Cir. 1958), *cert. denied*, 359 U.S. 959 (1959).

[31] Id. at 949–50. Other recent cases are discussed in Mueller, *Criminal Law and Procedure, 1958 Annual Survey of American Law*, 34 N.Y.U.L. REV. 83, 104–05 (1959); Mueller, *Criminal Law and Procedure, 1959 Annual Survey of American Law*, 35 N.Y.U.L. REV. (1960).

guess: Is all federal police questioning ultimately to be outlawed? Is it outlawed only if it postpones production before a magistrate?[32] If so, the federal police will have to time their arrests to one minute after the courts close their doors. A confession obtained prior to the reopening of the court's doors would be as lawful as the long questioning which produces it. To avoid such a subterfuge, the Court can hold only that a properly guarded and fairly conducted non-coercive questioning, with all cautions and rights extended, lasting only a very brief spell of time,[33] and a confession so produced, will be lawful, i.e., the confession will be admissible.[33a] Realities of police work seem to call for at least that much leeway, if for no other reason than to guide magistrates in properly conducting the preliminary hearing *and* to save a suspect, properly arrested without a warrant, whose innocence can be ascertained by a few questions, the embarrassment of a magisterial hearing. It is unrealistic not to admit that a magisterial hearing may severely and adversely affect a citizen's reputation. The further a suspect is shoved up on the ladder of criminal proceedings prior to ultimate determination of the issue, the greater is the adverse effect on his reputation.[33b]

Although some scholars fear that the Court is headed in the direction of extending its unreasonable delay-civilized standards test to govern state proceedings,[34] the Court certainly has not said *expressis verbis* that it even considered such a possibility.[34a] As late as 1951 the Court declared a state detention of twenty-five days prior to arraignment—the confession having been rendered on the fifth day—not to be violative of Fourteenth Amendment due process.[35] This is certainly more than a liberal measure,[36] and all indications are to the effect that the proven Fourteenth Amendment due process test will continue to be applied to the states, most of which are in basic agreement with the Supreme Court anyway, although professing to reject Mallory, *et al.*

## THE FORMS OF QUESTIONING

Disregarding the problem of unnecessary detention for questioning, we are now squarely faced with the forms which lawful or unlawful questioning may take. What type of questioning is actually being practiced by the police, and where is the limit of the permissible, i.e., where does unlawfulness begin, expressed through rejections of confessions in the elusive terminology of due process? Some day, perhaps, a line might be drawn between lawful and unlawful questioning of an arrestee in terms of inquisition and interrogation. So far these terms are little more than

---

[32] See Justice Reed's opinion in Porter v. United States, *supra* note 27.

[33] In *Mallory*, the Court said that Rule 5 (a) contemplates "a procedure that allows arresting officers little more leeway than the interval between arrest and the ordinary administrative steps required to bring a suspect before the nearest available magistrate." 354 U.S. at 453. The crucial words are "little more leeway." Read against the *Mitchell* case, phrased in terms of one willing to make a confession, here may lie the real answer to the troublesome question.

[33a] After completion of the manuscript so held in Goldsmith v. United States, 277 F.2d 335 (D.C. Cir. 1960), where Burger, J., strongly indicated that confessions made during a one and a half hour questioning with a one hour typing of the confession, with necessary interruptions, were not inadmissible, *id.* at 342–45, and held, moreover, that judicial permission may be granted for police to continue the interrogation while the suspect is in the marshal's custody after judicial hearing, and such later confession would stand. *Id.* at 340–42.

[33b] *Ibid.*, per Burger, J.

[34] Collings, *Criminal Law and Administration*, in 1957 ANNUAL SURVEY OF AMERICAN LAW 92, 109.

[34a] What is likely to happen, however, is that the Supreme Court will doubly extend the Elkins doctrine (Elkins v. United States, 364 U.S. 206 (1960); and see Rios v. United States, 364 U.S. 253 (1960), generated by Hanna v. United States, 260 F.2d 723 (D.C. Cir. 1958)), to Fifth Amendment confession cases and to federal supervisory (extra-constitutional) standards. Elkins v. United States, decided under the Court's federal supervisory power—but with strong references to the Fourth and Fourteenth Amendments—took the predicted step of overruling the (search and seizure) "silver platter" doctrine by holding that "evidence obtained by state officers during a search which, if conducted by federal officers, would have violated the defendant's immunity from unreasonable searches and seizures under the Fourth Amendment is inadmissible over the defendant's timely objection in a federal criminal trial." *Id.* at 223.

[35] Gallegos v. Nebraska, 342 U.S. 55 (1951).

[36] For Indiana's exclusion of a confession after a one hour delay, see Harness v. State, *supra note* 28.

epithets applied to a particular questioning procedure after it has been outlawed for whatever reasons.

Since police officers do not tell us when they violate the law or even when they are operating close to the line, we must search for evidence dehors the police blotter, the era of police boasting about third degree method having long passed.[37] We can judge only by what is taught to police officers in their training manuals, by what is revealed through the press, and by what occasionally gets into the courts.

The police manuals and textbooks consulted for this purpose would unquestionably find judicial endorsement. They speak of the reasonable opportunity which the law affords for questioning suspects. They warn against oppressive practices, generally not going overly into detail, but do not warn against employment of the typical investigators' tricks in questioning.[38]

At least occasionally, actual practice seems to vary from the standards taught at police academies. In the City of Chicago, in 1957, the sheriff's police in the Grimes Sisters murder case were reported to have held a suspect incommunicado for five days and to have *grilled* him severely, producing a confession which did not jibe with the physical facts.[39] Later similar scandals have occurred in Chicago and elsewhere so that the older disreputable police practices described by all the authors of the thirties may still be found, although, fortunately, on a much reduced scale.

It is this *grilling* in which we are here interested. I think that we may find four basic methods of *grilling* a suspect,—but I would not wish to attempt a differentiation in terms of interrogation and inquisition.

*(1) Questioning with Accompanying Brutality*

We shall start with the *grilling* in its most vicious form, the brutal coercion of a confession. There is no question whatsoever that any form of physical abuse to extract a confession (*third degree*[40]), or, indeed, any information, is and always has been highly unlawful in this country.[41] Charges of brutality on the part of the police are still frequently voiced and occasionally substantiated.[42] No statistics and no field research can establish how prevalent the practice is, but I suppose that the unashamed answers of a New York police lieutenant in the middle of the Twentieth Century are indicative of the situation in at least some police departments today:

"Q. And it was perfectly all right with you to have these prisoners beaten and knocked around, wasn't it?

A. Perfectly all right for them to be knocked down, yes, sir.

Q. And beaten? Is that right? It was in accordance with your wishes?

A. Not wishes.

[40] The origin of the term "third degree" is uncertain. Moreland takes it as derived from Russian interrogation practice, under which cross examination constituted the first degree, confrontation the second and severe physical duress the third. MORELAND, *op. cit. supra* note 5, at 91, citing Ripley's Believe It or Not. Webster's NEW WORLD DICTIONARY OF THE AMERICAN LANGUAGE 1516 (1953) indicates that the term might well be derived from the masonic initiation into the third degree, a traditionally rigorous exercise and test. (Like practices seem to prevail with some other fraternal organizations.) Another possible source is the *Peinliche Gerichtsordnung* of Empress Maria Theresia of Austria, of December 31, 1768 (*Constitutio Criminalis Theresiana*), which knew three degrees of suspicion and probable cause. The least degree of suspicion entitled the prosecution to "special investigation," the next higher degree of suspicion to an arrest, and the third degree of suspicion ("half proof") to application of torture. All three degrees together constituted the "inquisitorial procedure" which, of course, was conducted in secrecy. See LOHSING-SERINI, ÖSTERREICHISCHES STRAFPROZESSRECHT 15 (1952).

[41] Brown v. Mississippi, 297 U.S. 278 (1936).

[42] Among recent cases are: United States *ex rel.* Alvarez v. Murphy, 246 F.2d 871 (2d Cir. 1957); see also United States *ex rel.* Wade v. Jackson, 256 F.2d 7 (2d Cir.), *cert. denied,* 357 U.S. 908 (1958); United States v. Cummings, 154 F. Supp. 663 (D. Conn. 1956); People v. Speaks, 156 Cal. App. 2d 25, 319 P.2d 709 (1958), virtually unbelievable in this country.

[37] MORELAND, *op. cit. supra note* 5, at 95.

[38] E.g., HOUTS, FROM ARREST TO RELEASE 75–77 (1958); PUTTKAMMER, *op. cit. supra note* 28, §127. In general, see also MACHEN, THE LAW OF ARREST §45 (1950). DAX & TIBBS, ARREST, SEARCH AND SEIZURE 52, 98–101 (1946); SMITH, LAW OF ARREST, SEARCH AND SEIZURE 14 (1956).

[39] HOUTS, *op. cit. supra* note 38, at 77. In private conversation, I was informed by a sheriff's deputy that Houts is in error. The five day holding was done by the Chicago City Police.

Q. But you were satisfied?

A. Yes, sir."[43]

I should merely like to suggest that the criminal law with its sanctions against assault and battery is available and should be rigorously applied to violating officers. In fact, it might be worth considering an increase in the punishments for assault and battery committed during performance of official duties. Other possible protections can best be discussed below.

### (2) Questioning under Psychological Coercion

The next type of questioning relies on torment, the creation of mental stress, anxiety, tiring-out, etc., so as to induce the subject to make a confession. It is here where we are encountering major legal difficulties, there being no clear-cut guide by the Supreme Court, but only a score of sometimes hard-to-reconcile cases.[44] Having neither the time nor the inclination to reiterate what has been competently and repeatedly discussed in dozens of law review articles, I shall restrict myself to a summary: The official test of the Court still seems to be that of the *Ashcraft* line of cases which outlaws "inherent compulsion" in questioning, meaning sustained police pressure in the nature of mental torture, especially through relentless overbearing of the will—in short, inquisitorial methods.[45] But this objective test gains meaning only through what appeared to be a conflicting line of cases, starting with *Stein* v. *New York*,[46] which is regarded as having introduced a subjective standard. Stated differently, in my opinion *Stein* merely certified the rather obvious fact that what may be "inherently compulsive"

as to one suspect, may not be "inherently compulsive" as to another. In determining compulsiveness subjectively, the Court looks at a number of criteria, recently excellently summarized in a student note:

"1) number of questioners;

2) health, age, education and race of the defendant;

3) time held incommunicado;

4) delay before arraignment;

5) length of questioning, deprivation of refreshment, rest or relief during questioning;

6) threats or promises of benefit made;

7) hostility of questioners;

8) defendant's experience in ways of crime; and

9) living conditions during detention."[47]

Two recent examples may serve to demonstrate the test in action:

In *People* v. *Speaks*, the suspect was arrested shortly after she had had an epileptic seizure. She was kept up all night and questioned to exhaustion, was not informed of her constitutional rights, was not taken before a magistrate until six days after her arrest, was denied a phone call and an attorney, and was, during all this time, confined in a dark, damp, dingy basement cell together with drunks, and in a psychopathic ward together with psychopaths, was continuously interrogated for hours at a time, including at night time, was refused food and comforts, and was subjected to an electroencephalograph test for which needles were injected into her scalp, to

---

[43] Quoted in United States *ex rel*. Wade v. Jackson, 256 F.2d 7, 11 (2d Cir.), *cert. denied*, 357 U.S. 908 (1958).

[44] For a discussion of the trends, and especially the frolic and detour of Stein v. New York, 346 U.S. 156 (1952), see Cohn, *Federal Constitutional Limitations on the Use of Coerced Confessions in the State Courts*, 50 J. CRIM. L., C. & P.S. 265 (1959). See also Meltzer, *Involuntary Confessions—The Allocation of Responsibility Between Judge and Jury—A Comment on Stein v. People of the State of New York*, 21 U. CHI. L. REV. 317 (1954).

[45] Ashcraft v. Tennessee, 322 U.S. 143 (1944); Watts v. Indiana, 338 U.S. 49, 53–54 (1949).

[46] 346 U.S. 156, 185 (1952).

[47] Note, 33 NEB. L. REV. 507, 508 (1954), a comment on the *Stein* case, and reviewing all the appeals from state courts, since 1939; Stroble v. California, 343 U.S. 181 (1951); Gallegos v. Nebraska, 342 U.S. 55 (1951); Harris v. South Carolina, 338 U.S. 681 (1948); Turner v. Pennsylvania, 338 U.S. 62 (1948); Watts v. Indiana, 338 U.S. 49 (1948); Haley v. Ohio, 332 U.S. 596 (1947); Malinsky v. New York, 324 U.S. 401 (1944); Ashcraft v. Tennessee, 322 U.S. 143 (1944); Lyons v. Oklahoma, 322 U.S. 596 (1943); Ward v. Texas, 316 U.S. 547 (1942); Lisenba v. California, 314 U.S. 219 (1941); and numerous convictions reversed without opinion, a total of 17 cases on which the Court was divided and ten on which it was unanimous, between 1939 and 1954. The author also tabulated the voting records of the judges.

a depth of ¼ to ⅜ of an inch, producing intense pain. She confessed.[48] This case comes rather close to actual police brutality.

A case of more subtle mental torment arose in the Yale city of New Haven in 1954. Defendant, a negro with an eighth grade education, forty-eight years old, was suspected of murder and held incommunicado. The questioning police officer threatened the recalcitrant suspect (Rogers) with bringing in "for questioning Roger's [arthritic] wife if Rogers did not confess. He threatened to send the two foster children of the Rogerses, who were state wards, to an institution meanwhile," and "made a pretended telephone call on a dead wire to hold a car and officers in readiness to get Mrs. Rogers and the children. He then gave Rogers an hour to make up his mind whether to confess. At the end of that time he took the phone to pretend to order Mrs. Rogers and the children brought in. At this point Rogers gave in and made a confession."[49] Needless to say, such a method is highly unlawful and probably even constitutes inherent compulsion[49a] regardless of the subjective factors of the defendant's personality.[50]

(3) *Questioning with Trickery and Deceit*

The third method of questioning is marked by the use of trickery and deceit not amounting to compulsion, *i.e.*, not creating fear, anxiety or despair. The holdings are virtually unanimous that trickery and deceit on the part of the questioner, as long as not amounting to torment, are not unlawful.[51] *The Army Field Manual on Criminal*

*Investigation* does not advocate outright deceit, but it does endorse false emotional displays, false sympathies, and the like.[52] Similarly, Inbau, in his work on the subject, accepts the employment of false though realistic emotional displays during questioning,[53] and has practiced this method rather successfully himself.[54] He rationalizes that "at times the interrogator must deal with the criminal offender in a somewhat lower moral plane than that in which ethical, law-abiding citizens are expected to conduct their ordinary affairs."[55] The courts, *nolens volens*, appear to accept this reasoning. But even the moralist must agree that at least the *soft-touch* method is ethically unobjectionable. Merely by way of example, when a Scotland Yard Officer once had to interrogate a group of American sailors of the "gangster" or "bully" type, he employed the soft-touch method, talked about their mothers and girl friends and finally got them "in such a state of pathetic sentimentality and homesickness that one man broke down and wept,"—and confessed.[56]

The variations between deceit, sympathy falsely portrayed, false emotional display and the soft-touch method in its even less objectionable forms need not interest us any further since all these methods, so far, are judicially regarded as lawful.[57]

---

[48] People v. Speaks, 156 Cal. App. 2d 25, 319 P.2d 709 (1958).

[49] United States *ex rel*. Rogers v. Cummings, Reincke v. Tillinghorst, 154 F. Supp. 663 (D. Conn. 1956).

[49a] The Supreme Court decided the case just in time for insertion in this article. The test is, indeed, whether or not there was compulsion, i.e., overbearing of the will, and not whether the confession was trustworthy: Rogers v. Richmond, 81 S. Ct. 735 (1961) (with two justices dissenting).

[50] But see Edwards v. United States, 256 F.2d 707 (D.C. Cir. 1958), Bazelon, J., dissenting, where suspect was suffering from narcotics withdrawal pains, questioning to gain confession, holding transfer to hospital in abeyance until confession obtained, does not seem to amount to an unlawful torment.

[51] See Dession, Freedman, Donnelly, Redlich, *Drug-Induced Revelations and Criminal Investigation*, 62 YALE L.J. 315, 333, n.58 (1953), citing 3 WIGMORE,

EVIDENCE §841 (3d ed. 1949); INBAU, LIE DETECTION AND CRIMINAL INTERROGATION 175 (2d ed. 1948).

[52] DEPARTMENT OF THE ARMY, *op. cit. supra* note 7, at 51.

[53] INBAU, *op. cit. supra* note 12, at 105–149.

[54] Llewellen, *How to Make a Killer Confess*, Sat. Eve. Post, March 31, 1956, pp. 33, 99–100, an article on Professor Inbau.

[55] INBAU, *op. cit. supra* note 12, at 149. On a later occasion Inbau realized that, after all, the suspect may turn out to be just another law abiding citizen, rather than a criminal offender. Inbau, *The Confession Dilemma in the United States Supreme Court*, 43 ILL. L. REV. 442, 447 (1948), where he added "criminal suspects who may actually be innocent," but persisted in the "low plane" approach. See also *id.* at 451; and Inbau, *Law and Police Practice: Restrictions in the Law of Interrogation and Confession*, 52 Nw. U.L. REV. 77 (1957). This drew criticism from Judge Leibowitz in Leibowitz, *Law and Police Practice: Safeguards in the Law of Interrogation and Confessions*, 52 Nw. U.L. REV. 86 (1957).

[56] MARTIENSSEN, CRIME AND THE POLICE 74 (1951).

[57] "Sympathy falsely aroused," was condemned in Spano v. New York, 360 U.S. 315 (1959), but only

*(4) The Employment of Scientific Means or Devices During Questioning*

*(a) The polygraph.* There is, first of all, questioning with the aid of the polygraph, the so-called lie detector. We are here not interested in the question of admitting polygraph test results into evidence. Our problem is that of questioning with the aid of the polygraph to obtain confessions, admissions or information. While the experts lay great stress on the scientific perfection of the device during recent years,[58] courts are still reluctant to fully endorse questioning with the aid of the lie detector. (Are they, perhaps, merely using the scientific imperfection argument to avoid the issue of the ethical justification for probing man's innermost spheres?[59]) Test results, standing like admissions, are at least admissible in evidence when both parties had consented to such examination.[60] But since the defendant's protection is restricted to exclusion of the test results from evidence, seemingly the police may use the lie detector for questioning, i.e., as an investigative tool, and if only to scare a given suspect into making a confession before the test with this fearsome machine is actually conducted.[61] Such would, by some holdings, not amount to an unlawful interrogation practice.[62] In concluding

the subject of the polygraph interrogation, I should like to point to the *Statement of Principles Regarding Polygraph ("Lie Detector") Examinations*, adopted by the American Academy of Polygraph Examiners in 1957, which should dispel many doubts as to the intentions and motives of polygraph examiners, so that, at least in that respect, we need not be overly fearful.[63]

If we encounter objection to the employment of the polygraph in questioning suspects, it usually rests on two considerations: (1) the teleological, or foot-in-the-door argument, i.e., that once the practice receives outright sanctioning, the salesman will have his foot in the door and ultimately, through permissible comment at trial, we will add "lie detector sex offenders" to "fifth Amendment Communists."[64] The second consideration is an emotional one. It is powerful, though it rarely breaks loose from the subconscious strata: the polygraph chair (and, for that matter, the electroencephalograph chair) does not look unlike the electric chair!

*(b) Questioning with depth-psychiatrical methods.* The courts have been more explicit with respect to interrogations conducted with the aid of hypnosis, narcosis, or other forms of partial removal of inhibitions, especially when induced by the administration of drugs.[65] Confessions elicited by such methods have been struck down throughout,[66] notwithstanding that an odd conviction may be upheld where a drug administered to an addict in custody, to alleviate narcotic addiction withdrawal pains, may also have rendered

---

when accompanied by official pressure, fatigue or other factors.

[58] In general, see INBAU, *op. cit. supra* note 12; Levitt, *Scientific Evaluation of the "Lie Detector"*, 40 IOWA L. REV. 440 (1955).

[59] In general, see Silving, *Testing the Unconscious in Criminal Cases*, 69 HARV. L. REV. 686 (1956). For frank European standpoints see Kaganiec, *Lie Detector Tests and "Freedom of the Will" in Germany*, 51 Nw. U.L. REV. 446, 47 J. CRIM. L., C. & P.S. 570 (1957). See also 39 J. CRIM. L. & C. 665 (1949), for the French point of view.

[60] People v. Houser, 85 Cal. App. 2d 686, 193 P.2d 937 (1948); see also George, *Scientific Investigation and the Defendant's Rights*, 57 MICH. L. REV. 37 (1959). There is a paucity of holdings in point.

[61] Commonwealth v. Jones, 341 Pa. 541, 19 A.2d 389 (1941); State v. De Hart, 242 Wis. 562, 8 N.W.2d 360 (1943); see also Bennet, *The Arson Investigator and Technical Aids*, 49 J. CRIM. L., C. & P.S. 172, 176 (1958), for the experiences of the Detroit arson investigators.

[62] I.e., no coercion: People v. Sims, 395 Ill. 69, 69 N.E.2d 366 (1946); Brunner v. People, 113 Colo. 194, 156 P.2d 111 (1945).

[63] 48 J. CRIM. L., C. & P.S. 568 (1958).

[64] Silving, *op. cit. supra* note 59, at 692, n.39.

[65] In general, see Dession, Freedman, Donnelly, Redlich, *op. cit. supra* note 51; Muehlberger, *Interrogation Under Drug Influence*, 42 J. CRIM. L., C. & P.S. 513 (1951).

[66] E.g., Dugan v. Commonwealth, 333 S.W.2d 755 (Ky. 1960), and see George, *op. cit. supra* note 60, at 50, n.70, citing Leyra v. Denno, 347 U.S. 556 (1954); Lindsey v. United States, 237 F.2d 893 (9th Cir. 1956); State v. Lindemuth, 56 N.M. 257, 243 P.2d 325 (1952); People v. Leyra, 302 N.Y. 353, 98 N.E.2d 553 (1951); State v. Puseh, 77 N.D. 860, 46 N.W.2d 508 (1950). But psychologists or psychiatrists employing scientific tests may testify to the defendant's condition: People v. Esposito, 287 N.Y. 389, 93 N.E.2d 925 (1942); *but cf.* People v. Ford, 304 N.Y. 679, 107 N.E.2d 595 (1952).

the arrestee talkative enough for production of a confession.[67]

## SUMMARY OF THE LAW—THE CRUCIAL ISSUES—CONCLUSION

### The Law

We may now summarize: Federal officers may *probably* question a suspect in a civilized, non-coercive manner for a brief spell of time. Federal officers have a "little leeway," but, after an arrest without a warrant, may not cause unnecessary delay. This seems to imply a very limited right to ask questions. After an arrest with a warrant, the federal officer must produce the suspect promptly (forthwith) before a judge. Questioning in this case seems to be impermissible, nor, indeed, is it necessary. State officers may hold and question their suspects for a longer period—provided most probably that the evidence is not to be used in federal courts—, subject only to the prompt hearing mandates of their own state constitutions or statutes. Beyond that, federal due process under the Fifth and Fourteenth Amendments imposes limitations on the type and manner of questioning suspects. Whenever there is a right to interrogate, civilized standards must be followed. And while there is an absolute limit beyond which the questioner must never venture, most cases will probably be judged subjectively on the issue of coerciveness employed in questioning. Trickery and deceit alone will not invalidate a confession *ipso facto*, but mental and physical torment will.

Can law enforcement operate successfully within these restrictions? My answer would be yes, provided a number of caveats be observed.

1) The incompetent, unintelligent or untrained police officer does not have a chance to work successfully within these limits. As Inbau advocated strongly, police professionalisation is the answer on this point.[68]

2) Police attitude on the timing of the arrest must change materially. Many police officers "prejudge a suspect's guilt and make their arrest too soon."[69] Arrest, unless *flagrante delicto*, should not be made until the police have independently gathered enough information to warrant a binding-over to the grand jury by the examining magistrate.

3) Interviewing of a possibly concerned person has legal and psychological advantages over interrogation of an arrestee. The police ought to work more with interviews, less with interrogations.

4) Interviewing is successful only when the police enjoy the respect of the community. This respect it can gain by avoiding oppressive practices.[70] If one police officer is oppressive—and goes unpunished—the entire department will share the disrepute, and the community will be very reluctant to cooperate in responding to questions or otherwise.

---

[67] Sheedy, *Narcointerrogation of a Criminal Suspect*, 50 J. CRIM. L., C. & P.S. 118 (1958), commenting on People v. Townsend, 141 N.E.2d 729 (Ill. 1957), noted at 52 Nw. U.L. REV. 666 (1957); 24 BROOKLYN L. REV. 96 (1957). See also Griffith v. Rhay, 177 F. Supp. 386 (E.D. Wash. 1959).

[68] Inbau, *op. cit. supra* note 15, at 460.

[69] HOUTS, *op. cit. supra* note 38, at 76.

[70] Consider, for example, the simple device of informing an arrestee of his rights, perhaps even of posting them at the station house. This will create respect and rarely, if ever, interferes with the success of the investigation. Such is the new practice in New Orleans, see United States v. Sigler, 162 F. Supp. 256 (E.D. La. 1958), from which case note 4 is worth quoting:

A placard bearing the following information is now prominently displayed in each police station in the City of New Orleans:

"Right of Arrested Persons
"These Are Some of Your Rights Under the Laws of the United States and the State of Louisiana
"Right to Call Lawyer
" 'All persons arrested shall, from the moment of their arrest, be entitled to confer with counsel * * *.' (L.S.A.-R.S. 15:77)
"Right to Use Telephone
" 'They (arrested persons) shall be given the right and privilege of using the telephone in the jail or station or send a messenger for the purpose of communicating with counsel and with his friends and relatives for the purpose of securing counsel. They shall also have the right and privilege of using the telephone in the jail or station or send a messenger for the purpose of communication with any person, firm or corporation in order to secure their release by bail or parole.' (L.S.A.-R.S. 15:77)
"Right to Bail
" 'In all * * * cases (other than capital cases) the person accused shall be entitled to bail. The amount of the (bail) shall be fixed with consideration of the

5) The importance of confessions is overemphasized in America.[71] Independent preliminary leg and brain work, and especially scientific detection, are often more significant in solving a case than confessions.

## The Crucial Issues: Exclusion or Not

A question we posed at the outset remains unanswered. *Above and beyond* guaranteeing that convictions will not stand on untrustworthy evidence, is the exclusionary rule the best possible stimulus for obtaining from the police the desired response of civilized practices?

The Supreme Court has taken a thoroughly moral and typically American position: Even if trustworthy, it would be immoral for the state to utilize a confession obtained by what common mores, as ascertained by the Court, regarded as uncivilized. The government must not become *particeps criminis* to the wrongdoing of individual police officers. I do believe that most of our professional police officers are moral enough to

seriousness of the offense charged, the previous criminal record of the (person accused) and the probability or improbability of his appearing at the trial * * *.' (L.S.A.-R.S. 15:86)
"Right to Remain Silent
" 'No person shall be compelled to give evidence against himself in a criminal case or in any proceeding that may subject him to criminal prosecution * * *. No person under arrest shall be subjected to any treatment designed by effect on body or mind to compel confession of crime; nor shall any confession be used against any person accused of crime unless freely and voluntarily made.' (Article I, Section II, Louisiana [L.S.A.-] Constitution, 1921.")
The Massachusetts Attorney General has printed and distributed to police departments a pamphlet entitled "If you were arrested," for dissemination to arrestees. This pamphlet describes the arrestee's rights. Christian Science Monitor, Feb. 1, 1960, p2, cols. 6–8.
[71] Kennedy, *Some Practical Suggestions for the Taking of Criminal Confessions*, 48 J. CRIM. L., C. & P.S. 660 (1958); Schroeder, *New Procedures of Scientific Investigation and Protection of the Accused's Rights*, 49 J. CRIM. L., C. & P.S. 265 (1958); Edwards, *New Procedures of Scientific Investigation and the Protection of the Accused's Rights*, IV. B. I. Int. Acad. Comp. L. 5th Congr., Brussels, p. 189 (1958). On the efficient and intelligent investigation method of revenue agencies, see Murphy, *The Investigative Procedure for Criminal Tax Evasion*, 27 FORDHAM L. REV. 48 (1958).

go along with this reasoning or, at least, are conviction-eager enough to respond to the stimulus. If an individual officer is not responsive, he ought to be dismissed on short order.

But what if it could be established that exclusion has not yielded the expected results, that we have deceived ourselves all along? How else could civilized standards in conducting police interrogations be secured?

The ordinary criminal, civil, and administrative (disciplinary) remedies have been mentioned already. They are available now, and not even in conjunction with the exclusionary rule do they seem to constitute an effective remedy. (Or does the exclusionary rule work so well that in those jurisdictions there is no need to resort to the more direct remedies against violating officers?)

Nor should we expect relief by threatening imprisonment to police officers who violated civilized standards. Although the police usually are in favor of expanding the coverage of the criminal law, I do not think they would like such a new crime on the statute book. Moreover, privacy being essential for successful questioning,[72] proof of uncivilized practices, especially mental coercion, "beyond a reasonable doubt," would be hard to render. To void a conviction, on the other hand, the coercion need not be established beyond a reasonable doubt, so that the exclusionary rule seems preferable for practical reasons.

A third choice would lie in making police questioning a public matter, by permitting the public (and thus the press and ultimately perhaps newsreel and TV photographers) to be present.[73] But the price to be paid would be so high in terms of detriment to the suspect and the community (the investigating state authority) as to render such a plan worthless in practice. Semi-publicity might have greater promise, i.e., questioning conducted only if an attorney, relative or other confidant of the arrestee is present. Foreign countries, e.g., Sweden and Germany, have wider experience with the arrestee's right to call in a friend or relative, and we should be eager to

[72] Inbau, *op. cit. supra* note 15, at 447.
[73] See Mr. Justice Black's dissent in In re Groban, 352 U.S. 330, 340–43 (1957).

learn about their experiences. Immediately, of course, the question arises, how we should enforce this right to the presence of a confidant. By an exclusionary rule, or by what? *Quis custodiet custodes?* It is the same old problem!

This, finally, brings us to the problem of the right of representation by counsel at this preliminary stage of criminal procedure. It has been suggested that the mandatory presence of an attorney right after arrest will solve all our problems. (No one, so far, has suggested that a prospective arrestee should be warned to engage an attorney so that the waiting officer may then make an arrest.)

Mr. Allison has presented the arguments pro candidly and skillfully in a recent article. His points are:

"I. This is the only Way to Make Real the Recognized Rights and Safeguards that We Say an Accused Has Under Our Form of Government;
II. This Guarantee Will Help Prevent Use of Third Degree Methods and Extra-Legal Interrogations;
III. Advice of Counsel Early After Arrest Will Improve the Quality of Police Investigation;
IV. Counsel Early in the Proceedings Will Put the Poor Defendant on the Same Footing as Those Able to Pay;
V. Early Representation Will Enable the Defendant to Prepare His Defense, Thereby Affording Equal Justice."[74]

Law enforcement officers are opposed to such an extension of existing rights to representation because they

"desire to question the accused or consolidate their case by securing additional evidence unhampered by the professional tactics of an attorney. An attorney, if he were obtainable would advise the prisoner to answer no questions, in most cases he would secure the prisoner's immediate release on bail, in any event he would slow down tremendously the tactics which are occasionally employed during the period between arrest and the preliminary examination."[75]

The reality of the right to the assistance of retained counsel at the police inquest stage depends largely on the resolution of the issues already discussed. If police officers have no right to question their suspects, but must immediately surrender them to a magistrate, there is neither need nor opportunity to hail counsel to the station house. Procurement of counsel might cause delay beyond the time necessary for booking the prisoner, and a friendly police officer who would shelve the proceedings until the arrival of counsel might actually be violating federal due process.

But if and where a reasonable period for police questioning is accorded, the presence of an attorney in watch dog capacity will unquestionably prevent use of coercive police methods, whether or not there be need for any legal advice to the client. Therefore, my demands for postponing the arrest until the time when questioning of the suspect is no longer of paramount importance has even more validity if the right to presence of counsel at the station house is universally recognized.

What is the status of this right? The laws of the states vary widely, ranging all the way from a flat denial of either retained or appointed counsel at this preliminary stage to criminal penalty provisions against officers who fail to grant an arrestee the right to consult with retained counsel.[76] Until but a few years ago it could be safely said that

"the right of the defendant to obtain legal advice is almost wholly controlled by the discretion of the officers who have him in custody, and that an abuse by them of the right will bring no more than a judicial reprimand in form of a declaration that the officers have been overzealous in the performance of their duties."[77]

But in 1958, the Supreme Court felt compelled

---

[74] Allison, *He Needs a Lawyer Now*, 42 J. Am. Jud. Soc'y 113, 114, 115, 116, 118, 119 (1958).

[75] Moreland, *op. cit. supra* note 5, at 173.
[76] Ill. Rev. Stat. c. 38 §449.1.
[77] Note, *Right to Counsel Prior to Trial*, 44 Ky. L.J. 103, 107 (1955). The older law is nicely summarized in Moreland, *op. cit. supra* note 5, at 172–79.

to assert its powers over state police practice, under the due process clause of the Fourteenth Amendment. Seizing upon a dictum in *Powell* v. *Alabama* that the defendant "requires the guiding hand of counsel at every step in the proceeding against him,"[78] the Court in *Crooker* v. *California* added the dictum that

"state refusal of a request to engage a counsel violates due process not only if the accused is deprived of counsel at trial on the merits, ... but also if he is deprived of counsel for any part of the pre-trial proceedings, provided that he is so prejudiced thereby as to infect his subsequent trial with an abuse of 'that fundamental fairness essential to the very concept of justice.' "[79]

But the Court found that "the sum total of the circumstances here during the time petitioner was without counsel ... do not show petitioner to have been so 'taken advantage of' ... as to violate due process of law."[80] On a similar fact situation, and reaching the same result, the Court in *Cicenia* v. *Lagay* added that under its general supervisory power over the federal judiciary the result might well have been different.[81]

With these Fourteenth Amendment due process cases we now have a subjective test for the determination of unlawful refusal of the assistance of counsel at the police inquest stage (with respect to capital cases?). The test aims directly at the civilized practices—anti-coercion standard familiar to us from the cases dealing directly with questioning. Thus, in specific cases, subjectively judged, abusive denial of legal assistance, for coercive purposes, is one of the factors to be used—an important one at that—to determine coerciveness

of police practices in violation of the Fourteenth Amendment.[82] If we now ask ourselves the question how to enforce this right to counsel at the police inquest stage, we have, as in the folk song "Dear Lisa," reached the first stanza again. The circle is complete. Exclusion of the confession rendered in the absence of counsel or not?

But there remains one last possibility, not very obvious to Americans. We could deprive the police of all right to question their suspects and turn our lower judiciary and commissioners into French-style examining magistrates. At the magisterial inquest stage the right to be represented by counsel of choice, or, in many cases and jurisdictions, to have counsel assigned, is already an existing practice. The examining magistrate, however, would have to become an inquisitor. But this question we better defer until we hear from our European colleagues about their experience with the *juge d'instruction* or *Untersuchungsrichter*.

## Conclusion

Our views on questioning and confessions are still tainted by medieval traditions, when circumstantial evidence or witness' testimony never sufficed to convict a person. For the sake of his soul, the medieval defendant had to confess, whether he liked it or not, and capital execution without a confession would have been regarded as immoral everywhere, and as illegal in many continental jurisdictions.[83] Well, standards of morality have changed! We no longer hesitate to convict absent a confession, and rightly so. Hence, there is no longer a need for abusive questioning, or, indeed, in many cases for any questioning at all. A professional police renders its proof in a

---

[78] Powell v. Alabama, 287 U.S. 45, 68–69 (1932); see also Chandler v. Freytag, 348 U.S. 3 (1954). The history of the Court's use of the 14th Amendment to safeguard the right to representation by counsel in general, through the "traditional process of inclusion and exclusion," starting with Betts v. Brady, 316 U.S. 455 (1942), is retraced in Cash v. Culver, 79 S. Ct. 432, 435 (1959).

[79] Crooker v. California, 357 U.S. 433, 439 (1958), quoting, in part, from Lisenba v. California, 314 U.S. 219, 236 (1941).

[80] Crooker v. California, *supra* note 79, at 440. There were four dissents.

[81] Cicenia v. Lagay, 357 U.S. 504, 509 (1958).

[82] In general, see Allen, *op. cit. supra* note 13, at 10.

[83] Such was the philosophy of the Constitutio Criminalis Carolinae, the penal code of Emperor Charles V, whose jurisdiction extended over the Americas as well. During the 19th Century this code of 1533 still had subsidiary force in some remnants of the then defunct Holy Roman Empire, and as late as 1824 (the code's latest edition known to me) the torturing of suspects was regarded as more feasible and moral than either an acquittal, or a punishment without a confession. KOCH (ed.), HALS—ODER PEINLICHE GERICHTS-ORDNUNG KAISER CARLS V 6–12 (1824).

professional manner very much without the defendant's personal participation and not by what today is a morally and legally abusive practice.[84]

[84] After conclusion of this manuscript, the Supreme Court handed down its unanimous decision in Blackburn v. Alabama, 361 U.S. 199 (1960), finding that the extraction of a confession from a most likely insane and incompetent escapee from an insane asylum, in a session lasting more than seven hours, conducted in a dingy room filled with police officers, amounted to "an unconstitutional inquisition." The unanimity of the Court is noteworthy and lends encouraging support to the views expressed in this paper. See also note 49a, *supra*.

# Police Interrogation — A Practical Necessity

FRED E. INBAU

One completely false assumption accounts for most of the legal restrictions on police interrogations. It is this, and the fallacy is certainly perpetuated to a very considerable extent by mystery writers, the movies, and TV: whenever a crime is committed, if the police will only look carefully at the crime scene they will almost always find some clue that will lead them to the offender and at the same time establish his guilt; and once the offender is located, he will readily confess or disclose his guilt by trying to shoot his way out of the trap. But this is pure fiction; in actuality the situation is quite different. As a matter of fact, the art of criminal investigation has not developed to a point where the search for and the examination of physical evidence will always, or even in most cases, reveal a clue to the identity of the perpetrator or provide the necessary proof of his guilt. In criminal investigations, even of the most efficient type, there are many, many instances where physical clues are entirely absent, and the only approach to a possible solution of the crime is the interrogation of the criminal suspect himself, as well as others who may possess significant information. Moreover, in most instances these interrogations, particularly of the suspect himself, must be conducted under conditions of privacy and for a reasonable period of time; and they frequently require the use of psychological tactics and techniques that could well be classified as "unethical," if we are to evaluate them in terms of ordinary, everyday social behavior.

To protect myself from being misunderstood,

I want to make it unmistakably clear that I am not an advocate of the so-called "third degree," for I am unalterably opposed to the use of any interrogation tactic or technique that is apt to make an innocent person confess. I am opposed, therefore, to the use of force, threats, or promises of leniency—all of which might well induce an innocent person to confess; but I do approve of such psychological tactics and techniques as trickery and deceit that are not only helpful but frequently necessary in order to secure incriminating information from the guilty, or investigative leads from otherwise uncooperative witnesses or informants.

My position, then, is this, and it may be presented in the form of three separate points,[1] each accompanied by case illustrations:

*1. Many criminal cases, even when investigated by the best qualified police departments, are capable of solution only by means of an admission or confession from the guilty individual or upon the basis of information obtained from the questioning of other criminal suspects.*

As to the validity of this statement, I suggest that consideration be given to the situation presented by cases such as these. A man is hit on the head while walking home late at night. He did not see his assailant, nor did anyone else. A careful and thorough search of the crime scene reveals no physical clues. Then take the case of a women who is grabbed on the street at night

[1] The writer has presented and discussed these three points in various other published papers, both before and since they were presented at the International Conference on Criminal Law Administration in February, 1960. See: 43 Ill. L. Rev. 442 (1948); 52 Nw. U.L. Rev. 77 (1957); 3 Crim. L.Q. (Canada) 329 (1960); 3 N.U. Tri-Q. 3 (1961).

and dragged into an alley and raped. Here, too, the assailant was unaccommodating enough to avoid leaving his hat or other means of identification at the crime scene; and there are no other physical clues. All the police have to work on is the description of the assailant given by the victim herself. She described him as about six feet tall, white, and wearing a dark suit. Or consider this case, an actual recent one in Illinois. Three women are vacationing in a wooded resort area. Their bodies are found dead alongside a foot trail, the result of physical violence, and no physical clues are present.

In cases of this kind—and they all typify the difficult investigation problem that the police frequently encounter—how else can they be solved, if at all, except by means of the interrogation of suspects or of others who may possess significant information?

There are times, too, when a police interrogation may result not only in the apprehension and conviction of the guilty, but also in the release of the innocent from well-warranted suspicion. Here is one such actual case within my own professional experience.

The dead body of a woman was found in her home. Her skull had been crushed, apparently with some blunt instrument. A careful police investigation of the premises did not reveal any clues to the identity of the killer. No fingerprints or other significant evidence were located; not even the lethal instrument itself could be found. None of the neighbors could give any helpful information. Although there was some evidence of a slight struggle in the room where the body lay, there were no indications of a forcible entry into the home. The deceased's young daughter was the only other resident of the home and she had been away in school at the time of the crime. The daughter could not give the police any idea of what, if any, money or property had disappeared from the home.

For several reasons the police considered the victim's husband a likely suspect. He was being sued for divorce; he knew his wife had planned on leaving the state and taking their daughter with

her; and the neighbors reported that the couple had been having heated arguments, and that the husband was of a violent temper. He also lived conveniently near—in a garage adjoining the home. The police interrogated him and although his alibi was not conclusive his general behavior and the manner in which he answered the interrogator's questions satisfied the police of his innocence. Further investigation then revealed that the deceased's brother-in-law had been financially indebted to the deceased; that he was a frequent gambler; that at a number of social gatherings which he had attended money disappeared from some of the women's purses; that at his place of employment there had been a series of purse thefts; and that on the day of the killing he was absent from work. The police apprehended and questioned him. As the result of a few hours of competent interrogation—unattended by any abusive methods, but yet conducted during a period of delay in presenting the suspect before a committing magistrate as required by state statute—the suspect confessed to the murder. He told of going to the victim's home for the purpose of selling her a radio, which she accused him of stealing. An argument ensued and he hit her over the head with a mechanic's wrench he was carrying in his coat pocket. He thereupon located and took some money he found in the home and also a diamond ring. After fleeing from the scene he threw the wrench into a river, changed his clothes and disposed of the ones he had worn at the time of the killing by throwing them away in various parts of the city. He had hidden the ring in the attic of his mother's home, where it was found by the police after his confession had disclosed its presence there. Much of the stolen money was also recovered or else accounted for by the payment of an overdue loan.

Without an opportunity for interrogation the police could not have solved this case. The perpetrator of the offense would have remained at liberty, perhaps to repeat his criminal conduct.

2. *Criminal offenders, except, of course, those caught in the commission of their crimes, ordinarily*

*will not admit their guilt unless questioned under conditions of privacy, and for a period of perhaps several hours.*

This point is one which should be readily apparent not only to any person with the least amount of criminal investigative experience, but also to anyone who will reflect momentarily upon the behavior of ordinary law-abiding persons when suspected or accused of nothing more than simple social indiscretions. Self-condemnation and self-destruction not being normal behavior characteristics, human beings ordinarily do not utter unsolicited, spontaneous confessions. They must first be questioned regarding the offense. In some instances, a little bit of information inadvertently given to a competent interrogator by the suspect may suffice to start a line of investigation which might ultimately establish guilt. Upon other occasions, a full confession, with a revelation of details regarding a body, the loot, or the instruments used in the crime, may be required to prove the case. But whatever the possible consequences may be, it is impractical to expect any but a very few confessions to result from a guilty conscience unprovoked by an interrogation. It is also impractical to expect admissions or confessions to be obtained under circumstances other than privacy. Here again recourse to our everyday experience will support the basic validity of this requirement. For instance, in asking a personal friend to divulge a secret, or embarrassing information, we carefully avoid making the request in the presence of other persons, and seek a time and place when the matter can be discussed in private. The very same psychological factors are involved in a criminal interrogation, and even to a greater extent. For related psychological considerations, if an interrogation is to be had at all, it must be one based upon an unhurried interview, the necessary length of which will in many instances extend to several hours, depending upon various factors such as the nature of the case situation and the personality of the suspect.

The practical psychological requirement of privacy during a police interrogation calls, of course, for a consideration of the issue of an accused person's constitutional right to counsel. Does the right to counsel come into being at the time of arrest, or only at the time of trial, or perhaps at the time the judicial process begins (e.g., preliminary hearing, indictment, etc.)? And if the right to counsel starts at the time of arrest, or at some other stage prior to the trial itself, what about the legal validity of a confession obtained at a time when the accused was denied access to counsel? The answers to these questions are of considerable importance to all concerned.

If the right to counsel arises only at the time of trial, or even when the judicial process begins, as at a preliminary hearing or at the time of indictment, the police have at least some opportunity for an interrogation. On the other hand, if the right is considered to exist immediately upon arrest, the interrogation opportunity, for all practical purposes, is gone—because of the prevailing concept that the role of defense counsel is to advise his client, "keep your mouth shut; don't say anything to anybody."

That an accused person is entitled to counsel at the time of trial is a proposition that should and must stand unchallenged. It may also be conceded that the right to counsel should be considered to exist just as soon as the judicial process begins (e.g., preliminary hearing, indictment, etc.), although the case law over the years is to the effect that the right to counsel arises only in a proceeding that adjudicates guilt or innocence; in other words, it arises at the trial itself, and not at any pre-trial hearing.[2] However, there are several reasons for not extending the right beyond the judicial process stage. First of all, the constitutional right to counsel provision itself refers only to the right in "criminal *prosecutions*." Moreover, anyone exploring this right to counsel issue must also consider the United States Supreme Court decision in *Betts* v. *Brady*,[3] to the effect

[2] See Comment, 107 U. PA. L. REV. 286 (1958), and cases cited therein.

In Spano v. New York, 360 U.S. 315 (1959), the concurring opinion drew the "right to counsel" line at the point where the judicial process begins; in this particular case, upon the indictment of the accused.

[3] 316 U.S. 455 (1942).

that, with respect to indigent defendants, a state is under no due process requirement to appoint counsel in non-capital cases. As the majority opinion points out, the due-process line has to be drawn somewhere; otherwise counsel would have to be provided for an indigent person in a civil case involving a risk of property deprivation, since the due process guarantee prevails with respect to property as well as to life and liberty.

In my judgment the right to counsel at the time of trial, or even at the very start of the judicial process, should be accorded *and provided* to all indigent defendants, insofar as practicable, regardless of whether the case involves a capital or non-capital offense, or even if it amounts only to a misdemeanor. What I do object to is an extension of the right to arrestees, indigent or non-indigent, prior to the start of the judicial process. It is not constitutionally required, and practical considerations will not tolerate such an extension, and particularly so if the extension is supplemented by a rule of court that would nullify, as a violation of due process, a confession obtained during a period of police detention before the start of the judicial process. Moreover, sometime in the near future we will have to come to grips with this interrogation problem and consider the passage of legislation, by all the states as well as the federal government, which will specifically provide for a reasonable period of police detention for the interrogation of suspects who are not otherwise unwilling to talk.

The United States Supreme Court—or at least the majority thereof—has sensed the implications, insofar as the states are concerned, of a rule of law that would hold the right to counsel to exist at the time of arrest. The Court was confronted with this issue in the 1958 cases of *Crooker* v. *California*[4] and *Cicenia* v. *La Gay*,[5] in both of which state police officers had obtained confessions from arrestees who had previously requested but were denied the benefit of legal counsel. In 5-4 decisions the Court held that there was no due

[4] 357 U.S. 433 (1958).
[5] 357 U.S. 504 (1958).

process violation and that the confessions were therefore admissible in evidence.

It is of interest to note the consideration which the majority of the Court gave to the position urged upon it by defense counsel in these two cases: "It can hardly be denied," states the majority opinion, "that adoption of petitioner's position would constrict state police activities in a manner that in many instances might impair their ability to solve difficult cases." Also, according to the majority, "the doctrine suggested by petitioner would have a . . . devastating effect on enforcement of criminal law, for it would effectively preclude police questioning—*fair as well as unfair*—until the accused was afforded opportunity to call his attorney." The Court may well have added, "who would tell him to keep his mouth shut."

Regarding the routine advice of counsel to an arrestee to remain silent and refuse to answer questions put to him by the police, it is my suggestion that the legal profession give serious consideration to the adoption of an alternative practice, which would require counsel to say to his client, the arrestee: "Although you do not have to say anything, my advice to you is that you discuss this matter with the police and that you tell them the truth; I'll stand by to protect you from any harm or abuse." With the advent of such a change in the ethical concept of the role of counsel, we might then be able to say that all arrestees should be entitled to counsel from the time of their arrest. As matters now stand, however, public protection and safety require that we adhere to the present viewpoint that there is no right to counsel during the investigative, non-judicial stage of the case.

3. *In dealing with criminal offenders, and consequently also with criminal suspects who may actually be innocent, the interrogator must of necessity employ less refined methods than are considered appropriate for the transaction of ordinary, everyday affairs by and between law-abiding citizens.*

To illustrate this point, permit me to revert to the previously discussed case of the woman who was murdered by her brother-in-law. His confession was obtained largely as a result of the interrogator adopting a friendly attitude in questioning the suspect, when concededly no such genuine feeling existed; by pretending to sympathize with the suspect because of his difficult financial situation; by suggesting that perhaps the victim had done or said something which aroused his anger and which would have aroused the anger of anyone else similarly situated to such an extent as to provoke a violent reaction; and by resorting to other similar expressions, or even overtures of friendliness and sympathy such as a pat on the suspect's shoulder or knee. In all of this, of course, the interrogation was "unethical" according to the standards usually set for professional, business and social conduct. But the pertinent issue in this case was no ordinary, lawful, professional, business or social matter. It involved the taking of a human life by one who abided by no code of fair play toward his fellow human beings. The killer would not have been moved one bit toward a confession by subjecting him to a reading or lecture regarding the morality of his conduct. It would have been futile merely to give him a pencil and paper and trust that his conscience would impel him to confess. Something more was required— something which was in its essence an "unethical" practice on the part of the interrogator. But, under the circumstances involved in this case, how else would the murderer's guilt have been established? Moreover, let us bear this thought in mind. From the criminal's point of view, *any* interrogation of him is objectionable. To *him* it may be a "dirty trick" to be talked into a confession, for surely it was not done for his benefit. Consequently, any interrogation of him might be labeled as deceitful or unethical.

Of necessity, criminal interrogators must deal with criminal offenders on a somewhat lower moral plane than that upon which ethical, law-abiding citizens are expected to conduct their everyday affairs. That plane, in the interest of innocent suspects, need only be subject to the following restriction: Although both "fair" and "unfair" interrogation practices are permissible, nothing shall be done or said to the subject that will be apt to make an innocent person confess.

If all this be so, why then the withholding of this essential interrogation opportunity from the police? And we do, insofar as the stated law is concerned. It comes in the form of statutes or rules that require the prompt delivery of an arrested person before a magistrate for a preliminary hearing or arraignment. Moreover, the United States Supreme Court has decreed that in federal cases no confession is to be received in evidence, regardless of its voluntariness or trustworthiness, if it was obtained during a period of unnecessary delay in delivering the arrestee to a federal commissioner or judge for arraignment. In the federal jurisdiction of Washington, D. C., which must cope with a variety of criminal offences and problems similar to any other city of comparable size, this federal court rule has had a very crippling effect on police investigations.[6]

One incongruity of the prompt arraignment rule is this. It is lawful for the police to arrest upon *reasonable belief* that the arrestee has committed the offense, following which they must take him before a magistrate, without unnecessary delay, and charge him with the crime; but for legal proof of the charge, his guilt at the time of trial must be established *beyond reasonable doubt*. Moreover, when the accused gets into the hands of a magistrate for the preliminary hearing, the opportunity for an effective interrogation is ended, many times because of the advice he receives from his attorney to keep his mouth shut.

If we view this whole problem realistically, we must come to the conclusion that an interrogation opportunity is necessary and that legislative provision ought to be made for a privately con-

---

[6] In addition, some concern should be exhibited over the risk involved in freeing obviously guilty offenders as a result of the courts' efforts to discipline the police. For instance, following the Supreme Court's reversal of his rape conviction, and his release from custody, the defendant in Mallory v. U.S., 354 U.S. 449 (1957), committed two other offenses against female victims. For the latest one he was found guilty and sentenced to the penitentiary by a Pennsylvania Court. For further details, see INBAU & SOWLE, CASES AND COMMENTS ON CRIMINAL JUSTICE 643 (1960).

ducted police interrogation, covering a reasonable period of time, of suspects who are not unwilling to be interviewed, and that the only tactics or techniques that are to be forbidden are those which are apt to make an innocent person confess.

At one time it was fashionable in the United States for jurists and law professors to refer to the "Judges' Rules" which the English and Canadian courts have laid down for the "guidance" of police interrogators, and say: "If the British and Canadian police can be effective under such rules, then our officers have no cause to complain." Such naïveté seems to have dissolved since the appearance in print of the frank admissions of at least two prominent English police officials to the effect that the Judges' Rules could not be honored because of practical limitations. These writers actually revealed how the Rules were circumvented—by the simple devices of (a) postponing the time when the officers were satisfied of the guilt of the person they were interrogating, and (b) by pretending to search only for ambiguities when questioning a person already in custody.[7]

---

[7] One such acknowledgment was made by the Chief Constable of County Durham, England: St. Johnston, *The Legal Limitations of the Interrogation of Suspects and Prisoners in England and Wales*, 39 J. CRIM. L. & C. 89 (1948). Another such acknowledgment was made by the Commander of the Criminal Investigation Department, New Scotland Yard, London,

There are other ways to guard against abuses in police interrogation short of taking the privilege away from them. Moreover, we could no more afford to do that than we could stand the effects of a law requiring automobile manufacturers to place governors on all cars so that, in order to make the highways safe, no one could go faster than twenty miles an hour.

The only real, practically attainable protection we can set up for ourselves against police interrogation abuses (just as with respect to arrest and detention abuses) is to see to it that our police are selected and promoted on a merit basis, that they are properly trained, adequately compensated, and that they are permitted to remain substantially free from politically inspired interference. In the hands of men of this competence there will be a minimum degree of abusive practices. And once again I suggest that the real interest that should be exhibited by the legislatures and the courts is with reference to the protection of the innocent from the hazards of tactics and techniques that are apt to produce confessions of guilt or other false information. Individual civil liberties can survive in such an atmosphere, alongside the protective security of the public.

---

England: Hatherill, *Practical Problems in Interrogation*, in INTERNATIONAL LECTURES ON POLICE SCIENCE (Western Reserve Univ., 1956).

# Police Interrogation of Arrested Persons: A Skeptical View

"Questioning is an indispensable instrumentality of justice."
Justice Jackson, dissenting in
*Ashcraft* v. *Tennessee*, 332 U.S.
143, 160 (1944).

BERNARD WEISBERG

Should the police, in the course of criminal investigation, be entitled to interrogate an arrested person in privacy, without permitting him to communicate with a lawyer and prior to taking him before a judicial officer for a preliminary hearing? We would be hard put to explain to visitors from a legal Mars how such secret questioning in a police station fits into a system of criminal law which recognizes the privilege against self-incrimination and the right to counsel. Nevertheless, such questioning is common police practice in the United States. It is approved by leading authorities on criminal investigation and defended by responsible police administrators as necessary to effective law enforcement.

Such questioning is strikingly unlike the way in which a person accused of crime is treated in court. In court, with few exceptions, proceedings are public. In the police station, questioning is said to be effective only if it is conducted in privacy. In court, the defendant is entitled to the advice and support of a lawyer as well as family and friends. In the police station, the suspect is ordinarily not permitted to communicate with his family or a lawyer until his interrogation has been completed. In court, the defendant is entitled to know the charge against him and be confronted by adverse witnesses. In the police station, the suspect may not be told what crime the police

think he has committed, and he is frequently not charged with a crime until after he is questioned. If the police decide that he is innocent, he may be released without ever being charged with a crime. In court, the accused is informed of his right to counsel and right not to answer questions. In the police station, the police will probably not mention the subject of legal advice. Usually it is only after the questioning is completed and an oral statement is being reduced to writing that they will warn the prisoner that he is not required to answer their questions. In court, the defendant is presumed innocent. In the police station, the interrogator seeking a confession is likely to question a suspect on the hypothesis that he is guilty although the evidence is inconclusive. In court, an impartial judge and loyal counsel will protect the accused against badgering, questions based on false premises and other kinds of unfair cross-examination. The privilege against compulsory self-incrimination entitles him to avoid the witness stand entirely. In the police station, the interrogators are the only judges of what is proper questioning. They may try to trick their subject into making incriminating statements by falsely telling him that someone else has confessed and implicated him or by pretending to have physical evidence of his guilt. They may press him repeatedly, accuse him of lying or shout at him. They are likely to use the psychological pressures of isolation, prolonged questioning and various emotional appeals to encourage a confession. Since they are subject to no immediate supervision or disinterested observation, there is the danger that they will go further and use threats, deprive him of sleep or food or even use physical force in order to obtain a desired statement.

Proceedings in court are dominated by an insistence on procedural regularity. The conflict of interest between the accused and the prosecution is recognized and mediated by an impartial judge. Although the same conflict is present in more acute form in the police station, the suspect is left under the unsupervised control of investigators who naturally share the purposes and outlook of the prosecutor.

The law of police questioning, as we shall see, is compounded of incompleteness and indirection. It consists largely of rules about the admissibility of confessions and the requirement that arrested persons be promptly brought to court. Rather than directly regulating police interrogation practices, the law is vexed with the problem of providing effective remedies for the victims of improper police questioning.

Secret questioning by the police has characteristic aspects of illegality. Typically the suspect is held in violation of the general requirement that arrested persons be promptly brought before a judge, magistrate or commissioner. This postpones a preliminary hearing at which a judicial officer can advise the prisoner of his rights and decide whether there is enough evidence to justify holding him to answer a formal charge. Delay for the purpose of questioning encourages unlawful arrests without probable cause in the hope that station house interrogation will produce a confession or other useful evidence. When the prisoner is questioned, his right to bail and the advice of counsel are denied by the police for a period the length of which lies in their discretion. His right to a speedy trial is postponed. And if no one knows of the arrest, his isolation has the effect of postponing the right of habeas corpus.

It is also impossible to reconcile secret police questioning with the right to counsel and the privilege against self-incrimination. The right to counsel stands to ensure that an accused person, no matter what his economic position or degree

of sophistication, will understand his jeopardy and be able to defend himself intelligently. In these terms, it is hard to see any justification for postponing the right until after the period between arrest and appearance in court. It is during this period that a lawyer's advice is likely to have the most meaning and effect. Similarly, it is difficult to find a rationale for the privilege against self-incrimination which does not apply to police station questioning as well as examination in a court room.[1]

The secret questioning of arrested persons is defended simply with the argument that it is necessary to effective law enforcement. This view seems to be accepted by the public and at times by the courts. On the other hand, the argument against such interrogation practices has too often been rested on the danger of police brutality. Emphasis on the "third degree" has tended to obscure a number of difficult issues raised by pre-judicial police interrogation apart from the problem of abuses.

This paper will focus on the private questioning of persons in custody. It will not deal with the problem of determining when an arrest has taken place nor with interrogation prior to arrest. At the outset, we will examine the types of interrogation methods which are approved under professional police standards in the United States together with the argument that secret questioning is necessary for effective law enforcement. Part two will sketch the law of police questioning. The third section of this paper will consider the factual assumptions underlying the argument for secret questioning, the problems of empirical research and some relevant psychological and sociological factors. Part four will treat three secondary issues, the length of permissible interrogation,

[1] See BEISEL, CONTROL OVER ILLEGAL ENFORCEMENT OF THE CRIMINAL LAW: ROLE OF THE SUPREME COURT 86–107 (1955). The contrary argument is made in 3 WIGMORE, EVIDENCE §823 (3d ed. 1940). See also McNaughton, *The Privilege Against Self-Incrimination*, 51 J. CRIM. L., C. & P.S. 138, 151–52 (1960); Comment, *The Privilege Against Self-Incrimination: Does it Exist in the Police Station?*, 5 STAN. L. REV. 459 (1953); MAYERS, SHALL WE AMEND THE FIFTH AMENDMENT? 82–100 (1959).

when if at all the police should warn the prisoner of his rights and the exclusionary rules of evidence barring confessions obtained during unlawful police detention. The concluding sections will discuss the right to counsel in the police station and whether any pre-judicial interrogation by the police should be allowed.

## I. RECOMMENDED METHODS OF INTERROGATION AND THE ARGUMENT FOR SECRET QUESTIONING

It is playing Hamlet without the ghost to discuss police questioning without knowing what such questioning is really like. Terms such as "proper" and "fair" questioning are too often used without any explanation of what they mean in practice. What is needed is not another account of third degree horrors but an understanding of interrogation procedures which are approved by professional police standards in the United States. It is believed that the following summary of interrogation methods will give some content to the generalities in which the subject is usually discussed and serve as a preface to the ensuing discussion. It is based upon Part II of the leading police manual by Professor Fred Inbau and John Reid, *Lie Detection and Criminal Interrogation* (3d ed. 1953).

*Interrogation Methods*

The manual emphasizes the importance of avoiding threats, promises and abuses of any kind, methods which render a resulting confession involuntary or untrustworthy and "which no self-respecting officer can conscientiously defend." (p. 215)

The problem is how to elicit desired information from an untruthful subject. The recommended principles and methods assume no special equipment such as a lie detector. Instead, they are presented primarily for the average interrogator "who may be equipped with nothing more than his own good common sense and a fair understanding of human nature." (142)

"The principal psychological factor contributing to a successful interrogation is privacy. . . . [A] suspect or witness is more apt to divulge his secret in the privacy of a room occupied by only two persons than in the presence of five, ten, or twenty." (142) The interview should take place in a quiet room with as few distractions and police surroundings as possible.

"The less there is in the surroundings of an interrogation room to remind a criminal offender, suspect, witness, or other prospective informant that he is in police custody or jail, or that the penitentiary awaits, the more likely he is to make a frank statement. . . ." (147) Thus it is suggested that the room not have barred windows and noted that one police department purposely arranged its interrogation room with open windows so as to invite escape into an adjoining yard with no exit. It was found that once a guilty subject had unsuccessfully attempted to escape he usually confessed soon afterward.

Suspects may be classified into two groups, those whose guilt is definite or reasonably certain, and those whose guilt is doubtful or uncertain. The first group may be further classified in terms of the type of offense committed, the motivation and the offender's reaction. There are "emotional offenders . . . who commit crimes in the heat of passion, anger or revenge (e.g., assaults; killings; rape, or other sex offenses; etc.), and also persons whose offenses are of an accidental nature (e.g., the hit-run motorists)." (151) The emotional offender usually has strong guilt feelings. Thus "the most effective interrogation approach to use on him is one based upon sympathetic considerations." (151) But his urge to obtain relief by confession is opposed by the desire to avoid the legal consequences of his act. As time passes, and he is allowed to feel that he can escape undetected, the emotional offender may become less emotional and more rational. Therefore, the interrogator should not only sympathize with the offender and encourage the urge to confess, he should also persuade that subject that his guilt has been detected and that denials are useless. Thus it is effective for the interrogator to "display an air of confidence in the subject's guilt," to point out the circumstantial evidence against him, and to call attention to the physiological and psychological symptoms

155

of guilt. He must give no indication that he is influenced by what the subject may say in behalf of his innocence, even where the facts presented may indicate innocence; it is better initially to show no interest in exculpatory statements. By leading the offender to believe that he is exhibiting symptoms of guilt, his confidence in his ability to deceive can be destroyed or diminished and further resistance made to seem futile. Thus the interrogator will call the subject's attention to pulsation of the carotid artery in his neck, excessive activity of his "Adam's apple," dryness of the mouth, inability to look the interrogator "straight in the eye" or exhibitions of restlessness by leg swinging, hand tapping, foot wiggling and the like. ". . . [I]t is advisable to remind the subject that he doesn't feel very good inside; and that this 'peculiar feeling' (as if 'all his insides were tied in a knot') is the result of a troubled conscience. While making this statement it is well for the interrogator to touch or tap the subject's abdomen, as though it were the repository for the conscience to which the interrogator refers." (156) The subject who swears to his truthfulness, insists on his spotless record or who answers "not that I remember," can be told that in the interrogator's experience these are characteristic signs of lying.

Being careful to avoid the legal prohibition against promises of immunity or leniency as inducements, the interrogator may obtain an incriminating statement by sympathizing with the subject and telling him "that anyone else under similar conditions or circumstances might have committed a similar offense." (157) The subject is allowed to "save face" by the interrogator's assurances of sympathy and understanding. Such solicitations may "seem to cast a shadow over the subject's previously clear vision of the legal consequences of an exposure of his guilt." (158) Particularly in cases involving sex offenses, the offender will find it easier to confess as his guilt feelings are reduced by minimizing the moral seriousness of his offense. The interrogator may thus emphasize that the subject's sexual irregularity is not an unusual one, that it occurs frequently even among so-called normal or respectable persons, that the interrogator

has worked on cases involving much more offensive experiences, or "that the interrogator himself has been tempted to do, or almost or actually did do, the very sort of thing of which the subject is accused." (159) With the so-called "intellectual" type of subject, it may be helpful to refer to the Kinsey reports.

Condemning the victim or an accomplice may help the offender to justify the offense in his own mind and make it easier for him to confess. A rapist may be told that the victim was to blame for her provocative behavior. With an embezzler it may be helpful to condemn the employer for paying inadequate salaries. If an accomplice is blamed, or even government or society for allowing conditions conducive to such crimes, the offender may feel less responsible and find it easier to confess.

It is frequently essential to express friendship in urging the subject to tell the truth. Extending sympathy "by such friendly gestures as a pat on the shoulder or knee, or by a grip of a hand," telling the subject that "even if he were your own brother (or father, sister, etc.) you would still advise him to speak the truth," urging him to tell the truth "for the sake of his own conscience, mental relief, or moral well-being, as well as 'for the sake of everybody concerned,' and also because it is the only decent and honorable thing to do" (164), are gestures that "may produce a flood of tears along with the confession of guilt."

Compare the suggestion for "jolting" by the author of a different manual. The interrogator asks questions in a quiet almost soothing manner. Then ". . . the investigator chooses a propitious moment to shout a pertinent question and appear as though he is beside himself with rage. The subject may be unnerved to the extent of confessing. . . ."[2]

Another tactic is the "friend and enemy act" in which two interrogators alternate, one sympathetic and the other unfriendly. The subject may be thrown off balance and confess to the friendly questioner to retaliate against the colleague playing

[2] O'HARA, FUNDAMENTALS OF CRIMINAL INVESTIGATION 108 (1956).

156

the "enemy" role. It is also useful in some cases to invite the subject to admit to a partial lie by suggesting that his victim may have exaggerated the offense although the interrogator does not believe this. If the subject accepts the invitation to make a partial and less incriminating admission it becomes more difficult for him to continue to resist, having once acknowledged that he previously lied.

Some of the above methods are also applicable to the questioning of "non-emotional" offenders. Typical subjects of this type are "persons who have committed crimes for mercenary gain (e.g., robbery, burglary, etc.), and particularly those offenders who are repeaters or recidivists." (170) However, such subjects "experience little or no feeling of remorse, mental anguish, or compunction as a result of their criminal acts" and are thus less responsive to a sympathetic approach. Because they have a more realistic attitude, they are ordinarily more vulnerable to appeals to the logic of their situation, that is, a showing that their guilt can be or is established by evidence independent of their statements.

The questioner thus may point to the futility of resistance or appeal to the suspect's pride by flattery or a challenge to his honor. If efforts to obtain a confession are unavailing, an admission about another relatively minor offense may serve as a "wedge" which will lead to incriminating statements about the offense under investigation. Where two or more persons participated in the offense, a common technique is to play one against the other by leading each to believe that his accomplice has confessed and implicated him when this is not the fact; a method which another manual picturesquely calls "bluff on a split pair."[3] Similarly, the interrogator may pretend to have physical evidence which implicates the subject.

In interrogating suspects whose guilt is doubtful or uncertain, the examiner usually must decide whether to behave as though he believes the subject to be guilty or innocent or he may assume a neutral position. The first approach has the advantage of surprise and may "shock" the guilty subject into confession, but it has the disadvantage of

[3] *Id.* at 106.

putting the guilty subject on guard, and it may make an innocent subject too confused and excited to give helpful information. The second approach solves the latter difficulty and may encourage a guilty subject to "lower his guard" but makes it more difficult for the examiner to press the subject about his possible guilt. The interrogator who treats the subject as innocent or who takes a neutral attitude must determine whether he is lying; if so, then for interrogation purposes the subject may move into the category of those whose guilt is definite, or reasonably certain, although the experienced interrogator will know that an innocent person sometimes will lie in order to conceal an irrelevant indiscretion or circumstance which he fears would invite suspicion.

The advice for handling a person who refuses to answer questions is interesting. The examiner should concede the subject's right to remain silent but go on to point out the incriminating significance of his refusal. Then the interrogator should immediately ask some innocuous questions which may gradually lead to questions about the offense under investigation. The authors say,

"Except for the career criminal, there are very few persons who will persist in their initial refusal to talk after the interrogator has handled the situation in this suggested manner." (187)

The basic principles of interrogation of suspects and offenders are equally applicable to the questioning of witnesses or other prospective informants. A fearful witness should be assured of protection. A witness who refuses to cooperate in order to protect the offender or because his attitude is anti-police may be told that the offender has been disloyal; thus a wife may be told that her husband has been unfaithful.

"Ordinarily, however, some more effective measures are necessary. When all other methods have failed, therefore, the interrogator should accuse the subject of committing the crime (or of being implicated in it in some way) and proceed to interrogate him as though he were in fact considered to be the guilty individual. A witness or other prospective informant, thus faced with the possibility of a trial or conviction

157

for a crime he did not commit, will sooner or later be impelled to abandon his efforts in the offender's behalf or in support of his anti-social or anti-police attitudes." (195)

The author of a different manual makes a similar suggestion:

"Reverse Line-Up. This technique is applicable in crimes which ordinarily run in series, such as forgeries and muggings. The accused is placed in a lineup, but this time he is identified by several fictitious witnesses or victims who associated him with different offenses. It is expected that the subject will become desperate and confess to the offense under investigation in order to escape from the false accusations."[4]

The Inbau and Reid manual concludes with an analysis of the law of confessions. There is an extended discussion of the tests applied by the United States Supreme Court to the admissibility of confessions in state cases reviewed under the Fourteenth Amendment. The treatment of the "psychological coercion" cases concludes,

". . . there is nothing inherently wrong about a lengthy interrogation. It does appear, however, that during a lengthy interrogation time must be taken out for eating, drinking, and rest. As to just what is required will depend upon the particular case. The interrogator will have to exercise his own discretion as to what is reasonable under the circumstances."(208)

Compare the advice about lengthy interrogations in another police manual:

". . . .where emotional appeals and tricks are employed to no avail [the investigator] must rely on an oppressive atmosphere of dogged persistence. He must interrogate steadily and without relent, leaving the subject no prospect of surcease. He must dominate his subject and overwhelm him with his inexorable will to obtain the truth. He should interrogate for a spell of several hours pausing only for the subject's necessities in acknowledgement of the need to avoid a charge of duress that can be technically substantiated. In a serious case, the interrogation may continue for days, with the required inter-

[4] *Ibid.*

vals for food and sleep, but with no respite from the atmosphere of domination. It is possible in this way to induce the subject to talk without resorting to duress or coercion. The method should be used only when the guilt of the subject appears highly probable."[5]

Inbau and Reid point out 1) that the state courts have generally rejected the rule of *McNabb* v. *United States*[6] and will not exclude a confession obtained after failure to take a prisoner promptly before a magistrate as required by statute, 2) "the general rule that trickery and deception do not nullify a confession, regardless of the possible objection to such practices from a strictly moral viewpoint" (223) and 3) that except for the unusual statutory requirements found in Texas and the Uniform Code of Military Justice, it is not necessary to "warn an offender of his constitutional rights before obtaining his confession." (223)

The Inbau and Reid manual is an authoritative description of recommended interrogation techques. It appears to fairly reflect the substance and flavor of professional police literature.[7]

*The Argument for Secret Questioning*

The position that secret questioning is necessary for effective law enforcement has been summarized by Professor Inbau in this way:

"1. Many criminal cases, even when investigated by the best qualified police departments, are capable of solution only by means of an admission or confession from the guilty individual or upon the basis of information obtained from the questioning of other criminal suspects.

"2. Criminal offenders, except, of course, those caught in the commission of their crimes, ordinarily will not admit their guilt unless questioned under conditions of privacy, and for a period of perhaps several hours."[8]

[5] *Id.* at 112.
[6] 318 U.S. 332 (1943).
[7] See generally ARTHUR & CAPUTO, INTERROGATION FOR INVESTIGATORS (1959); KIDD, POLICE INTERROGATION (1940); MULBAR, INTERROGATION (1951); and O'HARA, *op. cit. supra* note 2.
[8] Inbau, *Restrictions in the Law of Interrogation and Confessions*, 52 Nw. U.L. REV. 77, 80 (1957). See also Inbau, *The Confession Dilemma in the United States*

He explains that the practical necessity for an interrogation does not exist in all cases and that ordinarily such questioning should not be the start of an investigation. A thorough investigation beforehand may turn up sufficient evidence to make a confession unnecessary and in other cases will help the interrogator obtain a confession and provide evidence to substantiate it. Questioning in privacy for "a reasonable period of time" is vital because self-condemnation is not normal human behavior. Very few confessions are likely to result from a "guilty conscience unprovoked by an interrogation." The subject should not be expected to divulge his secret unless he is questioned in privacy.

"For related psychological considerations, if an interrogation is to be had at all, it must be one based upon an unhurried interview, the necessary length of which will in many instances extend to several hours, depending upon various factors such as the nature of the case situation and the personality of the suspect.... [P]sychological considerations demand such secrecy. Moreover, to insist that all confessions be the result of 'reasoned choice' is to ignore the fact that a great many criminal confessions represent outbursts of emotion which one's reasoning power would tend to suppress."

"Lack of privacy during a criminal interrogation is comparable to a situation in which a surgeon tries to perform a serious operation out on a public street rather than in a properly equipped operating room. Each one has about an equal chance of a successful performance."

---

*Supreme Court*, 43 ILL. L. REV. 442 (1948); INBAU & REID, LIE DETECTION AND CRIMINAL INTERROGATION pt. II (3d ed. 1953), hereinafter cited as INBAU & REID, and Inbau, *"Fair Play" in Criminal Investigations and Prosecutions*, 3 Nw. Univ. Tri-Quarterly No. 2, p. 3 (1961). The summary of Professor Inbau's views in the following pages is based upon these sources.
Consider also Professor Inbau's view of the privilege against self-incrimination. It "exists mainly in order to stimulate the police and prosecutor into a search for the most dependable evidence procurable by their own exertions; otherwise there probably would be an incentive to rely solely upon the less dependable admissions that might be obtained as a result of a compulsory interrogation." INBAU, SELF-INCRIMINATION 6, 7 (1950).

Professor Inbau argues that use of the interrogation techniques described above is justified because:

1. Under the weight of authority in the United States, these methods of questioning are legally permissible.
2. Innocent persons are given sufficient protection since none of the methods described "are apt to induce an innocent person to confess a crime he did not commit," and the courts will not tolerate any questioning practices which fail to meet this standard.
3. These questioning practices can help to reduce the use of physical abuses, threats and promises by police officers who are "untrained and ill-equipped to conduct proper and effective interrogations."
4. Where serious crimes are involved which cannot be solved by gathering objective evidence, interrogation is necessary if the offenders are not to go free. This justifies the interrogator in dealing with "criminal offenders on a somewhat lower moral plane than that upon which ethical, law-abiding citizens are expected to conduct their every day affairs," or, put somewhat differently, "In dealing with criminal offenders, and consequently also with criminal suspects who may actually be innocent, the interrogator must of necessity employ less refined methods than are considered appropriate for the transaction of ordinary, everyday affairs by and between law abiding citizens."

Police opinion on the need for secret questioning in criminal investigation appears to be unanimous. Some of the strongest expressions of this view were occasioned by the Supreme Court's *McNabb* and *Mallory* decisions.[9] These rulings emphasized the duty of federal officers to take arrested persons before a committing officer without unnecessary delay. These cases hold broadly that a confession obtained by federal officers during an unlawful delay may not be used as evidence in a federal criminal trial. These decisions aroused sharp criticism from police and prosecutors throughout

[9] McNabb v. United States, 318 U.S. 332 (1943); Mallory v. United States, 354 U.S. 449 (1957).

the country. Each was followed by unsuccessful attempts at legislative reversal and congressional hearings at which law enforcement officials insisted that they could not function without the opportunity to interrogate arrested persons prior to their arraignment.[10]

˙ In 1943 hearings before a special subcommittee of the House Judiciary Committee, Major Edward J. Kelly, Superintendent of Police for the District of Columbia, testified that "the ruling in the *McNabb* case is one of the greatest handicaps that has ever confronted law enforcement officers" because it required that all arrested persons be promptly arraigned and charged with a crime without allowing the police an opportunity for interrogation.[11]

In 1957, Oliver Gasch, United States Attorney for the District of Columbia, testified before a special subcommittee of the House Judiciary Committee that the *Mallory* decision had created an emergency situation requiring immediate legislative action. He said,

"Without interrogation by the police of persons reasonably believed to have committed a crime, the police will be unable, in my judgment, to solve many serious crimes with which they and the community are confronted."[12]

In the same hearings, Robert Murray, District of Columbia Chief of Police, expressed the opinion that if *Mallory* stood it would result in a "complete breakdown in law enforcement in the District of Columbia." He predicted that the decision would also cause a "substantial rise in crime and a drastic reduction in the solution of major criminal cases."[13] William H. Parker, Chief of Police of Los Angeles, California, appearing for the legislative committee of the International Association of Chiefs of Police and, in his words, "to represent all local law enforcement in the United States" testified that *Mallory* "would destroy modern law enforcement as practiced and as preached today."[14]

In 1958, the same note was sounded in hearings before the Subcommittee on Constitutional Rights of the Senate Committee on the Judiciary. Police Chief Murray said,

"... most of the murders, the rapes, and robberies that I have come in contact with would have gone unsolved and unpunished under the Mallory decision."[15]

Deputy Chief Scott said that *Mallory* had resulted in an immediate increase in crime:

"Crime was reduced by this department by 35 per cent between 1953 and June 30, 1957. But immediately after the Mallory decision it began to rise in all categories, and, within 7 months had risen enough to almost cover the gains we had made in the first 6 months of 1957. Among these cases which happened during this time were street robberies, which rose about 20 per cent during these 7 months, and the crime of assault upon the victims of these robberies rose by 29 per cent."[16]

The police are not alone in the view that secret questioning is a necessary law enforcement tool. In an effort to overrule *McNabb*, the House of Representatives passed the Hobbs Bill three times.[17] In the closing minutes of the 85th Congress an amended version of the similar Willis-Keating Bill failed on a point of order in the Senate.[18] The

---

[10] Admission of Evidence in Certain Cases: *Hearings Before Subcommittee No. 2 of the House Committee on the Judiciary*, 78th Cong., 1st Sess., on H.R. 3690 (1943), hereinafter referred to as the *1943 House Committee Hearings;* Supreme Court Decisions: *Hearings Before the Special Subcommittee to Study Decisions of the Supreme Court of the United States of the House Committee on the Judiciary*, 85th Cong. 2d Sess., on the decision in the case of Mallory v. United States, Part 1 (1957), hereinafter referred to as the *1957 House Committee Hearings;* Confessions and Police Detention: *Hearings Before the Subcommittee on Constitutional Rights of the Senate Committee on the Judiciary*, 85th Cong., 2d Sess. (1958), hereafter referred to as the *March 1958 Senate Commitee Hearings;* and Admission of Evidence (Mallory rule): *Hearings Before a Subcommittee of the Senate Committee on the Judiciary*, 85th Cong., 2d Sess., on H.R. 11477, S.2970, S.3325 and S.3355, hereinafter referred to as the *July 1958 Senate Committee Hearings.*

[11] *1943 House Committee Hearings* at 1.

[12] *1957 House Committee Hearings* at 2. For Mr. Gasch's views in 1960, see text at note 58 *infra*.

[13] *Id.* at 34, 42.

[14] *Id.* at 89.

[15] *March 1958 Senate Committee Hearings* at 124.

[16] *Id.* at 133.

[17] The legislative history of the Hobbs bill is summarized in Inbau, 43 ILL. L. REV. 442, at 452, 453.

[18] The legislative history of the Willis-Keating bill is summarized in Hogan and Snee, *The McNabb-Mallory*

state courts have generally refused to adopt the McNabb Rule. (In 1960, Michigan became the first exception.[19]) The Uniform Arrest Act allows brief detention without requiring that the person held be produced before a magistrate.[20] Some state statutes sanction a fixed period of delay between arrest and arraignment.[21] The same court may hold detention for questioning illegal in a false arrest suit but in ruling on the admissibility of a confession describe a three-day incommunicado detention as proper.[22] And some courts have characterized "fair police questioning" as vital to effective law enforcement.[23] Although these actions do not represent a single position, each of them appears to reflect some agreement with the assumptions underlying the argument for secret questioning.

## II. THE LAW OF POLICE QUESTIONING

Do the police have the power under existing law to interrogate arrested persons in privacy for "a reasonable time" which may extend to several hours? Are the questioning practices described in Part I of this paper lawful? These issues are best discussed after a sketch of relevant legal principles.

The law in the United States which directly defines the powers of the police in questioning suspects and witnesses can be quickly stated. The police have the undoubted right to ask questions in the course of criminal investigation. However, unlike the courts, the police have no power to compel testimony. This is sometimes confused with the privilege against self-incrimination by references to an individual's "constitutional right" not to answer police questions. It is not unlawful to refuse to answer police inquiries and to do so it is not necessary to claim the privilege.

The real law of police questioning is found not in these propositions but in the indirect restrictions on pre-judicial interrogation imposed by the law of confessions and the general requirement that arrested persons be promptly produced in court.

### The Fourteenth Amendment Confession Cases

The law of confessions determines when the methods used by police to obtain an incriminating statement render it inadmissible as evidence of guilt. The traditional rule is that confessions must be "voluntary"; if obtained by physical force, threats or inducements, they may not be used in court. Wigmore's is the classic argument that the purpose of the rule is to exclude untrustworthy evidence.[24] Dean McCormick pointed to features of the rule indicating that it has the additional purpose of discouraging improper police conduct.[25] Since 1936, and the decision of the United States Supreme Court in *Brown* v. *Mississippi*,[26] the rationale of the law of confessions has become a constitutional issue. That case held for the first time that the use in a state court trial of a confession obtained by physical brutality violated the defendant's due process rights under the Fourteenth Amendment. Since then the law of confessions has undergone a dramatic development in a series of Supreme Court decisions holding that the use of improper methods of interrogation in obtaining a confession will make its admission in evidence a violation of federal due process whether or not it is involuntary under the traditional confession rule. The Fourteenth Amendment confession cases have weighed such circumstances as physical mistreatment, threats, deprivation of food and

---

*Rule: Its Rise, Rationale and Rescue,* 47 GEO. L.J. 1, 38–46 (1958); See also Note, *Prearraignment Interrogation and the McNabb-Mallory Miasma,* 68 YALE L.J. 1003, 1028–30 (1959).

[19] People v. Hamilton, 359 Mich. 410, 102 N.W.2d 738 (1960). The cases are collected at 19 A.L.R.2d 1331 (1951) and in INBAU & REID at 208–10.

[20] See Warner, *The Uniform Arrest Act,* 28 VA. L. R. 315 (1942); Foote, *The Fourth Amendment: Obstacle or Necessity in the Law of Arrest?* 51 J. CRIM. L., C. & P.S. 402 (1960); Foote, *Safeguards in the Law of Arrest,* 52 NW. U.L. REV. 16 (1957); Wilson, *Police Arrest Privileges in a Free Society: A Plea for Modernization,* 51 J. CRIM. L., C. & P.S. 395 (1960).

[21] See MO. STATS. ANNO., §544.170; R.I. GEN. LAWS, §12-7-13; S.C. CODE §17.261.

[22] Compare Fulford v. O'Connor, 3 Ill.2d 490 (1954), with People v. Kelly, 404 Ill. 281 (1949).

[23] Crooker v. California, 357 U.S. 433, 441 (1958); Cicenia v. La Gay, 357 U. S. 504, 509 (1958).

[24] 3 WIGMORE, EVIDENCE, §§822, 823 (3d ed. 1940).

[25] McCormick, *The Scope of Privilege in the Law of Evidence,* 16 TEX. L. REV. 447 (1938). See also McCormick, *Some Problems and Developments in the Admissibility of Confessions,* 24 TEX. L. REV. 239, 245 (1946).

[26] 297 U.S. 278 (1936).

sleep, prolonged interrogation, incommunicado detention, the failure of the police to warn the defendant of his right not to answer questions, the refusal to allow communication with counsel, the use of deception or trickery in questioning and failure to comply with statutes requiring that the prisoner be taken before a judicial officer promptly after his arrest. The decisions have been thoroughly analyzed elsewhere.[27] Only a few observations are necessary here.

The cases have reflected disagreement within the Court about the purpose of the constitutional rule. Thus the opinions have vacillated between the "trustworthiness" rationale of the traditional confession rule and an emphasis on enforcing "civilized standards" of police conduct.[28] The Court has refused to bar all confessions obtained during pre-arraignment interrogation of persons in custody[29] although one of the Justices has urged this step.[30] At times, the Court has insisted that the Constitution does not bar "fair" police questioning of persons denied access to counsel.[31] But the Court has also held that prolonged secret questioning is "inherently coercive."[32] Some opinions have spoken with a logic which, literally applied, would make all secret police questioning outlaw.[33] But even in opinions in which the

emphasis is on the conduct of the police, the Court has described the issue as one of "coercion," thus continuing to use the terminology of a rule which turns on the defendant's state of mind.

On reading the cases, one is struck by the handicaps under which the Court has labored in attempting to formulate the due process rule. Little is known about the psychology of interrogation and confession. The ambiguous concepts of coercion and free choice have invited dispute. And, judging from the opinions, the records in these cases usually contain very limited information about the circumstances of the interrogation and even less information about the defendant's state of mind. Under all of the circumstances, it is understandable that the determination in particular cases whether the defendant's will was "overborne" or the conditions of questioning "inherently coercive" has often provoked sharp disagreement.[34]

---

[27] Paulsen, *The Fourteenth Amendment and the Third Degree*, 6 STAN. L. REV. 411 (1954); Allen, *Due Process and State Criminal Procedures: Another Look*, 48 Nw. U.L. REV. 16 (1953); MAGUIRE, EVIDENCE OF GUILT c. 3 (1959). The cases are collected in Annot., 1 L.ED.2d 1735 (1957), supp., 4 L.ED.2d 1833 (1960), and in note 2 to the Court's opinion in Spano v. New York, 360 U.S. 315, 321 (1959).

[28] Compare Gallegos v. Nebraska, 342 U.S. 55 (1951), and Stein v. New York, 346 U.S. 156 (1953), with Ashcraft v. Tennessee, 322 U.S. 143 (1944), Watts v. Indiana, 338 U.S. 49 (1949), Spano v. New York, 360 U.S. 315 (1959), Blackburn v. Alabama, 361 U.S. 199 (1960), and Rogers v. Richmond, 81 S. Ct. 735 (1961).

[29] *Gallegos* and *Stein* cases cited note 28 *supra*. See also Lyons v. Oklahoma, 322 U.S. 596 (1944), and Brown v. Allen, 344 U.S. 443, 476 (1953).

[30] Justice Douglas, concurring in Watts v. Indiana, 338 U.S. 49, 56 (1949).

[31] *Crooker* and *Cicenia* cases cited note 23 *supra*.

[32] *Ashcraft* and *Watts* cases cited note 28 *supra*.

[33] "It is inconceivable that any court of justice in the land, conducted as our courts are, open to the public, would permit prosecutors serving in relays to keep a defendant witness under continuous cross examination for thirty-six hours without rest or sleep in an effort to extract a 'voluntary' confession. Nor can we, consistently with Constitutional due process of law, hold voluntary a confession where prosecutors do the same thing away from the restraining influences of a public trial in an open court room."
Ashcraft v. Tennessee, 322 U.S. 143, 154 (1944).

"A confession by which life becomes forfeit must be the expression of free choice. A statement to be voluntary of course need not be volunteered. But if it is the product of sustained pressure by the police it does not issue from a free choice. When a suspect speaks because he is overborne, it is immaterial whether he has been subjected to a physical or mental ordeal. Eventual yielding to questioning under such circumstances is plainly the product of the suction process of interrogation and therefore the reverse of voluntary. We would have to shut our minds to the plain significance of what here transpired to deny that this was a calculated endeavor to secure a confession through the pressure of unrelenting interrogation. The very relentlessness of such interrogation implies that it is better for the prisoner to answer than to persist in the refusal of disclosure which is his constitutional right. To turn the detention of an accused into a process of wrenching from him evidence which could not be extorted in open court with all its safeguards, is so grave an abuse of the power of arrest as to offend the procedural standards of due process."
Watts v. Indiana, 338 U.S. 49, 53, 54 (1949).

"The Fourteenth Amendment prohibits the police from using the private, secret custody of either man or child as a device for wringing confessions from them."
Haley v. Ohio, 332 U.S. 596, 601 (1948).

[34] Since the decision in Ward v. Texas, 316 U.S.

In all of the Fourteenth Amendment confession cases decided by the United States Supreme Court during the past 25 years, the defendant was questioned without · counsel being present. In some cases, his requests to communicate with a lawyer were denied; in others, attempts by lawyers to see him were barred. During these years a parallel line of decisions has dealt with the right to counsel itself, typically where the defendant was not represented at the trial stage and on that basis challenged the constitutionality of his conviction. The rule has developed that in capital cases the trial of an uncounselled defendant is barred by the Constitution. In other cases, the question is whether the defendant was denied a fair trial, considering the nature of the offense, his age, previous experience with the law and other factors bearing on his ability to intelligently defend himself.[35] The confession and right to counsel cases converged in *Crooker* v. *California*,[36] a capital case in which the defendant was held incommunicado and his requests for an opportunity to call a lawyer were denied by the police until he was questioned and a confession obtained. In a 5 to 4 decision, the Court held that under the circumstances the confession was not involuntary and also that the denial of counsel was not prejudicial for Fourteenth Amendment purposes. The majority opinion began from the premise that neither police detention and private questioning of arrested persons nor the failure of police to comply with local prompt production statutes suffice to render a confession so obtained "involuntary" under the Fourteenth Amendment. In holding the confession voluntary, the Court emphasized the defendant's age, intelli-

gence and education. He was 31 years old and a college graduate who had attended the first year of law school. The Court pointed out that he had taken a course in criminal law, had shown his awareness of the inadmissibility of the results of a lie detector test, had been warned before confessing that he did not have to answer questions and had indicated a full awareness of his right to be silent by the manner of his refusal to answer certain questions. In rejecting the distinct argument that the defendant had been denied his right to counsel, the Court recognized that for constitutional purposes the right to counsel is not limited to the trial of an accused but also protects a defendant during pre-trial proceedings if its denial is so prejudicial as to make the subsequent trial fundamentally unfair. The same circumstances which had been emphasized in holding the confession voluntary persuaded the majority that no such prejudice or unfairness was present in Crooker's case which came down to "a voluntary confession by a college-educated man with law school training who knew of his right to keep silent." The Court refused to accept the defendant's broad argument that every state denial of a request to contact counsel violates the constitutional right to counsel. Justice Clark said that the rule suggested would have a "devastating effect on enforcement of criminal law for it would effectively preclude police questioning—*fair as well as unfair*—until the accused was afforded opportunity to call his attorney."[37]

### The McNabb-Mallory Rule

In confession cases tried in the federal courts, the Supreme Court has imposed more stringent restrictions on police interrogation practices than in the Fourteenth Amendment cases. Starting in 1943 with *McNabb* v. *United States*,[38] the Court has established the rule that confessions are inadmissible if obtained by federal officers during an unlawful detention, that is, when they fail to take their prisoner before a committing officer without unnecessary delay following his arrest. The record

---

547 (1942), the Court has passed on the admissibility of confessions in twenty cases coming from the state courts. In only 2 of these cases was the Court unanimous on the result. *Spano* and *Blackburn* cases cited note 28 *supra*. In *Spano*, the Court divided 5 to 4 on the ground for decision. In *Blackburn*, Justice Clark concurred in the result. Disagreement in the confession cases is often phrased in terms of the proper scope of constitutional review of state court findings on the question of "voluntariness." This is the characteristic approach of dissenting opinions where the majority holds a confession inadmissible and reverses.

[35] The cases are collected at 93 L.ED. 137 (1950) and 2 L.ED.2d 1644 (1958).

[36] 357 U.S. 433 (1958).

[37] *Id.* at 441. See also Cicenia v. La Gay, 357 U.S. 504 (1958).

[38] 318 U.S. 332 (1943).

in the *McNabb* case indicated that federal officers, after arresting the defendants, had failed to take them promptly before a United States Commissioner or other committing officer as required by statute but had first interrogated two of them intermittently during a period of two days and the third continuously for five or six hours. The Court reversed the convictions on the ground that incriminating admissions obtained during this questioning had been improperly received into evidence. The Court read the federal statutes requiring prompt production of arrested persons before a committing authority as designed to avoid "all the the evil implications of secret interrogation of persons accused of crime."[39] Acting to vindicate this congressional policy and exercising its supervisory power over the administration of justice in the federal courts, the Court announced the doctrine that confessions obtained by federal officers during an unlawful detention are inadmissible even though they are "voluntary" under constitutional due process standards.

In the years that followed *McNabb* its seeming prohibition of all detention for purposes of questioning became clouded in uncertainty.[40] The unanimous opinion in *Mallory* v. *United States* put an end to the major questions about the *McNabb* rule. Mallory had been arrested as a rape suspect by the District of Columbia police. Instead of being taken directly before a committing magistrate, he was held at a police station for questioning, in the course of which he confessed. In holding the confession inadmissible, the Court ruled unanimously that Rule 5(a) of the Federal Rules of Criminal Procedure, which requires that an arrested person is to be taken "without unnecessary delay" before the nearest available commissioner or committing officer, does not permit delay for the purpose of questioning which "lends itself, even if not so designed, to eliciting damaging statements to support the arrest and ultimately his guilt."[41]

### The Prompt Production Statutes

In addition to the law of confessions, the other principal source of law on police questioning is found in the prompt production statutes which require that arrested persons be taken to court "without unnecessary delay," "immediately," or "forthwith."[42] Interpreting the most common provision, "without unnecessary delay," the *Mallory* case holds broadly that delay by federal officers for the purpose of questioning their prisoner is not permitted, although delay for such administrative procedures as "booking" is proper. The state court decisions have generally rejected the *McNabb-Mallory* rule and treat the violation of a prompt production statute only as a circumstance to be considered in deciding whether a resulting confession was voluntary.[43] These decisions indirectly sanction delay for the purpose of questioning by admitting a resulting confession. But the same court may hold such delay unlawful in a false imprisonment suit where the legality of the detention is the only question.[44] Similarly, the state courts have treated refusal to allow access to counsel and failure to warn the prisoner of his "rights" only as circumstances bearing on the question whether a confession was coerced.[45]

### The Legality of Secret Questioning

We return to the specific questions with which this section began. Professor Inbau's conclusion that state and local police who are not subject to *McNabb* and *Mallory* rule may lawfully question persons in privacy "for a reasonable time," which may extend to several hours, is based on the view that in a series of decisions between 1949 and 1953 the United States Supreme Court had returned to

---

[39] *Id.* at 344.
[40] Hogan & Snee, *op. cit supra* note 18.
[41] 354 U.S. 449, 454 (1957)

[42] The statutes are cited in note 7 to the Court's opinion in McNabb v. U. S., 318 U.S. 332, 342 (1943). The statutes are collected and reproduced at pp. 735 to 748 of the *March 1958 Senate Committee Hearings*.
[43] See references in note 19 *supra*.
[44] See cases cited note 22 *supra*.
[45] See, e.g., People v. Leyra, 302 N.Y. 353, 98 N.E.2d 553 (1951), and People v. Valletutti, 297 N.Y. 226, 78 N.E.2d 485 (1948).

the traditional confession rule of "voluntariness" or "trustworthiness" and had retreated from the position in some of its earlier cases that prolonged secret questioning is "inherently coercive."[46] This reading of the Fourteenth Amendment confession cases is arguable in view of the cases decided since 1953.[47] However it is not my purpose to dwell on the present boundaries of the constitutional rule. Varying facts make the cases difficult to generalize. The rule and its rationale are in the course of development and short run prediction seems a fruitless task.

There is a deeper problem. The legality of secret questioning does not depend on whether a court will exclude a resulting confession. If, in order to carry on such interrogation, the police arrest without probable cause, fail to observe the prisoner's right to prompt arraignment, deny his right to bail, violate a statute guaranteeing access to counsel, or postpone his right to habeas corpus by keeping his whereabouts unknown—if the police do any of these things, their interrogation is plainly unlawful. In several Fourteenth Amendment confession cases the Supreme Court has recognized that police delay after arrest for the purpose of questioning their prisoner violated one or more state laws. Indeed, one of the rules in these cases is that violation of a state prompt production statute will not by itself render a resulting confession inadmissible for Fourteenth Amendment purposes.[48]

The courts' refusal to apply an exclusionary rule to confessions obtained in violation of law does not make the interrogation practices lawful. Because the courts have thus far refused to apply such a rule and because public opinion fails to insist on the enforcement of state prompt production statutes, the widespread practice of detaining arrested persons for questioning prior to arraignment exists in a nether world of openly countenanced illegality.[49]

## The Legality of Deceptive Questioning

Another issue posed by the interrogation methods described in Part I of this paper is whether the techniques which call for the use of deception by police officers are legally permissible. Professor Inbau urges that they are and explains that innocent persons are protected adequately since none of the methods described "are apt to induce an innocent person to confess a crime he did not commit."

Do the questioning practices described adequately protect the innocent? In the abstract, it is not easy to see why a suspect would confess to a crime he did not commit merely because he is told that another person has confessed and implicated him or that the police have physical evidence of his guilt which does not in fact exist. On the other hand, perhaps a prisoner's sweetheart, told that he has been unfaithful, might thereby be given a motive for falsely accusing him.[50] And a suspect falsely charged with a number of crimes which he did not commit is apparently expected to discern an implied threat to be withdrawn upon confession to the specific offense under investigation.[51] What seems common sense may not be a reliable guide in these matters.

The legality of deceptive questioning is also debatable.[52] Once again, the courts have not dealt directly with the problem and the only law is found in the confession cases. The American decisions have generally refused to bar a confession although it was obtained by police deception or trickery, so long as the deception is not believed likely to produce an untrue confession.[53] However, this proposition may require qualification in the light

[46] INBAU & REID at 205–08.
[47] See especially *Spano, Blackburn,* and *Rogers* cases cited note 28 *supra.*
[48] Stein v. New York, 346 U. S. 156, 186–88 (1953).
[49] *Secret Detention By The Chicago Police,* a Report by the American Civil Liberties Union, Illinois Division (1959); Note, *Philadelphia Police Practice and the Law Of Arrest,* 100 U. PA. L. REV. 1182 (1952).

[50] INBAU & REID at 195.
[51] O'HARA, *op. cit. supra* note 2, at 106.
[52] As to the "ethics" of deceptive questioning, consider Professor Williams' comment on the second part of INBAU & REID:
"An Englishman's reaction to these procedures is generally squeamish; the American lawyer's tougher reaction is: 'Why not?'"
Williams, *Questioning by the Police: Some Practical Considerations* [1960] Crim. L. R. 325, 337.
[53] 3 WIGMORE, EVIDENCE, §841 (3d ed. 1940). But see Rogers v. Richmond, 81 S. Ct. 735 (1961), which casts constitutional doubts on this rule.

of standards applied by the United States Supreme Court in recent years to confessions in both federal and state cases. The emphasis in *McNabb* on the development of "civilized standards of procedure and evidence," could be applied to bar the use of trickery or deception to obtain a confession although the issue is not likely to arise in federal cases so long as *McNabb* and *Mallory* continue to exclude all confessions obtained by federal officers during a period of illegal detention without regard to the methods by which such confessions are obtained.

Two recent Fourteenth Amendment opinions indicate that the use of trickery and deception by police interrogators may create constitutional problems. In *Leyra v. Denno*,[54] the Court emphasized the fact that a psychiatrist employed by the police to question the defendant had interrogated him at length after misrepresenting himself as a physician desiring to give him medical relief from a painful sinus attack. In *Spano v. New York*, the Court held that the defendant's confession had been obtained by unconstitutional means under the following circumstances: The defendant had already been indicted. He surrendered after having been advised by counsel to answer no questions. He was then questioned almost continuously for approximately eight hours and his requests to see his lawyer were denied. He abandoned his refusal to answer any questions only after a policeman who was a boyhood friend repeatedly played on his sympathy by falsely telling him that a telephone call which the defendant had made to him had jeopardized the policeman's job and threatened disaster to the policeman's pregnant wife and three children. The court held that the defendant's "will was overborne by official pressure, fatigue and sympathy falsely aroused."[55]

Although the circumstances of these cases do not lend themselves to generalization, the opinions suggest reservations about any unqualified assertion that the use of deception in interrogation is lawful.

\* \* \*

[54] 347 U.S. 556 (1954).
[55] 360 U.S. 315, 323 (1959).

On the whole, police interrogation practices appear to be little governed by law. The principal legal restrictions are found in the confession cases. But it must be recognized that law which deals only with the admissibility of confessions has an extremely limited effect on police questioning practices. It applies only in a small fraction of the actual cases in which persons are arrested and questioned by the police. It may mean nothing to the large number of persons who are arrested and questioned but released without being charged with a crime, those who confess and plead guilty, and those who are tried on evidence other than a confession, perhaps evidence obtained from leads provided by a confession improperly obtained.

### III. QUESTIONS FOR RESEARCH

The argument for secret questioning is an argument from necessity, not from principle. No one says that such interrogation is good in itself but it is defended as a way of solving criminal cases which cannot be solved in any other way. The argument is based on factual assumptions and it calls for empirical proof which we do not have. Instead, the argument is rested entirely on the judgment of law enforcement officials. This judgment is entitled to great respect but cannot be accepted as conclusive. The police official characteristically reasons from individual cases, frequently those in which questioning produced a confession and which, in retrospect, he does not believe could have been solved in any other way. It is not, of course, possible to determine what might happen if the police were effectively denied the power to engage in secret questioning and thus compelled to stress or develop other methods of investigation. Like the rest of us, the police tend to be limited by the bounds of their experience. The established practice inevitably appears to be the only one that will work. Untried alternatives are dismissed without adequate evaluation.

The complexity of the phenomena and the practical difficulties of experimentation offer little encouragement to empirical study of the relationship between the variables of law enforcement and interrogation. Nevertheless, the police need for secret questioning does involve some problems which could be studied empirically and others which would be difficult to research but are useful to discuss because they emphasize how little we know of the facts.

1. The starting point for any empirical research should be the actual interrogation practices of the police. The problem here is not defining the questions but gaining access to the data. The goal should be to substitute systematically organized and objective descriptive data for the "common knowledge" of lawyers and newspapermen. Emphasis on the problem of the third degree has undoubtedly accounted for much police defensiveness in the face of proposals for objective observation of practices normally concealed from public view. The most ambitious empirical study of police practices in recent times tried to avoid the appearance of 'looking for wrongdoing' but what has been seen of the resulting report contains little useful information on interrogation practices.[56]

It should be possible to plan programs for impartial observation of police questioning practices which will win the cooperation of professional police administrators. Observers whose presence is unknown to those being viewed could watch and listen from behind one-way windows. Judging from the police manuals, the interrogation rooms of many police stations are already equipped for such observation. There would be difficulties but they should be solvable with the experience of social scientists who have handled similar problems in other fields.

2. How does a police force function when it is denied the right to use secret interrogation? How have the District of Columbia police adapted themselves to the *McNabb* and *Mallory* decisions? Are there other police departments which have

been forced by court decision or administrative changes to discontinue the questioning of suspects held incommunicado? In the 1957 House Committee hearings, Assistant Attorney General Olney said that despite the *Mallory* decision the police "cannot close up shop" and that if criminals were to be released the action would have to be taken by the courts in each case and not by action by the police in advance.[57] However, there are indications that the District of Columbia police have endeavored to comply with the Mallory rule in order not to hamper successful prosecutions. Oliver Gasch, the United States Attorney for the District of Columbia, told the 1957 House Committee hearings that the *Mallory* decision had created an emergency situation requiring immediate legislative action.[58] However, experience seems to have reduced his concern. In a 1960 address, Mr. Gasch criticized as "too speculative" the view that *Mallory* led to the subsequent sharp rise in crime in the District. He spoke with pride of his success in training District police officials to understand and follow the *Mallory* rule. Mr. Gasch said that *Mallory* questions are of controlling importance in less than five per cent of his criminal prosecutions[59] and that as the result of police department cooperation and the training program, District of Columbia police are making better cases by carrying on more extensive investigation prior to the arrest of suspects. He added that the accumulation of other evidentiary material has become standard operating procedure, reliance upon confessions has been minimized and police work generally has become more thorough and exact.[60]

[57] *1957 House Committee Hearings* at 187.

[58] *Id.* at 13.

[59] Compare Chief Murray's testimony in 1957 that perhaps as many as 90% of major crimes are solved after the subject is brought in and questioned. *1957 House Committee Hearings* at 43.

[60] Gasch, "Law Enforcement in the District of Columbia and Civil Rights," unpublished address of March 25, 1960, to Twelfth Annual Conference, National Civil Liberties Clearing House, Washington, D. C. The summary in the text is based on a mimeographed copy. Mr. Gasch's speech was reported in the Washington Post, March 26, 1960, p. D1.

The interesting lectures and discussions on the Mallory rule held by Mr. Gasch and members of his

[56] AMERICAN BAR FOUNDATION, THE ADMINISTRATION OF CRIMINAL JUSTICE IN THE UNITED STATES (Pilot Project Report) (1958). This unpublished seven volume report identifies some persons and places observed, and citations or quotations are forbidden. The pilot project study will be described in a book to be published in the near future. Remington, *Criminal Justice Research*, 51 J. CRIM. L., C. & P.S. 7, 18 (1960). The plan for the study is set forth in SHERRY & PETTIS, THE ADMINISTRATION OF CRIMINAL JUSTICE IN THE UNITED STATES (1955).

The *Mallory* decision has provided an unusual opportunity to study the effects of a change in the rules. Detailed information should be gathered about the ways in which the District of Columbia police have modified their investigation and questioning practices as a result of that change. Also, an opportunity for comparative study is afforded by the 1960 decision of the Michigan Supreme Court adopting the *McNabb-Mallory* rule.[60a]

3. The Phenomenon of Confession. There are many fascinating questions about the psychology of confession to crime. Some objective correlations between confessions and the conditions of interrogation might be illuminating. How often do interrogations produce confessions? How often are confessions obtained without an interrogation? Is it possible to generalize about the length and type of interrogation which is most likely to produce a confession in given types of cases or from given types of offenders? It would be interesting, for example, to know how often questioning produces a confession from previous offenders. The suspect who has already had brushes with the law is more likely to know of his right not to answer questions and to realize that incriminating statements will be used against him. Does this mean that confessions from professional criminals are more likely to be the result of special pressure or coercion? Does a subject who has once had a lawyer or a court explain that he need not answer police questions remember and act on this advice? What is the effect of advising the suspect of his rights at the outset of the interrogation or allowing him access to counsel promptly upon arrest? It is tempting to assume that advice of counsel or a caution will make questioning useless but it may be that more powerful tendencies are at work in the mind of the offender.

What are the psychological consequences of interrogation after arrest? Judges, like the rest of us, seem to know very little about this. They have been handicapped by the ambiguity of the concept of voluntary choice and by the typical paucity of information available to appellate court judges about the conditions of interrogation and the defendant's state of mind. The distinction between voluntary and coerced admissions is little help. As Justice Jackson pointed out, it is strange to speak of any confession as involuntary since any confession, even under duress, is the product of some deliberate choice.[61] He acknowledged that arrest, detention and questioning are inherently coercive and "put pressure upon the prisoner to answer questions, to answer them truthfully, and to confess if guilty." Instead of focusing on the pressure applied to the subject, he suggested that "the real issue is strength of character," whether the confession is the result of "free choice," or, put another way, whether the confessor was "in possession of his own will and self-control at the time of the confession." However, it is not clear what would be gained by asking about the defendant's strength of character, the degree of his self-control or his freedom to choose, instead of whether his admissions were voluntary.[62]

It is interesting to rethink the free will assumptions implicit in the idea of coercion in light of the modern view that the offender has a strong, unconscious urge to reveal himself.[63] The existence of some such tendency is observed in professional police literature.[64] Compare Wigmore's confident generalization:

"Every guilty person is almost always ready and desirous to confess, as soon as he is detected and arrested. . . . The nervous pressure of guilt is enormous; the load of the deed done is

---

staff with officers of the District Police Department are reprinted in *July 1958 Senate Committee Hearings* at 396–421. In his 1960 address, Mr. Gasch said that these lectures and discussions had been regularly repeated since they were first given in March, 1958.

[60a] People v. Hamilton, 359 Mich. 410, 102 N.W.2d 738 (1960).

[61] The summary of Justice Jackson's views in this paragraph is based upon his dissenting opinion in Ashcraft v. Tennessee, 322 U.S. 143, 156 (1944).

[62] For an analysis of the Fourteenth Amendment confession cases in terms of "objective" and "subjective" tests employed by the Court see Cohn, *Federal Constitutional Limitations on the Use of Coerced Confessions in State Courts*, 50 J. CRIM. L., C. & P.S. 265 (1959).

[63] See generally REIK, THE COMPULSION TO CONFESS (1959); ROGGE, WHY MEN CONFESS (1959).

[64] See INBAU & REID pt. II and references cited note 7 *supra*.

heavy; the fear of detection fills the consciousness; and when detection comes, the pressure is relieved; and the deep sense of relief makes confession a satisfaction. At that moment, he will tell all, and tell it truly. To forbid soliciting him, to seek to prevent this relief, is to fly in the face of human nature."[65]

The ultimate question about the psychology of confession in this context is the extent to which the experience of being isolated and interrogated after arrest operates as pressure on the prisoner to give admissions which are sought by his interrogators. To what extent this type of pressure could lead some persons to confess, although innocent, is one question. Another question is whether for some persons interrogation in isolation may not be the psychological equivalent of threats or force. It is hard to escape the suspicion that sustained secret interrogation by itself in many cases implicitly suggests kinds of pressure which should not be allowed.[66]

4. Apart from the incriminating statements which it produces, does secret questioning have other consequences which affect the efficiency of criminal investigation and prosecution? In the United States it is often said that police abuse of prisoners is one of the important causes of community distrust of the police.[67] Juries may reflect

[65] 3 WIGMORE EVIDENCE §851 at 319 (3d ed. 1940).

[66] "With a person behind bars, police have a certain leverage that is valuable. The fellow in handcuffs, without the immediate prospect of freedom, is likely to be quite voluble—if he believes it is the key to the jail door." MULBAR, INTERROGATION 35 (1951).

Consider also two contrasting judicial views: "A prolonged interrogation of an accused who is ignorant of his rights and who has been cut off from the moral support of friends and relatives is not infrequently an effective technique of terror." Blackburn v. Alabama, 361 U.S. 199, 206 (1960). "We are not ready to say that the pressure to disclose crime, involved in decent detention and lengthy examination, although we admit them to be 'inherently coercive,' are denied to a State by the Constitution, where they are not proved to have passed the individual's ability to resist and to admit, deny, or refuse to answer." Ashcraft v. Tennessee, 322 U.S. 143, 170 (1944) (dissenting opinion).

[67] See generally NATIONAL COMMISSION ON LAW OBSERVANCE AND ENFORCEMENT (The Wickersham Commission), REPORT ON LAWLESSNESS IN LAW ENFORCEMENT (1931).

community suspicions that police mistreatment of prisoners is frequent, tend to distrust police testimony and in some cases acquit guilty defendants. A more subtle corruption of the jury may also be traceable to interrogation practices. When the search for confessions becomes a principal tactic in police work and a large percentage of prosecutions depend on confessions, juries may come to feel that a charge unsupported by a confession is weaker than it really is. The jury thus may be unreasonably reluctant to convict unless the prosecution produces a confession.

It is important to learn more about public attitudes toward the police. Are there significant differences in attitude toward the police among various social, economic and racial groups?[68] What are the police practices, real or supposed, which underlie these attitudes? With information,

[68] See the interesting study of public attitudes toward the Los Angeles police force described in GOURLEY, PUBLIC RELATIONS AND THE POLICE (1953). This survey utilized a carefully constructed questionnaire which listed 22 topics dealing with various phases of police activity. The subjects were asked to choose among four alternative views on each topic. Three of the topics were the following:

*"Treatment of Suspects*

1. Respect constitutional rights of suspected criminals.
2. Use whatever degree of force found convenient.
3. Often conscienceless and brutal in performing duties.
4. Do not know.

*Protection of Innocent*

1. Careful not to arrest innocent persons.
2. Occasionally arrest innocent persons.
3. Indifferent whether persons arrested are innocent or not.
4. Do not know.

*Minority Groups*

1. Usually fair in dealing with minority groups.
2. Sometimes unfriendly in dealing with minority groups.
3. Definitely prejudiced against minority groups.
4. Do not know."

Among the trends observed in the data collected were these: persons over 55 were most favorably inclined toward the Los Angeles Police Department; men were more favorably inclined than women; whites more than Mexicans and Negroes least favorably inclined; those with least schooling were more favorably inclined with college graduates expressing the least approval;

it could become possible to discuss whether the elimination of secrecy in questioning prisoners would contribute to increased public confidence and consequent benefits to law enforcement which might outweigh the disadvantages seen by the police in such a move.

5. What is the relationship of secret questioning to police brutality? Secret interrogation in quest of a confession is usually described as the setting in which police brutality occurs. Here, too, closer analysis is needed. If investigation were possible, it might be discovered that a significant amount of police brutality is not, as often supposed, part of an attempt to secure a confession.

William Westley, a sociologist who closely observed a middle-western urban police department, reported that the use of violence was often justified by the police not as a means of coercing confessions but as a way of coercing respect. 73 officers, approximately 50% of all patrolmen in the city studied, were asked, "When do you think a policeman is justified in roughing a man up? The following table summarizes the answers:

| Type of Response | Frequency | Percentage |
|---|---|---|
| Disrespect for Police | 27 | 37 |
| When impossible to avoid | 17 | 23 |
| To obtain information | 14 | 19 |
| To make an arrest | 6 | 8 |
| For the hardened criminal | 5 | 7 |
| When you know the man is guilty | 2 | 3 |
| For sex criminals | 2 | 3 |
| | 73 | 100 [69] |

Professor Westley explains the responses in terms of the problems of the police who encounter continual hostility and criticism from the public and have as one of their major emotional needs securing respect from the public. His data suggest that the causes of police brutality are more subtle than is usually assumed.

Professor Westley describes the psychological plight of the policeman, responsible for enforcing laws about which the community often has mixed feelings, encouraged toward cynicism by his observations of corruption and the seamy side of life, prone to normal reactions of anger and the desire to punish wrongdoers, impatient with the delays and failures of the courts, and faced with a hostile and suspicious public. Rewarded poorly in status and pay, the police tend to identify as a group against the community whose suspicions and constant criticism are thought unjustified. Secrecy becomes a vital part of the policeman's code, particularly his unwillingness to be a "stoolie" who betrays the confidence or misdeeds of a fellow policeman. Westley asked 85 policemen representing all ranks how they thought the general public felt about the police. 73 per cent felt that the public was against and hated the police and 14 per cent thought that part of the public was for and part was against the police. Only 13 per cent thought that the public likes the police.[70]

William Whyte's study of a Chicago neighborhood observes:

"There are prevalent in society two general conceptions of the duties of the police officer. Middle-class people feel that he should enforce the law without fear or favor. Cornerville people and many of the officers themselves believe that the policeman should have the confidence of the people in his area so that he can settle many difficulties in a personal manner without making arrests. These two conceptions are in a large measure contradictory. The policeman who takes a strictly legalistic view of his duties cuts himself off

---

except for public servants, unskilled laborers were the occupational group most favorably inclined; among the lowest votes of confidence were those expressed by professional persons, students and housewives. Housewives answered "Do not know" most often; school teachers, especially females, rated police consistently lower than the average for all professionals, accountants consistently higher, entertainers generally thought poorly of the police as, with certain exceptions, did lawyers. The respondents were also invited to give free answers about personal contacts with policemen. Most of the unfavorable comments referred to unjustified tickets or arrests, rough treatment, inconsistency in traffic enforcement or unjustified questioning.

[69] Westley, *Violence and the Police*, 59 AM. J. SOCIOLOGY 34, 38 (1953).

[70] WESTLEY, THE POLICE: A SOCIOLOGICAL STUDY OF LAW, CUSTOM AND MORALITY 160 (1951) (unpublished Ph.D. thesis in the University of Chicago library). See also Westley, *Secrecy and the Police*, 34 SOCIAL FORCES 254 (1956) and NATIONAL COMMISSION ON LAW OBSERVANCE AND ENFORCEMENT, REPORT ON THE POLICE (1931).

from the personal relations necessary to enable him to serve as a mediator of disputes in his area. The policeman who develops close ties with local people is unable to act against them with the vigor prescribed by the law. . . .

"Observation of the situation in Cornerville indicates that the primary function of the police department is not the enforcement of the law but the regulation of illegal activities. The policeman is subject to sharply conflicting social pressures. On one side are the 'good people' of Eastern City, who have written their moral judgments into the law and demand through their newspapers that the law be enforced. On the other side are the people of Cornerville, who have different standards and have built up an organization whose perpetuation depends upon freedom to violate the law. Socially, the local officer has more in common with Cornerville people than with those who demand law enforcement, and the financial incentives offered by the racketeers have an influence which is of obvious importance. . . . He (the policeman) must play an elaborate role of make-believe, and in so doing, he serves as a buffer between divergent social organizations with their conflicting standards of conduct."[71]

We know too little of the values and attitudes of policemen and the social setting in which they live and work. And yet these matters have a vital bearing on the problems of criminal law enforcement and police practice. In short, we need a sociology and psychology not only for the criminal but for the police and public as well in order to escape the confines of conventional argument about police practices.

\* \* \*

In recent years we have been assured in some quarters that the people may be expected to decide major issues of personal liberty wisely once they are given "the facts." And it has become almost conventional to decry the lack of factual information available about police practices and the effect of legal restrictions on law

enforcement. The clarion call for research threatens to become a liberal platitude. However such empirical research as seems feasible will not take us very far in resolving the difficult issues about police interrogation powers. Information may be useful in tempering extravagant predictions that legal restrictions threaten a "breakdown in law enforcement." And a greater understanding of the sociology and psychology of the police and the public may be helpful in countering hostile stereotypes of the police interrogator as a Torquemada in modern dress.

But no amount of information can resolve the issues raised by secret questioning in the absence of some objective standards by which police efficiency can be judged. To give a crude example, are the police doing a satisfactory job if 50% of all robberies and 75% of all murders and rapes are solved and the offenders convicted? The police and the public are not accustomed to think in these terms. The police inevitably feel the strongest pressures and demands of the public in connection with individual cases. The policeman's world and needs are concrete and particular. The situations with which he deals are typically acute and not conducive to reflection about what the general rules ought to be. This is why the law has wisely insisted that other functionaries do the judging.

The way of the law is not easy. It is a truism that our system of criminal justice is willing to pay the price of letting ten guilty men go free in order to prevent one unjustified conviction. But this expresses an attitude and not a formula. The result may become less clear if the first number in the equation is known and turns out to be 100 or 1,000.

The law is abstract and often cold comfort in the face of the individual human crises which are the stuff of police work. But the solution of single crimes cannot be made the test for procedural rules. Experience indicates that a very substantial portion of all crimes cannot be solved nor is it necessary that they be solved in order to maintain reasonably orderly and secure communities.[72]

---

[71] WHYTE, STREET CORNER SOCIETY 136, 138 (1943).

[72] Schwartz, *On Current Proposals to Legalize Wire Tapping*, 103 U. PA. L. REV. 157 (1954).

Indeed it seems probable that the great bulk of crimes are never even reported to the police or, if reported, are disposed of summarily by a police decision not to proceed further.[73]

Police efficiency cannot be judged in a humane society by the results of particular cases. Once this is recognized, it becomes clear that the problem of the unwitnessed crime which seems unsolvable without a confession does not resolve the basic issues about police interrogation. Even if we knew the comparative frequency of such crimes and had some agreed standards for judging police efficiency, the more fundamental question would still remain: To what extent should police effectiveness be the ultimate test? The competing values of personal liberty are not entirely based on pragmatic reasoning.

## IV. Some Secondary Issues: The Length of Permissible Interrogation, Cautioning the Suspect and the Exclusionary Confession Rules

### The Length of Permissible Interrogation

For how long should the police be permitted to question an arrested person prior to taking him before a magistrate? This is a secondary question which is reached only after resolving the fundamental issue of whether any detention for police interrogation is to be allowed.[74] It is submitted that if we accept the propriety of such detention, then there is no rational basis for limiting its length except police discretion, subject to inevitably ineffective supervision by the courts.

The choice is between a specific time limit, such as 12 or 24 hours,[75] and a flexible standard, such

as "a reasonable time," which is intended to allow some interrogation. A specific time limit assumes the need for some questioning. It also recognizes that unlimited police questioning is inconsistent with personal liberty and pregnant with dangers of abuse. But a short time limit does not solve the problem of abuses. The possibility that prisoners may be mistreated in the course of police questioning arises primarily from the secrecy of the proceeding. A short time limit may only be a stopwatch which underlines the necessity for less leisurely methods. A specific time limit is also unsatisfactory from the point of view of the police because of its inflexibility. Any fixed amount of time is likely to be inadequate for the police in the most difficult cases. Any requirement designed for the most difficult cases tends to harden into a practice utilized in all cases, petty and serious alike. Unused power is the exception.[76]

---

[73] See Goldstein, *Police Discretion Not To Invoke the Criminal Process: Low-Visibility Decisions in the Administration of Justice*, 69 Yale L. J. 543 (1960).

[74] Delay in arraignment for other purposes such as collateral investigation or avoiding a warning to confederates is outside the scope of this discussion.

[75] This was the approach of some congressional proposals following the *Mallory* decision, e.g., S. 2432, 85th Cong., 1st Sess. (12 hour arraignment requirement to apply only in the District of Columbia) and S. 3355, 85th Cong., 2d Sess. (12 hour requirement plus additional time reasonably necessary where it is impossible to comply with the 12 hour requirement). A specific

time limit is also prescribed in a few state statutes. See references in note 21, *supra*. These proposals and statutes do not refer to interrogation and sanction it only by implication. But see the novel suggestion in Note, *Prearraignment Interrogation and the McNabb-Mallory Miasma*, 68 Yale L. J. 1003 (1959). The author proposes an amendment to Federal Rule 5(b) barring any interrogation prior to an arrestee's production before a federal commissioner. The commissioner would advise the prisoner that he is not required to answer questions. He would not tell him that any statement may be used against him, nor would the prisoner be told of his right to counsel, as this would be "premature." The prisoner would then be removed by the police who could question him for a maximum of 3 hours. The prisoner would again be brought before the commissioner, given the remaining advice now required by Rule 5(b), and given a physical examination if he alleges that violence was used.

[76] See generally *Secret Detention By The Chicago Police*, a Report by the American Civil Liberties Union, Illinois Division (1959). The Chafee report pointed out that the Washington police "have taken their time for investigating all sorts of run-of-the-mill offenses. The argument that civil liberties must go by the board when the State is in real danger hardly applies to the theft of a saxophone." See *1943 House Committee Hearings* at page 54. See also the case described at page 49 of the same hearings in which the prisoner was held two days for investigation after the theft of a wallet containing $2.50, a cheap watch and a pack of cigarets.

See the testimony of the Chief Postal Inspector of the Post Office Department during the 1957 House Committee Hearings. Mr. Stephens pointed out that in most postal theft cases the evidence is fairly conclusive before the defendant is taken into custody.

Although arbitrary from either point of view, a specific time limit would at least be clear. But it is doubtful whether a police department whose detention practices are now unlawful will comply with any new standard, however clear, if it does not in effect permit existing detention practices or if no new sanction is devised to ensure observance. Any rule which diverges sharply from present practice and the felt needs of the police is likely to lead to evasion. In other words, any time limit must not only be clear, it must also work. This means that it must be understood and accepted by the police.

Professor Inbau urges that the police be allowed a "reasonable" time for interrogating suspects. The interview must be "unhurried"; it may extend to several hours, "depending on various factors such as the nature of the case situation and the personality of the suspect."[77] In the 1943 House Committee hearings, Attorney General Biddle urged the adoption of a standard requiring arraignment "within a reasonable time." He suggested that this would allow some flexibility and discretion to the police and that any abuses of discretion would be checked by the courts as they worked out more specific rules on a case to case basis.[78]

But how are the courts to decide what is "reasonable?" Is the test to be whether the police feel that they have exhausted the possibilities of obtaining information by further interrogation? Is it to be whether they have had an adequate opportunity to try the sympathetic approach, the "friend and enemy act," "bluffing on a split pair" and the other formulae in the interrogator's guide? How many times should it be proper to urge the prisoner to confess before reasonable interrogation has come to an end? Is the reasonableness of the interrogation opportunity to be measured by the result? How many times should the police be "reasonably" entitled to press for an answer or refuse to accept explanations which they think false? Is the length of "reasonable" interrogation to vary directly or inversely with the determination of the prisoner to remain silent or persist in answers which the police disbelieve?[79]

Judges have no special expertise in the art of criminal investigation. They are not equipped to judge the necessities of investigation in specific cases. If governed by a flexible rule clearly intended to allow some police questioning, the courts would be reluctant to second-guess police strategy in any particular case. A flexible standard would thus lead the courts to defer to police discretion.

The issue is not how long the police shall be permitted to hold suspects before they account to a court but whether detention for the purpose of private questioning should be allowed at all. Once such detention is sanctioned in principle it seems impossible to formulate a limit on the duration of the interrogation which will eliminate the dangers of abuse or provide any effective judicial control over police discretion in dealing with arrested persons.

### Cautioning the Suspect

Should the suspect be informed of his rights before he is interrogated by the police? Generally, the American decisions have not required that police warn suspects that they are not required to answer questions. However, failure to caution is a circumstance which may be considered in deciding whether a resulting confession was voluntary.[80] In several Fourteenth Amendment confession cases, the failure of police interrogators to caution the defendant was one of the circumstances stressed by the United States Supreme Court in holding that subsequent confessions were obtained by unconstitutional means.[81]

---

Nevertheless he insisted that the *Mallory* decision would hamper investigations since "it would result, occasionally, in innocent people probably being charged. And, in addition, it would have the effect of charging the man first and then completing the investigation, instead of the other way around." *1957 House Committee Hearings* at 96.

[77] 43 ILL. L. REV. 442, 450 (1948).

[78] *1943 House Committee Hearings* at 27 *et seq.*

[79] Consider the application of a standard of "reasonableness" to the facts of Spano v. New York, note 28 *supra*, where the defendant persisted on his attorney's prior advice in refusing to answer questions and confessed only after almost 8 hours of questioning and four separate sessions with his policeman boyhood friend.

[80] Wilson v. United States, 162 U.S. 613 (1896).

[81] See, e.g., Watts v. Indiana, note 28 *supra*.

It appears that police practice in the United States does not ordinarily include cautioning suspects in custody before they are questioned. The Inbau and Reid manual emphasizes that in the absence of such a specific requirement, it is unnecessary for an interrogator to "warn an offender of his constitutional rights before obtaining his confession."[82] Testimony in the 1957 House Committee hearings indicated that in Washington, D. C., the practice was to inform a suspect at the time that oral statements are reduced to writing that he is not obliged to make any statement but no warning was given before or during his interrogation. Police officials said that a caution before questioning would lead the subject not to make any incriminating statements. Chief Murray said,

"I think as we go out and pick up a man for rape or murder and if we tell him, in effect, that anything you tell me may be sufficient to put you in jail, I don't think he is going to tell us very much."[83]

The Chief Postal Inspector of the Post Office Department thought that warning a suspect of his rights "would be, in effect, suggesting to the individual in many cases that he should not make a statement. I don't believe that it would be in the interests of reliable law enforcement."[84]

It would be interesting to know whether the usual assumption about the effect of a caution is borne out by experience. The United States Attorney for the District of Columbia advised the March, 1958, Senate Committee hearings that he had recently suggested to District of Columbia police officials that all arrested persons be warned prior to any interrogation that they are not required to make a statement and that any statement might be used against them. He believed that the suggestion would be adopted.[85] It should be possible to find out whether since that time the District of Columbia police have followed the practice of cautioning suspects before questioning and how, if

at all, this has affected the number and types of statements obtained.

The Judges' Rules under which the British police operate provide that an investigating officer may question any person, whether suspected or not, but whenever he has made up his mind to charge a person with a crime he must first caution the subject before asking any questions or any further questions, as the case may be. Rule No. 3 broadly prohibits questioning persons in custody even after they are cautioned.[86] But it is not clear whether the Judges' Rules are now followed by the British police or whether the judges themselves enforce the rules. There are indications that it is common practice for the British police to question without cautioning persons they have decided to charge and also to question suspects in a police station.[87] Moreover we are told that the British

<hr>

[82] INBAU & REID at 223.
[83] *1957 House Committee Hearings* at 37.
[84] *Id.* at 100.
[85] *March 1958 Senate Committee Hearings* at 108. See also references cited note 60 *supra*.

[86] The Judges Rules as amended through 1957 are reprinted in an appendix to DEVLIN, THE CRIMINAL PROSECUTION IN ENGLAND (1958). They may also be found in MORIARTY, POLICE LAW 65–67 (14th ed. 1957). See also L. R. (1918) 1 K.B. 539; 6 POLICE JOURNAL 342, 353 (1933).
[87] Commander Hatherill of the New Scotland Yard Criminal Investigation Department says that it is his practice to postpone giving a caution in the course of interrogation by the expedient of deferring his decision to charge a suspect. He says that he charges a suspect "before I reached the point where I felt there would be no further doubt in anybody's mind." HATHERILL, INTERNATIONAL LECTURES ON POLICE SCIENCE, SECOND INSTITUTE OF THE LAW-MEDICINE CENTER, WESTERN RESERVE UNIVERSITY 37 (1955). See also memorandum of Professor Harry Street in the *March 1958 Senate Committee Hearings* at 13, 15.
Lord Justice Devlin indicates that it may not be so easy to avoid the rules in this way since counsel can object on the ground that the police officer at a certain point must have decided to charge the accused and therefore should have administered a caution before proceeding further. "If the evidence which the police had up to this point was strong and clearly pointed to the accused, the officer will find it difficult to maintain under cross-examination that he had not yet made up his mind to charge the accused. In practice, the Judge tends to make his own assessment of the evidence; and if he thinks it strong enough, he will not put much value on assertions by the police officer that he was still in doubt." DEVLIN, *op. cit. supra* note 86, at 34–36.
The 1929 Report of the Royal Commission on Police Powers and Procedure, CMD. No. 3297, recognized that the Judges Rules, by making the warning requirement turn on the interrogator's decision to charge, invite tactical delay by the police. The Commission concluded that since the purpose of the Rules is to

judges "at the present time tend to wink at breaches of the Rules, at any rate if the charge is a serious one" and that "it is no longer the practice to exclude evidence obtained by questioning in custody."[88]

It is hard to see any justification in principle for not ensuring that every person in imminent jeopardy of a criminal charge knows of his right not to answer questions and his right to counsel. These rights are probably more important at the police stage of criminal proceedings than at any other time. However, as the English experience just described indicates, any rule which requires a caution inevitably invites avoidance. Even if it is tied to an objective event such as the commencement of interrogation or the time of arrest, the probable conflict of testimony about whether a required caution was in fact given makes satisfactory judicial enforcement doubtful. Any rule requiring a warning is also likely to be ineffectual

since the significance and effect of a warning depend primarily on emphasis and the spirit in which it is given. A warning can easily become a meaningless ritual.[89]

Putting enforcement difficulties to one side, it is easier to say that some warning should be given than to determine when this should be done. The Judges Rules regard the officer's decision to charge the suspect with the crime or his arrest as the critical time. But it may be that a lesser degree of suspicion should bring the principle into play. If there are compromising circumstances, although suspicion has not ripened yet into accusation, interrogation of the suspect is likely to become a quest for incriminating admissions and the logic of the right to silence should require a warning.[90]

The idea of the caution seems to reflect an uneasy recognition of the fact that the roles of interrogator and suspect are antagonistic. The interrogator has the advantage of authority, sophistication and, after arrest, physical control over the suspect. The notion that he should precede questioning with a caution suggests that the interrogator should act to protect the interests of the suspect at the same time that he is attempting to obtain damaging statements from him.[91] But

---

inform persons that they are not obliged to make incriminating statements the spirit of the Rules requires a caution at the outset of an interview.

Professor Williams describes a number of recent cases in which the police appear to have detained suspects for questioning and to have carried on interrogation of persons in custody. Williams, *Questioning by the Police: Some Practical Considerations*, [1960] CRIM. L. R. 325, 328–31.

[88] Williams, *op. cit. supra* note 87, at 328, 331. Recently a committee of British lawyers reported that forms of "brain washing" are used in British police station interrogations. The report describes practices resembling the "friend and enemy act" (see INBAU & REID at 165). *Preliminary Investigation of Criminal Offences*, a Report by Justice (The British section of the International Commission of Jurists) (1960), reprinted in [1960] CRIM. L. REV. 793; New York Times, January 29, 1961, p. 71. The report will be presented to the Royal Commission on Police whose formation was announced in December, 1959. The Commission has been directed to examine the role and responsibilities of the British police and their relationship to the public. This will be the first such study since that of the historic Royal Commission of 1929. It is interpreted as a response to deteriorating relations between the British police and the public following "some widely publicized cases in which policemen were accused of unnecessary violence or even found implicated in crimes." New York Times, December 17, 1959, p. 75. One British observer has expressed regret that the Commission does not intend to consider police interrogation powers and practices except insofar as they affect public confidence in the police. Editorial, [1960] CRIM. L.R. 293.

[89] ". . . [W]e cannot give any weight to recitals which merely formalize constitutional requirements." Justice Douglas in the plurality opinion in Haley v. Ohio, 332 U.S. 596, 601 (1948). Fikes v. Alabama, 352 U.S. 191, 193 (1957), indicates that a caution, along with the other circumstances of an interrogation, must be considered in the light of the defendant's mentality and experience.

[90] S.3325, 85th Cong., 2d Sess., introduced by Senator Morse, during the post-*Mallory* congressional debate, would have gone further than the Judges Rules. This proposal provided that every person accused or suspected of a crime, whether or not in custody, should not be questioned without first being informed of the nature of the offense, his right to have counsel present, his right not to make any statement and that any statement could be used against him in a criminal prosecution. Any statement obtained without such a warning would be inadmissible. Compare the views of the 1929 Royal Commission, note 87 *supra*.

[91] Compare Lord Justice Devlin's view: "The real significance of the caution is that it is, so to speak, a declaration of war. By it the police announce that they are no longer representing themselves to the man they are questioning as the neutral inquirer whom the good citizen ought to assist; they are the prosecution and are without right, legal or moral, to further help from the

this cannot effectively substitute for the loyalty of counsel or the disinterestedness of a judge. The chief significance of the caution may well be that it serves to remind the police officer that he is subject to legal and moral limitations in dealing with his prisoner and thus counteracts to some extent the attitudes which are so easily engendered by his position of authority over the suspect.

### The Exclusionary Confession Rules

Characteristically, much of the discussion about police interrogation practices in the United States has focussed on the question of remedies for a person from whom the police have obtained a confession by improper means. The common law of coerced confessions and tort remedies for false imprisonment and assault have proved inadequate to deal with the problem of interrogation abuses.[92] The resulting concern has been reflected in the development of the Fourteenth Amendment confession rules and the *McNabb-Mallory* doctrine. Both lines of cases have produced sharp disagreement paralleling the controversy about the exclusionary rule which bars unlawfully seized evidence from criminal trials. Excluding a confession obtained during unlawful detention (or during prolonged questioning) and evidence obtained in an unlawful search both involve a deliberate rejection of evidence not shown to be false and in many instances shown independently to be reliable proof of guilt. This is also true of a coerced confession which under common law standards is inadmissible despite independent corroboration.[93] The confession rules and the rule on unlawfully seized evidence are defended on the grounds that 1) they are the only effective sanctions against violations of personal rights by law enforcement officials, and 2)

they protect the integrity of the judicial process since the admission of such evidence would make the courts participants in the process of obtaining convictions by unlawful means. In both cases the rule is attacked on the grounds that 1) it frees guilty persons because of the misconduct of enforcement officials, 2) in practice, it does not result in better police discipline and 3) it protects only a small number of the victims of police misconduct since the rule has no effect when such persons are not charged with a crime or if charged plead guilty. It is said that the exclusionary rules are ineffective to stop abuses because an investigator may still use improper methods in order to obtain leads to other admissible evidence.

The arguments for and against the exclusionary rules have been stated fully elsewhere[94] and will not be repeated here. But here too dependable information could assist discussion along fresh lines. To what extent do the police use prohibited methods to obtain admissions which they know will not be admissible but which they hope will lead to other evidence? What is the effect of the exclusionary rules, including the rule on coerced confessions, in plea and sentence bargaining between the prosecution and defense? As stated earlier, it should be possible to study the effects of the *McNabb* and *Mallory* decisions on the methods of operation of the FBI and the District of Columbia police, as well as the effects of *People* v. *Hamilton* in Michigan. Is it true that "the average police officer is not sensitive to the decision of a court rejecting a defend-

---

accused; no man, innocent or guilty, need thereafter reproach himself for keeping silent, for that is what they have just told him he may do." DEVLIN, *op. cit. supra* note 86, at 37.

[92] NATIONAL COMMISSION ON LAW OBSERVANCE AND ENFORCEMENT, REPORT ON LAWLESSNESS IN LAW ENFORCEMENT (1931); Foote, *Tort Remedies for Police Violations of Personal Rights*, 39 MINN. L. REV. 493 (1955).

[93] 3 WIGMORE, EVIDENCE, §§856–58 (3d ed. 1940).

[94] See *Memorandum on the Detention of Arrested Persons and Their Production Before a Committing Magistrate*, prepared by some members of the Bill of Rights Committee of the American Bar Association and submitted May 15, 1944 to Sub-Committee No. 2 of the Committee on the Judiciary, House of Representatives. This memorandum, apparently prepared by Professor Chafee, is reprinted in the *1957 House Committee Hearings*, the *March 1958 Senate Committee Hearings*, at 69 A.B.A. REPORTS 274 (1944) and in DOCUMENTS ON FUNDAMENTAL HUMAN RIGHTS 483 (Chafee ed. 1951). See also Hogan and Snee, *op. cit. supra* note 18; Barrett, *Personal Rights, Property Rights, and the Fourth Amendment*, [1960] SUPREME COURT REV. 46; 8 WIGMORE, EVIDENCE, §§2183, 2184 (3d ed. 1940); Waite, *Police Regulation by Rules of Evidence*, 42 MICH. L. REV. 679 (1944); and Inbau, *The Confession Dilemma in the United States Supreme Court*, 43 ILL. L. REV. 442 (1948).

ant's confession?"[95] Taken literally, this statement would apply to the use of force as well as interrogation free of violence. On the other hand, there are indications that the police are keenly aware of judicial rules of exclusion and attempt to adjust their investigating practices so as not to hamper successful prosecution.[96] The "average police officer" may not be sensitive to the problems in this field, but the attitudes of his superiors and the policies which they enforce count for much more.

Information about the effects of the exclusionary rules in practice will not resolve the issue. There is no calculus to indicate at what point the community will insist that the rules be changed because of the number of apparently guilty persons whom they set free. Nor is there any formula which can demonstrate the success or failure of the exclusionary rules in curbing police misconduct. But factual information could temper extravagant predictions that the rules threaten a breakdown in law enforcement.

## V. THE RIGHT TO COUNSEL IN THE POLICE STATION

Should an arrested person be entitled to counsel before or during any interrogation by the police? Perhaps the question is more properly put, should arrested persons be denied the right to counsel prior to preliminary hearing? At issue are three distinct questions, 1) whether the police should be permitted to deny an arrested person's request to communicate with a lawyer, 2) whether the police should be under an affirmative duty to advise arrested persons before questioning that they are entitled to communicate with counsel at any time and 3) whether the arrestee who does not know a lawyer or have the money to employ one should be assisted in finding counsel or furnished with counsel at public expense before he is questioned.

The importance of counsel during the period be-

tween arrest and production of the prisoner in court has been well stated and need not be rehearsed here.[97] The reasons for the right to counsel during the later stages of criminal proceedings apply with even greater force to the period during which a potential defendant is in the custody of police who have not yet accounted to a court. The suspect may not know of his legal rights. Even if he does, he probably needs professional advice to correctly evaluate his position. Early intervention by a lawyer can reduce the likelihood of abuses. He can also reduce the impact of discrimination against the poor and those who are less equipped by experience or education to understand their rights. As Professor Chafee said, "A person accused of crime needs a lawyer right after his arrest probably more than at any other time."[98]

Writing in 1955, a student of the right to counsel observed, "Strangely enough, it is impossible to say just when the right to counsel begins."[99] The 1958 decisions of the Supreme Court in *Crooker* v. *California*[100] and *Cicenia* v. *LaGay*[101] mark an important beginning in this field. In *Crooker*, a bare majority of the Court rejected the broad argument that the constitutional right to counsel should apply generally during police interrogation proceedings. But the reasoning of the decision may foreshadow a far-reaching development in the direction urged by Crooker's counsel. The Court's formulation of the constitutional rule has a broad ring. ". . . [S]tate refusal of a request to engage counsel violates due process not only if the accused is deprived of counsel at trial on the merits . . . but also if he is deprived of counsel for any part of the pretrial proceedings, provided that he is so prejudiced thereby as to infect his subsequent trial

[95] Inbau, *op. cit. supra* note 94, at 461.
[96] See the *Mallory* lectures given by the U. S. Attorney's staff to the District of Columbia police, cited note 60 *supra*. See also the testimony of William H. Parker, Los Angeles Chief of Police, in the *1957 House Committee Hearings* at 71 *et. seq.*, especially at 72 and 87.

[97] Allison, *He Needs a Lawyer Now*, 42 J. AM. JUD. SOC'Y 113 (1958); Rothblatt & Rothblatt, *The Right to Counsel and to Prompt Arraignment*, 27 BROOKLYN L. REV. 24 (1960).
[98] Chafee Report, cited note 94 *supra*, at 47.
[99] BEANEY, THE RIGHT TO COUNSEL IN AMERICAN COURTS 127 (1955). There are a few exceptions. Some state statutes make it a crime to prevent an arrested person from communicating with a lawyer. CAL. PENAL CODE §825 (1959); ILL. REV. STATS. c. 38, §477 (1959); MO. STATS. ANNO. §544.170 (1953).
[100] 357 U. S. 433 (1958).
[101] 357 U. S. 504 (1958).

with an absence of that fundamental fairness essential to the very concept of justice."[102] Crooker was undoubtedly adversely affected since counsel might have strengthened his resolve not to answer questions, shortened his interrogation by seeking habeas corpus or explained rights which he may not have understood. But the Court took a different view. Crooker was not "prejudiced" since his case was one of "a voluntary confession by a college educated man with law school training who knew of his right to keep silent." The rule of *Crooker* appears to be that the defendant is prejudiced by the denial of counsel if he does not know of his right not to answer police questions. The companion case of *Cicenia* v. *LaGay* supports this view. Justice Harlan's opinion in *Cicenia* is curiously lacking in information about Cicenia such as we are given about Crooker. In substance, all that the Court says about Cicenia is that he consulted a lawyer before surrendering to the police and during his questioning his requests to see his lawyer were refused as were his lawyer's requests to see him. As the Court of Appeals observed in *Griffith* v. *Rhay*,[103] Cicenia was presumably advised of his rights since he had consulted counsel before surrendering.

If this reading of *Crooker* is correct, then every suspect in police custody who does not know of his right not to answer police questions has the constitutional right to talk to a lawyer before he can be interrogated. The presumption against waiver of the constitutional right can cast *Crooker* protection around one who does not request counsel since his failure to ask for a lawyer may buttress the defendant's argument that he did not know his rights.[104] Paradoxically, the prisoner like Crooker

or Cicenia who requests counsel will be in a weaker position to claim the right to counsel since it will be easier to infer that he was sophisticated enough to know of his right to silence.

This is the reading of *Crooker* adopted by the Court of Appeals in *Griffith v. Rhay*. Griffith was a murder suspect who was interrogated and confessed while a hospital patient following serious surgery and while under the influence of a narcotic and analgesic drug. Although he was warned at the outset of the questioning that anything he said could be used against him, he was not told that he did not have to answer, nor was he asked if he had a lawyer or told that a lawyer could be provided if he desired. He did not ask for a lawyer. The court held that Griffith was prejudiced by the absence of counsel since there was no indication that he knew of his right to remain silent, counsel would undoubtedly have advised him of the right and, under the circumstances, would probably have advised him to remain silent. His failure to request counsel was not treated as a waiver since there was no indication that he knew of his right to counsel and, even if he did, he was not in physical and mental condition to intelligently waive the right. The use of a confession based on admissions obtained during his interrogation was held a violation of constitutional due process.

The argument for excluding counsel from the police station is simply that if the suspect talks to a lawyer he will be advised not to answer any questions. This assumption is implicit in Justice Clark's statement in *Crooker* that to "preclude police questioning—*fair as well as unfair*—until the accused was afforded opportunity to call his attorney" would have a "devastating effect on enforcement of criminal law."[105] Similarly, in *Cicenia* Justice Harlan said that to adopt the defendant's

---

[102] 357 U.S. 433, 439 (1958). Compare the Court's statement three years earlier that due process is denied by the assignment of counsel "at such time and under such circumstances as to preclude the giving of effective aid in the preparation and trial of a capital case." Reece v. Georgia, 350 U.S. 85, 90 (1955).

[103] 282 F.2d 711 (9th Cir. 1960) *cert. denied*, 5 L.Ed. 2d 373 (1961).

[104] This is not inconsistent with the statement in *Crooker* that "coercion seems more likely to result from the state denial of a specific request for opportunity to engage counsel than it does from state failure to appoint counsel immediately upon arrest." 357 U.S.

433, 438. That point is made in discussing the admissibility of the confession.

Query, since the *Crooker* rule turns on whether the defendant knows of his right to silence, can the police safely exclude counsel by administering a caution? If so, then the cases requiring that the right to counsel be waived intelligently should put the burden on the police to show more than a perfunctory warning. See text at note 89, *supra*.

[105] 357 U.S. 433 at 441.

position "would constrict state police activities in a manner that in many instances might impair their ability to solve difficult cases."[106] The police officials who testified at the 1944 and 1947 House Committee hearings on the *McNabb* and *Mallory* cases said that an arrested person will generally not answer any questions after he had been advised by a lawyer or by the "tier lawyers" in a jail.[107] Justice Jackson said that any lawyer "worth his salt" will tell his client to say nothing to the police.[108]

It would be interesting to know how often and in what type of cases lawyers do advise cooperation and full disclosure. Since silence inevitably invites suspicion, it is not unreasonable to suppose that in many cases where the suspect is innocent his lawyer will advise him to answer questions in order to clear himself as quickly as possible and assist the police. Moreover, the lawyer's advice may be different if he is present at the interrogation. It is one thing to dispense general advice to a suspect from whose interrogation the lawyer will be barred and quite a different matter to counsel silence or answers to particular questions when the lawyer hears them as they are asked.

But there seems no reason to doubt that counsel will ordinarily advise silence where he learns that his client is guilty or, although innocent, endangered by compromising circumstances and probably also when he lacks sufficient information to form a considered judgment.[109] This would make the work of the police more difficult. Introducing counsel into police station questioning would have the practical effect of giving life to the privilege against self-incrimination prior to the judicial stage of criminal proceedings. From the police point of view, it would have the effect of making interrogation after arrest impossible in the very cases in which it is most likely to help them find the offender. The problem of counsel in the police station thus brings us back to the initial question, whether any pre-judicial interrogation by the police should be allowed.

## IN CONCLUSION: SHOULD ANY PRE-JUDICIAL QUESTIONING OF ARRESTED PERSONS BE ALLOWED?

The modern police function of preliminary criminal investigation and interrogation of suspects is an unusual instance of discretionary administrative power over persons unregulated by judicial standards. As Lord Justice Devlin has shown, it is only in modern times that the police have inherited the responsibility for investigating crimes and initiating prosecutions.[110] In Britain, by the early 19th century, this function had been successively passed on by the grand jury and in turn by the magistrates as the procedures of each became judicial in character. Except for the British Judges Rules and the law of confessions, the English and American courts have not attempted to define the interrogation powers of the police. In large measure police station questioning in the United States is governed only by the self-imposed restraints of the police and by limited judicial action in the small number of cases in which police conduct becomes a litigated issue.

Whatever the reasons for their circumspection, the failure of the courts to assume supervisory powers over police interrogation practices remains an anomaly. It is sometimes grounded on the American separation of judicial and executive powers. But this doctrine has not prevented the courts from developing judicial standards for other administrative agencies.

Measured by legal standards, the most unique feature of police station questioning is its characteristic secrecy. It is secrecy which creates the risk of abuses, which by keeping the record incomplete makes the rules about coercion vague and difficult to apply, which inhibits the development of clear rules to govern police interrogation and which contributes to public distrust of the

---

[106] 357 U.S. 504 at 509.

[107] *1943 House Committee Hearings*, at 6, *1957 House Committee Hearings*, at 36.

[108] Watts v. Indiana, 338 U.S. 49, 59 (1949) (concurring opinion).

[109] In Griffith v. Rhay, the Court of Appeals said "In view of [the defendant's] physical condition, the possible effect of the demerol, and the seriousness of the charge and penalty, ... an attorney would probably also have advised him to refuse to talk." 282 F.2d 711, 717.

[110] DEVLIN, *op. cit. supra* note 86, c. 1.

police. Secrecy is not the same as the privacy which interrogation specialists insist is necessary for effective questioning. Inconspicuous recording equipment or concealed observers would not detract from the intimacy between the interrogator and his subject which is said to increase the likelihood of confession.

No other case comes to mind in which an administrative official is permitted the broad discretionary power assumed by the police interrogator, together with the power to prevent objective recordation of the facts. The absence of a record makes disputes inevitable about the conduct of the police and, sometimes, about what the prisoner has actually said. It is secrecy, not privacy, which accounts for the absence of a reliable record of interrogation proceedings in a police station. If the need for some pre-judicial questioning is assumed, privacy may be defended on grounds of necessity; secrecy cannot be defended on this or any other ground.

Secrecy should be prohibited. The method must be comprehensive and complete. Many of the various proposals to use sound recordings or motion picture cameras deal only with admissions which the prosecution wishes to use in evidence.[111] To be effective, the rule should require a record from start to finish of any interrogation in a police station sealed and certified by an independent observer of the entire proceeding. The subject need not be aware of the presence of the observer or the recording equipment.

Problems come immediately to mind. Who would the observers be and how would their continued independence be assured? Would the presence of observers in time become generally known and make suspects aware that their interrogation was being recorded? If this happened would the frequency of confessions actually be reduced? Is there a strange concern about the ethics of "eavesdropping," even when the procedure is likely to benefit the prisoner? Would the general requirement of a record eventually produce pressure for further change in the direction of magisterial inter-

rogation? The questions seem difficult; however, the interests involved are of sufficient importance to justify the investment of considerable effort and ingenuity to find solutions.

Once it becomes possible to speak factually about police station interrogation proceedings, three principal benefits may be anticipated. First and foremost is the elimination of obvious abuses. The problem of abuses is still a very real one. Continued charges of prisoner mistreatment and insistence on secrecy make it impossible to accept police claims that the third degree is a thing of the past. Moreover interrogation methods which eschew violence may nevertheless involve other abuses which are morally and psychologically equivalent to physical force. The relationship between the interrogator and his prisoner inevitably invites abuses not because policemen are any more brutal than the rest of us but because the officer's natural indignation at crimes of violence, his position of relative sophistication and control over the prisoner, the absence of disinterested observation and, above all, the frustration of suspended judgment all lead him to justify the use of means which would be rejected if exposed to public scrutiny.[112] Professor Inbau finds ethically unobjectionable the use, when dealing with persons suspected of crime, of less refined methods than are appropriate for ordinary relationships among law-abiding citizens. As an ethical principle, the limits of this view are not immediately apparent.

Wigmore saw the problem very clearly when discussing the privilege against self incrimination:

"The exercise of the power to extract answers begets a forgetfulness of the just limitations of that power. The simple and peaceful process of questioning breeds a readiness to resort to bullying and to physical force and torture. If there is a right to an answer, there soon seems to

---

[111] See e.g., 3 WIGMORE, EVIDENCE, §851a (3d ed. 1940), suppl. p. 102.

[112] Consider the following views of one thoughtful police official:
"Officers who have formed definite opinions as to guilt or circumstances may innocently exert a strong influence on the statements of witnesses whom they interrogate. Furthermore, when investigators allow theories of situations to form before there are sufficient facts disclosed to support them, they are likely to find their subsequent investigation restricted to a

be a right to the expected answer, that is, to a confession of guilt."[113]

It is asking too much of the most disciplined of men to grant virtually unlimited discretion to the interrogator in such a situation without the guidance and restraint of clear rules, disinterested observation and eventual public scrutiny. The rules against coercion and promises are manifestly inadequate for this purpose.

The second benefit which may be expected from the elimination of secrecy in police station interrogation is the clarification of the rules about coercion and voluntariness. The very concept of

pressure is unsatisfyingly vague. With complete records and a concrete understanding of what police interrogation practices are actually like, the courts will have a greater opportunity to clarify the rules in general and agree about their application in particular cases. The facts may also be helpful to the courts and legislatures in developing rules to affirmatively define police interrogation powers.

Lord Justice Devlin recognizes that the breadth of administrative discretion found in police interrogation practices is inconsistent with the values of a democratic society. He judiciously suggests that the system works in large part because of the average Englishman's confidence that his police will behave fairly. The appointment, since he wrote, of a Royal Commission to study the deteriorating relationship between the police and the public may foreshadow some qualification in this conclusion.[114] In the United States, it is difficult to discern the same degree of mutual confidence between police and public which our British cousins have enjoyed. Eliminating secrecy in police station questioning could go far to build public confidence in the police, the kind of confidence to which the police should be entitled and which in the long run may prove a more powerful aid to effective law enforcement than the most refined methods for obtaining confessions.

Beyond the problem of secrecy is the ultimate question, whether any pre-judicial interrogation should be allowed. Such proceedings are irreconcilable with the privilege against self-incrimination and the right to counsel. Whether the police need such powers in order to function effectively is a matter of conjecture. Because such questioning has become established practice, albeit without legal sanction, any suggestion to abolish it and completely judicialize the handling of arrested persons will seem unrealistic. And yet, in the span of history, it is only yesterday that official torture was abolished. And we may yet see wider interest in experiments aimed at increasing personal liberty in the field of criminal law enforcement.

---

search for facts to lend support to the ill-conceived theory. . . .

"Many hazards instantly appear when a criminal investigation centers upon certain suspects because of theories prematurely entertained. The most troublesome of these hazards is that of premature arrest. Arrests of this character are not made by reason of a logical analysis of supporting facts, but they occur by reason of the influence of the preconceived theory, strengthened in part by other conjectures such as the probability of the suspect escaping the immediate jurisdiction, or as in many instances, the hope that by severe grilling the suspect may be brought to the point of putting his own neck in the noose by confessing his crime. In every instance of premature arrest it eventually becomes apparent that there is not sufficient real evidence to support a specific charge. This condition leads to further compromising situations, and the effect of the troublesome factors are forestalled or delayed by resorting to other questionable practices, thus setting off a chain of illegal action that may run the gamut of condemned practices, from the filing of unjustified vagrancy charges with exorbitant bail, through incommunicado confinement to escape the writ of habeas corpus; coercive grilling, in the hope of securing a confession; third degreeing when coercion fails; and even on up to actual 'framing,' which has too frequently occurred.

"Policemen, in their eagerness to detect crime and to apprehend and bring criminals to justice, are inclined to overlook the importance of separation of governmental function as a safeguard of personal liberty. They are wont to usurp the prerogatives of the judiciary in fixing the guilt or innocence of the accused, and in eagerness to assert this pseudo authority will resort to practices that are questionable or highly irregular if not actually illegal."

KOOKEN, ETHICS IN POLICE SERVICE 54, 55 (1957).

[113] 8 WIGMORE, EVIDENCE, §2251, at 309 (3d ed. 1940).

[114] See references in note 88 *supra*.

# Police Interrogation Privileges and Limitations Under Foreign Law

## Canada

G. ARTHUR MARTIN

It is trite law that a policeman whose duty it is to inquire into alleged offences has the right to question persons likely to be able to give him information. The earlier English cases however made a sharp distinction between the right of a police officer to question a person when he was merely conducting an investigation and his right to question a person whom he had already taken into custody or had decided to charge.

In *R. v. Knight and Thayre*,[1] Channel, J., said:

"It is, I think, clear that a police officer or anyone whose duty it is to inquire into alleged offences as this witness here, may question persons likely to be able to give him information, and that, whether he suspects them or not, provided he has not already made up his mind to take them into custody. When he has taken anyone into custody and also before doing so when he has already decided to make a charge, he ought not to question the prisoner. A magistrate or judge cannot do it and a police officer certainly has no more right to do so. I am not aware of any distinct rule of evidence, that if such improper questions are asked the answers to them are inadmissible, but there is clear authority for saying that the Judge at the trial may in his discretion refuse to allow the answer to be given in evidence and in my opinion that is the right course to pursue."

The person questioned however had a common law right to keep silent and not incriminate him-self.[2] The Canadian courts however from a very early time have uniformly held that a statement made by an accused, if made voluntarily, is admissible notwithstanding that it is made while in custody in answer to questions put by the police.[3]

The Supreme Court of Canada in *Boudreau v. The King*[4] held that such statements are admissible if made voluntarily in the sense that that term is used by Lord Sumner in *Ibrahim v. The King*[5] where the principle is stated as follows:

"It has long been established as a positive rule of English criminal law, that no statement by an accused is admissible in evidence against him unless it is shewn by the prosecution to have been a voluntary statement in the sense that it has not been obtained from him either by fear of prejudice or hope of advantage exercised or held out by a person in authority."

There was however a considerable body of authority prior to the judgment of the Supreme Court of Canada in *Boudreau v. The King, supra*, that *as a matter of law* a statement made by an accused in answer to questions by the police in circumstances where he was either in actual custody or where the police had made up their mind to charge him was not admissible unless the statement was preceded by a warning that he was not obliged to answer.

In *Gach v. The King*[6], Taschereau, J., speaking for the majority of the court said:

[1] 20 Cox C.C. 713 (1905).

[2] "Section 110 is clearly an invasion of the common law right of a subject to remain silent lest he incriminate himself." Stewart, J., in Greathead v. Newcastle, 107 Can. C.C. 363, 366 (1954).
[3] R. v. Elliott, 3 Can. C.C. 95 (1899); R. v. Day, 20 O.R. 209 (1890).
[4] 94 Can. C.C. 1 (1949).
[5] [1914] A.C. 599, 609.
[6] [1943] S.C.R. 250, 254, 79 Can. C.C. 221, 225.

"There is no doubt that when a person had been arrested, all confessions made to a person in authority, as a result of questioning, are inadmissible in evidence unless proper caution has been given. This rule which is found in Canadian and British law is based on the sound principle that confessions must be free from fear, and not inspired by a hope of advantage which an accused may expect from a person in authority."

The present position is authoritatively stated in the judgment of Kerwin, J. (now C. J. C.), in the *Boudreau* case as follows:[7]

"The mere fact that a warning was given is not necessarily decisive in favour of admissibility but, on the other hand, the absence of a warning should not bind the hands of the Court so as to *compel* it to rule out a statement. All the surrounding circumstances must be investigated and, if upon their review the Court is not satisfied of the voluntary nature of the admission, the statement will be rejected. Accordingly, the presence or absence of a warning will be a factor and, in many cases an important one."

Mr. Justice Rand, in his judgment in the *Boudreau* case, recognizes the competing interests of effective police investigation of crime on the one hand and the protection from abuse of power on the other:

"No doubt arrest and the presence of officers tend to arouse apprehension which a warning may or may not suffice to remove, and the rule is directed against the danger of improperly instigated or induced or coerced admissions. It is the doubt cast on the truth of the statement arising from the circumstances in which it is made that gives rise to the rule. What the statement should be is that of a man free in volition from the compulsions or inducements of authority and what is sought is assurance that that is the case. The underlying and controlling question that remains: Is the statement freely and voluntarily made? Here the trial judge has found that it was. It would be a serious error to place the ordinary modes of investigation of crime in a straight-jacket of artificial rules; and the true protection against improper interrogation or any kind of pressure or inducement is to leave the broad question to the Court. Rigid formulas can be both meaningless to the weakling and absurd to the sophisticated or hardened criminal; and to introduce a new rite as an inflexible preliminary condition would serve no genuine interest of the accused and but add an unreal formalism to that vital branch of the administration of justice.

"I do not mean to imply any right on the part of the officers to interrogate or to give countenance of approval to the practice; I leave it as it is, a circumstance frequently presented to Courts which is balanced between a virtually inevitable tendency and the danger of abuse."[8]

The burden of proving to the satisfaction of the trial judge that a statement made by the accused was voluntarily made in the above sense is upon the Crown.[9] When a statement is tendered the trial judge holds a "trial within a trial" or as it is commonly called a *voire dire* in the absence of the jury. If the prosecution discharges the onus of proving that it was made voluntarily the statement is admitted in evidence. The weight to be attached to a statement admitted as voluntary is for the jury. If the Crown does not discharge the onus of proving it was made voluntarily the statement is ruled inadmissible and no more is heard of it.

The length of time over which questioning is conducted and the manner in which it is carried out are relevant factors in the subsequent determination of the voluntary nature of a confession.

---

See also Sankey v. The King, 48 Can. C.C. 97: "It should always be borne in mind that while, on the one hand questioning of the accused by the police, if properly conducted and after warning duly given, will not *per se* render his statement inadmissible, on the other hand, the burden of establishing to the satisfaction of the Court that anything in the nature of a confession procured from the accused while under arrest was voluntary always rests with the Crown." Per Anglin, C. J. C., at p. 101.

[7] Boudreau v. The King, 94 Can. C.C. 1, 3 (1949).

[8] *Id.* at 8.

[9] R. v. Thompson, [1893] 2 Q.B. 12, 17 Cox C.C. 641.

In *R. v. Howlett*[10] the Ontario Court of Appeal quashed the conviction of the accused because the only evidence consisted of a statement which the Court held had been obtained by police interrogation of a coercive nature over a three hour period. In the more recent case of *R. v. Nye*[11] the same court held that a statement made by appellant was made voluntarily although appellant had been questioned at intervals by the police over a period of about twelve hours while in custody. The court held that throughout this period no improper inducement had been held out to the accused to make a statement nor was she threatened in any way. In *R. v. Fitton*[12] the Supreme Court of Canada on appeal by the Crown reversed the judgment of the Ontario Court of Appeal ruling inadmissible a statement made by the accused because in the opinion of that court it was obtained by questions put by police officers that were in the nature of cross-examination in that the questions of the police had suggested that several items in an earlier statement made by accused were false. Rand, J., said:

"Questions without intimidating or suggestive overtones are inescapable from police enquiry; and put as they were here, they cannot by themselves be taken to invalidate the response given. The question still remains: was the statement made through fear or hope induced by authority?"[13]

It would appear from the recent decisions that the courts are taking a more liberal attitude than heretofore with respect to lengthy police interrogation providing that the questions are not such as to imply a threat.[14] The Canadian courts have not adopted a hard and fast rule that a statement made during a period of detention that is illegal is necessarily inadmissible. It is a circumstance and a cogent circumstance to be considered, and no

doubt illegal detention of the accused, unless satisfactorily explained by the prosecution, would raise a strong presumption that a statement made during that period was obtained by duress.

In *Chapdelaine v. The King*[15] the Quebec Court of Appeal rejected a statement made by accused where the circumstances were such as to indicate that the police had held the accused incommunicado for the purpose of inducing her to make a confession of guilt. The Court said:

"The duty of the officers was to bring this woman to Court within a reasonable delay. They had no authority to keep her *incommunicata*, whether she asked for a lawyer or not. It is obvious that the purpose of this incarceration was to create suspense in the mind of the accused, which could undermine a stronger mind than hers. It is true that she was not otherwise ill-treated but a display of kindness with, at times, a show of authority and usurped power, in such an environment, which amounted part of the time to solitary confinement was not without its effect—and this was sought.

"It is a remarkable coincidence that the accused was allowed to see a solicitor the day she signed a confession. Before that, she was not seen by friends or relatives, though they had come to headquarters."

An accused who has been arrested on a criminal charge has the right to retain counsel immediately, and any interference with this right by the police would suggest an improper purpose in so doing which would cast doubt on the voluntary nature of a statement subsequently made by the prisoner.[16]

[10] [1950] O.R. 181, 96 Can. C.C. 182.
[11] 122 Can. C.C. 1 (1958).
[12] [1956] S.C.R. 958, 116 Can. C.C. 1.
[13] 116 Can. C.C. at 6.
[14] *But cf.*, the judgment of the British Columbia Court of Appeal in R. v. Eaton, 117 Can. C.C. 375 (1957).

[15] 72 Can. C.C. 209, 211–12 (1933).
[16] R. v. Dick, 87 Can. C.C. 101, 112 (1947).
"The suggestion that any detective or other police officer is justified in preventing or attempting to prevent a prisoner from conferring with his counsel is a most shocking one. The suggestion that counsel, if he is permitted to confer with his client who is in custody, might thereby obstruct the police in the discharge of their duties is even more shocking. The prisoner is not obliged to say anything and the lawyer is entitled to advise him of that right. The lawyer is an officer of the Court and it is the function of the courts to administer justice according to the law. To prevent an officer of the Court from conferring with the prisoner who in due course may appear before it, violates a right of the prisoner which is fundamental to our system for the

The prisoner should not be denied his right to communicate with his relatives.[17]

It must be borne in mind that in Canada prose-

cuting counsel does not take part in the investigation of crime except in an advisory capacity to the police. The courts have laid it down on more than one occasion that it is the duty of prosecuting counsel to present fairly and dispassionately all the credible evidence that is available to the Court whether the evidence is for or against the accused.[18] In *R. v. Chamandy*[19] Mr. Justice Riddell, speaking for the Ontario Court of Appeal, said:

> "It cannot be made too clear, that in our law, a. criminal prosecution is not a contest between individuals, nor is it a contest between the Crown endeavouring to convict and the accused endeavouring to be acquitted; but it is an investigation that should be conducted without feeling or animus on the part of the prosecution, with the single view of determining the truth."

administration of justice." (Per the report of the Honourable Mr. Justice Roach of the Ontario Court of Appeal sitting as a Commissioner appointed by the Attorney-General under §46 of the POLICE ACT, R.S.O. 1950, c. 279, to investigate a complaint made against the conduct of the police.)

[17] "There is one further matter that deserves comment. A person who has been arrested should not be held incommunicado. We do not find it necessary to find as a fact that the infant plaintiff was denied his right to communicate with his father at the first reasonable opportunity. If, however, the father of the infant plaintiff was refused permission by the Sergeant of Police to see his son at any time before the charge came on for hearing in Court, such practice cannot be justified in this or in any other case. A person in custody should never be denied his right to communicate with his relatives at the earliest reasonable opportunity so that he may avail himself of their advice and assistance. That right ought to be recognized and given effect in all cases, and care should be exercised by police authorities to see that it is not wholly disregarded." Koechlin v. Waugh & Hamilton, [1957] O.W.N. 245, 249.

[18] Lemay v. The King, [1952] S.C.R. 232, 102 Can. C.C. 263; Boucher v. The King, [1957] S.C.R. 16, 110 Can. C.C. 263.
[19] 61 Can. C.C. 224, 227 (1934).

# England

## GLANVILLE L. WILLIAMS

### THE JUDGES' RULES

Americans who feel dissatisfaction with certain methods of police questioning sometimes look at the English Judges' Rules to see if there is any lesson to be learned from them. Perhaps there is a lesson, though not one that appears on the surface.

The Judges' Rules were originally formulated in 1912, with additions in 1915, and an important interpretation in 1930. Although the Rules are nine in number, the gist of them may be stated in two propositions.

1. When a police officer has made up his mind to charge a person with a crime, he should caution

him in the usual words: "Do you wish to say anything in answer to the charge? You are not obliged to say anything unless you wish to do so, but whatever you say will be taken down in writing and may be given in evidence."

2. A person in custody must not be questioned.

Violation of these rules confers a discretion on the judge to exclude from evidence a statement made by the accused.

### The Caution

The first rule is not a serious impediment to the police. When the police question a suspect, he is usually ready to answer their questions in order to try to assuage their suspicions. They need not administer the caution until they have obtained sufficiently incriminating statements to satisfy them of guilt. But even if the caution is uttered before this point, it will not usually inhibit replies. When the police officer has persistently questioned a suspect, thus bringing him to the point where he is ready to make a statement, the utterance of the caution is unlikely to alter matters.

The requirement of the caution pays lip service to the doctrine that an accused person has a right to silence, while not effectively safeguarding that right. Let us imagine what form of words would be needed if criminals were really to be advised of the best mode of exercise of their privilege. A policeman would have to say to every possible culprit (not merely to a person who had already doomed himself by replies to questions): "You need not reply to my enquiries, and in your own interest you should consult a lawyer before answering any of them." This warning has only to be phrased to make apparent its incompatibility with the successful performance of the functions of the police.

### The Rule Against Questioning in Custody

The other rule, against questioning in custody, does not clearly appear from the Judges' Rules as they were formulated in 1915. Indeed, Rule 3 states that "persons in custody should not be questioned without the usual caution being administered" which seems to imply that if the caution is administered, questioning is permissible. However, some judges even before 1915 had excluded statements obtained by interrogation in custody, whether upon caution or not. The true intent of the Judges' Rules was finally settled by a police circular issued by the Home Secretary with the approval of the judges in 1930. The circular states:

"His Majesty's Judges have advised as follows:—Rule (3) was never intended to encourage or authorise the questioning or cross-examination of a person in custody after he has been cautioned, on the subject of the crime for which he is in custody, and long before this Rule was formulated, and since, it has been the practice of the Judge not to allow any

answer to a question so improperly put to be given in evidence."

### The Practice of the Police

This interpretation may now be said to be a dead letter. Notwithstanding the circular, the police still interrogate persons in custody, and the judges admit the resulting confessions in evidence.

These facts are not generally acknowledged in England, and need to be demonstrated in slightly more detail. As an illustration, take the incident related by Mr. G. H. Hatherill in an address to the Royal Empire Society. Since Mr. Hatherill bore the impressive title "Commander (Crime)" at Scotland Yard, and told the story with some pride as an example of police practices, it may be taken as a confession by the police of what they do. Early on Christmas Day, 1944, a young woman was found murdered at Dagenham. Mr. Hatherill sent out his detectives to bring in to the police station the dead girl's young men—six or seven—with orders not to tell them why they were to go there but to note their behaviour. "Having all been torn away from their Christmas dinners, all but one of them wanted to pull down the police station. The odd man raised no difficulties, and when asked to get into the car said: 'I shall have a ride, anyway.' He eventually confessed to the murder."

Action of this type could be accounted efficient and proper police work if each suspect were given to understand that he was accompanying the police freely. However, it was doubtless part of the ruse in this instance, as in sundry others, to give each suspect the impression that he was under compulsion, in order to frighten him into confessing if he were the real culprit. Such action undoubtedly constitutes a false imprisonment.

Sir Ronald Howe, who was formerly a Deputy Commissioner at Scotland Yard, wrote that "the Judges' Rules are so much a part of the detective's training that it is a very rare thing for him to disregard them." But Sir Ronald had just stated his opinion that according to the Rules "a man taken into custody may not be questioned at all until [a] caution has been administered."[1] This is the wording of Rule 3, but it has long been known to contain a misleading implication. As was pointed out before, according to the interpretation adopted by the judges in 1930, Rule 3 was never intended to encourage or authorise the questioning or cross-examination of a person in custody after he had been cautioned.

Later in his article, the author gave details of the methods used by the police in questioning those whom they had "pulled in" on suspicion of crime. They will give the suspect a nice, strong cup of tea with plenty of sugar in it, express sympathy for his plight, and try by every means to get his confidence. "Most suspects, especially those new to the game or being questioned about a serious crime like murder, are only too eager to confide in somebody, and if the questioning policeman shows himself a decent chap, anxious to be fair, he will quite often be the confidant." It seems evident from the reference to the "questioning policeman" that the Home Secretary's circular of 1930 is regarded as a dead letter.

The way in which the police behave when they think the circumstances require it is illustrated by the case of Rowland in 1946. Rowland was suspected of murder, and was awakened at 11 p.m. by two police officers who told him to get up and dress. He was told that an inspector wanted to see him at the police station. He was taken to the police station and arrived there at 11:30 p.m. According to the evidence of the police themselves, he was questioned for two hours, and then had his statement taken down and signed, which took forty minutes; this would have meant that Rowland got to bed, in the police station, at ten minutes past two in the morning. Only after he had made his statement was he charged with anything. According to Rowland's own evidence, the period of questioning was substantially longer.

There can be no doubt that this action by the police was illegal. English law knows no "detention for questioning" short of arrest, and the act of taking Rowland to the police station without his consent was an illegal arrest because the reason for it was not stated at the time. It is surprising that, when Rowland was put on trial, his statement made in answer to the improper questioning was admitted in evidence without comment from the presiding judge or even protest from his own counsel.

## The Attitude of the Judges

These and other instances indicate that detention for questioning, and questioning after arrest, are still practised by some police forces, without serious check. To add to the anomaly, it seems from the reported cases that the judges have given up enforcing their own rules, for it is no longer the practice to exclude evidence obtained by questioning in custody. In 1930, when the judges' opinions were reported in the Home Secretary's circular, it was broadly true that the custom of the judges was not to allow any answer to questions addressed to a person in custody to be given in evidence. Earlier, in *Voisin*, the Court of Criminal Appeal had laid it down as a general principle that the confession was admissible though obtained as a result of questioning in custody; but a judge might exclude it in the particular case on grounds of unfairness. Thereafter the judicial attitude toughened, and between the wars the general practice was to exclude the confession; but since about 1950 they have almost uniformly been admitted.[2]

Our toleration of this situation in England raises serious doubts of our *bona fides* in prohibiting police interrogation of persons seriously suspected of crime. Thurman Arnold showed, in a penetrating and amusing study, that the criminal process embodies conflicting values, and he concluded that "the public administration of criminal justice is not a method of controlling crime. It is rather one of those problems which must be faced by those who desire to control crime."[3] So likewise with the ban on interrogation by the police. A

---

[1] See Sir Ronald Howe's article in *John Bull*, March 8, 1958.

[2] See May, 36 Cr. App. R. 91 (1952); Wattam, 36 Cr. App. R. 72 (1952); Bass, [1953] 1 Q.B. 680; Joyce, [1957] 1 W.L.R. 140; and *compare* Mills, [1947] K.B. 297.

[3] THE SYMBOLS OF GOVERNMENT c.6 (1935).

traditional principle of "fairness" to criminals, which has quite possibly lost some of the reason for its existence, is maintained in words while it is disregarded in fact. When judges both assert that the police should discipline themselves, and yet admit evidence that has been obtained by lack of the judicially-imposed discipline, the stultification of our professions becomes patent.

### ARGUMENTS IN FAVOUR OF ALLOWING THE POLICE TO DETAIN FOR QUESTIONING

The reader may be expecting at this point, from the pen of an English lawyer, a vigorous denunciation of the police and of the judges, and a plea for a return to the Judges' Rules as interpreted in 1930. What ought to be considered, however, is whether these Rules are a workable part of the machinery of justice. Perhaps the truth is that the Rules have been abandoned, by tacit consent, just because they are an unreasonable restriction upon activities of the police in bringing criminals to book.

Take the facts in *Voisin*,[4] one of the first cases after the formulation of the Judges' Rules where the Rules were in effect ignored by both the police and the judges. The accused had been detained for questioning by the police on suspicion of murder, but the police had not at that time decided to charge him with the crime. (Indeed, others were detained on the same suspicion, though subsequently released.) As part of the questioning, the police asked the accused if he would have any objection to writing down the two words "Bloody Belgian." He replied, "Not at all," and then wrote down "Bladie Belgiam." These words were his death-warrant, for the body of the murdered woman had had a label attached to it with the two words spelt in the same way as the accused now spelt them. The trial judge admitted the evidence, notwithstanding that the accused had not been cautioned and was in custody at the time; and the Court of Criminal Appeal affirmed the conviction.

From every point of view except the legal one,

[4] [1918] 1 K.B. 531.

the action of the police in this case was perfectly proper. It is true that a number of innocent persons were subjected to the inconvenience of detention in the police station for questioning, but this was surely a lesser evil than that a dangerous murderer should be left at large in society. The request addressed to Voisin was not likely to entrap an innocent man; on the contrary, it gave the accused an opportunity of convincing the police of his innocence, if he were innocent, for then his handwriting and spelling would have been different from the writing on the label.

In the same way, the action of the police in the case related by Mr. Hatherill was socially justified. It may be, in retrospect, a source of mortification that one has missed one's Christmas dinner, and an even greater misfortune that six men should have missed their Christmas dinners. But the evil is infinitely less than that a murderer should go free.

This same incident seems to show the need for some power of detention for evidentiary purposes on reasonable suspicion, distinct from the power of arrest. It is true that, in many cases, the police are able to act effectively without powers of detention. They may interrogate a suspect in his house, with his reluctant consent, or they may prevail upon him to attend for questioning in the police station. But these methods are not always adequate. A common method of solving crime is to use the *modus operandi* index and compile a list of all criminals who are known to use the methods employed in committing the crime under investigation; the list is then narrowed by excluding all those who for one reason or another could not have been responsible—as where they do not correspond with the description given by witnesses, or can produce a satisfactory alibi. The process frequently leaves a number of suspects. A witness may be shown photographs of these suspects, and he may pick out one, who is then put in an identification parade; if he is identified as the criminal, there may be sufficient evidence to charge him. Suppose, however, that the witness cannot make up his mind between two photographs? The police may wish to bring in the two suspects to stand in identification parades, but it seems clear that the law of arrest is unsuitable to achieve this end. An arrest supposes that a charge is made and that the accused will be brought before a magistrate as the first step in legal proceedings. But it would be improper to bring a man before a magistrate merely with the evidence that either he or someone else committed the crime. The machinery of arrest is inappropriate until suspicion has been focussed on a single person.

It may be conceded that hardship may be caused to persons who have previously been convicted of crime if they are subject to detention and police interrogation merely because some one else has committed a crime by a similar method. A former criminal who is now trying to lead an honest life may have his new career gravely jeopardised by such action on the part of the police. Thus a power of detention for questioning would certainly need to be used with wisdom and restraint. But this is not necessarily a reason for withholding the power from the police altogether. It should, of course, be limited to crimes of some gravity, and also subject to a limit of duration, and other safeguards to be suggested presently.

### OTHER CONSIDERATIONS OF POLICY

English lawyers tend to regard it as axiomatic that the police should not interrogate persons in custody, and they rarely enquire into the reason for the prohibition. Historically, it seems to have owed its origin to the indignation caused by judicial inquisition in political cases.

The King's Council of the seventeenth century provided a striking parallel with the secret police of modern tyrannies. It had its spies in every locality; it arrested and imprisoned persons on the slightest suspicion; and it issued orders to justices of the peace who interrogated suspects under torture.[5] These excesses of governmental power burnt into the racial memory of the Anglo-American peoples. It was by way of reaction against them, as well as against the general

[5] NICHOLAS, PROCEEDINGS AND ORDINANCES OF THE PRIVY COUNCIL xlvi–xlvii, 129 (1837).

severity of the criminal law, that the opinion came to be accepted in the early years of the nineteenth century that a magistrate should not interrogate an accused person. In 1848, this self-restraint was translated into law.

During the course of the nineteenth century, judges assumed that what was forbidden to the magistrate as a judicial officer was also forbidden to the police, and occasionally they excluded evidence obtained by the questioning of suspects in custody. But there is no compulsion about this logic, for the considerations of policy are different. It may be indecorous for a judge to question an accused person, and it may offend our sense of fairness to send an accused person to prison for refusing to answer incriminating questions; but neither of these issues is involved in questioning by the police.

The rule against police questioning cannot be explained by saying that such questioning may result in untrue confessions, for it can sometimes be demonstrated that the confession is true. Where the confession discloses details of the crime which only the criminal could have known, its authenticity is beyond doubt; yet some judges have excluded such a confession if it was the result of questioning by the police.

A possible argument against the questioning of prisoners is that the possession of this power tempts the police to do their job in an unsatisfactory way. One of the remarkable features of police practice in England, which impresses Continental observers, is the short space of time that is allowed to elapse between the arrest of an offender and his appearance in court and subsequent trial. Whereas, in many European countries, a defendant may languish in prison for as much as a year without trial,[6] this would be unheard of in England. The

[6] See, for France and Belgium, the instances given by ENSOR, COURTS AND JUDGES 35 (1933); DENNING, FREEDOM UNDER THE LAW 10 (1949). Dr. Otto John was kept in custody in West Germany for nearly eleven months before the opening of his trial on November 12, 1956. These prolonged detentions are especially significant when combined with police interrogation. Cardinal Mindszenty, who was tried before the People's Court in Budapest in 1949, put in a formal plea which stated that he had been interrogated in custody and in court

reason sometimes suggested is that the English police generally build up their evidence before making the arrest, so that very shortly after making the arrest they are ready with their evidence in court. On the Continent, the tendency is to arrest the suspect as the first step, in order to interrogate him; and the interrogation may be continued for weeks or months. Nevertheless, the abuses of Continental procedure are not a necessary element in police questioning. Under English law, the police only have a few hours in which to question the arrested suspect before bringing him before a magistrate. Even if the principle were conceded that the police may properly question a person in custody, a short time-limit would obviously be placed upon such questioning in order to avoid prolonged detention without trial.

Perhaps the real reason why we in England are afraid to allow the police to question persons accused of crime is that we fear the very efficiency of the proceeding. Few criminals can remain completely silent under persistent questioning; and if they answer, they are likely to give themselves away, if only by making statements which can be disproved, or statements which are inconsistent with a defence afterwards set up for them at the trial. A considerable number will confess. Sir Patrick Devlin in his Sherrill Lectures pointed to the remarkable proportion of confessions among those convicted of homosexuality between consenting adults—94 percent—where apart from the confession it would often have been extremely difficult to convict. He pointed out that in Scotland, where the judges are more active in

preventing police questioning, only one person out of nine convicted of homosexuality made a written admission.[7] One may well feel that the practice of prosecuting homosexual acts between adults is mistaken, but that has nothing to do with the general question whether the police should be allowed to use efficient methods for enforcing the law.

A strict ban on interrogating persons in custody would place a strain upon the self-restraint of the police. The duty of the police is to detect criminals, and they are generally allowed to address questions to every quarter where they hope to obtain information. It may seem strange that they should be supposed not to ask questions of the one person who is central to the whole investigation. To tie the hands of the police on a "sporting theory of justice" has a debilitating effect upon morale. As Sir Ronald Howe has said, "it is essential to effective police action that the police should be convinced that, when they have spent many hard days and nights tracking a suspect down, he should be properly dealt with." This consideration would seem to suggest a modification of the Judges' Rules, or of their interpretation, to allow some questioning in custody.

It must also be remembered that when the preliminary enquiry comes to be held, the prosecution will be forced to come out into the open with the details of its case against the accused. This is as it should be, for it would not be right for the accused to be taken by surprise at the trial. Yet there is no apparent unfairness in trying to obtain certain information from the accused before the preliminary enquiry, while he is still in the dark about the details of the prosecution's case. After the enquiry, the accused will be able to adjust his tale to fit the known facts.

For these important reasons, a complete prohibition of the questioning of those who are strongly suspected is difficult to enforce against the police, and, if it were strictly enforced, might breed a dangerous attitude of cynicism. The police may well ask themselves whether society can be so interested in the conviction of offenders, if it with-

---

for 40 days. Pastor Dinov, who was eventually acquitted by a People's Court in Sofia in 1949, was questioned for two months in prison, sometimes by a single questioner, sometimes by teams. Torture is not necessary to procure confessions if unlimited and practically unceasing questioning is permitted, for no ordinary person can stand it, especially when the prisoner has his resistance lowered by lack of warmth, lack of food, and lack of sleep, and is compelled to remain standing during the questioning. Mr. Stypulkowski, who wrote his experiences in his book INVITATION TO MOSCOW (1951), had to endure 141 examinations, of which some lasted for fourteen hours at a time. See also BECK & GODIN, RUSSIAN PURGE AND THE EXTRACTION OF CONFESSION (1951).

[7] DEVLIN, THE CRIMINAL PROSECUTION IN ENGLAND 58–59 (1958).

holds from the officers of the law one of the most potent means (and often the only means) of obtaining the evidence necessary for a conviction.

But, it may be said, the arguments for allowing the police to question a suspect do not justify them in taking him to the police station, where he feels himself to be isolated and at their mercy. Why should not the police do their questioning in the suspect's own home, before arresting him? This would certainly be the better practice wherever possible, even though it may not be so likely a way of securing a confession. Yet there are occasions when questioning, if it is to be done at all, must be done in custody. Where the crime is a grave one, and the suspicion already strong it may not be safe to leave the suspect unarrested. Or the matter on which the accused is questioned may not have come to the knowledge of the police until after he has been arrested. Or, again, the accused may be in custody on one charge, when it is desired to interview him on another.

### THE MECHANICAL RECORDING OF CONFESSIONS

The trend of the foregoing argument is that questioning in custody is an essential part of police investigation where the author of a crime cannot otherwise be detected, and, consequently, that it should be legalised and at the same time controlled. At the moment, English Judges maintain in theory an idealist rule, while conniving at police practices which set it at defiance.

One point needing attention is the possibility of providing for the mechanical recording of confessions. The present practice is for a statement to be written out either by the accused or by the police officer and signed by the accused. But a confession is admissible in evidence even though it has not been reduced to writing, or even though the accused withholds his signature, provided that the judge holds that it was properly obtained. In such circumstances there is likely to be a collision of evidence between the accused and the police as to what exactly the accused said. Often there will have been no shorthand note of an interview with the defendant in which he is alleged to have ad-

mitted guilt, and the court will have to make up its mind between the two versions of what passed. Where two police officers have interrogated the accused, the practice, approved both judicially and by the Home Office, is for the two officers to consult together after the interview when preparing their notes of what was said.[8] They may even prepare a joint note.[9] But it is strongly argued that this is unfair to the accused, since, instead of possibly three versions of the actual words used, the two police officers are ranged solidly upon one side of the fence, and the accused upon the other.[10]

Even where the statement is reduced to writing and signed by the defendant, the position is by no means satisfactory, because the statement does not show the questions by which particular answers were prompted. When an answer is obtained to a question, the question is not recorded separately in the written statement, but is embodied in the answer, though the wording was that of the interrogating officer and not that of the accused. If a leading question elicits a monosyllabic answer, it may be subtly misleading to write the result as though the statement implied in the question emanated from the accused.

These difficulties could be obviated if the interview were tape-recorded, so that the court of trial could, in case of challenge, ascertain precisely what the accused said. It is true that tapes can be tampered with, but this danger could be met by requiring the tape to be sealed by the accused person and deposited for transcription with an officer of the court.

Probably the most serious difficulty in the way of the proposal is that the police may fear that the presence or suspected presence of a recording instrument will inhibit the answers of suspected persons. A similar fear explains why the police, in interviewing a suspected person, do not write down his answers at the time; they do not want to let the suspect realise that he is dictating evidence against himself. Perhaps the difficulty would be

[8] Bass, [1953] 1 Q.B. 680; Home Secretary's circular to Chief Constables, No. 172/54, dated August 30, 1954.

[9] DEVLIN, *op. cit. supra* note 7, at 50.

[10] R. Kenneth Cooke in [1954] CRIM. L. REV. 833.

met if it were standard practice for the police, in interviewing any witness in connection with suspected crime, to carry a little attache case which, placed in an inconspicuous position, would record the conversation without drawing too much attention to itself. If this were a generally known and accepted part of police practice, it might not exercise too damping an effect upon investigations, and it would add greatly to the reliability of any evidence that results. At any rate, when the accused person is ready to make a statement there would seem to be little difficulty in recording his voice; and this is already done in Israel in the case of all major crimes.

## SAFEGUARDING AGAINST ABUSES

The practice of interrogation by the police is certainly open to the possibility of abuse. The police, convinced that they have got the right man, may sometimes regard themselves as morally justified in extorting a confession in order to keep an evil-doer under lock and key. The interrogation may be accompanied by promises or threats which would render the confession inadmissible if they could be proved in court, but which are afterwards denied by the officers concerned. A defendant is in a peculiarly weak position when he makes allegations of this kind against the police. The word of two officers, whose character appears to be above suspicion, will almost always be preferred to that of a person accused of crime. Yet it is known that some policemen are dishonourable, and policemen are occasionally found in the courts to have given false evidence.

It is sometimes suggested that an accused person should be entitled to see his lawyer before answering any questions by the police, and indeed that he should have a right to the presence of his lawyer during questioning. This would certainly operate as a substantial safeguard against illegality, but there is one fact that makes it impracticable. As soon as a lawyer is introduced on the scene, he advises his client to answer no questions. Thus if a lawyer were admitted the whole proceeding would be stultified. In *Voisin*, for example, it would quite possibly have resulted in the acquittal of a

dangerous murderer, for a legal adviser would not have allowed Voisin to write the fatal words.

From the lawyer's point of view, the advice he gives his client to refuse a statement is reasonable. Not knowing the evidence in the hands of the police, it would be highly dangerous to the defence to allow the accused to be questioned.

The defending lawyer's job is to befriend his client and (subject to a few overriding restrictions imposed by professional ethics) to give him the best advice in his own interest. The lawyer is entitled to assume the innocence of his client when all appearances are against him. It has been the experience of centuries that this arrangement is necessary to protect the innocent and to redress the lack of balance between the power of the State and that of the subject. As part of his function, the defending counsel will make full use of the rule that an accused person need not answer until a *prima facie* case has been established against him—and even then is obliged to answer only in the sense that he is put under the practical necessity of defending himself. We look upon this rule as an important part of the protection given by law to the liberty, dignity and privacy of the subject, notwithstanding that this sometimes makes the task of the prosecution harder. Still, considerations of liberty, dignity, and privacy must give way to some extent to the practical necessities of law enforcement, and for this reason it is necessary to maintain the present position under which a person who is in the custody of the police has no legal right to have his lawyer present while he is making a statement. The Royal Commission on Police Powers and Procedure recommended that in cases where the attendance of friends and legal advisers is open to no objection, the deponent should always be offered the option of having them present. But it seems that in practice the police invariably take the view that the presence of an outsider is open to objection.

For the same reason, it would be impracticable to require that the questioning of a person in custody should take place in the presence of a magistrate. Such a proceeding would be regarded as judicial, and there would be an irresistible demand that the accused should be given the right to legal representation and advice. Besides, the English police technique of friendliness and cups of tea could hardly be used to produce confessions if there had to be a formal hearing before a magistrate. From the point of view of the police, the most effective interrogation is one conducted in privacy.

It would, however, be a step towards preventing possible abuses if the accused were removed from the custody of the police. Only long familiarity causes us to accept without surprise the arrangement under which a suspect is placed in the absolute power of those whose duty it is to obtain evidence against him. Consider: we employ police to investigate crime, and expect them to attain a measure of success in the apprehension and conviction of criminals; at the same time, we allow those who are arrested to remain for a time in the custody of the police themselves. The result can be seen in cases like *Rowland,* which was discussed above, where interrogation of the suspect went on far into the night. The situation is a particularly dangerous one where the crime charged is that of an attack on a policeman, for here the *esprit de corps* of the Force is aroused, and the police are tempted to exceed proper limits.

The conclusion is that where a local jail is available, it should be made a rule that persons arrested should be lodged forthwith in this jail rather than in a police cell. This would mean that the physical safety of the accused person would be the responsibility of a different set of officials from the police. The police could be given a reasonable opportunity to question the accused in private in the prison, but the door would have the usual grid through which a prison warder might occasionally look. Thus the accused person would have some feeling of security against possible illegal violence on the part of the police, and the trustworthiness of confessions would be increased. The arrangement would also be to the advantage of the police because they could more easily refute charges of impropriety.

Whatever may be thought of these particular suggestions, there can hardly be any doubt that the general subject of questioning by the police needs to be reconsidered in the light of present needs and present practices. So long as there is pressure upon the police to keep down the rate of crime, they are likely to ignore restrictions which they feel to be unreasonable.

# *France*

## ROBERT VOUIN

According to the French penal procedure, the police may interrogate an *arrested* person, in the case of a crime or a flagrant delict, prior to taking him before the Public Prosecutor.[1]

Apart from the case of a flagrant delict, a preparatory inquiry may be opened on request of either the Public Prosecutor or the victim of the

offence. In this case, the examining magistrate can issue against the *accused* person: (1) a summons or mere invitation to appear freely before the judge; (2) a warrant or an order given to the public forces to bring the accused person before a judge; (3) a committal order for the head-watchman of the jail to receive the accused person; or (4) a warrant for arrest, an order given to the public forces to identify and arrest an escaped accused, in order to take him to jail.[2] Irrespective of the nature of the warrant delivered against the accused,

[1] CODE OF PENAL PROCEDURE (hereinafter C.P.P.), arts. 63, 64.

[2] C.P.P., art. 122.

he cannot be interrogated by the police. But the examining magistrate, in the process of the preliminary investigation, may give rogatory commissions to the police ("commissions rogatoires"), that is to say, may entrust a judicial police officer with the responsibility of assuming a certain part of the inquiry; however, the interrogation of the accused cannot be included in such commissions.[3] By virtue of this situation, a person may be heard by a judicial police officer as a *witness*, before being brought before the judge to be indicted.

Thus, in France, a person may be heard or interrogated by a judicial police officer before being brought before a magistrate ("Procureur de la République" or "Juge d'Instruction") in two situations: (1) in the case of a person who has been heard first as a witness by a judicial police officer, on a rogatory commission from a judge; (2) in the case of a person arrested in a case of a crime or a flagrant delict. In both cases, the French law grants an effective guarantee to the person who has been heard or interrogated in this manner by the judicial policer officer, but this guarantee is not always the same.

In France, the suspected person enjoys an effective protection as soon as he is brought before the examining magistrate as an accused. From that time, actually, he is not only excused from taking an oath to tell the truth, but also he may require the help of a barrister. The latter must be convoked by the judge to every interrogatory, permitted to study the briefing, and allowed to communicate freely with his client any time he desires.[4] As these protections do not facilitate their task, the examining magistrate and the police might be tempted to put off their application, delaying as long as possible the time when the suspected person is the object of a formal inculpation. But the jurisprudence has reacted against this trend by formulating a rule that the Penal Procedure Code has just adopted.

According to Article 105 of this Code, "the examining magistrate in charge of a preliminary investigation, as well as the magistrates and the judicial police officers acting upon a rogatory commission, cannot (otherwise it would not be valid) hear as witnesses persons against whom serious and concordant incriminating evidences exist, when this hearing would result in eluding the defence guarantees."

Thus, when a judicial police officer hears a person as a witness, upon a rogatory commission, and when serious and concordant incriminating evidence appear against this person, he must immediatly put an end to this person's interrogatory, because the latter, liable to be incriminated, cannot be interrogated from then on but by the magistrate, and must be brought before him at once.

Actually the whole difficulty lies in knowing what must be understood by "serious and concordant incriminating indicia," and the policemen affirm that this difficulty is not unsubstantial. But it is always possible for the judicial police officer, when he has discovered incriminating indicia which seem to him "serious and concordant" to bring the matter to the judge. Besides, the jurisprudence specifies what we must understand by these indicia by stating, for instance, that the inculpation could sometimes be delayed, as in the *Dominici* case,[5] even though, in the *Fesch* case, the preliminary investigation procedure was declared null and void because it was delayed too long.[6]

Several kinds of persons may be delayed for 24 hours at the disposal of the judicial police officer who is in charge of the inquiry, in case of a crime or a flagrant delict. But only the persons against whom serious and concordant incriminating indicia exist may be kept on a close watch for 24 additional hours, upon the decision of the "Procureur de la République." Now, any person kept on a close watch, in case of a crime or a flagrant delict, may be interrogated by the judicial police officer within the 24 hours allowed. At the end of the time allowed, the person must be discharged or brought before the "Procureur de la République."

The result is that, in the *preliminary* investigation for a crime or a flagrant delict, a person may

[3] C.P.P., arts. 81, 151, 152.
[4] C.P.P., arts. 114, 118.

[5] Cass. Crim., Sem. Jurid. 1954.11.8351 (1954).
[6] Cass. Crim., Sem. Jurid. 1955.11.8851 (1955).

be interrogated by the judicial police officer during two periods of 24 hours each, even if serious and concordant incriminating indicia exist againt him. This solution, opposed to the solution of the Article 105 of the same Code, may be explained by the special nature of the crime or the flagrant delict, which allows and even demands a specially fast procedure, in which the certainty of guiltiness makes possible a restriction of the guarantees granted to the defence.

Thus, if it is asked what limitation may be supplied to the right of the police to interrogate an arrested person before bringing him before the competent magistrate, the French law supplies the question with two different answers. It does not limit the delay for this interrogatory to a reasonable time; it does not prescribe to reduce it in order to help any useless slowness. The French law, depending on the cases, prescribes to put an end to the police interrogatory, either when serious and concordant incriminating indicia are disclosed against the interrogated person, or when this person has been delayed against his will for 24 or 48 hours. And these two different solutions seem equally justified.

Because of certain abuses of the police investigation, the question had been raised in France whether the assistance of a barrister should be permitted to a suspected person as early as his police interrogatory and prior to any actual judicial procedure. The new Penal Procedure Code has admitted this assistance to the suspected person by a defence counsel during the prehearing period only under very strict conditions.

According to the Code, in the case of a flagrant crime, the "Procureur de la République" may summon a warrant against any person suspected of having participated in the offence. He interrogates at once the person who is thus brought before him, and this person "if he reports himself, accompanied by a defence counsel, ... may be interrogated only in the presence of the latter."[7]

This procedure, according to the text, applies only "if the matter has not been referred to the examining magistrate yet." But it concerns an interrogatory by the "Procureur de la République" and not by a judicial police officer. The assistance of a defence counsel during the interrogatory is a privilege granted to the suspected person who spontaneously reports himself before the magistrate. But this privilege is granted to this person only if his spontaneous appearance is the consequence of a warrant summoned against him.

We can see that this assistance is very limited. Defence counsel (barristers) do not ask for it to be extended, because they don't care to assist their clients during the police phase of the procedure. Actually, it is still too early, the Code being in force only since March 2, 1959, to say what an institution which has not had a chance to prove itself yet is worth.

If a person suspected of having committed a crime was delayed by the police during an illegal extended period and if, during the illegal extension of the delay, he confessed he was the author of the crime, it is certain his confession could not be considered as a proof of the crime and should be set aside in the proceedings in court. As a matter of fact, the proof is free in France, on the understanding it has been legally secured and legally brought forward in court.

[7] C.P.P., art. 70.

## Germany

WALTER R. CLEMENS

### INTERROGATION OF THE SUSPECT BY THE POLICE SUBSEQUENT TO HIS PRELIMINARY ARREST

Under Section 163 of the German Code of Criminal Procedure (hereinafter called CCP), the police are bound to investigate criminal offenses and take all measures that permit of no delay, with a view to preventing collusion in the case. Within the scope of this duty they are authorized to make a preliminary arrest of suspects, provided requirements of Section 127(i) or (ii), CCP,[1] are complied with.

However, the right to a deprivation of liberty effected by the police is subject to limitations, as well as a review by the judge, according to the provisions of Article 104 of the Basic Law for the Federal Republic dated May 23, 1949,[2] and Section

128, CCP, supplementing and implementing the provisions of the Basic Law.[3]

Within the time-limit between the arrest by the police of the suspect and the date when he must be brought before the judge under Section 128, CCP, the police may collect evidence of every description and, in particular, interrogate him. This authorization stems from their duty, imposed upon them under Section 163, CCP, to investigate offenses. Naturally, such questioning of the preliminarily detained person can turn out to be detrimental to him. On the other hand, it can be advantageous, because under Section 128(i), CCP, the police are authorized to release him, which they are always bound and prepared to do, if the evidence gleaned by them, and in particular the interrogation of the arrestee, has rebutted the strong suspicion prevailing against him.

The suspect can defeat his interrogation by the police (as well as by the prosecutor or judge) by taking advantage of his privilege of silence, conceded to him under Section 136, CCP.[4]

To begin with, the right of the police to interrogate the suspect subsequent to his preliminary arrest is subject to certain restrictions as regards the mode of interrogation. Section 136a, CCP,[5]

[1] This provision is set forth in full in my paper on police detention and arrest privileges, which appears in Part I of this volume.

[2] It reads as follows:

"(i) The freedom of the individual may be restricted only on the basis of a formal law and only with due regard to the forms prescribed therein. Detained persons may be subjected neither to mental nor physical ill-treatment.

"(ii) Only a judge is entitled to decide on the admissibility and extension of a deprivation of liberty. In the case of any such deprivation which is not based on the order of a judge, a judicial decision must be obtained without delay. The police may, on their own authority, hold no one in their own custody beyond the end of the day following the arrest. Further details are to be regulated by the law.

"(iii) Any person temporarily arrested on the suspicion of having committed a punishable act must, at the latest on the day following the apprehension, be brought before a judge who shall inform him of the reason for the arrest, interrogate him, and give him an opportunity to raise objections. The judge must, without delay, either issue a warrant of arrest, setting out the reasons therefor, or order the release.

"(iv) A relative of the person arrested or a person enjoying his confidence must be notified without delay

of any judicial decision ordering or extending the deprivation of liberty."

[3] The latter provision reads as follows:

"(i) The preliminarily arrested person, unless set free at once, shall without delay, at the latest on the day following the apprehension, be brought before the judge (Amtsrichter) who has jurisdiction in the district where the apprehension took place; he shall inform him about the reasons for the arrest, examine him and give him an opportunity to raise objections.

"(ii) If the judge holds the arrest not to be justified or its reasons no longer existent, then he orders the release. Otherwise he will issue a warrant of arrest."

[4] See my paper on the privilege against self-incrimination, which appears in Part IV of this volume.

[5] This provision reads as follows:

"(i) The freedom of determination and manifestation of the defendant's will shall not be impaired through ill-treatment, fatigue, subjecting to bodily trespass, application of drugs, through torturing, de-

which is binding on the judge, the district attorney, and the police at all stages of the proceedings, prohibits certain methods of interrogation determined to be immoral.

This provision—which incidentally applies also to the hearing of witnesses according to Section 69(iii), CCP—was inserted in the CCP through an amendment in 1950.[6]

Prior to 1950 the CCP, originating in the year 1877, contained no provisions outlawing certain methods of interrogation. Such provisions appeared to be unnecessary, because the law presupposed as a matter of course that the German judges, public prosecutors, and police officers would refrain from dubious interrogation methods.

The sad experiences during the time of the Nazi regime (1933 to 1945), in the course of which the use of force and other disreputable methods was quite common, in particular during interrogations to which the suspect had to subject himself before the police, justly demanded that a recurrence of such disgraceful happenings should be banned by the provisions of Section 136a, CCP.

It must be emphasized that this provision contains not only a prohibition against specific interrogation methods, but also an unequivocal prohibition against using in evidence statements of the defendant which were obtained in violation of the first-mentioned prohibition. The ban on the use of such evidence applies even in the event that the defendant has given his consent.

It might be of interest that Section 136a, CCP, has received a broad interpretation on the part of the courts and the law professors. Thus the German Federal Supreme Court[7] and part of the legal teaching profession[8] have taken the view that obtaining a statement from the suspect through the use of a so-called "lie detector" falls under the ban of Section 136a(i), CCP, and that such a statement cannot, under Section 136a(iii), be used in evidence. The Bavarian Supreme Court[9] goes even farther. In a judgment rendered in 1951 it held:

"It does not appear out of place to interpret the provision of Section 136a, CCP, as the legal manifestation of the will of the law-maker going beyond the wording of the statute to rule out in a trial the use of evidence obtained through *immoral* means."

Also any wilful violation of Section 136a (i and ii), CCP, is punishable under Section 343 Criminal Code, which deals with the extortion of statements.

Moreover, the right of the police to interrogate the suspect subsequent to his preliminary arrest is subject to certain time limits. These are laid down in Section 128(i), CCP, which says that the arrestee must be brought before the judge without delay ("unverzüglich"), at the latest on the day following his preliminary arrest. This provision is the result of an amendment made in 1950.[10] The former text of this provision merely required the "bringing of the arrestee before the judge *without delay*," without providing for a specific time limit. This statutory phrase gave rise to a dispute which persisted for some decades as regards the interpretation of the term "without delay." The police,

---

ceiving, or hypnosis. Coercion may only be used to the extent permitted by the Criminal Procedure Statute. Threats with any measure outlawed under its provisions and the promise of any advantage not provided for by the law is prohibited.

"(ii) Measures impairing the memory or discernment of the defendant are not allowed.

"(iii) The prohibitions enacted in paras. (i) and (ii) are binding regardless of the consent of the defendant. Statements obtained in violation of this prohibition must not be used in evidence, not even with the consent of the defendant."

[6] Art. 3, No. 51 des Gesetzes zur Wiederherstellung der Rechtseinheit auf dem Gebiet der Gerichtsverfassung, der Bürgerlichen Rechtspflege, des Strafverfahrens und des Kostenrechts vom 12 Sept. 1950 (Art. 3, No. 51 of the Law dated September 12, 1950, on the Restoration of Legal Unity in the Field of Court Constitution, Administration of Civil and Criminal Justice and Law Costs).

[7] 5 Entscheidungen des Bundesgerichtshofs in Strafsachen 333 ( Decisions of the Federal Supreme Court in Criminal Matters).

[8] For instance: KLEINKNECHT-MÜLLER, KOMMENTAR ZUR STRAFPROZEBORDNUNG (Commentary on the CCP) §136(a) n.3(c) (4th ed.) and EBERHARD SCHMIDT, LEHRKOMMENTAR ZUR STRAFPROZESSORDNUNG (Instructional Commentary of the German Code of Criminal Procedure) pt. II, §136(a) n.9 (1957).

[9] Entscheidungen des Bayerischen Obersten Landesgerichts in Strafsachen (Decisions of the Bavarian Supreme Court in Criminal Matters) 460 (1951).

[10] Art. 3, No. 50 of the Law dated September 12, 1950. For complete citation to Law, see note six, *supra*.

following a dubious practice, used to interpret this term as entitling them to detain the arrestee as long as appeared necessary to them for the purpose of gleaning the complete incriminating evidence. Grave objections were justly raised against such practice. In 1922 they culminated in a judgment rendered by the Frankfort/Main Appellate Court[11] which interpreted the words "without delay" to mean that the appearance before the judge had to take place at the latest on the day following the apprehension, and that a prolonged delay for the purpose of procuring further evidence was improper.

Also the Reichsgericht (Supreme Court of the former Deutsche Reich) rendered a decision in 1932,[12] in which it said that as a rule the bringing of a preliminarily arrested person before the judge must take place at the latest on the day following the apprehension. During the period subsequent to 1933 this decision was open to strong criticism. A report by the Chief of the Berlin Criminal Police which appeared in 1934[13]—that means at the beginning of the Nazi regime—denounced the decision as completely out of place, and went on to say

"that an end had to be put to the excessive esteem of individualistic interests, and neglect of collectivistic interests which had carried fatal irresolution into the ranks of the police, hamstringing many of them in the impetus of the first action. Not only had the constitutional protection of the right of liberty to be taken into account, but much the more so the state's general interest in the interpretation of the words 'without delay.' For this very reason the arrestee would often have to put up with a police detention in excess of the 24-hours limit. On this a clear legal rule must be demanded."

In spite of this criticism the predominating police practice subsequently adhered to the decision of the Reichsgericht. However, the conflict of opinions on the interpretation of the words "without delay" did not come to an end until after the new phrasing of Section 128, CCP, in 1950.

For the purposes of an interrogation (or the collection of other evidence), the police, according to the present wording of Section 128(i), CCP, may detain a suspect arrested by them at the latest until the expiration of the day following his apprehension, whereupon he shall be brought before the appropriate judge. In the event his interrogation (or the collection of other evidence) has already been finished prior to that time, he shall be brought before the judge even earlier, that is, immediately upon completion of the inquiries. The infraction of these rules will constitute an illegal deprivation of liberty.

Going beyond the time-limit laid down in the law is not permitted, not even with the consent of the arrestee.[14]

It may be emphasized that the police are not entitled to detain the defendant on any ground whatsoever if he was arrested on the strength of a judicial warrant. In such case they are obligated, as is prescribed by Section 114(b), CCP, to take him before the judge "without delay," at the latest during the day following his apprehension, without being authorized, according to the prevailing and correct opinion, to delay the commitment by procuring evidence, or interrogating the arrestee. Neither are the police authorized to release the arrestee, because his arrest had not been ordered by them, but by the judge.

## THE DEFENSE OF THE SUSPECT DURING THE PRELIMINARY PROCEEDINGS

Section 137, CCP, provides that at any stage of the proceedings—which includes the police or district attorney's investigations—the suspect can avail himself of the aid of a defense counsel. The latter's communication with the arrested defendant, however, is subject to certain limitations, laid down in Section 148, CCP, which reads:

[11] JURISTISCHE WOCHENSCHRIFT (Weekly Law Journal) 1058 (1922).

[12] 135 Entscheidungen des Reichsgerichts in Zivilsachen 161 (Decisions of the Reichsgericht in Civil Matters).

[13] Quoted in KAUFMANN, DER POLIZEILICHE EINGRIFF IN FREIHEITEN UND RECHTE (The Police Encroachment upon Liberties and Rights) 78 (Frankfort/Main 1951).

[14] See KLEINKNECHT-MÜLLER, op. cit. supra note 8, at §128 n.3.

"(i) Written and oral communication with counsel is permitted to the arrested defendant.

"(ii) As long as the court case is not opened the judge may refuse written communications, if he is not permitted to look into them.

"(iii) Until the same moment the judge, unless the arrest is based only on danger of escape, can order the talks with counsel to take place in his presence or the presence either of a deputy or of a commissioned judge. . . ."

Hence, the arrestee can confer with counsel orally or in writing prior to his first police interrogation. He can defeat the restrictions laid down in Section 148(ii) and (iii), CCP, by taking advantage of his privilege of silence, conceded to him under Section 136, CCP.

Furthermore, counsel is in principle not entitled to attend the interrogation by the police or prosecution of either the defendant or other persons.

Pursuant to Section 147, CCP, however, counsel (and counsel alone; the defendant has no such right) is entitled to the inspection of the minutes of the district attorney and the police regarding the interrogation of the defendant and the opinions of the experts. Such right is granted him even during the initial stages of the investigation.

These far-reaching restrictions imposed upon counsel have met with vehement criticism in Germany of late. At the German Lawyer's Meeting in May, 1959, the president of the Federal Supreme Court supported this criticism by saying:[15]

"I agree that the position of counsel is too weak in our Code of Procedure, and that it must be built up strongly. Especially during the preliminary proceedings counsel will have to take a more active part, and no doubt his status as a whole will have to be raised. . . . That counsel may attend at the police interrogation, that he is supposed to attend at the prosecutor's interrogation, that he is allowed to ask questions, all this . . . I think is a matter of course."

There is good reason for entertaining hopes that very soon the position of counsel for the defense during the preliminary proceedings will be considerably fortified by way of an amendment of the law, and especially that he will be granted the right to be present at the police and district attorney's interrogations of his client, the witnesses and the experts, and to communicate with the defendant at any stage of the procedure without any supervision on the part of the judge or other persons.

In German criminal procedure it is counsel's function to help the defendant by having him exonerated, that means in the first place to obtain his acquittal or, if not, a sentence which is as lenient as possible. He is prohibited from acting to his client's detriment. In other words, he holds a one-sided party position. The public prosecution, on the other hand, is under German law an authority which is bound to be impartial. They will, therefore, ascertain under Section 160(ii), CCP, not only all incriminating, but also all exonerating and mitigating circumstances. Section 296(ii), CCP, even goes as far as entitling the public prosecution to make appeals and other remedies under the law in favor of the defendant. Such rights and duties of counsel and prosecution prevail at all stages of the criminal proceedings, hence also during the preliminary proceedings.

As the district attorney is the sole master of the preliminary proceedings (that means the proceedings prior to the presentation of the written charge to the trial judge), the part played by counsel for the defense can only be relatively restricted during this stage of the proceedings. Heinrich Henkel,[16] Professor of Criminal Law at the University of Hamburg, has rightly pictured that part as follows:

"In regard to his investigation-activities counsel is limited to submitting the exonerating material which has come to his knowledge, to the public prosecutor. He is not entitled to make his own investigations running parallel to those of the public prosecutor.

"The dividing line which must be drawn between the preparing and assisting activities of counsel on one hand, and the investigation-activities of the public prosecutor on the other hand, can, it is true, hardly be ascertained in

[15] ANWALTSBLATT (Lawyers' News) 209 (1959).

[16] STRAFVERFAHRENSRECHT (Law of Criminal Procedure) 211 (1953).

general terms; here the merits of the individual case must prevail, and the various objectives of the parties must be considered, at all events, however, the sole and exclusive responsibility of the public prosecutor for this stage of the proceedings. Certainly, counsel may not only accept enlightenment in the matter (through the defendant, his relations and friends), but also inquire who might be a witness to the facts. However, as a rule he is not permitted to question witnesses, as the latter would mean an encroachment upon the investigating activities of the public prosecutor, and might possibly expose counsel to the suspicion of influencing witnesses within the meaning of Section 159, 160 of the German Criminal Code."

The position of counsel during the course of the preliminary proceedings, as set out, appears to be too weak. It should be fortified considerably by way of a change of the law.

### Utilization of a Confession Made by the Defendant During his Illegal Preliminary Police Detention

As was mentioned above, the police may interrogate the defendant, preliminarily detained by them, without delay, at the latest until midnight of the day following the apprehension. A confession made to the police by the defendant at a moment subsequent to this time-limit has therefore been brought about in violation of statutory provisions.

This, however, does not necessarily mean that the judge is prevented from using it as evidence. This will occur only if the statute prohibits the use of such evidence.

While there is in the CCP no prohibition against using as evidence a confession which the defendant made to the police after the expiration of the time-limit provided for in Section 128, CCP, such confession can in principle be used with the qualification that the judge, within the scope of the free evaluation of evidence (Section 261, CCP), can refrain from using it[17] in an individual case.

[17] This matter is dealt with in a report concerning "The Exclusionary Rule with Respect to Illegally Seized Evidence" which appears in Part II of this volume.

The legal position is different in a case where the confession was brought about through ill-treatment, fatiguing or similar illegal devices. The above-mentioned statutory prohibition under Section 136a, CCP against using the evidence applies to such a case.

### Conclusion

In the light of the foregoing observations the three questions posed for discussion in connection with this topic[18] can be answered as follows:

(1) Under German law the police are authorized to interrogate a preliminarily detained suspect at the latest until the end of the day following his apprehension. This provision is satisfying and has not given rise to objections.

The commitment-limit provided for in Section 128, CCP, does not appear to be too long, and there is as yet no need for shortening it, which indeed cannot be recommended, because by doing so the police would in many instances have no sufficient chance to clear up the facts to such extent as would enable the judge, once the arrestee has been brought before him, to make his decision forthwith, without being compelled to make further inquiries himself as to whether a warrant of arrest appears necessary. There is no need either for prolonging the above-mentioned time-limit.

In comparison to a statute providing that the bringing of the suspect before the judge shall be effected "without delay" (the legal requirement in Germany prior to 1950) or "within a reasonable time," it is felt that the present German law, on account of its lack of ambiguity, should be given preference.

(2) Under German law the arrestee is entitled—and should be entitled everywhere—to get in touch with counsel immediately following his preliminary arrest, and by all means prior to his first police interrogation. The rights of counsel during this stage of procedure, however, are, as was shown, too restricted under German law and should be broadened.

The legal and ethical rules to be respected by

[18] The questions are set forth in the introduction to Part III of this volume.

prosecutor and counsel at this procedural stage should be the same as in the subsequent court proceedings, because the preliminary and the subsequent court proceedings represent one organic entity.

(3) A confession made by the defendant during his illegal police detention should not—following German law—be suppressed in principle, but only if it was obtained through immoral means, e.g. duress.

# Israel

HAIM H. COHN

A person arrested without a warrant must be taken forthwith to the nearest police station, and if the arrest was lawful, the officer in charge of the police station takes that person into custody; "otherwise, the arrested person shall be at once released."[1] Where he is detained, he must be brought before a magistrate within 48 hours of his arrest; if he has not been brought before a magistrate within 48 hours, he must be released.[2]

A police officer of or above the rank of inspector or specifically authorized in that behalf, may examine orally any person, whether in custody or not, who is supposed to be acquainted with the facts or circumstances of any offence in respect of which such officer is enquiring; the person so examined is bound to answer truly all questions put to him by the officer, other than questions the answer to which would have a tendency to expose him to a criminal charge.[3] Where, however, a person makes a confession to have committed an offence, such confession is not admissible in evidence against him unless the prosecution has adduced evidence to prove the circumstances in which it was made and the trial judge is satisfied that it was made freely and voluntarily.[4]

The precaution invariably taken by the police to ensure that the statement made by a person in custody should be free and voluntary, is strict compliance with the English Judges' Rules.[5] Thus, where a police officer has made up his mind that a person in custody is likely or liable to be charged with an offence, he first cautions him that he is not under any obligation to make a statement or to say anything, but that any statement he may choose to make will be taken down in writing and may be given in evidence; and where that person then expresses the desire to make a statement, he is invited to do so in his own words, and may not be cross-examined or asked questions except for the purpose of removing ambiguity in what he has actually said. Although, in ordinary criminal procedure, the Judges' Rules are not yet part of the law of Israel (any more than they are part of the law of England[6]), they were enacted in Israel as binding law for military police investigations,[7] and are to be incorporated in a new code of criminal procedure which is at present in the process of being drafted. But whether these Rules are binding law or only rules for the guidance of the police, it is well established that a court may reject a confession as not freely or voluntarily made, although the Judges' Rules were in fact duly complied with, and a court may find a confession to be free and voluntary although the

[1] Criminal Procedure (Arrest and Searches) Ordinance §§7 & 8, Laws of Palestine cap. 33.
[2] *Id.*, §10.
[3] Criminal Procedure (Evidence) Ordinance §2, Laws of Palestine cap. 34.
[4] Evidence Ordinance §9, Laws of Palestine cap. 54.

[5] Archbold's Pleading, Evidence and Practice in Criminal Cases 422 (34th ed. 1959).
[6] *Id.* at 424.
[7] Military Jurisdiction Act, 5715-1955, §§266–69, reproduced in English in United Nations Yearbook on Human Rights for 1955, at 142.

Judges' Rules have not in fact been complied with.[8] The question whether a confession was free and voluntary is a pure question of fact to be determined by the trial judge upon the evidence before him, and the defendant is entitled to the benefit of any doubt remaining in the mind of the trial judge.[9]

Although the requirement that it should be free and voluntary applies under the statute only to the "confession by the accused that he has committed an offence,"[10] the courts in Israel have always applied it to any statement made by the accused while he was in police custody, the reason being that if the prosecution produces such a statement in evidence, presumably it produces it for the purpose of incriminating the accused. The rule would probably not be applied if such statement were produced in evidence by the defence (but no case is reported in which this question has actually arisen).

Police interrogation of persons in custody is conducted as a matter of course. When such persons are brought before a magistrate, they are sometimes heard to complain that although they have been in police custody for two days already, they have not once, or only once, been questioned; on the other hand, it is a frequent occurrence that magistrates are asked by the police for further remands because it is desired to obtain a further statement from the person in custody. In most cases, however, in which a further remand is asked for purposes of police interrogation, it is because of apprehensions on the part of the police that the person in custody might, if set at liberty, interfere with or improperly influence other witnesses or conceal or destroy material evidence.

The question of the admissibility of a statement made to the police while the person making the statement was in unlawful custody, e.g. where the 48 hours' period had elapsed and he had not been brought before a magistrate, has never arisen

in Israel. It is submitted that the rules applying to statements made in lawful custody, *a fortiori* apply to statements made in unlawful custody; but, apart from that, any unlawfulness of the arrest or of the custody should have no direct bearing upon the question whether the statement was made freely and voluntarily—the less so as in many cases the prisoner is not, at the time he makes the statement, aware of the fact that he is unlawfully detained, such unlawfulness deriving not unfrequently from purely formal defects in warrants of arrest. There are civil, criminal and administrative remedies open to a person who was unlawfully arrested or unlawfully detained, but it is not one of those remedies that a statement he made while in unlawful custody must for this reason be rejected *in limine*.

On the other hand, the physical conditions under which a person is detained, the time of the day or night at which his statement is taken, the length of time during which it was taken, or the number of times it was asked of him—have all been held to have a direct bearing upon the question whether the statement was or was not free and voluntary. Statements were rejected which were given four hours after the person had first been cautioned and refused to speak[11]; or which were given in the middle of the night, whether after long hours of interrogation or upon his being suddenly awakened out of his sleep.[12] The argument that all police custody involves *ipso facto* some measure of duress and that no confession made in such custody should ever be admitted in evidence,[13] would, if accepted, lead to most serious handicaps in the administration of justice and does not appear, at any rate as a generalisation, to be justified on the facts. The only proper and just method of proceeding would appear to be that each statement be considered on its own merits, according to the particular circumstances under

---

[8] MILITARY JURISDICTION ACT, 5715-1955, §478; Muflah v. Attorney-General, 3 Piskei Din 31 (1949).

[9] Grossberger v. Attorney-General, 8 Piskei Din 182, 188 (1954).

[10] EVIDENCE ORDINANCE §9, LAWS OF PALESTINE cap. 54.

[11] Attorney-General v. Aharonovitz, 10 Piskei Din 599, 604 (1956).

[12] Goldstein v. Attorney-General, 10 Piskei Din 505, 545 (1956).

[13] See, e.g., REPORT OF THE SEMINAR ON THE PROTECTION OF HUMAN RIGHTS IN CRIMINAL LAW AND PROCEDURE (U.N. Doc. ST/TAA/HR/2). The seminar was held in Baguio City, Philippines, in 1955.

which, and the motives for which, it was actually made.

The principle underlying the rejection of non-voluntary confessions is that such confessions are likely to be untrue, whereas a voluntary confession may reasonably be taken to be true, as no person will wilfully make a statement against his interest.[14] It is as well to bear in mind that the issue before the court when considering the admission or rejection of a statement made by a person in custody, is not whether the police misconducted themselves and ought to be penalized, but solely whether the statement as such is or is not reliable and credible.

As to the right of persons in custody to have the advice of counsel prior to their interrogation, it is provided that any advocate charged with the defence of an unconvicted prisoner may have access to him on any day and at any reasonable hour, care being taken that the prisoner may see his legal advisers without the presence of any other person.[15] The procedure followed is that the person in custody notifies the officer in charge of the prison or other place of detention, on a form to be provided to him for that purpose, that he wishes to see a certain advocate and charge him with his defence; that advocate is then notified by the police accordingly, and if he wishes to see the person in custody, he is given the necessary facilities. The same applies to an advocate charged by friends or relatives of the arrested person with his defence, provided the arrested person agrees to execute a power of attorney for that advocate. It happens very frequently that a person in custody refuses to make any statement to the police so long as he has not seen a lawyer, in which case his refusal is usually taken down in writing to be signed by him, and often produced in evidence at his trial. It has also happened that persons in custody agreed to make a statement on condition that their counsel be present, in which case counsel is invited to be present, with the not infrequent result that eventually, on counsel's advice, no statement is forthcoming.

[14] 3 WIGMORE, EVIDENCE §§822–23 (3d ed. 1940).
[15] Rules 260 and 263, Prison Rules, 1925, as amended in 1945.

It is noteworthy, and at first sight alarming, that in almost every major trial where it is sought to produce in evidence a statement given to the police by the accused while in custody, the defence raises objection to the effect that the statement was improperly obtained. The cases in which those objections were upheld are very rare; and in the few cases in which such a statement was rejected, it was not necessarily owing to any proven misconduct on the part of the police, but because of the trial judge's doubt whether the statement was free and voluntary or perhaps given under some misconception on the part of the accused that there was some duty on him to make it. As the law imposes on the prosecution the burden to prove positively that any such statement was made freely and voluntarily, there can not, either legally or tactically, be any harm in putting the prosecution to its proof; and it can easily happen that a perfectly admissible statement is rejected because the trial judge is not satisfied with the quantum of proof adduced by the prosecution as to the circumstances in which it was made, or because the accused, testifying on his own behalf (in what is known as the "little trial" on the admissibility of the statement), succeeded in raising a doubt in the judge's mind as to whether his evidence or that of the police witness was to be preferred. But even if the statement is held to be admissible, the case of the accused has not in the least been prejudiced by his false accusations against the police (trial in Israel not being by jury, but by professional judges only).

Nor is it considered unethical for a defence lawyer to advise his client that the admission in evidence of his statement should be contested. A lawyer will advise his client on what grounds it *may* be contested, and he need not be suspected of doing more than that; if his advice is clear and intelligible, he will receive his instructions promptly. It would, of course, be unethical for the lawyer to suggest to his client a fabricated story; but not only persons with some experience as defendants in criminal cases, but also readers of trial accounts in newspapers, will be apt to do their own fabricating and instruct their lawyers as if in good faith. As a matter of conjecture it is not unrealistic to assume that many of the stories of police misconduct for the consumption of the courts are concocted in prison, where the more experienced veterans place their masterminds at the service of the uninitiated. The damage undeservedly done to the reputation of the police force in general, and the officers involved in particular, by the publicity attending the "little" as all trials, whatever their ultimate outcome, should not pass unnoticed.

In the eyes of many a judge, the refusal to make a statement to the police at the first opportunity is some indication either that the accused wished to conceal what he knew and did not cooperate with the police, or that he had some good reason not to make a statement. Considerations of this kind have been held not to be sufficient to corroborate other evidence, let alone to be evidence in their own right; they cannot even, standing alone, be sufficient reason to negative the credibility of the accused as a witness; but it is no use denying their existence. It is, therefore, not surprising that many advocates encourage their clients to make statements to the police when asked to do so, even while in custody; generally speaking, however, an advocate will not advise a person in custody to make a statement or to refuse to do so, until he himself has heard his client's story. It is in any event entirely proper for an advocate to advise his client not to make a statement but to exercise his right to remain silent.

Insofar as prosecuting counsel are concerned, it is an unwritten rule that there should be no contact between a person in custody and any member of the prosecuting staff (other than police), except upon the express request of the person in custody. No statement of any person suspected of crime is ever taken by prosecuting counsel, nor is any such person ever interrogated by prosecuting counsel except in court. Where the prosecution desires to have a statement made to the police clarified or amplified, police are instructed to request a further statement from the person in custody, provided the trial has not yet started. Any meeting between prosecuting counsel and an accused person before the trial, in the absence of the judge or of defending counsel, even for purposes of a pre-trial conference, would render the prosecutor liable to disciplinary action (all prosecuting counsel in Israel are civil servants). Similar rules apply to the contact between prosecuting counsel and witnesses for the defence, although the contact between counsel for the defence and witnesses for the prosecution is considered legitimate, so long as no attempt is made to exercise undue influence upon them.

In conclusion, it should be noted that in Israel even the full confession of the accused, although found to have been made freely and voluntarily, is not, if made out of court, sufficient to support a conviction; there need not be corroborative evidence, but the confession must be shown, by some other evidence, to be at least probably true and to fit in with the proven circumstances surrounding the acts confessed to.[16] No such evidence is required to support a plea of guilty in court; it is just another safeguard against illegal police interrogation, superimposed by the judiciary on the safeguards already provided for by the legislature.

[16] Anderlarsky v. Attorney-General, 2 Pesakim 87, 88 (1949).

# *Japan*

HARUO ABE

## POLICE INTERROGATION SUBSEQUENT TO ARREST AND PERMISSIBLE DELAY PRIOR TO ARRAIGNMENT

Should the police be permitted an opportunity to interrogate an arrested person prior to taking him before a judicial officer for a hearing? If so, should the provision for delay due to police interrogation be general (*e.g.*, a "reasonable time" or "without unnecessary delay") or specific (*e.g.*, four hours, twelve hours, or twenty four hours)? The answer depends upon how far one goes with idealism. If the arrest should be regarded as the terminal of criminal investigation or if the suspect should not be regarded as evidential means, the right of the police to interrogate the arrested person should be denied. Again, if one insists that rigorous limitation be placed on police interrogation, the permissible delay should be prescribed by a general term with very strict interpretation or by a specific term of a few hours.

In Japan the statutes and practices have dealt with this problem in a very realistic manner. In conducting criminal investigations, most Japanese investigators, whether the police or public prosecutors, are very anxious to obtain confessions rather than circumstantial evidence. Consequently, ordinary criminal investigators in Japan believe that one of the most important functions of the criminal investigator is to interrogate an arrested person prior to taking him before a judicial officer. The Japanese system of procedure subsequent to arrest will not be well understood without a deep insight into the psychological background of the investigators.

In Japan the principal investigating agencies are the police and the public prosecutors. They cooperate and divide the work of investigation between them; the former collect evidence in a crude form, whereas the latter refine and supplement it from a legal standpoint. When a suspect is arrested by the police, he is usually taken to the police station where he may be detained for 48 hours from the time of arrest. During the period of 48 hours the police may interrogate him from time to time; if he confesses, the confession may be reduced to a written statement.[1] It is unlawful for the police to detain him beyond this limit. If the police need to detain an arrested suspect longer, they must take him to a public prosecutor within 48 hours from the time of arrest together with evidence showing reasonable grounds to support the suspicion of guilt.[2] Otherwise the police must release the suspect at the expiration of the 48 hours period.

The public prosecutor who receives the suspect must immediately inform him of the charges against him and of his right to counsel and give him an opportunity for explanation.[3] The public prosecutor makes investigation, usually by questioning the suspect and other persons, to obtain further evidence supporting the suspicion of guilt. His major reliance upon personal evidence, however, does not mean that he pays little attention to physical or real evidence. If the public prosecutor believes that the grounds for detention of the suspect are reasonable, he shall within 24 hours from the time of receiving the suspect request a judge to issue a warrant for detention.[4] If he fails to make the request within the prescribed period or if the judge does not issue a warrant upon the request, the prosecutor is obliged to release the suspect, unless during the same period he institutes a prosecution by filing a written information against the suspect.[5] Thus the total period during which the investigators may interrogate the suspects without a warrant for detention may be at most 72 hours from the time of arrest.[6]

[1] CODE OF CRIMINAL PROCEDURE, art. 198 (1948).
[2] *Id.*, arts. 203, 204.
[3] *Id.*, art. 205.
[4] *Id.*, art. 205.
[5] *Id.*, art. 205.
[6] *Id.*, art. 205, par. 2.

However, this does not mean that the police have free rein to interrogate around the clock during the period.

The judge who has been requested to issue a warrant for detention shall hear the suspect and decide on the necessity and ground for detention.[7] The hearing is closed to the public. The period of detention secured by a warrant of detention is no longer than ten days.[8] However, the judge may extend it at the request of the public prosecutor. The total period of such extension should not exceed ten days[9] except that, when certain serious crimes are involved, an additional extension period not exceeding five days is permissible.[10] The public prosecutor is required to carry out the investigation within this period[11] and to decide whether or not there is sufficient evidence to support the prosecution of the detained suspect. If the prosecutor is convinced of the guilt of the suspect, he may file a written information with the court to open prosecution. The suspect has no right to be released on bail during this detention period unless and until a prosecution be instituted against him.

Recently a minority of progressive lawyers has been criticizing the present statutes for allowing investigators too much freedom. Clearly influenced by the development of the confession rule in American federal courts,[12] these lawyers contend that the 72 hours delay legalized under the Japanese system is clearly improper. The opinion of the United States Supreme Court in the *Mallory* case[13] and the dissenting opinion of Edgerton, C. J., in the *Netoyer* case,[14] seem to encourage the radical views of the lawyers who doubt the lawfulness of such statutes and practices as allowing the detention to be used for criminal interrogation.

However, such extremely idealistic views are not popular among the majority of Japanese lawyers who find in the present statutes a practical compromise between idealism and realism. The author is inclined to support the popular view for the following five reasons:

(1) At the present stage of scientific criminal investigation confession is still one of the most important sources of evidence;

[7] *Id.*, art. 207.
[8] *Id.*, art. 208, par. 1.
[9] *Id.*, art. 208, par. 2.
[10] *Id.*, art. 208a. This provision was newly adopted in 1953. So far, no such additional detention has been requested or permitted under this new provision.
[11] The following table, constructed from the data published in MINISTRY OF JUSTICE, THE 84TH ANNUAL STATISTICAL REPORT OF PUBLIC PROSECUTION FOR 1958 (1959), shows the number of persons received by all public prosecutor's offices in 1958 and detained for various periods for investigation. Where a suspect is detained more than once, his detention period is calculated as the total of those detentions.

[12] *Cf.* Abe, *Jihaku ni kansuru Eibeiho jo no Shogensoku (Anglo-American Rules on Confession)*, KEISATSU KENKYU (The Police Studies) Vol. 29, No. 8, p. 15; *Id.*, Vol. 29, No. 10, p.3; Vol. 29, No. 11, p.45 (1958); *Id.*, Vol. 30, No. 1, p.96; Vol. 30, No. 6, p.29 (1959) (a comparative analysis of the development of the confession rule from the standpoint of a Japanese lawyer).
[13] Mallory v. United States, 354 U.S. 449 (1957).
[14] Netoyer v. United States, 250 F.2d 31 (D.C. Cir. 1958).

| Detention Period | Prosecuted | | Not Prosecuted | Others | Total |
|---|---|---|---|---|---|
| | Trial | Non-Trial | | | |
| Not detained............. | 40,919 | 184,490 | 292,453 | 140,326 | 658,188 |
| Within 5 days............. | 9,171 | 4,908 | 6,325 | 2,177 | 22,581 |
| Within 10 days............ | 54,616 | 18,246 | 26,997 | 13,206 | 113,065 |
| Within 15 days............ | 5,859 | 975 | 2,214 | 857 | 9,905 |
| Within 20 days............ | 14,985 | 1,169 | 4,562 | 1,948 | 22,664 |
| Over 20 days.............. | 411 | 28 | 57 | 21 | 517 |
| Total.................. | 125,961 | 209,816 | 332,608 | 158,535 | 826,920 |

(2) Japanese judges are reluctant to convict an accused upon circumstantial evidence;

(3) Under the Japanese substantive criminal laws, where rules of presumption have very limited room to function, it is highly difficult to prove *mens rea* of the accused;

(4) The public prosecutor in Japan must make a "quasijudicial" decision in that he has to be well convinced by the evidence supporting the probable conviction of the accused before he decides to institute a prosecution;

(5) In Japan, people expect the public prosecution to maintain a very low "not guilty" rate (less than 1%).[15] If the prosecution made it the rule to prosecute suspects upon *prima facie* evidence and raised the "not guilty rate" over 1%, the prosecution would be severely criticized by public opinion and the legislature.

What is stated above does not mean that we should be content with the unsatisfactory reality.[16] On the contrary, the author agrees with the

---

[15] The following table shows the "not guilty" rates in recent years in Japan.

[16] *Cf.*, Abe, *The Role of Public Prosecutors in a Modern Society*, in KAINO (ed.), SAIBAN (Trial) 115, 129 (1959) (in Japanese). In this article the author pointed out as follows: "It is the tradition of placing too much emphasis upon confession which is hampering the growth of this scientific spirit. In Japan it appears that the police, public prosecutors, and the judges are very fond of confessions. Among the police there are still those who regard a "fist" as the best lie-detector. It is a shame that a distinguished public prosecutor should give hell to the suspect in order to obtain a confession. Among judges there are those who do not like to pronounce "guilty" except upon confession. In the technical terminology of criminal investigation, to force the accused to confess is called to make him 'break down.' Today, a good many people still think that a good criminal investigator is a person who is skilled in making a suspect 'break down' (i.e., compelling him to talk in exhaustion). If every one depends upon confession, criminal investigation does not grow up. It is true that forcing to confess is an easier and more convenient method than gathering physical evidence by walking around. But unless one decides to give up obtaining confession and rely on physical evidence, the modernization of criminal investigation cannot be expected. To abstain from self-incriminating evidence and to give up obtaining confession may result in temporary inefficiency of investigation, but the prosecution and the police will not mature without going through this thorny path."

---

contention of Professor Kaino, one of the most progressive scholars in Japan, who wisely suggested that we should be able to reach the ideal of criminal justice only through a painful period in which sly criminals escape justice wholly unpunished, and that the privilege against self-incrimination, though seemingly obstructive, has a disciplinary effect on the development of scientific

THE NUMBER OF THE ACCUSED PRONOUNCED "NOT GUILTY" AFTER FORMAL TRIAL IN THE COURTS OF FIRST INSTANCE

| Year | Defendants Finally Adjudicated in Ordinary Courts of First Instance | Not Guilty* | % |
|---|---|---|---|
| 1953 | 115,354 | 1,202 | 1.0 |
| 1954 | 109,696 | 869 | 0.8 |
| 1955 | 124,037 | 925 | 0.7 |
| 1956 | 124,179 | 710 | 0.6 |
| 1957 | 106,351 | 566 | 0.5 |
| Total | 579,617 | 4,272 | 0.72 |

* Defendants pronounced "not guilty" do not comprise those who were excused from punishment or acquitted because of statutes of limitation, etc. See Abe, *The Role of Public Prosecutors in a Modern Society*, in KAINO (ed.), SAIBAN (Trial) 115, 116 (1959) (in Japanese).

and. circumstantial investigations.[17] However, the author believes that the ideal should be reached step by step. The first step should be to train the police in scientific and civilized techniques of criminal interrogation rather than to prohibit the police from depending on the confession of the suspect. For this purpose the use of the "polygraph,"[18] for example, is highly recommended. There are many Japanese cases in which the timely use of the polygraph has led to successful investi-

---

[17] See Abe, *Self-Incrimination—Japan and the United States*, 46 J. CRIM. L., C. & P.S. 613, 624 (1956).

[18] It appears that techniques and devices of polygraphy in Japan have been greatly improved by Mr. Yoshimasa Imamura and his colleagues in Scientific Police Research Institute. One of the characteristics of the Japanese lie-detector is its sensitivity to galvanic skin reflex. For the development of lie-detection techniques in Japan see Imamura *et al.*, *Development of Lie-detection Techniques in Japan*, 11 SCIENCE AND CRIME DETECTION, (No. 2) 228 (1958) (in Japanese).

gation.[19] In a few cases Japanese courts have used polygraph records in weighing the trustworthiness of the defendant's testimony.[20]

## THE RIGHT OF THE ARRESTED PERSON TO COUNSEL

### Right to Counsel in General

The Constitution of Japan guarantees the right of the accused[21] and the arrested person[22] to counsel. The Code of Criminal Procedure specifically provides[23] for the privileges of the arrested person to counsel. According to the provisions of the law, an arrested person is entitled to counsel prior to the hearing before the detention judge, whereas he has no right to the public counsel to be appointed by the court unless and until prosecution be formally instituted against him.

### Communication Between Counsel and Arrestee and Its Restrictions

The principle of free communication between counsel and arrestee is statutorily established in Japan.[24] Counsel may communicate with and personally interview an arrested person without being monitored or having any one present.[25] There are two major exceptions to the principle. In the first place, it is provided that certain measures may be prescribed by law or the rules of the Court to prevent the escape of the arrested person or the destruction of evidence.[26] Thus far, however, no such restrictions have ever been prescribed except for the case where the arrested person is on the premises of a court.[27] Secondly, investigating officials may designate the date, place and time of interview, if such designation is necessary for investigation and only if it is made prior to the opening of the public prosecution.[28] Despite the proviso warning "that such designation should not unreasonably restrict the right of the suspect to prepare for defense," Japanese investigators are prone to utilize this privilege of designation to the extremity. In certain cases involving election law violation, bribery or racketeering, investigators often feel the necessity

[19] It is reported that from May, 1956, to July, 1959, 1,211 cases were tested by means of the polygraph. Data of polygraphic experiments are collected in series of publications (in Japanese) by The Scientific Police Research Institute.

[20] Decision of the Kyoto District Court, Fukuchiyama Branch, March 5, 1959 (prosecution for larceny; polygraphic records received); decision of the Chiba District Court, Yokaichi Branch, May 28, 1958 (prosecution for rape-murder; polygraphic records received).

[21] THE CONSTITUTION OF JAPAN, art. 37, par. 3: "At all times the accused shall have the assistance of competent counsel who shall, if the accused is unable to secure the same by his own efforts, be assigned to his use by the State." The original Japanese term for "the accused" is *keiji hikokunin* which literally means "criminal defendant." The word "the accused" being used in the official translation is, therefore, inaccurate and misleading, because the word "accused" may imply also the status of a person who has been accused but not yet formally indicted. In Japanese legal terminology *keiji hikokunin* or "the criminal defendant" does not include *higisha* or "the suspect" which means one who has been investigated but not yet formally prosecuted by a written indictment (or more exactly a written "information").

[22] *Id.*, art. 34: "No person shall be arrested or detained without being at once informed of the charges against him or without the immediate privilege of counsel. . . ."

[23] CODE OF CRIMINAL PROCEDURE, art. 30 (right of defendant, suspect and their relatives to assign the counsel); arts. 203, 204 (mandatory requirement of informing the arrested person of the right to counsel).

[24] *Id.*, art. 39. It should be noted that the restriction of communication and interview by the order of the court under article 80 of the Code of Criminal Procedure does not extend to the privilege of counsel to communicate with or interview an arrested person. For the translation of article 81, see note 29, *infra.*

[25] *Id.*, art. 39, par. 1: "The accused or the suspect placed under physical restraint in any way may, without having any official bystander present, have an interview with his defense counsel or any other person who is going to be his defense counsel upon request of the person who is entitled to appoint defense counsel . . . and may deliver or receive any documents or any other thing."

[26] *Id.*, art. 39, par. 2: "With regard to the interview and delivery or receipt of things prescribed in the preceding paragraph, such measures may be provided by law or ordinance (including the Rules of the Court; the same shall apply hereinafter) as are necessary for preventing the escape of the accused or the suspect, the destruction or concealment of evidence, or the delivery or receipt of those things which may hinder the safe custody of the accused or the suspect."

[27] THE RULES OF THE SUPREME COURT, art. 30.

[28] CODE OF CRIMINAL PROCEDURE, art. 30, par. 3: "The public prosecutor, public prosecutor's assistant officer and judicial police official . . . may, when it is necessary for investigation, designate the date, place and time of interview and delivery or receipt of things mentioned in Paragraph 1 only prior to the opening of public prosecution, provided that such designation should not unreasonably restrict the right of the suspect to prepare for his own defense."

of restricting free communication between the arrested person and outside people. In such cases investigators ask the court to issue an order to restrain free communication between the arrestees and outside persons other than the counsel.[29] But since this order does not restrain the approach of the counsel to arrestees, public prosecutors usually attempt to go one step further by invoking the provision authorizing investigators to designate the time and place for interviewing.

The degree to which public prosecutors utilize the privilege of restraining the interview varies from place to place[30] and from case to case. In small or middle-sized towns, where there is no perceivable tension between defense lawyers and investigators, public prosecutors seldom use this privilege of restriction. However, in large cities, such as Tokyo or Osaka, where there is some tension between defense counsel and criminal investigators, public prosecutors frequently use their privilege. Should the public prosecutor, for example, invoke this privilege in a case involving election law violation in Tokyo, the average practice would be as follows: During the ten day period of detention a defense lawyer would be permitted to interview the arrestee only once. If the detention were to be extended beyond the ten day limit, he would be entitled to see his client once more. This means that an arrested person may personally communicate with his counsel six

times during a 20 day detention period if he has three defense lawyers. In cases where a designation of date for interview is made, the average time for one interview is usually about 15 to 20 minutes.

The practice of restraining interview has naturally been arousing considerable feeling of dissatisfaction among progressive lawyers.[31] Some bar associations have passed resolutions requesting public prosecutors to exercise within reasonable limits their privilege of restraining interview. The Federation of Japanese Bar Associations also made a declaration[32] urging investigators not to abuse their privilege of restraining interview.

Thus far, there have been only a few Supreme Court decisions regarding the legitimate limitation of the investigator's privilege of restraining interview.[33] They indicate that the Supreme Court has been rather reluctant to handcuff investigators in exercising this privilege.

It should be noted that the law[34] provides for the recourse to a judicial remedy in the form of "*jun kokoku*" (quasi minor-appeal) to the court. This quasi appeal may be taken by a person who is not content with the restraining measure taken by investigators for hampering the interview between counsel and arrestee. It is reported that recently a few progressive lawyers took recourse to this provision. But no cases have ever been reported where the measures taken by investigators were set aside by the court. The proper solution of this problem seems to be not in judicial control but in the sense of humanity existing in the minds of criminal investigators.

### Ethics of Counsel Concerning Free Communication with an Arrestee

To destroy or conceal evidence in criminal cases of others constitutes a crime under the Japanese

[29] *Id.*, art. 81: "When there is reasonable ground to suspect that the accused under detention may escape or destroy evidence, a court may, upon request of a public prosecutor or on its own initiative, forbid him interview with other persons than those prescribed in Art. 39, Par. 1, examine documents and other things he may deliver to or receive from such persons, forbid him to deliver or receive them, or seize them. However, he shall not be forbidden to receive food nor shall it be seized."

[30] It was reported that out of 10,808 suspects, for whom detention was requested by the Tokyo District Public Prosecutors' Office from January to June, 1951, 821 (or about 7.6%) were those against whom orders to forbid the interview with outside people (except their counsel) were issued by the court. There were, however, many districts where the percentage of the issuance of such orders was less than 1%. For details see MINISTRY OF JUSTICE, CRIMINAL AFFAIRS BUREAU, A SURVEY OF THE ADMINISTRATION OF THE CODE OF CRIMINAL PROCEDURE AND THE SUGGESTIONS TO ITS AMENDMENTS (Materials on Prosecution, No. 33) 83 *et seq.* (1952) (in Japanese).

[31] See, *e.g.*, Ozu, *Improper Restrictions on the Interview of Counsel with the Accused or the Suspect*, 51 JURIST 14 (1954) (in Japanese).

[32] *Id.* at 17.

[33] Vol. 7, No. 7 Sup. Ct. Crim. Rep. 1474 (2d Petty Bench 1953), prosecution for bribery, four times of interview in a few minutes each held "improper" (dictum); Decision of the Supreme Court (2d Petty Bench, April 20, 1955) designation of the date of interview on the very day when the accused was indicted, held not necessarily unlawful.

[34] CODE OF CRIMINAL PROCEDURE, art. 430.

Penal Code.[35] If a defense counsel instigates or helps an arrestee to destroy or conceal evidence, the counsel is punishable under the Code. Investigators sometimes complain that there are cases, though very few, where defense counsel instigate or help arrestees to obstruct investigation.[36] However, since the communication between counsel and arrestee is not monitored, it is impossible to ascertain whether such complaints are true or not. The key to securing fairness on the part of counsel in free and secret communication between counsel and arrestees must be sought in the ethics of lawyers and the mutual trust between counsel and investigators. The days when the arrestees were detained *incommunicado* have passed. But the days of sound practice of free communication being established upon the mutual trust between counsel and investigators will not come very soon.

## LEGAL REMEDIES FOR AN ACCUSED PERSON WHO CONFESSED DURING AN ILLEGAL DETENTION PERIOD

What legal remedies should be available to an accused person who confessed to a crime during a period of police detention which extended beyond prescribed limits? Should he be entitled to have the confession suppressed?

These questions seem to be somewhat academic to Japanese lawyers because in practice there has been (and perhaps "there will be") no actual case where a Japanese prosecutor has ever attempted to introduce in evidence a confession which was obtained during a period of detention which extended beyond prescribed limits.

However, there was a case where the admissibility of a confession obtained by a police officer during an illegal detention was in question.[37] In this case the Supreme Court held that the written confession should not be regarded simply as null and void even if it had been made during an illegal detention. In another case, where the time of counsel's interview with the suspect under police detention was limited to two or three minutes and the admissibility of the confession made during the detention was challenged, the Court held that the confession was admissible because the illegality of the interview procedure did not affect the voluntariness of the confession.[38] From these precedents it may be inferred that the Supreme Court of Japan has been taking the position that "voluntariness" is the sole or most important criterion for the admissibility of a confession. In some cases a detention beyond prescribed limits may psychologically distort the voluntariness of a confession, but illegal extension of detention does not logically insure the involuntariness of a confession obtained during illegally prolonged detention. Under the Japanese system a confession obtained during "unreasonably prolonged" detention is presumed to be involuntary and inadmissible;[39] but a detention extended beyond prescribed limits does not necessarily mean "unreasonably prolonged" detention, unless the extension be made for such a long period as to have a torturing effect upon the detained person.[40] Most judges and public prosecutors seem to agree with the position of the Supreme Court, but majority opinion among scholars and private lawyers appears to be against the position of the Court. The author also favors this latter opinion.

---

[35] PENAL CODE OF JAPAN, art. 104.

[36] Several cases in which defense lawyers appeared to abuse their privilege of free communication with the arrestees are reported in MINISTRY OF JUSTICE, CRIMINAL AFFAIRS BUREAU, A SURVEY OF THE ADMINISTRATION OF THE CODE OF CRIMINAL PROCEDURE AND THE SUGGESTIONS TO ITS AMENDMENTS (Materials on Prosecution, No. 33) 56 *et seq.* (1952) (in Japanese). Also see Ozu, *op. cit. supra* note 31, at 16, reporting five cases in which counsel allegedly abused their right to free communication as experienced by Mr. Okazaki, during his 3 years and 7 months activities as a public prosecutor in Tokyo.

[37] Vol. 6, No. 10 Sup. Ct. Crim. Rep. 1245 (3d Petty Bench 1952).

[38] Vol. 7, No. 7 Sup. Ct. Crim. Rep. 1474 (2d Petty Bench 1953).

[39] THE CONSTITUTION OF JAPAN, art. 38, par. 2; CODE OF CRIMINAL PROCEDURE, art. 319, par. 1.

[40] There is a case where the Supreme Court held that a confession based upon another confession which had been made in a preliminary hearing after more than 40 days detention was not a "confession made after prolonged detention." Vol. 2, No. 10 Sup. Ct. Crim. Rep. 1209 (2d Petty Bench 1948).

# *Norway*

ANDERS BRATHOLM

In Norway the police have power to question a witness or a suspected person. But neither the witness nor the suspected person has any duty to make a statement, apart from giving his name, address and position.[1]

If a witness chooses to make a statement to the police, he is obliged to tell the truth, if he can do so without exposing himself or one of his relatives to danger of being punished or losing the respect of his fellow citizens.[2] A suspect can, however, without penalty make a false statement.

If the questioning implies that the witness is suspected of the crime in question, he is in the same legal position as an expressly suspected person and can, accordingly, make a false statement without risking being held criminally responsible.

The police have no duty to draw the attention of a suspect to the fact that he need not make a statement or that everything he says may be taken down and used as evidence against him. On the contrary, if the suspect declines to make a statement, the examining officer can draw his attention to the fact that his refusal could be considered as a circumstance which weighs against him. The same applies if the accused refuses to make a statement in court.[3]

As far as witnesses are concerned, it is laid down in the regulations for the Public Prosecuting Authority that the police shall inform a witness, who is not obliged to give a statement on ground of his relationship to the suspect, about his right in this respect. Otherwise, the police have no duty to inform the witness about his right to decline to answer questions.

It is made clear in the Criminal Procedure Act, and in the regulations which apply to the police, that no form of pressure must be brought to bear on a person being questioned.[4] There are, however, few regulations as to *how* the questioning shall take place. But it is understood that the questioning cannot be carried out under such conditions, or last so long, that the interrogated person is exposed to undue strain. To question him at night or for many hours without a pause, would in most cases be considered impermissible. It happens, however, in practice, especially in serious cases, that suspected persons have to undergo somewhat long and exhausting questioning, but really overwhelming strain is avoided. A confession obtained as a result of improper questioning will, as a rule, be admitted in evidence.[5]

The statement of a suspected person (or a witness) to the police is, as a rule, taken down and read over to him, and, in most cases, signed by him.

It is generally held that Section 332 of the Criminal Procedure Act does not permit the reading in court of the statement of the accused to the police, but in practice this interdiction has been of little significance. As a rule the police officer who took down the statement will give evidence in court with respect to what the accused told him. In this connection, the officer usually reads through the statement just before he enters the courtroom.[6]

The accused person has the opportunity to have counsel in attendance during police questioning, but it is seldom that this happens in practice in

---

[1] CRIMINAL CODE OF 1902, §§167, 333.
[2] *Id.*, §167(2).
[3] CRIMINAL PROCEDURE ACT OF 1887 (hereinafter called CPA), §260.

[4] CPA, §§256–58.
[5] See BRATHOLM, NORDISK TIDSSKRIFT FOR RETTSVITENSKAP (NORTHERN JOURNAL OF LAW) 109 (1959).
[6] Andenaes contends, and supports his contention with very convincing arguments, that the CPA can reasonably be interpreted in such a way that the police report in most cases can be read in court as a supplement to the oral statement of the officer. See his article in POLITIEMBEDSMENNENES BLAD (THE JOURNAL OF POLICE OFFICIALS) 149, 158 (1958).

211

any case during the time before or just after his arrest.[7]

A person who is arrested must, if at all possible, be brought before an examining judge within the end of the day after his arrest, if the police have not set him at liberty within this time.[8] Strictly speaking he should be brought before a magistrate at the earliest possible opportunity, and at the latest within the next day. But in practice it is seldom that his appearance before the court takes place before about 24 hours have passed.[9]

While the accused person is in custody, he is more or less frequently questioned by the police, either in prison or at the police station. The accused can refuse such questioning, but in practice it seldom happens that he does so. A refusal would in most cases worsen his position.[10] Questioning both before and after remand in custody can take place without witnesses. According to Swedish law, a witness must be present, if at all possible, during the police questioning.[11] A policeman can serve as a witness.

[7] See BRATHOLM, PAAGRIPELSE OG VARETEKTSFENGSEL (ARREST AND DETENTION BEFORE TRIAL) 92, 263–64 (Oslo 1957).

[8] CPA, §§235, 236.

[9] Sometimes the time limit is exceeded without a valid reason. See BRATHOLM, op. cit. supra note 7, at 263. Evidence, or a confession, obtained during such a period, is valid. A survey of the arrest and remand provisions in CPA is given in my paper on police detention and arrest privileges, which appears in Part I of this volume. A more detailed survey may be found in the author's article, *Arrest and Detention in Norway*, 108 U. PA. L. REV. 336 (1960).

[10] If it turns out that the remanded (or prosecuted) person was innocent, he is, as a rule, entitled to compensation by the State for economic loss caused by his imprisonment (or by the prosecution). Such a claim is in first instance generally decided upon by the Magistrate's Court. CPA, §§469–71.

[11] THE SWEDISH PROCEDURE ACT OF 1942, c. 23, §10.

# PART FOUR

# The

# Privilege

# Against

# Self-Incrimination

In the preparation of their papers dealing with the privilege against self-incrimination, the Conference participants were asked to consider four general questions:

(1) Is the privilege worthy of retention?

(2) If retained, what should be its scope, and what limitations, if any, should be applied in its interpretation?

(3) Under a system of dual sovereignties (e.g., federal and state), should each sovereign include within the privilege granted by it the possibility of incrimination under the laws of other sovereigns?

(4) To what extent does the concept of the privilege prevail in foreign countries? Is its absence compensated for in any other way? Has its absence led to abuses by police and prosecution?

The papers dealing with these and related problems are reproduced in the following pages. A brief summary of the American law with respect to the privilege appears at the outset. This is followed by the policy-oriented papers of the two American participants in the Conference who discussed self-incrimination, Professor John T. McNaughton of the Harvard Law School and Louis C. Wyman, former Attorney General of New Hampshire. Part IV then concludes with reports by the seven foreign authorities concerning the status of the privilege against self-incrimination in their countries.

# The Privilege Against Self-Incrimination: Principles and Trends

CLAUDE R. SOWLE

## Sources of the Privilege

In the United States, the privilege against self-incrimination is pervasive. The privilege is explicitly recognized not only in the Federal Constitution[1] but also in the constitutions of 48 of our states.[2] The two remaining states, Iowa and New Jersey, achieve the same result in different ways. Iowa, in the absence of an express constitutional provision, reads the privilege into the due process clause of its constitution.[3] New Jersey, on the other hand, grants the privilege by statute.[4]

Perhaps the most familiar wording of the privilege is that found in the Fifth Amendment to the Federal Constitution, which provides, among other things, that "No person . . . shall be compelled in any criminal case to be a witness against himself. . . ." Many of the states, in wording their privileges, have copied the federal provision. Others have not.[5] Yet, both in general purport and in basic interpretation, all of the privileges, federal and state, essentially point in the same direction.

Although, because of their pervasiveness and rough uniformity, convenience might suggest that we mentally allow the various privileges to coalesce, an accurate discussion of "the" privilege in this country, in the broad sense, demands a threshold recognition that each of the 51 individual privileges marches forward with sturdy independence. Thus, each privilege is available only in the jurisdiction granting it. Of course, to claim anything more for the various state privileges would be to undermine prevailing constitutional notions of the proper role to be played by the individual states, both among themselves and in their relations with the federal government. And, although something more, in theory at least, might have been claimed for the federal privilege, it has been settled law for well over one hundred years that the Fifth Amendment privilege against self-incrimination, just as the other provisions of the Bill of Rights, is binding only upon the Federal government. As the United States Supreme Court reiterated near the turn of the century in *Brown v. Walker*, "[T]he [Federal] Constitution does not operate upon a witness testifying in the state courts, since we have held that the first eight amendments are limitations only upon the powers of Congress and the federal courts, and are not applicable to the several states, except so far as the Fourteenth Amendment may have made them applicable."[6]

A review of the sources of the privilege would be incomplete without at least a brief consideration of the Court's reference, in *Brown v. Walker*, to the Federal Constitution's Fourteenth Amendment. For present purposes, the significant clauses of that amendment are these:

1) "No State shall make or enforce any law

---

[1] U. S. Const. amend. V.

[2] The state constitutional provisions are cited and quoted in 8 Wigmore, Evidence §2252 n.3 (3d ed. 1940).

[3] See Amana Society v. Selzer, 94 N.W.2d 337, 339 (Iowa 1959).

[4] State v. Zdanowicz, 69 N.J.L. 620, 55 Atl. 743 (1903). See also State v. White, 27 N.J. 158, 168–69, 142 A.2d 65, 70 (1958).

[5] For a brief summary of the language of the various constitutional provisions, see the text at notes 2 to 7 of McNaughton, *The Privilege Against Self-Incrimination*, which appears immediately following this article.

[6] 161 U. S. 591, 606 (1895). See also Feldman v. United States, 322 U. S. 487, 490 (1943).

which shall abridge the privileges or immunities of citizens of the United States";[7] and

2) "nor shall any state deprive any person of life, liberty or property without due process of law...."[8]

In the context of our discussion, these clauses translate into the following questions:

1) Is the privilege against self-incrimination a "privilege" or "immunity" of United States citizens which the states may not abridge? and

2) Should a state deny one his life, liberty or property without making the privilege available to him, would such a deprivation be without due process of law and hence a violation of the Fourteenth Amendment?

The short, well-known, fifty-year-old answer to both of these questions is "no"; the privilege against self-incrimination, as embodied in the Fifth Amendment, is not made applicable to the states by virtue of either of these clauses of the Fourteenth Amendment.[9]

The Supreme Court's narrow reading of "privileges" and "immunities" is acceptable to most as a correct adherence to the limited role accorded those terms by precedent. However, the Court's conclusion that the privilege is not inherent in due process is, to many, a debatable interpretation of that constantly expanding phrase. That this question probably will be revisited is evidenced by the fact that when the issue last came before the Supreme Court fourteen years ago, the minority favoring recognition of the privilege as a basic demand of Fourteenth Amendment due process had grown from one to four justices.[10]

Nor is the question stripped of practical significance by virtue of the fact that each state already has a privilege of its own. A decision that the Fourteenth Amendment required state recognition of a privilege against self-incrimination would permit the Supreme Court to become, for the first time, an overseer of state activities touching upon the privilege. And, although one might expect this oversight to be both benevolent and restrained, thus resulting in the fashioning of a Fourteenth Amendment privilege which would be something less than a mere carbon copy of the Fifth Amendment privilege,[10a] the potential of such a new federal power could not, of course, be ignored.

## THE GENERAL SCOPE OF THE PRIVILEGE

Let us move from our review of the sources of the privilege into a brief and very general discussion of its scope.

The privilege, irrespective of the differences in wording which mark its various sources, seems clearly to bestow its protection upon a defendant on trial in a criminal case. However, it is ironic to note parenthetically that even as recently as 75 or 80 years ago, he who stood accused of a crime was the very one who did not need the protection of any such privilege. For, until the latter half of the nineteenth century, when legislatures began to change the testimonial status of the accused, the defendant was not a competent witness either for or against himself.[11]

Upon leaving the area of the accused and moving into the domain of the ordinary witness, the problems of interpretation become more difficult. One must strain a bit with the words of the various privileges in order to bring within their ambit a witness who is not, at the time he invokes the privilege, a defendant in a criminal case. To refine the problem in terms of a question: Is the privilege available to one who does not have the

[7] U. S. CONST. amend. XIV, §1.
[8] Ibid.
[9] Twining v. New Jersey, 211 U. S. 78 (1908).
[10] See Adamson v. California, 332 U. S. 46 (1947). Four members of the present Court also apparently hold this view. See the dissenting opinions of Mr. Justice Black, in which the Chief Justice and Mr. Justice Douglas concurred, and Mr. Justice Brennan, in which the Chief Justice also joined, in Cohen v. Hurley, 81 S. Ct. 954, 963, 974 (1961).

[10a] But see the dissenting opinion of Mr. Justice Brennan in Cohen v. Hurley, 81 S. Ct. 954, 978 (1961) ("I would hold that the full sweep of the Fifth Amendment privilege has been absorbed in the Fourteenth Amendment. In that view the protection it affords the individual . . . against the State, has the same scope as that against the National Government. . . .").
[11] For a discussion of this change and the reasons therefor, see 2 WIGMORE, EVIDENCE §579 (3d ed. 1940). The various statutes are collected in 2 id. §488 n.2.

status of an accused but who is asked, under oath, to relate facts which, if divulged, might directly or indirectly result in his henceforth becoming an accused? Words such as "In all criminal prosecutions, the accused shall not be compelled to give evidence against himself," and, to a lesser extent, words such as "No person shall be compelled in any criminal case to be a witness against himself," seem either to compel or at least to suggest strongly that the privilege is available to a criminal defendant and to no one else. However, the cases are to the contrary. Out of a mixture of history, precedent and policy has come the well established doctrine that the ordinary witness is privileged not to answer incriminating questions.[12] Moreover, he not only may leave such questions unanswered at any stage of a judicial proceeding, criminal or civil, but also he may invoke his privilege in connection with other official proceedings, such as administrative hearings and legislative investigations.[13]

Since the various constitutional privileges accord protection to any "person," or to the "accused,"

or to a "witness," this would seem to imply that the privilege is not available to non-human entities. And the cases, which are not numerous, clearly point in this direction. Corporations were the first bloodless creatures to feel the sting of this literal reading of the privilege, and the rule there fashioned imposed upon the corporation a duty to deliver up its books and records for official inspection even though corporate criminality might thereby be disclosed.[14] Moreover, the net was held to be sufficiently large to catch also the agent who holds in a representative capacity corporate documents which incidentally disclose the agent's own criminality. He cannot, according to the rule, interpose a personal claim of privilege and thereby lock up the corporate file cabinets.[15] However, for some time the rationale of these corporate decisions was not completely clear. Were they primarily an outgrowth of the visitorial powers normally reserved to the sovereign who permits the corporation to be born? Or were they based upon a strict reading of the constitutional phraseology and its history? Clarification came in a 1944 decision of the United States Supreme Court which denied the privilege to an unincorporated association—a labor union. In this decision, *United States v. White*, the Court stated: "The test . . . is whether one can fairly say under all the circumstances that a particular type of organization has a character so impersonal in the scope of its membership and activities that it cannot be said to embody or represent the purely private or personal interests of its constituents, but rather to embody their common or group interests only."[16] The *White* case thus makes it clear that the general rule has a base much broader than the state's visitorial power over corporations.[17] However, the language of the decision, in seeming to place emphasis upon the size and impersonal nature of the artificial

[12] 8 WIGMORE, EVIDENCE §2252 (1)(a) ("A clause exempting a person from being 'a witness against himself' protects as well a *witness* as a *party accused* in the cause; that is, it is immaterial whether the prosecution is then and there 'against himself' or not. So also a clause exempting 'the accused' protects equally a mere witness.").
[13] See In re Lemon, 15 Cal. App.2d 82, 59 P.2d 213 (1936) ("When the Fifth Amendment to the Constitution of the United States was first proposed by Mr. Madison, the proposed provision read, 'No person . . . shall be compelled to be a witness against himself.' The accounts of the debates show that this was deemed to be too broad and the proposal was amended by adding the words 'in any criminal case.' . . . The wording of the proposal as amended may not have been happily chosen for undoubtedly the privilege intended to be given was the common-law privilege against self-incrimination in any proceeding, civil or criminal, and the courts have liberally construed the various constitutional provisions to confer such privilege. As stated by Wigmore in section 2252, at page 834, the variety of phrasing found in the various Constitutions 'neither enlarges nor narrows the scope of the privilege as already accepted, understood, and judicially developed in the common law.' The privilege then is . . . accorded to all witnesses in all proceedings and has no relation to the rights of parties. . . ."). See also McCarthy v. Arndstein, 266 U. S. 34 (1924) (civil proceeding); Emspak v. United States, 349 U. S. 190 (1955) (legislative hearing); Smith v. United States, 337 U. S. 137, 150 (1949) (administrative proceeding).

[14] Wilson v. United States, 221 U. S. 361 (1911).
[15] *Id.* at 382.
[16] 322 U. S. 694, 701 (1944).
[17] The principle has been applied to a political party, Communist Party of the U. S. v. Subversive Activities Control Board, 223 F.2d 531 (D.C. Cir. 1955), to a partnership, United States v. Onassis, 133 F. Supp. 327 (S.D. N.Y. 1955), and to the board of trustees of the Bail Fund of Civil Rights Congress of New York, Field v. United States, 193 F.2d 86 (2d Cir. 1951).

entity, rather than upon the mere fact of its non-human shell, raises certain additional questions. For example, is the privilege still available to the small partnership, or to the close corporation spawned by promises of tax savings?[18] Suffice it to say that although the basis of the rule and the direction in which it is proceeding have become clear, the exact scope of the doctrine is far from a settled question.

Our discussion thus far has indicated that, for purposes of analysis and clarity, the privilege can and should be divided into two parts: (1) the privilege of an accused person and (2) the privilege of an ordinary witness. Perhaps it will now be profitable to discuss separately and in slightly more detail these two branches of the privilege.

### THE PRIVILEGE OF THE ACCUSED

As indicated above, the words of the various constitutional provisions clearly cover the defendant in a criminal case. However, to record accurately the dimensions of this shelter for the accused, one must take cognizance, also, of those statutes which, during the last century, wiped away the testimonial incompetence of the criminal defendant. This legislation did not merely bestow competency where previously there was none. It usually provided, in addition, that notwithstanding his newly-won status, the accused could elect not to utilize it, that is, he could be called as a witness at his own request and not otherwise.[19] This, of course, is something more than the ordinary witness's option to pick and choose, at his peril,

among a field of incriminating as well as non-incriminating questions. It is, instead, a somewhat broader shield, a shield designed to accomplish a complete prohibition of inquiry, if the accused so elects. Thus, the statutes granted something more than a mere privilege against self-incrimination; they granted, instead, a privilege not to testify at all. Perhaps a question is appropriate at this point: Is this broader privilege of the accused not to testify at all, as opposed to the narrower privilege of the ordinary witness not to incriminate himself, merely a creature of legislative grace, and thus subject to legislative withdrawal? Or, on the other hand, are these statutes actually codifications of a broader constitutional privilege for the accused? Demands for a narrowing of the privilege may someday cause legislatures to present this question to the courts.[20]

Upon returning from conjecture as to the status of these statutes to the more immediate problem of their interpretation, we at once meet the question of who can qualify as an accused person. Is the term to be read narrowly and thus limited to one against whom formal criminal proceedings have been instituted? Or are the statutes broad enough to cover also the potential defendant — for example, the prime suspect who is ordered to appear before the grand jury or at the coroner's inquest? Although there is some authority to the contrary, most courts read the term "accused" literally; hence, the suspect, or potential defendant, cannot refuse to be sworn, although he may, of course,

---

[18] In In re Subpoena Duces Tecum, 81 F. Supp. 418, 421 (N.D. Cal. 1948), the court refused to apply the *White* doctrine to a small family partnership. The court stated: "It may be that some partnerships, which have a large number of partners . . . might . . . take on the habilaments of an association or corporation. But certainly this small family partnership does not reach such a stature." Compare In Re Greenspan, 187 F. Supp. 177 (S.D. N.Y. 1960) (denied privilege to corporation of which Greenspan was sole shareholder).

[19] The words of ILL. REV. STAT., ch. 38, §734, are typical: "No person shall be disqualified as a witness in any criminal case or proceeding by reason of his interest in the event of the same, as a party or otherwise . . . : Provided, however, that a defendant in any criminal case or proceeding shall only at his own request be deemed a competent witness. . . . "

[20] One court has considered the question and held that the broader privilege of the accused has a constitutional foundation. See United States v. Housing Foundation of America, 176 F.2d 665, 666 (3d Cir. 1949) ("Compelling the defendant Westfield to take the stand and to testify in a criminal prosecution against him is so fundamental an error that the judgment must be reversed and a new trial ordered. . . . The error made arises from confusing the privilege of any witness not to give incriminating answers with the right of the accused not to take the stand in a criminal prosecution against him. Both come within the protection of the . . . 5th Amendment . . . The plain difference between the privilege of witness and accused is that the latter may not be required to take the stand at all. We need only say in this case that the accused was required to take the stand and to testify over his objection and in violation of his right protected both by the Constitution and the common law.").

refuse to answer all incriminating questions which are put to him.[21]

Let us assume, however, that we have a situation in which an accused, on trial for a criminal offense, has decided to invoke his privilege to remain off the stand. To what extent can the prosecution seek to dent or perhaps even to strip away part of this suit of armour which encases the defendant?

Much energy has been expended by prosecutors in an effort to persuade the courts to limit the privilege of the accused to freedom from testimonial compulsion, thus leaving the prosecution free to compel the defendant's assistance in connection with the production of non-testimonial evidence. Under this dichotomy, the defendant could not, of course, be compelled to take the stand and testify (or to produce in court, under judicial order, private papers and perhaps other objects); however, the accused could be compelled to stand up in court in order to facilitate a witness's identification of him, to display a scar, to don certain apparel, to assume a certain position and, perhaps, even to provide a specimen of his handwriting or his voice. If generalization is possible in this uncertain borderland of the privilege, it is to the effect that the prosecutors have met with a fair degree of success. The efforts of defendants to block such courtroom demonstrations (and, in the same vein, to suppress the results of demonstrations and tests conducted outside the courtroom) frequently have been unavailing.[22] However, the decisions are far from uniform. Professor McCormick, in an attempt to bring order out of apparent conflict, has suggested that some courts appear to draw a line between enforced passivity on the part of the accused and enforced activity on his part. That is, they have regarded as unprivileged those things involving

passive submission, while recognizing as privileged those activities requiring the active cooperation of the accused.[23] Inasmuch as this shadowy corner of the privilege provides an ideal battleground for those who would limit the privilege and those who would expand its scope, we can safely assume that it will be productive of conflict for some time to come.

In another area of potential limitation upon the privilege, defendants have met with considerably more solicitude, particularly at the hands of the legislatures. Many jurisdictions, in an effort to minimize the disagreeable legal consequences flowing from an invocation of the privilege, have provided by statute that the failure of the accused to take the stand shall not be made a subject of comment and shall not create any presumption against him.[24] However, in recent years the outcry for repeal of such legislation has been substantial, and several states have seen fit to allow comment, although, to be sure, the inference thus permitted is merely a prop under other evidence pointing toward guilt, rather than a substitute for it.[25] Moreover, it should be noted that those who would do away with the no-comment statutes must be something more than merely effective lobbyists. They must also contend with the courts, for several statutes permitting comment have been declared unconstitutional on the ground that to comment is to coerce, and to coerce is to compel, albeit in a somewhat indirect way.[26]

In concluding our discussion of the privilege of

---

[21] In re Lemon, 15 Cal. App.2d 82, 59 P.2d 213 (1936); Post v. United States, 161 U. S. 583, 587 (1894). *Contra*: State v. Allison, 116 Mont. 352; People v. Gillette, 126 App. Div. 665, 111 N.Y.S. 133 (1908) (for later legislative and judicial developments concerning the New York situation, see People v. Steuding, 185 N.Y.S.2d 34 (App. Div. 1959)).

[22] The cases are collected in INBAU, SELF-INCRIMINATION: WHAT CAN AN ACCUSED PERSON BE COMPELLED TO DO? (1950). See also MAGUIRE, EVIDENCE OF GUILT §2.04 (1959).

[23] See MCCORMICK, EVIDENCE §126 (1954).

[24] For example, Illinois provides: "[The defendant's] neglect to testify shall not create any presumption against him, nor shall the court permit any reference or comment to be made to or upon such neglect." ILL. REV. STATS., ch. 38, §734.

[25] California effected the change by constitutional amendment (" . . . in any criminal case, whether the defendant testifies or not, his failure to explain or to deny by his testimony any evidence or facts in the case against him may be commented upon by the court and by counsel, and may be considered by the court or the jury. . . ." CALIF. CONST., Art. I, §13.). Iowa has a statute permitting comment.

[26] See In re Opinion of the Justices, 300 Mass. 620, 15 N.E.2d 662 (1938), and State v. Wolfe, 64 S.D. 178, 266 N.W. 116 (1936). *Contra*: State v. Baker, 115 Vt. 94, 53 A.2d 53 (1947), and State v. Ferguson, 226 Iowa 361, 283 N.W. 917 (1939).

the accused, let us focus our attention upon the defendant who, rather than remaining mute, elects instead to take the stand in his own behalf. The cases hold that by offering himself as a witness, the accused thereby assumes an obligation to respond to all relevant inquiries concerning the crime charged.[27] The phrase, "relevant inquiries concerning the crime charged," is broader than might at first appear. Thus, it may include within its coverage not only questions directly related to the offense with which the defendant is charged, but also inquiries concerning other unprosecuted misdeeds of the accused, so long as such extrinsic offenses appear to bear upon some aspect of the principal crime, such as motive, intent, premeditation, and so forth.[28] Generalization becomes more difficult, however, when we inquire into the propriety of questioning the defendant concerning misconduct which bears directly upon the question of his credibility, and thus only indirectly upon the question of his guilt. Some courts permit such questioning, thus requiring that the defendant witness step out entirely from behind his shield.[29] Other courts hold, however, that once the prosecutor begins to inquire into criminal conduct of the defendant bearing solely upon his truth-telling potential, the accused may, by a claim of the privilege, turn away the questions.[30]

### The Privilege of the Ordinary Witness

To round our our discussion of the privilege, let us turn now to a discussion of the privilege of the ordinary witness.

Although, again, generalization is difficult and perhaps may be misleading, I will risk the following statement of the scope of protection usually accorded an ordinary witness: An ordinary witness, unlike the accused, cannot refuse to take the stand; however, once on the stand, the ordinary witness is privileged not to disclose facts involving criminal liability, or its equivalent, in the jurisdiction in which the disclosure is sought. Or, to state the rule negatively: The ordinary witness cannot be required to give answers or to furnish, and authenticate by his oath, personal documents which will create the danger of his conviction of a crime in the jurisdiction seeking such answers or documents.

Further formulation of the doctrine can perhaps best be achieved by a consideration of what is not covered by the witness's privilege.

The reference to "criminal liability" and to "conviction of a crime" in the foregoing statement of the witness's privilege is a reflection of certain basic limitations which find general support in the cases. Thus, the courts hold that the witness must give answers which might subject him to civil liability, at least so long as the civil liability involves penalties intended to be remedial rather than punitive.[31] Moreover, the witness generally is not privileged to shrink from answers which, although nonincriminating, would tend to disgrace or degrade him.[32]

However, the most limiting aspect of the general rule, at least potentially, is that portion which holds that the witness is not protected against factual disclosures which create a danger of criminal liability in jurisdictions other than the one in which the privilege is claimed. By virtue of this limitation, the privilege is thus not available to a witness in a state or federal proceeding who fears incrimination only under the laws of a foreign country,[33] or to a witness in a state proceeding who fears incrimination only under the laws of another state or under federal law,[34] or to a witness in a federal proceeding who fears incrimination only under state law.[35] Several additional comments concerning this portion of the general rule seem to be in order. For one thing, the earlier decisions supporting this limitation are leavened by allusions to the remoteness of potential prosecution

---

[27] 8 Wigmore, Evidence §2276(2) (3d ed. 1940).
[28] *Ibid.*
[29] People v. Casey, 72 N.Y. 393, 398, 399 (1878).
[30] State v. Bragg, 140 W.Va. 585, 601–02, 611, 87 S.E.2d 689, 700, 704 (1955).

[31] Boston & M. Ry. Co. v. State, 75 N.H. 513, 77 Atl. 996 (1910); 8 Wigmore, Evidence §2254 (3d ed. 1940).
[32] In re Vince, 2 N.J. 443, 67 A.2d 141 (1949); 3 Wigmore, Evidence §987 (3d ed. 1940).
[33] Republic of Greece v. Koukouras, 264 Mass. 318, 164 N.E. 345 (1928).
[34] See Jack v. Kansas, 199 U.S. 372 (1905).
[35] Hale v. Henkel, 201 U. S. 43 (1906).

in another jurisdiction.[36] However, later decisions leave one with the feeling that, although the aspect of remoteness was once looked upon as a question of fact, it has now hardened into a presumption of law.[37] We should also note that the limitation imposed by the general rule is clearly an outgrowth of policy, for the words of the various constitutional provisions certainly do not compel such a result. Thus, it is not surprising that there is some authority contrary to the general rule. The following statement from a 1947 decision of the Supreme Court of Michigan captures the rationale of the minority courts:

"We are of the opinion that the privilege against self-incrimination exonerates from disclosure whenever there is a probability of prosecution in State or federal jurisdictions. . . . It seems like a travesty on verity to say that one is not subjected to self-incrimination when compelled to give testimony in a State judicial proceeding which testimony may forthwith be used against him in a federal criminal prosecution."[38]

A highly practical comment may be appropriate at this point: Because court and counsel generally are not free to compel the witness to disclose the exact geographical locus of his fear, the limitation we are discussing may be more apparent than real. Reality swiftly returns, however, when the so-called witness immunity statutes, which are discussed below, come into play.

Assuming, then, that the witness possesses a privilege of the approximate scope just suggested, it is appropriate to consider next the test to be applied by the courts in determining when a particular question may go unanswered on the ground that a response would tend to incriminate the witness.

It is a general rule in the state courts that an invocation of the privilege will be sanctioned only where it appears probable that the witness has

committed a crime under the law of the forum and that the fact called for constitutes or forms an essential part of that crime.[39]

In the federal courts, on the other hand, the witness will find that his refusals to answer are considered in light of somewhat more liberal criteria. There, the witness is free to conceal not only incriminating facts but also clues or leads to such facts, that is, sources or means by which evidence of the witness's criminal complicity may be obtained. The United States Court of Appeals for the Third Circuit recently set forth the federal approach in these terms:

"It is enough [to justify a claim of the privilege] that the trial court be shown by argument how conceivably a prosecutor, building on the seemingly harmless answer, might proceed step by step to link the witness with some crime . . . and that this suggested course and scheme of linkage not seem incredible in the circumstances of the particular case. . . . In performing this duty, the judge cannot be a skeptic, but must be acutely aware that in the deviousness of crime and its detection, incrimination may be approached and achieved by obscure and unlikely lines of inquiry."[40]

Closely related to our present discussion is the problem of waiver. Just as a witness may balk too soon, so too may he balk too late. Thus, one can observe today an increasing tendency on the part of the well-coached witness to stop early lest he be enticed onto the trail of a transaction which, under the doctrines of waiver, he may be forced to follow through to its bitter end. One might properly characterize this current spate of witness timidity as unduly cautious, and perhaps even improper, in light of the established doctrine that waiver occurs only where the witness has disclosed at least one incriminating fact concerning a particular transaction.[41] But perhaps as the definition of "incriminating" tends to become broader, it

---

[36] See, e.g., Brown v. Walker, 161 U. S. 591, 606 (1896).

[37] See, e.g., United States v. Murdock, 284 U.S. 141 (1932).

[38] People v. Den Uyl, 318 Mich. 645, 651, 29 N.W.2d 284, 287 (1947). To the same effect, see Com. v. Rhine, 303 S.W.2d 301, 304 (Ky. 1957), and State ex rel Mitchell v. Kelly, 71 S.2d 887 (Fla. 1954).

[39] The cases are collected and discussed in McCORMICK, EVIDENCE §129 (1954).

[40] United States v. Coffey, 198 F.2d 438, 440 (3d Cir. 1952). See also Hoffman v. United States, 341 U.S. 479, 488 (1951).

[41] See 8 WIGMORE, EVIDENCE §2276(1) and (2)(b) (3d ed. 1940).

supports in its wake a correspondingly broad concept of waiver.[42] At any rate, the waiver-motivated refusals proceed apace and with a minimum of judicial interference.

A discussion of the privilege of the ordinary witness would be incomplete without at least brief reference to a significant by-product of the so-called witness immunity statutes which have been enacted by both the federal and state governments.[43] Under such a statute, the government involved may grant to a witness immunity from prosecution growing out of any testimony given by the witness. After thus removing the danger of incrimination, the sovereign involved may compel the witness to disclose fully the details of any matters or transactions under investigation. Of course, the breadth of this immunity may be somewhat illusory. A particular state can do no more than grant immunity from prosecution by it; it cannot, of course, grant immunity from prosecution by other states or by the federal government. On the other hand, the federal government, at least in areas of national concern, may grant immunity against both federal and state prosecution;[44] however, as a matter of policy, it may not always choose to do so.

Let us take the case, then, of a witness who, under a grant of immunity from state prosecution, is compelled to answer questions put to him by state authorities. Although the information given cannot later afford the basis for a state prosecution of the witness, quite possibly the information may subsequently be utilized elsewhere — for example, in a federal court prosecution of the witness for violations of federal law incidentally disclosed in his state testimony. Notwithstanding this forbidding possibility, the witness generally will not be permitted to invoke his state privilege since he has been granted full immunity against subsequent state prosecution.[45] Nor can he invoke his federal privilege since, under United States Supreme Court rulings mentioned earlier, the Fifth Amendment is available only in federal proceedings.[46] Moreover, the federal government, according to the Supreme Court, is entitled to use, in a subsequent federal prosecution, testimony compelled by state authorities under a grant of immunity from state prosecution.[47] It readily can be seen, then, that our witness is on the horns of an uninviting dilemma: Either (1) he can, notwithstanding the grant of state immunity, refuse to answer, whereupon he may be jailed by the state for contempt, or (2) he can answer the state authorities, whereupon he may find that he has in effect confessed himself into a federal penitentiary. Thus, a state government and the federal government—two independent sovereigns acting legally within their respective spheres of authority—can, by virtue of the total effect of their separate actions, deny to a witness his general privilege not to incriminate himself, although both sovereigns are constitutionally required to preserve just such a privilege.[48]

[42] This is particularly true if waiver is held to occur when one discloses a fact he properly could have withheld under claim of privilege.

[43] The statutes are collected in 8 WIGMORE, EVIDENCE §2281 (3d ed. 1940).

[44] See Ullmann v. United States, 350 U.S. 422 (1956), and Reina v. United States, 81 S. Ct. 260 (1960).

[45] See Jack v. Kansas, 199 U.S. 372 (1905).

[46] See notes 9 and 10 *supra*. See also Knapp v. Schweitzer, 357 U.S. 371 (1958).

[47] Feldman v. United States, 322 U.S. 487 (1944).

[48] The difficult problems in this area are fully explored in Knapp v. Schweitzer, 357 U.S. 371 (1958), and Mills v. Louisiana, 360 U.S. 230 (1959).

# The Privilege Against Self-Incrimination: Its Constitutional Affectation, Raison d'Etre and Miscellaneous Implications

JOHN T. McNAUGHTON

The other day I was told by a scientist of an experiment in Professor Spemann's laboratory in Freiburg: Biologists removed from the pre-embryo of a lizard those cells which were ordained to be the lizard's *tail*. They grafted the stolen lizard cells onto the pre-embryo of a frog, grafting them on at a point where the frog's *nose* was destined to emerge. After the requisite period of time passed, the tadpole and then frog appeared. What do you suppose the frog had where its *nose* belonged? A lizard's—

*—nose!*

The privilege against self-incrimination has, I sometimes suspect, the awe-inspiring quality of those life cells. To a person observing its operation from distant space, the conclusion would be inescapable that the privilege contains a consciousness of the whole organism of a legal proceeding, and, while retaining some of its own unique characteristics, miraculously transmogrifies, adapts, assimilates to supply the organism what it needs.

One does not condemn the lizard's tail cells for producing a nose on the frog's face any more than one blames a blind man for reading with his hands. One should not blame the privilege against self-incrimination for demonstrating its infuriating capacity to frustrate an otherwise untrammeled inquisitor by supplying, in its own way, the absent decencies.

However, things are not this simple.

The privilege is not always ideally suited to supply what the organism needs (the frog would have fared better with a *frog's* nose). And the privilege sometimes supplies more than the organism needs. Like the mysterious life cells—which sometimes lose their sense of purpose and run riot, perhaps accounting for the disease called cancer—the mysterious privilege against self-incrimination, unguided by any clear purpose, sometimes runs riot.

### ["*The*" *Privilege Is Many Things*]

All of this being the case, an assignment to discuss the privilege is a difficult one. There is, of course, no "the" privilege. The privilege is many things in as many settings. The privilege is a prerogative of a defendant not to take the stand in his own prosecution; it is also an option of a witness not to disclose self-incriminating knowledge in a criminal case, and in a civil case, and before a grand jury and legislative committee and administrative tribunal. It may also be a privilege to suppress substances removed from the body or admissions made in prior judicial proceedings or to the police. It is sometimes held to apply beyond incrimination under domestic law to incrimination under foreign law (but not to disgrace or to embarrassment of one's friends). It is applied to excuse nondisclosure of political and religious crimes; and it is applied to excuse nondisclosure of common-law crimes of violence. Beatniks, bums and ex-convicts are allowed to claim the privilege; so are persons whose habits of nonconformity are less obnoxious.

"The" privilege is lurking in all of these settings, and more. I have not time to treat all of the problems which come to mind. I have selected only two to discuss in any detail today. The first is [A] the role of the privilege as a constitutional doctrine. My thought in this regard is to assess the strength and nature of the strait jacket in which we find ourselves. The second is [B] the policy of the privilege. I will probe its purpose, which, like the purpose embedded in a life cell, determines its functions in new sets of circumstances.

First—

## [A.] THE PRIVILEGE AS A CONSTITUTIONAL DOCTRINE

The federal Constitution and the constitutions of all but two states[1] include language relating specifically to self-incrimination. The language of the 5th Amendment, known to you all, is "No person . . . shall be compelled in any criminal case to be a witness against himself . . . ." This language appears verbatim in 16 state constitutions.[2] It appears with immaterial substitutions of synonymous words in 14 more state constitutions.[3] Different language coming to the same thing, but more clearly applying only to an accused in his own prosecution, exists in the constitutions of 11 other states.[4] That language, with insignificant variations, is, "In all criminal prosecutions, the accused shall not be compelled to give evidence against himself."

Accounted for therefore are 41. To the "left" of those 41 states are Iowa, which has no express provision but reads the privilege into its due process clause,[5] and New Jersey, which stubbornly insists that the privilege there is solely a creature of statute.[6] To the "right" are seven states with provisions not too different from the Massachusetts language, "No subject shall . . . be Compelled to accuse, or furnish evidence against himself.'"[7]

## [Federal Provision Originally Narrow]

There is little to explain what the drafters of the federal Constitution meant by their words. We have a few indicia, however.[8] We have the words themselves. And we have the scant legislative history, the varying phraseologies used by the many states, and the practice of official questioning of suspects (not under oath) which continued for decades after the federal and many other constitutions were adopted. The probabilities, in my opinion, substantially favor the conclusion that the constitutional protection was originally intended only to prevent return to the hated practice of compelling a person, in a criminal proceeding directed at him, to swear against himself.[9]

This protection, until the end of the 19th century, was not litigated partly for the reason that for most of that time in most jurisdictions criminal defendants were submerged in a large class of persons disqualified as witnesses because of interest. The question of the application of the

---

[1] Iowa and New Jersey. See text at notes 5 and 6.

[2] Alaska, Arizona, Arkansas, California, Florida, Hawaii, Idaho, Michigan, Minnesota, Nevada, New York, North Dakota, Ohio, South Carolina, West Virginia, Wisconsin. Also, Canal Zone and Puerto Rico.

[3] Colorado, Illinois, Indiana, Maryland, Missouri, Montana, Nebraska, New Mexico, Oregon, South Dakota, Vermont, Virginia, Washington, Wyoming.

[4] Alabama, Connecticut, Delaware, Kentucky, Maine, Mississippi, North Carolina, Pennsylvania, Tennessee, Texas, Utah.

[5] See Amana Society v. Selzer, 94 N.W.2d 337, 339 (Iowa 1959).

[6] See State v. White, 27 N.J. 158, 168–69, 142 A.2d 65, 70 (1958).

[7] Georgia, Kansas, Louisiana, Massachusetts, New Hampshire, Oklahoma, Rhode Island. The *Georgia* language—"No person shall be compelled to give testimony tending in any manner to criminate himself" —first appeared in the constitution of 1877. The *Kansas* provision—"No person shall be a witness against himself"—was in the original constitution adopted in 1859. The *Louisiana* provision is the same as the federal with this clause added: " . . . or in any proceeding that may subject him to criminal prosecution . . . ." This broad form first appeared in the constitution of 1879. The *Massachusetts* language appears in text above. It antedated the federal constitutional provision by nine years. The *New Hampshire* constitution, except for a missing comma, has the Massachusetts provision. It dates from 1784. *Oklahoma's* constitution, dating from admission of the state to the Union in 1907, states that "No person shall be compelled to give evidence which will tend to incriminate him . . . ." The *Rhode Island* language is, "No man in a court of common law shall be compelled to give evidence criminating himself." The word "criminating" was substituted for "against" between October 9 and November 18, 1841, during conventions preliminary to the adoption of the state's first constitution in 1842.

[8] For a discussion of these items of historical evidence, see the authorities cited in note 20 *infra*.

[9] See Silving, *The Oath* (pts. I & II), 68 YALE L. J. 1329, 1527 (1959), for an historical and analytical treatment of the role of the oath—the "self-curse"—in various legal systems including our own.

narrow constitutional clause never arose. The broader protection—of witnesses, and in civil cases—was given during the first years of this nation solely on the basis of well-established common law, without reference to constitutions. For example, prior to 1868 the privilege had been mentioned in only 15 reported federal cases,[10] and in none of those cases was the Constitution referred to, although in one of the cases a number of authorities, including an English statute, were cited by counsel for the witness.[11] State constitutional provisions were invoked by counsel in several state cases during the early and middle 19th century. However, an Arkansas case in 1853 was the first to assert that the constitutional privilege extended beyond the accused to a *witness* in a criminal case,[12] and an Indiana case in 1860 was the first to declare that the constitutional privilege applied in a *civil* case.[13]

[10] United States v. Saline Bank, 26 U. S. (1 Pet.) 100 (1828); United States v. Darnaud, 25 Fed. Cas. 754 (No. 14918) (C.C.E.D. Pa. 1855); United States v. Dickinson, 25 Fed. Cas. 850 (No. 14958) (C.C. Ohio 1840); Sanderson's Case, 21 Fed. Cas. 326 (No. 12297) (C.C.D.C. 1829); Bank of the United States v. Washington, 2 Fed. Cas. 741 (No. 940) (C.C.D.C. 1828); United States v. Craig, 25 Fed. Cas. 682 (No. 14883) (C.C.E.D. Pa. 1827); Devaughn's Case, 7 Fed. Cas. 560 (No. 3837) (C.C.D.C. 1824); United States v. Lynn, 26 Fed. Cas. 1036 (No. 15649) (C.C.D.C. 1822); United States v. Miller, 26 Fed. Cas. 1254 (No. 15772) (C.C.D.C. 1821); United States v. Smith, 27 Fed. Cas. 1158 (No. 16332) (C.C.Conn. 1809); Ex parte Lindo, 15 Fed. Cas. 556 (No. 8364) (C.C.D.C. 1807); United States v. Burr, 25 Fed. Cas. 38 (No. 14692e) (C.C. Va. 1807); United States v. Moses, 27 Fed. Cas. 5 (No. 15824) (C.C.D.C. 1804); Neale v. Coningham, 17 Fed. Cas. 1266 (No. 10067) (C.C.D.C. 1802) (dissent); United States v. Gooseley, 25 Fed. Cas. 1363 (No. 15230) (C.C. Va. 1790?).

[11] United States v. Miller, 26 Fed. Cas. 1254 (No. 15772) (C.C.D.C. 1821). Curiously, the *federal* constitutional privilege was applied by a *state* court, in Higdon v. Heard, 14 Ga. 255 (1853), to a civil party against whom equitable discovery was sought. At that time there was no constitutional privilege in Georgia, and the court held that the common law privilege was inapplicable because of a Georgia statute requiring that discovery relating to gaming be made. The court said that the effect of the federal constitutional privilege was not to privilege disclosure in the state civil proceeding but rather to prevent the use in a subsequent prosecution of the self-incriminating disclosures compelled.

[12] State v. Quarles, 13 Ark. 307 (1853).

[13] Wilkins v. Malone, 14 Ind. 153 (1860).

## [From Counselman to Arndstein to Quinn]

In the federal sphere, it was not until after Congress tampered with the privilege and the resulting immunity statute was put to the test in 1892 that it had to be decided whether the privilege as applied to a *witness* in a criminal proceeding was assured by the Constitution or merely by the common law. The Supreme Court in *Counselman v. Hitchcock* held that the privilege of a witness before a grand jury was constitutionally guaranteed and was therefore beyond the power of the legislature to alter.[14] On the facts, this holding was an easy exegesis because the testimony sought might have exposed Counselman to prosecution for the very crimes being investigated by that grand jury—perhaps to an indictment by that grand jury. The dictum was broad, however. It was that "[t]he object [of the constitutional provision] was to insure that a person should not be compelled, when acting as a witness in any investigation, to give testimony which might tend to show that he himself had committed a crime."[15]

*Counselman* was cited three decades later by the Court in *McCarthy v. Arndstein* to support the further holding that the privilege as applied in *civil* judicial proceedings was also constitutionally guaranteed.[16] And after another generation of three decades, the Court in 1955, consistent with its expanding philosophy of the privilege if not with the federal constitutional language (nor

[14] 142 U. S. 547 (1892).

[15] *Id.* at 563.

[16] 266 U. S. 34, 40, 42 (1924). Mr. Justice Brandeis, delivering the opinion of the Court, said, "The government insists, broadly, that the constitutional privilege against self-incrimination does not apply in any civil proceeding. The contrary must be accepted as settled. The privilege is not ordinarily dependent upon the nature of the proceeding in which the testimony is sought or is to be used. It applies alike to civil and criminal proceedings, wherever the answer might tend to subject to criminal responsibility him who gives it. The privilege protects a mere witness as fully as it does one who is also a party defendant. It protects, likewise, the owner of goods which may be forfeited in a penal proceeding. See *Counselman* v. *Hitchcock* .... [Arndstein, a bankrupt being examined as to his assets pursuant to statute] may, like any other witness, assert the constitutional privilege; because the present statute fails to afford complete immunity from prosecution."

arguably, with what was the common law), surprised no one when in *Quinn v. United States* and *Emspak v. United States* it held that a witness before a legislative committee could find sanctuary in the third clause of the 5th Amendment.[17]

Thus the constitutional privilege by the cases mentioned has been extended to all official interrogations except perhaps those by the police.[18] And by *Hoffman v. United States*, as will be indicated later,[19] it has been extended to disclosures the protection of which I am sure would have shocked the early judges.

### [A Strait Jacket, Retail]

The series of decisions by the Court illustrates, I think, a statement attributed to Mr. Justice Frankfurter. In response to a student's question whether courts make law, the then Professor Frankfurter is reported to have said, "Legislatures make law wholesale. Courts make law retail." In this series of cases, the Court "retailed" Congress out of the "wholesale" business.

The constitutional strait jacket is on.

Indeed, although there are a few areas in which a few tucks could be taken—for example, a redefinition of "incrimination" to include disgrace, personal harm, foreign risks and the like; or a holding that the plea of privilege itself "tends to incriminate"; or inclusion of the taking of body fluids—it is difficult to see how the next generation can continue the pace and deliver anything significant say in 1984, a year already marked for reasons not unrelated to our discussions in this Northwestern University Law School centennial celebration.

With the decisions of the last 70 years in mind, I cannot and do not take the position that the privilege against self-incrimination, as we now know it, is not a constitutional doctrine. *It certainly is.* Nor do I suggest that the law on the complex subject should be controlled by a literal reading of 15 words penned five generations ago. *It certainly should not.* My point, rather, is one which I am by no means the first to make.[20] It is quite simply that, except for the narrow proscription of compulsory sworn testimony from an accused in a criminal proceeding directed at him, the privilege has become a constitutional doctrine only piece by piece and relatively recently. And in the process, the constitutional privilege has incorporated and exceeded the common law privilege against self-incrimination.

### [Three Conclusions]

Now, three conclusions follow:

—[1] One is that any statements in judicial opinions which justify recognition of the privilege on the ground that the Founding Fathers might otherwise be shocked at the treatment being accorded their great Charter are nonsense. Not one in a hundred modern privilege cases falls within their 5th Amendment intentions.

—[2] The second conclusion is that the fact that the privilege is now a constitutional doctrine does not really put us in an escape-proof strait jacket. While the principle is now largely off limits to legislatures (the only bodies equipped to deal with the problem in a comprehensive way), it is obviously not beyond change. In this year 101 of

[17] Emspak v. United States, 349 U. S. 190 (1955); Quinn v. United States, 349 U. S. 155 (1955). Construing the more inclusive state constitutional language mentioned earlier at note 7, both Massachusetts and New Hampshire late in the 19th century had held that the privilege applied in behalf of witnesses before legislative committees. Emery's Case, 107 Mass. 172, 9 Am. Rep. 22 (1871); State v. Nowell, 58 N. H. 314 (1878). The Wisconsin court, in In re Falvey, 7 Wis. 630 (1858), had avoided such a holding, pointing out that historically there was no privilege applicable before parliamentary inquiries and that the statute authorizing the inquiry granted immunity from subsequent use of the facts disclosed in any event. See CUSHING, ELEMENTS OF THE LAW AND PRACTICE OF LEGISLATIVE ASSEMBLIES IN THE UNITED STATES 397 (2d ed. 1863). Cushing held that there was no privilege in parliamentary inquiries, but that disclosures could not be used as evidence in criminal prosecutions.

[18] See text at note 56.

[19] See text at note 58.

[20] See, e.g., MAYERS, SHALL WE AMEND THE FIFTH AMENDMENT 183–227 (1959); Corwin, *The Supreme Court's Construction of the Self-Incrimination Clause*, 29 MICH. L. REV. 191, 191–96 (1930); Pittman, *The Fifth Amendment: Yesterday, Today and Tomorrow*, 42 A.B.A.J. 509 (1956).

For contrary views on the scope of the original constitutional doctrine, see Franklin, *The Encyclopédiste Origin and Meaning of the Fifth Amendment*, 15 LAW. GUILD REV. 41 (1955); Note, *Applicability of Privilege Against Self-Incrimination to Legislative Investigations*, 49 COLUM. L. REV. 87, 90–94 (1949).

Darwin's "Origin of Species," we must recognize that the privilege, perhaps by a series of what Judge Frank called "creative misunderstandings," has evolved and continues to evolve apace.[21] The pace is set by the Supreme Court of the United States, and the state supreme courts, like metal shavings in a magnetic field, fall into pattern.

—[3] The third conclusion is that the privilege, receiving as it does no guidance from the constitutional language, must receive guidance from some underlying policy or policies—from some deeply felt sentiments worthy of constitutional recognition.[22]

So to the second part of my paper:

[21] "The critics of the Supreme Court, however, in their over-emphasis on the history of the Fifth Amendment privilege, overlook the fact that a noble privilege often transcends its origins, that creative misunderstandings account for some of our most cherished values and institutions; such a misunderstanding may be the mother of invention." Frank, J., dissenting in United States v. Grunewald, 233 F.2d 556, 581 (2d Cir. 1956), *rev'd*, 353 U.S. 391 (1957). The social value of such "misunderstandings" is emphasized by Holmes: "If truth were not often suggested by error, if old implements could not be adjusted to new uses, human progress would be slow." Holmes, The Common Law 37 (1881).
Dealing with an analogous point, Mr. Justice Frankfurter had the following to say: "Law is a social organism, and evolution operates in the sociological domain no less than in the biological. The vitality and therefore validity of law is not arrested by the circumstances of its origin. What Magna Carta has become is very different indeed from the immediate objects of the barons at Runnymede. The fact that scholarship has shown that historical assumptions regarding the procedure for punishment of contempt of court were ill-founded, hardly wipes out a century and a half of the legislative and judicial history of federal law based on such assumptions." Green v. United States, 356 U. S. 165, 189 (1958) (concurring opinion). And Mr. Justice Brennan, speaking of the development of the federal rule excluding unconstitutionally obtained evidence, recognized the role which may be played by judicial mistake: "[T]he Court in Boyd v. United States, [116 U. S. 616 (1886),] and in subsequent cases has commented upon the intimate relationship between the privilege against unlawful searches and seizures and that against self-incrimination. This has been said [by Wigmore] to be erroneous history; if it was, it was even less than a harmless error; it was part of the process through which the Fourth Amendment, by means of the exclusionary rule, has become more than a dead letter in the federal courts." Abel v. United States, 362 U.S. 217, 255 (1960) (dissenting opinion).
[22] On the point of guidance (or lack of it) given the courts by the policies of the privilege against self-incrimination, Professor Kalven had this to say: "[T]he

[B.] THE POLICY OF THE PRIVILEGE

There is no agreement as to the policy of the privilege against self-incrimination. Indeed, almost as many purposes have been suggested as there are exceptions to the hearsay rule, or as there are uses for a screw driver. Compare the screw driver. The screw driver at our house is used to pry tops off cans, to gouge holes in wood, to dig pits for tulip bulbs, to score lines and occasionally even wrong-end-to to drive tacks. Once, after hearing strange noises, I searched the house for a prowler who was not there, clutching a screw driver in my fist. But those things are not what a screw driver is *for*. Better suited for those purposes are the lid-flipper, chisel, trowel, pencil, hammer and knife respectively. A screw driver was created and survives as a tool because it is the thing best suited to drive screws.

Now consider the privilege against self-incrimination. Here are the dozen policies which have been advanced as its justification.[23]

law and the lawyers despite endless litigation over the privilege have never made up their minds just what it is supposed to do or just whom it is intended to protect.... [S]ince the privilege is enshrined in the Bill of Rights, has a long history, and has complex potentialities, it cannot quite so readily be assumed that attempts to use it today against a new problem are obviously beyond its traditions or legitimate potentialities." Kalven, *Invoking the Fifth Amendment: Some Legal and Impractical Considerations*, 9 Bull. Atom. Scientists 181, 182–83 (1953).
[23] The following books, reports, opinions and articles are presented alphabetically by author. Each deals favorably or unfavorably with one or more of the policies stated in my list in the text. As the reasons for the privilege are presented in the text below, the appended footnotes indicate the authors to whose writing I suggest you go for useful comment on the point.
American Bar Association Committee on Improvements in the Law of Evidence, *Report*, 63 Reports of the American Bar Association 570, 591 (1938).
ALI Model Code of Evidence rules 201(1), 203, comment on 201(1) (1942).
Bentham, Rationale of Judicial Evidence (1827), 7 The Works of Jeremy Bentham 446–47, 449, 451–52, 454–55, 466 (Bowring ed. 1843).
Boudin, *The Constitutional Privilege in Operation*, 12 Law. Guild Rev. 128, 149 (1952).
Cardozo, J., in Palko v. Connecticut, 302 U.S. 319, 325–26 (1937).
Chafee, The Blessings of Liberty 186–90 (1956).
Clapp, *Privilege Against Self-Incrimination*, 10 Rutgers L. Rev. 541, 542–50 (1956).

Field, J., in Wilson v. United States, 149 U.S. 60, 66 (1893).

Fisher, *The Fifth Amendment and Forced Confessions*, 71 CHRISTIAN CENTURY 945 (1954).

Fortas, *The Fifth Amendment: Nemo Tenetur Prodere Seipsum*, 25 CLEV. B.A.J. 91, 98–99 (1954).

Frank, J., dissenting in United States v. Grunewald, 233 F.2d 556, 580–82, 587–91 (2d Cir. 1956), *rev'd*, 353 U.S. 391 (1957).

GRISWOLD, THE FIFTH AMENDMENT TODAY 7–9, 61, 75 (1955).

Kalven, *Invoking the Fifth Amendment: Some Legal and Impractical Considerations*, 9 BULL. ATOM. SCIENTISTS 181, 182–83 (1953).

Livingston, *Introductory Report to the Code of Criminal Procedure*, 1 WORKS OF EDWARD LIVINGSTON ON CRIMINAL JURISPRUDENCE 332, 355–56 (1873).

MAGUIRE, EVIDENCE OF GUILT 12–14 (1959).

Martin, J., in Aiuppa v. United States, 201 F.2d 287, 300 (6th Cir. 1952).

MAYERS, SHALL WE AMEND THE FIFTH AMENDMENT 229–31 (1959).

McCORMICK, EVIDENCE 156, 253, 255–56 (1954); *Law and the Future: Evidence*, 51 Nw. U. L. REV. 218, 221–22 (1956).

McKenna, J., dissenting in Wilson v. United States, 221 U.S. 361, 393 (1911).

Meltzer, *Required Records, the McCarran Act, and the Privilege Against Self-Incrimination*, 18 U. CHI. L. REV. 687, 689–99, 701 (1951).

Moreland, *Historical Background and Implications of the Privilege Against Self-Incrimination*, 44 KY L.J. 267, 274–76 (1956).

NEW JERSEY COMMITTEE ON THE REVISION OF THE LAW OF EVIDENCE, REPORT TO THE SUPREME COURT 58 (1955).

NEW YORK CONSTITUTIONAL CONVENTION COMMITTEE, 9 PROBLEMS RELATING TO JUDICIAL ADMINISTRATION AND ORGANIZATION 920, 922–24, 926, 928–30 (1938).

Pound, *Legal Interrogation of Persons Accused or Suspected of Crime*, 24 J. CRIM. L. & C. 1014, 1015, 1017 (1934).

Pittman, *The Colonial and Constitutional History of the Privilege Against Self-Incrimination in America*, 21 VA. L. REV. 763, 783 (1935).

Ratner, *Consequences of Exercising the Privilege Against Self-Incrimination*, 24 U. CHI. L. REV. 472, 484, 487–89 (1957).

STEPHEN, 1 A HISTORY OF THE CRIMINAL LAW OF ENGLAND 342–43, 441–42, 535, 543–44, 565–66 (1883) (views first expounded in 1 JURIDICAL SOCIETY'S PAPERS 456, 470 *et. seq.* (1857)).

TRAIN, COURTS, CRIMINALS, AND THE CAMORRA 19 (1912).

Warren, C. J., in Quinn v. United States, 349 U.S. 155, 161–62, 164 (1955).

Weinstein, *The Law's Attempt to Obtain Useful Testimony*, 13 J. OF SOCIAL ISSUES 6, 9 (1957).

8 WIGMORE, EVIDENCE §2251 (3d ed. 1940).

WISCONSIN COMMITTEE ON TRIAL PROCEDURE, REPORT TO AMERICAN INSTITUTE OF CRIMINAL LAW AND CRIMINOLOGY (WISCONSIN BRANCH) (1910).

[*Three Makeweights*]

[1] *One:* It protects the innocent defendant from convicting himself by a bad performance on the witness stand.[24]

[2] *Two:* It avoids burdening the courts with false testimony.[25]

[3] *Three:* It encourages third-party witnesses to appear and testify by removing the fear that they might be compelled to incriminate themselves.[26]

These first three reasons may have something to them. The screw driver handle after all does drive tacks. But are they not obvious makeweights?[27]

[24] Discussed in Clapp, Field, Livingston, Meltzer and Ratner.

[25] Discussed in Frank and Meltzer.

[26] Discussed in Chafee, Maguire, Meltzer, Ratner and Wigmore.

[27] [1] The nervous-innocent-person argument can have application only to criminal defendants; the privilege does not protect civil parties and third-party witnesses, nervous or otherwise, from being called to the witness stand. There is of course always a chance that an innocent criminal defendant, by his poor witness-stand performance, will convict himself. To take the stand with such a possibility, however slight, in mind must be a frightening experience. But does the risk of a miscarriage of justice for this reason exceed the risk of a miscarriage of justice because of the inference which will surely be drawn from the defendant's failure to testify? Probably not. Strangely enough, then, the privilege in the mass of cases of frightened innocent defendants (if it influences them at all) probably has a net tendency to seduce them into convicting, not saving, themselves by their silence.

[2] The privilege does not at a bargain price give the tribunal significant *protection against false testimony*. Consider first [a] where the privilege is *waived*: There are practical considerations, including the inference usually drawn from the claim of privilege, which often press reluctant defendants to testify and reluctant witnesses to answer incriminating questions. The testimony given in these instances may or may not be perjured. It is not more likely to be truthful because of the existence of the waived privilege. Then consider [b] where the privilege is *claimed*: There certainly are situations where, but for the privilege, the tribunal would be given perjured testimony. But there are also situations where, but for the privilege, the tribunal would be given truthful testimony. The question here is, Does the privilege, in the instances where it is claimed, on balance leave the trier of fact in a better or worse position for purposes of finding truth? This question was faced and decided, rightly in my opinion,

### [*The "Futility" Argument*]

[4] *Four:* The privilege is a recognition of the practical limits of governmental power; truthful self-incriminating answers cannot be compelled, so why try.[28]

This argument may deserve more attention than I give it in this paper. But I am unwilling to accept the idea that the limits of the principle of compulsory testimony shall be set without regard for the *legitimacy* of the witness' refusal to disclose. Furthermore, I do not agree that this futility argument applies to enough witnesses in enough situations to account for anything approaching the present privilege against self-incrimination: Is it clear that most witnesses in most situations would elect to remain silent or to perjure themselves in order to avoid making self-incriminating

disclosures? Nor am I persuaded by the collateral point that because many people would provide perjurious answers it is intolerably unfair to insist upon disclosure from the honest witness. And, finally, what problems of Game Theory, of Brinkmanship, do we invite if we admit to witnesses at large that the limits of compulsory disclosure are at the point where they no longer succumb to the threat of punishment?

I like to think—though I may be wrong—that the latent merits in this Reason 4 may be found not in the *fact* of contumacy but rather in the *justifications* for it. The justifications, if any, appear elsewhere in the list of reasons.

### [*Appeals to Prejudice and Reverence*]

[5] *Five:* The privilege prevents procedures of the kind used by the infamous courts of Star Chamber, High Commission and Inquisition.[29]

[6] *Six:* It is justified by history, whose tests it has stood; the tradition which it has created is a satisfactory one.[30]

These last two statements are platitudes. They are not reasons at all—at least not in the sense that they provide us with a rationale useful in deciding future difficult cases.[31]

---

when the disqualification of interested persons as witnesses was abolished. Evidence may be biased or even perjured. But it should not be excluded on this ground, especially not at the option of the interested witness. From the point of view of truth-finding, it is better to hear a witness, cross-examine him, and give his testimony whatever weight it appears to deserve. To the extent that the avoidance-of-perjury argument is aimed not at improving the quality of information available to the court, but rather at avoiding the inhumanity of putting the witness in the position where he is for practical purposes forced to lie, to commit a serious crime against God, the point is covered explicitly in Reason 11.

[3] The argument that the privilege *encourages testimony* of course has no application to the criminal defendant, who must appear in court anyway and who, if he testifies, waives his privilege. The argument has little or no application to parties in civil litigation, whose presence and testimony for practical purposes are compelled by tactical considerations. Those who advance this argument do so only with respect to third-party witnesses. And, as to them, there is not much reason to think that a potential witness, *with* a choice whether or not to appear at the inquiry, would be influenced to do so by the existence of the privilege. It is no pleasure to have to claim the privilege—to run the risk of having it denied and to bear the consequences of the inferences drawn from the claim if it is allowed. Indeed, if, as this argument implies, the value of the privilege is to be measured in terms of total information gotten from third-party witnesses, the privilege probably produces for the court a net loss. This is so because a person *without* a choice whether to appear—one who cannot avoid appearing—may be excused by the privilege from giving information which otherwise might be extracted.

[28] Suggested in Meltzer.

[29] Discussed in Bentham, McCormick and Warren.

[30] Discussed in Bentham, Griswold, Maguire, McKenna and Warren.

[31] [5] The naked association of compulsory self-incrimination with the unpopular *Star Chamber* produces no valid conclusion. Not everything about the Court of the Star Chamber or the other inquisitional courts was bad (they were, for example, quite efficient!). The requirement of self-incrimination, if it is bad, is bad for reasons not stated in this argument. To the extent that the argument is elliptical—intending to assert that there should be interrogation only after formal presentment, or that interrogations should be humane, or that proceedings which further "bad" law are bad—the argument is more specifically made elsewhere.

[6] The argument that the privilege is good because it is supported by *history* and by the *constitutions* must be treated with deference. The statement is true. And if the question is whether the privilege should be abolished in its entirety, it properly puts the burden of proof on the iconoclast. But the argument, without particulars, is not meaningful when the question is how to construe the privilege in particular cases. It is, as I said in the text, a platitude which, in judicial

[*Off-Point Arguments*]

[7] *Seven:* The privilege preserves respect for the legal process by avoiding situations which are likely to degenerate into undignified, uncivilized and regrettable scenes.[32]

[8] *Eight:* It spurs the prosecutor to do a complete and competent independent investigation.[33]

Reasons seven and eight are merely statements, in less satisfactory terms, of more basic rationales to be mentioned at the end of the list.[34]

In my opinion, the policies central to the privilege against self-incrimination can be identified by discussing only the four reasons yet to come. I offer for your consideration my analysis of those reasons, an analysis in which I still have some confidence despite the wounds it suffered from the rapiers of my colleagues at the Harvard Law School who were kind enough to read an early draft of this paper.

[*The 5th as a 1st Amendment Privilege*]

[9] *Nine:* The privilege aids in the frustration of "bad laws" and "bad procedures," especially in the area of political and religious belief.[35]

This reason has appeal, especially now in what most of us hope is the twilight of an era of irresponsible legislative investigating committees and especially when we recognize that the history of the privilege clearly shows that it sprang from attempts to frustrate valid (but bad) belief-control laws.

The reason is difficult to handle.

On the one hand, it seems clear that the privilege is useful to frustrate official inquiries which have

---

opinions, is an acceptable substitute for reasons. True, with expert opinion on the policy of the privilege in such discord, it is unlikely that the majority of an appellate court could agree on a statement of meaningful reasons; and, more important, it is likely that the bar and public to which the judicial opinion is addressed will accept the reference to history with much less criticism than they would any set of particular reasons the court could devise. Nevertheless, palatable as it may be, Reason No. 6 is no more than an appeal to reverence just as, in Reason No. 5, reference to the Star Chamber is an appeal to prejudice. The real reasons must be found elsewhere.

[32] Discussed in Clapp, Frank, Maguire, Meltzer, N.Y. Committee and Stephen.

[33] Discussed in Chafee, Clapp, Maguire, Meltzer, N.J. and N.Y. Committees, Stephen and Wigmore.

[34] [7] The privilege does contribute to *respect for the legal process.* But respect is derivative. Any respect engendered by the privilege is respect reflecting favorable opinion as to the values honored by the law in this area of its fact-finding procedures. Those values, unstated in this argument, must be the reasons for the privilege.

[8] The argument that the privilege is good because it spurs the prosecutor to make an *independent investigation,* it should be noted, has no significant application to claims of privilege by parties or witnesses in civil proceedings or by third-party witnesses in criminal trials. Its reasoning is limited to claims by defendants in criminal cases and by suspects in preliminary inquisitions. But more important: The argument, al-

though phrased in terms of what the privilege *encourages,* obviously intends to imply only that there is something bad which the privilege *deters.* Assuming the truth of the implied proposition that existence of the privilege does cause additional independent investigation, can this additional investigation be the aim of the privilege? It cannot be. The ultimate objective, other things being equal, cannot be to require the prosecutor to do his job in a hard rather than an easy way! On the contrary, other things being equal, it is quite desirable that the prosecutor and the police allocate their limited resources so as to seek out the evidence most easily obtainable and most indicative of truth.

What is the hidden meaning in the argument? [a] Does it relate to *efficiency*? Is it that absent such an independent investigation some cases will come out wrong, presumably acquitting guilty defendants? No. The privilege is not given to the accused in order to guarantee that the state's case against him will be better. [b] Does the hidden meaning of the argument relate to *conduct toward the accused*? Yes, surely it does. The proponents of the argument reason as follows: [i] Government should acquire evidence necessary for prosecution of criminals; [ii] government should not have the right to get evidence from the suspect; therefore, [iii] government should get evidence from "independent investigation." This conclusion, which as indicated *sprang from* the principle that government should not have the right to get evidence from the suspect, is then advanced as a reason for the principle that government should not have the right to get evidence from the suspect! The reasoning is of course circular.

The fundamental question remains: Why not have the right to get the evidence from the suspect? Because it would upset the "fair" state-individual balance or would lead to the successful prosecution of "bad laws"? Because it is not humane or may lead to torture? The true reasons are only negatively implied.

[35] See Boudin, Chafee, Frank, Kalven, Griswold, Pittman and Stephen.

*evil* objectives only because it is useful sometimes to frustrate official inquiries *no matter what* the objectives. Does the law wish to tolerate a device the purpose of which is to make law unenforceable? Well, we know that the law does not exclude such a possibility. That is one of the principal functions of the jury, especially in criminal cases.[36] But the law would be foolish if it put the discretion to frustrate, the safety valve, in the hands of the person least likely to use it properly—the witness being compelled to disclose, the person whose interest it is to thwart the proceeding no matter how "good" its objective. There seems to be no escape from the conclusion that one who employs the privilege solely to frustrate a valid proceeding is misusing the privilege, that he is in fact practicing a form of civil disobedience.

On the other hand, civil disobedience is sometimes honorable. Consider the civil disobedience of Jesus Christ, George Washington, Mahatma Gandhi and Albert Bigelow, the Quaker who in 1958 attempted to sail his boat, the "Golden Rule," into the Eniwetok testing grounds. (The civil disobedience of Willard Uphaus, a person well-known to this afternoon's other American panelist, Attorney General Wyman, is now attending the judgment of history.) Civil disobedience frequently leads to improvements in the law. Should persons who are less frank than say Gandhi about their disruptive objectives—perhaps because to them martyrdom offers no irresistible appeal—be condemned out-of-hand for achieving their ends by misusing the privilege against self-incrimination?

Things being as they are in some grand jury and legislative committee inquiries, I am satisfied that this Reason No. 9 cannot be dismissed. Adequate 1st Amendment protections are absent: There is no solid tradition of official self-restraint in the "anti-belief" area and no established privilege not to disclose matters related closely to religious, political and moral belief and activities.[37]

[36] Professor Henry Hart was the author of the following dictum: "It is important to proper administration of the law that the public believe in the humanity and justice of decisions. This value the law seeks to serve partly through the institution of the jury trial. The jury, representing 'the people,' is deliberately inserted as a kind of cushion between the individual on the one hand and the coercive power of the state on the other. The jury, always in criminal cases, and within broad limits in civil cases, is allowed to thwart the law's commands—in effect to find the facts untruthfully—if it is not satisfied with the justness of the commands as applied to the case in hand." Hart and McNaughton, *Evidence and Inference in the Law*, 87 DAEDALUS: J. AM. ACAD. OF ARTS & S. 40, 50 (1958).

The suggestion has been made that, historically, the two devices of the jury and the privilege combined to frustrate "bad law." "This privilege against self-incrimination . . . was insisted upon as a defensive weapon of society and society's patriots against laws and proceedings that did not have the sanction of public opinion. In all the cases that have made the formative history of this privilege and have lent to it its color, all that the accused asked for was a fair trial before a fair and impartial jury of his peers, to whom he should not be forced by the state or sovereign to confess his guilt of the fact charged. Once before a jury, the person accused needed not to concern himself with the inferences that the jury might draw from his silence, as the jurors themselves were only too eager to render verdicts of not guilty in the cases alluded to." Pittman, *The Colonial and Constitutional History of the Privilege Against Self-Incrimination in America*, 21 VA. L. REV. 763, 783 (1935).

[37] Such a "1st Amendment privilege" may just now be in its infancy. See Barenblatt v. United States, 360 U.S. 109 (1959) (5 to 4 decision), for a discussion of Watkins v. United States, 354 U.S. 178 (1957), Sweezy v. New Hampshire, 354 U.S. 234 (1957), and other cases in point. In Barenblatt v. United States, the petitioner, a teacher, refused to answer questions asked by a subcommittee of the Un-American Activities Committee. The questions related to his present and past membership in the Communist Party, his past membership in certain organizations, and whether he knew a certain person "as a member of the Communist Party." The opinion at page 126 recognized a qualified privilege: "Undeniably, the First Amendment in some circumstances protects an individual from being compelled to disclose his associational relationships. However, the protections of the First Amendment, unlike a proper claim of the privilege against self-incrimination under the Fifth Amendment, do not afford a witness the right to resist inquiry in all circumstances. Where First Amendment rights are asserted to bar governmental interrogation resolution of the issue always involves a balancing by the courts of the competing private and public interests at stake in the particular circumstances shown." Later, at page 134, the opinion concluded that "the balance between the individual and the governmental interests here at stake must be struck in favor of the latter, and that therefore the provisions of the First Amendment have not been offended." See also Uphaus v. Wyman, 360 U.S. 72 (1959) (5 to 4 decision), involving the refusal on 1st Amendment grounds to produce records before the state attorney general, who was authorized by joint resolution of the legislature to conduct investigations.

I am reluctant therefore to condemn the "misuse" of the device which has always been particularly effective to frustrate "belief probes" and which is often the only device available to do the job. I am reluctant even though the device is much too blunt and thus is available to frustrate proper as well as improper proceedings, proper as well as improper questions.

It should be acknowledged, however, that the "1st Amendment" reason for the 5th Amendment privilege is by definition limited to free-speech, -religion and -assembly situations. It has no application in normal day-to-day criminal investigation and prosecution. None. If the judges would only recognize this one truth and treat the "1st Amendment" 5th Amendment cases separately, at least half of the confusion and nine-tenths of the emotion enmeshing the privilege against self-incrimination would be dissipated.

(Ask yourselves: How many civil libertarians in this audience would be concerned—really concerned—with the 5th Amendment privilege if there were an adequate 1st Amendment privilege? And how many criminal lawyers here represented are delighted to have the 1st Amendment-5th Amendment confusion continue so your clients can undeservedly reap its harvest?)

---

The records allegedly showed the names of persons who had attended a "World Fellowship" camp, a camp at which a number of Communists spoke. Uphaus' conviction for contempt was affirmed.

Compare Bates v. City of Little Rock, 361 U.S. 516 (1960), in which a refusal to make disclosure was upheld on 1st (via 14th) Amendment grounds. Little Rock and North Little Rock passed tax ordinances requiring local organizations to disclose their members and contributors. The custodians of the NAACP records were convicted and fined for refusing to make the disclosures. The repressive effect of the ordinance upon the NAACP and its members was uncontraverted. The Supreme Court reversed the convictions, holding that "the municipalities have failed to demonstrate a controlling justification for the deterrence of free association which compulsory disclosure of the membership lists would cause." *Id.* at 527. Compare also Talley v. California, 362 U.S. 60 (1960), in which it was held unconstitutional to punish a person for failure to comply with an ordinance requiring handbills to bear the names and addresses of the persons responsible for them.

### [Privilege to Commit Crime?]

The next reason for the privilege may be a hybrid, sharing some attributes with Reason 9 just mentioned and some with Reason 12 yet to come. Or it may be no reason at all. I tender it gingerly and (at the present stage of my thought on the subject) without approval. It is—

[10] *Ten:* The privilege, together with the requirement of probable cause prior to prosecution, protects the individual from being prosecuted for crimes of insufficient notoriety or seriousness to be of real concern to society.

The concern here is mainly with the "fishing expedition," with what Wigmore called the "unlawful process of poking about in the speculation of finding something chargeable."[38]

The pure "poking about" fishing expedition has a peculiar odious characteristic: The fishing expedition, if allowed, could put all or any of us in jail!

Each of us, after all, is a criminal more or less.[39] But as to most of our crimes we are, practically speaking, the indispensable threshold witnesses.

---

[38] 8 WIGMORE, EVIDENCE §2250, at 284 (3d ed. 1940).

[39] H. L. Mencken pointed out that "society, in order to protect the weak and botched against the bold and original, has had to proclaim certain human acts, under certain circumstances, as too dangerous to be permitted, and hence as what we call criminal. Most of us aspire to the majority of those acts in secret, and some of us commit them surreptitiously, but the man who performs them in such a manner that the fact becomes notorious is a menace to the security of the rest of us, and we go through the solemn hocus-pocus of seizing him and trying him, and pump up indignation over his rascality, and finally visit upon him the thing called punishment." Mencken, *A Mencken Chrestomathy*, in VOICES IN COURT 540 (Davenport ed. 1958).

And Professor Schwartz made the following observation: "The paradoxical fact is that arrest, conviction, and punishment of every criminal would be a catastrophe. Hardly one of us would escape, for we have all at one time or another committed acts that the law regards as serious offenses. Kinsey has tabulated our extensive sexual misdeeds. The Bureau of Internal Revenue is the great archive of our false swearing and cheating. The highway death statistics inadquately record our predilection for manslaughter. 100% law enforcement would not leave enough people at large to build and man the prisons in which the rest of us would reside." Schwartz, *On Current Proposals to Legalize Wire Tapping*, 103 U. PA. L. REV. 157 (1954).

There is just no one who knows nearly as much as we ourselves about *where* to go to find *what* evidence of *which* crimes! It could go without saying that the law does not intend that all of these crimes be prosecuted. The existence of the great majority of them is known only to their perpetrators and perhaps to persons in pari delicto or who for other understandable reasons prefer that the misdeed be forgotten. A system of criminal law enforcement which punished, or even detected, all such crimes would be insufferable. Similarly, it would be a frightening situation if the system were constructed so that the prosecutor had it within his power to select from all of the crimes of all of us the ones to pursue. A license to wiretap our brains could, as I indicated a moment ago, put us all, or any chosen ones of us, in the dock if not in a cell.

The place to nip this specter may be in the bud— by depriving the state of authority to compel self-incriminatory disclosures. The probable-cause requirements, with the privilege tacitly built in, prevent the fishing expedition in regular criminal proceedings. Sometimes, however, in grand-jury, legislative and administrative-agency inquiries, where there is no probable-cause requirement, there is only the privilege to perform this function.

Only two reasons remain. In them, I suggest, must be found the essence of policy of the privilege against self-incrimination applicable in the normal day-to-day criminal investigation and prosecution.

### [Avoidance of Inhumane Treatment]

[11] *Eleven:* The privilege prevents torture and other inhumane treatment of a human being.

An aspect of civilization is an aversion to the knowing infliction of suffering—an aversion to cruelty. Modern man insists that beef cattle be killed in a humane way and he is revolted by the method used on geese to produce *pate de foie gras*. He no longer hangs his felons in public (if at all), and he no longer takes the rod to his child.

What bearing does all this have on the privilege against self-incrimination?

This: The law, it is said, will not authorize compulsory disclosure if the situation falls within a class in which inhumane force is likely to be brought to bear to overcome the person's reluctance to disclose or where the private interests affected are so great that it would be inhumane to compel it.

[a] *"Third degree" methods*[40] employed by the ancient continental inquisitional courts of course fall within the proscribed kinds of force. And the torture occasionally employed by the antecedents of our own criminal courts is unacceptable to us today. It is said that a modern American court or grand jury or investigating agency or legislative committee or some new creation authorized to compel disclosures might, but for the privilege, revert to such barbaric practices. This I simply do not believe. I dismiss the argument.

[b] Short of torture, what abuses of the witness loom? There is *browbeating* or *bullying*.[41] When a legal right to an answer exists, one can expect the presiding official to allow the questioner wide latitude in his attempts to extract relevant information of any kind from a witness reluctant for any reason. The latitude, at least in legislative-committee and grand-jury investigations and in hearings before magistrates, frequently includes bullying and browbeating. This of course is quite obnoxious to civilized sensitivities. Perhaps there is something to the thought that when the state is putting questions, the answers to which will disclose criminal activities by the witness, we are very likely to find an especially high insistence checked by an especially high reluctance and consequently too frequent resort to verbal abuse rather than to orderly contempt proceedings in an attempt to break the stalemate. If so, the privilege against self-incrimination has found a partial justification.

### [A Reluctant Witness' Trilemma]

[c] What about the feeling that it is inhumane

[40] See A.L.I. Code, Bentham, Cardozo, Chafee, Clapp, Griswold, Maguire, Mayers, McCormick, Moreland, N.J. Committee, Pittman, Pound, Stephen and Train.

[41] See A.B.A. Committee, A.L.I. Code, Bentham, Cardozo, Chafee, Clapp, Mayers, Meltzer, N.Y. Committee, Pound and Stephen.

to force a witness to *choose among the three horns of the triceratops* (harmful disclosure, contempt, perjury)?[42] The first thing to observe is that the problem is not peculiar to the situation in which self-incriminatory disclosure is demanded. In one degree or another it is a problem inherent in the principle of compulsory testimony. Witnesses reluctant for whatever reason face this trilemma.

[i] The distinguishing point where self-incriminatory disclosures are demanded, according to some people, seems to be that the trilemma may be resolved in favor of *disclosure*! That is, that the witness' "will" will have been broken. Or, put another way, that the witness will have been forced to do a "stultifying" thing.[43]

Is there an elusive something to this point?

The thought seems to be that, whereas a truly voluntary confession of wrongdoing does the confessor immense psychological good, its opposite produces the opposite. The point, it seems to me intuitively, has merit, if any, only when the disclosure is [A] a confession, [B] made involuntarily, [C] of conduct reprehensible in the witness' own mind, [D] by a witness whose ability psychologically to rehabilitate himself—to "live with" his having done the reprehensible thing—will be impaired by adding to his *commission* of the reprehensible act his *admission* that he committed it. Perhaps I should add, as another relevant factor, the audience to which the disclosure is made: [E] The larger and the more comprehending this audience is and the more important the opinions of this audience are to the witness, the more "stultifying" the disclosure would seem to be.

The elusive something, then, that there may be to this "self-stultification" point is in any event very limited. At the very most it applies only to unambiguous confessions of quite reprehensible misdeeds—not to "clues" and the like, remotely implying minor turpitude.

[ii] According to others, the point which distinguishes the compulsion of self-incriminatory disclosures seems to be that the trilemma will probably be resolved by the witness in favor of

*perjury*, and that this is an "intolerable invasion of his 'personality'."[44] The thought is that it is inhumane to force a religious witness to violate his sacred oath—to commit a crime against God. And I suppose that a kindred argument could be presented that it is inhumane to force *any* witness, religious or otherwise, to violate the "categorical imperative"—to break faith with his rational commitment to truth-telling as a necessary moral principle.

Before I received the responses of my colleagues to the early draft of this paper, I believed that this inhumanity-of-coerced-perjury point was not too important. I am still of that mind with respect to the agnostic and atheistic witness. I underestimated, however, the importance attributed by many to the religious consideration. Perhaps my reaction was the result of my own experiences with witnesses in action. Perjury is commonplace. It is too commonplace to be thought of by the average witness as a soul-destroying experience. In any event, the religious argument could in many circumstances be met in a manner more sensible than a grant of privilege. It could be met by eliminating the oath—a procedure followed, I understand, quite commonly on the Continent.

[d] Last of the inhumanities the avoidance of which is said to justify the privilege is that of compelling a witness to commit the "unnatural act" of *inflicting injury on himself*.[45] True, Shakespeare considered it important that the king be forced to drink the very wine he had poisoned to kill Hamlet, and Olsen and Johnson thought it necessary to have the slain duck fall on the hunter's head. The element of hoist-with-his-own-petard incongruity, which in legitimate drama provides poetic justice and in vaudeville creates humor, on a witness stand undoubtedly produces an increment of cruelty. However, it is by no means clear to me that that increment of cruelty, by itself,

[42] See Bentham, Frank, Martin and Meltzer.
[43] Suggested by Fisher and Frank.

[44] United States v. Grunewald, 233 F.2d 556, 591 (2d Cir. 1956)(Frank, J., dissenting), *rev'd* 353 U.S. 391 (1957). See Silving, *supra* note 9, at 1346, for a report of the views to this effect of Franciscus Memmius, expressed in 1698 as a result of an inquiry ordered by Pope Innocent XII.
[45] See Frank, Griswold, Meltzer, Stephen and Weinstein.

comes to much. Nor is it clear to me that the cruelty incident to compelling a witness to harm himself outweighs the need for disclosure in enough cases to justify unqualified privilege whenever self-incrimination is involved.

### [*Right to be Let Alone and to a Fair Fight*]

[12] *Twelve:* The privilege contributes toward a fair state-individual balance by requiring the government to leave the individual alone until good cause is shown for disturbing him and by requiring the government in its contest with the individual to shoulder the entire load.[46]

There is a strong policy in favor of government's leaving people alone, and there is a complementary strong policy which demands that any contest between government and governed be a "fair" one. It follows that the government should not disturb the peace of an individual by way of compulsory appearances and compulsory disclosures which may lead to his conviction unless sufficient evidence exists to establish probable cause. Obviously, if the individual's peace is to be preserved, the government must obtain its prima facie case from sources other than the individual. According to Dean Wigmore, there was a moment in the early 1600s when the privilege, in its primordial state, was assumed to go no further than this; it was not doubted that a suspect could be made to respond to questions once he was properly accused; it was just that a person could not be compelled to provide the *first* evidence against himself.[47]

The principle was not long so limited, in any event.

In the 1641 flood, which ostensibly was aimed at the fishing expedition and which therefore swept away the Courts of Star Chamber and High Commission and of course the hated oath ex officio, the ground was washed from under all compulsory self-incrimination.[48] Since 1680 it has been assumed that, even though probable cause has been established (and the peace of the individual may be disturbed to the extent that he is required to stand trial), nevertheless the government cannot compel self-incriminatory disclosures.

That not only the oath ex officio but all authority to compel self-incriminatory disclosures was extinguished in the final decades of the 17th century may be attributable to the revolution in political thought which was occurring at the time. The sovereign king was being supplanted by the sovereign individual. This philosophy, dominant now for three centuries, naturally nurtures the concept that the individual may not be conscripted to assist his adversary, the government, in doing him in. It would not be a "fair fight."[49]

(It might be worth saying in this connection that the original privilege against self-incrimination probably was, in the time of the emancipation of the individual from tyranny of kings, "one of the great landmarks in man's struggle to make himself civilized."[50] This opinion was stated by Dean Erwin Griswold in a speech directed at the excesses of (what I have called) "belief probes" in the early- and mid-1950s. The language has been quoted frequently by the courts. I remind you, however, that times, problems and especially

[46] See Bentham, Clapp, Fortas, Griswold, Pound and Ratner.
[47] 8 Wigmore, Evidence §2250, at 293–96 (3d ed. 1940).
[48] 8 *id.* §2250, at 292–93.

[49] Jeremy Bentham called this argument the "fox hunter's reason." Bentham, Rationale of Judicial Evidence (1827), 7 The Works of Jeremy Bentham 454 (Bowring ed. 1843). That the feeling is part of our culture is confirmed by the unwritten code which governs every fight in the great American morality plays, the TV westerns. Inroads on this sentiment have slowly been made in litigation on the civil side. Inroads are not yet perceptible on the criminal side.
[50] Griswold, The Fifth Amendment Today 7 (1955). The dean, in his speech delivered at this centennial celebration on May 13, 1960, confirmed, I think, that he is a "Reason Niner" (for explanation, see my text *supra* at and following note 35). It is out of respect for the freedom-of-belief arguments he and others persuasively present that I urge the development of an adequate *1st* Amendment privilege—one which would precipitate the mud out of the *5th* Amendment water. However, since there is not yet such a 1st Amendment privilege to which they can resort and since the privilege against self-incrimination at its beginning certainly performed a Reason 9 function, my chances of persuading "Reason Niners" to relinquish their grip on the fringes of the 5th Amendment are probably about as good as those of persuading Southerners to quit calling themselves Democrats.

the privilege against self-incrimination have changed almost beyond recognition in the past three centuries. Today our nation is one of expanding, mixing and mobile populations, complex interdependencies, shortening cultural roots and, incidentally, a homicide rate 10 times that in England. I suggest that, in this context, the privilege against self-incrimination—at least in its modern shape, doing much more than frustrating "belief probes" —may be an expensive gesture indeed. It may in most applications be an example of man's casuistic insistence upon being civilized to a fault.)

Well, those are the dozen reasons given.

The reasons, obviously, are not mutually exclusive; there is much overlapping. Furthermore, the proponents and detractors of the dozen reasons have not always put them just as I have, and have frequently gone into much more detail in their discussions, but I think that this list of 12 exhausts the reasons for the privilege against self-incrimination appearing in legal literature. Unless, of course, we add two, with the significant numbers 0 and 13, which are, Number 0, that the privilege has *no* justifying policy;[51] and, Number 13, that much, much more testimony should be privileged anyway, so we should accept the privilege against self-incrimination, crude as it is, and be thankful for small favors.

The former needs no explanation. The latter needs a good deal of explanation because it is possible that it is at this point where those for and those against the privilege against self-incrimination really join issue.

### [Reason Number 13?]

This much I will say today about "Reason 13": The present system of compulsory attendance and disclosure is unbearably inflexible. It is based on the black-and-white idea that practically speaking the only limit to testimonial compulsion is relevancy, with little regard given by the law to the inconvenience of attending and none to the risks

[51] See TRAIN, COURTS, CRIMINALS, AND THE CAMORRA 19 (1912); WISCONSIN COMMITTEE ON TRIAL PROCEDURE, REPORT TO AMERICAN INSTITUTE OF CRIMINAL LAW AND CRIMINOLOGY (Wisconsin Branch) (1910); ALI MODEL CODE OF EVIDENCE, comment on rule 201(1) (1942).

to reputation, fortune, friends and even life which can be wrought by compelling a human being to make a disclosure which might be of only the slightest legitimate importance to the inquisitor.

A paper could be given on this point alone.[52]

[52] Since the early days of Elizabeth I, when one ran serious risk of a suit for maintenance if he testified in a case, things have changed drastically but by almost imperceptible degrees. Now one may be jailed or sued for failure to attend or testify. The reasoning is that "[t]he right to sue and defend in the courts is the alternative of force. In an organized society it is the right conservative of all other rights, and lies at the foundation of orderly government." Chambers v. Baltimore & Ohio R.R., 207 U.S. 142, 148 (1907) (Moody, J.). And "[t]he suppression of truth is a grievous necessity at best . . .; it can be justified at all only when the opposed private interest is supreme. . . ." McMann v. SEC, 87 F.2d 377, 378 (2d Cir. 1937) (L. Hand, J.).

As a consequence there are very few rules which permit nondisclosure on grounds that compulsory disclosure would invade an interest *of the witness*—that is, on grounds that disclosure would cause undue harm *to the witness* or to something or someone dear to him. There seems to be a privilege not to disclose theological opinions, and there may be a privilege not to disclose trade secrets. The husband-wife incompetency, in one of its formulations, is a privilege of one spouse not to testify against the other. In many jurisdictions there lingers a privilege not to submit to physical examination. That, unless we admit the privilege against self-incrimination to the category, is all. There is no clear-cut privilege not to disclose political opinions (see note 37 *supra*). Nor is there a privilege against disclosing facts which tend to lead to self-degradation, -assassination or -bankruptcy. There is no privilege against doing in a mother, brother or child, or against making disclosures which will lead to the felling of a favorite tree or to the gassing of a beloved dog.

The law takes the position that the relationship between the degree of materiality of the evidence and the degree of anguish caused the witness by its disclosure is irrelevant. Even the catchall Rule 45 of the Uniform Rules of Evidence ignores this consideration. Disclosure must be made.

A useful purpose would be served by a thorough analysis of the whole concept of compulsory testimony. Among the questions to be asked are: (1) What are the "hard-core" areas in which the need for information or the harm to the witness is always so great or so small as to require that disclosure be compelled or privileged, as the case may be? (2) How should the judge inform himself adequately to exercise discretion intelligently—a significant problem even where disclosure even to the judge is resisted by the witness? (3) To what extent would "judge-shopping" and loss of respect for the courts result from discretion being exercised in one way by one judge and in another way by another judge? (4) What difficulties in planning a case would be caused by the fact that parties cannot know in advance whether the affected evidence will be admitted? (5)

It should be noted, however, that the injustice caused by this inflexibility of the system is not, on balance, alleviated by the privilege. The privilege itself is inflexible; it is unqualified. Even when limited to its proper uses, it is far too broad: In order to insure that a great private interest is protected when the public need for information is small, it denies a great public need when the private interest is small. Also, being limited to self-incrimination, the privilege is too narrow to alleviate the injustices of the inflexible system in other areas where public need conflicts with private interests. It is both too broad and too narrow to have a positive net value.

It should be clear by now that the policy underpinning the privilege is anything but clear. The most I can hope to have achieved is to have "left the darkness entirely unobscured." That was the remark reportedly made by Whitehead about an exposition by Russell. Perhaps a little more than that is possible. I can give you my own view, good at least for the present moment, in capsule form.

---

In what respect are the criteria different in courts, grand juries, and legislative committees?

The analysis might produce conclusions, for example, that legislative investigating committees should have no power to compel disclosures at all, and that judges in courts should have wide discretion in any particular instance to excuse or compel disclosure as the balance of need for information and private interests of the witness appears to indicate.

Compare the statements of Circuit Judge Edgerton and Professor McCormick with respect to the related question of privileged communications:

"I think a communication made in reasonable confidence that it will not be disclosed, and in such circumstances that disclosure is shocking to the moral sense of the community, should not be disclosed in a judicial proceeding, whether the trusted person is or is not a wife, husband, doctor, lawyer, or minister." Mullen v. United States, 263 F.2d 275, 281 (D.C. Cir. 1958) (Edgerton, J., concurring).

"Even if we concede that there is ground for some protection for these privileged confidences greater than the interest of secrecy for such unprivileged relations as parent and child, brother and sister, or employer and confidential secretary, it surely goes too far to place the screen before such protected confidences without regard for what the countervailing need for the evidence may be in the interest of justice. A wholesale rule of privilege whatever the need for disclosure is a crude and clumsy handling of the problem." McCormick, *Law and the Future: Evidence*, 51 Nw. U. L. Rev. 218, 220–21 (1956).

## [*The "Real" Reasons*]

It is my opinion that the privilege, like the screw driver, is *used* for all sorts of reasons, most of them having little or no relation to its purpose. The significant purposes of the privilege remaining after the 1st Amendment albatross has been cut free (as it must be before the matter can be discussed rationally[53]) are two: [1] The first is to remove the right to an answer in the hard cores of instances where compulsion might lead to inhumanity, the principal inhumanity being abusive tactics by a zealous questioner.[54] [2] The second is to comply with the prevailing ethic that the individual is sovereign and that proper rules of battle between government and individual require that the individual not be bothered for less than good reason and not be conscripted by his opponent to defeat himself.[55]

Now, finally, to a quick expression of opinion on a miscellany of points:

### [c.] MISCELLANEOUS PROBLEMS

[1] In what proceedings should the privilege apply? It follows from the purposes of the privilege just mentioned that the privilege should be available only in proceedings in which the government is the interrogator. That is, it plays little or no role in normal civil litigation. It serves one or both of its principal policies, mainly as to suspects but also as to third-party witnesses, in criminal proceedings of all kinds. It probably plays its most important role in free-wheeling legislative investigations where both policies of the privilege are applicable and, incidentally, where there is rarely a demonstrable need for the disclosure.

### [*Privilege in the Police Station?*]

[2] Does the privilege apply in the police station? No, it does not.[56] But this is a quibble. Both

---

[53] See the discussion of Reason 9 *supra* in text at note 35.

[54] This is included in Reason 11 *supra*.

[55] This is Reason 12 *supra*.

[56] Since police have no legal right to compel answers, there is no legal obligation to which a privilege in the technical sense can apply. That is, it makes no sense to say that one is privileged not to disclose—that one is

policies of the privilege which I accept, as well as most of those which I reject, apply with full force to insure that police in informal interrogations not have the right to compel self-incriminatory answers. Whether the result is reached by pointing out the elementary fact that police have not been given the authority to compel disclosures of any

kind or whether the result is put on the ground that the person questioned is "privileged" not to answer makes little difference. Answers should not be compelled by police. There is a desperate need for an acceptable substitute for police interrogation of suspects. I hope that this conference will contribute something toward that need.

---

excused from the legal consequences of contumacy—when there are no legal consequences of contumacy.

The contrary arguments—those favoring extension of the privilege to police interrogations—should be stated, however. There are several: (1) That, while there is *no* legal obligation to disclose to police, the police may successfully misrepresent that there *is* such a legal obligation; and that, while there may be no *legal* sanction for contumacy in a police investigation, there may be an *illegal* one, and that the methods to compel disclosure threatened or used by police may be more fearsome than those threatened or used by a court. Since police, like courts, are agents of the state, the argument runs, it would not be illogical to hold that any self-incriminating disclosures obtained by police as a consequence of coercion or of successful misrepresentation that disclosure was obligatory be treated in the same manner as self-incriminating disclosures improperly obtained by a court. (2) That American police in their investigations perform the function of the old English committing magistrate, before whom the privilege did apply. (3) That, although constitutional language in this area is not too helpful, the self-incrimination clause in no instance grants, in terms, a "privilege" to be free from legal compulsion, but in most instances states simply that the person shall "not be compelled to give evidence against himself." The objective of police interrogation of a suspect is of course to induce him in a sense to give evidence against himself. (4) That the confessions doctrine has not yet in all jurisdictions been extended to exclude evidence of coerced *admissions* of facts or of *silence* from which one might infer guilt, as contrasted with evidence of coerced *confessions* admitting all elements of the crime. According to the argument, the privilege should be extended to exclude evidence of such admissions and silence.

Federal decisions on the point are in conflict despite Bram v. United States, 168 U.S. 532 (1897). In that case (at 542) Mr. Justice White declared that, "In criminal trials, in the courts of the United States, wherever a question arises whether a confession is incompetent because not voluntary, the issue is controlled by that portion of the fifth amendment to the constitution of the United States commanding that no person 'shall be compelled in any criminal case to be a witness against himself.' " The *Bram* case, a curious one in which the "coerced confession" seems to have been neither a confession nor coerced and, furthermore, one in which the statement was obtained by an officer of a foreign government, purports to be a square holding that coerced confessions are excluded by the privilege against self-incrimination. The *Bram* case was cited with approval in Bullock v. United States, 122 F.2d

213, 215 (D.C. Cir. 1941) (dictum of Edgerton, J.), and the same result was reached in Brock v. United States, 223 F.2d 681 (5th Cir. 1955). Nevertheless, dicta in a number of federal cases treat the point as still undecided. E.g., United States v. Carignan, 342 U.S. 36, 41 (1951); Upshaw v. United States, 335 U.S. 410, 414 n.2 (1948); Helton v. United States, 221 F.2d 338, 341 (5th Cir. 1955). In one federal case there is dictum clearly implying that the privilege has no application to police interrogations. Wood v. United States, 128 F.2d 265, 268 (D.C. Cir. 1942).

State cases are similarly in conflict. See, e.g., People v. Simmons, 28 Cal.2d 699, 716, 719, 720, 172 P.2d 18 (1946) (privilege applies); People v. Shroyer, 336 Ill. 324, 168 N.E. 336 (1929) (privilege applies); People v. Fox, 319 Ill. 606, 150 N.E. 347 (1926) (privilege does not apply); State v. Height, 117 Iowa 650, 91 N.W. 935 (1902) (privilege applies); Claflin v. State, 154 Kan. 452, 119 P.2d 540 (1941) (privilege applies); People v. Owen, 154 Mich. 571, 118 N.W. 590 (1908) (privilege does not apply); Matter of Schmidt v. District Attorney, 225 App. Div. 353, 357, 8 N.Y.S.2d 787 (1938) (privilege applies); Abston v. State. 139 Tex. Cr. 416, 417, 141 S.W.2d 337 (1940) (privilege applies); Owens v. Commonwealth, 186 Va. 689, 43 S.E.2d 895, 898 (1947) (privilege does not apply).

Both the Model Code of Evidence (Rule 203) and the Uniform Rules of Evidence (Rule 25) would extend the privilege to police interrogations in the following language: "[E]very natural person has a privilege, which he may claim, to refuse to disclose in an action or *to a public official* of this state or any governmental agency or division thereof any matter that will incriminate him...." (Emphasis added.) The Model Code (Rule 232) and the Uniform Rules (Rule 38) continue that "Evidence of a statement or other disclosure is inadmissible against the holder of the privilege if the judge finds that he had and claimed a privilege to refuse to make such disclosure but was nevertheless required to make it." For such provisions to serve their desired beneficial purpose, present methods of police questioning would have to be altered drastically, causing without doubt a substantial reduction in effectiveness. Procedures would have to be adopted to insure that the suspect was made aware of his privilege, perhaps by a warning such as that used in England and required by the Code of Military Justice, 10 U.S.C. §831(c) (Supp. V, 1958). It might also require a right to counsel and a verbatim record of proceedings at the interrogation. On these points, see Meltzer, *Required Records, the McCarran Act, and the Privilege Against Self-Incrimination*, 18 U. Chi. L. Rev. 687, 695–98 (1951); Pound, *Legal Interrogation of Persons Accused or Suspected of Crime*, 24 J. Crim. L. & C. 1014 (1934.)

## [*Two-Sovereignty Rule*]

[3] What about the two-sovereignty rule? The domestic interrogator is not spurred by any "conviction hunger" when the requested disclosure incriminates only under foreign law; so the risk of inhumane treatment is not unusually high. The government questioning and the witness being questioned are not "at war" where the only incrimination is under foreign law; so the sentiments establishing "rules of battle" are inapplicable. Assuming my assessment of the policies underlying the privilege to be correct, then, the privilege has no relevancy where no crime of the forum is involved, where disclosures involving foreign crimes are of no more interest to the interrogator than any other disclosures compelled of the witness.

It might be added that even if my analysis of policies is wrong, and the purpose of the privilege is to excuse the witness from the unpleasantness, the indignity, the "unnatural" conduct of denouncing himself, there is a strong argument that incrimination under foreign law should nevertheless be disregarded. Recognition of such a risk as a basis for privilege would put the interrogating sovereign in the position of being unable, even by granting the fullest immunities within its power, to compel what may be essential information. This result may not be intolerable, but it is quite inconvenient.

A solution to the problem, at least where it appears that there has been cooperation between the local inquisitors and foreign prosecutors, appears to be emerging. It is not to privilege disclosure but rather in some manner to prevent its use by the foreign government.[57]

## [*What "Tends to Incriminate"?*]

[4] What, for purposes of the privilege, "tends to incriminate"?[58] Any fact requested of a criminal defendant by the prosecution at his trial, if relevant, is on the prosecution's own assumption incriminating. It of course does not follow that a criminal defendant should be spared having the questions put to him and having to plead the privilege. The incorporation of this fringe benefit, however, another accident in the development of the constitutional/common-law privilege, is sensible enough. But what is the rule of general application? It should be this: A fact tends to incriminate only [a] if its disclosure would increase the probability that the witness will be convicted of a crime, and [b] if after its disclosure the witness will be in substantial danger of conviction of the crime. This definition could, of course, extend to any "clue" fact which increases the probability that a "subordinate" fact will be discovered and thus that an "ultimate" fact, and the "crime," will be proved. The difficulty here nowadays lies in the failure of the courts, first, to adhere to the test that the risk be *substantial*,[59] and, second, to require that the claimant make a decent *showing* that the test has been met. The progeny of *Hoffman v. United States* have distended the privilege so far that it is now virtually impossible to think of a question in any way relevant to a criminal investigation to which any witness could not successfully plead the privilege.[60] Indeed, it is now difficult logically to avoid the conclusion that the plea of privilege itself tends to incriminate![61]

[57] Discussion of this possibility, most recently suggested by Mills v. Louisiana, 360 U.S. 230 (1959), is the main object of a recent article of mine. McNaughton, *Self-Incrimination Under Foreign Law*, 45 VA. L. REV. 1299 (1959).

[58] The leading case on this point is Hoffman v. United States, 341 U.S. 479 (1951).

[59] See Emspak v. United States, 349 U.S. 190, 203 (1955) (dissenting opinion of Harlan, J.); Hinds v. John Hancock Mut. Life Ins. Co., 155 A.2d 721, 735–36 (Me. 1959) (Webber, J.: "So many persons have claimed the privilege in recent years for reasons based upon political convictions or upon their personal philosophy as to the proper scope of inquiry and examination rather than upon honest fear of self-incrimination, that the probabilities that might otherwise have tended to support such a presumption [that the plea was in good faith] have been greatly diminished.").

[60] See, e.g., Courtney v. United States, 236 F.2d 921 (2d Cir. 1956), which applies the principle of Hoffman v. United States, note 58 *supra*. A witness before a grand jury refused to name persons to whom he was forced by business considerations to pay small amounts of tribute. His conviction for contempt was reversed on the ground that disclosure would supply clues which might lead to his conviction for not filing information returns required by the Internal Revenue Code. This possibility of incrimination played no part in the witness' refusal to answer and was not even unearthed until after his appearances before the grand jury.

[61] See the writings of Professors Byse, Kalven and Ratner on the point. They would all, as I read them,

permit a plea of privilege when the true answer would be "No" to the question, "Are you now or have you ever been a member of subversive organization *A*?" Professor Ratner would allow the plea on the straightforward ground that, if privilege could be pleaded only when the true answer would be "Yes," then the plea of privilege would itself provide the very clue against which the privilege was designed to protect. That is, the plea would itself be self-incriminating. Ratner, *Consequences of Exercising the Privilege Against Self-Incrimination*, 24 U. CHI. L. Rev. 472, 490 (1957). Professor Kalven takes essentially the same position. UNIVERSITY OF CHICAGO ROUND TABLE, Aug. 23, 1953, p. 4. Professor Byse apparently would allow the plea, although the true answer would be "No," only if the question as to subversive organization *A* was in a *series* of questions—for example, as to membership in subversive organizations *A, B, C, D*, etc.—at least one of which (say as to *C*) would call for a truthful answer of "Yes." His reasoning seems to be that the *contrast* between the plea of privilege as to question *C* and the negative answers as to questions *A, B* and *D* serves to equate the plea with a "Yes" answer. Byse, *Teachers and the Fifth Amendment*, 102 U. PA. L. REV. 871, 876 (1954).

There is of course merit to the observations of these scholars. Their proposal that a witness be permitted in effect to employ "ringer" or "red herring" pleas in order to dilute the clue-giving nature of the plea may be justified. It is similar to the device used in Arabian Nights: Putting an *X* on every door deprives the *X* on the door of the intended victim of its significance. On the other hand, that we are driven by logic to such devices might suggest that the whole concept of allowance of privilege to avoid "clues" has gotten entirely out of hand.

Compare the point made by Dean Griswold. He suggests that a plea of privilege is proper (at least if the question relates to membership in the Communist Party) because a truthful "No" answer may put the witness in the position where "in his own interest he may have to undertake to state and explain his membership and activities in the various front organizations." GRISWOLD, THE FIFTH AMENDMENT TODAY 19 (1955).

Compare also a quite different kind of "No" answer. This phenomenon appears where a question is asked the answer to which *negatively* has incriminating implications. Thus if it is known that a crime was committed at noon in the northeast quadrant of a circle and that the witness was somewhere in the circle that noon, the fact that he was *not* then in the *southwest* quadrant is, by a process of subtraction, an incriminating fact. Or if it is known that the witness was in the northeast quadrant at some time during the day, the fact that he was *not* there at *6 p.m.* is, by the same process of subtraction, an incriminating fact. The privilege properly covers such "subtractive" facts. It is important to distinguish from this type of question, which usually appears in a pin-pointing series and each of which truly elicits an incriminating fact, the question mentioned earlier which usually appears in an open-ended series and which does not involve the subtractive process.

*[Immunity Statutes]*

[5] How broad must an immunity be? The Supreme Court in *Counselman v. Hitchcock* said that an immunity statute, "to be valid, must afford absolute immunity against future prosecution for the offense to which the question relates."[62] This has been assumed to be the law. It should not be, however. The "fruit of the poisonous tree" doctrine has sufficed in the areas of search and seizure[63] and wiretap.[64] While the considerations are not exactly the same, that doctrine should suffice here. A statute which proscribes the use, directly or indirectly, of the compelled disclosure should be held constitutional.

In conclusion—

*[The Desirable Course]*

[6] What would I like to see done with the privilege?

Well, first, let me emphasize that one does not advise surgery lightly—not unless the need is patent. Furthermore, one does not, when he performs the surgery on one part of the body, do it without regard for the impact on other parts of the body. The same is true of surgery on an institution integral to the legal organism. As Judge Learned Hand, speaking of the institution of trial by jury, once said, "Like much else in human affairs, its defects are so deeply enmeshed in the system that wholly to disentangle them would quite kill it."[65]

Nevertheless, I wish for surgery.

Before I wished too much change in the privilege itself, however, I would be pleased to see one or

---

See Communist Party v. Subversive Activities Control Board, 223 F.2d 531, 548–49 (D.C. Cir. 1954), *rev'd on other grounds*, 351 U. S. 115 (1956) ("a witness cannot refuse to take the stand on the ground that pleading the privilege will itself tend to incriminate him").

[62] 142 U. S. 547, 586 (1892).

[63] Silverthorne Lumber Co. v. United States, 251 U. S. 385 (1920).

[64] Nardone v. United States, 308 U. S. 338, 341 (1939) (this case was the source of the "fruit of the poisonous tree" phrase).

[65] Jorgensen v. New York Ice Machinery Corp., 160 F.2d 432, 435 (2d Cir. 1947).

more developments along these lines: [a] First, some form of a 1st Amendment privilege, which would relieve the 5th Amendment privilege of its illicit but apparently necessary burden in "belief probes."[66] [b] Second, a grant of some discretion to judges to compel or excuse disclosures as the competing interests indicate.[67] And [c], third, elimination of the oath for criminal suspects and defendants (and perhaps elimination of penalties for false testimony and contempt by them as well).

Those developments should come first.

Then, as for the privilege itself, [a] I would like to see a reversal in the constitutional drift—and if necessary constitutional amendment in jurisdictions where amendment is not out of the question—with a hope that all that would eventually remain of the privilege would be its function as a complement of the requirement of probable cause. That is, one would be privileged, as John Lilburn insisted, not to provide the *first* evidence against himself. [b] I would leave the witness-abuse problem entirely to the due process clause, with *Rochin v. California*[68] and the offspring of *Brown v. Mississippi*[69] providing the starting points for reasoning. Such a rule would be almost as prophylactic and much less wasteful. It would not flush the baby down the drain with the bath water.

The changes would probably stir emotions only during a relatively short transitional period. Like the medieval citizens who at first clung to trial by ordeal and raised the equivalent of "due process" objections to jury fact-finding,[70] we would probably adjust to and prefer the new procedures. Scholars meeting at the *bi*centennial of Northwestern University School of Law in the year 2060 would look back and wonder what the fuss was all about.

[66] See note 37 *supra* for evidence of the Supreme Court's struggle with this problem.

[67] See note 52 *supra* on this point. Wigmore suggests that the trial judge has inherent power "to decline to compel production [of a document] where in the case in hand the document's utility in evidence would not be commensurate with the detriment to the witness . . . ." He cites no authority. 8 Wigmore, Evidence § 2211 (3d ed. 1940). A minor addition to Uniform Rule of Evidence 45 would achieve the objective suggested in the text.

[68] 342 U. S. 165 (1952).

[69] 297 U. S. 278 (1936). The principle was applied most recently in Spano v. New York, 360 U. S. 315 (1959), and in Blackburn v. Alabama, 361 U. S. 199 (1960).

[70] Plucknett, A Concise History of the Common Law 125 (5th ed. 1956).

# A Common Sense View of the Fifth Amendment

LOUIS C. WYMAN

Almost every state in the United States has a constitutional privilege against self-incrimination.[1] This privilege is commonly known by the general public as "The Fifth Amendment" in recognition of the Fifth Amendment to the United States Constitution which affords the privilege to participants in federal proceedings. The United States constitutional privilege does not extend to state proceedings, but the privilege is available under the constitutions of most states.[2] For the sake of simplicity, the privilege against self-incrimination will be referred to herein as "The Fifth Amendment" without regard to whether its application in a particular case derives from federal or state constitutional provisions.

There is little doubt but that application of the Fifth Amendment today has deteriorated to a point where judicial decision limiting its abuse is sorely needed. One need do no more than read the daily newspaper to realize that witnesses before investigating committees of Congress and the states, before grand juries, and in judicial and administrative proceedings generally are often utilizing the Fifth Amendment not to prevent incriminating themselves, but to protect others, or as a thinly veiled way of expressing their contempt for or opposition to the questioner. It is unfortunate that authorities of no less stature than Erwin N. Griswold, Dean of the Harvard Law School, have

to some extent encouraged an unnecessarily broadened interpretation of the Fifth Amendment which impedes rather than aids sensible application of constitutional principles in this area.[3]

It is settled law—if indeed it can be said that with the current vogue of divided and concurring opinions and an atmosphere of rapidly changing judicial concepts the law itself is settled—that the privilege against self-incrimination is personal to the witness and cannot be used to protect against the unpleasantness of informing on others.[4] Similarly, a person who claims the Fifth in refusing to answer has no right to do so privately or to prevent the questioner from making the fact public knowledge.[5] That there may follow from such a course of action certain consequences adverse to the financial, spiritual, physical or moral interests of the claimant may be unfortunate, yet this cannot and should not alter the seriousness and real significance of the claim by any witness.[6]

Under present judicial decisions, claiming the Fifth Amendment probably does not require a conclusion that the witness has been guilty of a crime. However, it is submitted that the very least it can mean, if the Fifth Amendment is to continue to be an effective constitutional arm of the Bill of Rights,

[1] 8 WIGMORE, EVIDENCE §2252 (3d ed. 1940).

[2] See Wyman v. DeGregory, 101 N.H. 171, *cert. denied*, 360 U.S. 717 (1959); In re Pillo, 11 N.J. 8, 93 A.2d 176 (1952); Twining v. New Jersey, 211 U.S. 78 (1908); Jack v. Kansas, 199 U.S. 372 (1905); Brown v. Walker, 161 U.S. 591 (1895).

[3] See GRISWOLD, THE FIFTH AMENDMENT TODAY (1955).

[4] Rogers v. United States, 340 U.S. 367 (1951); Hale v. Henkel, 201 U.S. 43, 69 (1906); McCORMICK, EVIDENCE 269 (1954); 58 AM. JUR., *Witnesses*, 49.

[5] Brown v. Walker, 161 U.S. 591 (1895); Kiewel v. United States, 204 F.2d 1 (8th Cir. 1953); Nelson v. Wyman, 99 N. H. 33, 105 A.2d 756 (1954); United States v. Nesmith, 121 F. Supp. 758 (D.D.C. 1954).

[6] Brown v. Walker, 161 U.S. 591 (1895). See also 8 WIGMORE, EVIDENCE §2255 (3d ed. 1940):

"To invoke the sentiments of lofty indignation and of courageous self-respect against the arbitrary methods of royal tyrants and religious bigots, holding an inquisition to enfore cruel decrees of the prerogative, and torturing

is that if the witness answered he might furnish a link in a chain of evidence that might lead to his prosecution for a crime not outlawed by the statute of limitations. The word "conviction" has not been used at this point. It is conceivable that facts might be elicited through questioning that, in the mind of the witness, might give him genuine apprehension that those responsible for prosecution in the jurisdiction involved might think he had committed a crime. If this were so, then should the witness be compelled to answer out of his own mouth, he would perforce expose himself to the risk and even the probability of prosecution—the very situation which the Fifth Amendment was designed to prevent.[7]

However, the fact that people may well look askance at a witness invoking the Fifth Amendment should not change the responsibility of the judiciary to stop the abuse of the Fifth by numbers of witnesses and, in the process, to halt the deterioration of public respect for the law which such abuses have demonstrably created.[8] For example, when Dave Beck, the West Coast labor leader, refused on the grounds of the Fifth Amendment even to acknowledge the presence or identity of his own son, it was the natural reaction of most Americans that if this is the law, the law must be "a ass, a fool."

There is no need for this state of the law. Under

existing decisions of the Supreme Court such a refusal may understandably be construed as resting upon fear of the application of the doctrine of waiver, although the Supreme Court has said in *Rogers v. United States:*

> "As to each question to which a claim of privilege is directed, the court must determine whether the answer to that particular question would subject the witness to a 'real danger' of further crimination."[9]

While the responsibility of the trial court is clear, it is submitted that too few trial judges have been willing to utilize this discretionary authority to enforce a reasonable restraint upon exercise of the privilege. A "real danger" is not a mere possibility of danger.

*Rogers v. United States* arose out of a federal grand jury investigation in Colorado. Books and records of the Communist Party of Denver were the subject of inquiry. Jane Rogers, subpoenaed *duces tecum* as treasurer of the Communist Party of Denver, testified that, by virtue of her office, she had been in possession of membership lists and dues records of the Party. Under examination, Mrs. Rogers denied having possession of the records, saying she had turned them over to someone else, but she refused to identify the person to whom she had given the books, stating in court as her only reason, "I don't feel that I should subject a person or persons to the same thing I'm going through." She was thereupon found in contempt, committed to the custody of the marshal, and spent the night in jail. The next day she appeared with her counsel before the Grand Jury and claimed the Fifth Amendment in refusing to disclose the person to whom she had given the books and records. The District Court's ruling that her refusal was not privileged and her sentence of four months in jail was affirmed by the United States Supreme Court on the theory that the Fifth Amendment claim was an afterthought, coming only after she had voluntarily testified relative to her status as an officer of the Communist Party of Denver. In short, she had waived any right to claim the Fifth on that

---

their victims with rack and stake, is fitting and laudable and moves men with a just sympathy. But to apply the same terms to the orderly everyday processes of the witness-stand, in a community governing itself in freedom by the will of the majority and having on its statute-book no law which was not put there by itself and cannot be repealed tomorrow—a community, moreover, cursed above others by constant evasion of the law and by overlaxity of criminal procedure,—this is to maltreat language to enervate virile ideas, to abuse true sentiment, to degrade the Constitution, and to make hopeless the correct adjustment of the best motives of human nature to the facts of life. Were it not so serious in its implications, it would be as ludicrous a spectacle as if one were to devote a colossal fortune to founding a hospital for the care of ablebodied vagrants, or to recite Milton's Ode to the Nativity at the birth of a favorite feline's litter."

[7] Hoffman v. United States, 341 U.S. 479, 486 (1951); Blau v. United States, 340 U.S. 159 (1950).

[8] *Cf.*, O'Conor, *The Fifth Amendment: Should a Good Friend Be Abused?*, 41 A.B.A.J. 307 (1955).

[9] 340 U.S. 367, 374 (1951). See also 8 WIGMORE, EVIDENCE §2275 (3d ed. 1940).

subject. In so holding, the Supreme Court said, *inter alia*, that:

"To uphold a claim of privilege in this case would open the way to distortion of facts by permitting a witness to select any stopping-place in the testimony."[10]

And later in the opinion:

"Disclosure of a fact waives the privilege as to details."[11]

This decision has expectedly resulted in situation after situation where attorneys have advised witnesses before investigating committees that the only safe course is to claim the Fifth Amendment very early in the questioning. This results in scandalously remote refusals, such as failure to acknowledge whether or not it is snowing outside, a declination which occurred in the course of an investigation in New Hampshire. It was considered virtually hopeless to transfer this refusal to the courts because of the noticeable reluctance on the part of the judiciary in the last few years to look behind the claim of the Fifth Amendment and to reject it when clearly unreasonably invoked. In a court's discretion this might be done *in camera* in jury cases or off-the-record in issues to court, but it should be done.

Curiously, there has developed a trend of editorial, law review, and academic comment in the direction of an excessive tenderheartedness toward the motley coterie of Fifth Amendmenteers. One disturbing aspect of this trend is that this nation grew to its present position of material wealth and military power from strength of character and firmness of principle by processes foreign to such an attitude toward pleas of self-incrimination. Our forefathers wisely inserted the Fifth Amendment in our Constitution in an attempt to prevent inquisitions of the types so common in Europe at that time and to protect accused citizens against being compelled to incriminate themselves under torture. It was never intended to license perjury, to exculpate contempt, or to defeat the orderly processes of constitutional judicial procedure, as occurs when a witness claims the Fifth Amend-

ment to protect others and not himself, or when he has committed no crime and knows it and, as anyone can see from the question itself, he reasonably risks no prosecution for crime from his answer.

Some have suggested that the Fifth Amendment should now be construed solely in terms of subjective possibilities implicit in the subject-matter (i.e., leaving it up to the witness to make a final determination) of the question,[12] but if this view is carried to the point of judicial confirmation, for all practical purposes a witness might take the Fifth Amendment with impunity almost in answer to any possible question because his subjective decision would leave no objective basis for rejection.

No one wants to destroy for others or for himself the protection against compulsory self-incrimination that is the plain meaning of the Fifth Amendment. At the same time, as a lawyer, member of a State Judicial Council, and for three-quarters of a decade Attorney General of a State, I have become increasingly aware of growing public disrespect (particularly among adolescents) for law and order, and mounting public cynicism toward the courts' handling of the Fifth Amendment.[13] It takes nothing from you or me to require by judicial interpretation that the claim of the Fifth Amendment shall mean nothing more and nothing less than that there are reasonable grounds to believe that a truthful answer if given might lead to conviction or prosecution for the commission of a crime within the jurisdiction of the questioning authority not outlawed by the statute of limitations. If it be urged that one consequence of such a judicial interpretation is obloquy of a wit-

---

[10] 340 U.S. at 372.
[11] *Id.* at 373.

[12] See Ratner, *Consequences of Exercising the Privilege Against Self-Incrimination*, 24 U. Chi. L. Rev. 472, 490 (1957) ("In order to enforce the policies of the privilege a witness must be free to invoke it whenever the question is improper, regardless of what his actual answer would be. . . . If a question is innocent on its face and is not designed to elicit incriminating information, the witness may invoke the privilege provided he can show that one of the possible answers which is not too remote or fanciful, would be incriminating. In making this showing he may refer to extrinsic matters such as his own reputation and the reputations of persons referred to in the question.").

[13] See, e.g., the comic strip "Dick Tracy," circa December, 1959.

ness who claims the Fifth Amendment, candid observation requires recognition of the fact that refusal to answer because to answer might incriminate must involve a certain measure of moral obloquy *per se*. At the very least, it means that the witness may be unduly sensitive to fears of a risk of prosecution even though not guilty of any crime. It cannot mean less than this for the claim of the privilege can also mean that he *has* committed a crime for which he might be convicted (and which is not outlawed by the statute of limitations).

Maudlin sentimentality implicit in the view that "horrors" are heaped upon individual witnesses by being required to take the Fifth Amendment publicly, because the public generally takes a dim view of the claim, particularly when the witness is a member of the academic fraternity or in public service, should not becloud the issue. Historically, the shoe was on the other foot when the subject-matter of investigation was economic cartels, big business, lobbying, or other fields.[14] Not so, however, when investigations have been probing to determine the existence of subversion within and without the academic community. It seems as though every time the state would inquire into whether (or not) anyone within the academic community has conspired, advocated or taught the overthrow or destruction of state or nation by force, violence or unlawful means, a type of academic paranoia manifests itself, routinely supported by such organizations as the Fund for the Republic, the American Civil Liberties Union, and others. Apparently issues of loyalty and security continue to be violently controversial at home or in the halls of Congress when involving an element of compulsion.[15]

[14] See Black, *Inside a Senate Investigation*, Harper's Magazine, February, 1936.

[15] See the Annual Reports of the American Civil Liberties Union, 1952 to 1959. See also Porter, *The Supreme Court and Individual Liberties*, 48 KY. L. J. 48 (1959).

There may well develop a difference in terms of judicial application of the Fifth Amendment to compulsory testimony, between the "ordinary crimes" such as larceny, embezzlement, robbery, murder and the like, and crimes such as treason, sabotage, espionage

Motivation for the clamor of protestation, most prolific amongst the academic community, chronically includes such editorial columns as the *St. Louis Dispatch*, the *New York Times*, the *Washington Post*, and the *Denver Post*, and is usually along one of the following lines:

(a) The cry of academic freedom that the campuses of America are cloistered incubators in which governmental inquiry must not tread lest it discourage the fruits of dissent that ripen on the tree of intellect.[16]

(b) Those who urge that freedom of speech and thought generally is a mainstay of the strength of America; that no one in his right mind in a free society would choose Communism or be subversive; and that the remedy (keeping abreast of potential subversion) is worse than the malady (subversion) itself.

(c) Those who assert that America is the last refuge of proud individualism against state authority and that compulsory disclosures invade individual rights of privacy without reasonable justification, namely, without a showing that state or national security is sufficiently endangered.

(d) Those to whom the First Amendment (much less the Fifth) is akin to Valhalla and who urge that freedom of speech, of press, and of religion, entirely prohibits such inquiry for all practical purposes (including the oft-expressed views of no less than Justices Black and Douglas on the Supreme Court itself[17]).

(e) Those who contend that the personal infamy and attendant harmful consequences to claiming the Fifth Amendment publicly (such as loss of job, harm to reputation or community standing, etc.)

and subversion which are recognized as involving a design to destroy both the Constitution and the courts themselves. It is not unreasonable to suggest a more stringent restriction upon availability and application of the Fifth Amendment when testimony relates to crimes of the latter category.

[16] See Sweezy v. New Hampshire, 354 U.S. 234 (1957); 1 EMERSON & HABER, POLITICAL AND CIVIL RIGHTS IN THE UNITED STATES 730 (2d ed. 1958).

[17] See DOUGLAS, THE RIGHT OF THE PEOPLE (1958); Black, J., dissenting, in American Communications Ass'n v. Douds, 339 U.S. 382, 445 (1950), and Dennis v. United States, 341 U.S. 494, 579 (1951); Solter, *Freedom of Association*, 27 GEO. WASH. L. REV. 653 (1959).

should justify extension of the Fifth Amendment so that anyone faced with such a loss may properly plead the Fifth in refusing to answer.

During the days of reaction against certain excesses on the part of occasional individual investigating committee chairmen or members, critics vociferously voiced other objections, such as guilt by association, hysteria, character assassination, and the like. Not as much is heard of these clichés nowadays, largely because some of the sources have apparently felt that they had severely restricted investigatory powers in the field of subversion. Recently, since the High Court reaffirmed state authority to investigate subversion in the *Uphaus* case,[18] the prime editorial line has been to urge that a consequence is to revive the era of the "Fifth Amendment Communist" and other understandable if lamentable descriptive epithets of frustrated investigators. Unfortunately, the intolerance of the liberal left and its blindness to fact when commenting upon objects of antipathy provably exceeds in unfairness and abuse of due process the worst excesses of those who upon occasion stirred up the situation in the first place. This editorial theme gains momentum from the desire of most persons to be free from governmental observation in their private lives and natural reluctance to inform upon others or to expose others to such superintendence, a human weakness not indigenous to America alone.

While the Fifth Amendment itself expressly refers to criminal cases, its application to non-criminal proceedings such as Congressional and state fact-finding investigations is compelled from its nature. There would be little to commend such a restrictive interpretation as would hold that witnesses testifying under oath in extra-judicial proceedings might be compelled to testify without restriction upon the use of their testimony in a subsequent criminal prosecution. However, it is submitted that a re-examination of the present status of the Amendment is imperative. It has been construed and interpreted out of context with its plain and historically intended meaning,

with a consequent dilution of both its effect and the respect of citizens for the law.

Members of the bar, whether lawyers or judges, need to face squarely up to the fact that the Fifth Amendment is being repeatedly and intentionally used by witnesses to cover up a multitude of improper objections from contempt to perjury.[19] This is not good for the cause of American jurisprudence, since public confidence in the law and in our courts is shaken by such antics. The witness who seeks not to protect himself personally but to use the Fifth Amendment as a means for protecting others, does so contrary to the settled principle that it is a privilege personal to the witness alone.[20] Likewise, the claim of the Fifth Amendment as a device to protect against conscientious recriminations or to decline to reveal sources of information, to avoid publicity, or as a matter of personal principle, is an abuse. The problem is a serious one because it affects the moral fiber of basic American principles; moreover, continued loose construction of the Amendment gives aid and comfort to those individuals who with malice aforethought abuse the privilege, seeking to frustrate, defeat and stultify the vital fact-finding function of Congress or state legislatures.[21]

A grant of immunity from prosecution will effectively eliminate applicability of the Fifth Amendment, whether or not the testimony to be elicited might expose the witness to prosecution in another, separate jurisdiction.[22]

But this is an expensive proposition, for the witness is granted full and complete immunity in respect to anything he may have done concerning which he responsively testifies. For this reason, in most situations relating to possible subversive activities, the grant would and should be made only to a witness who is believed to possess con-

---

[18] Uphaus v. Wyman, 360 U.S. 72 (1959), 100 N.H. 436, 130 A.2d 278, 101 N.H. 139, 136 A.2d 221 (1957).

[19] See TAYLOR, GRAND INQUEST 201 (1955); Williams, *Problems of the Fifth Amendment*, 24 FORDHAM L. REV. 19 (1955); 8 WIGMORE, EVIDENCE, §2279 (3d ed. 1940).
[20] Rogers v. United States, 340 U.S. 367 (1951); United States v. Murdock, 284 U.S. 141 (1931).
[21] See Noonan, *Inferences from the Invocation of the Privilege Against Self-Incrimination*, 41 VA. L. REV. 311 (1955); 8 WIGMORE, EVIDENCE §2272a (3d Ed. 1940).
[22] DeGregory v. Wyman, 100 N.H. 163, 513, 101 N. H. 82, 171, *cert. denied*, 360 U.S. 717 (1959).

siderable information concerning the activity of others.[23]

It becomes increasingly obvious in attempting to achieve a commonsense application of the Fifth Amendment as applied to disclosures elicited by questioning in investigations, that certain fundamentals need to be remembered. Among these are the fact (1) that an investigation is an investigation and is not a prosecution[24]; (2) mere fact-finding questioning concerning what happened or what was in fact said or done is neither prior censorship nor an injunction to conformity, nor a charge nor an indictment[25]; (3) empirical denials of ultimate facts under investigation by witnesses cannot be permitted to preclude relevant cross-examination to test the truth of the denials nor shift to the investigating agency the burden of establishing probable cause for further questioning to the satisfaction of the witness.[26]

Constitutional amendment limiting the scope of the Fifth Amendment is unnecessary. The limitation should come from judicial interpretation. As Mr. Justice Frankfurter has so aptly indicated,

the ultimate final answer to any judicial problem in the United States is the word of the Supreme Court of the United States.[27]

What appears to be needed specifically is:

A. A Court decision radically limiting the doctrine of waiver. This can be achieved by a reversal or strict limitation upon *Rogers v. United States*,[28] and thus neither a witness nor his counsel would fear going to the threshold of an incriminating question before claiming the Fifth Amendment.[29] It is the doctrine of waiver that in large measure has led to so much public ridicule and contempt, for when, as the Lord Chancellor of Great Britain has written in comment upon the Alger Hiss case, a witness takes the Fifth Amendment on the question of whether he plays tennis or is a member of the American Legion, for fear of waiver, it is carrying things too far.[30] In this connection, it should make no difference whether the witness has denied or affirmed essential criminal facts in his previous answers. He should be permitted to take the Fifth in not replying to any question without fear that his previous answers shall constitute a waiver of his right to later claim the Fifth Amendment, *provided always* that the requirements of the next sub-paragraph (B) exist in the claim of the Fifth.

B. Judicial decision should affirm that a plea of the Fifth Amendment means that the witness, acting honestly, has reasonable grounds to believe that if he answered truthfully such an answer might furnish a link in a chain of evidence that *might* lead to his conviction or prosecution for a crime not outlawed by the statute of limitations. The decision should affirm explicitly that the link is not in the realm of speculative possibility but

---

[23] *Cf.*, N.H. REV. STATS. ANNOT., c. 588 (1959); DeGregory v. Wyman, *supra* note 22.

[24] Uphaus v. Wyman, 360 U.S. 72 (1959).

[25] See briefs in Wyman v. Sweezy, 100 N.H. 103 (1956).

[26] See Ex Parte Senior, 37 Fla. 1, 19 So. 652, 656 (1896); Wyman v. Sweezy, 100 N.H. 103, 108 (1956) (" 'It is not always easy to distinguish teaching or advocacy in the sense of incitement from teaching or advocacy in the sense of exposition or explanation.' *Dennis* v. *United States*, 341 U.S. 494, 572. The distinction is one of fact. The defendant's denial that he advocated, taught or in any way furthered the aim of overthrowing constitutional government by force or violence in his lecture is simply his determination of that fact, which the committee could believe or not as it saw fit. The witness could not by his answer impose upon the investigating committee the burden of producing evidence that a doctrine aimed at the violent overthrow of existing government was in fact advocated by him before it could inquire of him concerning the lecture."). Curiously, this undeniable fundamental appears to have been ignored in the concurring opinion of Justices Frankfurter and Harlan in *Sweezy* v. *New Hampshire*, 354 U.S. 234 (1957), where the empirical denials of the witness Sweezy seem to have been accepted at face value and considered as having foreclosed further investigation in the nature of cross-examination. This point, though not involving the Fifth Amendment directly, is capable of similar application and should be cleared up.

[27] "Such a judgment must be arrived at in a spirit of humility when it counters the judgment of the State's highest court. But, in the end, judgment cannot be escaped—the judgment of this Court." Frankfurter, J., concurring, in Sweezy v. New Hampshire, 354 U.S. 234, 266 (1957).

[28] 340 U.S. 362 (1951).

[29] This would constitute a substantial adoption of the English law. See Annot., *Self-Incrimination, Waiver*, 95 L. ED. 2d 354, 360 (1951); Annot., *Self-Incrimination—Waiver as to Details*, 147 A.L.R. 255, 263 (1943).

[30] JOWITT, THE STRANGE CASE OF ALGER HISS 142 (1953).

rather of discernible and reasonable probability, reasonably obvious to the trial court or questioner on the face of the record. The decision should reaffirm that a claim of the Fifth Amendment for reasons beyond the foregoing, whether tested by the question or tested by the possible answer, is improper and—as Chief Justice Marshall once said—"in conscience and in law as much a perjury as if he had declared any other untruth upon his oath."[31] (This requirement assumes that the resolution empowering the investigating agency has been found to be constitutional and the question itself relevant thereto.)

C. State legislation empowering the granting of immunity to the witness when it seems necessary and advisable to do so.

D. Specific judicial disapprobation and limitation upon use of the Fifth Amendment for subjective reasons of conscience, dislike of the questioner or the question, or disinclination to inform on others.

E. Legislation establishing for federal and state agencies the judicial transfer that applies in New Hampshire, *i.e.*, that whenever a witness declines to answer or refuses to obey a subpoena or to produce documents, the administrative agent or committee may then transfer the matter by petition to any Justice of the Superior Court, who shall then continue with the matter in court as though the original proceedings had been commenced in court. In this way, long and protracted delays in judicial determination of constitutionality, relevancy, and appropriateness of the claim of the Fifth Amendment, may be promptly secured and the witness assured of constitutional protections in the process.[32]

A liberal injection of judicial common sense into the never-never land that has repeatedly characterized invocation of the Fifth Amendment in recent years is genuinely needed, particularly in the field of legislative and congressional investigations. Such a doctrine would be a step forward for American jurisprudence, and would do much to restore public confidence in the law. Carefully phrased and properly handled in the trial court, it will neither limit nor destroy any of our essential or traditional freedoms.

---

[31] United States v. Burr, 25 Fed. Cas. 38 (1807).

[32] N.H. REV. STATS. ANNOT., c. 491, §§19 and 20:

"19. *Petition.* Whenever any official or board is given the power to summon witnesses and take testimony, but has not the power to punish for contempt, and any witness refuses to obey such summons, either as to his appearance or as to the production of things specified in the summons, or refuses to testify or to answer any question, a petition for an order to compel him to testify or his compliance with the summons may be filed in the superior court, or with some justice thereof.

"20. *Procedure.* Upon such petition the court or justice shall have authority to proceed in the matter as though the original proceeding had been in the court, and may make orders and impose penalties accordingly."

# The Privilege Against Self-Incrimination
## Under Foreign Law

## Canada

G. ARTHUR MARTIN

### INTRODUCTION

Under the British North America Act of 1867,[1] which united the various British Colonies in North America in a federal union, legislative power was divided between the central authority, the Parliament of Canada, and the legislatures of the component provinces. The residual legislative authority to make laws "for the peace order and good government of Canada" is vested in Parliament but, in addition, the B.N.A. Act grants exclusive legislative jurisdiction to Parliament to legislate in relation to matters coming within certain enumerated classes of subjects. By section 91, clause 27, the Parliament of Canada is given exclusive legislative jurisdiction in relation to the "Criminal Law, except the constitution of the courts of criminal jurisdiction, but including the procedure in criminal matters." By section 92 of the B.N.A. Act, each of the provinces is given legislative jurisdiction in relation to matters coming within a number of specified classes of subjects including "(13) Property and Civil Rights in the Province" and "(16) Generally all matters of a merely local or private nature." Among the enumerated classes of subjects assigned to the provincial legislature is "(15) The imposition of punishment by fine, penalty, or imprisonment for enforcing any law of the province made in relation to any matter coming within any of the classes of subjects enumerated in this section."

In *Proprietary Articles Trade Association v. A. G. Can.*[2] Lord Atkin, speaking for the Judicial Committee of the Privy Council, in discussing the power of Parliament to create new crimes said:

"In their Lordships' opinion s.498 of the Criminal Code and the greater part of the provisions of the Combines Investigation Act fall within the power of the Dominion Parliament to legislate as to matters falling within the class of subjects, 'the criminal law including the procedure in criminal matters' (s.91, head 27). The substance of the Act is by s.2 to define, and by s.32 to make criminal, combines which the legislature in the public interest intends to prohibit. The definition is wide, and may cover activities which have not hitherto been considered to be criminal. But only those combines are affected 'which have operated or are likely to operate to the detriment or against the interest of the public, whether consumers, producers or others'; and if Parliament genuinely determines that commercial activities which can be so described are to be suppressed in the public interest, their Lordships see no reason why Parliament should not make them crimes. 'Criminal law' means 'the criminal law in its widest sense': *Attorney-General for Ontario v. Hamilton Street Ry. Co.*, [1930] A.C. 524. It certainly is not confined to what was criminal by the law of England or of any Province in 1867. The power must extend to legislation to make new crimes. Criminal law connotes only the quality of such acts or omissions as are prohibited under appropriate penal provisions by authority of the State. The Criminal quality of an act cannot be discerned by intuition; nor can it be discovered by reference to any standard but one: Is the act prohibited with penal consequences? Morality and criminality are far from

[1] 30 & 31 VICT., c.3 (U.K.).
[2] [1931] A.C. 310, 323–4.

co-extensive; nor is the sphere of criminality necessarily part of a more extensive field covered by morality—unless the moral code necessarily disapproves all acts prohibited by the State, in which case the argument moves in a circle. It appears to their Lordships to be of little value to seek to confine crimes to a category of acts which by their very nature belong to the domain of 'criminal jurisprudence'; for the domain of criminal jurisprudence can only be ascertained by examining what acts at any particular period are declared by the State to be crimes, and the only common nature they will be found to possess is that they are prohibited by the State and that those who commit them are punished."

On the other hand, the provinces have the legislative jurisdiction by virtue of section 92(15) to affix penalties to their own competently enacted legislation in order to enforce it. The power of the provinces to impose penalties to enforce their legislation with respect to matters committed to them has resulted in the development of a body of law which is sometimes called "Provincial Criminal Law."[3] In *R. v. Yolles*,[4] Porter, C.J.O., said:

"It is, however, one of the powers exclusive to the Province, to impose penalties for the enforcement of its own statutes. Such penal statutes of the Province have been variously designated as 'provincial criminal law,' 'quasi-crimes' or offences of a civil nature. They undoubtedly have the essential characteristic of criminal law in that they are penal."

Where the constitutional validity of such enactments is brought into question the courts must examine the legislation to ascertain its true purpose. The provinces cannot under the guise of inflicting a penalty for the violation of an enactment of a regulatory nature prohibit conduct as *contra bonos mores* and thereby encroach upon the exclusive jurisdiction of Parliament to create crimes.[5]

The courts will examine "the pith and substance" of the legislation no matter what form it may take. There may be an area in which the jurisdiction of Parliament and that of the provinces may overlap, that is to say, a province may validly legislate in relation to a matter in its provincial aspect notwithstanding that Parliament might properly legislate in relation to the same matter from a federal aspect. In this situation the provincial legislation remains valid unless and until it is superseded by federal legislation *in pari materia*. If the Provincial and Dominion enactments come into conflict the Provincial legislation is superseded or abrogated to the extent that it conflicts with the Dominion legislation.[6]

An excellent illustration of the division of legislative jurisdiction between the Dominion and the Provinces is afforded by the judgment of the Ontario Court of Appeal in *R. v. Yolles*. The regulation of Highway Traffic is within the legislative jurisdiction of the provinces.[7]

Section 29(1) of the Ontario Highway Traffic Act[8] provides that:

"Every person is guilty of the offence of driving carelessly who drives a motor vehicle on a highway without due care and attention or without reasonable consideration for other persons using the highway."

The Dominion Criminal Code[9] by section 221(1) provides that everyone who is criminally negligent in the operation of a motor vehicle is guilty of an indictable offence.

The definition of criminal negligence contained in section 191 of the Criminal Code requires the *showing* of a wanton or reckless disregard for the lives or safety of other persons.[10]

[3] Re McNutt, 47 S.C.R. 259, 21 Can. C.C. 157 (1912); Saumur v. Recorder's Court, [1947] S.C.R. 492, 494.
[4] 123 Can. C.C. 305, 318 (1959).
[5] R. v. Hayduk, [1938] O.R. 653, 71 Can. C.C. 134.

[6] "There can be a domain in which provincial legislation may overlap in which case neither legislation will be ultra vires if the field is clear, but if the field is not clear and the two legislations meet the Dominion legislation must prevail: see *G.T.R. v. A.G. Can.*, [1907] A.C. 65." Lord Tomlin in A.G. Can. v. A.G. B. C., [1930] A.C. 111, 118.
[7] Provincial Secretary of P.E.I. v. Egan, [1941] S.C.R. 396, 76 Can. C.C. 227.
[8] R.S.O., c. 167 (1950), as reenacted by 1955 (ONT.) c.29, §4.
[9] 1953–54 (CAN.) c.51.
[10] "191(1) Every one is criminally negligent who (a) in doing anything, or (b) in omitting to do anything that it is his duty to do shows wanton or reckless disregard for the lives or safety of other persons."

The Ontario Court of Appeal held that section 29(1) was valid provincial legislation in relation to the control of traffic on highways in the province and that it was not "in pith and substance" legislation in relation to criminal law. Moreover, there was no conflict between the provincial legislation and section 221 of the Criminal Code which made the criminally negligent operation of a motor vehicle a crime since by definition criminal negligence requires "recklessness," a different mental attitude to the one required to constitute the offence of driving carelessly.[11]

This brief description of the provincial power to create "offences" and the power of parliament to create "crimes" is of necessity fragmentary, but some description of the Canadian federal system is necessary in order to understand, in the discussion which follows, the enactments with respect to the abolition of the privilege against self incrimination in its federal and provincial aspects.

### Self-Incrimination in Canada

It is necessary to distinguish between the position of an *accused* person at his trial on a criminal charge and the position of a mere *witness*. The *accused* at his trial on a criminal charge is not a compellable witness, and no questions can be put to him by the court or the prosecutor unless he chooses to become a witness in his own behalf.[12] Section 4 of the Canada Evidence Act [13] provides as follows:

"(1) every person charged with an offence and, except as in this section otherwise provided, the wife or husband, as the case may be of the person so charged, is a competent witness for the defence, whether the person so charged is charged solely or jointly with any other person."

"(5) the failure of the person charged, or of the wife or husband of such person, to testify, shall not be made the subject of comment by the judge, or by the counsel for the prosecution."

Where the accused does testify on his own behalf he may of course by cross-examination be required to incriminate himself in respect of the offence charged, and since he puts himself forward as a credible person he may therefore be questioned as to whether he has been previously convicted.[14] He may not, however, be cross-examined as to previous misconduct which has not led to conviction unless such acts are relevant to the charge against him, as they may be if they are relevant to the issue of identity or to negative accident or innocent intent.[15]

Parliament has, however, with respect to offences created under federal statutes, occasionally made the accused a compellable witness at the instance of the prosecution.[16] Moreover, in respect of prosecutions for provincial offences in Ontario, the accused is a compellable witness for the prosecution. The Ontario Evidence Act by Section 1(a) defines "action" as including "a prosecution for an offence committed against a statute of Ontario or against a by-law or regulation made under any such statute" and section 5 provides:

"The parties to an action, and the persons on whose behalf the same is brought, instituted, opposed or defended shall, except as hereinafter otherwise provided, be competent and compellable to give evidence on behalf of themselves or of any of the parties and the husbands and wives of such parties and persons shall except as hereinafter otherwise provided, be competent and compellable to give evidence on behalf of any of the parties."[17]

---

[11] *Cf.*, Re Dodd, [1957] O.R. 5, 116 Can. C.C. 337, where the same court held that §48(1) of the Ontario Highway Traffic Act was in conflict with §285(2) (now §221(3)) which creates the offense of leaving the scene of an accident with intent to escape liability, civil or criminal, and hence was superseded thereby.

[12] "Such person is not a compellable witness and therefore cannot be directly called upon to testify by or on behalf of the Crown." Osler, J.A., in R. v. D'Aoust, 5 Can. C.C. 407, 3 O.L.R. 653 (1902). 8 WIGMORE, EVIDENCE §2268(2) (3d ed. 1940).

[13] R.S.C., c.307 (1952).

[14] *Id.*, §12; R. v. D'Aoust, *supra* note 12; R. v. Dorland, [1948] O.R. 913, 92 Can. C.C. 274, *leave to app. ref'd*, 93 Can. C.C. 135.

[15] Koufis v. The King, [1941] S.C.R. 481, 76 Can. C.C. 161.

[16] See, for example, R. v. Fee, 13 O.R. 590 (1887), where under a provision in the Canada Temperance Act the accused was compelled to testify at the instance of the prosecution. See also R. v. Pantelidis, 79 Can. C.C. 46 (1942).

[17] The Ontario Evidence Act, R.S.O., c.119 (1950). In practice, this right does not appear to be used by the prosecution.

The common law privilege protecting a *witness* from answering questions which may tend to incriminate him has been abolished in respect of proceedings over which the Parliament of Canada has legislative jurisdiction by the Canada Evidence Act, subject to the protection afforded by section 5 thereof whereby if the witness objects to answering the answer cannot be used in subsequent proceedings. Section 5 reads as follows:

"(1) No witness shall be excused from answering any question upon the ground that the answer to such question may tend to criminate him, or may tend to establish his liability to a civil proceeding at the instance of the Crown or of any person.

"(2) Where with respect to any question a witness objects to answer upon the ground that his answer may tend to criminate him, or may tend to establish his liability to a civil proceeding at the instance of the Crown or of any person, and if but for this Act, or the Act of any provincial legislature, the witness would therefore have been excused from answering such question, then although the witness is by reason of this Act, or by reason of such provincial Act, compelled to answer, the answer so given shall not be used or receivable in evidence against him in any criminal trial, or other criminal proceeding against him thereafter taking place, other than a prosecution for perjury in the giving of such evidence."

A similar provision exists in the Ontario Evidence Act dealing with matters over which the Province has legislative jurisdiction. Section 7 provides as follows:

"(1) A witness shall not be excused from answering any question upon the ground that the answer may tend to criminate him, or may tend to establish his liability to a civil proceeding at the instance of the Crown or of any person or to a prosecution under any Act of the Legislature.

"(2) If, with respect to any question, a witness objects to answer upon any of the grounds mentioned in subsection 1, and if, but for this section or any Act of the Parliament of Canada,

he would therefore have been excused from answering such question, then, although the witness is by reason of this section or by reason of any Act of the Parliament of Canada compelled to answer, the answer so given shall not be used or receivable in evidence against him in any civil proceeding or in any proceeding under any Act of the Legislature."[18]

The other provincial legislatures have enacted similar statutes;[19] however, the common law privilege of refusing to answer questions which may tend to criminate the witness seems to have been retained in Newfoundland and Prince Edward Island with respect to proceedings over which the provinces have jurisdiction.[20]

It is quite clear from the terms of the Canada Evidence Act that a witness who is compelled to answer questions in a provincial proceeding by virtue of a provincial enactment is protected in respect of his answers in relation to a subsequent criminal prosecution for a crime under a federal statute.[21] Under the Ontario Evidence Act the witness who is compelled to answer in a proceeding over which the province has jurisdiction is protected in respect of his answer in relation to a subsequent prosecution for the violation of a provincial enactment. Similarly, by virtue of the Act, if in any proceeding over which the Parliament of Canada has jurisdiction the witness is

[18] It will be noted that the Canada Evidence Act provides that if the witness objects to answer his answer shall not be receivable in evidence against him in any proceeding *thereafter* taking place. The Ontario Evidence Act merely states that the answer if objected to shall not be receivable in evidence against him in *any* proceeding. It might therefore be arguable that although an accused is a compellable witness for the prosecution in a provincial prosecution, nevertheless if he objected to answer on the ground that his answer would tend to criminate him that answer is protected and is not receivable in evidence against him in the very proceeding before the court.

[19] R.S. Nova Scotia, c.88, §55 (1954); R.S. New Brunswick, c.74, §7 (1952); R.S. Manitoba, c.75, §7 (1954); R.S. Alberta, c.102, §8 (1955); R.S. British Columbia, c.113, §5 (1948).

[20] R.S. Newfoundland, c.120, §3 (1952); R.S. Prince Edward Island, c.52, §6 (1951).

[21] R. v. Harcourt, 53 Can. C.C. 156 (1929); R. v. Simpson & Simmons, 79 Can. C.C. 344 (1943), *leave to app. to Sup. Ct. of Can. ref'd*, 80 Can. C.C. 78. A *fortiori* if the answer is compelled under a federal statute.

compelled to answer over his objection, the witness is protected in respect of that answer in relation to a subsequent prosecution for a violation of a provincial enactment. The witness is thus protected in respect of his answer whether the answer is made in a proceeding over which Parliament has jurisdiction or whether the proceeding is one over which the province has jurisdiction, and he is protected against its use in respect of a subsequent prosecution for the violation of either a provincial enactment or a federal statute.

It is quite clear that the witness is protected in respect of the subsequent use of his answers only if he objects, and the court or other tribunal is not required to advise the witness of his rights. In *R. v. Tass*[22] Kerwin, J., (now C.J.C.) said: "[T]he matter seems quite clear that if the person testifying does not claim the exemption, the evidence so given may be later used against him, and this notwithstanding the fact that he may not know of his rights." Moreover, the Canada Evidence Act applies to all proceedings where a witness may be lawfully examined under oath and is not restricted to judicial proceedings. In *R. v. Mazerall*[23] the accused was charged with the offence of conspiring to violate the Official Secrets Act, and evidence was admitted of answers given by the accused in reply to questions put to him before a Royal Commission consisting of the Honourable Mr. Justice Kellock and the Honourable Mr. Justice Taschereau constituted by an Order in Council under the provisions of the Inquiries Act[24] with power to require witnesses to give evidence under oath. Prior to being examined before the Royal Commission, Mazerall had been taken into custody by an officer of the Royal Canadian Mounted Police and was detained in custody in the police barracks in Ottawa under the authority of an Order in Council purporting to be made under powers conferred upon the Governor General in Council by the War Measures Act.[25] The Order in Council empowered the Minister of Justice, if satisfied that, with a view to preventing any

particular person from communicating secret and confidential information to an agent of a foreign power or otherwise acting in a manner prejudicial to public safety, it was necessary so to do to make an order that such person be interrogated and detained. While still in custody under the order the accused was brought before the Royal Commission and was examined on oath. Both the trial court and the Court of Appeal held that the accused's answers under oath given without objection before the Royal Commission were admissible on his trial for conspiracy. The court clearly recognized the distinction between the so-called confession rule and the privilege of a witness against self-incrimination. With respect to evidence given under oath by a witness it was not necessary for the prosecution to establish that the answers were freely and voluntarily made, nor would their admissibility be affected, as would statements made to the police by inducements or threats held out or exercised by the police while in their custody.

It is quite clear that documents which are produced under the compulsion of a statute are not protected by section 5 of The Canada Evidence Act even though their production is objected to.[26] But while the documents are not protected against use by the prosecution in a subsequent criminal proceeding against the witness, they must be proved independently of the evidence of the witness as to which objection was taken.[27]

[22] 87 Can. C.C. 97, 99 (1946).
[23] 86 Can. C.C. 137, *id*. 321 (C.A.) (1946).
[24] R.S.C., c.99 (1927).
[25] R.S.C., c.206 (1927).

[26] R. v. Simpson & Simmons, 79 Can. C.C. 344 (B.C.C.A.) (1943), *leave to app. to the Sup. Ct. of Can. ref'd*, 80 Can. C.C. 78. ("That section is limited by its express terms to an answer by a witness to a question and says nothing whatever about the use of incriminating documents produced by a witness under compulsion and after objection. This section therefore can have no application to the facts of this case and could not and cannot be invoked by Simpson to protect him from the use of those documents against him at his trial." Sloan, J.A., 79 Can. C.C. 344, 353.)
[27] "I am satisfied with the admissibility of the books and documents in question at the trial but yet another aspect of the matter remains to be dealt with *i.e.* the method of proof of these documents. No difficulty is found on this score with relation to the books of account of James Maynard Ltd. They were admittedly proved *aliunde* by the evidence of the witness Worsley." Sloan, J.A., in R. v. Simpson & Simmons, 79 Can. C.C. 344, 357 (1943).

Under both Dominion and Provincial legislation there are many statutes which create administrative tribunals with all the powers of a court to summon witnesses and to require them to give evidence under oath with respect to the matter under investigation.[28] These investigations are frequently followed by prosecutions for serious crimes such as conspiracy to defraud, arson, theft of securities, combinations in restraint of trade and other offences. The abolition of the privilege of a witness to refuse to answer criminating questions enables these tribunals to subject a person suspected of illegal acts to a most searching examination which often enables a case to be built up against him. In *R. v. Barnes*[29] the accused after his committal for trial on a charge of manslaughter was served with a subpoena requiring him to give evidence before the coroner.[30] The Ontario Court of Appeal held that the accused was a compellable witness. The Court held that the fact that Barnes was a defendant in criminal proceedings in which he was not a compellable witness did not entitle him to exemption in other proceedings. The judges, however, were widely separated in their views as to the propriety of such action on the part of the authorities. Meredith, C.J.C.P., said:

"If the proceedings in the Coroner's Court are now carried on for the purpose only of extracting from the appellant a confession or information such as would lead to his conviction of the crime he is charged with, they would be not only illegal but also inexcusable."

On the other hand Riddell, J., said:

"Much has been said as to the alleged hardship upon Barnes in being compelled to give evidence—it is, however, to be hoped that we have not yet arrived at the point that one accused of crime has so many and so high rights that the people have none. The administration of our law is not a game in which the cleverer and more astute is to win, but a serious proceeding by a people in earnest to discover the actual facts for the sake of public safety, the interest of the public generally."

The result of the abolition of the privilege against self incrimination when used as a means of obtaining evidence upon which to base a criminal charge has been to impair substantially the traditional concept that a person suspected of a crime has the right to refuse to furnish evidence against himself through his own testimonial utterances. It would seem, in the interest of fairness, that in all cases a witness subject to interrogation under oath ought at the very least to be advised of his right to object and the exemption flowing therefrom.

---

[28] Some examples of this type of legislation may be found in the following statutes: The Ontario Securities Act, R.S.O., c.351, §§21, 23 (1950); this statute authorizes the appointment of a person or persons to make investigation into the affairs of companies trading in securities and other matters. The Fire Marshal's Act, R.S.O., c.140 (1950), authorizes the Fire Marshal to conduct an investigation into the cause, origin or circumstances of any fire for the purpose of determining whether it was the result of carelessness or design and to report to the Crown Attorney the result of the findings, and for this purpose he has the right to summon witnesses to give evidence under oath. The Combines Investigation Act, R.S.C., c.314 (1952), authorizes the Director of Investigation or a member of the Restrictive Trade Practices Commission appointed under the Act to order that any person present in Canada be examined on oath where a breach of the Act is suspected. The Excise Act, R.S.C., c.99 (1952), empowers certain officers to conduct inquiries into matters relating to the excise and to summon witnesses and require them to give evidence under oath. R. v. Denmark, 72 Can. C.C. 9 (1939).

[29] 36 Can. C.C. 40 (1921).

[30] The Corners Act, R.S.O., c.70, §18(1) (1950), provides that where a person has been charged with a criminal offence arising out of a death, an inquest touching the death shall be held only upon the direction of the Attorney-General. Under §25(1) the Coroner has the same power to summon witnesses and to punish for refusing to give evidence as a court. Section 25(4) provides that a witness shall be deemed to have objected to answer any question upon the ground that his answer may tend to criminate him and the answer so given shall not be used or be receivable in evidence against him in any trial or other proceeding against him there-after taking place other than a prosecution for perjury. The effect of §25(4) is of doubtful validity in so far as it purports to affect the admissibility of answers in subsequent criminal proceedings. Section 5 of The Canada Evidence Act applies thereto, and that Act requires the witness to take objection. R. v. Mottola & Vallee, 124 Can. CC. 288 (1959).

# *England*

GLANVILLE L. WILLIAMS

### THE WITNESS'S PRIVILEGE

As an English lawyer I think of the privilege against self-incrimination as the privilege of a witness to refuse to answer a question which may incriminate him. In England, this privilege has not caused anything like the difficulty it has in the United States, largely perhaps because we do not have anti-communist laws and investigations— we have Communists, but think they are best left alone. If a question were ever to arise in the course of a public investigation whether a witness were a Communist, he could not refuse to answer on the ground of self-incrimination, since the profession of Communism is not a crime.

Subsidiary reasons why we hardly ever hear of the privilege against self-incrimination in England are the following. We do not have grand juries trying to build up evidence by inquisitorial procedure. The police get their evidence by voluntary statements, and they prefer it this way. Public life is relatively honest, so that there is not much corruption to investigate. We do not have the difficulty arising from the federal structure. We do not have the waiver rule, so that the witness can make his claim to privilege whenever he wishes. Finally, the judge will disallow the claim unless there is a substantial danger of prosecution.

### THE DEFENDANT'S PRIVILEGE

The title of the present symposium refers to a principle which has been subsumed in American legal thought under the same name as the witness's privilege. This is the privilege of an accused person not to be questioned in court without his offering himself for the purpose. In my opinion, it is not aptly called a privilege against self-incrimination, since it is both more and less than that. On the one hand, a defendant who does not offer himself

for questioning cannot be questioned at all—he has a privilege not only to refrain from incriminating himself by specific answers but to avoid being asked the questions. On the other hand, a defendant who does offer himself for questioning no longer has any privilege against self-incrimination in respect of the crime with which he is charged.

The present rule in England on the subject of questioning the defendant to a criminal charge remains the compromise settled by the Criminal Evidence Act, 1898. The defendant may elect to give evidence, and if he does so, he is sworn and liable to cross-examination like an ordinary witness, except that he cannot generally be cross-examined upon his previous convictions. Counsel for the Crown may not comment upon the defendant's failure to give evidence, but the judge may. Although at first judges were chary of commenting, they have come more and more to do so, and the result is that the privilege to testify conferred upon defendants by the Act of 1898 has considerably increased the chance of convicting the guilty.

· It still occasionally happens that a judge takes the traditional view that the defendant to a criminal charge is entitled to maintain silence and, accordingly, either fails to draw the jury's attention to the fact that the accused has not given evidence or even directs the jury not to take that fact against the accused. A striking illustration was the direction of Devlin, J., in the trial of Dr. Adams in 1957. Counsel elected not to call the defendant, and the judge directed the jury strongly against attaching any significance to the defendant's silence, maintaining that such reticence should never be thrown into the scales on the side of the prosecution. This certainly does not represent the ordinary judicial view. It should also be noticed that there was much evidence before the court as to what had happened on the occasions in question: it was perhaps not a case where vital information was evidently in the possession of the defendant which he was withholding from the court.

The decision whether to call the accused places a heavy burden of responsibility upon counsel for the defence. By hypothesis, it has been held that there is a case to answer, so that the accused is involved in considerable suspicion. If the accused gives evidence, his answers or demeanour may tell heavily against him. If he keeps out of the witness box, the judge may make this a matter of adverse comment. Occasionally, however, the strategy of keeping the defendant out of the witness box is brilliantly successful, if the defending counsel can think of a plausible excuse for doing so. At the trial of Merrett for murdering his mother, counsel for the defence explained the accused's silence by thanking God that "there are people who would rather go to their death with their lips sealed than that they should speak a single word that would reflect on the name of a mother." The Scottish jury, deprived of the opportunity of hearing Merrett and not liking to condemn the reason for it, brought in a verdict of "not proven." The sequel was unfortunate, for Merrett later murdered both his wife and his mother-in-law.[1]

A defendant who elects to give evidence and who then lies is technically subject to prosecution for perjury, but it is not the ordinary practice to prosecute for this. It seems, however, that occasionally prosecutions take place.[2]

*The submission of "no case"*

A defending counsel who is in a dilemma whether to call his client or not can sometimes save himself a difficult decision by making a successful submission of "no case to answer" (in effect a motion for directed verdict or dismissal). The submission is made at the close of the prosecution's case and must be immediately ruled upon by the judge or magistrate, as the case may be. If the ruling is in favour of the submission, the case will immediately come to an end—if the trial is on indictment,

a formal acquittal will be taken from the jury upon the judge's direction. Thus the accused will be saved from making any answer.

The question to be considered upon the submission of "no case" is whether it would be proper, on the evidence already heard, to convict the accused if he makes no answer. In other words the question is whether the prosecution has given reasonable evidence of the matters in respect of which it has the burden of proof. As the rule was judicially expressed, no case appears unless there is "such evidence that if the jury found in favour of the party for whom it was offered, the court would not upset the verdict."[3]

The rule serves two principal purposes. In the first place, it operates to control the jury, reducing the possibility of capricious verdicts. It is true that a capricious verdict may be upset on appeal, but a defendant is better off to have the charge dismissed at the trial. In the second place, the rule gives effect to the principle that a man is not compelled to answer a charge unless he is involved in a degree of suspicion. It is an important adjunct to the defendant's privilege of silence during the trial; indeed, it is only where the defendant succeeds on a submission of "no case" that he is perfectly safe in exercising his privilege of silence.

An illustration of the conditions in which the submission may be successful is supplied by the case of *Atter*.[4] The facts given in evidence by the prosecution were that a prostitute was found murdered; the accused admitted he had been with her shortly before her death, and a magazine was found in his room which told a story of a motiveless murder remarkably similar to the killing of the prostitute. On a submission made by counsel for the defence, Devlin, J., directed the jury to return a verdict of Not Guilty. The learned judge explained to the jury that an accused person had a right to demand that the prosecution's case against him should be proved before he went into the witness box. The evidence here was mere suspicion, and "you cannot put a multitude of suspicions together and make proof out of it."

[1] See T. B. Smith in [1954] CRIM. L.R. 500.
[2] WILLIAMS, THE PROOF OF GUILT 67 n. (2d ed. 1958).

[3] Parratt v. Blunt, 2 Cox C.C. 242 (1847).
[4] *The Times*, March 22, 1956; [1956] CRIM. L.R. 289.

256

Formerly, the right to submit no case was qualified in the case of joint trials. It was held that one of two or more persons jointly tried could not claim to be released from the proceedings for insufficiency of evidence against him until all the evidence for the other defendants was finished.[5] But these rulings, which never had much sense in them, have been forgotten and departed from.[6] The position now is that one of co-defendants can submit "no case" as if he were indicted alone.

There is at least one respect in which the law is in an unsatisfactory state. If counsel for the defence makes a submission of "no case," the theory is that the judge is bound to rule upon it and to rule in the defendant's favour if there is no case to answer. However, there is some danger for counsel in making the submission, because if it is overruled the jury may misunderstand what has passed and think that the judge is convinced of the guilt of the accused. Thus the submission is not generally made unless it has a good chance of success. Another reason why the submission might not be made in the past was that the accused might not be represented, and although this is now unlikely in a trial on indictment, it may happen in summary trials. One might think that a defendant should not be the worse off if no submission is made on his behalf, for this is a situation where the judge should look after the interest of the defendant and take the point himself if he thinks that the prosecution have not produced sufficient evidence to be answered. This opinion is, indeed, accepted to the extent that a judge is allowed to take the point of his own motion.[7] But he is not regarded as bound to do so, and no criticism is made of his conduct if he allows the trial to take its course.

This distinction has an important consequence if the case goes up on appeal. If a submission of "no case" has been made and wrongly rejected by the presiding judge, the judge is regarded as having erred in point of law, and accordingly the defendant may appeal to the Court of Criminal Appeal on this ground. Now the rule with regard to appeals on questions of law is that the appeal must be allowed unless the case can be brought within the proviso to section 4(1) of the Criminal Appeal Act, 1907. The usual statement of the effect of the proviso is that the Crown has to show that, on a right direction, the jury *must* have come to the same conclusion—a rule which in this context means that the appeal must succeed, since on a right direction, namely a direction to the jury to return a verdict of Not Guilty, the jury must have come to the opposite conclusion from the one it did.[8]

Contrast the situation where there is no submission. Here the judge does not make an error of law in allowing the trial to proceed, and an appeal against conviction cannot adopt the same argument as where there has been a submission. An appeal may be taken on the ground that there was a "miscarriage of justice," an expression which includes cases where the verdict was unreasonable having regard to the evidence. However, in deciding this question the Court of Criminal Appeal will look at the whole evidence, including the evidence given by the defence in chief and elicited from the witnesses for the defence on cross-examination.[9] It may be that a defective case for the prosecution will thus be aided by admissions made by the accused on cross-examination or by evidence given against him by his co-defendant.

At one time it was clearly settled that this liberty to look at the evidence as a whole applied only where there had been no submission. If there were a submission of "no case" which was wrongly rejected, the Court of Criminal Appeal regarded itself as not entitled to look at evidence subsequently received. This was laid down in *Joiner*.[10] In a number of subsequent cases the distinction has been blurred, the Court saying that it is always entitled to look at the evidence as a whole. However, in all the cases in which this dictum occurs, the point seems to have been obiter.[11]

---

[5] Carpenter v. Jones, (1828) M. & M. 198 n.; 173 E. R. 1130 n.; Martin, 17 Cox C.C. 36 (1889).

[6] Abbott, [1955] 2 Q.B. 497 (C.C.A.).

[7] George, 1 C.A.R. 168 (1908), 25 T.L.R. 66, 73 J.P. 11.

[8] See the judgment of Lord Goddard, C.J., in Abbott, *supra* note 6.

[9] Jackson, 5 C.A.R. 22 (1910).

[10] 4 C.A.R. 64 (1910).

[11] See H. Calvert in 1958 CRIM. L.R. 232.

Accordingly, it is still open to the Court of Criminal Appeal to follow the explicit authority of *Joiner*. The decision in *Joiner* seems, indeed, to be logically necessary if the law is not to be at odds with itself. If the trial judge is under a duty to accept a submission and stop the case, it ought not to affect the rights of the accused if the case is improperly allowed to continue. Nor is it only a matter of logic, for a denial of the principle of *Joiner* would put an undesirable responsibility on counsel for the defence. Suppose that his submission that there is no case to answer is overruled by the trial court. He may go on with the case by calling evidence for the defence, but, if *Joiner* is wrong, will take the risk that this further evidence may complete the prosecution's case. The alternative is for him to take no further part in the proceedings and to appeal against conviction. But the risk here is that the appeal court may uphold the decision that there was a case to answer and may therefore affirm the conviction, the defendant having in fact been convicted without being heard. It is unlikely that a defending counsel would be prepared to take this second risk, so that he is almost compelled to proceed with the case. And the effect of this may be that the accused is dislodged from his position of silence.

It would be satisfactory in point of legal principle if the decision in *Joiner* were re-established; but, in addition, it may be suggested that there should be no legal distinction between cases where a submission is made and where it is not. The duty of the presiding judge is to see that justice is done, whether application is made by counsel for the defendant or not.

### Searching the body of the accused

In American legal writing, the concept of the privilege against self-incrimination has been applied to medical examinations of accused persons by police surgeons, the use of stomach-pumps, and such like. In England we should not think of these problems as raising an issue of self-incrimination; they relate merely to the limits on the powers of the police in relation to detained persons. Although there is little authority, it can be said with some confidence that the use of force against the body of a detained person for the purpose of obtaining evidence is an illegal battery. There is, however, a common-law power to search arrested persons (the police have not tried to assert that this extends to a search of the body, as distinct from a search of the clothes or exterior); and magistrates have a statutory power to authorise the taking of fingerprints.

# France

ROBERT VOUIN

A fundamental general rule of French penal procedure is that nobody is bound to accuse himself, that no one is obliged to give evidence against himself. Although it may be necessary to denounce crimes committed by someone else, according to the Penal Code, the guilty person's confession can never be legally demanded.[1] All the more, this confession can never be extorted through torture or any kind of violence. Nor can it be obtained, according to the French jurisprudence, by surprise or by trickery or through some stratagems incompatible with the right to a fair trial.

However, to understand the true state of the law, one must consider its application in several concrete settings.

[1] C.P.P., art. 62.

Whenever, in the course of a judicial investigation, it becomes necessary to establish or to check on the identity of a person, the person is bound to lend himself to whatever operations are demanded by the investigation or checking.[2] Thus, it is certain that the judicial police officer may take a picture of the person involved and may take his fingerprints as well.

Since 1954, French legislation has authorized, when it is a matter of verification for a crime, a delict, or a traffic accident, blood tests to determine whether the act was committed "under the influence of a state of intoxication." Such tests, in any case where they may be useful, also may be carried out on the victim (who may be the guilty person). Of course, the question is whether a person has to lend himself to the checking necessary to determine how much alcohol is in his blood. According to the law, "these verifications are compulsory in any case of crime, delect or accident followed by a death."[3] However, it does not seem admissible that blood testing should be imposed upon a person who refuses it absolutely. However, a person, by his refusal, sets against himself a presumption which may be retained among all the other data of proof.

Several years ago, the question was raised in France whether an interrogatory under narcotics (narcoanalysis or narcodiagnosis) may be used in the judicial procedure. It is quite certain that this method cannot be used by the judicial police in order to obtain confessions or accusations. But it can be used by psychiatrists in carrying out a mental examination of the accused person. The best solution is to decide that the doctor may use all the means of his art, and consequently have recourse to psychoanalysis under narcotics, when he wants to have a diagnosis either to try to cure a sick person or to answer a question asked by the judge concerning penal responsibility. However, in either situation, the examination should be conducted under the condition that the physician must never, because of medical secrecy, convey to the judge any confessions or accusations he might have obtained while examining the person.[4] However, this opinion is not admitted by everybody, and the problem, which is not linked solely to the use of narcotics but is raised by every mental testing, has not yet received a solution which would be certain or final in the French legislation or jurisprudence.

It was provided by the "Code d'Investigation Criminelle" (Criminal Investigation Code), and it has just been confirmed by the Penal Procedure Code, that the accused person can never be a witness in his own trial, and, if he makes some statements in front of his judges, he does not have to do it under oath. Otherwise, he might have to choose between perjuring himself or accusing himself. The French law saves him from the necessity of this choice by excusing him from the oath and, in so doing, sets aside the possibility of an accused person getting a penal sentence for false testimony.

The French law does punish the person who, possessing proof of the innocence of a person prosecuted for a crime or delict, does not produce spontaneously his testimony to the justice. However, the person responsible for a prosecution, as well as his collaborators and accomplices, is not subject to this obligation of testifying in behalf of the innocent person. To provide otherwise would require the person responsible for a false prosecution to accuse himself of a crime.[5]

By the same decree, a similar exemption is granted to the parents and relatives—up to the fourth degree of relationship—of accused persons, their collaborators and accomplices. In addition, the decrees which mention the obligation of reporting crimes and attempted crimes do not punish any refusal to report them when it is the doing of the perpetrator's parents or relatives.[6] And, in the same way, the accused person's close relatives do not speak under oath when they have to appear in the trial.[7]

[2] C.P.P., art. 61.

[3] CODE DES DEBITS DE BOISSONS ET DES MESURES CONTRE L'ALCOOLISME, art. 1, §88.

[4] *Cf.*, H. Donnedieu de Vabres, 29 REVUE INTERNATIONALE DE POLICE CRIMINELLE 25 (1949) and Vouin, Rec. Dalloz, Chronique, 101 (1949).

[5] C.P.P., art. 63.

[6] C.P.P., art. 62.

[7] C.P.P., arts. 335 and 448.

On the other hand, witnesses who testify under oath cannot be excused for any personal reasons from fulfilling the obligations imposed upon them by the oath. Thus, the witness will bring upon himself punishment for false testimony in case he violates his oath, even if he lies only to protect himself from possible prosecutions.[8] Should this witness be allowed to refuse his testimony under the excuse that he should not be put under the obligation of accusing himself? That remedy, in the French opinon, would be worse than the evil.

According to the Criminal Investigation Code of 1808, a full account of the charge had to be made by the "ministére Public" at the beginning of the trial in the Assize Court, and the president was allowed to interrogate the accused person only after each witness's testimony and on the ground of this testimony. However, a different practice actually was established. In fact, the account of the charge was never made, and the president would interrogate the accused, in front of the jury, about the facts with which he was being charged.[9] Actually, this interrogatory was a cause of abuses. Most certainly, the accused person had the possibilty of not answering, but in this case, the president alone was speaking, and too often he had the appearance of a prosecutor. The jurisprudence slowly reacted, deciding that a sentence was invalid when it had been pronouned by an Assize Court the president of which, in the process of the trial, had before the proper time spoken out concerning his feelings with respect to the guilt of the accused.[10]

This solution is quite justified, because the president of the French Assize Court and his two assessors, since 1941, participate in the jury's deliberation on the guilt of the accused person. So it has been maintained by the Penal Procedure Code of 1958, according to which the president interrogates the accused and gets his statements, that, under penalty of invalidity, the president "has

the duty not to show his opinion on guilt."[11] One may object that it would have been better to omit completely the accused person interrogatory by the president and reinforce the account of the charge by the "ministére public."

Under the authority of the Code of 1808, the judicial procedure for the preliminary investigation, the purpose of which was to determine whether sufficient evidence existed to justify a trial of the accused person, was consonant with the old inquisitorial type of procedure, that is, it was a written, secret, and "non contradictoire" procedure. This system was greatly modified by the law of December 8, 1897. Under this law, the accused person, if he so desires, may be helped during the investigation period by a barrister who is invited to each interrogatory and who is allowed to study beforehand the dossier of the procedure. Moreover, the barrister is permitted to communicate freely, at any time, with his client.

This procedure is unanimously viewed, in France, as an elementary guarantee of the rights of the defense. Consequently, it has been retained without discussion by the Code of 1958.[12] However, one may ask himself very seriously whether the principle of the "instruction contradictoire" is really justified. In fact, to the extent that the accused person participates in the preliminary examination, he may, later on, feel embarrassed to question its results before the jurisdiction of judgment. During the preparation of the new Code, it had been offered to make "contradictory" the expert's report carried out in the process of the preliminary investigation.[13] However, this provision was not incorporated because the barristers very clearly stated that they would rather not have the defense participate in the expert's report in order to be able later on to criticize freely the expert's conclusions. The objection seems right. But, if it is accurate, it should be put forward as well against the very principle of the "instruction contradictoire."

[8] Cass. Crim., Rec. Dalloz 1918.1.36 (1914).
[9] *Cf.*, Vouin, REVUE DE SCIENCE CRIMINELLE 43 (1955).
[10] Cass. crim., Bull. Crim. No. 476 (1956).

[11] C.P.P., art. 328.
[12] C.P.P., arts. 114 and 118.
[13] *Cf.*, Vouin, REVUE DE SCIENCE CRIMINELLE 243 (1956).

# Germany

WALTER R. CLEMENS

In the German law of procedure—not only civil and criminal, but also administrative, labour, social, etc.—the rule "nemo tenetur se ipsum accusare" has been generally accepted for well over one century. It is based on the ethical concept that the procedural interest in the exploration of the truth must stand back behind the higher valued interest of the individual to be protected from any coercion to self-incrimination. It is the purpose of this report to show how this principle is legally ruled in the field of criminal procedure.

## THE PRIVILEGE OF THE DEFENDANT

### Privilege of silence

This subject matter is covered by section 136 of the German Code of Criminal Procedure (hereinafter called CCP). This section deals only with the interrogation of the defendant by the judge. As the expression of a general principle, though, it is held to apply also to his interrogation by the public prosecutor and the police.[1] It reads:

"(i) At the beginning of the first interrogation the defendant shall be informed about the nature of the charge. He shall be asked if he wants to reply to the charge.

"(ii) The interrogation shall give the defendant an opportunity to remove the grounds for suspicion prevailing against him and to put forward the facts which speak in his favor.

"(iii) During the first interrogation of the suspect an inquiry shall also be made into his personal status."

[1] See EBERHARD SCHMIDT, LEHRKOMMENTAR ZUR STRAFPROZEBORDNUNG (1957), Vorbemerkung 6 vor §133, Teil II (Instructional Commentary of Criminal Procedure, part II, preliminary note no. 6, §133, 1957).

### (a) *Privilege of silence ad rem*

Section 136(i), CCP, points out quite clearly that the defendant—who incidentally cannot be heard as a witness under German law, and hence cannot make a sworn statement in a case against himself—is under no obligation to answer the charge, i.e., to make a statement ad rem. Rather, he is entitled to refuse to answer the charge or keep silent from the beginning.

It is a contested question whether the defendant who does not take advantage of his privilege of silence is under procedural law obligated to tell the truth. The predominant and correct opinion of the law teachers[2] answers this question in the negative. However, the discussion about the defendant's duty to tell the truth appears to be useless anyway, because the CCP provides for no means of forcing him into telling the truth or changing an untrue statement.

And at any time he is allowed to revoke both his preparedness and his refusal to make a statement, as well as a former statement, especially a confession.

### (b) *Privilege of silence ad personam*

It appears to be uncontested that under procedural law the defendant is not obligated to give particulars, let alone correct particulars, pertaining to his personal status. The former Reichsgericht,[3] however, and some legal theorists[4] take the view that such obligation can be deduced from the substantive law, namely section 360(8) of the German Criminal Code (hereinafter called CC). This provision penalizes him who before a

[2] See EBERHARD SCHMIDT, *op. cit. supra* note 1, §136 n.11–13.
[3] 72 Entscheidungen des Reichsgerichts in Strafsachen 30 (decisions of the Reichsgericht in Criminal Matters).
[4] See KLEINKNECHT-MÜLLER, KOMMENTAR ZUR STRAFPROZESSORDNUNG, 4 Auflage, Anmerkung 2a zu §136 (Commentary of Criminal Procedure, §136 n.2a, 4th ed.).

competent authority or a competent official makes an incorrect declaration or refuses a declaration with regard to his name, his status, his calling, his business, his residence or his nationality. The question whether this provision is applicable to the defendant who has violated it in the course of a procedure against himself, should—contrary to the Reichsgericht—be answered in the negative.

This follows from the generally accepted legal concept of the "collision of interests" which says that a less valuable interest must stand back when it comes into conflict with a higher-valued interest. Beyond dispute, the privilege of silence ad rem as laid down in section 136(i), CCP, is higher in value than the average person's duty to give true particulars ad personam, established in section 360(8), CC, which penalizes the offender only with a fine up to 150 Deutsche Marks or with detention up to six weeks. Now in practice the enforcement of a true statement ad personam will in many cases violate and even defeat the higher-valued privilege of silence ad rem, because true particulars often throw light upon the identity of the offender and hence incriminate him ad rem and contrary to the statute. The predominant opinion[5] is therefore that the defendant has no duty—neither under procedural nor under substantive law—to answer or to answer correctly in regard to his particulars, and is not punishable under section 360(8), CC, if he refuses a declaration ad personam or gives false particulars.

(c) *Consequences of refusal to answer or of false statements.*

As mentioned, the CCP does not attach detrimental consequences to the silence or deliberate falsehood ad rem or ad personam of the defendant. This is not to say, however, that such demeanor should be always irrelevant in the sphere of substantive law. Adverse consequences of such nature are for example the following:

(i) Stubborn or insolent denials of the defendant can influence sentence, as is justly held by the Federal Supreme Court, especially in several decisions rendered in 1951.[6] In view of the fact that the defendant is not obligated under the law to make a confession, and any pressure used in this connection is prohibited, the Federal Supreme Court rules it to be inadmissible to assess a more lenient punishment only on account of a confession, and a more severe punishment only on account of a denial. Yet it justly takes the view that the court in considering the stubborn denial of a defendant is free to draw its conclusions as to the degree of his personal guilt, especially as to his lack of repentance and dangerous criminal character. For this reason, the Federal Court goes on to say, the judge may deny mitigating circumstances or may make no allowance for the period of custody undergone awaiting trial or may impose a stiffer sentence.

(ii) The Federal Supreme Court[7] further holds that the silence or denial of a defendant may constitute or increase the danger of collusion and so may be relevant to the grant of a warrant of arrest.

(iii) Finally, the willingly false statement of the accused may constitute another criminal offense.[8] For instance if he in his defense declares the sworn incriminating statement of a witness to be a lie, this may incur punishment under section 164, CC (false accusation), or section 185 and following of the Criminal Code (defamation, slander, etc.).

*Other aspects of the privilege*

In the absence of a clear legal ruling criminal courts and law teachers have stretched the protection of the suspect from self-incrimination beyond his privilege of silence, and have developed the principle that the suspect is under no obligation to make an *active* contribution[9] to his conviction.

[5] See EBERHARD SCHMIDT, *op. cit. supra* note 1, §136 n.9, and HENKEL, STRAFVERFAHRENSRECHT (Law of Criminal Procedure) 223–24.

[6] 1 Entscheidungen des Bundesgerichtshofs in Strasfsachen 103, 105 (Decisions of the Federal Supreme Court in Criminal Matters), and MONATSSCHRIFT FÜR DEUTSCHES RECHT (German Law Monthly) 440 (1951).

[7] MONATSSCHRIFT FÜR DEUTSCHES RECHT 532 (1952).

[8] See KLEINKNECHT-MÜLLER, *op. cit. supra* note 4, §136 n.3.

[9] See BELING, DIE BEWEISVERBOTE ALS GRENZEN DER WAHRHEITSERFORSCHUNG IM STRAFPROZESS (The Evidential Prohibitions in Criminal Proceedings as Limits to the Search for Truth) 11 (1903).

In application of this principle the Reichsgericht[10] does not think it the suspect's duty to furnish a specimen of writing for the purpose of contriving a comparison of writings within the meaning of section 93, CCP, and it is generally accepted[11] that the suspect is not under the obligation, laid down generally in section 94, CCP, to surrender objects which might be of importance as evidence or are subject to confiscation.

While not being under an obligation to make an *active* contribution to his conviction, as was said above, yet the suspect is under an obligation to maintain a *passive* attitude in regard to measures which are instrumental in his conviction, i.e., he must tolerate them. His consent is not necessary. This applies in particular to his bodily examination as provided in section 81a, CCP, and to the taking of a blood-test (with the restriction that detriments to his health shall not ensue), and further to the taking of pictures and fingerprints, measurements and other modes of action under section 81c, CCP, as well as the seizure of letters and telegrams written by him or addressed to him under section 99, CCP, the search of his dwelling under section 102, CCP, etc.

### THE PRIVILEGE OF THE WITNESS

*The privilege of silence*

Section 55, CCP, provides:

"(i) Every witness can refuse information as to all questions the answer to which might incur prosecution for himself. . . .

"(ii) The witness shall be advised on his privilege to decline to answer questions."[12]

The question whether this provision applies also to the interrogation of the witness by the district attorney or the police is generally answered in the affirmative as far as paragraph (i) is concerned. It is, however, generally answered in the negative respecting paragraph (ii),[13] which appears unfortunate but cannot be helped de lege lata.

Section 55(i) establishes—other than section 136(i) for the defendant—no general right of the witness to decline to answer, but only the limited right to refuse information on any facts the description of which might incur punishment against himself. Section 55(i) is the outcome of the already mentioned basic principle that nobody is obligated to incriminate himself. The provision serves to protect the witness only, not the defendant, so that—according to the opinion of the Federal Supreme Court,[14] which, however, is not uncontested—a review on law does not lie on the defendant's behalf if the court has failed to advise the witness on his privilege of silence according to section 55(ii) CCP.

The declaration of the witness that he would take advantage of his privilege of silence is just as revocable as his declaration that he would make a statement.[15] If it is only at the trial that a witness who prior to it had been heard by the district attorney or the police refuses to give evidence, then the court is, under section 252, CCP, prohibited from using his former statements. This applies also to the evidence of a witness who, contrary to section 55(ii), CCP, was not advised properly.[16]

Section 55(i) does not permit the witness to conceal from the court a fact endangering himself if he has not taken advantage of his privilege of silence. Rather is he in such case bound—this is, in contrast to the defendant—to tell the whole truth; and he will, under the CC, incur punishment by giving false evidence.

*Other aspects of the privilege*

The witness can refuse his consent to a bodily examination and the taking of blood for the same

---

[10] 15 Entscheidungen des Reichsgerichts in Strafsachen 320.

[11] See BELING, *op. cit. supra* note 9, and EBERHARD SCHMIDT, *op. cit. supra* note 1, §94 n.17.

[12] An important supplementing provision to §55 is §56, CCP. It says that the facts on which the witness grounds his privilege must be supported by evidence to the satisfaction of the court, and that the solemn declaration of the witness on oath is sufficient for that purpose.

[13] As to details, see EBERHARDT SCHMIDT, *op. cit. supra* note 1, §52 n.15.

[14] 1 Entscheidungen des Bundesgerichtshofs in Strafsachen 39.

[15] 63 Entscheidungen des Reichsgerichts in Strafsachen 302 and EBERHARD SCHMIDT, *op. cit. supra* note 1, §52 prelim. n.9.

[16] 20 Entscheidungen des Reichsgerichts in Strafsachen 186.

reasons as he can under section 55(i), CCP, refuse his testimony. This is provided for in section 81c(i), CCP. He is also not under the obligation to surrender objects which might have evidential value or are subject to confiscation (section 95(ii), CCP). However, the CCP does not go as far as to spare the witness such search or confiscation as might result in his criminal prosecution. Such action he is bound to tolerate, just like the suspect.

## The Privilege of the Expert

Under section 76(i), CCP, the expert is entitled to refuse to give his opinion for the same reasons as entitle a witness to refuse to make a statement, especially under section 55(i), CCP. So, all that in this connection was said about the witness will apply here correspondingly. A farther-reaching protection of the expert is not provided for by the CCP.

## Privileges of Other Persons

On behalf of persons other than the suspect, the witness, and the expert, a protection, within the scope of criminal proceedings, from self-incrimination is out of the question and therefore not provided for by the CCP. It is true that this statute does grant some other privileges of silence. These rights, however, have no bearing on the concept of the privilege against *self*-incrimination, because their objective is not to afford the privileged persons protection from self-incrimination, but protection from the incrimination of others, especially near relations, from conflicts of conscience, etc.

It is for this reason that the near relations of the suspect have under section 52, CCP, in principle been conceded the privilege of silence. Again, under section 55(i), CCP, the witness is entitled to refuse to answer if, otherwise, a near relation would be jeopardized with criminal prosecution. And under section 53 certain persons who are under the pledge of secrecy, e.g., clergymen, defense counsel, lawyers, doctors, etc., have also been granted the privilege of silence, unless they have been released from their duty to professional discretion.

## Summary

In the light of the foregoing observations, the following summary of the German law can be made:

The CCP affords the defendant, the witness, and the expert a very extensive protection from self-incrimination. This protection is founded on a basic principle which has been generally acknowledged for more than a century and has in the Federal Republic become an integral part of the general sense of justice. Therefore it must be maintained unrestrictedly, all the more so since nobody, as far as is known, has demanded to narrow or repeal the relevant provisions after the breakdown of the Nazi-regime.

Within the Federal Republic of Germany, the Law of Criminal Procedure is exhaustively covered in the CCP, that is on a federal basis. As a result the German Länder, according to the provisions of the Basic Law, have no right to enact law pertaining to this matter. Thus, in the absence of a competitive sphere of legislative jurisdiction between the Bund (Federation) and the Länder, no problems of dual sovereignty can arise in this area in the Federal Republic of Germany.

# *Israel*

## HAIM H. COHN

In his classic outline of the history and policy of the privilege against self-incrimination, Wigmore categorically states that the origin of the privilege was purely local (17th century—England) and that "in the other legal systems of the world it had no original place."[1] It is not so much in order to disprove that statement, nor to suggest that the Anglo-American concept of the privilege against self-incrimination may have been influenced by ancient Middle Eastern institutions, but rather in order to show how deeply this concept is entrenched in Israeli legal consciousness, that a short account is given of its origins in the law of ancient Israel.

The rule that no man may incriminate himself was first distinctly enunciated by Rava, who lived in exile in Babylon in the 4th century A.D.,[2] in the following terms: "a man is nearest to himself, and no man calls himself a wrongdoer."[3] Later jurists have separated the two component parts of this rule from each other and have laid down the second part of the rule as a general prohibition of self-incrimination;[4] but the two parts of the rule have to be read together for a proper understanding of its origin.

Both near relatives and wrongdoers are incompetent witnesses. The incompetency of near relatives was based on an interpretation of the scripture[5] to the effect that a man may not be put to death either for the sins of his parents or of his children or because of, that is, on the testimony of, his parents or children.[6] The incompetency of

wrongdoers was derived from the scripture, "put not thine hand with the wicked to be an unrighteous witness,"[7] which was read to mean that the wicked are bound to be unrighteous witnesses and therefore are incompetent.[8] It appears that incompetency to testify was not generally regarded as a disqualification which one should do one's best to remedy, but rather as a welcome cause to evade the onerous duty of testifying. Not only was the punishment for false testimony very severe (namely the same punishment to which the accused had been liable, had he been convicted[9]), but if the accused was convicted of a capital offence, "the hands of the witnesses shall be first upon him to put him to death."[10] In addition, there may have prevailed then, as there prevails today, very good reasons for a potential witness not to get implicated in judicial proceedings. There cannot, at any rate, be any doubt that potential witnesses tried to disqualify themselves from testifying by asserting that they had committed this or the other offence or that they were leading dissolute lives, so as to bring themselves within the category of the "wicked" who had to be presumed to be "unrighteous" witnesses. It was in order to cure this mischief that Rava laid down his rule: as far as the incompetency of near relatives was concerned, none is nearer to a man than he himself, and if his near relatives are incompetent to testify against (or for) him, *a fortiori* must he be incompetent to testify against (or for) himself; but as far as the incompetency of wrongdoers is concerned, no man may be heard to assert that he is a wrongdoer *so as to disqualify himself as a witness.*

The incompetency to testify in one's own favour dates from a period earlier by at least two centuries than Rava's time. There is, for instance, a Mishnaic[11] text to the effect that the presump-

---

[1] 8 WIGMORE, EVIDENCE §2251 at 304 (3d ed. 1940).
[2] At exactly the same time, Roman law provided specifically for judicial examination of accused persons under torture: THEODOSIAN CODE BOOK IX Title 35 (De Quaestionibus) at 250 (Pharr Trans.).
[3] Talmud Sanhedrin 9, 1.
[4] See, e.g., Rashi (Shlomo Yitzhaki) in his Commentary to Talmud Yebamot 25, 2.
[5] Deuteronomy 24, 16.
[6] Talmud Sanhedrin 27, 2.
[7] Exodus 23, 1.
[8] Talmud Sanhedrin 25, 1; Baba Kama 72, 2.
[9] Deuteronomy, 19, 19.
[10] Deuteronomy, 17, 7.
[11] The Mishna is the earliest part of the Talmud and was finally completed about 200 A.D.

tion that a woman is violated by the enemy while held as a prisoner cannot be rebutted by the solemn oath of her husband that "her hand did not move out of my hand from the day the enemy entered Jerusalem until he left," because nobody is a witness in his own cause.[12] (It was, on the other hand, always recognized that a man must be heard in his own defence, albeit not as a witness; and the Mishnaic law was that even after sentence had been pronounced, proceedings had to be reopened up to five times if the accused wished to argue something in his favour, provided it was an argument of substance.[13]) There was, thus, nothing revolutionary in Rava's ruling that a man is not competent to disqualify himself as a witness by his own testimony: although self-incriminating, this testimony was in his own favour, because its purpose was to be released from the duty of testifying in another cause. In a different context, the same Rava even reduced the *ratio* of the prohibition of bribery to the formula, "no man will convict himself"—meaning that, having received a bribe, the judge might identify himself with the donor and thus become a judge in his own cause.[14]

Nor was there anything surprising in the subsequent evolution of Rava's rule into a general prohibition of self-incrimination. Indeed, the prior existence of a rule against self-incrimination, although not yet expressly formulated, may be deduced from several Mishnaic texts. Thus, a biblical instance of questioning a person accused of crime and obtaining his confession ("And Joshua said unto Achan: make confession and tell me now what thou hast done; hide it not from me. And Achan answered Joshua and said: indeed I have sinned…and thus and thus have I done"[15]) was interpreted in the Mishna as if the confession had been asked for and made only after trial and conviction and not before, and then only for the purpose of expiating the sin before God so as not to be revisited again after death.[16] Later jurists

[12] Talmud Ketubot, 27, 2.
[13] Talmud Sanhedrin 42, 2.
[14] Talmud Shabbat 119, 1; Ketubot 105, 2.
[15] Joshua 7, 19–20.
[16] Talmun Sanhedrin 43, 2.
The confession of sin in repentance before God is, of course, always encouraged and at certain times (the

dismissed this and similar biblical stories simply as exceptions to the general rule,[17] although not a single instance of the application of any such rule occurs in the Bible.[18]

Or, where witnesses to a deed testified that at the time they had witnessed the deed they were incompetent for reason of their sinfulness, their evidence as to their witnessing the deed was held admissible and that as to their incompetency was held inadmissible.[19] Or, where a man came forward and said that he had killed a woman's husband, that woman could not, on the strength of such evidence, be allowed to remarry.[20]

The question thus arose whether a man's statement may be divided so that only the self-incriminating part would be inadmissible, whereas the neutral part would be admissible in evidence. In the case of the self-confessed murderer of the woman's husband, for instance, one school held that the confession would be admissible as evidence of the husband's death, but not of his murder by the confessor; another school held that the confession was indivisible and inadmissible for any purpose.[21] There finally emerged a rule that the neutral part of a confession is admissible only for the purpose of corroborating other independent evidence: thus, where the issue requiring proof is the death of a man, the evidence of a witness to the death may be corroborated by that part of the confession of the killer which testifies to the death having occurred; but the killing can never be

day of atonement) even prescribed. But these confessions have no legal significance and are not admissible in evidence against the confessor or at all; it is a sin even to remind a man who has confessed before God of the misdeeds he had confessed to: Maimonides, Teshuva, 7, 8. (For a similar rule, *cf.* Canons 1755, 1757, Corpus Juris Canonici.)
[17] Maimonides, Sanhedrin, 18, 6.
[18] It is worthy of note that Lilburn, defending himself against the claim by the judges that he was, although an accused, under obligation to be examined, relied on the law of God for his refusal to answer (3 HOWARD'S STATE TRIALS 1315); but he gave no particular text in the scriptures as authority for his proposition, except Christ's trial by Pilate, and there stood at once corrected by the judges (See 8 WIGMORE, EVIDENCE §2250 n.103).
[19] Talmud Ketubot 18, 2.
[20] Talmud Yebamot 25, 1.
[21] Talmud Yebamot 25, 2.

proved by the confession of the killer even where corroborated by the evidence of one independent witness, because at least two witnesses are required, and the confessor is not a witness against himself.[22]

At about the time of the Mishna another rule had been laid down to the effect that the admission by a party to a suit that a debt was owed by him was tantamount to the evidence of a hundred witnesses.[23] This was well established law when Rava first enunciated his rule; and the fact that the concept of the prohibition of self-incrimination had existed and been recognized before Rava formulated the rule with regard to the competency of witnesses is also apparent from the way in which the conflicts between valid admissions and invalid confessions had been solved. Thus, where a man admitted to have raped or seduced a woman, or to have stolen a chattel, he could not on the strength of such admission be adjudged to pay a fine or otherwise be punished but would be held liable to pay damages to the injured party.[24] Or, where a man said to two others, "I have stolen a sum of money from either the one or the other of you, but do not know from whom," he was held to be liable to both; another school held that where a man had admitted to have stolen money, and several persons came forward, each claiming that the money had been stolen from him, the stolen money was to be deposited in court, and the thief would not have to pay more than once.[25]

In later times, the rule that the confession to a criminal act would serve as a civil cause of action, but would not be admitted as evidence in criminal proceedings, was applied to confessions of arson,[26] embezzlement,[27] the taking of usurious interest,[28] and, by analogy, of adultery—the confessing wife losing her claim to maintenance and other monetary benefits, but not her status as a married woman, and incurring no liability to be divorced or punished on the strength of her confession only,[29]

An early authority poses the question whether the injunction of the scripture, "Ye shall have one manner of law,"[30] should not be read to prohibit any distinction between civil and criminal law with regard to admissions and confessions; the question is answered in the negative, because the scripture itself says in civil causes, He shall pay, but in criminal causes, He shall die.[31]

The reasons underlying the rule against self-incrimination were at various periods differently expounded. The earliest version appears to be that as the scripture expressly commands, "at the mouth of two witnesses, or three witnesses, shall he that is worthy of death be put to death, but at the mouth of one witness he shall not be put to death"[32] —no one may be condemned otherwise than on the evidence of witnesses, as distinguished from the evidence of himself.[33] Maimonides adds a reason of his own, holding that a court may not inflict punishment on a man only because of his having confessed to a crime: "maybe his mind is disturbed in this matter, or maybe he is one of those melancholy and depressed persons who look forward to dying and are apt to run a sword through their bodies or throw themselves from a roof, and maybe such a person comes forward and confesses to a crime which he did not commit, so as to be put to death."[34] Another reason given was based on the words of the prophet that all souls are the Lord God's,[35] hence no admission by which a man may forfeit his life can be of any effect, his life being not his own but God's to dispose of, whereas his property is his own, and he may dispose thereof in any way he likes, including by the admission of debts.[36] Still another theory propounded was that if confessions were accorded any probative value in criminal proceedings, courts might be inclined to overvalue them, as King David did,[37] and thus be

[22] Hameiri on Sanhedrin 1, 1 (13th century).
[23] Talmud Gittin 40, 2; Kiddushin 65, 20 *et aliunde*.
[24] Talmud Ketubot 41, 1.
[25] Talmud Baba Metzia 37, 1.
[26] Rashba (Shlomo ben Aderet), 13th century.
[27] Mordehai (Mordehai ben Hillel Ashkenazi), 13th century.
[28] Ritba (Yomtov ben Avraham of Sevilla), 14th century.

[29] Maimonides, Ishut, 24, 18, (12th century).
[30] Leviticus 24, 22.
[31] Tossefta Shevuot 3, 7 (completed about 600 A.D.).
[32] Deuteronomy 17, 6.
[33] Tossefta Sanhedrin 11, 3.
[34] Maimonides, Sanhedrin 18, 6.
[35] Ezekiel 18, 4.
[36] Radbaz (David ben Zimra), 16th century.
[37] 2 Samuel 1, 16: "And David said unto him, Thy

guilty of a dereliction of their own fact-finding duty.[38] Later jurists pointed out the real difference between civil admissions and criminal confessions to be that by an admission, an obligation was created which had only to be enforced by the court; whereas the conviction of a criminal offence was not in the nature of the enforcement by the court of an obligation voluntarily undertaken by a party but of a creation by the court of the party's liability.[39]

With the emancipation of the Jewish communities and the loss of domestic criminal jurisdiction, the rule prohibiting all self-incrimination has be-

---

blood be upon thy head; for thy mouth hath testified against thee, saying I have slain the Lord's anointed."
[38] Joseph Ibn Migash (11th century).
[39] Levush Mordehai (Mordehai Epstein), 19th century.

come obsolete. In the new State of Israel, the English common law privilege has replaced the ancient Jewish law prohibition: self-incrimination is no longer regarded as unlawful *per se*, but is now left to the free choice of the individual concerned. But any suggestion that even the privilege should now be abolished and a person be made compellable to give evidence incriminating himself, would—whatever the weight and substance of the reasons prompting such reform—find no countenance in Israel. Although no part of a formal constitution, the principle is, in the words of Cardozo, "so rooted in the traditions and conscience of our people as to be ranked as fundamental"; and any attempt to further restrict its scope and application would be denounced as incompatible with democracy and the rule of law.

# *Japan*

## HARUO ABE

### HISTORICAL BACKGROUND[1]

It is not easy to realize the true picture of the Japanese system designed for protecting human rights against illegal or unfair exercise of investigating authority without having some preliminary knowledge about the historical background of the Japanese legal system. This is particularly true for an accurate understanding of the concept of the privilege against self-incrimination in Japan. Therefore, a brief account of the democratizing process of the Japanese system is given.

#### *Historical Sketch up to 1889*

From the 8th century down to the 1860's criminal justice in Japan was profoundly influenced by

[1] See also Abe, *Self-Incrimination—Japan and the United States*, 46 J. CRIM. L., C. & P.S. 613 (1956).

Chinese legal tradition. Ancient Chinese laws had been adopted and modified by feudal precedents and ordinances. The thought and philosophy basic to the administration of criminal justice were the result of a mixture of traditional Japanese morals under feudalism and the Japanese interpretation of Confucian ethics.

Since the 1860's the Japanese system of criminal justice has experienced two revolutionary changes. The first one occurred in the 1870's, following the Meiji Restoration, under the influence of European legal culture, and the second one started in 1946 following the termination of World War II, under the influence of Anglo-American legal tradition.

In 1868 the Tokugawa Shogunate's Government collapsed and was succeeded by the more enlightened government of the Emperor Meiji. However, it took time for the new government to sweep away all the feudalistic remnants. For example, it was not until 1879 that legalized torture was entirely abolished. Beating and "Stone Holding" were common techniques employed to extort confessions from prisoners.[2] In the "Stone Holding" torture the prisoner was forced to sit upon a corrugated wooden seat, holding heavy flat stones of about 100 pounds each in his lap. Astonishingly enough, the criminal statutes of the 1870's retained the provisions for torture devices. Moreover, Article 318 of the Revised Criminal Code of 1873 provided that "the accused shall be found guilty by the conviction of the court based upon his confession." This provision, which declared the principle of "no conviction without confession," helped to enthrone confession as "the queen of evidence."

In 1876, being urged by Professor Boissonade, who had been invited from France by the Japanese Government to codify and modernize the legal systems of Japan, the government changed the wording of Article 318 of the Revised Criminal Code to provide that "the accused shall be found guilty by evidence."[3] This was the first step toward reformation. In 1879 the age-old torture system was statutorily abolished. In 1880 the Criminal Procedure Law drafted by Professor Boissonade after the model of French law was enacted. Thus, under the influence of the European culture of the 19th century, the new Japan gradually paved its way to the modernization of its legal system.

### Development under the Old Japanese Constitution

Even prior to World War II Japan had a constitutional law which was to some extent based upon the principles of the rule of law and representative government. The Imperial Constitution of 1889 provided for the separation of powers and contained a limited bill of rights. Under the Imperial Constitution criminal justice was administered under the law as enacted by the national legislature. However, Japan was far from being a modern democratic country in that she was

[2] For the details of the torture techniques employed in the feudal ages and prewar days in Japan see Abe, *op. cit. supra* note 1, at 613–619.

[3] For the event which moved Prof. Boissonade toward such action see Abe, *op. cit. supra* note 1 at 616 n.14.

reigned over and ruled by the Emperor, who was regarded as an incarnate deity and the ultimate source of sovereign power. The principal characteristic of this old regime was its compromise between the ideal of modern constitutionalism and the traditional principle of government by the Emperor. Under such constitutional monarchy the principle of the rule of law could not command its full implementation. The civil rights of the subjects were sometimes restricted by the administrative superiority of the Emperor's Government. It should be noted also that leading politicians and jurists in those days could not realize fully the significance of the rôle of the bill of rights.

Under the Imperial Constitution of 1889, the Penal Code of 1907 and the Code of Criminal Procedure of 1890 were enacted. The latter was replaced by the Code of Criminal Procedure of 1922. Judging from the wording of the new statutes, there seemed to be no substantial difference between the modernized criminal justice of Japan and that of a European country. Criminal justice based on these new laws was strongly influenced by German legal theories and considerably colored by the liberalism of the 19th century. For instance, the new system adopted the accusatorial system and the principle of trial on evidence. Thus, although the blueprint of the machinery of criminal justice under the new system was not too unsatisfactory, the practice went along in a direction divergent from that originally expected. The practice of coercing confession became rather common among the police; prisoners were kept "incommunicado" quite often; and the preliminary examination, which was kept secret from the public, became a sort of "Star Chamber" affair.

### Reform under the new Constitution of 1947

The governmental system of Japan underwent a fundamental change when the "Constitution of Japan" came into force in 1947. This occurred during the occupation of the Allied Powers following the termination of World War II. Under the new Constitution, with the adoption of a revised parliamentary system, the establishment of the principle of a parliamentary cabinet and the securing of the complete independence of the judiciary, a democratic government has been established. The Emperor has descended from the position of incarnate god and has lost his political power. He is now nothing but "the symbol of the State and the unity of the people." Under the new regime the principle of the rule of law in its pure and perfect form has been embodied in the existing legal system through the constitutional guarantee of fundamental human rights and the creation of a system of judicial review over administrative and legislative action. With the establishment of the revised governmental system under this new Constitution, Japan has achieved the appearance of a modern democratic state at least from the legal aspect. It was against this historical background that the present code, the Code of Criminal Procedure of 1948,[4] was enacted. The functions of the reformed machinery of criminal justice in Japan can be appreciated only in the new light of the postwar regime.

As was mentioned before, the former Code of Criminal Procedure of 1922 was based in its entirety on European (particularly German) law, whereas the present Code of Criminal Procedure of 1948, which was enacted under the new Constitution of 1947, has largely adopted Anglo-American devices to protect human rights. The new Code is still based, however, on the Continental tradition of law in its general scheme. Thus, it may be said that the present system of criminal justice in Japan is a mixture of Continental (especially German) and Anglo-American traditions of law.

### PARTICULAR PROBLEMS CONCERNING THE PRIVILEGE AGAINST SELF-INCRIMINATION IN JAPAN

#### Is the Privilege Worthy of Retention?

Is the privilege against self-incrimination worthy of retention? Despite the strong antagonism of Japanese criminal investigators toward the privilege, most Japanese lawyers seem to agree that the privilege is worthy of retention with or without qualifications. Article 38 of the Japanese Constitution proudly declares that "No person shall be

[4] THE CODE OF CRIMINAL PROCEDURE (Law No. 131, July 10, 1948; enforced on January 1, 1949).

compelled to testify against himself...." Under the present criminal procedure, a suspect is entitled to be notified of the privilege against self-incrimination before being interrogated.[5] Thus, in starting interrogation most Japanese investigators reluctantly murmur the following prototype phrase: "You don't have to answer, if you don't want to." It is contended that such a mechanical warning does not help very much. The suspects may even take it as an ironical challenge. But there is no doubt that such a warning helps to remind the investigators themselves of their obligations to respect the privilege against self-incrimination.

In an article published a few years ago the author analyzed the concept of the privilege against self-incrimination in Japan from various angles and pointed out the high disciplinary effects of this constitutional device.[6] The author has no intention of reiterating all the discussions presented in the previous article. In this chapter, therefore, only highlights of the current issues in Japan will be given.

#### The Privilege Against Self-Incrimination and the Right to Cross-Examination

It is submitted that Japan was so hurried in adopting the concept of privilege against self-incrimination that she overlooked the possible imbalance between the privilege and the whole structure of traditional criminal justice.

Under Anglo-American law it has been well settled that once the accused has taken the witness stand he is assumed to have waived his privilege against self-incrimination and may be cross-examined by the prosecution with respect to what he stated in the direct examination. Strangely enough, Japanese law did not adopt this rule when it imported the concept of the privilege against self-incrimination. Under Japanese law a defendant is incompetent as a witness. This means that he

[5] THE CODE OF CRIMINAL PROCEDURE, art. 198, par. 2: "In the case of questioning mentioned in the preceding paragraph [i.e., questioning of a suspect by a public prosecutor, public prosecutor's assistant officer or judicial police officer], the suspect shall, in advance, be notified that he is not required to make a statement against his will".

[6] See Abe, op. cit. supra note 1.

cannot be sworn as a witness even though he may be willing. He may of course testify without taking an oath if he does so voluntarily; but since he is not sworn, he may conceal the truth or make a false statement without risking perjury.[7] Thus, he enjoys an absolute privilege even to refuse to answer the questions propounded by the prosecution or the judge with regard to the ambiguous points contained in his statement; the court is not allowed to consider the mere fact that the accused failed to answer by invoking his privilege. Such particular status of law strengthens the privilege against self-incrimination into a privilege of silence or even a privilege of false statement. Unquestionably this is impairing the spirit of even-handed justice.

## The Privilege Not to Identify Oneself

In interpreting the concept of the privilege against self-incrimination, most Japanese judges have been taking the position that the privilege should include the right to withhold one's own name and any other information which might identify oneself. Should the name of the accused be regarded as something which tends to incriminate him? Under Anglo-American law this question will generally be answered in the negative, except in particular cases where falsifying a name constitutes the essential part of a crime; in general, a name, although it is something of primary importance to investigators or the triers, is only a remote fact which rarely tends to incriminate a person. Under Japanese law, however, most judges and progressive scholars are prone to interpret this privilege as being in the accused's extreme favor. They adopt the concept in its logical pureness, eliminating or disregarding all the qualifications which have been imposed upon the concept in its long historical development under the Anglo-American system.

[7] *Cf.*, THE PENAL CODE OF JAPAN, art. 169: "When a witness, who has been sworn in accordance with law, gives false testimony, imprisonment at forced labor for not less than three months nor more than 10 years shall be imposed." In this connection it may surprise Anglo-American lawyers to learn that in civil actions, while the parties can be sworn, should they give false testimony it would not constitute a crime of perjury since the provision concerning that crime applies only to witnesses, not to parties. *Cf.*, THE JAPANESE CODE OF CIVIL PROCEDURE, arts. 336 *et seq.*, esp. arts. 338 and 339.

There have been many cases in which accused persons have not disclosed their names throughout the proceedings; most judges have taken such practice as a matter of course.

The first challenge to this practice was made in 1951 by the Sapporo High Court in the case of a communist appellant who, in filing the appeal, used the signature "Unknown X," which was not recognized as an ordinary signature required by the rules of criminal procedure. The court dismissed the appeal, holding that in filing an appeal the appellant was not entitled to use such a meaningless signature as a means of invoking the privilege against self-incrimination.[8] The reasoning was substantially based on the theory that because he actively asked the appellate court for a judicial remedy, he, as the moving party, should reveal his name. However, the opinion of the court was criticized as conservative even by the judiciary on the theory that it required the appellant to make an unnecessary feudalistic courtesy in exercising his own right to appeal.

The second challenge was made in 1952 by the same high court in a case where the counsel filed an appeal in the names of three communist appellants "Unknowns X, Y and Z". The court dismissed the appeal as against procedure, holding in substance (a) that the privilege against self-incrimination might be invoked only at the stage of the main proceedings and with respect to the facts concerning crimes; (b) that the privilege did not authorize the appellants to conceal their names at the stage of preparing the main proceedings; (c) that the notification of appointment of the counsel made in the names of "Unknowns X, Y and Z" was illegal; (d) and that the appeal filed by the counsel illegally appointed was null and void.[9]

The theory proposed by the high court decision was confirmed by a recent Supreme Court decision. In 1957 the Supreme Court dismissed an appeal taken by communist defendants from a decision of the Tokyo High Court affirming a decision of the Chiba District Court which held

[8] Vol. 4, No. 5 High Courts Crim. Rep. 512 (Sapporo High Court 1951).
[9] Vol. 5, No. 10 High Courts Crim. Rep. 1653 (Sapporo High Court 1952).

that the notification of appointment of a counsel undersigned with defendants' jail numbers was null and void. In that case the court held that one's own name should not be regarded as a fact tending to incriminate oneself concerning which the accused had the constitutional privilege of non-disclosure.[10]

However, the view advocated by these judicial precedents has not been very popular among the majority of scholars and judges, although it has been enthusiastically accepted by practical-minded lawyers and investigators. It appears that in Japan the function of the privilege against self-incrimination is far-reaching, because most judges are (a) still giving the phrase "against himself" in Article 38 of the Constitution as broad an interpretation as "against his will on any ground" and (b) allowing the witness himself to judge the probability of self-incrimination.[11]

## The Statutory Duty of Disclosure in the Quasi-Public Relationship

Does the privilege against self-incrimination excuse the statutory duty of disclosure in the quasi-public relationship? This problem appears to have been of vital importance under American law.[12] It is becoming important also in Japan, where there are a great number of administrative statutes which comprise specific provisions imposing upon citizens the duty to file reports, to keep records, to disclose records for official inspection, and to answer questions asked by administrative officials with respect to matters of quasi-public importance.[13] It is obvious that the draftsmen of these statutes were aware of the problem regarding the relationship between the privilege of non-disclosure

[10] Vol. 11, No. 2 Sup. Ct. Crim. Rep. 804 (Grand Bench 1957).

[11] Vol. 6, No. 8 Sup. Ct. Crim. Rep. 975 (Grand Bench 1952).

[12] See, for example, Note, *Quasi-Public Records and Self-Incrimination*, 47 COLUM. L. REV. 838 (1947); Strasheim, *Agreements and Obligation to Waive the Right Against Self-Incrimination*, 32 NEB. L. REV. 577 (1953).

[13] *E.g.*, THE INCOME TAX LAW, arts. 63, 64, 70; THE CORPORATION LAW, arts. 48, 49; THE NARCOTICS CONTROL LAW, arts. 37–50, 53, 72; THE GAS SUPPLY ENTERPRISE LAW, arts. 21–29, 46, 47, 58, 59.

and the statutory duty of disclosure, because some of those provisions requiring administrative reports or records contain a precautionary proviso that "the prescribed authority of questioning and inspection should not be interpreted as granted for criminal investigation."[14] However, because as a matter of fact in most cases an administrative investigation may reveal the facts tending to incriminate the subject person, this proviso has only abstract meaning.

Recently the problem of the constitutionality of the provisions requiring incriminating disclosure has been discussed in several cases. In 1948, a licensed custodian of narcotics was prosecuted under the Narcotics Control Law for his failure to record an unlawful delivery of narcotics. The Niigata District Court and the Tokyo High Court held that the defendant was not guilty because, owing to the privilege against self-incrimination, he should not be compelled to record the unlawful delivery of narcotics. The prosecution appealed from the decision of the high court. In 1954 the Supreme Court reversed the decision of high court, holding that, despite the privilege against self-incrimination, the defendant had the duty of recording the illegal delivery of narcotics because he had consented to be controlled by the Narcotics Control Law when he applied for a position as a licensed narcotics custodian.[15] This decision appears to have relied on the so-called "waiver by consent" theory.

Two years later the Supreme Court again held that the provision of the Narcotics Control Law requiring the recording of illegally handled narcotics was constitutional despite Article 38, Par. 1, of the Constitution.[16] In this case the Court relied upon the reasoning that the law imposing the duty of recording was constitutional because such control was required from the standpoint of public health. The theoretical basis of this reasoning appears to be (a) the consideration of the quasi-public relationship between the custodian of narcotics

[14] See, *e.g.*, THE INHERITANCE TAX LAW, art. 60, par. 4.

[15] Vol. 8, No. 7 Sup. Ct. Crim. Rep. 1151 (2d Petty Bench 1954).

[16] Vol. 10, No. 7 Sup. Ct. Crim. Rep. 1173 (Grand Bench 1956).

and the state and (b) the so-called "generic class of acts" theory as proposed by Wigmore.[17]

Some other precedents also were based substantially upon the "generic class of acts" theory. For example, in a case where the issue was the constitutionality of the Alien Registration Law requiring the alien who had illegally entered Japan to apply for registration, the Supreme Court held that the law imposing the duty did not infringe upon the privilege against self-incrimination because the law imposed only the duty to apply for registration, not the duty to disclose incriminating facts.[18]

There are also a few high court decisions which are based substantially on the same theory and support the constitutionality of tax law provisions which required incidentally self-incriminating facts. For example, in a tax law violation case the Nagoya High Court held that the provision of the Corporation Tax Law, which punished the maker of a falsified income report, did not infringe upon the privilege against self-incrimination although the income had been illegally obtained by black marketing, because the provision required the report on the income itself, not the report on the illegal source of the income.[19]

Recently the dilemma between the privilege against self-incrimination and the quasi-official duty of disclosure has been highlighted by a series of inferior court decisions concerning the constitutionality of a sort of "hit and run" provision in Article 67, Par. 2, of the Road Traffic Control Law Enforcement Ordinance.[20]

The Road Traffic Control Law, Article 24, Par. 1, provides: "In case where death or injury of a person or destruction of property has been caused by the traffic of a vehicle, horse or tram-car, the driver, crew or other worker thereof shall aid the victim and take other necessary measures in accordance with the provisions of ordinance." In amplifying this provision of law the Road Traffic Control Law Enforcement Ordinance, Article 67, Par. 2, further provides: "In the event that the driver of the vehicle, horse or tram-car mentioned in the preceding paragraph (or the crew or other workers thereof in case of an accident of the driver) has taken the measures prescribed by the preceding paragraph and does not find a police officer on the scene of accident, he shall immediately inform a police officer of the police station exercising jurisdiction over the place of the accident about the substance of the accident and the measures taken according to the same paragraph and shall receive directions from the officer as to whether he may continue to drive or leave the scene of accident." The first challenge to the constitutionality of Article 67, Par. 2, of the Ordinance was made in 1949 by the Kobe District Court, Amagasaki Branch. In a "hit and run" case, where the defendant left an injured pedestrian helpless, the court held that Article 67, Par. 2, of the Ordinance was unconstitutional, because it required the defendant to disclose the details of the accident, thereby possibly leading to his incrimination for negligent homicide.[21] In the same year, however, an opposing view was expressed by the Kobe District Court[22] and the Kagoshima Summary Court.[23] The former ruled that the provisions were constitutional on the ground that they were administrative provisions aimed at the maintenance of public welfare and had nothing directly to do with Article 38 of the Constitution. The latter supported the constitutionality of the provisions on the theory that the necessity of the public welfare might restrain the constitutional privilege against self-incrimination.

---

[17] 8 WIGMORE, EVIDENCE §2259(c) (3d ed. 1940).

[18] Vol. 10, No. 12 Sup. Ct. Crim. Rep. (Grand Bench 1956). Also see Vol. 12, No. 1 Sup. Ct. Crim. Rep. 1 (1st Petty Bench 1958) holding that to request under the threat of punishment the presentation of an alien registration certificate does not violate art. 38, par. 1 of the Constitution, even if the request were made by the public officer for the purpose of criminal investigation of the name and residence of the alien.

[19] Vol. 4, No. 7 High Courts Crim. Rep. 704 (Nagoya High Court 1951); see also Vol. 5, No. 2 High Courts Crim. Rep. 160 (Tokyo High Court 1952).

[20] THE LAW FOR THE ENFORCEMENT OF THE ROAD TRAFFIC CONTROL LAW (Cabinet Ordinance No. 261 of 1953 with the latest amendment by Cabinet Ordinance No. 254 of 1958).

[21] Decision of the Kobe District Court, Amagasaki Branch, May 28, 1959, 189 HANREI JIHO (Law Reports Times) 6 (1959).

[22] Decision of the Kobe District Court, June 22, 1959, 195 HANREI JIHO (Law Reports Times) 8 (1959).

[23] Decision of the Kagoshima Summary Court, July 7, 1959, 195 HANREI JIHO (Law Reports Times) 9 (1959).

Both of these appear to depend upon the theory that even a constitutional right may be restrained by the necessity of public welfare, and the former has a slight implication of the "generic class of acts" theory.

One month later the holdings for constitutionality were rebutted by another decision rendered by the Akita District Court, Yuzawa Branch.[24] This court emphasized the short linkage between the required disclosure and the possible prosecution which may result from the data disclosed and declared the unconstitutionality of Article 67, Par. 2, because of its substantial compulsion to self-incriminating statement.

Recently, however, an eclectic view for constitutionality was propounded by the Utsunomiya District Court. In a "hit and run" case where the defendant, after giving emergency aid to two persons he injured, drove away without reporting to the police, the court held that Article 67, Par. 2 was constitutional insofar as it could be interpreted to require the defendant to inform the police of such facts as do not directly tend to incriminate him.[25] Under this theory it is enough for a driver hitting a person to inform the police of the fact of the accident without disclosing his name by personally reporting or anonymously telephoning or sending a message to the police. It should be noted also that in the course of reasoning the court made the following criticism of the traditional justification of "hit and run" statutes: It is improper to restrict the privilege of non-disclosure in the name of public welfare; if so, one might totally deny the privilege in criminal procedure because of the public nature of the criminal procedure which is designed to

maintain welfare and security of the community. Thus, until the Supreme Court says its last word on this complicated problem, the ado over the constitutionality of "hit and run" provisions will continue.[26]

## Major Differences Between American and Japanese Concepts of the Privilege Against Self-Incrimination

*Immunity Statutes and the Privilege Against Self-Incrimination*

In the United States "Immunity Statutes" seem to have been one of the most effective weapons of investigating authorities in their fight against organized crime that is guarded with the privilege against self-incrimination.[27]

In Japan there have been no remarkable movements toward enactment of such immunity

[24] Decision of the Akita District Court, Yuzawa Branch, Aug. 19, 1959, 198 HANREI JIHO (Law Reports Times) 20 (1959).

[25] Decision of the Utsunomiya District Court, Oct. 17, 1959 (not yet published). Also see Decision of the Tokyo District Court (the 17th Division), Dec. 14, 1959, which expressed another eclectic view for the constitutionality of article 67, par. 2, on the theory that under the provisions a person may be punished for his failure to make a required report, but that such a report is inadmissible as evidence against him if the incriminating disclosure is made under the threat of punishment. However, this qualification does not satisfactorily function as a guaranty in cases where the disclosure is used as a clue.

[26] Thus far no Supreme Court decision on this issue has been handed down. However, it should be noted that recently the Osaka High Court (Decision of Osaka High Court, Dec. 22, 1959) reversed the Kobe District Court decision, note 21 *supra*, and held the provisions to be constitutional on the theory that the provision should be interpreted to require the report which helps to identify the accident (*e.g.*, date, place, and an outline of the accident and the name of the victim) but not to require the report concerning the circumstances which tend to show negligence on the part of a driver. The reasoning of the court complies by and large with the view of Assistant Professor Fujiki of Tokyo University as expressed in his recent article *Dorokotsu Torishimari Ho Shiko Rei 67-Jo 2-Ko to Mokuhiken* (*Art. 67, Par. 2 of the Road Traffic Control Law Enforcement Ordinance and the Right to Non-Disclosure*) Vol. 12, No. 8 KEISATSU GAKU RONSHU (Police Science Review) 12 (1959). Judge Urabe expressed an opposing view to Mr. Fujiki's in his article *Jiko o okoshita Jidosha Untenshn no "Jiko no Naiyo" Hokoku Gimu to Mokuhiken* (*Duty of Reporting the "Substance of an Accident" by the Driver who Caused the Accident and the Right to Non-Disclosure*), 20 HANREI HYORON (Law Reports Review) 3 (1959). He maintained that the broad wording ("Substance of the Accident") does not permit the limited interpretation as suggested by Mr. Fujiki and suggested a legislative specification of the wording. It should be noted that a legislative change is contemplated in accordance with the view of Judge Urabe. See also Tamiya, *Jidosha Jiko no Hokoku Gimu to Mokuhiken* (*Duty of Reporting an Auto Accident and the Right to Non-Disclosure*), 189 JURIST 24 (1959), a useful comment on the recent decisions on this subject with specific reference to American cases on "hit and run" statutes.

[27] See, *e.g.*, Comment, *Immunity from Self-Incrimination Under the Federal Compulsory Testimony Act*, 46 J. CRIM. L., C. & P.S. 679 (1956).

statutes. Since the enactment of the Federal Compulsory Testimony Act of 1954, Japanese lawyers have been aware of the practical significance of the device. However, it is generally with academic interest that most Japanese lawyers regard it. The reason why the Japanese draftsmen are rather apathetic to this seemingly attractive device to control unbridled use of the privilege against self-incrimination is psychological rather than logical. The wisdom on which "immunity statutes" are based is very simple. A child who has broken a window in conspiracy with his friends may say to the angry mother: "I will tell you who did it if you don't punish me, Mommy." And if the mother is very anxious to know, she may give immunity to her child and say: "O.K. Johnny, I won't punish you. Then tell me honestly who did it." This is the psychology of the immunity system. Perhaps Japanese government lawyers are too austere to relinquish their prosecuting authority in such a psychological game of give and take.

### Denial of the Privilege Against Self-Incrimination to Public Officials

Although Japanese law expects public officials to cooperate with criminal investigations,[28] it does not go so far as to require public officers to waive their privilege against self-incrimination. Ethically, doubt has been expressed as to the propriety of permitting a witness to refuse to give testimony tending to subject him to subsequent prosecution, especially where a public officer as a witness invokes the privilege to cloak alleged malfeasance in office. Legally, however, public officials fully enjoy the privilege against self-incrimination, even when they are prosecuted for crimes closely related to their official duties. Strangely enough, there have been no movements toward legislation designed to restrict the privilege of government officials. Since there is no particular psychological factor hampering such legislation the reason for this legislative hesitance may be attributed to the fact that Japanese lawyers have been unfamiliar with this

[28] *Cf.,* THE CODE OF CRIMINAL PROCEDURE, art. 239, par. 2, which provides: "When a government or public official in exercise of his function believes that an offense has been committed, he must lodge an accusation."

type of legislation. Very few lawyers in Japan have been aware of the fact that in some states of the United States there are statutes and precedents which, under the threat of dismissal, compel government officials to waive their immunity with regard to matters within the scope of their duties.[29] However, it is foreseen that the day will come when the draftsmen of Japanese law will be fully aware of the possibility of this type of legislation and start to move toward it.

### Non-Testimonial Disclosures and the Privilege Against Self-Incrimination[30]

Should the privilege against self-incrimination excuse a person from producing a writing in his possession? If so, to what extent? Anglo-American law has answered the question in the affirmative, although it has been making continuous efforts to limit the scope of the privilege, which has been improperly far-reaching. In the course of these efforts, official documents and corporation records have been removed from the protection of the privilege on the basis of the "personal nature doctrine" or "public or quasi-public record doctrine."

However, most Japanese lawyers will doubt the rationale of the Anglo-American rule that a person shall be protected from the compulsory production of writing just as a person shall be protected from the coercive taking of evidential utterance from his lips. Once an incriminating piece of information has been embodied voluntarily in documentary material, the compulsory production of the material will be far less painful to the person who has given the information than the compulsory taking of the information from his lips.

Under Japanese law, the scope of compulsory

[29] See, *e.g., Note,* 64 HARV. L. REV. 987 (1951); *Note, Claim of Immunity from Self-Incrimination by Public Officers,* 64 U.S.L. REV. 561 (1930); NEW YORK CONSTITUTION, art. 1, §6 (as amended and effective Jan. 1, 1939); Canteline v. McClellan, 282 N.Y. 166, 25 N.E.2d 972 (1940); Christal v. Police Comm'n, 33 Cal. App. 2d 564, 92 P.2d 416 (1939); Goldway v. Board of Higher Educ., 37 N.Y.S.2d 34 (1942); Drury v. Hurley, 339 Ill. App. 33, 88 N.E.2d 728 (1949); LA REV. STAT., tit. 33, §2426 (1950).
[30] The points made here appeared in substantially the same form in Abe, *op. cit. supra* note 1, at 627-29.

search and seizure is interpreted to cover "any articles" whatsoever which the court believes should be used as evidence or liable to confiscation.[31] The phrase "any articles" has been interpreted to comprise any sort of real or documentary evidence which will be relevant and admissible in a court. Japanese law has no rule excluding documentary evidence simply because of its self-incriminating nature. The requirement of a warrant or an order of the court is a guaranty against a possible misuse of the system of compulsory production of articles.

In the United States the problem of compulsory taking of physical evidence, such as blood tests, alcoholic intoxication tests, etc., has been much discussed also under the topic of self-incrimination.[32] However, most Japanese lawyers will doubt the reason why this type of disclosure should be covered by the privilege against self-incrimination. Experience shows that the admission of such type of physical evidence has the most pleasing effect of killing the need for confession and of stimulating scientific investigation. Again a more flexible approach under the Japanese law will be noted.[33]

### REEXAMINATION OF DUALISM OF STATE AND FEDERAL JURISDICTIONS AFFECTING THE SCOPE OF THE PRIVILEGE

In the eyes of Japanese lawyers the rule of dualism of state and federal jurisdictions as affecting the privilege against self-incrimination appears

[31] Cf., THE CODE OF CRIMINAL PROCEDURE, arts. 99, 102 and 218.

[32] It should be noted here that Professor Inbau concluded from his historical survey of the development of the privilege that it was originally designed to prohibit "the practice of extracting incriminating statements from accused persons." INBAU, SELF-INCRIMINATION: WHAT CAN AN ACCUSED PERSON BE COMPELLED TO DO? 5 (1950).

[33] Under the Japanese law the problem of the admissibility of physical evidence is answered expressly in the affirmative by the provisions concerning "evidence by inspection (kensho)" and "expert evidence (kantei)." See THE JAPANESE CODE OF CRIMINAL PROCEDURE, arts. 128 et seq., especially art. 218, par. 2, providing for the taking of finger prints, foot prints, or photographs of the accused, and art. 167 providing for the possibility of confining the accused in a certain place if necessary for an expert examination, e.g., for an insanity test. To prevent misuse, all these means of compulsory taking of physical evidence are subject to

to be somewhat strange. The American federal rule of "dualism" established by the Murdock[34] case and elaborated by the Feldman[35] case "cuts into the very substance of the Fifth Amendment"[36] and is "subversive of the spirit and letter of the Bill of Rights."[37]

Let us ask, "What is the rationale of the dualism in the privilege against self-incrimination?" Wigmore's view was that (a) the privilege is not substantially curtailed by the dualism because the danger of prosecution is remote and (b) the difficulty of ascertaining what is criminal in another jurisdiction should make a different rule impractical.[38] Are these two cornerstones of the dualism still sound today? The world has become much narrower than in the days of Wigmore. Not only the world but also the universe is becoming smaller. The technique of communication has made remarkable progress. Testimony in a court may be communicated to every corner of the country in a few hours through a network of mass-media, such as radio, television and newspapers. The police network also will be quick enough to detect new pieces of evidence against the witness using his testimony in a court as a clue. On this new basis a state witness might be prosecuted in a federal court and vice versa. Under such circumstances, it is not practical to say that a state and a federal jurisdiction are foreign to each other, as much the same relation as between "China" or "Peru" and the United States[39]; nor is it proper for a federal court to pretend to be "blind" to the laws and facts of a state jurisdiction and vice versa. The development of legal publications and the possibility of using legal experts are enabling state courts to know the law of a federal jurisdiction and vice versa. Now

judicial control in the form of warrants or orders of the court. In the Japanese courts physical evidence taken by these means is evaluated as the most reliable and scientific basis of fact finding. The witnesses lie often, but the things and circumstances do not.

[34] United States v. Murdock, 284 U.S. 141 (1931).

[35] Feldman v. United States, 322 U.S. 487 (1944).

[36] Id. at 498 (dissenting opinion of Black, J.).

[37] McAllister, J., in In re Watson, 293 Mich. 263, 284, 291 N.W. 652, 661 (1940).

[38] WIGMORE, EVIDENCE §2258 (3d ed. 1940).

[39] Id., §2258.

that the two cornerstones of the dualism have lost their significance, is there any other reason for insisting on dualism?

It was noteworthy that the *DiCarlo*[40] and the *Adams*[41] cases proceeded a few steps toward a realistic solution of this problem, but did not reach it.

[40] United States v. DiCarlo, 102 F. Supp. 597 (N.D. Ohio 1952).
[41] Adams v. Maryland, 347 U.S. 179 (1954).

A fallacy of dualism appears most clearly in the application of immunity statutes. It is extremely unreasonable that a witness should be compelled to testify under an immunity statute in one jurisdiction while risking prosecution in another jurisdiction. This means trapping a person with a seemingly lawful device. A practical and realistic step toward the elimination of this fallacy is urgently desired.

# *Norway*

## ANDERS BRATHOLM

No precise doctrine regarding self-incrimination is to be found in Norwegian or Scandinavian law as is the case in Anglo-Saxon law, but certain of the principles which are derived from the Anglo-Saxon doctrine are applicable in the Scandinavian countries. Thus a person who is charged or accused has no duty to give a statement (apart from his name, position and address) to the police or to the court, and he can make a false statement without being liable to punishment.[1] He cannot confirm his statement by oath.

A witness, as a rule, has a duty to give a statement in court and to confirm his statement by oath. If the questioning implies that the witness is suspected of an offense, he can demand to be charged, and then he has no duty to answer. Nor has he a duty to answer if his answer will expose him to the danger of losing the respect of his fellow citizens.[2]

When the question arises as to what extent the accused in other ways has a duty to cooperate with the solution of the case in view, the legal position

in Norway (and in the other Scandinavian countries) is very dubious in many respects. Thus the extent to which an accused person may be subjected to various forms of frisking, tests, and so on, is somewhat vague.

According to the Norwegian Criminal Procedure Act it is permitted to search a person who on reasonable grounds is suspected of having committed an act for which the maximum statutory penalty is higher than a fine, if there is reason to believe that the search will lead to the discovery of evidence against him.[3]

Although the Criminal Procedure Act has no clear provisions on the point, it is assumed that the right to search also includes an examination of *the body* of the accused. The aim for such an examination may be to find scratches, bites, punctures caused by a hypodermic needle, and the like, on the body of the accused.[4] It is characteristic of this examination that it only has to do with the *external* condition of the body and that it does not exceed the process of observation.

The legal position is more doubtful when it comes to the question of the admissibility of performing an operation or the like on the accused, in order to obtain evidence against him. Examples of

[1] PENAL CODE OF 1902, §167.
[2] CRIMINAL PROCEDURE ACT OF 1887 (hereinafter called CPA), §177. See also PENAL CODE, §167.

[3] CPA, §221.
[4] It is generally held that CPA, §221, authorizes such an examination of the body of the accused.

such actions are gynecological examinations, stomach pumping, blood tests, etc. As regards blood tests, there is a clear authority in the motoring laws permitting the testing of a person whom there is good reason to suspect of having driven a motor vehicle in an intoxicated condition.[5] (A person who has, when driving, more than 0.5 promille (per thousand) concentration of alcohol in the blood is considered as intoxicated[6] and is usually sentenced to at least 21 days imprisonment.) The general opinion in Norway is that the provision in respect of blood tests in the motoring laws is practical and important to the clearing up of the case, and that it does not constitute any unreasonable invasion of the rights of the person charged.

Corresponding provisions in respect of blood tests are found in Danish and Swedish law.

It is not clear to what extent the police have the right to take a blood test from persons other than those who are suspected of having driven a motor vehicle in an intoxicated condition. In practice, however, a blood test is sometimes taken in such a case, and there has been, as far as I know, no occasion when the person involved has opposed the test. At any rate, the courts have not been faced with the problem of the legality of such an examination undertaken against the wishes of the person tested.

Furthermore, it is doubtful how far an accused person may be subjected to similar forms of corporal examination or operation.

One might perhaps say that it is the current Norwegian law that operations or the like on an accused person, in order to obtain evidence against him, can only be undertaken against his will when authority for the procedure exists in the *written* law. In this connection it can be mentioned that some years ago the Supreme Court decided that a woman suspected of having undergone an illegal abortion could not be compelled to submit to gynecological examination.[7]

Physical examination of the accused can involve a fourth type of evidence, the so-called evidence of identity (fingerprints, photographs, confronting with witnesses, handwriting tests, etc.). In this field, too, we have no clear legal provisions in Norway. However, the question whether an accused person is bound to give fingerprints did come before the Supreme Court in 1929 and 1935, and in both cases the court decided that the accused was so bound.[8] The court reached its decisions mainly by analogous reasoning, recalling the provision in the criminal law that an accused person is bound to give his name, position and address.[9]

With regard to the other forms of evidence of identity, there is no legal precedent, but it may surely be assumed that the accused is also bound to permit his photograph to be taken, submit to confrontation, etc.[10] In practice accused persons do not generally protest against partaking of such examinations.

Finally another type of investigation will be dealt with: The use of the lie-detector, narcoanalysis and similar chemical or technical media whose purpose is to solve the question of guilt. In Norway these measures have not hitherto been employed during investigations. Moreover, it is probably not permissible to employ them, even if the accused person consents to the measure.

In recent years the question of the permissibility of such measures has been discussed at some length by professional men in the Scandinavian countries,[11] and it seems to be the general view that the measures should be entirely excluded from the systems of criminal law, at any rate until they have reached a higher degree of reliability than is the case today.

It must be added that narcoanalysis has been undertaken in a number of cases in Denmark and in Sweden in connection with psychiatric observation of the accused, but the purpose has not been to bring to light whether the accused has committed the crime he was suspected of but rather to gain information concerning his state of mind. The

---

[5] THE LAW OF MOTOR VEHICLES OF 1926, §17.
[6] *Ibid.*
[7] Norsk Retstidende (Nor. Law Rep.) 204 (1936).

[8] Norsk Retstidende (Nor. Law Rep.) 221 (1929) and 1088 (1935).
[9] PENAL CODE, §333.
[10] See BRATHOLM, PAAGRIPELSE OG VARETEKTSFENGSEL (Arrest and Detention Before Trial) 258 (Oslo 1957).
[11] See references in BRATHOLM, *op. cit. supra* note 10, at 258 n.39.

accused has, of course, in all cases consented to the narcoanalysis.

It may be mentioned that in Norway there is no exclusionary rule, and there is reason to believe that evidence obtained by illegal means in most cases will be admitted.

In conclusion one may say that although in Norway—as in the other Scandinavian lands—there is no doctrine corresponding to that in Anglo-Saxon law on self-incrimination, there is in these countries a limit to what the accused may be subjected to. But at present it is far from clear in many types of cases where the line should be drawn. The absence of a fixed doctrine has brought it about that the accused—and in some cases counsel as well—are not aware of the possible rights of a charged person in this respect, and this again leads to the fact that problems seldom arise in practice. Most persons, when charged, consent to the inquiry desired by the police, because they believe that it is their duty to cooperate. Many, too, are anxious to avoid the aggravation of suspicion that would be caused by refusal to submit to investigation. As contact with Anglo-Saxon law improves, there is good reason to believe that more and more persons will become aware of the problem of self-incrimination, and thus more attention will be devoted to it in theory and in legislation. In that connection it can be mentioned that a committee was appointed a couple of years ago with the responsibility of drafting a new criminal procedure act for Norway.[12]

[12] The chairman of the committee is Professor Johs. Andenaes, Director of the Institute of Criminology and Criminal Law, Oslo.

HARUO ABE, Public Prosecutor, Ministry of Justice, Tokyo. Mr. Abe has had extensive experience both in the prosecution of criminal cases and in the drafting of penal legislation. He holds a Master of Laws degree from Harvard University and has contributed articles to American as well as Japanese legal periodicals. He is the co-author of *Glueck Hanzai Yosokuho Nyumon* (An Introduction to the Glueck Prediction Method) (Tokyo 1959) and *Taiho, Koryu, Hoshaku* (Arrest, Detention and Release on Bail) (Yokogawa ed. Tokyo 1958).

FRANCIS A. ALLEN, Professor of Law, University of Chicago. Professor Allen was formerly a member of the law faculties of Northwestern and Harvard Universities and from 1946 to 1948 served as Law Clerk to the late Mr. Chief Justice Fred M. Vinson of the United States Supreme Court. He is a frequent contributor to legal periodicals and was a prime mover in the drafting and adoption of the 1961 Illinois Criminal Code. Professor Allen is presently serving as Chairman of The Attorney General's Committee on the Administration of Federal Justice for Criminal Indigents.

ANDERS BRATHOLM, Professor of Law, University of Oslo. Professor Bratholm studied criminology and law as a postgraduate student at New York University. During the spring term of 1960, he was a Visiting Professor in the Law School of the University of Pennsylvania. Professor Bratholm is the author of *Paagripelse og Varetektsfengsel* (Arrest and Detention Before Trial) (Oslo 1957), as well as numerous articles.

WALTER R. CLEMENS, Head Officer, Ministry of Justice, State of Hamburg. Dr. Clemens has served as a member of the Court of Appeals of Hamburg and has an option to return to the bench at any time. He is the author of numerous articles in German legal periodicals.

HAIM H. COHN, Justice of the Supreme Court of Israel. Mr. Justice Cohn previously served as Attorney General, Director General of the Ministry of Justice, and Minister of Justice of Israel. From 1957 to 1959, he was a member of the United Nations Commission on Human Rights and, in 1951, he was Chief Israeli Delegate to the United Nations Conference on International Criminal Jurisdiction. Justice Cohn is a frequent contributor to Hebrew legal periodicals.

CALEB FOOTE, Professor of Law, University of Pennsylvania. A former member of the faculty of the University of Nebraska Law School, Professor Foote was Walter E. Meyer Visiting Research Professor of Law at Harvard University during the 1960-61 academic year. He has written extensively in the field of criminal law and procedure and is a Consultant to the United Nations' Division of Human Rights.

FRED E. INBAU, Professor of Law, Northwestern University. Long active in the field of scientific evidence, Professor Inbau served from 1933 to 1938 as a member of the staff of the Scientific Crime Detection Laboratory of Northwestern University School of Law, and from 1938 to 1941 as Director of the Chicago Police Scientific Crime Detection Laboratory. He is the author of *Cases and Comments on Criminal Justice* (1960) (with Claude R. Sowle); *Lie Detection and Criminal Interrogation* (3d ed. 1953) (with John E. Reid); and *Self-Incrimination: What Can an Accused Person Be Compelled To Do?* (1950).

G. ARTHUR MARTIN, Q.C., Member of the bars of British Columbia and Ontario, with offices in Toronto. Mr. Martin for many years has specialized in trial and appellate work in the criminal law field and, in the course of his career, has appeared as counsel for the defense in thirty-eight murder cases. He is Lecturer in Criminal Law and Procedure, Osgoode Hall Law School, Toronto.

FRANK J. McGARR, Member of the Chicago Bar. Prior to his entrance into private practice in 1958, Mr. McGarr served as First Assistant United States Attorney for the Northern District of Illinois. He is a member of the law faculty of Loyola University in Chicago.

JOHN T. McNAUGHTON, Professor of Law, Harvard University. Prior to joining the Harvard faculty, Professor McNaughton was Editor of the Pekin (Ill.) *Daily Times*. Since 1957, while a member of the Harvard faculty, he has served as Assistant District Attorney of Middlesex County, Massachusetts. Professor McNaughton, who has written extensively in the field of evidence law, recently completed a revision of Volume 8 of *Wigmore on Evidence*. Currently on leave of absence from Harvard, he is serving as Deputy Assistant Secretary of Defense for International Security Affairs.

GERHARD O. W. MUELLER, Professor of Law, New York University. Professor Mueller is Director of the Comparative Criminal Law Project at New York University and Editor-in-Chief of *The American Series of Foreign Penal Codes*. A frequent contributor to both American and foreign legal periodicals, he also served as Editor of *Essays in Criminal Science* (1961).

MONRAD G. PAULSEN, Professor of Law, Columbia University. Professor Paulsen previously served on the law faculties of the University of Minnesota, Indiana University, and the University of Utah. He is the co-editor, with Professor Sanford H. Kadish, of a forthcoming casebook on criminal law.

ROBERT VOUIN, Professor of Criminal Law in the Faculty of Law of the University of Paris. Professor Vouin formerly served on the law faculties of the University of Bordeaux and the University of Poitiers. He is the author of a number of books and is a frequent contributor to legal periodicals in France and elsewhere.

FRANK J. REMINGTON, Professor of Law, University of Wisconsin. From 1950 to 1956, Professor Remington served as a member of the technical staff and Advisory Committee for the new Wisconsin Criminal Code. He is a Special Consultant and member of the Advisory Committee for the American Law Institute's Model Penal Code as well as Project Director of the American Bar Foundation's Survey of the Administration of Criminal Justice in the United States.

CLAUDE R. SOWLE, Associate Professor of Law, Northwestern University. Professor Sowle is the author of *Cases and Comments on Criminal Justice* (1960) (with Fred E. Inbau) and is Editor-in-Chief of the *Journal of Criminal Law, Criminology and Police Science*. He also serves as Training Consultant to the Chicago Police Department.

BERNARD WEISBERG, Member of the Chicago Bar. Mr. Weisberg is General Counsel of the American Civil Liberties Union, Illinois Division. Prior to commencing the practice of law in Chicago in 1953, he served as Law Clerk to Mr. Justice Tom C. Clark of the United States Supreme Court. Mr. Weisberg was one of the authors of *Secret Detention by Chicago Police*, a 1959 report by the Illinois Division of the ACLU.

GLANVILLE L. WILLIAMS, Reader in English Law, University of Cambridge, and Fellow of Jesus College, Cambridge. Professor Williams is a Barrister of the Middle Temple and a Fellow of the British Academy. During 1959-60, he served as the first Walter E. Meyer Visiting Research Professor in the School of Law of New York University. Professor Williams had written extensively; his books include *The Sanctity of Life and the Criminal Law* (1956), *The Proof of Guilt* (1958), and *Criminal Law: The General Part* (1953).

O. W. WILSON, Superintendent of Police, Chicago. Superintendent Wilson was for many years Professor of Police Administration and Dean of the School of Criminology of the University of California at Berkeley. Before joining the California faculty, he served for eleven years as Chief of Police in Wichita, Kansas. Superintendent Wilson is the author of several books as well as numerous articles.

LOUIS C. WYMAN, Member of the New Hampshire Bar, with offices in Manchester, and former Attorney General of New Hampshire. In addition to practicing law in Massachusetts, Florida and New Hampshire, Mr. Wyman has served as counsel to two Congressional committees. He is a past President of the National Association of Attorneys General of the United States.

## Date Due